*Benedetto Accolti and the*
*Florentine Renaissance*

# Benedetto Accolti and the Florentine Renaissance

ROBERT BLACK

*Lecturer in Modern History,*
*University of Leeds*

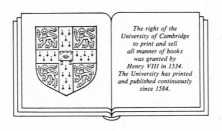

The right of the
University of Cambridge
to print and sell
all manner of books
was granted by
Henry VIII in 1534.
The University has printed
and published continuously
since 1584.

CAMBRIDGE UNIVERSITY PRESS

*Cambridge*

*London New York New Rochelle*

*Melbourne Sydney*

Published by the Press Syndicate of the University of Cambridge
The Pitt Building, Trumpington Street, Cambridge CB2 1RP
32 East 57th Street, New York, NY 10022, USA
10 Stamford Road, Oakleigh, Melbourne 3166, Australia

© Cambridge University Press 1985

First published 1985

Printed in Great Britain at the University Press, Cambridge

Library of Congress catalogue card number: 84–27498

*British Library Cataloguing in Publication Data*
Black, Robert
Benedetto Accolti and the Florentine Renaissance.
1. Accolti, Benedetto 2. Humanists – Italy –
Biography
I. Title
001.2'092'4   PA85.A3/

ISBN 0 521 25016 1

# Contents

*To Nicolai Rubinstein*

# *Preface*

The contribution of Florence's humanist chancellors to Renaissance culture is well known: not only were Salutati and his successors preeminent scholars in their own right but as leaders of the Florentine humanist movement they deserve much credit for making Florence one of the great centres of Renaissance civilization. Of these humanist chancellors, least recognition has gone to the Aretine, Benedetto Accolti, whose term of office lasted from 1458 until his death in 1464. This neglect goes back to the fifteenth century. After a successful career as a lawyer, Accolti devoted only the last few years of his life to the humanities, and when he died at the age of forty-nine, he was just beginning to establish himself in the first rank of humanists; his sudden death prevented him from circulating his two recently completed Latin compositions, which, to judge from surviving manuscript copies, were not widely read in the fifteenth century. His history became a standard work on the first crusade only in the sixteenth century when it was printed in several editions and translated into Italian, French, German and Greek, whereas his dialogue comparing antiquity and modern times was not generally known before the end of the seventeenth century, when interest in the *querelle des anciens et des modernes* led to its publication in several editions. Adequate recognition may also have been denied to Accolti because little has been known of his life. He did not collect his own letters, so that the usual principal source for the biography of humanists, their Latin correspondence, has not been available for the study of Benedetto Accolti; indeed, only two private letters, both brief and informal compositions in Italian, have survived.

Nevertheless, Accolti's interest as a major personality in mid-fifteenth century Florence and his importance in the development of Italian Renaissance culture should not be overlooked. Accolti's deep commitment to humanist studies, which eventually led him to abandon a lucrative legal career in order to become Florentine chancellor, illustrates the vital role that his native city, Arezzo, had in nurturing many of the leading figures of the early Renaissance. Medieval Arezzo had been more notable as a cultural than as an economic centre, and by the fifteenth century, despite subjugation to Florence accompanied by a deep economic slump, Arezzo was able to preserve its educational traditions. Arezzo's significance as a centre of learning in the thirteenth and early fourteenth centuries is well known: not only was there a major Aretine university in the thirteenth century but Geri d'Arezzo was one of the leading figures in pre-humanism at the turn of the fourteenth century. It is less well known that the Aretine tradition of classical scholarship and education continued throughout the fourteenth and early fifteenth centuries and prepared the ground for the emergence of a remarkable succession of Aretine humanists including Bruni, Marsuppini, Tortelli, Aliotti, Griffolini and Benedetto and Francesco Accolti.

Accolti's work as Florentine chancellor sheds light on the political world of Florence in the mid-fifteenth century. The chancellor was Florence's senior civil servant, not a political official; nevertheless, the exclusion of the chancery from politics was an ideal in Florence, not always a reality. Unlike his successor, Bartolomeo Scala, Accolti had no ambition to become a political heavyweight; yet he did in fact sometimes exercise an influence on policy, particularly by virtue of his legal knowledge and authority. The discovery of unknown documents (published here as Appendix IV) shows not only the limitations of Medicean control over foreign policy in the early 1460s but also Accolti's occasional independent influence. Accolti's own relationship with the Medici was a problem for him and perhaps even for the Medici themselves. Evidence has been found to suggest that he never achieved intimacy with Cosimo or his sons; his principal aim was to maintain his position as chancellor, and in the increasingly divided regime which ruled Florence in the 1460s Accolti seems to have attempted to develop connections with both the Medici and their opponents. He might have found it easier to gain support from the Medici's rivals, and yet he never gave up hope of a rapprochement with the Medici themselves.

Accolti's principal interest as Florentine chancellor was in administration and in the humanities; indeed, he emerges as one of the major reformers in the history of the Florentine chancery. Following the almost complete collapse of the chancery under Poggio from 1453 to 1456, Accolti restored administrative reforms first envisaged under Bruni and realized under Marsuppini but allowed to lapse at the end of Marsuppini's life. Moreover, he introduced a number of novel procedures which considerably improved the efficiency of the chancery. It may be surprising that previous chancellors, albeit distinguished humanists, had gone only a short way to introducing the new learning into the records of the chancery; a concern with the classical revival not only led Accolti to secure a permanent place for italic script in the Florentine chancery and to revive a lofty classical style in public letter writing which had been achieved under his predecessor Marsuppini but allowed to lapse under Poggio, but in fact credit goes to Accolti for extending classical Latin prose style beyond the public letters of the commune to diplomatic records and to the debates of the deliberative assembly, the *pratica*. For modern historians Accolti's reforms are perhaps unfortunate, since he and his assistant undertook extensive rewriting of records which has rendered them problematic and less valuable as historical sources; however, his reforms were considered of the greatest importance by his contemporaries, who not only praised his work as chancellor unstintingly but also doubled his salary. Under Accolti a spirit of reform entered the Florentine chancery, and in one sense the important reforms of his successor Scala were the legacy of Accolti's term as chancellor.

Previous humanist chancellors had played an important role in public life not so much as leading political figures but rather as official apologists for Florentine diplomacy. Accolti similarly made a notable contribution as public spokesman in foreign policy, particularly on behalf of Florentine diplomacy in the face of the Turkish menace. It has sometimes been believed that growing commercial interests in the East led Florence to oppose efforts to launch a crusade after the fall of Constantinople in 1453. Such views, however, oversimplify Florence's diplomatic position in the 1450s and 1460s. In an earlier study,[1] I attempted to show that, as a Christian state, Florence could not ignore the call to a crusade of a truly determined pope such as Pius II; further examination of the sources has now verified this conclusion, showing moreover that Florentine support for Pius II's crusade was part of Florence's anti-Venetian diplomacy. Accolti was responsible as chancellor for Florentine crusading apologetics, and his history of the first crusade was his major contribution to Florentine diplomacy during Pius II's pontificate, attempting not only to prove Florence's sincere devotion to the Christian cause but also to prevent the pope from becoming the pawn of Florence's rival, Venice.

Accolti's support for the crusade was more than an official duty; a deeply religious man, he had a profound personal concern for the plight of Eastern Christianity. It is often overlooked that traditions of pilgrimage and crusade to the holy lands were long established in Tuscany and by no means moribund in the fifteenth century. Moreover, there was a circle of ardent crusading enthusiasts in Renaissance Florence, centring on Agnolo and Donato Acciaiuoli, with whom Accolti can be connected. Accolti's history was part of the vast humanist literature stimulated by the Turkish menace in the fourteenth, fifteenth and sixteenth centuries, and not all these writings were the products of sincere religious feelings or dedication to the crusading cause. Like his fellow humanists, Accolti was attempting

[1] 'La storia della prima crociata'.

to demonstrate his excellence in an established genre of apologetic literature, but that is not to deny his deep religious motivations as well.

It has been possible to reconstruct the detailed historical circumstances
in which Accolti's principal works originated. Evidence has been found to
suggest that his dialogue was written in competition with an old Aretine
enemy, Francesco Griffolini, who, Accolti hoped, could be prevented from
returning to Florence and becoming a protégé of the Medici. With his
dialogue he wanted to gain an entrée into Medicean circles for himself
instead, just as with his history he hoped to take advantage of Medicean
support for Pius II's crusade in early 1464. But these two works have an
importance in their own right and deserve to be recognized as outstanding
humanist compositions of the mid-fifteenth century. The dialogue is the
first extended work in Western literature expressly devoted to the quarrel
of the ancients and moderns, anticipating the development of this theme in
the seventeenth and eighteenth centuries. The dialogue also made a
notable contribution to religious thought in the early Renaissance: Accolti
is one of the earliest humanists to make an explicit connection between the
history of culture and the history of the church, a link which became
characteristic of Erasmian and Protestant thought in the sixteenth century;
moreover, Accolti was able to take an almost exclusively historical view of
the development of the church, unlike his medieval predecessors who
tended to study ecclesiology in terms not only of history but also of
prophecy, analogy and syllogistic logic. Accolti's history is significant not
only for highlighting the importance of the Turkish question, but also
because it reveals many of the preconceptions and attitudes which early
humanists took to the writing of history. A study of Accolti's historical
methods suggests that it is not appropriate to regard the early humanists as
critical historians; rather, their work was the culmination of the rhetorical
tradition of historiography established in antiquity and continued
throughout the Western middle ages. Accolti's most important contribution to the development of humanist historiography was as one of the
early representatives of Renaissance medievalism. Nothing could be
further from the truth than the often repeated generalization that the
Renaissance humanists repudiated their medieval past in favour of
antiquity. During the fifteenth century there was in some humanist circles
a growing 'revolt of the medievalists' which sought to establish the middle
ages as a period worthy of historical study. Along with Bruni, Biondo and
Donato Acciaiuoli, Accolti deserves credit as one of the founding fathers of
the Renaissance medieval revival which was to culminate in the work of
the greatest Italian Renaissance medievalist, Carlo Sigonio, and ultimately
led to Muratori himself.

In the view of his contemporary Vespasiano da Bisticci, Benedetto
Accolti deserved a biography. 'There would be many things about Messer

Benedetto worth recording for posterity', he wrote, 'which I shall leave to whoever wants to take the trouble to write his life.'[2] The present work is intended to fill this gap.

I should like to thank the British Academy, the University of Leeds, the University of London and the United States–United Kingdom Educational Commission for the financial support which they have provided at various stages in my research. I should also like to express my gratitude to the staff of the Archivio di Stato, Biblioteca Nazionale Centrale, Biblioteca Laurenziana and Biblioteca Riccardiana in Florence, of the Archivio di Stato, Archivio della Fraternità dei Laici, Archivio Capitolare and Biblioteca Comunale in Arezzo, and of the Warburg Institute in London for their assistance in my research. I am extremely grateful to Alison Brown, Rab Hatfield, Bill Kent, Dale Kent, Paul Oskar Kristeller, Anthony Molho and John Stephens for their help and for the many bibliographical and archival references which they have generously given me. I am particularly grateful to Frank Dabell, not only for references, but also for helping me to gain access to Italian publications in recent years when my time in Arezzo and Florence has been very limited. I have a special debt to Daniela De Rosa, who has shared with me some of the conclusions of her research on the Florentine chancery under Poggio before she had herself published her many important discoveries; without her great generosity my discussion of Accolti's election to the Florentine chancellorship and of his term as chancellor would have been entirely inadequate. I owe a great debt to my wife, Jane, for advice on many aspects of the Italian Renaissance, and most particularly for her knowledge of political thought, Roman law and the Italian jurists. My greatest debt, however, is to my teacher and friend, Nicolai Rubinstein, who introduced me to the complexities of research in Italian history and Renaissance studies, and whose erudition has solved countless particular problems and has been a constant source of inspiration to me over the past fifteen years; his example has always been a reminder of my own shortcomings, and although it may be presumptuous to associate my own work with such a scholar, nevertheless my sense of obligation is so great that I should like to dedicate this book to him.

*School of History, University of Leeds,*  R.D.B.
*March, 1984*

[2] Vespasiano, *Vite*, i, 598.

# Abbreviations

| | | |
|---|---|---|
| Cat. | Catasto | |
| Cento | Consiglio del Cento, registri | |
| CP | Consulte e Pratiche | |
| CSopp | Corporazioni religiose soppresse dall'Impero Francese | |
| DelSA | Deliberazioni, Signori e Collegi, Speciale autorità | |
| Dipl. | Diplomatico | |
| LC | Legazioni e commissarie. Elezioni ed istruzioni ad oratori | |
| LF | Libri Fabarum | |
| Mss | Manoscritti | |
| MAP | Mediceo avanti del Principato | |
| MRep | Miscellanea Repubblicana | |
| Miss. | Missive, Prima Cancelleria | |
| MissOr | Missive Originali | |
| Miss2ª | Missive, Seconda Cancelleria | |
| Not.A. | Notarile Antecosimiano | |
| Provv. | Provvisioni, registri | |
| Resp. | Responsive | |
| RVdO | Risposte Verbali d'Oratori | |
| BLF | Biblioteca Laurenziana, Florence | |
| BMF | Biblioteca Marucelliana, Florence | |
| BNF | Biblioteca Nazionale Centrale, Florence | |
| CPass | Carte Passerini | |
| CSopp | Conventi Soppressi | |
| Magl. | Magliabecchiano | |
| Palat. | Palatino | |
| Panc. | Panciatichi | |
| PG | Poligrafo Gargani | |
| BRF | Biblioteca Riccardiana, Florence | |
| Big. | Bigazzi | |

*Milan*

| | |
|---|---|
| ASM | Archivio di Stato, Milan |
| SPEFi | Sforzesco, Potenze estere, Firenze |
| BAM | Biblioteca Ambrosiana |

*Vatican City*

| | |
|---|---|
| BV | Biblioteca Apostolica Vaticana |
| Ott.Lat. | Ottoboniano Latino |
| Urb.Lat. | Urbinate Latino |
| Vat.Lat. | Vaticano Latino |

*Venice*

ASV                    Archivio di Stato, Venice

## Publications

| | |
|---|---|
| ASI | *Archivio storico italiano* |
| ASL | *Archivio storico lombardo* |
| AMAPet | *Atti e memorie dell'Accademia Petrarca di scienze, lettere ed arti in Arezzo* |
| BHumRen | *Bibliothèque d'humanisme et renaissance* |
| BollRCA | *Bolletino del Rotary Club di Arezzo* |
| BSenSP | *Bolletino senese di storia patria* |
| BIHR | *Bulletin of the Institute of Historical Research* |
| DBI | *Dizionario biografico degli italiani* |
| EHR | *English Historical Review* |
| GStLI | *Giornale storico della letteratura italiana* |
| IMU | *Italia medievale e umanistica* |
| ItS | *Italian Studies* |
| JHI | *Journal of the History of Ideas* |
| JWCI | *Journal of the Warburg and Courtauld Institutes* |
| NRivSt | *Nuova rivista storica* |
| PG | *Patrologie grecque* |
| PP | *Past and Present* |
| Rin. | *Rinascimento* |
| RIS | *Rerum italicarum scriptores* |
| RQ | *Renaissance Quarterly* |
| RSI | *Rivista storica italiana* |
| SR | *Studies in the Renaissance* |
| Galletti | Benedetto Accolti, *Dialogus de praestantia virorum sui aevi*, in *Philippi Villani liber de civitatis Florentiae famosis civibus*, ed. G. Galletti (Florence, 1848), 105–28. |
| Recueil | Benedetto Accolti, *De bello a christianis contra barbaros gesto*, in *Recueil des historiens des croisades. Historiens occidentaux*, v (Paris, 1895), 529–620. |

# Arezzo in the early Renaissance

## (i) Political and economic life

The history of Benedetto Accolti's native city, Arezzo,[1] followed a characteristic pattern for a Tuscan city-state at the end of the middle ages: rapid expansion was succeeded by internal disruption, leading to loss of independence and prolonged civic decline. The climax of the Aretine commune's growth had been reached during the thirteenth century and was followed by almost a century of factional conflict and foreign war, culminating in the surrender of Arezzo to Florence in 1384. Florentine rule brought an end to overt political turmoil, but it also coincided with an economic depression from which Arezzo did not begin to recover until at least the sixteenth century.

---

[1] The fundamental source for Aretine history before 1384 is Pasqui's *Documenti*; the prefaces to the first three volumes provide the best available narrative of Aretine history before Florentine rule. The most recent general history is M. Falciai, *Storia di Arezzo* (Arezzo, 1928). A guide to the families who composed the Aretine patriciate is Lazzeri, *Guglielmino Ubertini*, 241–305. The most important sources for and works dealing with Aretine political history before 1384 are, after Pasqui, Giovanni L. De Bonis, *Liber inferni Aretii*, ed. A. Bini and Bartolomeo di Gorello, *Cronica dei fatti d'Arezzo*, ed. A. Bini and G. Grazzini, in RIS², xv, 1; *Annales Aretinorum maiores et minores*, ed. *iidem*, RIS², xxiv, 1; A. Bini, 'Arezzo ai tempi di Dante', AMAPet, n.s. ii (1922), 1–57; G. Marri Camerani, *Statuto di Arezzo (1327)* (Florence, 1946); G. Fatini, 'L'ultimo secolo della repubblica aretina', BSenSP, xxxi (1924), 61–106; L. Romanelli, *La presa di Arezzo per Enguerrando VII sire di Coucy nel 1384* (Arezzo, 1887); P. Durrieu, 'La prise d'Arezzo par Enguerrand VII, Sire de Coucy', *Bibliothèque de l'École des chartes*, xli (1880), 161–94; D. Bini, 'Il conflitto secolare tra i communi di Arezzo e di Firenze fino all'assoggettamento del primo al secondo', AMAPet, xxx–xxxi (1941), 55–73; Lazzeri, *Aspetti*, 79–100. The principal article on Aretine political history in the fifteenth century is Pasqui, 'Una congiura'. There has been more interest in recent scholarship on Aretine economic, financial and social history in the fourteenth and fifteenth centuries, for which some works of importance are Benigni, 'Fonti'; Carbone, 'Note'; Varese, 'Condizioni'; Cherubini, 'Schede'; Dini, 'Lineamenti'; Lazzeri, *Aspetti*; A. Fanfani, 'Costi e profitti di un mercante del '300', NRivSt, xviii (1934), 412–22; F. Melis, 'Lazzaro Bracci', AMAPet, n.s. xxviii (1965–7), 1–18; *idem*, 'Uno sguardo al mercato dei panni di lana a Pisa nella seconda metà del Trecento', *Economia e storia*, vi (1959), 321–65; *idem*, 'L'economia delle città minori della Toscana', in *Le zecche minori toscane fino al xiv secolo. Atti del terzo convegno internazionale di studi* (Pistoia, 16–19 September 1967),

For most of the thirteenth century Arezzo had prospered and its commune had grown stronger, but Arezzo's rise brought the commune into conflict with neighbouring towns, especially Florence and Siena, and in 1289 Arezzo was decisively defeated by Florence at the battle of Campaldino. This humiliation was followed by more than twenty years of dissension among Arezzo's leading families. Two factions, called the Verdi and the Secchi, emerged and eventually the Secchi prevailed, installing their leader, Guido Tarlati, bishop of Arezzo, as despot in 1312. The *signoria* of Guido Tarlati temporarily restored Arezzo's prestige: he built a new circuit of walls which greatly enlarged the city, restored Arezzo's dominions in the countryside, introduced a new silver and copper currency and replenished the city's treasury. He reached the highpoint of his career when he crowned Louis of Bavaria as emperor in Milan in 1327, but he died a few months later, bequeathing the *signoria* to his brother, Pier Saccone. Arezzo's fortunes again waned under Pier Saccone, who was reduced to such desperation by the armies of Perugia and Florence and by plots among the Aretine patriciate that in 1337 he sold the city to Florence. This first period of Florentine dominion, however, was shortlived: in July 1343 internal dissension in Florence gave Aretines the opportunity to regain their freedom and restore an independent communal regime, which was now dominated by patrician Guelf families such as the Bostoli who had opposed the Ghibelline *signoria* of the Tarlati.

But the new Guelf commune did not bring stability to Arezzo. The city was now continuously under threat from the Tarlati and other exiled Ghibellines, and the regime was plagued by divisions among its leading members. The death-throes of the Aretine republic occupied the decade from 1375 to 1384, when, besides undergoing seven changes of regime and three rebellions, the city was sacked twice by the troops of mercenaries.[2] The end was finally reached in 1384 when the condottiere Enguerrand de Coucy put Arezzo up for sale. At first he approached the Sienese, but while they dithered he concluded a deal with the Florentines, who took possession in November 1384.

Florentine rule, now permanently established, brought greater tranquillity to political life in Arezzo than the Aretines had been able to achieve themselves. The Aretine commune had failed to control the feudal magnates both in the city itself and in the nearby countryside. Before 1384 the

13–40, esp. 34–6; Cherubini, *Signori*, 313–92; *Idem*, 'Inventario dei beni del "piccolo borghese" aretino Agnolo di Bartolo detto Panciola', *Signori*, 495–500; A. Molho, 'A note on Jewish moneylenders in Tuscany in the late Trecento and early Quattrocento', in *Renaissance Studies in Honor of Hans Baron*, ed. *idem* and J. A. Tedeschi (Florence, 1971), 99–117; Herlihy and Klapsich-Zuber, *Les toscans*; *idem*, 'Fiscalité et démographie en Toscane (1427–1430)', *Annales*, xxiv (1969), 1313–37.

[2]  Arezzo underwent a grave economic crisis as a result of this political and military upheaval: cf. Cherubini, *Signori*, 321ff.

Tarlati and the Ubertini had possessed strongholds in the countryside from which they could easily make sorties against the city; indeed, the Tarlati's fortified castle, Pietramala, which was only six miles from Arezzo, had provided Enguerrand de Coucy and his ally, Marco Tarlati, with a base for launching their assault on Arezzo in 1384. The feudal families had over-shadowed and finally eclipsed the commune: first Guglielmo Ubertini had been effective ruler of Arezzo until his death at Campaldino in 1289; then came the *signorie* of Guido and Pier Saccone Tarlati; in the end it was the attempt of Pier Saccone's son Marco to establish himself as despot with the help of Enguerrand de Coucy which precipitated the surrender of Arezzo to Florence in 1384. Florentine military resources far outstripped anything that the Aretine commune could have mustered, and so the Florentine regime had greater success against the feudal magnates of Arezzo. Some were forced to submit their possessions in the countryside to Florence[3] and dangerous fortresses near the city were razed.[4] Indeed, one suspects that the very high rate of taxation at which the feudal nobility were assessed after 1390 not only reflected their position as the region's dominant class[5] but was in part an attempt at discriminatory or even punitive action by Florence against a class which included many of its former enemies from the Tarlati, Ubertini and other Ghibelline families.[6] Florence pacified the magnates of Arezzo and its countryside not only by overt force and through financial discrimination but also by diplomacy: in return for Florentine protection and recognition of their feudal rights, the Ubertini of Chitignano in the Casentino became the perpetual allies of Florence in 1384, thus preserving a semi-independent lordship for themselves until the eighteenth century.[7]

The main threat to Florentine rule and to domestic tranquillity in Arezzo came from the wars with Milan and Naples in which Florence was embroiled for more than half a century after the end of Aretine indepen-dence in 1384. Members of the Tarlati family led the armies of Giangaleazzo Visconti, duke of Milan, to the walls of Arezzo in 1390, no doubt in the hope of regaining some kind of control over the city; this attempt, however, came to nothing, as did further schemes of Giangaleazzo's to foment revolt in Arezzo in 1400.[8] More serious was the civic unrest in Arezzo provoked by Florence's deteriorating relations with Ladislas of Naples in 1408 and 1409. A policy of exiling large numbers

---

[3] *Annales Aretinorum Maiores*, RIS², xxiv, 1, p. 97, n. 1.
[4] *Ibid.*, 108; Bruni, *Historiae*, 239. For more references to Florentine subjugation of Aretine magnates in 1384, cf. Cherbuini, *Signori*, 202, n. 2.
[5] Cherubini, 'Schede', 6.
[6] For a list of the Aretine nobles included in the *lira* of 1390, cf. *ibid.* 8–9. The nobles may not actually have paid these taxes: cf. Carbone, 'Note', 187–8.
[7] Cherubini, *Signori*, 202ff.
[8] Cf. Bruni, *Historiae*, 247–9; Brucker, *Civic World*, 172–3.

of potential rebels had been used to underpin Florentine rule in Pisa since 1407, and in 1408 a similar policy was suggested for Arezzo; it was rejected then as counterproductive, but the events of 1409 led the Florentines to change their minds.[9] As Ladislas prepared an invasion force against Florence at the beginning of the year, Florentine intelligence uncovered allegedly treasonable activities by a number of friars and at least one layman in Arezzo.[10] In May 1409 Ladislas appeared before the walls of Arezzo with his army but the major insurrection for which he had hoped failed to occur;[11] a plot to betray Arezzo to him was uncovered, resulting in the execution of one conspirator.[12] A more important result was that Florence now introduced the policy of mass exile used in Pisa, turning at least a hundred Aretines out of their homes.[13] Exile on this scale led to incidents of injustice, mistaken identity, rapine and fornication,[14] and growing hostility to Florentine rule provoked two large-scale conspiracies in Arezzo: the first in September 1409 was led by the Bostoli family, the second in December by the Albergotti.[15] Both plots failed and were followed by numerous executions;[16] Florence then continued the policy of exiling potential rebels until 1414 when, with Ladislas's death, the danger to Florentine rule in Arezzo once again receded. The bitterness which was the legacy of these years, however, lived on in the memories of Aretines and was at least in part responsible for another attempt to overthrow Florentine rule in Arezzo twenty years later in 1431. The power of the Bostoli and Albergotti had been curtailed as a result of the events of 1409, but a prominent Aretine from a feudal family, Conte Mariotto di Biagio Griffolini,

[9]  *Ibid.*, 214–16.
[10] ASF, Otto di Guardia, 10, fol. 53r (16 April 1409): scribatur capitaneo custodie civitatis Aretii quod dictum officium extitit informatum quod quidam civis civitatis Aretii nomine Cerretta conditionis mediocris qui habet tres filios ex quibus duorum nomina ignoramus sed ambo videtur quod sint ad servitia Regis Ladislai et tertius vocatur Bernardus qui a pluribus mensibus citra de quindecim diebus in quindecim dies praticavit venire ad civitatem Florentie et quod dictus Ceretta pluries usus fuit dicere verba que dicto officio generant maximam suspitionem. Proinde stet attentus circa praticam dicti Cerette . . . fol. 69r (18 May 1409): scribatur capitaneo custodie civitatis Aretii quod ad aures dicti officii de novo devenit quod in regulis fratrum que sunt in civitate Aretii sunt certi fratres de partibus regni seu subditi Regis Ladislai qui verbis satis inhonestis utuntur. Proinde sollicite inquirat de predictis et eos expellat de eius iurisdictione. fol. 72r (24 May 1409): scribatur capitaneo custodie civitatis Aretii comendando eum de gestis circa fratres religiosos forenses qui erant in civitate Aretii. I am grateful to Dr P. J. Jones for directing me to this volume. Cf. Brucker, *Civic World*, 215.
[11] Pasqui, 'Una congiura', 4, n. 1.        [12]  *Ibid.*
[13] Brucker, *Civic World*, 216; ASF, Otto di Guardia, 10, fol. 78v (10 June 1409): [they elect] ser Bartolomeum Bambi Ciay notarium florentinum in notarium et officialem ad consignandum Aretinos et Castilionenses relegatos in civitate[m] Florentie.
[14] Cf. *ibid.*, vol. 80r (14 June 1409).
[15] Pasqui, 'Una congiura', 4, n. 1; *Cronica di Iacopo Salviati*, in *Delizie*, xviii, 331ff. For suspicions of other members of the Bostoli and Albergotti families in the early summer of 1409, cf. ASF, Otto di Guardia, 10, fol. 80r, 82v, 83r.
[16] Pasqui, 'Una congiura', 4, n. 1.

who had been one of Arezzo's most eminent citizens and merchants in the 1420s, attempted in 1431 to betray the city to the forces of the duke of Milan led by the condottiere Niccolò Piccinino. Once again, however, the conspiracy failed and Griffolini and a number of his associates were apprehended and summarily executed.[17]

Despite these occasional incidents, political life in Arezzo in the early fifteenth century was usually tranquil, in marked contrast to the last years of self-government. The Florentines had been proud to number Arezzo among their possessions, and when the surrender was announced in November 1384, the entire city of Florence was reported to have taken to the streets, lighting bonfires and holding jousts for the whole day.[18] Aretines did not prove to be intractable subjects, and so Goro Dati, writing in the early fifteenth century, was probably speaking for most Florentines when he proudly called Arezzo a 'great acquisition' which was 'useful for the city of Florence'.[19] In his history of Florence, Dati provided an interesting description of Arezzo, particularly emphasizing its natural amenities:

The city of Arezzo is very old, and according to ancient chronicles it was a noble city even before the Romans came to Tuscany. It is situated near the river Arno, which rises in the Casentino over Pratovecchio in a mountain called Falterona; the river Tiber, which flows to Rome, also originates in this mountain. The city of Arezzo is forty miles from Florence, a distance which can be travelled in one day. Its site is strong and well-placed, descending from the hill on which the citadel is located and spreading below onto a plain furnished with many springs of running water. The nearby countryside is flat rather than hilly and possesses more fine land than anywhere else in that region. For there is an abundance of grain, oats and fine game. The town is well situated and has good air, and it begets men of keen intellect.[20]

Aretines may have acquiesced in Florentine rule in the knowledge that Florentine power would help to prevent the turbulent events of 1375 to 1384 from recurring; however, it is doubtful whether many Aretines rejoiced at their subjugation to Florence, especially since Florentine rule coincided with a severe economic recession in Arezzo. Arezzo, like the rest of Tuscany, had reached the height of its medieval prosperity in the thirteenth and early fourteenth centuries, when the area enclosed by its third set of walls suggests a population perhaps as high as 20,000.[21] The Black Death and the political and military crises of the fourteenth century

---

[17] *Ibid.* 3–19. Mariotto Griffolini's declared motives for conspiring against Florence were oppressive tax burdens and fear of renewed mass exile in Arezzo: cf. *ibid.*, 16. His taxes in fact more than doubled between 1423 and 1429: cf. ASA, Lira, 6, fol. 10v and 7, fol. 17r. For more details about Mariotto, his family and his conspiracy, cf. *infra*, pp. 186ff.

[18] Cf. *Diario d'anonimo fiorentino*, in *Documenti di storia italiana*, vi (Florence, 1876), 456.

[19] G. Dati, *Istoria di Firenze*, ed. L. Pratesi (Norcia, 1904), 36.

[20] *Ibid.*, 30.     [21] Herlihy and Klapisch, *Les toscans*, 180.

reduced the population by as much as two thirds, so that by 1390 the city's population was only about 7000.[22] Apart from in Pistoia, Florentine rule coincided with declining population in its larger subject cities,[23] and Arezzo was no exception, by 1427 its population having fallen to 4123.[24] In the first forty years of Florentine rule, thus, the population of Arezzo fell by perhaps a third, which amounted to a decline of just over 1% a year.[25] Although not as great as the catastrophic decline suffered by Pisa between 1406 and 1427, which was 2.34% a year,[26] the continued population decline in Arezzo could have had only the most serious effect on the economic life of the city. Indeed, the communal government of Arezzo was aware of the consequences for the Aretine economy of the depopulation of the city and countryside, and strenuous efforts were made to attract foreigners to settle in Arezzo. It became normal practice to offer prospective citizens five years exemption from all communal taxes,[27] and as a result a considerable number of new citizens were created from the end of the fourteenth century.[28] Evidently, however, these efforts by the Aretine government to offset the falling population did not meet with much success, at least until the second quarter of the fifteenth century when the decline was finally arrested and the population levelled off at about 4500.[29]

The clearest indication of economic depression in Arezzo is the decline in the average wealth of Aretine households during the fifteenth century. Whereas in 1423 the average wealth of a household was 455 florins, by 1443 it had fallen to 250 florins and by 1480 it reached a nadir of 200

---

[22]  In 1387 and 1390, there were respectively 1645 and 1776 households in Arezzo (Varese, 'Condizioni', 62–3), so that the approximate population was between 6500 and 7200.

[23]  Herlihy and Klapisch, *Les toscans*, 177–81.

[24]  *Ibid.*, 664. On *ibid.*, p. 180, the authors give the figure of 1183 hearths from the *catasto* of 1427; my own count, based on ASF, Cat. 273 (1429), gives 1191 hearths.

[25]  Herlihy and Klapisch, *Les toscans*, 180.          [26]  *Ibid.*

[27]  Cf. e.g. ASA, Provv. 1, fol. 12r (11 December 1385): . . . propter guerras et scandala hactenus orta et agitata in civitate et comitatu Aretii ipsa civitas et comitatus sunt civibus et incolis vacuati et volentes quantos possibile est forenses et aliengenos allicere et ipsam civitatem et comitatum habitatoribus instaurare . . . providerunt . . . quod quicumque forensis . . . veniet deinceps ad habitandum et standum cum sua familia in civitate vel comitatu Aretii intelligatur esse et sit exemptus liber . . . ab omnibus et singulis oneribus . . . comunis Aretii . . . infra quinque annos.

[28]  Cf. *ibid.* fol. 37v–38r, 39r–v, 42v, 57r–v, 60r, 73v.

[29]  Varese ('Condizioni', 62–3) gives the following numbers of households on the basis of which Aretine population can be estimated:

| Year | Households | Estimated population |
|------|-----------|---------------------|
| 1436 | 1336 | 5300 |
| 1443 | 1087 | 4300 |
| 1450 | 1110 | 4500 |
| 1458 | 1128 | 4500 |
| 1467 | 1217 | 4900 |
| 1480 | 1274 | 5100 |
| 1490 | 973 | 3900 |

florins.[30] As a result of this increasing poverty, the total wealth of the population declined from 529,000 florins in 1423 to 271,500 florins in 1443, reaching a nadir of 219,200 florins in 1490.[31] Indeed, this decline in wealth during the fifteenth century is all the more striking when it is contrasted with the population, which has been seen to have been more or less stable after 1427.[32] A further measure of the drastic decline of Arezzo as a city in the later middle ages is provided by the number of notaries at work there during the fourteenth and fifteenth centuries. Legal contracts, deeds of procuration, testaments and innumerable other acts regarding almost all aspects of economic and civic life were recorded by notaries, whose records of matriculation into the Aretine guild of lawyers and notaries have survived for this period. Whereas in 1346, just before the Black Death, there were about 150 notaries matriculated in the guild,[33] by 1364 there were about 50[34] as there were still in 1390,[35] but by 1447 their numbers had fallen to about 30,[36] evidence of the degree to which the whole of civic life in Arezzo had wound down by the fifteenth century.

One symptom of Arezzo's worsening condition in the early Renaissance was the malaise of the city's commerce and industry. Arezzo did manage to beget one important international merchant, but Lazzaro Bracci's meteoric rise at the turn of the fifteenth century testifies more to his special entrepreneurial talents than to the buoyancy of Aretine commerce and industry,[37] which had never made the city into a major mercantile centre in the later middle ages. Evidence of this comes not only from the study of a merchant such as Simo d'Ubertino[38] but also from the relatively small contribution made by Arezzo's leading merchants and industrialists to Aretine direct taxation in 1390.[39] In the early 1420s, the largest foreign venture was mounted by Mariotto Griffolini, involving trade with Budapest in Hungary;[40] after this collapsed in the mid-1420s with losses in the region of 5000 florins,[41] Aretines seem to have been less active abroad. In 1427 the only two Aretines with substantial business interests outside Florentine territory were Griffolini, who had ventures in Ancona and Rome,[42] and Paolino di Messer Niccolò, who was involved in commerce at Avignon and Rome.[43] By 1427 business consisted mainly of local shops and trades; even Francesco di Baccio Bacci, the richest man resident in

[30] *Ibid.*, 50, 62–3.   [31] *Ibid.*, 50.   [32] Cf. p. 6, n. 29, *supra*.
[33] ASA, Dott. Not. fol. 32r–33v   [34] *Ibid.*, fol. 34r–37r.
[35] Cherubini, 'Schede', 13.   [36] ASA, Dott. Not. fol. 34v, 35v, 36r–v.
[37] Cf. Lazzeri, *Aspetti*, 101–25; Melis, 'Lazzaro Bracci', AMAPet, n.s. xxxviii (1965–7), 1–18; Fanfani, 'Costi', NRivSt, xviii (1934), 412ff.
[38] Cherubini, *Signori*, 325.   [39] *Idem*, 'Schede', 6–8.
[40] ASF, Cat. 201, fol. 334 bis r, 426r.   [41] *Ibid.*, fol. 334 bis r, 426 r.
[42] *Ibid.*, fol. 334r, 334 bis r, 426r.   [43] *Ibid.*, 202, fol. 153r–v.

Arezzo, was merely a successful shopkeeper,[44] and of the thirty-five
Aretine households with wealth greater than 1000 florins in 1427–9,[45]
twenty-four were retailers and manufacturers operating one or more local
businesses, which included thirteen woollen cloth shops,[46] four apothecary shops,[47] three leather shops,[48] three silk shops,[49] four general mer-

[44] *Ibid.*, 203, fol. 359r, 372r. On the Bacci, cf. M. Salmi, 'I Bacci di Arezzo nel sec. xv e la loro cappella nella chiesa di San Francesco', *Rivista d'arte*, ix (1916), 224–37; Ginzburg, *Indagini*; G. Goretti Miniati, 'Alcuni ricordi della famiglia Bacci', AMAPet, n.s. viii–ix (1930), 92–103; Lazzeri, *Ubertini*, 273–4.

[45] These were, according to ASF, Cat. 273 (Sommario della città di Arezzo): Gregorio Marsuppini, capital (*valsente*) of 13,049 florins; Francesco di Baccio Bacci, 10,147 fl.; Michele di Conte Marsuppini, 5758 fl.; Tuccerello di Cecco, 5592 fl.; Mariotto di Biagio Griffolini, 4823 fl.; Lippo di ser Niccolò Lippi, 3561 fl.; Jacopo di Tome, 2723 fl.; heirs of Agnolo di Biagio da Pantaneto, 2532 fl.; heirs of Vanni di ser Niccolò, 2489 fl.; Antonio di Donato da Pantaneto, 2082 fl.; Paolino di Messer Niccolò, 2007 fl.; Francesco di Ghirigoro di Giovanni, 1920 fl.; Monna Mattea di Simone di Ghino, 1705 fl.; Michele di Santi Accolti, 1584 fl.; Agnolo di Bartolomeo, 1524 fl.; Urbano di Guido, 1389 fl.; Nanni and ser Paolo di ser Bartolomeo, 1388 fl.; Nanni and Bartolomeo di Matteo, 1353 fl.; Guaspare di Maestro Ciechino, 1338 fl.; Andremo di Landuccio Albergotti, 1329 fl.; Giovanni di Nicola Sinigardi, 1316 fl.; Nanni di Jacopo, 1275 fl.; Giuliano di Agnolo di Maggio, 1263 fl.; Buono di Giovanni, 1236 fl.; Mattea di fu Carcastione di Duccio, 1236 fl.; Damiano di Giovanni Marzi, 1173 fl.; Cristofano del Tortello, 1154 fl.; Pippo di Piero di Dottino de' Gozzari, 1146 fl.; Antonio di ser Giovanni, 1136 fl.; Agnolo di Giovanni, 1125 fl.; Mariotto di Bettino, 1123 fl.; Francesco di Messer Giovanni di ser Baldo, 1091 fl.; Piero di Giovanni di ser Agnolo, 1090 fl.; heirs of Mariotto di Nanni, 1054 fl.; Jacopo di Niccoletto Albergotti, 1015 fl.; Giovanni di ser Antonio, 1016 fl.

[46] Owned by: Chiaromanno di Gregorio Marsuppini, in partnership with Mariotto di Biagio Griffolini (*ibid.*, 201, fol. 334r); Tuccerello di Cecco (*ibid.*, 202, fol. 630r, 631r); heirs of Agnolo di Biagio da Pantaneto (*ibid.*, fol. 406v); Francesco di Ghirigoro di Giovanni (*ibid.*, 203, fol. 199v); sons of Agnolo di Bartolomeo (*ibid.*, 200, fol. 195v); Urbano di Guido in partnership with heirs of Simo di Panco (*ibid.*, 202, fol. 567r, 569r, 578v); Nanni and Bartolomeo di Matteo (*ibid.*, 201, fol. 1138r); Guaspare di Maestro Ciechino (*ibid.*, 203, fol. 821r); sons of Nanni di Jacopo (*ibid.*, 201, fol. 1015r); Damiano di Giovanni Marzi (*ibid.*, 203, fol. 164r); Mariotto di Bettino (*ibid.*, 201, fol. 527v–529v); Piero di Giovanni di ser Agnolo (*ibid.*, 202, fol. 182v); heirs of Mariotto di Nanni in partnership with Giovanni di Antonio di Pace (*ibid.*, 203, fol. 209r).

[47] Owned by Francesco di Baccio Bacci (*ibid.*, fol. 359r, 372r); Mariotto di Biagio Griffolini (*ibid.*, 201, fol. 333r, 334r bis, 426r–v); Guaspare di Maestro Ciechino in partnership with Donato di Piero (*ibid.*, 203, fol. 823r); Giuliano di Agnolo di Maggio (*ibid.*, 688r bis).

[48] Owned by Agnolo di Bartolomeo (*ibid.*, 200, fol. 194r, 195v); Mariotto di Bettino (*ibid.*, 201, fol. 527v–529v); Giovanni di ser Antonio in partnership with Agnolo di Nanni (*ibid.* 203, fol. 665r).

[49] Owned by Buono di Giovanni, in partnership with Cusume di Nanni di Jacopo (*ibid.*, 200, fol. 722r, 726r; 201, fol. 1015r); Agnolo di Giovanni (*ibid.*, 200, fol. 324r, 329r); Nanni and ser Paolo di ser Bartolomeo with Agnolo di Gionta (*ibid.*, 201, fol. 985v).

chandise shops,[50] two banks,[51] one butcher's shop,[52] one haberdasher's shop,[53] and one metal shop.[54]

Many Aretines were slow to adjust to the more limited and different opportunities available in commerce and industry in the fifteenth century, and the continued prominence of the wool industry in this period points to a conservatism among Arezzo's business community which looked back to better days when the manufacture of woollen cloth had been the mainstay of their prosperity.[55] Indeed, the kind of mercantile ethos which developed at the height of Arezzo's medieval economic growth had not waned by the fifteenth century. Not to mention the large majority of rich Aretines who were by vocation businessmen, an interest in commerce was also shown by professional men, such as the notary ser Paolo di ser Bartolomeo, who, besides investing in two separate companies, arranged for his nephew to work in a shop in Pesaro;[56] another example is the lawyer Gregorio Marsuppini, who, besides his investments in the Medici bank in Florence, had business dealings with other leading Florentine families such as the Strozzi, Serristori, della Luna, Peruzzi, Baroncelli, Parenti and Capponi.[57] Even a nobleman such as Conte Mariotto Griffolini was involved in four separate business ventures.[58] A few richer Aretines were not involved in business, but there were often circumstances to discourage or prevent commercial activity: Antonio di Donato da Pantaneto, who had capital of 2082 florins in 1429, was an eight-year-old orphan,[59] whereas Mattea di Simo di Ghino[60] and Mattea fu di Carcastione di Duccio,[61] with capital of 1706 and 1236 florins respectively in 1429, were widows of over seventy. One Aretine, evidently too old himself for business, certainly wished that his dependants would show more enterprise:

I have reached the decrepit age of eighty-six or thereabouts, wrote Giovanni di Nicola Sinigardi in 1427, and am almost always ill, and with good reason, and am afflicted and able to do nothing. I have five children by the grace of God and Our Lady. I have one daughter who is a young widow; and at home with me I have two more married daughters whose husbands have little inclination for earning; and

---

[50] Owned by Francesco di Baccio Bacci (*ibid.*, 203, fol. 359r, 372r, 398r); Michele di Conte Marsuppini (*ibid.*, 201, fol. 550r); Lippo di ser Niccolò (*ibid.*, 201, fol. 285r); Francesco di Ghirigoro di Giovanni (*ibid.*, 203, fol. 197r bis).
[51] Owned by Mariotto di Biagio Griffolini in partnership with Pippo di Piero di Dottino de' Gozzari (*ibid.*, 202, fol. 122r, 123r); Jacopo di Tome (*ibid.*, 201, fol. 988r).
[52] Owned by Nanni and Bartolomeo di Matteo (*ibid.*, fol. 1135r).
[53] Owned by Giovanni di ser Antonio (*ibid.*, 203, fol. 665r).
[54] Owned by Nanni di Jacopo (*ibid.*, 201, fol. 1008r).
[55] Cf. Lazzeri, *Aspetti*, 108–12; R. Davidsohn, *Geschichte von Florenz. Anmerkungen und Exkurse zum zweiten Teil* (Berlin, 1896–1927), 11; Herlihy and Klapisch, *Les toscans*, 295, 297, 299; Dini, 'Lineamenti', 3–22.
[56] ASF, Cat. 201, fol. 985v, 986r, 988r.       [57] *Ibid.*, 203, fol. 644v–647v.
[58] *Ibid.*, 201, fol. 328r–334 bis r, 424r–427r; 202, fol. 122r, 123.
[59] *Ibid.*, 200, fol. 17r.       [60] *Ibid.*, 201, fol. 776v.       [61] *Ibid.*, fol. 496r.

the other two are sons who stand about doing nothing useful for themselves or for the family.[62]

Deep-rooted traditions, however, were unable to save Arezzo's wool industry from near collapse by the end of the fifteenth century,[63] and mercantile conservatism did not prevent, and indeed probably exacerbated, the general depression in Aretine business which intensified in the course of the fifteenth century. In 1427 liquid capital in Arezzo amounted to 96,406 florins, comprising 33.5% of the total wealth of the city.[64] By 1490, on the other hand, the total liquid capital of Arezzo was only 38,488 florins, and comprised merely 17.6% of the total wealth.[65] Evidently there was a flight to the land taking place in Arezzo during the fifteenth century.

Arezzo had always been the centre of an important agricultural region in Tuscany. Indeed, the district surrounding Arezzo was the most predominantly agricultural region under Florentine rule in 1427. This is clear in the first place from the distribution of population in Aretine territory compared with elsewhere in Tuscany. In the Aretine district there were 4.7 rural dwellers for every city dweller, whereas the ratio for the Florentine countryside was 3.4 to 1, for the Pisan countryside 2.47 to 1, for the Pistoian countryside 2.65 to 1, for the Volterran countryside 1.16 to 1 and for the Cortonan countryside 1.42 to 1.[66] The predominance of agriculture is also clear from the distribution of wealth in Arezzo and its countryside compared with the rest of Tuscany. The city of Arezzo accounted for only 48.5% of the total wealth of the Aretine district, whereas the city of Florence accounted for 84.7% of the total wealth of its region, the city of Cortona for 71.9% of its regional wealth, the city of Pistoia for 60%, the city of Pisa for 77.2% and the city of Volterra for 73.1%.[67] Indeed, it is hardly surprising therefore that Goro Dati singled out Arezzo's wealth as an agricultural centre in his description, making a particular point of the rich, well-irrigated land surrounding the city.[68]

A striking feature revealed by the recent comprehensive study of the Florentine *catasto* of 1427 is the enormous contrast in wealth between

---

62   *Ibid.*, 203, fol. 664r: Esso Giovanni è divenuto in età decrepita, cioè d'anni 86 o circa, e quasi sempre infermo casgionevole e doglioso e in niente poderoso di sua persona con cinque figliuoli a piacer di dio e della Nostra Signoria. Fra' quali è una femina, vedova e giovane. Et 'a in casa con secho due nore fanciulle, e loro mariti sono con pocho aviamento o industria d'alcun guadangno. E gli altri due suo' figliuoli attendono a darsi tempo sanza fare alcuna utilità né per loro né per la casa.

63   Dini, 'Lineamenti', 15–20.      64   Herlihy and Klapisch, *Les toscans*, 664.

65   Varese, 'Condizioni', 51–3.      66   Herlihy and Klapisch, *Les toscans*, 231.

67   *Ibid.*, 664.

68   Cf. p. 5, *supra*. On the economy of the Aretine countryside, cf. also G. Cherubini, 'Aspetti della proprietà fondiaria nell'aretino durante il xii secolo', ASI, cxxi (1963), 3–40; *idem, Una comunità dell'Appennino dal xii al xv secolo* (Florence, 1972); *idem, Signori*, esp. chs. ii, iv, vi, xiii; *idem*, 'Le campagne aretine alla fine del medioevo', BollRCA, 836 (17 February 1975), reprinted in *Contributi*.

Florence and the rest of its subject towns and territories. Florentines comprised only 14.1% of the population of Tuscany, yet they possessed 51.2%
of the total landed wealth, 78% of the total liquid capital and 67.4% of the
total wealth.[69] Like the rest of Florentine subject territories in the fifteenth
century, Arezzo was a depressed area in comparison with Florence.
Aretines were far poorer, only thirty-five Aretines in 1429 having capital
of 1000 florins or more.[70] This was in contrast to more than eight hundred
Florentines, who constituted 8.3% of taxpayers in Florence,[71] whereas the
thirty-five Aretines comprised 2.8% of taxpayers in Arezzo.[72] Depression
in contrast to Florence is also suggested by Aretine shop rents, which
usually did not exceed nine florins a year,[73] whereas in Florence equivalent
shops were often let for thirty-five florins.[74] Dowries too in Arezzo were
much smaller than in Florence, where among rich citizens they usually
exceeded 1000 florins in the fifteenth century.[75] In contrast, most rich
Aretines expected to provide about 300 florins for their daughters, a figure
which had apparently remained about the same since the mid-fourteenth
century.[76] Piero di Giovanni di ser Agnolo, who had capital of 1090
florins, had to repay a dowry of 240 florins.[77] The silk merchant, Buono
di Giovanni, who had capital of 1236 florins in 1429, wrote, 'I shall soon
be obliged to marry my grown daughter; she will cost me, to provide a
dowry and pay the wedding expenses, about 400 florins.'[78] Buono later
declared that her dowry had in fact been 300 florins, leaving 100 florins,
which was a usual figure, for wedding expenses.[79] Only the richest Aretine,
Gregorio Marsuppini, is known to have received the substantially larger
sum of 600 florins as dowry for his Genoese wife.[80]

Certainly during the fifteenth century the Florentine government did

[69] Herlihy and Klapisch, *Les toscans*, 243.    [70] Cf. p. 8, *supra*.
[71] Cf. Martines, *Social World*, 35, who says that this represented 8.3% of Florentines. The
*valsenti* cited by Martines include all deductions including those for members of the
family and cannot be compared precisely with the *valsenti* of Aretines (cf. p. 12,
*infra*). If the *valsenti* of Aretines had included all deductions, there would have been a
greater contrast between Arezzo and Florence.
[72] In Florence, the richest 2.8% had *valsenti* of nearly 4000 florins or more: cf. Martines,
*Social World*, 365–78.
[73] Cf. ASF, Cat. 200, fol. 18r; *ibid.*, 201, fol. 351r, 529v, 555r, 769r, 1010r, 1135r; *ibid.*,
202, fol. 408v; *ibid.*, 203, fol. 352r, 359r, 665r, 697v.
[74] Cf. G. Brucker, *Renaissance Florence* (New York, 1969), 24, 282.
[75] Cf. *idem*, 'The Medici in the fourteenth century', *Speculum*, xxxii (1957), 11; Martines,
*Social World*, 37–8; Herlihy and Klapisch, *Les toscans*, 414–15.
[76] Cf. Cherubini, *Signori*, 317.    [77] ASF, Cat. 202, fol. 176r.
[78] *Ibid.*, 200, fol. 732r: E più 'o d'incharicho la mia fanciulla grande da marito del tempo
. . . la quale mi chostarà in darli la dota et mandarla a marito circha a fiorini 400 d'oro.
[79] *Ibid.*, fol. 738v. For Aretine wedding expenses, cf. *ibid.*, 203, fol. 383r: A Maestro
Lionardo di Messer Giovanni Roselli 'o [i.e. Francesco Bacci] promessi per dota di la mia
figliola di fiorini cinquecento . . . E per spese mi bisogna per lei per fornimenti et spese
fiorini 100.
[80] *Ibid.*, fol. 647v.

little to mitigate this inequality in the distribution of wealth throughout their dominions. In fact, the system of taxation which Florence developed during the fifteenth century could only have worked to exacerbate the contrast between Florence and its subject town of Arezzo. In Florence direct taxation was based on the *catasto*, which was a means of establishing liability to forced loans (*prestanze*). The head of each household in Florence had to submit a *portata* (tax return) declaring all his capital assets and liabilities, which were then subtracted from assets and, after allowing for dependants and the value of the family house, the resulting sum, known as the *valsente*, was then subject to a forced loan of 0.35%.[81] In Arezzo a different system was used. Aretines were required to submit a *portata* of all their capital assets and liabilities, which were then subtracted from assets and the remainder, or *valsente*, was the basis for determining tax. After 1427 Aretines like Florentines were allowed to subtract the value of their house from their assets, but unlike Florentines they were never allowed to deduct an allowance for dependants. In Arezzo, moreover, the procedure for determining tax on the basis of the *valsente* was more severe than the system used in Florence. Before 1490 only 80% of an Aretine's *valsente* was subject to tax; after 1490, it was 75%. Before 1427 the rate of taxation was one florin for every 540 florins of this portion of the *valsente*; after 1427, it was one florin for every 600 florins. This amounted to 1.54%, then 1.33% of an Aretine's *valsente* that he had to pay in taxes.[82] Aretines therefore were more heavily taxed than Florentines in three ways: (1) theirs was an actual tax, not a forced loan as in Florence, eventually to be refunded at interest; (2) they were not permitted to make deductions for dependants; (3) their rate was higher: 1.54%, then 1.33% in contrast to 0.35%. Aretines had to pay a heavy price for the political stability that they gained under Florentine rule.

### (ii) Educational and intellectual traditions

One feature of Arezzo particularly stressed by Goro Dati was its lively intellectual life. Surprising though it may seem that a city of between four and five thousand in the midst of a great economic depression should have produced citizens of outstanding scholarly attainments, nevertheless it is a fact that Arezzo was one of the great cradles of learning during the Renais-

[81] On the Florentine *catasto*, cf. Herlihy and Klapisch, *Les toscans*, 48ff.
[82] On Aretine taxation in the fifteenth century, cf. Benigni, 'Fonti'; Carbone, 'Note'; and Varese, 'Condizioni', 39–49. For a system of taxation similar to the one used in Arezzo, cf. E. Fiumi, *Storia economica e sociale di San Gimignano* (Florence, 1961), 1976. For further examples of heavier taxation in the Florentine dominions than in Florence itself, cf. A. Molho, *Florentine Public Finances in the Early Renaissance* (Cambridge, Mass. 1971), 28ff.

sance. This intellectual eminence embraced not only classical studies, poetry and literature but also extended to professions such as medicine and especially law. Indeed, the University of Florence, where the usual subjects of the medieval curriculum such as law, medicine and theology were taught, employed more teaching staff of Aretine origins than from any other Italian city.[83] Despite the prominence of Aretines in law and medicine, fifteenth-century Arezzo is most noteworthy as the home of many of the outstanding figures of the early Renaissance. The central personality, indeed, of early fifteenth-century Florentine humanism, Leonardo Bruni, was an Aretine; although Bruni emigrated to Florence and became a Florentine citizen, he had nevertheless received his education in Arezzo, and he continued to have close ties with his native city, where he owned two houses and at least one large estate.[84] Another important figure in the early Renaissance was Poggio Bracciolini, who received his education from the age of eight in Arezzo.[85] Both Bruni and Poggio were Florentine chancellors, and another chancellor of Aretine birth was Carlo Marsuppini, who, as professor of poetry and rhetoric in the Florentine university for many years, had a formative influence on many subsequently distinguished Florentine humanists, including Alamanno Rinuccini, Matteo Palmieri, Donato Acciaiuoli, Cristoforo Landino and Bartolomeo Scala.[86]

Bruni and Marsuppini were key figures in the fifteenth-century Greek revival, as was another Aretine, Giovanni Tortelli, who combined proficiency as a humanist with professional training in philosophy and theology. Tortelli travelled together with two fellow Aretines in 1435 to Constantinople, where he remained for two years studying Greek. After his return to Italy, he translated the life of St Athanasius into Latin and undertook the first humanist translation of Aristotle's *Posterior Analytics*; he was an intimate friend of many leading humanists of his day, including Bruni, Marsuppini and Valla, who dedicated to him the famous *Elegantiae*, and his own major work was an enormous treatise in twenty-four books, *De orthographia*, which was as much an historical, topographical and philosophical study of Latin vocabulary, diction and usage. As a philologist, Tortelli was second only to his friend Valla in the early Renaissance, but as a librarian he was in a class of his own. Entrusted by Pope Nicholas V with the enormous task of organizing the papal library, Tortelli personally made the first catalogue, consisting of more than nine thousand entries; as the first Vatican librarian, Tortelli had considerable

[83] Cf. B. Barbadoro, 'Gli umanisti aretini', *Annali della cattedra petrarchesa*, viii (1938), 127ff.

[84] Cf. Martines, *Social World*, 117–23.

[85] Cf. Walser, *Poggius*, 7, 327.     [86] On Marsuppini, cf. *ad indicem*.

command of papal patronage, commissioning on behalf of the pope translations from Greek, copies of Latin classics and original humanist works.[87]

Another important Aretine humanist of the mid-fifteenth century was Francesco Griffolini, son of the executed nobleman and international merchant, Mariotto di Biagio Griffolini. Francesco Griffolini made a distinguished contribution to the Greek revival during the fifteenth century. Working mainly as a translator of the Greek classics, he made Latin versions of more than a hundred and twenty of Chrysostom's homilies, the *Heroicus* of Philostratus, Lucian's oration on calumny, and, most important, the last eight books of the *Iliad* and the entire *Odyssey*, thus completing the enterprise which had been left incomplete by Valla's death in 1457 and providing the first humanist translation of the Homeric epics. Griffolini achieved greatest renown however for his translations of two spurious works, the letters of Diogenes the Cynic and the letters of the pseudo-Phalaris, the latter of which especially was widely circulated and read during the Renaissance. Griffolini spent his entire adult life in exile from his native city of Arezzo; nevertheless there is evidence that he owed his passionate love of the classics to the Aretine tradition of humanist scholarship.[88]

Many Aretine humanists were intimate friends, and contact among them was maintained above all through the efforts of the humanist scholar and Benedictine monk, Girolamo Aliotti. Unlike his more illustrious contemporaries, Aliotti remained in Arezzo for most of his life, but he was an indefatigable correspondent, keeping in touch with Aretine friends who through his efforts were not allowed to drift apart. His own major contribution to the *studia humanitatis* was his Latin correspondence, which he collected in ten books in 1472, adding two more books in 1473. Besides this, he was the author of a number of Latin orations as well as a dialogue on the virtues of the monastic vocation, a treatise on monastic education and a tract on the future of the church.[89]

The strength of the humanist tradition in fifteenth-century Arezzo is admirably illustrated by the interests of the famous teacher of Marsilio Ficino, Niccolò Tignosi. Although a native of Foligno, Tignosi emigrated in the 1430s to Arezzo where, having taken a wife from the Aretine patriciate and established a medical practice, he soon became a citizen and played a part in Aretine public life in the mid-fifteenth century. By profession a physician and by education an Aristotelian natural philosopher,

[87] On Tortelli, cf. Mancini, 'Tortelli'; the studies by O. Besomi, M. Regoliosi, M. Rinaldi and M. Cortesi, IMU, ix (1966), 75–121, 123–89; xii (1969), 129–96; xiii (1970), 95–137; xvi (1973), 227–61; xxii (1979), 449–83; R. P. Oliver, 'Giovanni Tortelli', in *Studies presented to David Moore Robinson*, ii (St Louis, 1953), 1257–71; Ginzburg, *Indagini*, 18ff.
[88] On Griffolini, cf. pp. 185ff, *infra*.      [89] On Aliotti, cf. his *Epistolae*.

nevertheless Tignosi was remarkable among early fifteenth-century scholastics for his interest in and extensive knowledge of the humanities. Not only did he choose for commentary humanist translations of Aristotle's *Posterior Analytics*, *Nicomachaean Ethics* and *De anima*, but in his commentaries he made frequent citations of classical Latin historians and poets as well as of contemporary historical events. He showed a humanist's awareness of the revival of culture in his own age, particularly in the fields of painting, sculpture and eloquence, and he composed four purely humanist works: a panegyric of Cosimo de' Medici, a lamentation of the fall of Constantinople, an account of the origins of his native city of Foligno and an exhortation, based on precedents from ancient and modern history, against declaring war with too much haste. Tignosi had contacts with many of the leading figures of Italian humanism and especially notable was his close friendship with many of the renowned humanists from his adopted city of Arezzo, where he must have acquired much of his passion for the humanities.[90]

Goro Dati was not alone in recognizing the preeminence of Arezzo as a cradle of learning in the fifteenth century. An Aretine vernacular poet of the mid-fifteenth century, Stefano Gambino, wrote a long vernacular poem celebrating the distinguished intellects of Arezzo, including Bruni, Marsuppini, Tortelli, Griffolini and Benedetto and Francesco Accolti.[91] In his funeral oration for Leonardo Bruni, Poggio Bracciolini declared,

All learned men owe the greatest debt to that city [of Arezzo], which seems to be the home of the muses in our times; indeed, they have cultivated and enhanced the study of the humanities and of wisdom.[92]

Goro Dati attributed this intellectual distinction to Arezzo's particularly fine air, but perhaps a more important factor was the attitude of the

---

[90] On Tignosi, cf. Sensi, 'N. T. da Foligno', who publishes critical editions of five shorter works, *Expugnatio Constantinopolitana*, *Quod tarde bella suscipienda sint*, *De laudibus Cosmi*, *In illos qui mea in Aristotelis comentaria criminantur* and *De origine fulginatum*, 423–95; A. Rotondò, 'Niccolò Tignosi da Foligno', Rin. viii (1958), 217–55; E. Berti, 'La dottrina platonica delle idee nel pensiero di Niccolò Tignosi da Foligno', in *Filosofia e cultura in Umbria tra medioevo e rinascimento. Atti del quarto convegno di studi umbri* (Gubbio, 1966), 533–65; Thorndike, *Science and Thought*. Neither Sensi nor Rotondò has investigated Tignosi's activities as an Aretine citizen, and I hope to publish documents regarding him which I have found in Arezzo.

[91] *Versi di Gambino d'Arezzo con un carme di Tommaso Marzi*, ed. O. Gamurrini (Bologna, 1878), 32–6, 68–70. On Gambino's life, cf. the introduction by Gamurrini, *ibid.*, x–xx; on his works, *ibid.*, xx–xxviii, and G. Fatini, 'Il culto di Dante in Arezzo', AMAPet, n.s. ii (1922), 200–8. He was described by Aliotti as 'historiarum, et antiquitatis indagator curiosus' in his *Epistolae*, i, 526. Besides the ms. of his verses published by Gamurrini, there is another in the Bodleian Library, Canonici, Italici, 52. There is an unpublished letter by Aliotti about Gambino in BLF, 90 superiore, 346, fol. 133v–134r.

[92] Bruni, *Epistolae*, ed. Mehus, i, p. cxix.

Aretine patriciate, who encouraged scholarship and classical learning. Notable were the remarks included in his tax return of 1427 by Gregorio Marsuppini about the activities of his learned son Carlo, who, he wrote, 'at the age of twenty-nine years is a student of poetry, philosophy and other learned disciplines, as well as of Greek and Latin. This afore-mentioned scholarship is for honour, not for earning.'[93] Not dissimilar was the attitude of Mariotto Griffolini, who acted as a patron of learning in Arezzo in the 1420s, when he gave financial support and encouragement to the young and impoverished Girolamo Aliotti, who was thereby enabled to continue his humanist studies.[94]

Throughout the early Renaissance the sympathy of the Aretine patriciate for scholarship and classical learning was translated into direct action by the commune, which went to considerable trouble and expense in running a civic grammar school and engaging a master to teach the Latin language and the classics to the youth of Arezzo.[95] In 1387, shortly after the loss of Aretine independence in 1384, the commune granted a local Latin teacher, Bernardo di Miglio, a tax exemption in order to keep him in Arezzo,[96] and the next year they set about finding a public grammar teacher by establishing a commission of citizens, which attempted to encourage the noted Aretine classical scholar and friend of Salutati's and Petrarch's, Domenico di Bandino;[97] they were unable to draw him away from Florence, but they managed to elect a younger Aretine, Francesco di Feo di Nigi (b. 1355).[98] This was to prove a particularly felicitous appointment, and Francesco di Feo was to serve as public Latin and classics teacher in Arezzo for twenty-nine years, from 1389 to 1399, 1403 to 1413 and 1419 to 1428.[99] Francesco must have been a particularly inspired teacher, and besides his being the probable Latin master of Leonardo Bruni, his terms

---

[93] ASF, Cat. 203, fol. 647v: Carlo è d'età de' anni xxviii. Studia in poesia, philosophia et altre scientie et in greco et latino, le quali scientie sopradecte sono d'onore et non di guadagnio.

[94] Aliotti, *Epistolae*, i, 191–2.

[95] I am preparing a study of grammar school education in Arezzo in the Renaissance. The following is a list of those teachers employed by the commune in the late fourteenth and early fifteenth centuries: Francesco di Feo di Nigi (1389–99), Domenico di Bandino (1399–1402), Francesco di Feo (1403–13), Domenico di Bandino (1414–15), Niccolò di Duccio d'Arezzo (1415–16), Giovanni di Ercole da Montepulciano (1416–18), Francesco di Feo (1419–28), Antonio di Simone di Niccolò d'Arezzo (1428–30), Marco di Giovanni di Simo d'Arezzo (1432–4), Antonio di Salimbene da San Severino (1435–8) Guillaume de Jean de Bourges (1440–7), Giovanni di Antonio Tami d'Arezzo (1449–54).

[96] ASA, Provv. 1, fol. 107v, 109r–v. Cf. H. Baron, 'The year of Leonardo Bruni's birth', *Speculum*, lii (1977), 611.

[97] ASA, Provv. 2, vol. 16r–v, 18r–v. On Domenico, cf. p. 19, *infra*.

[98] ASA, Provv. 2, fol. 28v, 29r, 34v–35r, 46r.

[99] *Ibid.*, fol. 62r–v, 64v, 65v, 139v, 156r–157r; *ibid.*, 3, fol. 46v–47r, 107v–108r, 120v–121r, 149r–150v; *ibid.*, 4, fol. 4r; *ibid.*, 5, fol. 4v–5r, 7v, 34r, 253v–54r, 256v; *ibid.*, 6, fol. 44v, 56r.

of appointment also coincide with the formative years of most of the great Aretine humanists of the early Renaissance – Poggio, Marsuppini, Tortelli, Aliotti, the Accolti brothers – and he probably also supervised the very early education of Francesco Griffolini. Domenico di Bandino also served the commune from 1399 to 1401 and 1414 to 1415,[100] indicating the high standard of classical education available in Arezzo in the early Renaissance, and there is evidence that Aretine grammar teachers required their pupils to study and even purchase entire texts of classical authors.[101]

This Aretine scholarship in the Renaissance period was the culmination of an earlier educational tradition little less outstanding in its day. Arezzo's population was never more than 20,000 in the middle ages, and yet the commune had its own university in the thirteenth century; the importance which medieval Aretines placed on learning is highlighted by comparing thirteenth-century Arezzo with Florence, which, notwithstanding a population of as many as 100,000, had no university. The University of Arezzo was closely connected with the University of Bologna, so that the pre-eminence of law in the university was to be expected. What was more peculiarly Aretine was the important role played in the university curriculum by rhetoric, which was taught in Arezzo with an unusually extensive reference to classical literature.[102] Grammar and rhetoric were taught outside the university, and boys are known to have studied classical authors such as Terence at school in Arezzo.[103] One early fourteenth-century teacher of grammar, Goro d'Arezzo, wrote an elementary Latin vocabulary list and set of grammar rules, a treatise on the principles of orthography in which he quoted Priscian and Vergil, and a commentary on Lucan.[104] It was from this background that a figure of crucial importance for the Renaissance emerged: Geri di Federigo d'Arezzo. Geri d'Arezzo's role in establishing Renaissance humanism is comparable only to Lovato Lovati's in Padua, and his attainments are a tribute to the cultural traditions built up in Arezzo during the middle ages. Geri was probably born in the 1260s or 1270s, the son of a notary and himself a lawyer. Most of his works are lost or survive only in fragments, but what remains shows a remarkable knowl-

[100] *Ibid.*, 3, fol. 172r, 206v; *ibid.*, 5, fol. 116r, 142v, 254r, 256r.
[101] Cf. ASF, Magistrato dei pupilli avanti del principato, 6, fol. 50v (16 January 1393 (ab inc.)): the *ufficiali dei pupilli*, guardians of Giovanni di fu Bartolomeo di ser Spinello of Castiglion-Fiorentino, hearing that Giovanni needs 'unius Luchani pro studiendo ipsum librum et quod magister Nicholaus de Aretio vendidit et dedit dicto Johanni unum librum Luchani bonum et chorectum pro pretio florenorum decem auri', order that Maestro Niccolò d'Arezzo be paid 10 florins for the book from Giovanni's estate. I am grateful to Dr R. Mueller for this reference.
[102] Cf. Wieruszowski, 'Arezzo', 347ff., 382.
[103] Cf. R. Weiss, *Il primo secolo dell'umanesimo* (Rome, 1949), 128.
[104] Cf. BNF, Panc. 68, fol. 1r–20r; *ibid.*, Magl. viii, 1412, fol. 29v–35r, and especially fol. 30r and 35r for citations of classical authors; British Library, Harleian, 1458.

edge of classical antiquity. It is clear that he attempted to model his Latin writing style directly on classical authors, rejecting at least in part the medieval traditions of *dictamèn*. He knew certain classical texts which were little known in the middle ages, such as Pliny's letters, and he exercised critical judgement on ancient texts, realizing for example that the *Gallic Wars* was a genuine work of Caesar's. He revived classical literary genres such as the dialogue, and on the model of classical authors he collected his own correspondence, thus anticipating Petrarch. Moreover, he formed his own circle of humanist friends similar to Mussato's and Lovati's group in Padua.[105]

Geri d'Arezzo was one of the founders of a movement which transcended civic boundaries, as was recognized by Salutati and Zabarella, both of whom, writing at the end of the fourteenth century, placed Geri alongside Mussato as one of the initiators of the revival of letters.[106] After Geri, however, classical scholarship in Arezzo suffered a setback, owing largely to the collapse of the Aretine commune in the early fourteenth century which led to the temporary closure of the university. Nevertheless, the Aretine intellectual tradition remained vital and an interest in classical studies continued; in fact, Arezzo was the only centre of learning in Italy to maintain a continuous tradition of humanist scholarship from the earliest days of pre-humanism until the full bloom of the Renaissance in the fifteenth century. One early fourteenth-century Aretine, Simone della Tenca, who was a collector of manuscripts of classical authors, owned copies of Justin, Sallust and Terence, of Cicero's *De officiis*, *De oratore*, *De amicitia*, and *Disputationes tusculanae* in addition to other Ciceronian treatises and orations, of Palladius's *De re rustica*, of Seneca's *Epistolae morales* and tragedies with Nicholas of Trevet's commentary, and of such rare works as Pliny's letters, Livy's *Decades* with Nicholas of Trevet's commentary and Apuleius's *De deo Socratis*.[107] Of particular importance was the bequest made by Simone of part of his library in 1338 to the Dominican convent in Arezzo,[108] thereby giving future generations the opportunity of studying a wide variety of classical authors;[109] moreover, even in the troubled years of the mid-fourteenth century, there are numerous references to Aretine teachers of grammar who thus encouraged the

---

[105] On Geri d'Arezzo and his circle, cf. Weiss, *Il primo secolo*, 53–66, 105–33; *idem*, 'Lineamenti per una storia del primo umanesimo fiorentino', RSI, lx (1948), 349–66; *idem*, 'The dawn of humanism in Italy', BIHR, xlii, 11–12; Wieruszowski, 'Arezzo', 380–2.

[106] Cf. Weiss, 'Dawn of humanism', 2.

[107] Cf. Pasqui, 'Raccolte', 128ff.; *idem*, 'La biblioteca', ASI, ser. 5, iv (1889), 250ff.; Weiss, 'Lineamenti', 358.

[108] Cf. Pasqui, 'Biblioteca', 251–2; for the Franciscan library in San Francesco, cf. *idem* in *Miscellanea francescana*, iii (1888), 73–81, and 'Raccolte', 138–9.

[109] *Ibid.*, 142–3.

generation of Aretines following Geri and Simone to carry on their commitment to classical studies.[110] Geri's son, Federigo, wrote Latin verse epistles like his father; he corresponded with Petrarch, who sent him a letter on the hidden moral significance of Vergil; and he composed Italian poems, one of which was an invective castigating Florence for having been associated with Catiline.[111] Domenico di Bandino, mentioned already as one of Arezzo's communal grammar teachers, composed an enormous encyclopedia, *Fons rerum memorabilium*, and was notable for his efforts to recover and collect classical manuscripts, an interest which he shared with some of his contemporaries in Arezzo.[112] Bartolomeo di Giovanni Marzi, an Aretine physician, owned Cicero's *De officiis* and *De inventione* and Ovid's *Metamorphoses*.[113] Another Aretine, Giovanni Lippi, was asked for some Ciceronian texts by Salutati, who praised him for his 'great abundance of books'.[114] The commune too was active during the early fifteenth century in preserving Aretine libraries, on one occasion providing funds for the Dominicans to put their collection in order.[115] Another Aretine who played an important role in the transmission of classical authors was the notary and scribe, Giovanni Aretino, now identified as Giovanni di Cenne di Nome d'Arezzo, who belonged, together with Bruni, Poggio, Niccoli and Traversari, to the Florentine humanist *avant garde* in the early fifteenth century; Giovanni was one of the earlier students of Greek in the fifteenth century, but his greatest achievement was to lead the revival of interest in pre-Gothic (*antiqua* or Carolingian) minuscule script and to share the credit, along with Poggio, for originating humanist script, which he passed on to future generations of scribes in Florence and Venice.[116]

The emphasis which Aretines placed on their educational traditions in the early fifteenth century is demonstrated by a letter in which Girolamo Aliotti wrote, 'Our fatherland has always been considered the wet-nurse of the best minds' and 'its milk' has been 'the teachers and instructors of

---

[110] Cf. G. degli Azzi, 'Documenti sui maestri di grammatica in Arezzo nei secoli xiv e xv', AMAPet, n.s. xii–xiii (1932), 117–20.

[111] Cf. BLF, 90, 13 (inferiore), fol. 26r; Weiss, *Il primo secolo*, 59, 66, 105; C. and L.Frati, 'Indice delle carte di Pietro Bilancioni', *Il propugnatore*, n.s. iv, pt 1 (1891), 167; G. Franceschini, 'Schede per una storia della cultura aretina nell'età dell'umanesimo', AMAPet, n.s. xxxvi (1952–7), 292.

[112] On Domenico di Bandino, cf. T. Hankey, 'Domenico Bandino of Arezzo', ItS, xii (1957), 110–28; *idem*, 'The library of Domenico di Bandino', Rin. viii (1957), 177–207; *idem*,'The successive revisions and surviving codices of the *Fons Memorabilium Universi* of Domenico di Bandino', *ibid.*, xi (1960); 3ff.; *idem* in DBI, v, 707–9; R. Sabbadini, *Le scoperte dei codici latini e greci* (Florence, 1905–14), ii, 179–90.

[113] Pasqui, 'Raccolte', 45.          [114] *Ibid.*, 46.          [115] *Ibid.*, 43.

[116] On Giovanni Aretino's work as a scribe, his identification and a full bibliography, cf. now G. Nicolaj Petronio, 'Per la soluzione di un enigma: Giovanni Aretino copista, notaio e cancelliere', *Humanistica lovaniensia*, xxx (1981), 1–12.

grammar' employed at public expense.[117] The public records of the commune abound in similar references to this Aretine tradition of classical learning which, it was argued, had made Arezzo famous and should be perpetuated by continuing to maintain a grammar school at public expense.[118] Aretines wanted to keep the tradition of grammar and rhetoric alive in part as a memento of the great university where the other important subjects of the medieval curriculum had been taught,[119] and in fact they had attempted unsuccessfully to revive their university in the mid-fourteenth century, when their imperial privilege to have a university was renewed by Emperor Charles IV.[120] However, what is an even more impressive testimony to the tenacity and vitality of Aretine educational traditions is that in 1452, during the Italian tour of Emperor Frederick III, the Aretines secured another renewal of the imperial privilege;[121] after a further decade of discussion and and preparation,[122] they in fact reopened their university in 1464, when the first roll of teaching staff were appointed,[123] and this Aretine university then continued to function throughout the rest of the fifteenth century and at the beginning of the sixteenth.[124] In the early Renaissance, Aretines were keenly aware of their loss of prestige in becoming subjects of Florence, and they recognized that they had fallen far behind other cities in wealth, but they took consolation in the remarkable Aretine cultural heritage which they were proud to have maintained over so many generations.[125]

[117] Aliotti, *Epistolae*, i, 73–7.

[118] Cf. e.g. ASA. Provv. 2, fol. 16r; *ibid.*, 4, fol. 4r; *ibid.*, 5, fol. 34r, 107r; *ibid.*, 6, fol. 119v, 203r; *ibid.*, 7, fol. 33v; *ibid.*, 8, fol. 2r; *ibid.*, QCanc. 2, fol. 12r–13v; *ibid.*, 3, fol. 7r, 8r.

[119] ASA, Provv. 5, fol. 107r (8 December 1413): prefata civitas aretina consueverit ab antiquo studium habere in omni scientie facultate quo infiniti ipsius cives per diversas mundi partes honorabantur et patrie multe redundabant comoditates, et cupientes ipsum studium iuxta posse suscitare . . . the priors elect a new grammar teacher.

[120] Cf. A.Moretti, 'L'antico studio aretino', AMAPet, n.s. xiv–xv (1933), 317.

[121] ASA, Provv. 9, fol. 138r–140r, 143r–v.

[122] *Ibid.*, 10, fol. 58v–59r, 218r; 11, fol. 89v–90r.

[123] *Ibid.*, fol. 154r–v, 156r–157r.

[124] The revival of the Aretine university is unknown to contemporary scholars of the Italian universities (cf. P. Denley, 'The social function of Italian Renaissance universities', *Town and Gown: The University in Search of its Origins. CRE Information*, lxii (1983), 48), although this was briefly referred to by Moretti ('L'antico studio', AMAPet, n.s. xvi–xvii (1934), 128–30) and Pasqui (*Documenti*, ii, 294). G. Nicolaj Petronio, 'Notariato aretino tra medievo et età moderna: collegio, statuti e matricole dal 1339 al 1739', *Studi in onore di Leopoldo Sandri* (Rome, 1983), 652, n. 94, is aware that the imperial privilege was renewed and that doctorates were granted, as were Moretti and Pasqui, but like them does not cite the appointment of teaching staff; she also questions how long the university remained open. There is a long and important series of unpublished documents regarding this unknown Renaissance university in the Archivio di Stato of Arezzo, which I hope to study and publish in the near future.

[125] ASA, Provv. 5, fol. 34r (3 April 1411): attento quod utilissimum et necessarium est ut civitas Aretina scientificis repleatur hominibus quorum virtutibus et scientia non solum divitiis verum etiam fama perempnia divina favente clementia civitas antedicta fuit in preteritum sublimata et inter ceteras famosissimas civitates nomen assumpsit . . .

Like his compatriots, Benedetto Accolti was heir to all these legacies of Arezzo's history in the early Renaissance; Accolti and his family were not only beneficiaries of the intellectual fruits of the Aretine educational tradition but were considerably affected by economic, social and political conditions in Arezzo, and it is no exaggeration to say that their fortunes were substantially shaped by Aretine history in the later middle ages and early Renaissance.

# 2

# The Accolti family

In the later middle ages, there were two main branches of the Accolti family, one in Arezzo and one in Florence;[1] in the thirteenth and fourteenth centuries, it was the Florentine Accolti who were prominent in public life, whereas in the fifteenth century it was the Aretine line, that of Benedetto himself, which achieved renown. The Florentine Accolti were a Guelf mercantile family who rose to prominence during the political upheavals of the second half of the thirteenth century. One line of the Florentine Accolti descended from Spinello Accolti, who matriculated as a merchant in 1235 and was a resident of Borgo San Jacopo in the Sesto of Oltrarno.[2] This branch of the family were members of the new regime which ruled Florence from 1250 to 1260, Maffio di Spinello having taken part in the battle of Montaperti in 1260 and his brother Accolto di Spinello having been a member of the general council of 1256. Maffio was a member of the general council of 1280, and it seems that Spinello had at least one other son, Bocca, who is recorded in 1273 as the purchaser of some land beyond the walls of the Oltrarno.[3] Other Accolti then living in Oltrarno were Messer Amato di fu Accolto Accolti and Filippo Accolti.[4] They may have been related to the famous banking family, the Bardi, who lived in Oltrarno too: one of Nepo di Messer Bardo de' Bardi's neighbours in 1269 was Guido Accolti, who, perhaps at this point called Guido Accolti de' Bardi, was elected *podestà* of Pistoia in 1297.[5] The Accolti of Oltrarno remained loyal Guelfs, as was realized by Emperor Henry VII, who in 1313 condemned Gherardo di Colto from Oltrarno as a rebel;[6] but

---

[1]  For Accolti elsewhere in Tuscany, cf. *Delizie*, vii, 216, 230, 238, 241 and xi, 64; BNF, PG, 16.
[2]  ASF, Mss. 348, fol. 13v; G. Richa, *Notizie istoriche delle chiese fiorentine* (Florence, 1754–62), ix, 3.
[3]  *Il libro di Montaperti*, ed. C. Paoli (Florence, 1889), 75; *Delizie*, vii, 198, and ix, 97; D. M. Manni, *Osservazioni sopra i sigilli* (Florence, 1739–86), xxvi, 103–9.
[4]  BNF, PG, 16; ASF, Mss. 348, fol. 13v.
[5]  *Delizie*, vii, 209; *Le consulte della repubblica fiorentina*, ed. A. Gherardi (Florence, 1896–8), ii, 592–3.
[6]  *Delizie*, xi, 125.

like many other ardent supporters of the Guelf party, this line of the Accolti family had lost power in Florence by the end of the fourteenth century, when, for example, ser Alessandro Colti from the quarter of Santo Spirito (the new name for the Sesto of Oltrarno) was unsuccessful in 1381 in a scrutiny for communal offices.[7]

Another line of the Accolti family lived north of the Arno, in the Sesto of Borgo. Like the Accolti of Oltrarno, they were Guelfs and they became leading members of the regime which reformed the Florentine constitution at the turn of the thirteenth century, this branch of the family including among its members two Gonfaloniers of Justice and seven priors between 1296 and 1324. Cino, a merchant, was a member of the general council in 1278 and in 1283 was elected by the Signoria as one of the supervisors of the *estimo*; in 1293 he was appointed treasurer of the Romagna by Pope Martin IV and in 1296 he became Florentine Gonfalonier of Justice. His son Lotto, also a merchant, was enrolled in the Arte della Seta, the silk merchants' guild.[8] Lapo di Ugo Bonacolti, like Cino, was a member of the general council in 1278, and in 1290 he was appointed one of the treasurers of the Florentine militia; Caraccio di Ugo Bonaccolti, Lapo's brother, was a prior in 1298, as was Caraccio's son, Cione, in 1320.[9] Vanni Accolti was Gonfalonier of Justice in 1304, and in 1313, like Gherardo di Colto from Oltrarno, he was condemned as a rebel by Henry VII.[10] Messer Filippo Accolti, Vanni's son, who was a lawyer, was a prior in 1318 and 1323.[11] Messer Teghia Buonaccolti, also a lawyer, was a prior three times, in 1317, 1322 and 1324, and one of the speakers at the Parlamento of July–August 1343.[12] Giovanni Colti was a councillor and ambassador in 1342,[13] but the Accolti of Borgo like the line from Oltrarno seem to have suffered along with other prominent Guelfs after the more popular regime of 1343 gave a greater role to the minor guilds; unlike other Guelf families, they never reestablished themselves after the period of minor guild predominance from 1343 to 1382, so disappearing from Florentine history by the end of the fourteenth century.[14]

The Accolti of Arezzo, like their Florentine namesakes, took part in the public life of their commune during the thirteenth century; similarly the upheavals of fourteenth-century Italian political and social life appear to

---

[7] *Ibid.*, xvi, 252.
[8] Davidsohn, *Geschichte von Florenz*, II, ii, 234; IV, ii, 298; *Anmerkungen* to IV, ii, 93; *Delizie*, ix, 52, 332; BMF, C 1, fol. 212v.
[9] *Delizie*, ix, 52; *Consulte*, ed. Gherardi, i, 393; BMF, C 1, fol. 213v, 230v.
[10] *Ibid.*, fol. 218v; *Delizie*, xi, 125.
[11] Marchionne Stefani, *Cronaca fiorentina*, ed. N. Rodolico, RIS², xxx, 1, 124, 131; BMF, C 1, fol. 229v, 233r.
[12] *Ibid.*, fol. 228v, 232v, 234r; *Delizie*, xiii, 203.   [13] *Ibid.*, 188.
[14] Buonaccolto di Francesco Buonaccolti, e.g., was unsuccessful in 1382 for the *tre maggiori*: cf. *ibid.*, xvi, 167.

have disturbed and even uprooted the Aretine Accolti, but, unlike the
Florentine family, they managed to regain much of their earlier standing in
the commune by the early fifteenth century. Nero Accolti, who is
mentioned in the treaty of 1251 between Florence and the Guelfs of
Arezzo, was a magnate,[15] but later Aretine Accolti were not nobles, frequently belonging to guilds of professionals such as physicians and
notaries, as well as being merchants and money lenders.[16] The family may
originally have immigrated to Arezzo from the Casentino, the mountain-
ous region between Florence and Arezzo: by the beginning of the fourteenth century, ser Accolto di Accolto del Riccio had immigrated to
Arezzo from Faltona, a village in the Casentino; moreover, in the mid-
fourteenth century the Aretine line from which Benedetto Accolti
descended had moved from Arezzo to Pontenano, a village near Faltona.
Ser Accolto di Accolto del Riccio matriculated in the Aretine guild of
notaries and became an Aretine citizen; he died sometime between 1347
and 1352,[17] leaving three sons, of whom one, Maestro Gregorio, was a
physician.[18] Although after Nero Accolti it seems that the Aretine Accolti
were no longer nobles, nevertheless they appear to have enjoyed a high
social position in Arezzo; thus, Catarina and Cecilia Accolti belonged to
the convent of Santa Maria di Pionta near Arezzo, to which a number of
Tuscan noble families such as the Bardi, Adimari, Cerchi, Bostoli and
Sassoli had entrusted their unmarried daughters.[19]

The earliest known direct ancestor of Benedetto Accolti was
Benevenuto, whose son Accolto appears as a prosperous merchant and
money lender in Arezzo during the 1320s.[20] Accolto di Benevenuto had
died by 1330 when his son Matteo is referred to as 'Matteus quondam
Accolti de Aretio'.[21] Matteo, who seems to have maintained the prosperity
established by his father,[22] had himself died by 1353, when a dispute over
his estate had to be settled by arbitration.[23] Matteo had four sons, Santi,
Grazia, Ugolino and ser Donato, three of whom remained in Arezzo: Santi
and Grazia were mentioned there in 1366 as were Grazia and Ugolino in

---

[15]  BCA, 12, fol. 1v bis; BMF, A 135, fol. 124v.
[16]  Cf. ACA, 598, fol. 115v–116r, 117r; 601, p. 90.
[17]  BCA, 12,fol. 1v bis; ASA, Dott. Not. fol. 22v, 32v; ACA, 602, p. 211; 603, fol. 50v; 604,
       fol. 74r; 605, fol. 50r; 608, fol. 81r; 610, fol. 10r; 611, fol. 7v. Cf. *ibid.*, 597, fol. 67v.
[18]  ASF, Mss. 348, fol. 13v; BNF, PG, 16; Marzi, *La cancelleria*, 230; ACA, 598, fol. 122r.
       Another physician in the family was Maestro Uberto Accolti, mentioned in 1311: cf.
       BMF, A 135, fol. 124v.
[19]  ASF, Not. A. G 837 (1350–1), fol. 58r. Nuns tended to come from good families because
       a dowry was required: cf. Hay, *The Church*, 62.
[20]  Cf. ACA, 598, fol. 6v, 115v–117r; 611, fol. 28r, 47r; 617, fol. 116v; BCA, 12, fol. 1v bis.
[21]  ACA, 617, fol. 8v.
[22]  *Ibid.*, 598, fol. 116r–v; 608, fol. 10r; 611, fol. 28r; 612, fol. 52r–v, 61r, 82v; 617, fol.
       8v, 116v. Cf. *ibid.*, 597, fol. 12v and 67v.
[23]  ASF, Not. A. G 837 (1352–4), fol. 71v, 100r.

1371, 1382 and 1383.[24] It has been seen, however, that Arezzo underwent a series of political crises during the fourteenth century, and it is possible that these upheavals led a number of members of the Accolti family to seek their fortunes outside their native city; although travel and migration were normal features of medieval Italian life, it is still no exaggeration to regard the Accolti of Arezzo as an unsettled family after the mid-fourteenth century. Matteo di Accolto's fourth son, ser Donato, emigrated from Arezzo to Pistoia, where he practised as a notary.[25] Matteo's two grandsons, Santi di Grazia and Ugolino di Grazia, left Arezzo not for Pistoia but for Pontenano in the Casentino, on the Alpe di Santa Trinita, about ten miles northwest of Arezzo, where they had become permanent residents by 1385.[26] These direct ancestors of Benedetto Accolti were not the only members of the Accolti family to leave Arezzo during the fourteenth century. Maestro Gregorio di ser Accolto di Accolto del Riccio da Faltona, the physician, had emigrated from Arezzo to Florence by 1320, when he had become a member of the Florentine guild of physicians and apothecaries. In the 1330s Maestro Gregorio lived in the parish of Sant'Apollinare in the Sesto of San Pancrazio in Florence, and he was still resident there in 1351, when he is mentioned in the tax register for the quarter of Santa Croce (into which the Sesto of San Pancrazio had been incorporated). He established himself quickly in Florence, becoming a captain of Orsanmichele in 1324 and marrying into an old Florentine family, the Compagni, in 1337. As a member of the *gente nuova* he seems to have risen too rapidly in Florentine society, for along with other recent immigrants he was disqualified from holding public office in Florence in October 1346. Maestro Gregorio perhaps then contemplated returning to Arezzo, where in 1353 he bought a house in the Borgo Marciani in the quarter of Porta di Foro[27] and where he lived until at least 1360.[28]

The migrations of the Accolti family during the thirteenth and fourteenth centuries often coincided with periods of particularly rapid social, political or economic change in Arezzo. It was in the midst of the Aretine commune's rapid expansion at the end of the thirteenth century that the

---

[24] BMF, A 135, fol. 124r–v.

[25] ASF, Not. A. A 64, fol. 17v, 19r, 85r; A 65, fol. 1r.

[26] ASF, Cap. 52, fol. 49r. Pontenano had become a *feudum* of the Aretine commune in 1256: cf. Pasqui, *Documenti*, ii, 306–9; Cherubini, *Signori*, 68.

[27] ASF, Mss. 348, fol. 13v; Marzi, 230; BNF, PG, 16; ACA, 602, p. 211; *ibid.*, 604, fol. 74r; *ibid.*, 605, fol. 50r; *ibid.*, 610, fol. 10r; ASA. Not.A. G 837 (1352–4), fol. 89r; ASF, Provv. 33, fol. 126v; 34, fol. 93v–94r. For the last two references I am indebted to Dr J. Najemy.

[28] Cf. A. Ugolini, *Maestro Gregorio d'Arezzo e le sue rime* (Livorno, 1901), 8–9; E. Malvestiti, 'Medici e medicine nel xiv secolo: Maestro Gregorio d'Arezzo', BollRCA, 866 (1 April 1977), reprinted in *Contributi*, 15. On Maestro Gregorio as a poet, cf. *infra*, p. 44.

line of the family from Faltona in the Casentino emigrated to Arezzo, along with numerous other immigrants. Maestro Gregorio's move from Arezzo to Florence, which probably occurred sometime between 1300 and 1320, coincided with the collapse of public order in the wake of Aretine defeat in the battle of Campaldino, the struggle for power in Arezzo between the Verdi and Secchi factions and the rise of the Tarlati despotism. It was during the weak government of the Guelf regime which attempted to return Arezzo to communal government from 1343 until 1384 that Benedetto Accolti's ancestors, Santi di Grazia and Ugolino di Grazia, left Arezzo, perhaps in search of refuge in the hills of the Casentino. In fact, some of the early fourteenth-century Accolti in Arezzo were Ghibellines,[29] which suggests that Santi and Ugolino could possibly have had political motives for moving to Pontenano after 1343, when Arezzo had come under a Guelf regime.

The peregrinations of the Accolti family did not end in Pontenano, a barren and remote mountain village, which could have offered them little more than refuge. Sometime after 1391, Ugolino di Grazia moved to Perugia in Umbria, on the other side of the Apennines from Pontenano, where he raised his two sons, Michele and Paolo, born in 1389 and 1392.[30] On the other hand, Santi di Grazia, Ugolino's brother and Benedetto Accolti's grandfather, spent the rest of his life in Pontenano, where he owned a house and a small farm, consisting of four plots of arable land, four plots of timber, one plot suitable for mixed farming, four meadows, four vineyards and a paddock. This farm was held on perpetual lease from the fraternity of Santa Maria of Arezzo for three *staia* (bushels) of grain a year; it was subject to a tithe of one and a quarter *staia* of grain a year payable to the parish of Pontenano, so that, with a total yield of grain of approximately thirteen or fourteen *staia* a year, this was a poor farm in comparison with some owned by other fourteenth-century Aretines.[31]

Santi di Grazia had two sons, the eldest of whom, Grazia, was born in 1363. Grazia, like his father Santi, had neither a profession nor a trade,[32] but Santi di Grazia's other son, Michele, who was born in 1375 and was Benedetto Accolti's father, clearly had more ability than his brother Grazia. For three generations no one in this line of the Accolti family had had a profession, and so Michele di Santi was taking an important step when in the 1390s he decided to cross the Apennines from Pontenano and go to Bologna to study law. He may have felt that, in studying for a profession, he was reestablishing family traditions from the early fourteenth

---

[29]  BMF, A 135, fol. 124v. For a similar migration from Arezzo as a result of political turmoil and Ghibelline associations, cf. Cherubini, *Signori*, 319–36.
[30]  BMF, A 135, fol. 123r–124v; ASF, Cat. 201, fol. 768r–v.
[31]  ASA, PdB, 3, fol. 574r–v.
[32]  ASA, PdB, 3, fol. 577r: Grazia suo fratello . . . non sa arte né mestieri niuno.

century, when at least five members of the Accolti family in Arezzo belonged to the professional classes; however, earlier members of the Aretine family are known to have been either notaries or physicians and so law was a departure for Michele. It is perhaps a measure of the confidence which Michele's family placed in his abilities that they were willing to meet the expenses of a legal education in Bologna lasting at least five years, all the more so as Michele's father Santi is known not to have been rich. Michele lived up to his family's expectations and became the first of a long succession of Accolti lawyers in February 1399, when he passed his private and public examinations in civil law at Bologna.[33] He may have had a doctorate in canon law too, but it is not known where or when it was conferred.[34]

Michele's legal career soon made him much more prosperous than his elder brother Grazia, with whom he shared his father's small patrimony in Pontenano. Professional success soon made him feel that he was supporting not only his own family but Grazia's as well; sardonically he wrote in 1419 that the only useful members of his and Grazia's family of some fifteen persons were himself and the slave girl.[35] Grazia's contribution came from the income of land only; to his inheritance at Pontenano he added a farm at Salutio in the Val d'Arno Casentinese, four miles northwest of Pontenano and two and a half miles east of the Arno, which became his main source of income.[36] Grazia was able to declare only the modest capital of 458 florins in 1429,[37] whereas Michele, through his professional earnings, became a substantial landowner in the course of the early fifteenth century. He acquired farms at Tulliano in the Val d'Arno Casentinese, beside the Arno, a mile and a quarter northeast of Salutio, and at Lorenzano, two miles south of Tulliano along the Arno. At Bagnena, beyond the Arno valley in the foothills of the Alpe della Badia di Santa Trinita, five miles west of the Arno and two and a half miles east of Pontenano, Michele acquired nine farms, four let on short-term leases and five on perpetual leases, as well as one at Poggibaldi near Tulliano which he owned in partnership with Giovanni di Francesco da Valenzano.[38]

Farming in the Arno valley was more profitable for Michele than in the hills of the Casentino, which is rocky, rugged country, in marked contrast to the rich, low-lying and well-irrigated land of the Val d'Arno

---

[33] *Il 'liber secretus iuris caesarei' dell'Università di Bologna*, ed. A. Sorbelli (Bologna, 1938–42), i, 127.

[34] In 1427 some of his law books were 'libri . . . di decretali': cf. ASF, Cat. 201, fol. 359r.

[35] ASA, PdB, 3, fol. 577r: et in tucto fr'amendoi [the households of Michele and his brother Grazia] 'anno bocche quindici tutte de' inutili se non è Messer Michele e la schiava.

[36] *Ibid.*, 574v–575r; ASA, Cat. 3, fol. 212r–213r.

[37] ASF, Cat. 273, fol. 23r.

[38] ASA, PdB, 3, fol. 575r–577r; ASA, Cat. 3, fol. 208r–211r; ASF, Cat. 201, fol. 355v–358v.

Casentinese. Michele's lands in Bagnena and Pontenano were typical of
the hills of the Casentino – mainly meadow, forest and vineyard, with a
small proportion of arable land, whereas his property in Tulliano,
Lorenzano and Poggibaldi resembled most farms in the Val d'Arno
Casentinese, with a high proportion of arable land. Michele obtained the
largest yields from his farms at Tulliano and Poggibaldi in the Val d'Arno
Casentinese. His property at Tulliano, which was farmed by Marco di
Lando da Valenzano in exchange for a loan of twelve florins, two *lire*, a
pair of oxen worth eighteen florins and sixteen *staia* of grain, yielded
100 *staia* of grain and ten barrels of wine a year, while his land in
Poggibaldi, farmed by Antonio di Donato with his son Donato di Antonio
for a loan of twelve florins, thirty-seven *staia* of grain, a pair of
oxen worth sixteen florins and twenty farm animals, yielded 100 *staia* of
grain and five barrels of wine a year. On the other hand, for all his property
in the Casentine hills, which consisted of a considerably greater area than
his land in Poggibaldi and Tulliano, he received only 86½ *staia* of grain a
year.[39]

Pontenano like the rest of the Casentine hills is accessible only by a
winding, rocky road, which must have been closed for most of the winter
and even today is extremely difficult to use. This region had little to offer
Michele, who, moreover, could hardly have contemplated a legal career in
a desolate mountain village. Grazia too, with his farm at Salutio in the
richer Val d'Arno Casentinese, was no longer dependent on his patrimony
in Pontenano, and it seems that sometime between May 1408 and July
1409 he and his brother Michele returned to Arezzo.[40] Conditions there,
it has been seen, had become more settled under Florentine rule, in contrast
to the years leading up to 1384, when Michele's and Grazia's father and
uncle had retreated to Pontenano. Arezzo was Michele's and Grazia's
ancestral city, and it was natural for them to attempt to resettle there.
Indeed, Arezzo attracted back the other itinerant branch of the Accolti
family who had been in Perugia since the 1390s but who in 1426 returned
to Arezzo, where they were received as citizens and remained resident until
at least the seventeenth century.[41] The long-standing connection of the
Accolti family with Arezzo accounts for the ease with which they reestablished themselves there in the fifteenth century. Michele and Grazia soon
took a place among the governing classes of the city, acquiring houses and

[39]  *Ibid.*, fol. 353v–358v.
[40]  Michele and Grazia were not subject to Aretine taxation as late as 30 April 1408 (cf. ASA,
     Daz. 46, *passim*) but were included among Aretine taxpayers after 1 July 1409 (cf. *ibid.*,
     47, fol. 171r).
[41]  ASF, Cat. 201, fol. 768r–v; BMF, A 135, fol. 119r–127r. Similarly the Aretine Simo
     d'Ubertino, having emigrated to Pisa in the Aretine troubles of the 1380s, returned to
     Arezzo in 1385: cf. Cherubini, *Signori*, 334.

property there, and Michele quickly married a member of a prominent Aretine family.

After the coming of Florentine rule in 1384 Arezzo maintained a degree of self-government. Florence sent two of its own citizens to be captain and *podestà* of Arezzo with responsibility for administering justice, maintaining order, providing defence and preserving Florentine rule,[42] but much local administration remained in the hands of Aretines themselves, who continued to choose most of their other officials. The method of filling communal offices in Arezzo, which was similar to that used in Florence, consisted of two stages: first, *imborsazione* or *reforma*, in which citizens were declared eligible for office and their names placed in purses; second, *estrazione*, in which names of citizens were drawn from the purses to fill offices. *Reforme* took place every three years during the first years of Florentine rule in Arezzo, but at the beginning of the fifteenth century the interval between *reforme* was lengthened to five years; *estrazioni* took place whenever an office was due to be filled.[43]

In 1412 both Michele and Grazia were declared eligible for communal office, Grazia's name being placed in the purse for the priorate and Michele's in the purses for the offices of rector of the fraternity of Santa Maria della Misericordia, captain of the Guelf party and member of the council of sixty. Michele first held office as a member of the general council in 1413; in 1417 he was again on the general council and he became one of the Guelf members of council of sixty in 1418, the year in which he also first served as a prior. Grazia first held office on the general council in 1418, and in the following year he was a prior as well as one of the four officials in charge of dowries. Michele was again on the general council in 1421; in 1421–2 he was once more a Guelf member of the council of sixty and in 1424 he was a prior for the second time.[44] Prominent citizens were called upon to introduce legislation and resolutions in the Aretine general council, and Michele acted in this capacity as communal spokesman several times during his term on the council in 1417–18;[45] he was also one of the sixteen citizens chosen to negotiate with the captain of Arezzo early

[42] There is a brief account of Aretine government at the beginning of Florentine rule (up to 1396) in G. Guidi, *Il governo della città-repubblica di Firenze del primo Quattrocento* (Florence, 1981), iii, 40–5. The Florentine administration in Arezzo was military and judicial, consisting in 1387 of a captain, a judge qualified in civil law, 5 notaries, 4 domestic servants, 6 cavalrymen, 30 infantry and a mounted bugler: cf. ASF, CdC, 49, fol. 19r. For the Florentine role in Aretine direct and indirect taxation, cf. Benigni, 'Fonti', and Carbone, 'Note'.

[43] For the regulations used to fill communal offices in Arezzo under Florentine rule, cf. Guidi, *Il governo*, iii, 40–5, for the end of the fourteenth century and ASF, Tratte, 861, 862, 870 for the fifteenth century.

[44] Cf. ASF, Tratte, 870, Imborsati e capitoli (1412), not foliated; ASA, Estr. 6, fol. 56r, 132v, 145r, 146r, 148r, 159r, 163r, 184v, 187r, 190r, 229v; *ibid.*, 7, fol. 14v, 52r, 69r.

[45] ASA, Provv. 5, fol. 217r–v, 223r–v, 227v, 228r.

in 1417 about a reduction or cancellation of indirect taxation (*gabelle*) in the city,[46] and eleven years later in 1428 he served on another committee, this time to negotiate with the captain of Arezzo regarding law and order in the Aretine countryside.[47] His legal experience and knowledge helped in his work as a communal negotiator, and in 1416 the commune was so grateful for his efforts on their behalf that they voted to cancel tax arrears owed by him and his brother Grazia.[48]

The role in communal life which Michele and Grazia Accolti took in the 1410s and 1420s was moderately active, comparable to that of one branch of a family such as the Marsuppini. In the period between 1400 and 1427 nine members of this branch of the Marsuppini family held the offices of prior seven times and captain of the Guelf party twice, and were thirteen times on the general council;[49] during the same period, Michele and Grazia, the only eligible members of the Accolti family, held the priorate three times, and were on the general council four times and on the council of sixty twice. The Accolti family had been established in Arezzo by the mid-thirteenth century, considerably earlier than the Marsuppini, who had moved to Arezzo from Quarata in the countryside at the beginning of the fourteenth century;[50] the Marsuppini, however, had managed to prosper under the communal regime of 1343 to 1384, in contrast to the Accolti, who had withdrawn from Aretine public life at that time. It is possible that the position of the Accolti family in fifteenth-century Arezzo was not what it had been before 1343, for Aretine families of comparable antiquity to the Accolti, such as the Lippi, had a noticeably greater role in communal life after 1384 than the Accolti: between 1389 and 1427, for example, Angelo di Paolo Lippi was a prior eleven times, a captain of the Guelf party nine times, a member of the general council eight times and a member of the council of sixty three times.[51]

Michele's wealth too may have eased the reentry of the Accolti family into Aretine social and political life. In the *catasto* of 1429 Michele declared assets worth 1584 florins, 9 *soldi*, making him the fourteenth richest man in Arezzo and placing him amongst the richest 1.2% of Aretines.[52] Michele's wealth enabled him to own a house in Arezzo comparable in value to those of other leading Aretines. His house, together

[46] *Ibid.*, fol. 209v.      [47] *Ibid.*, 6, fol. 23r.      [48] *Ibid.*, 5, fol. 181v.
[49] ASA,Estr. 4,fol. 131v; *ibid.*, 5, fol. 28v, 38v, 46v, 53r, 67r, 80v, 99r, 114r, 116v, 164r; *ibid.*, 6, fol. 5v, 10r, 79r, 96r, 118r, 190r; *ibid.*, 7, fol. 31v, 54v, 66v, 75v, 83r, 120v.
[50] On the Marsuppini, cf. Pasqui and Viviani, *Guida*, 211–12; E. Gamurrini, *Istoria genealogica* (Florence, 1668–85), i, 117–24; BMF,C 61 (Memorie della famiglia Marsuppini); Lazzeri, *Ubertini*, 275–6.
[51] ASA, Estr. 1, fol. 2v, 14r, 17r, 65r, 67r, 110r, 117v; *ibid.*, 4, fol. 44v, 54v, 77r, 108r, 123r, 128r, 146r; *ibid.*, 5, fol. 14v, 19v, 23r, 53r, 96v, 148v, 164r, 164v; *ibid.*, 6, fol. 86v, 105v, 142r, 174r, 208v, 217v, 229v; *ibid.*, 7, fol. 2r.
[52] ASF, Cat. 273, fol. 36v.

with two shops on the ground floor, was worth about 250 florins,[53] just as Giovanni di ser Antonio, who in the 1429 *catasto* was the thirty-fifth richest Aretine, had a house and three shops worth 200 florins and Monna Mattea di Simone di Ghino, in 1429 the thirteenth richest Aretine, owned a house and two shops worth 250 florins.[54]

Wealth attracted wealth, and so in 1408 Michele was able to marry Margherita, the daughter of Messer Rosello di ser Fino Roselli of Arezzo. Michele received a dowry of 300 florins from Margherita;[55] such a dowry was a substantial amount, comparable, as has been seen, to the dowries of other leading Aretines, and it indicates the respect commanded in Arezzo by Michele.[56] Another sign of Michele's prominent social position in Arezzo can be seen in the social rank of the Roselli family. The fourteenth-century Aretine verse chronicler, ser Bartolomeo di ser Gorello, referred to the Roselli as one of the most notable of Aretine families, and a road in the quarter of Porta di Borgo was named Borgo dei Roselli.[57] In the early fifteenth century the Roselli were still prominent in Arezzo. In 1427 Maestro Lionardo di Messer Giovanni Roselli, Messer Rosello di ser Fino's grandson, married a daughter of Francesco di Baccio Bacci.[58] The Bacci were one of the best Aretine families; Francesco, who had received in 1402 the large dowry of 400 florins for his wife Filippa di Gualtieri di Donato Alfini,[59] was, according to the 1429 *catasto*, the second richest Aretine and he gave Lionardo Roselli the even larger dowry of 500 florins for his own daughter.[60]

Michele Accolti also began to acquire land in and near Arezzo. The countryside round Arezzo, up to about one mile from the city walls, was called the *camparie*, up to about five miles, the *cortine*, and in 1427 Michele had land in both these districts, as well as in the city itself. In the city he had a garden in the Contrada delle Carbonaie, for which he received an annual rent of five *lire*. In the *camparie* at Traitone, he had two plots of arable land as well as two more at Strada di San Biagio, all of which were farmed by Domenico del Budda d'Arezzo for a loan of eight florins, yielding fifty *staia* of grain a year. In the *cortine* he bought a vineyard in Pieve di San Giovanni a Capolona, six miles northwest of Arezzo, for ten florins, as well as a house there. He himself supervised the cultivation of the vineyard and used the house as his country residence, 'per habitare del detto Misser Michele in villa', as he wrote in his tax return. The vineyard

---

[53] ASF, Cat. 201, fol. 351r.
[54] *Ibid.*, 203, fol. 665r; *ibid.*, 201, fol. 769r. Cf. Varese, 'Condizioni', 53.
[55] BCA, 12, fol. 3r.      [56] Cf. p. 11, *supra*.
[57] Bartolomeo di ser Gorello, *Cronica*, RIS², xv, 1, 18–19. For the Borgo dei Roselli, cf. ASF, Cat. 202, fol. 170r; *ibid.*, 810, fol. 736r. On the Roselli family, see Lazzeri, *Ubertini*, 258–60, and *infra*, pp. 33–5, 38–9, 42, 44, 48.
[58] ASF, Cat. 203, fol. 383r.      [59] ASF, Not.A. A 47, fol. 211r.
[60] ASF, Cat. 203, fol. 383r.

yielded forty barrels of wine a year, replacing his vineyard at Lorenzano in the Casentino as his family's main source of wine. Michele also acquired a farm at Milisciano, beside Pieve di San Giovanni a Capolona, consisting of two houses, a garden, thirty-four plots of land, a field and a plot of land for mixed cultivation; he also had two other plots of land at Milisciano, one arable, the other a vineyard.[61]

In a number of ways, therefore, Michele Accolti led the life of an Aretine patrician by the 1420s; nevertheless, Michele's line of the Accolti family had spent much of the second half of the fourteenth century away from their native city, and so it is not surprising that Michele preserved a certain detachment from Arezzo. In 1427 he retained strong ties with the Casentino, where most of his land was still located. Moreover, Michele's farmland in and near Arezzo did not prove to be as productive as his farms in the Casentino; from the farms at Traitone, Strada di San Biagio and Milisciano he received an annual income of less than one hundred *staia* of grain, in contrast to his farms in the Casentino, from which he received more than three hundred *staia* of grain a year.[62] The rest of Michele's family retained strong ties with the Casentino too. All the property owned by his brother Grazia was in the Casentino,[63] and Michele's niece, Fia, was married by her father Grazia to Giovanni di Stefano, a resident of Salutio in the Val d'Arno Casentinese.[64] Grazia's son Agnolo (b. 1401)[65] matriculated in the Aretine guild of lawyers and notaries in 1421[66] but it was at least ten years before he gained prominence as a notary both in the Aretine diocese[67] and commune;[68] he spent the early part of his career building up a practice in the Casentino, where he appears to have been one of the principal notaries in the 1420s and 1430s.[69] It has been noted moreover that the great majority of the Aretine patriciate in the fifteenth century had interests in the mercantile life of the city;[70] Michele Accolti, on the other hand, had investments only in agriculture, and his reluctance to invest in Aretine business may suggest that he was inclined to keep aloof from the everyday life of the city. The location of Michele's house too suggests a certain distance from the heart of Aretine communal life. Permanently

---

[61]  Cf. ASA, PdB, 3, fol. 575r–577r; Cat. 3, fol. 208r–211r; ASF, Cat. 201, fol. 351r–355r; BCA, 34, fol. 252r.

[62]  Cf. ASF, Cat. 201, fol. 351v–358v.      [63]  *Ibid.*, 203, fol. 628r–630r.

[64]  *Ibid.*, fol. 630v.      [65]  *Ibid.*      [66]  ASA, Dott. Not., fol. 50r.

[67]  Cf. ASF, Not.A. A 46 and 48, which are devoted to Agnolo's work for the Aretine diocese after 1434, and in particular A 46, fol. 20v, where he is called 'notarius et scriba episcopalis curie aretine'.

[68]  He was named as chancellor of the communal fraternity of Santa Maria della Misericordia on 20 December 1446: cf. ASF, Not.A. P 290 (1441–6) not foliated.

[69]  Cf. ASF, Not.A. A 45 (1429–35), which was almost completely devoted to his clients in the Casentino, and A 47 (1436–41), which is no longer so exclusively devoted to work there but in which his clients from there still occupy an important place.

[70]  Cf. pp. 7–10, *supra*.

established Aretine patrician families such as the Bacci, Albergotti, Marsuppini or Sinigardi tended to live in the centre of the city within the circle of the thirteenth-century walls;[71] Michele's house, on the other hand, was in the Contrada of San Lorentino, near the Porta di San Lorentino, one of the two northern gates of the city. The Contrada of San Lorentino was located between the site of the old thirteenth-century walls, corresponding today to Via Garibaldi, and the new fourteenth-century walls built by Guido Tarlati. This part of the city enclosed much farmland and in the fifteenth century was still largely the outskirts of Arezzo.[72]

It has been pointed out that the fourteenth century had an unsettling effect on the Accolti family; although two branches of the family during the more stable fifteenth century reestablished themselves permanently in Arezzo – those descended from Michele's uncle Ugolino di Grazia and from his brother Grazia di Santi – nevertheless Michele Accolti, Benedetto's father, did not come to regard Arezzo as his only home. Indeed, by 1416 Michele had a house and was living in Florence.[73] Michele established residence in Florence to pursue his profession as a lawyer, practising with Florentine lawyers, taking employment on cases in Florence and teaching at the Florentine university. In May 1414, Michele and the famous Florentine lawyer and legal commentator, Paolo di Castro, were engaged to settle a dispute between the Conti Gherardesca and Florence's subject city of Pisa.[74] In April 1416 Michele was elected to read civil law for four months at the University of Florence at an annual salary of seventy florins.[75] Michele and Guglielmo di Francesco Tanagli, another prominent Florentine lawyer, were opposing advocates in a case during 1425.[76] In Florence on 24 September 1427, Michele and three lawyers practising in Florence, Giovanni di ser Girolamo da Gubbio, Guglielmo di Francesco Tanagli and Tommaso della Bordella, arbitrated a case regarding the Barbolani family from Montaiuto.[77] It may be assumed therefore that by 1416 Michele had an active legal practice in Florence and was matriculated in the Florentine guild of lawyers and notaries.[78]

Michele's entry into Florentine legal circles may have been facilitated by his father-in-law, Messer Rosello di ser Fino Roselli, himself a well-known lawyer. The marriage between Michele Accolti and Margherita

[71] Pasqui and Viviani, *Guida*, 209ff.; ASF, Cat. 203, fol. 657r.
[72] ASA, PdB, fol. 576v; Pasqui and Viviani, *Guida*, 231. Michele later identified the same house as being located in the *contrada* of Ruga Mastra: cf. ASA, Cat. 3, fol. 208r and ASF, Cat. 201, fol. 351r.
[73] BCA, 34, p. 252: copy of a document of 4 May 1416 attested by ser Cristoforo di Francesco de' Bezzoli di Arezzo: 'Actum Florentiae in Populo Sancti Appollinaris videlicet in domo habitationis . . . Michaelis'.
[74] BCA, 12, fol. 6v; T. Dempster, *De etruria regali* (Florence, 1723–4), ii, 318.
[75] Park, 'Readers', 273.     [76] BNF, Landau Finaly, 98, fol. 69r–73v.
[77] BNF, PG, 16.     [78] Cf. Martines, *Lawyers*, 501.

Roselli in 1408 was, it has been observed, a union of two Aretine patrician families, but it was just as much a professional match, helping to advance Michele in his legal career. Rosello had received his doctorate in civil law from Bologna, where he taught law in the 1380s; in the 1390s he taught in the Florentine university, enrolled in the Florentine guild of lawyers and notaries, built up a private legal practice in Florence and became a Florentine citizen.[79] It was perhaps Rosello's Florentine connections that gave Michele Accolti a start in Florence.

Nevertheless, Michele was not the first member of the Accolti family to emigrate from Arezzo to Florence; it has been pointed out that during the fourteenth century Maestro Gregorio di ser Accolto di Accolto del Riccio da Faltona moved from Arezzo to Florence to set up a medical practice.[80] In fact, an even closer connection exists between Michele and Maestro Gregorio. In Florence, Michele first lived in the parish of Sant'Apollinare in the quarter of Santa Croce. Sant'Apollinare or Pulinari, suppressed in 1755, would today have been at the southern end of Via del Proconsolo, on the north side of Piazza San Firenze, between Via Vigna Vecchia and Via dell'Anguillara. In 1427 Michele was living in the same area, now near the church of San Procolo, in a house rented from Alessandro Covoni. San Procolo stood at the intersection of Via Pandolfini and Via de' Giraldi, a few hundred yards northeast of Sant'Apollinare. Sant'Apollinare was in fact the parish in which Maestro Gregorio Accolti had lived in Florence, and it is possible that Michele chose to live there to reestablish his ties with the earlier Accolti of Arezzo resident in Florence.[81]

It is interesting that both Michele and Maestro Gregorio had links not only with Arezzo but with the Casentino. The Casentino consists of hills and valleys surrounding the river Arno as it rises in the Monte di Falterona and flows south to Arezzo. One natural egress from this region is to proceed south along the Arno into the valley surrounding Arezzo, a route

---

[79]  *Ibid.*, 498; *Statuti*, ed. Gherardi, 357–8, 359–60, 362–3, 371, 372.

[80]  Cf. p. 25, *supra*.

[81]  ASF, Cat. 201, fol. 359v: 'Et sta al presente el detto Misser Michele in Arezzo apresso a Sam Proculo in casa d'Alessandro Covoni. Pagha di pisgione fiorini 30 l'anno.' There was no church of San Procolo in Arezzo. Michele, at the beginning of his tax return (*ibid.*, fol. 351r), said that he 'habita al presente a Fiorenza. In Arezzo è dela contrada di Ruga Mastra dela Porta di Fuori . . . la quale casa, quando el detto Messer Michele è Arezzo, è per suo habitare. Et al presente nella detta casa non habita persona.' Moreover, the Covoni were a well-known Florentine, not Aretine, family, and there was a church of San Procolo in Florence; obviously Michele mistakenly wrote Arezzo instead of Florence. On Sant'Apollinare and San Procolo, cf. E. Repetti, *Dizionario geografico-fisico-storico della Toscana* (Florence, 1833–45), ii, 275; R. Ciullini, 'Di una raccolta di antiche carte e vedute della città di Firenze', *L'universo*, v (1924), 590–4 and 13 maps. For Maestro Gregorio's residence, cf. Marzi, *La cancelleria*, 230; BNF, PG, 16. Maestro Gregorio and Michele Accolti both lived in the same quarter and *contrada* of Arezzo: Ruga Mastra in Porta di Foro: cf. A. Ugolini, *Maestro Gregorio d'Arezzo et le sue rime* (Livorno, 1901), 8–9, and ASF, Cat. 201, fol. 351r.

along which Michele must have gone to visit his farms and bring their produce home to Arezzo. Another way out is to go north along the Arno through the valley between Monte di Falterona and Pratomagno, continuing all the way to Florence. Michele Accolti could just as easily have attended to his property in the Casentino living in Florence as he had been able to do living in Arezzo.

Economic conditions in Arezzo probably influenced Michele's decision to seek his fortune in Florence, for Arezzo, as has been pointed out, suffered a severe depression under Florentine rule in the fifteenth century. Indeed, the assets of Aretine lawyers in 1429[82] provide graphic proof of the advantages of pursuing a legal career in Florence as opposed to Arezzo:

| | |
|---|---|
| Messer Gregorio di Domenico Marsuppini | 13,049 florins[83] |
| Messer Michele di Santi Accolti | 1584 florins[84] |
| Messer Benedetto di Giovannozzo | 801 florins[85] |
| Messer Gusime di Filippo Paganelli | 498 florins[86] |
| Messer Jacopo Roselli | 473 florins[87] |

Three of the five Aretine lawyers thus had assets worth less than 1000 florins and two, less than 500 florins. Of the other two, Michele Accolti had almost double the wealth of Benedetto di Giovannozzo whereas Gregorio Marsuppini was in a class by himself, and it is noteworthy that both Gregorio Marsuppini and Michele Accolti lived not in Arezzo but in Florence. As the prosperity of his fellow citizens declined in the fifteenth century, Michele's wealth rose; in 1419 there were seventy-six Aretines with higher tax assessments than his and in 1423 there were still sixty-nine, but by 1436 there were only nineteen, showing the very tangible benefits of a successful career in Florence.[88]

In the 1410s and 1420s Michele Accolti seems to have divided his time between Florence and Arezzo: he had houses in both cities; his legal practice appears to have been in Florence, yet he fulfilled the duties of an Aretine citizen, serving as a communal official in Arezzo nine times between 1413 and 1428. In fact, Michele's ties with both cities were put to use by the Aretine commune, who elected him their ambassador to Florence, where he spent fifteen days in February 1417, gaining Florentine approval and confirmations of Arezzo's civic ordinances,[89] as well as negotiating various minor matters on behalf of the commune;[90] he was

---

[82] According to ASF, Cat. 273, fol. 23v, 36v, 10r, 12r, 33v.
[83] Cf. ASF, Cat. 203, fol. 643r–647v.   [84] Cf. *ibid.*, 201, fol. 351r–359v.
[85] Cf. *ibid.*, 200, fol. 770r–773v.
[86] Cf. *ibid.*, fol. 931r–933r; ASA, Dott.Nott. fol. 34v.
[87] Cf. ASF, Cat. 201, fol. 42r–43r.
[88] ASA, Lira, 5, fol. 17r; 6, fol. 33r; 7, fol. 35r; 8, fol. 38r.
[89] ASA, Provv. 5, fol. 211r, 212r; BCA, 12, fol. 6v.
[90] ASA, Provv. 5, fol. 211v; Entr. Usc. 40, fol. 85v.

also sent as ambassador to Florence in 1424 to protest against proposals to make the Aretines pay for the armament of their citadel.[91] It was perhaps his dual life which finally led to the division of his and his brother Grazia's property. In fifteenth-century Italy, it was not unusual for sons to retain their father's property in common after his death; sometimes this meant that they actually lived together, but just as often they could have separate residences.[92] Michele and Grazia Accolti both had their own houses in Arezzo, and yet they did not at first divide their property after coming from Pontenano. There was perhaps no inconvenience in communal ownership as long as both brothers were mainly resident in Arezzo, but as Michele became more involved in Florence with his legal practice, they decided to obtain a formal division, which took place in 1423.[93] As the elder brother, Grazia took most of their father's patrimony in Pontenano; the remaining lands there they continued to own in partnership, Grazia receiving two thirds of the income, Michele one third; and each brother retained the property which he himself had purchased.[94] The division, however, was very much a legal convenience, and Michele always maintained close ties with his brother Grazia and his family. In 1429, for example, he complained to a friend in Florence that he had to make onerous contributions to the support of Grazia and his family,[95] and in the 1430s he allowed his nephew, Agnolo di Grazia, to use his house in Arezzo for his notarial practice.[96]

Michele never became the most eminent lawyer of his day in his native city of Arezzo, where he was always outshone by his illustrious compatriot, Angelo de' Gambiglioni, and his long periods of absence from Arezzo even placed him behind a lesser figure such as Benedetto di Giovannozzo,[97] but in Florence he established himself as one of the more notable practising lawyers in the 1420s and 1430s. One sign of his solid professional reputation was his appointment as a judge outside Florence: in 1429 he was elected *podestà* of Perugia and, in the same year, *podestà* of Volterra.[98] Michele used friendships he had made among Florentine citizens to advance his legal career. One such acquaintance was Forese Sachetti, a Florentine citizen of moderate importance in governing circles. While serving in Perugia as *podestà*, Michele wrote to Sachetti, 'You have

---

[91]  *Ibid.*, 48, fol. 195v.
[92]  On households and their structure among Florentine families, cf. Kent, *Household and Lineage*, 21–117.
[93]  ASA, Lira, 6, fol. 33r; cf. *ibid.*, Cat. 3, fol. 208r–213r.
[94]  *Ibid.*; ASF, Cat. 201, fol. 353r–355r.     [95]  Published *infra*, pp. 39–40, n. 115.
[96]  ASF, Not.A. A 47, fol. 29v, 33r, 187r.
[97]  Cf. ASA, Provv. 6, fol. 21v–30v, where in December 1428 and January 1429 Michele was the commune's third choice after Angelo Gambiglioni and Benedetto di Giovannozzo as their legal negotiator with Florence in a dispute over taxation.
[98]  BCA, 12, fol. 6v–7r.

made my interests your own by your good will and have thus guided my affairs; so I ask you to recommend me ardently to the new officials of the university and especially to those who are your intimate friends, and when you see your new *podestà*, recommend me to him.'[99] Michele's greeting to the new *podestà* of Florence may have been a courtesy extended to a fellow judge serving in a foreign town; his request to be recommended to the Florentine officials of the university was obviously made in the hope of gaining a reappointment to teach law in Florence.

Michele succeeded in obtaining a teaching post again at the University of Florence, where he read civil law in the academic years 1429–30, 1431–2, 1432–3 and 1434–5.[100] His salary varied between 120 and 150 florins a year,[101] so placing him in the second rank of university teachers of law in Florence, behind men of national reputation such as Messer Sallustio di Messer Guglielmo da Perugia and Messer Lodovico di Maestro Santi da Roma, who commanded as much as 500 florins a year, but ahead of junior staff who were paid sixty florins or less a year.[102] Michele's reputation as a lawyer in Florence during the 1430s was sound, as is shown by Vespasiano da Bisticci's recollection of him as a 'solennissimo dottore',[103] and during that period his commitments there grew to such an extent that he was no longer able always to discharge his duties as a citizen in Arezzo: although his name was drawn for the priorate and for the general council in Arezzo, Michele was absent from Arezzo on both occasions and so did not take up office. Indeed, in 1433 Michele's name was drawn for the highest communal office in Arezzo, the *caput scripte* (the Aretine equivalent of the Florentine Gonfalonier of Justice), but again he was absent from Arezzo.[104]

Michele's position at the end of his life was unsettled. He was an expatriate Aretine living most of the time in Florence where he pursued an active and successful legal career; yet unlike his father-in-law Rosello Roselli, he never became a Florentine citizen, nor did he acquire any property in or near Florence, only renting a house there for thirty florins a year.[105] Indeed, his eldest daughter, Agnesa, did not marry a Florentine, but took a husband from Castiglion-Aretino (subsequently known as Castiglion-Fiorentino), Giovanni d'Agnolo di Pietro, who received from Michele a dowry of 300 florins and a trousseau worth sixty florins.[106] Perhaps it was economy which dissuaded Michele from seeking a Floren-

[99] The letter is published by Flamini, *Lirica toscana*, 578; the autograph manuscript is ASF, CSopp, 78, 325, n. 107. The letter is to be dated 1429 when Michele was *podestà* of Perugia.
[100] Park, 'Readers', 284–91; cf. *Statuti*, ed. Gherardi, 413–14.
[101] Park, 'Readers', 284–91. [102] *Ibid.*, 268–303. [103] Vespasiano, *Vite*, i, 595.
[104] ASA,. Estr. 8, fol. 58r, 61v, 115v, 119r, 159v, 162r–163r.
[105] Cf. pp. 30ff, *supra*. [106] ASF, Cat. 201, fol. 359v.

tine husband for his daughter, for 300 florins would have been a small
dowry in Florence in the fifteenth century, whereas in Arezzo it was no less
than dowries provided by many other patricians. Michele too did not give
up public life altogether in Arezzo in the 1430s; although he declined to
become a prior, *caput scripte* and a councillor, he did serve on the general
council in 1429, 1430 and 1432.[107] After 1435 he seems to have retired
from teaching in Florence, perhaps because of the chronic illness from
which he suffered throughout the 1430s,[108] returning to Arezzo, where he
was a member of the general council in 1438 and *caput scripte* in 1439,[109]
so holding at last Arezzo's highest magistracy just two years before his
death. The standing in Arezzo finally achieved by Michele at the end of his
life is clear from a resolution passed by the Aretine general council on 18
February 1441, three days after his death, when, 'in view of the laudable
and cherished memory of the renowned and excellent doctor of laws
Messer Michele di Santi of Arezzo', the council voted the sum of ten florins
'for his remains . . . to be honoured at his funeral by the commune of
Arezzo . . . in order to provide the very best example to others'.[110]

Nevertheless, in Florence Michele's status had always been equivocal,
which could hardly be uncommon in a society in which citizenship, the
right to public office and even social rank depended on ancestral links with
a city. Michele's social position derived from the antiquity of the Accolti
family in Arezzo, and so it is not surprising that, although his professional
career was in Florence, he did not achieve Florentine citizenship and
retained ties with Arezzo, where he and his family belonged to the city's
patriciate. There were other Aretines who led this kind of double life in
both Florence and Arezzo. Gregorio Marsuppini, although he had extensive investments in Florentine commerce, still owned farmland only in the
*cortine* and *camparie* of Arezzo.[111] Leonardo Bruni, although he had been
given Florentine citizenship, retained two houses in Arezzo and at least one
large estate at Quarto outside Arezzo.[112] The sons of Rosello Roselli,
Michele Accolti's brothers-in-law, themselves Florentine citizens, still had
their property in and near Arezzo. Antonio di Rosello had a house in

---

[107] ASA, Estr. 8, fol. 35v, 96r, 127r.     [108] Cf. *ibid.*, fol. 159v, 162r–163r; 9, fol. 51v.
[109] *Ibid.*, fol. 46v, 85r. Michele was commissioned by several members of the Marsuppini
family in Arezzo to write a *consilium* on a legal dispute on 28 April 1434: cf. ASA, Atti
civili, 14, fol. 28v. I am grateful to Mr Frank Dabell for this reference.
[110] ASA, Provv. 7, fol. 76v (19 February 1440 (ab inc.)): . . . visa laudabili et recolenda
memoria famosissimi et egregii legum doctoris domini Michelis Sanctis de Acoltis de
Aretio qui migravit a seculo cuius laudabilis memoria in eternum veniet et bonum esset
quod per commune Aretii honoretur sibi corpus in funere suo de aliquibus certis ut aliis
prebeatur exemplum optimum. *Ibid.*, fol. 77r: . . . quod . . . priores possint spendere in
et pro honoratione corporis recolende memorie dicti domini Micaelis usque in
quantitatem fl. decem . . . For the payment of these funeral expenses, cf. ASA, Entr. Usc.
69, fol. 88v.
[111] ASF, Cat. 203, fol. 644r–v; cf. Martines, *Social World*, 127–31.     [112] *Ibid.*, 117–23.

Arezzo and farmland in the Aretine countryside; he never owned property in or near Florence, acquiring farmland away from Arezzo only in 1442 as part of the dowry of his Paduan wife. Bernardo di Rosello, still a Florentine citizen, lived in Arezzo, where he owned a house and farmland; all the land he purchased after 1430 was near Arezzo and in the 1430s he opened a wool and leather shop in Arezzo. Rinaldo and Battista di Rosello, also Florentine citizens, lived in Arezzo, where they owned a house in common with their brother Antonio, where Rinaldo was a partner in an Aretine company as well as working for another Aretine firm, and where Battista was a grain dealer and book-keeper; all Rinaldo's and Battista's farmland was in the countryside of Arezzo too.[113]

Michele Accolti established a way of life which was carried on after his death in 1441 by his son Benedetto, who, having become a lawyer, divided his time between a professional career in Florence and commitments to his native city of Arezzo. There is one other feature of Benedetto Accolti's life which may perhaps have had its roots in his father's interests. Benedetto Accolti became an important humanist in Florence, and there is perhaps some evidence that his father Michele had had an interest in Latin letters too. Three of Michele's personal letters – all addressed to Forese Sachetti – have survived; two of these are written in Italian and were simple letters of recommendation, similar to countless others written in Florence during the fifteenth century.[114] The third is also a letter of recommendation, but this one is written in Latin. Michele's letter, composed in 1429, was not written in the most up-to-date classical Latin, using *quod*, for example, instead of the infinitive for indirect speech. Nevertheless, it was unusual for a layman who was not a humanist or grammar teacher to write a personal letter in Latin by the fifteenth century, and the letter has a number of literary flourishes, such as 'iam diu experientia certissima luce clarius percepi' and 'me servitorem vestrum intrinsice dilexit et diligit non proximis operibus meis sed propter immensam clementiam vestram'.[115]

---

[113] ASF, Cat. 36, fol. 47r–v, 151r–v; 37, fol. 1152r–1154v; 358, fol. 42r–v, 161r–v; 452, fol. 74r, 155r–v; 665, fol. 698r, 780r–781r; 701, fol. 205r–206v.

[114] For the first letter, cf. pp. 36–7, *supra*. All three letters were severely damaged by the flood of 1966; the manuscripts have now been restored, but are no longer completely legible. The text of the unpublished Italian letter is: *Verso*: Magnificho et potenti viro Foresi de Sachettis de Florentia honorando capitaneo civitatis . . . * singularissimo. *Recto*: Magnifice et potens vir maior mi singularissime. I'o sentito che nella vestra corte è preso uno Lorenzo chiamato Rassina da Rassina per certa rasgione, el quale è mio intimo amicho. Et però vi priegho quanto posso che vi piaccia averlo rachomandato et questo mi riputarò in grande piacere dela magnificentia vestra, alla quale stretissi-mamente mi racommando. Datum Florentie die viiii[a] ianuarii. Vester maior servitor, Michael de Aretio, legum doctor. (*illegible) Source: ASF, CSopp, 78, 325, n. 132.

[115] The text of the Latin letter is: *Verso*: Magnifico viro Foresi de . . . * ectis de Florentia honorando capitaneo Aretii domino et benifactori fideliter honorando. *Recto*: Magnifice vir et domine mi singulariter honorande. Quia iam diu experientia certissima luce clarius percepi quod magnificentia vestra me servitorem vestrum intrinsice dilexit et diligit non

The letter is not written in the matter-of-fact Latin characteristic of notarial documents or legal opinions and treatises; its style is similar to that used in letters written by Aretine grammar teachers,[116] and shows that Michele not only had had a thorough grounding in grammar and classical authors but also continued to make use of his early education in later life. Michele on this occasion was trying to cut a dash, and this letter may suggest that he was an amateur student of classical authors who bequeathed his interest in Latin letters to his son Benedetto.

proximis operibus meis sed propter immensam clementiam vestram, ideo humillissime supplico et exoro ut placeat favores vestros solitos michi impendere taliter quod officiales libre onus debitum omnibus perpenso et maturo iudicio pensatis michi imponant, et maxime habito respectu ad onus maximum familie mee et fratris mei ob cuius substentationem efficitur disturbatio et laboribus et oneribus michi quasi importabilibus quotidie me incessanter expono. Profecto mi tediosum et laboriosum est valde, quod michi a magnificentia vestra adscribam ad gratiam singularem. Insuper egregium virum et multiplici virtute refertum dominum Antonium de Aretio latorem presentium in fratrem . . . * et honorandum ad proximos lares pro aliquibus diebus pro quibusdam suis agendis remeantem supplico tota affectu ut habere placeat favorabiliter recommissum, prout in vestra magnificentia continuo et . . . * spero cui prodesse me suum servilem recommictitur. Datum Perusii die xviii februarii. Vestre magnificentie fidelis . . . * Michael de Pontenano . . . * Aretii . . . * recommendatione . . . * (*illegible) Source: ASF, CSopp, 78, 325, n. 279. Like the letter published by Flamini (cf. p. 37, n. 99, *supra*), this letter is to be dated 1429.

[116] Cf. e.g. ASA, Provv. 4, fol. 4r (letter of Maestro Francesco di ser Feo, 13 May 1403).

# 3

# *Benedetto Accolti's early life and works*

Benedetto Accolti was born in 1415, the third child of Michele di Santi Accolti and Margherita di Rosello Roselli. His elder brother Antonio was born in 1410 and his sister Agnesa in 1413. He had three younger brothers: Francesco, born in 1416; Donato, in 1421; and Giovanni, in 1423.[1] His two younger sisters, Tommasa and Nanna, were born between 1427 and 1441.[2] Two of Accolti's brothers died in their youth: Antonio between 1430 and 1445, and Giovanni between 1443 and 1456.[3]

Benedetto Accolti was depicted as a man of preeminent intelligence by Vespasiano da Bisticci, who particularly praised his memory, declaring that it was a marvel, unequalled by any of his contemporaries.[4] This prodigious intellect was an endowment shared by his equally brilliant brother, Francesco. Their father, Michele, must have been a man of considerable ability to restore his family from the oblivion of the Casentine hills to social prominence in Arezzo and forge for himself a prosperous legal career in Florence without the benefit of a previous legal tradition in his family. On their mother's side, Benedetto and Francesco benefited from the intellectual versatility of the Roselli family. Their grandfather, Rosello, the son of a notary, had become one of the leading lawyers of Florence by the turn of the fifteenth century; he was the founder of a veritable legal dynasty, numbering many lawyers in succeeding generations. The Roselli family was distinguished too by a remarkable series of Italian poets in the fifteenth

---

[1] ASF, Cat. 201, fol. 359v.

[2] Neither was mentioned *ibid.*, and 1441 is the date of Michele's death: cf. p. 58, *infra*.

[3] ASF, Not.A. A 45, fol. 15r–v, where Antonio is mentioned as a witness on 3 August 1430; *ibid.*, P 290 (1441–6), not foliated, 19 November 1445, where he is not listed as one of the Accolti brothers giving their sister Tommasa in marriage to Francesco Lippi. ASA, Cat. 7, fol. 212v ff., where Giovanni submits his return with his brothers in 1443; ASF, Not.A. S 1190 (unbound, unfoliated), where he is not mentioned as one of the brothers dividing Michele's estate on 25 April 1456. Neither Antonio nor Giovanni apparently died in Arezzo, as their deaths are not recorded in the Libri dei morti of the Aretine fraternity of Santa Maria della Misericordia (AFL, 886 (1420–33), 887 (1433–57)).

[4] Vespasiano, *Vite*, i, 595.

century, and members of the family showed an interest in Latin letters as
well.

In addition to the intellectual family life which the Accolti brothers
enjoyed, credit for stimulating their keen intellects must go particularly to
their native city of Arezzo, where, it has been seen, a vital educational tradition continued to flourish in the early fifteenth century. It is probable
that Benedetto and Francesco Accolti profited from the superior education available at the Aretine communal grammar school, and under the
guidance of excellent teachers such as Francesco di Feo and Domenico di
Bandino their precocious talents developed in similar directions: they both
gained recognition as Latin scholars and humanists; they both published a
considerable amount of Italian verse; and they both became civil and
canon lawyers. Their upbringing was supervised closely by their father
Michele, who, having established himself as one of the leading lawyers in
Florence, wanted his sons, according to Vespasiano, to follow him as
lawyers, this time with the kind of professional entrée which he himself
had been unable to enjoy.[5] They received further help from their father's
legal library, which consisted of thirty-six volumes of civil law texts,
decretals, commentaries and *consilia*. Valued at 290 florins, it constituted
a considerable collection,[6] and, available as it was from the beginning of
their studies, it saved the brothers from having to gather a collection one
volume at a time, just as collections of law books handed down from past
generations probably contributed to the emergence of other legal dynasties
in medieval and Renaissance Italy. Benedetto and Francesco probably
received encouragement in their legal studies from members of the Roselli
family too. Three of their mother's brothers were practising lawyers during Benedetto's and Francesco's youth: Giovanni, Francesco and Antonio
Roselli; also their mother's sister was married to an Aretine lawyer, Guido
Lamberti. Four cousins on their mother's side were practising lawyers as
well: Jacopo and Rosello di Giovanni Roselli, Giovanni di Battista Roselli
and Giovanni di Antonio Roselli.[7] Moreover, by becoming lawyers
Benedetto and Francesco could expect the esteem of their fellow citizens in
Arezzo, where law was the preeminent profession.[8]

---

[5]  *Ibid.*      [6]  ASF, Cat. 201, fol. 359r.
[7]  On the Roselli family as a legal dynasty, cf. ASF, Not. A. A 45, fol. 19r–20v; *ibid.*, A 49,
     fol. 180r; *ibid.*, A 51, fol. 86v–87r; *ibid.*, A 55, fol. 148r; *ibid.*, Cat. 359, fol. 870v; BNF,
     PG, 1735; BCA, 50, fol. 30r, 197r; AFL, 886, fol. 97r; BCA, 55, fol. 267r–v; *Statuti*, ed.
     Gherardi, 414, 419–20, 427–8, 444, 462; M. Borel d'Hauterive, *Le monarque de la
     sagesse* (Paris, 1869); G. Pancirolo, *De claris legum interpretibus* (Leipzig, 1721), 361–4,
     444; Flamini, *Lirica toscana*, 276–86.
[8]  Cf. Wieruszowski, 'Arezzo', 329–30, 342ff.; E. Besta, *Fonti: Legislazione e scienza
     giuridica*, part 2, in *Storia del diritto italiano*, i (Milan, 1923), 857–82, for numerous
     Aretine lawyers of the fourteenth and early fifteenth centuries, of whom Francesco
     Albergotti (d. 1376) and Angelo Gambiglioni (d. 1451) were the most famous.

Benedetto and Francesco Accolti chose to study at the University of Bologna, the leading centre of legal studies in Italy during the middle ages. Bologna was the university at which Michele Accolti had studied, and the Accolti brothers may also have chosen Bologna for their legal education because their cousin, Francesco Roselli, had till recently been a professor of canon law and a practising lawyer there.[9] One year apart in age, it was obviously convenient for both brothers to attend the same university; they took with them their father's legal library, a substantial part of which, unfortunately, was lost on their return home from Bologna.[10] Benedetto studied both civil and canon law at Bologna, and on 20 July 1437 he was given a private oral examination in civil law by three professors at Bologna, Niccolò Ghislardi, Niccolò de' Santi and Battista da San Pietro. The examiners reported that he gained great distinction in the examination and they passed him unanimously.[11] He probably took the course to become a doctor of canon law by three years' additional study, since he was later referred to as a doctor of both laws.[12] As the public examination in law was a formality, it was not uncommon to postpone it for several years, and Benedetto's took place in Bologna on 30 June 1440.[13]

Michele Accolti apparently used his position in the Florentine university to obtain teaching posts there for his sons, Benedetto and Francesco; according to Vespasiano, it was his particular wish for them to work under him in Florence.[14] Even before he had received his doctorate, Benedetto was appointed on 11 October 1435 to lecture there in *ius civile extraordinarium* at a salary of twenty florins a year.[15] He also taught at Bologna in 1437, the year in which he received his degree there in civil law.[16] The next year, 1438–9, he was again teaching in Florence, at the same salary of twenty florins a year that he had received in 1435.[17] For the next session in Florence, however, his salary was increased to sixty florins,[18] perhaps in recognition of the experience as a university teacher he had gained over the previous five years. Accolti's precocious accomplishments in law gained early recognition in his native city of Arezzo, where, between May 1438 and April 1439, he was appointed at the age of twenty-three to serve as

---

[9] ASF, Cat. 359, fol. 870v; on a visit home to Arezzo in the autumn of 1430 he was struck down by plague and died on 27 October 1430: cf. ASF, Not.A. A 45, fol. 19r–20v; AFL, 886, fol. 97v.

[10] ASA, Cat. 7, fol. 221r.

[11] *Il 'Liber secretus'*, ed. A.Sorbelli (Bologna, 1938–42), ii, 150–1.

[12] E.g. cf. ASF, CP, 56, fol. 1r; on this course, cf. Martines, *Lawyers*, 82.

[13] *Il 'Liber secretus'*, ii, 174; cf. Martines, *Lawyers*, 88–9.

[14] Vespasiano, *Vite*, i, 595.     [15] *Statuti*, ed. Gherardi, 441–2.

[15] A. Sorbelli, *Storia della Università di Bologna* (Bologna, 1944–7), i, 242.

[17] ASF, Monte Comune, 1285, fol. 90r, for which I am grateful to Professor A. Molho.

[18] Park, 'Readers', 296; *Statuti*, ed. Gherardi, 444.

legal adviser to a commission of citizens established to draw up new statutes for the city of Arezzo.[19]

1435 to 1440 were years of waiting for Benedetto Accolti, who by the age of twenty had already begun to assume family responsibilities, acting on one occasion in 1435 as his father's procurator.[20] He had obviously mastered the academic law curriculum by the same date, when he had first been engaged at the Florentine university as a lecturer. However, he could not practise law in Florence until he reached twenty-five, the minimum age for matriculation into the Florentine guild of lawyers and notaries.[21] In the meantime, he occupied himself with other pursuits, one of which was composing and publishing Italian verse, a pastime which he shared with his brother Francesco.[22] The Accolti brothers were heirs to a long tradition of vernacular poets in Arezzo,[23] several of whom were leading exponents of the *dolce stil nuovo* at the beginning of the fourteenth century. One member of the Accolti family, Maestro Gregorio di ser Accolto, who has already been mentioned as a resident of both Arezzo and Florence, achieved some distinction as an Italian poet in the fourteenth century,[24] and they may also have been following the example of some members of the Roselli family, several of whom were poets in the fifteenth century. Their uncle, Antonio Roselli, the famous canonist, wrote a poem on the corruption of the contemporary church;[25] another uncle, Bernardo, was the author of a didactic *canzone*, suggesting remedies for the caprices of fortune.[26] But as vernacular poets Antonio and Bernardo were outshone by their nephew, Rosello di Giovanni Roselli, Benedetto Accolti's cousin, who was the author of an important collection of Tuscan poetry; modelled on Petrarch's famous example, Rosello's *canzoniere*, which he himself compiled, consisted of fifty-six sonnets, four *canzoni*, two *sestine* and ten ballads, and was one of the largest and most significant collections of the early fifteenth century.[27]

Seven of Benedetto Accolti's Italian poems survive, of which six are *capitoli* in *terza rima* and one is a *canzone*.[28] Three of the *capitoli* form a

---

[19] ASA, Provv. 6, fol. 335r. For the circumstances leading to the compilation of the new statutes, cf. *ibid.*, fol. 293r; the new statutes appear *ibid.*, fol. 335r–340r.

[20] ASA, QCanc. 2, fol. 18v (29 October 1435).     [21] Martines, *Lawyers*, 32.

[22] On Francesco Accolti's poetry, cf. M.Messina, 'Le rime di Francesco Accolti', GStLI, cxxxii (1955), 173–233; *idem*, 'Francesco Accolti di Arezzo', Rin. i (1950), 308–12.

[23] Cf. G. Fatini, 'Il culto di Dante in Arezzo', AMAPet, n.s. ii (1922), 139ff. and Flamini, *Lirica toscana*, for the traditions of Aretine vernacular poetry in the fourteenth and fifteenth centuries.

[24] Cf. Ugolini, *Maestro Gregorio*, and Malvesti, cited *supra*, p. 25, n. 28.

[25] Ed. A. Lumini, *Scritti letterari*, ser. 1 (Arezzo, 1884), 159–63; cf. Flamini, *Lirica toscana*, 276, 494, 572–3, 724–6 and *infra*, pp. 221–2.

[26] *Ibid.*, 277, 515, 726.

[27] *Ibid.*, 278–86, 403–10, 490–2, 499–501, 518–19, 574, 726–31.

[28] Critical ed. by Jacoboni, 'Rime', 241–302.

series of love poems; another *capitolo* is an invective against an anonymous detractor; the longest poem is a verse treatise on the nature of friendship; and the final *capitolo* is a panegyric of the Virgin. The *capitolo* on
friendship was Accolti's entry to the famous Certame Coronario of
1441,[29] and it must have been composed after the love poems, since in it
Accolti refers to his frivolous early years when he wrote verses on 'what he
knew of love'.[30] The invective was possibly written in this same period
when Accolti enjoyed more leisure time; it was clearly not written much
later, since a manuscript of it bears the date 1445–8.[31] The encomium of
the Virgin was probably written in 1450, the date ascribed to it in the
earliest surviving manuscript.[32] Like the poetry of his brother Francesco
and his cousin Rosello, Benedetto's verse was highly regarded in the
fifteenth century. Vespasiano da Bisticci declared that he had a good style
in writing Italian poetry,[33] praising in particular the gracefulness of his
verse, and his poems achieved considerable popularity soon after they
were composed; indeed, two manuscripts of them are known to have been
copied in the 1440s, two more in the 1450s, five others may be attributed
to the middle of the fifteenth century, and there are thirty-two fifteenth-
century manuscripts in all.[34]

Accolti's four love poems form a series, depicting the sufferings endured
by the poet in the course of a frustrated infatuation and recording the
lessons which he drew from these experiences. In the *capitolo* 'Po' che 'l
cieco furor', which, according to the caption in several manuscripts, was
composed for 'a lover of his', the poet asks either Cupid or his beloved to
put an end to his sufferings, to which, however, both remain insensitive. In
the *capitolo* 'Quell'antico disio', he calls upon death to release him from
his torments, vividly depicting his forthcoming encounter in the under-
world with legendary aggrieved lovers who will commiserate with him.
His *capitolo* 'Quando el foco d'amor' is devoted to a lesson learnt from his
amorous experience, namely that death is a benefit, offering release from
worldly suffering and admittance to celestial bliss. His *canzone*
'Giovanetti leggiadri e pellegrini', which narrates the course of his infatuation from first encounter to final frustration, is presented to teach others
to spurn love and to offer sympathy to those who have suffered like him.

---

[29] On the Certame, cf. P. Rajna, 'Le origini del Certame Coronario', in *Scritti varii . . . in
onore di R. Renier* (Turin, 1912), 1027–56; A. Altamura, *Il Certame Coronario* (Naples,
1952); Flamini, *Lirica toscana*, 3–51; G. Mancini, *Vita di L. B. Alberti* (Florence, 1911),
200ff.; *idem*, 'Un nuovo documento sul c.c.', ASI, ser. 5, ix (1892), 326–42; Holmes,
*Florentine Enlightenment*, 103–5; G. Gorni, 'Storia del C.C.', Rin. xii (1972),
135–81.

[30] Jacoboni, 'Rime', 286. The earliest ms. containing all four love poems, BRF, 1939, is
dated 1443–6 (*ibid.*, 242, 263, 265, 269, 277).

[31] *Ibid.*, 242, 282.    [32] *Ibid.*, 297.    [33] Vespasiano, *Vite*, i, 597.

[34] Cf. Jacoboni, 'Rime', 241–2, 263, 265, 269, 277, 282, 285, 297.

The invective is directed by Accolti against 'someone who has defamed him', and in it the poet invokes numerous curses upon his enemy. The *capitolo* on friendship is a didactic work, arguing that true friendship can arise only from the pursuit of virtue, which produces mutual admiration between friends. His last poem, 'Donna del cielo', portrays the Virgin's omnipotence and infinite mercy, concluding with a personal prayer to her from Accolti himself.

Neither the *canzone* nor the encomium of the Virgin contains any complex or developed literary subject matter. Although the *canzone* has a didactic purpose, attempting to dissuade the reader from the attractions of carnal love, it is written in a popular vein, as is the panegyric of the Virgin, in which Accolti expresses religious sentiments widely held in the later middle ages. Accolti's remaining five poems, on the other hand, are more intricate works of literature, based on classical Latin and humanist sources. In the *capitolo* 'Po' che'l cieco furor', Accolti uses the classical commonplaces, love's arrow and blind Cupid (vv. 14, 37–9, 64–7); he also describes the torments of Narcissus, using Ovid's *Metamorphoses* (II, vv. 356ff.) as a source. The second love *capitolo*, 'Quell'antico disio', makes use of even more complex literary subject matter, reworking Boccaccio's *Amorosa visione*, a long didactic poem which was well known in Florence during the fifteenth century.[35] Accolti used the section of *Amorosa visione* which recounted the torments suffered by lovers made famous in classical and medieval literature such as Dido, Tristan and Isolde and Laodamia, deriving the series of aggrieved lovers in this *capitolo* entirely from this part of *Amorosa visione*.[36] 'Quando el foco d'amor', the last of Accolti's love *capitoli*, makes still more extensive use of classical sources; its contents are philosophical, and it has been suggested that verses 52 to 81 of Accolti's poem derive from verses 240 to 288 of Juvenal's tenth satire.[37] However, closer examination shows that Juvenal and Accolti shared a common source, namely, the first book of Cicero's *Disputationes tusculanae*. The philosophical content of Accolti's poem is entirely based on Cicero, as the *capitolo* is actually an adaptation into Italian verse of selected passages of the *Tusculan Disputations*.[38] His longest and most

[35]  Ed. V. Branca (Florence, 1944). For its circulation, cf. the mss. listed *ibid.*, ix–xvii, which are mainly Florentine.
[36]  Cf. 'Quell'antico disio', vv. 67–82 and *Amorosa visione*, ix, 31–3, xi, 38–51, xx, 43–88, xxii, 7–42, 55–88, xxiii, 40–88, xxiv, 1–42, xxv, 13–60, xxvii, 1–48, 52–78, xxviii, xxix, 1–30, 40–2, xxxiv, 80–2.
[37]  Flamini, *Lirica toscana*, 347.
[38]  Juvenal, e.g., does not mention Pompey's ignominious flight from Italy nor the plight of his children, which Accolti took from *Disp.tusc.* I, xxxv, 86. Cf. 'Quando el foco', vv. 43–270 with *Disp.tusc.* I,xxxi, 75, xxxiv,83–4, xxxv–xxxvi,85–6, xxxvii,89–91, xxxviii,91, xxxix,93–4, xl,96–7, xli,97–9, xlvii–xlix,116. Jacoboni, 'Rime', 276, noted that the beginning of the speech by Socrates was derived from *Disp.tusc.* but did not

involved poem, the *capitolo* 'Se mai gloria' on the theme of friendship, is philosophical too; in this work Accolti reworked another Ciceronian philosophical dialogue, *De amicitia*, into Italian verse.[39] Accolti's last poem, the invective 'O tu che se' di tal superbia pieno', also has a classical source: Ovid's invective *In Ibin*. This poem has an intricate literary structure as well, putting to use techniques of classical rhetoric; in it Accolti followed the procedures of *epideixis*, the rhetoric of praise and blame, making particular use of *amplificatio*, which was the method of embellishing an argument or concluding an oration. Accolti's poem is an amplification of Ovid's *In Ibin*,[40] *amplificatio* being frequently used as a technique of composition in panegyric.[41]

In the *canzone* 'Giovanetti leggiadri e pellegrini', Accolti says that in his youth he devoted himself to the study not only of law but also of letters:

> Quando nel primo giovinile stato
> Da Dio e da natura fui condotto,
> Volsi la mente sotto
> Studio di legge e litteral dottrina,[42]

and indeed his poems testify to his erudition in the humanities from an early age. Both Benedetto and his brother Francesco quickly gained distinction as humanists, and the tradition of classical scholarship and education which continued to flourish in Arezzo in the early fifteenth century must have fired their enthusiasm for the humanities. It was also due to their father Michele's amateur interest in Latin letters that they developed a precocious talent for the classics, and further evidence of the importance attached to humanist studies in the Accolti household is provided by Benedetto's younger brother Donato. Donato, who was six years younger than Benedetto, enjoyed a less active life than his two elder brothers, spending most of his time in Arezzo where he had a modest career in public life. Not a scholar of Benedetto's or Francesco's stature, Donato did compose a description of the city of Florence in Italian verse,[43] and in 1444 he wrote a brief life of a soldier in the service of Niccolò Piccinino in reason-

realize that the rest of the poem was too. She observed, 270–1, that Accolti missed the irony of Callimachus's epigram on Cleombrotus, but it was Cicero who missed Callimachus's meaning and whom Accolti was copying (*Disp.tusc.* I, xxxiv,84).

[39] Cf. 'Se mai gloria', vv. 61–351, and *De amicitia*, v,18–xii,40, xiv,48–51, xvi,58–xxi,78, xxiii,87–8, xxv,93–4, xxvii,100–1.

[40] Cf. 'O tu che se', vv. 4–36 with *In Ibin*, 107–24; cf. Flamini, *Lirica toscana*, 528–9.

[41] Cf. *Rhet. ad Her.*, II,xix,30; II,xxx,47–9; III,viii,15.    [42] Jacoboni, 'Rime', 278.

[43] Biblioteca Capitolare, Pescia (Pistoia), Scaff. XXIII, palch. VI op. 11, n. 11, fol. 147r–148v; cf. P. O. Kristeller, *Iter Italicum* (London, 1963–7), ii, 68, 557, who gives the following description: Descriptio Florentine civitatis edita per Donatum Accoltum Arretinum inc. Fluentia Firenze hora si noma, a poem. I have been unable to see the ms. because the Biblioteca Capitolare is now closed and the collections have been put in storage.

ably correct humanist Latin, which he dedicated to his more learned brother Francesco.[44] Moreover, members of the Roselli family were interested in the study of Latin letters. Antonio Roselli, Benedetto's uncle, was the author of several Latin orations,[45] and his brother Bernardo served as chancellor to the count of Urbino in the early fifteenth century, which suggests that he may have had some classical education.[46] Rosello di Giovanni Roselli also demonstrated knowledge of the classics in his poems, two of which are in part paraphrases, in part translations, of Juvenal's third and tenth satires;[47] Rosello composed as well a few Latin verses and a Latin prose letter, in which he paid some attention to humanist style.[48]

Unfortunately, none of Benedetto Accolti's early Latin prose compositions has survived;[49] nevertheless, his ability to write classical Latin earned him recognition as a humanist as early as 1436, when, at the age of twenty-one, the great humanist Poggio Bracciolini wrote to him, praising his command of Latin.

Your letters have delighted me, he said, and I admire your ability to write with eloquence, ornament and fluency . . . In every period of history very few authors can with any justice be called eloquent. I see that you have made great strides in this discipline, and I congratulate you for devoting your intellect to the cultivation of letters, which not only can prove profitable but may also win you esteem.

[44] BV, Ott.Lat. 1863, fol. 291r–292r: Anno millesimo quadrigentesimo quarto de mense Junii. *Inc.* [P]lerosque huius orbis viros fasces divitias potentates doctrinas accumulare imspeximus pariter unius hore spatium auferre . . . *Expl.* Donatus Arretinus de morte et appensione fortissimi Antonelli equitis ad dominum Franciscum fratrem attice quidem doctrine virum eruditissimum. Francesco Accolti had studied Greek under Filelfo, probably between 1434 and 1438: cf. DBI, i, 104;L. Landucci, 'Un celebre scrittore aretino del sec. xv', AMAPet, vii, 2 (1887), 50; C. Corso, 'Francesco Accolti', BSenSP, lxii–lxiii (1955–6), 23ff.
[45] BAM, C 145 inf., fol. 141r–146r: D. Antonii Roxelli utrisque iuris Monarchae oratio pro principio studii in civitate Florentiae. *Inc.* [A]rbitrabar sacro santae militantis ecclesiae . . . *Expl.* Qui vivit et regnat in saecula benedictus; *ibid.*, fol. 291r: Gratiarum actio pro militari dignitate adepta per clarissimum Monarcham D. Antonium Rosellum. *Inc.* [I]n maximum quam decus christianissime Princeps . . . *Expl.* et studia mea illum suscipere coegerint et ego imo etc.
[46] ASF,Cat. 37, fol. 1154v. Although he was not a notary, his work as a chancellor sometimes earned for him the title 'ser': e.g. *ibid.*, Not.A. A 46, fol. 7v. Cf. Flamini, *Lirica toscana*, 277.
[47] *Ibid.*, 490–2, 499–501.     [48] Ed. *ibid.*, 608–10.
[49] The two Latin epigrams, attributed to Benedictus Aretinus, in Biblioteca Civica, Verona, 280 (1366), fol. 17v (cf. G. Biadego, *Catalogo . . . dei manoscritti della B. C. di Verona* (Verona, 1892), 183) are probably poems by his grandson, Cardinal Benedetto Accolti, who wrote numerous similar epigrams: cf. *Carmina illustrium poetarum italorum* (Florence, 1719), i, 1–7; *Carmina quinque hetruscorum poetarum* (Florence, 1562), 129–36. Biadego attributes this manuscript to the fifteenth century, which would make Cardinal Benedetto's (b. 1499) authorship impossible, but the hand, although more characteristic of the late fifteenth century, could also date from the early sixteenth century.

In the same letter Poggio praised Accolti for his study of the great ancient philosophers, 'to whose works', he wrote, 'you devote yourself continuously',[50] and indeed Accolti's Italian poetry testifies to the intensive study of classical authors alluded to by Poggio.

In his development as a humanist, the most powerful influence on Accolti was exercised by Leonardo Bruni, the leading figure of the Florentine humanist world in the 1430s and early 1440s. As an expatriate Aretine living in Florence, Bruni apparently took a special interest in Accolti as the son of a fellow countryman who demonstrated a prodigious talent for the humanities. At the time of Bruni's death in 1444 Accolti was described as his very close friend; he was immediately sent a copy of Poggio's funeral oration on Bruni from Rome, where Poggio was employed as a papal secretary.[51] He was a close friend too of Bruni's son, Donato, whose grief in 1444 he was reported to have shared; it was hoped that both Donato Bruni and Accolti would derive mutual consolation from Poggio's panegyric.[52] Accolti moreover was the dedicatee of Carlo Marsuppini's elegy on the death of Bruni, a Latin poem which is primarily a consolation for the young Accolti on the loss of his mentor, Bruni.[53] Marsuppini declares that, although grief and death are inevitable and human knowledge is impotent in the face of death, nevertheless literature is undying and so the man of letters is rendered immortal by his writings: 'thus, Leonardo, your name will be celebrated for innumerable years'. From his native city of Arezzo and even more from his adopted home of Florence, Marsuppini continues, Bruni has received the highest honours, and, 'if celestial rewards are given according to merit, you, Leonardo, will now go to join the Elysian company'; with Dante, Petrarch, Boccaccio and Salutati as your guides and companions, 'you will swell the holy chorus, the learned multitude'. These consolatory verses were aptly directed to the young Accolti, who seems to have grieved particularly over Bruni's death.[54]

The close ties between Bruni and Accolti are clear not only from these testimonies of Accolti's grief in 1444; as a humanist Accolti would follow the path which had been established by Bruni, who was not only his

---

[50] *Epistolae*, ii, 97–101.  [51] Alioti, *Epistolae*, i, 91.  [52] *Ibid.*
[53] Cf. BAM, Trotti, 373, fol. 41v: Karoli Aretini pro obitu Leonardi viri doctissimi ad Benedictum Iurisconsultissimum elegia incipit. Besides this ms., in which the elegy occupies fol. 41v–45r, the poem is also preserved in Biblioteca Corsiniana, Rome, Corsini 582 (45 C 17), fol. 102r ff. The elegy was published in *Carmina illustrium poetarum italorum*, vi (Florence, 1720), 267–71, but with the dedication to Accolti omitted.
[54] BAM, Trotti 373, fol. 43v: Sic, Leonarde, tuum nomen celebrabitur annos/ Innumeros; obitu gloria maior erit . . . [fol. 44r] Si bene pro meritis celestia munera reddunt,/ Ibis ad Elysios nunc, Leonarde, viros./ Occurretque tibi redimitus tempora Dantes,/ Qui canet infernas et super astra vias./ [fol. 44v] Advenietque simul multa gravitate Petrarcha,/ Boccatiusque simul, Collutiusque simul./ His ducibus venies, florent ubi gramine campi,/ Augebisque pios agmina docta choros. Cf. *Carmina*, 269–70.

mentor but also his model and paragon. In his elegy, Marsuppini
mentioned to Accolti only one specific literary achievement of Bruni's, his
history of Florence,[55] and this echoes a personal opinion of Accolti's, who
considered this to be Bruni's greatest literary work. Accolti later sought to
emulate Bruni the historian in his own two principal humanist compositions; his *Dialogue* was written to prove that recent times too had their
great men and deeds,[56] which was one of the principal themes of Bruni's
history of Florence.[57] Moreover, in his second major composition, a history of the first crusade, Accolti was following a route which had first been
opened by Bruni in his Florentine history: the writing of medieval history.
Accolti's fascination with the middle ages seems to have been sparked off
by Bruni, who was the champion *par excellence* of the post-classical era,[58]
and as a humanist and historian, Accolti took Bruni as his model. The seed
of medievalism, planted in Accolti by Bruni, however, bore fruit only many
years later in Accolti's mature works; nevertheless, even Accolti's first
compositions, his Italian poems, showed the strong influence of Leonardo
Bruni. Bruni had been the leading figure in the revival of Cicero in
fifteenth-century Florence, not only with his life of Cicero, *Cicero novus*,[59]
but also with his use and imitation of Cicero's writings such as *De oratore*,
*Disputationes tusculanae* and *De natura deorum*,[60] so that Accolti was
following his example by popularizing *De amicitia* and *Disputationes
tusculanae* in his poetry. Bruni had also drawn inspiration from Cicero in
his campaign as champion of the *vita activa*, and similarly Accolti in his
poem on friendship based a defence of the active life and a condemnation
of the contemplative, conceived on the Brunian model, on a passage from
Cicero's *De amicitia*:

> It is natural and useful for everyone to have
> Human intercourse and to flee the
> Solitary life . . . [61]

At the end of his life, Bruni moreover had taken particular interest in

---

[55]  BAM, Trotti, 373, fol. 42r: Quidve tuam prodest scripsisse Fluentie claram/ Historiam?
     . . . [fol. 44r] Huius [sc. Florence's] et hystoria est per te decursa, sed ipsum/ In medio
     cursu mors inimica rapit. Cf. *Carmina*, 267, 270.
[56]  Cf. Ch. 8, *infra*.          [57]  Bruni, *Historiae*, 3–4.
[58]  Cf. Baron, *Crisis*², esp. 191–211, 225–69, 279–90.
[59]  Cf. E. Fryde, 'The beginnings of Italian humanist historiography: the "New Cicero" of
     Leonardo Bruni', EHR, xcv (1980), 533–52.
[60]  Cf. R. Sabbadini, in GStLI, xcvi (1930), 131ff.; V.Rossi, *Il Quattrocento* (Milan, 1933),
     105–7; Baron, *Crisis*², 229–32, 513–14; J. Siegel, ' "Civic Humanism" or Ciceronian
     Rhetoric?', PP, xxxiv (1966), 14ff; F. Tateo, *Tradizione e realtà nell'umanesimo italiano*
     (Barin, 1967), 236–40; D. Marsh, *The Quattrocento Dialogue* (Cambridge, Mass.
     1980), 1–37.
[61]  Jacoboni, 288; cf. *De amicitia*, v, 19; xxiii, 87–8. On Bruni's Ciceronian defence of the
     active life, cf. esp. H. Baron, 'Cicero and the Roman civic spirit in the middle ages and the
     early Renaissance', *Bulletin of the John Rylands Library*, xxii (1938), 72–97.

defending the merits of the vernacular. He had upheld its historical pedigree in the face of criticism from Flavio Biondo, who maintained that modern Italian was a corruption of classical Latin.[62] Bruni also wrote lives in Italian of Dante and Petrarch in the 1430s to demonstrate the capacity of the vernacular to express serious philosophical, literary and historical ideas.[63] At that time Bruni seems to have been the centre of a learned circle in Florence one of whose preoccupations was the defence of the vernacular. Like Bruni, other members of this group published works which showed that the vernacular was appropriate for serious discussion. These included Matteo Palmieri, whose treatise on political theory, *Della vita civile*, which was published at this time, demonstrated that political ideas from Cicero, Aristotle, Quintilian and the medieval Italian jurists could be discussed in Italian;[64] Alberti made a similar point by publishing his treatise *Della famiglia* in Italian at about this time.[65] It would seem that Accolti too was a member of this group led and inspired by Bruni: much of his poetry, which was in fact written at this time, was based on weighty classical and humanist sources, and a work such as the *capitolo* 'Quando el foco', demonstrating as it did that Cicero's *Disputationes tusculanae* could be adapted to Italian verse, deserves to stand beside *Della vita civile* and *Della famiglia* as an attempt to show how questions from classical moral philosophy could be discussed in the vernacular.

In endeavouring to defend the Italian language, Accolti worked in close cooperation with Alberti, who organized a public vernacular poetry competition, under the patronage of Piero di Cosimo de' Medici; the Certame Coronario was held in the Florentine cathedral on 22 October 1441 in the presence of Pope Eugenius IV with ten papal secretaries acting as adjudicators. The theme was true friendship, 'la vera amicizia', and Benedetto Accolti's entry, the *capitolo* 'Se mai gloria', based as it was on Cicero's *De amicitia*, again demonstrated his concern with establishing the claims of the vernacular to an equal place beside classical Latin. Several other competitors also wrote serious philosophical poems; however, the adjudicators did not consider any of the entries worthy of the laurel crown, and so the whole affair ended on a disappointing note.[66] Nevertheless, the Certame Coronario did help to publicize the efforts on behalf of the vernacular by humanists such as Accolti, who deserves a place alongside Alberti as one of the early protagonists of the vernacular classicized on the

---

[62] On the dispute between Bruni and Biondo over the vernacular, cf. Biondo, *Scritti inediti*, 115–30; Bruni, *Epistolae*, ii, 62–8; Baron, *Crisis*[1], i, 303–6, ii, app. 7; Holmes, *Florentine Enlightenment*, 104–5.

[63] Cf. Baron, *Crisis*[2], 337–9, 344–6.

[64] For a full discussion of Palmieri's use of sources, cf. Warner, 'Political ideas'. For its date, cf. Baron, *Crisis*[1], ii, 583ff.

[65] Cf. Baron, *Crisis*[2], 348–50.   [66] Cf. p. 45, *supra*.

Latin model. It is well known that the Italian language was greatly enriched in vocabulary and syntax during the fifteenth century through the efforts of Alberti, who advocated a reformed vernacular on the model of classical Latin and who was probably the author of the first Italian grammar, which he based on the analogy of classical Latin grammar;[67] it should perhaps be pointed out that the poets who participated in the Certame Coronario also contributed to this important development in the history of the Italian language, and that one of them was Benedetto Accolti, whose contribution to the competition achieved a wide circulation in the fifteenth century.

Accolti's close association with Florentine humanism in the 1430s is also clear from the direct influence exercised on him by Matteo Palmieri, who, besides belonging to Bruni's circle, was a pupil of Accolti's friend, Carlo Marsuppini. Palmieri in *Della vita civile* usually followed Cicero's *De officiis*[68] but diverged at one point by stressing that 'friendship (*amicizia*) is the protection, defence and stability of every state',[69] and that loss of friendship among the citizens was the cause of the fall of the Roman Empire: 'those who, united in friendship, had tamed all the world and given laws to all nations, by their own discords, destroyed themselves entirely; such being the fruits of friendship, it must with diligence be sought and preserved among men'.[70] Similarly Accolti in his poem on friendship went beyond Cicero's *De amicitia* in making, like Palmieri, friendship the opposite of civil discord:

> And as much as through discord and the poison
> Which is born therein everything is ruined,
> So through friendship it flourishes and becomes serene.
> And . . . that friendship . . . without which the world would be lost,
> That is, highest concord, . . . unites the citizens
> For the benefit of the fatherland . . .[71]

Palmieri's distinctive emphasis on the importance of friendship in political life seems to have been adopted by Accolti, whose poem on friendship, written only a few years after the publication of *Della vita civile*, thus shows the influence of the most important text on political theory to emerge from the world of Florentine humanism in the early fifteenth century.

Besides Bruni, Alberti and Palmieri, Accolti was closely associated in his youth with another great figure of Florentine humanism: Poggio Bracciolini, who, it has been seen, wrote to Accolti as early as 1436

[67] Cf. Baron, *Crisis*[2], 350.    [68] Cf. Warner, 'Political ideas', 10–11.
[69] *Della vita civile*, 139; cf. Warner, 'Political ideas', 40.
[70] *Della vita civile*, 140; cf. Warner, 'Political ideas', 41.
[71] Jacoboni, 'Rime', 296–7; cf. *De amicitia*, vii, 24.

praising his accomplishments in the humanities. At this time Poggio declared that Accolti was one of his closest friends;[72] and it is clear that Poggio shared with Bruni the role of mentor to Accolti during these years. Accolti found Poggio's works as a humanist useful in his own studies of the classics and therefore considered himself in Poggio's debt; Poggio, for his part, denied that he had done anything very substantial to help Accolti, but said he was willing, in view of his own affection for Accolti, to accept his gratitude.[73] Poggio used his position as Accolti's counsellor not only to praise his excellence as a humanist but also to encourage him in the further pursuit of eloquence, which, Poggio predicted, would allow Accolti to rise to the peak of dignity and honour.[74]

At the best of times it could not always have been easy to have two mentors, and the late 1430s were probably not an altogether smooth road for Accolti, particularly as relations between Poggio and Bruni were not always harmonious.[75] Since the 1420s Bruni had reigned supreme among humanists in Florence, particularly after his reappointment as chancellor in 1427, but in the 1430s with the arrival of the papal curia in Florence, Bruni had to share the limelight with papal secretaries of equal stature as humanists, such as Poggio and Biondo. Perhaps some of the ill feeling generated by this coexistence can be detected in Bruni's and Biondo's controversy over the vernacular; indeed, humanists in Florence at this time came closest to open altercation on the occasion of the Certame Coronario. Alberti chose the papal secretaries as adjudicators because he felt they needed to be shown that Latin was not the only language in which serious ideas could be expressed. However, when the secretaries, refusing to award the laurel crown, suggested that the vernacular had not yet attained the stature of classical Latin, the competitors and organizers were furious, maintaining that the adjudicators had been motivated solely by envy. Over this issue, Accolti stood with Bruni and Alberti against the papal secretaries, Biondo and Poggio, who also took Biondo's side in the controversy over the origins of the vernacular.[76] Nevertheless, Accolti managed to keep Poggio's goodwill throughout these years. Apparently endowed not only with a formidable intellect but also with a placid temperament and a likeable nature, Accolti had, according to Vespasiano, an especially genial and gracious manner with everyone,[77] a description which was echoed by Poggio himself, who wrote that he 'was endowed with the greatest geniality, making everyone like him to a truly remarkable degree'.[78]

---

[72] Poggio, *Epistolae*, ii, 221.    [73] *Ibid.*, 100–1.    [74] *Ibid.*, 100.
[75] In 1439, e.g., relations between Poggio and Bruni were strained, and Bruni accused Aliotti of turning Poggio against him: cf. Aliotti, *Epistolae*, i, 25–9.
[76] Cf. Walser, *Poggius*, 258–62, for Poggio's views on the vernacular.
[77] Vespasiano, *Vite*, i, 596.    [78] Poggio, *Epistolae*, ii, 222.

Poggio gave Accolti the benefit of his wisdom not only with regard to his activities as a humanist but also concerning his legal studies. Indeed, Accolti's versatility in both these fields of learning struck Poggio. 'It is indeed the sign of a formidable intellect,' he wrote to Accolti, 'that you have mastered two disciplines, either of which is difficult and arduous to comprehend; indeed, you have made yourself the equal of those even who devote themselves entirely to only one of these subjects.' Law was an especially difficult subject to understand, according to Poggio, because there were so many differing opinions and so much disagreement among lawyers; there were countless volumes of commentary to entangle the reader in webs of contradiction. Legal writings were padded with so much superfluous verbosity that they required a lifetime of dedication from even the quickest of readers. The writings of lawyers lacked all stylistic refinements; modern jurists appeared entirely ignorant of the eloquent works of their ancient predecessors. They were so deeply engrossed in refuting the opinions of their colleagues that they seemed to have lost all sight of the truth. Accolti's interest in both law and the humanities struck Poggio as remarkable, for, as far as he was concerned, the two disciplines had nothing in common; indeed, law was nonsense according to Poggio because it was entirely devoid of eloquence.[79]

Although a number of well-established humanists were lawyers, the choice of a career in law by a humanist such as Accolti still seemed remarkable in the 1430s. Indeed, Poggio was probably speaking for other humanists then living in Florence when he derided Accolti's chosen career. Bruni himself wrote in exactly the same vein regarding law to Niccolò Strozzi, as did Lapo da Castiglionchio, another Florentine humanist connected with the papal curia, to Roberto Strozzi,[80] and it is unlikely that any of these humanists would have spared Accolti their barrage of vituperation against law. Indeed, the time had passed when humanists such as Salutati had been able to feel sympathy for law because of its close relations in the academic curriculum to the *studia humanitatis*. In the thirteenth and fourteenth centuries, rhetoric had often been closely associated with law in Italian universities, and it has been observed that very often early humanists such as Lovati and Geri d'Arezzo were lawyers.[81] However, the humanist movement passed at the end of the fourteenth century largely into the hands of professional rhetoricians, notaries and grammar teachers; these experts in grammar and rhetoric had moved away from the *ars dictaminis* to the direct study of classical authors, and were particularly sensitive to classical Latin style. Moreover, having no more affiliation to

---

[79] *Ibid.*, 97–100.
[80] *Disputa*, ed. Garin, 8; *Reden und Briefe*, ed. Müllner, 258–9.
[81] Cf. Weiss, 'Dawn of Humanism', BIHR, xlii (1969), 2ff.

the legal profession, they were now freer to attack lawyers for their allegedly barbarous Latin style; indeed, humanists such as Poggio or Bruni, whose work as secretaries was closely related to the notarial profession, probably resented the superior social status as well as the greater wealth and political influence of lawyers.

Poggio warned Accolti of 'the common weakness of many lawyers who abuse the law, inflicting injury for the sake of pecuniary gain'. In Poggio's eyes, the judgements of most lawyers were determined by their fees, and almost all lawyers entered the legal profession to satisfy their avarice; he was certain, on the other hand, that Accolti, whose excellent character burned with the love of virtue, stood out from the common multitude of lawyers and would spurn any source of dishonest profit.[82] All this must surely have tried Accolti's genial and apparently phlegmatic disposition. His grandfather, his father, three of his uncles and three of his cousins were all lawyers; both he and his brother Francesco had devoted themselves for at least five years to law when in 1436 Poggio let fall this shower of insults upon, it must have seemed, Accolti's own family. Accolti had the misfortune to appear in humanist circles at a time when relations between humanists and lawyers were particularly strained, and his experiences at the hands of humanists such as Poggio and Bruni had a profound effect on him. Later in life, in fact, Accolti lost interest in law, and it is possible that the abuse to which he had been subjected since his youth eventually proved effective.[83]

Nevertheless, neither Bruni nor Poggio could have expected Accolti, with a formidable legal tradition behind him on both sides of his family, to abandon the study of law forthwith at their behest. Poggio's actual advice to Accolti was to combine his two interests as much as possible. 'Make sure', Poggio urged, 'that you embellish the law with eloquence, which provides the greatest possible refinement to life.' Poggio was a man of considerable political experience; having started life as the son of a humble farmer, he had built up a substantial private fortune by the late 1430s, when he came into close contact with Accolti. He had enough sense to see the practical advantages of a legal career, and he urged Accolti to devote all his energies to the study of law, 'which will provide the wealth necessary to safeguard human life'. Writing with the sincerity born of personal experience, Poggio warned Accolti of the miseries of poverty. 'I would not want you to follow the teachings of that philosophy', he admonished Accolti, alluding to Stoicism, 'which upholds that happiness consists only of virtue, for many things besides virtue are needed to lead a civilized life . . . People often give lip-service to the virtues of poverty, with no knowledge of what it is like themselves. For it is the hardest and most grievous

---

[82] Poggio, *Epistolae*, ii, 98–100.    [83] Cf. pp. 113–14, *infra*.

experience to be poor and indigent, having to beg with a face full of dejection for the necessities of life.'[84] Such words were aptly directed at the young Benedetto Accolti, who had spent his youth in circumstances of prosperity, if not of great wealth. By the time he was born in 1415, his father Michele had established a successful legal career; he had never had to suffer the penury of life in the remote hills of the Casentino, where his father had spent his youth. Indeed, Accolti probably received similar strictures about the miseries of poverty from his father, who, Vespasiano noted, was so keen for him to make his way in the legal profession.

With pressure and encouragement coming from all sides, Benedetto Accolti must have been eager to embark on a full career as a practising lawyer as he neared his twenty-fifth birthday in 1440, when he would finally be eligible to join the Florentine guild of lawyers and notaries. On 4 April 1440 Accolti was duly matriculated in the Florentine Arte di Giudici e Notai, sponsored by his father and his father's colleague in the Florentine university, Giovanni di Girolamo da Gubbio.[85] Accolti's immediate matriculation on his twenty-fifth birthday reflects the influence that his father was able to exert as a long-standing guild member and an eminent figure in Florentine legal circles; this was the kind of advantage which Michele himself had been unable to enjoy. Benedetto's early matriculation may also indicate his own impatience to embark upon a full-time legal career which had been denied him because of his youth since 1435, when he had first become the colleague of older, fully established lawyers in the Florentine university.

There are other signs of Accolti's frustration with the progress of his legal career in 1440. At the very time of his matriculation in the Florentine guild of lawyers, Poggio, then resident in Florence with the papal curia, wrote to friends in Siena recommending Accolti for an appointment to teach law in the University of Siena.[86] Accolti evidently felt that his merits were insufficiently appreciated in Florence. 'Benedetto Accolti, an extremely learned lawyer', wrote Poggio to the chancellor of Siena, 'has so much legal ability that in my opinion he should doubtless be compared to the legal pundits of antiquity. But it often happens that someone's merits are appreciated least of all in his own homeland.' Accolti seems to have been particularly conscious that his age might be an impediment to an appointment in Siena, suggesting perhaps that his youth had become a sore point during the previous five years in Florence. 'Nor is it a question of age,' Poggio assured the chancellor,

---

[84] Poggio, *Epistolae*, ii, 98–100.
[85] ASF, Arte di giudici e notai, 126, fol. 45r–v; for Giovanni di Girolamo as one of Michele's colleagues in the Studio, cf. *Statuti*, ed. Gherardi, 438–40.
[86] Poggio, *Epistolae*, ii, 220–2, 228–31.

for a given number of years are not what matter but rather knowledge of the law. If you were making an appointment to govern your republic, in which the welfare of the state were at stake, then perhaps someone of mature years would be needed, who would combine prudence with the most extensive practical experience. But since it is a question of civil law and giving lectures on law in public, what is relevant is not age but knowledge and intelligence, both of which Benedetto already enjoys in abundance. We have seen about us the many doting, ignorant, stupid old men and, on the other hand, mature, qualified young men, whose virtues more than compensate for their tender age. Indeed, Benedetto has already passed the age at which many bishops and cardinals are created.

Another source of discontent may have been the small salary of sixty florins that Accolti was receiving then in Florence, where he was still one of the junior members of the teaching staff, and he may have felt that the time had come for him to enjoy some of the monetary rewards of a legal career depicted by Poggio four years earlier. Indeed, in his letter, Poggio made a particular point of saying that pecuniary recompense had nothing whatever to do with Accolti's wish to leave Florence, which suggests that the very opposite was true. Accolti, moreover, may have been sensitive to the dubious reputation enjoyed in Italy by the University of Florence, which, by the fifteenth century, 'had fallen distinctly behind the first-rate and even some of the second-rate universities'.[87] In his letters Poggio actually made a particular point of Accolti's desire to play a part in a 'celebrated theatre, where he could gather the fruits of his own labours. He could do this most easily, he thinks, by working in one of those universities enjoying a preeminent reputation, especially at Siena, which commands such particular esteem within this circle of universities.' Indeed, Poggio went further in his praise of the University of Siena and by implication in his criticism of the Florentine university in a letter to another Sienese friend, in which he declared that 'Accolti wished to work in the Sienese university because at that time it was flourishing more than other universities'. Moreover, Poggio hoped that Accolti's appointment would stimulate greater enthusiasm for humanism in Siena. 'Benedetto of Arezzo is an extremely learned lawyer,' he wrote to his Sienese friend, evidently a humanist himself, 'and he has also gained great distinction in our own field of study [viz. the humanities]. It is my opinion that, although he is second to none in his knowledge of law, he is superior to many in eloquence . . . On behalf of the kind of learning in which you delight, I beseech you to give him your support.'

Poggio wrote two of his letters of recommendation to Siena on 8 April 1440, only four days after Accolti had matriculated in the Florentine guild of lawyers. It may seem strange that Accolti was considering a career in Siena at the very time he had become eligible to work as a practising lawyer

---

[87] Park, 'Readers', 271.

in Florence. But it must be remembered that Accolti had no strong ties to any particular Italian city. The ancestral links of the Accolti family with Arezzo had been greatly weakened in the fourteenth century and in the fifteenth they were never fully repaired by Michele Accolti. With loyalties already divided among the Casentino, Arezzo and Florence, there was little to hold Accolti back from seeking his fortunes in Siena.

Accolti was not in fact appointed to the University of Siena; nevertheless, the year 1440–1 would still be a milestone in his life. He seems to have put to one side thoughts of seeking a career outside Florence; as a member of the Florentine guild of lawyers, he would devote all his energies to building up a legal practice there. Up to 1441 he had divided his time between law and the humanities; now he was to turn his full attention to legal practice and teaching. Until 1441 he had been the bachelor son of a prosperous lawyer able to provide for his needs, free from any weighty family responsibilities. However, on 15 February 1441 his father Michele died[88] and Benedetto was left, or would be by 1445, the eldest son of the Accolti family. His younger brother Francesco was still free to seek his fortune as an itinerant lawyer throughout the cities of north Italy, a career which he embarked upon soon after 1441.[89] As head of the Accolti family, on the other hand, Benedetto now had responsibilities to his younger brothers and sisters in Arezzo, and it would have proved much more difficult for him to work in Ferrara or Milan than it would for his brother Francesco. In the hard years after 1441 Benedetto Accolti perhaps looked back with nostalgia to his youth in the late 1430s, when he had had so much more time to devote to his most profound interest, the *studia humanitatis*.

---

[88]  AFL, 887, fol. 47r; his uncle Grazia died on 21 October 1444: cf. *ibid.*, fol. 62v.
[89]  For a summary of Francesco Accolti's legal career, cf. DBI, i, 104–5.

# 4

## Accolti in Florence and Arezzo in the 1440s and early 1450s

The Certame Coronario of October 1441 with its inconclusive outcome was a discouraging experience for the competitors, and Benedetto Accolti was perhaps fortunate in having an intellectual life which extended beyond the now somewhat soured humanist circles of Florence. He had just become fully qualified to practise law and he now devoted all his efforts to establishing a legal practice in Florence. In the five or six years following 1441 Accolti appears to have laid his humanist studies to one side, his father Michele's death in 1441 having led him to concentrate on the serious business of building up a legal career to help to support his widowed mother and brothers and sisters. Michele Accolti had left an estate worth about 1600 florins; this would provide an annual income of perhaps just over 100 florins,[1] which would be a useful supplement to a professional income but nothing like enough to maintain the Accolti family at the standard of living provided by Michele with his earnings as a lawyer. Moreover, Benedetto had two younger unmarried sisters, Tommasa and Nanna, whose dowries would eventually reduce substantially the capital inherited from his father. After his father's death in 1441 Accolti must have felt that he had little time for an unremunerative pastime such as the humanities.

Accolti's legal career advanced during the early 1440s, and after his unsuccessful attempt to move to Siena in 1440 he showed no more signs of wishing to leave Florence for a number of years. He taught civil law at the university throughout the 1440s, and his salary rose rapidly from the sixty florins that he had been receiving up to 1442. For the academic year 1442–3 he was given a rise to ninety florins, which placed him in the middle rank of the teaching staff, behind Benedetto Barzi and Domenico Martelli but ahead of juniors such as Girolamo Machiavelli and Tommaso Deti. For the 1443–4 session he was given a further rise to 120 florins, placing him at the head of the roll in civil law along with Domenico

---

[1] For the value of Michele's property, cf. p. 30, *supra*; in the 1427 *catasto*, income was regarded as 7% of capital.

Martelli, whom, however, he was soon to leave behind. For he was given another rise of eighty florins for the session 1444–5, placing him at the undisputed head of the civil law staff, a position which, insofar as payment records have survived, he did not relinquish.[2] Benedetto Accolti therefore by the age of twenty-nine had reached a position of greater eminence in the university than his father Michele had ever achieved. Besides his greatly increased earnings, moreover, another old source of dissatisfaction with Florence was quickly removed in the 1440s. In the 1430s he had been unable to supplement his income from teaching with earnings from private legal practice; after 1441, however, he was able as a member of the Florentine guild of lawyers to practise law in Florence and he is known to have begun working for Florentine families during this period.[3]

By the mid-1440s Accolti was understandably more content with his life in Florence than he had been in the late 1430s. His high salary now allowed him to look for a wife, whom he found in Laura di Messer Carlo Federighi. His marriage to her in 1446[4] further strengthened his ties with Florence, for the Federighi were a prominent Florentine patrician family, living in the parish of San Pancrazio in the quarter of Santa Maria Novella; most of the family had houses in the Via degli Orefici, today called Via dei Federighi, or in the Piazza di San Pancrazio.[5] In the fourteenth century the family were members of the greater guilds, mainly as wool merchants, apothecaries and bankers;[6] the first member of the family to enter Florentine public life was Federigo di Arrigo, an apothecary, who belonged to the Signoria in 1325.[7] His son Tommaso was the first in the family to gain political prominence, being a member of the Signoria four times in the mid-fourteenth century.[8] Tommaso's nephew, Francesco di Lapo, who was Laura Federighi's grandfather, was one of the leaders of the so-called oligarchic regime at the turn of the fifteenth century. He was a member of the Balìa of 1381; Gonfalonier of Justice in 1382 and 1405; and a member of the Dieci di Balìa in 1389, 1393, 1396 and 1404. He was captain of Arezzo in 1385 during the difficult period immediately after the establishment of Florentine rule there in 1384, and represented Florence in negotiations with the Tarlati family over the surrender of their fortress Pietramala to Florence. In 1386 he was Florentine ambassador to Bologna and Venice; in 1390, again ambassador to Venice as well as to Alberto d'Este; and in 1396, ambassador to Vicenza. Francesco Federighi died in

---

[2] Park, 'Readers', 297–303. Cf. ASA, Estr.9, fol. 144r; 10, fol. 20r–v, 26v; ASF, Monte Comune 2364, fol. 101v, for reference to which I am indebted to Professor A. Molho.

[3] ASF, Dip., Famiglia Baldovinetti, 3 October 1446.

[4] ASF, Mss. 348, fol. 14r; BNF, PG, 16.

[5] BNF, CPass. 187, n. 51, fol. 1v; ASF, Cat. 42, fol. 446r; *ibid.*, 620, fol. 320r; *ibid.*, 671, fol. 376r.

[6] BNF, CPass. 8, fol. 95r; 187, n. 51, fol. 2r.       [7] *Ibid.*, 8, fol. 95r.       [8] *Ibid.*

1411,[9] and his leading position in the regime was assumed not so much by his eldest son Jacopo, who, although a prior in 1407 and Gonfalonier of Justice in 1425, devoted himself mainly to the wool business,[10] but rather by his younger son Carlo, Laura's father and Benedetto Accolti's father-in-law. Carlo became a lawyer and established a legal practice in Florence in the 1410s; he taught in the Florentine university during the 1410s, 1420s and 1430s, and frequently worked as a legal adviser to the Florentine government. However, most of his energies were devoted not so much to law as to Florentine public life, for Carlo Federighi belonged to the inner circle of the regime from the 1420s until his death in 1449, a position where he remained during and after the political turmoil in Florence of the 1420s and 1430s which resulted in the ascendancy of the Medici. In the period 1429 to 1434 he was a speaker in sixty sessions of the *pratica*; he was Gonfalonier of Justice in 1444 and a prior in 1417 and 1424; he was appointed to the Dieci di Balìa for the Lucchese War in 1429; he was four times one of the Dodici Buonuomini and three times one of the Sedici Gonfalonieri. He enjoyed a distinguished career as a Florentine diplomat: in 1420 he was one of the commune's ambassadors at the departure of Pope Martin V from Florentine territory; in 1422 he went as Florentine ambassador to the Sultan of Egypt in order to secure Florentine trading rights in the Eastern Mediterranean; in 1434 he was one of the Florentines chosen to receive Pope Eugenius IV when he arrived on Florentine territory in flight from the condottiere of the duke of Milan, Niccolò Piccinino; and in 1439 he went as Florentine ambassador to Emperor Albert, who created him count palatine.[11] Laura Federighi's uncle, Benozzo, was a prominent member of the Florentine church as a canon of the Florentine cathedral after 1403 and as bishop of Fiesole from 1421 until his death in 1450; in 1422 he was recommended to the pope by the Florentine government to become a cardinal and again in 1445 to become archbishop of Florence.[12] In the mid-fifteenth century the family also enjoyed a high social position in Florence, as is shown by marriages which they contracted with established patrician families such as the Gondi, Bartoli, Rucellai, Panciatichi, Lenzi and Bartolini.[13]

Marriage into a prominent Florentine family was a considerable departure from the way of life hitherto followed by the Accolti family. Michele Accolti had lived and worked in Florence, but in other ways he

[9]  *Ibid.*, 8, fol. 95r; *ibid.*, 187, pp. 25–7; *ibid.*, 187, n. 51, fol. 2r; cf. Brucker, *Civic World*, 267.
[10]  BNF, CPass. 8, fol. 95r; 187, p. 25–7.
[11]  ASF, Mss. 250, fol. 700r; *ibid.*, 266, fol. 37v–38r; BNF, CPass. 187, n. 51, fol. 2v–3r; Brucker, *Civic World*, 269, 505; Kent, *Rise of the Medici*, 206, 231; Rubinstein, *Government*, 24, 237–8; Park, 'Readers', 276–7.
[12]  BNF, CPass. 187, n. 51, fol. 4r–5r.
[13]  *Ibid.*, 8, fol. 95r; 187, p. 25–7; cf. Kent, *Rise of the Medici*, 182.

remained an outsider; indeed, while he was alive his eldest daughter
Agnesa had married not a Florentine but a native of Castiglion-Aretino.
Now five years after his death his eldest surviving son married the daughter
of an eminent Florentine, and this was to prove the first stage of a process
whereby Benedetto Accolti was to become more and more intimately
associated with Florence.

Considerations of social status aside, Accolti's connection with the
Federighi would be an asset in his legal career; not only was his father-in-
law Carlo a prominent Florentine lawyer, but as a leading statesman he
commanded influence in Florence which may have made Accolti the envy
of other aspiring lawyers there. Indeed, the real question is not so much
why Accolti undertook a marriage from which he had everything to gain,
but why he was accepted into the Federighi family at all. The marriage was
certainly a legal alliance; Carlo and Michele Accolti had been colleagues in
the Florentine university,[14] and Carlo must have recognized the qualities in
Benedetto Accolti which promised a brilliant legal career from an early
age. Even more important was Carlo Federighi's relative poverty compared to other leading Florentine patricians. His main concern had never
been a lucrative legal practice; his real interest was public life and he left
the pursuit of wealth to his elder brother Jacopo and his nephews Federigo,
Paolo and Domenico. In the 1420s, 1430s and 1440s Carlo's assets of
about 1700 florins, consisting of land holdings and shares in the Florentine
funded debt (the Monte), were almost always exceeded by liabilities, so
that he was usually charged only a nominal sum by the Florentine tax
officials.[15] He was unable to provide the large dowries of 1000 florins or
more expected by other Florentine patrician families, and he arranged for
Laura, his eldest daughter, to have a dowry of 500 florins by investing in
the Monte delle Doti (dowry fund).[16] As an Aretine, Benedetto Accolti and
his family were accustomed to considerably smaller dowries than those
given in Florence; in fact, Laura's 500 florins would have been a large
dowry by Aretine standards.

Nevertheless, Florentines were sensitive to the point of obsession about
family history and lineage and so it must be wondered why a patrician
family such as the Federighi were willing to accept a 'new man' such as
Accolti. In fact, the *gente nuova* was not a homogeneous social class in
later medieval Florence.[17] Stigma was often attached in Florence to new

---

[14] *Statuti*, ed. Gherardi, 438–40; Park, 'Readers', 273, 276, 277.
[15] ASF, Cat. 42, fol. 446r–447r; *ibid.*, 76, fol. 65r–v; *ibid.*, 365, fol. 366r–v; *ibid.*, 405, fol.
199v–200r; *ibid.*, 460, fol. 280v–281v; *ibid.*, 495, fol. 99v–100r; *ibid.*, 620, fol. 320r–v;
*ibid.*, 671, fol. 376r–379v.
[16] ASF, Monte delle doti, 1, fol. 94v, 151r.
[17] On the *gente nuova* in the fifteenth century, cf. Kent, *Household and Lineage*, 16–17,
217–18, 255–6, who gives further bibliography for the fourteenth century in n. 47, p. 17;
Kent, *Rise of the Medici*, 212–22.

families, but this was particularly so in the case of families such as the Pucci, Cocchi-Donati or Serristori who had recently risen from the lower social ranks in Florence itself. With respect to *gente nuova* moving into Florence, a distinction should be drawn between peasants or rustics without notable family background upon whom Florentines since the days of Dante had heaped abuse, and established patrician families from other Italian cities such as the Panciatichi from Pistoia, who were able to bring with them to Florence much of the social rank enjoyed in their native city. It is likely that the Federighi did not regard Benedetto Accolti, who was a patrician in Arezzo, in the same way as they might have done a member of a newly risen Florentine family.

Moreover, Benedetto Accolti may have enjoyed the advantage of a direct link with Florence. Family lineage in Florence not only provided an entrée into patrician society but also had a constitutional significance, admitting citizens to public office on the grounds that their ancestors had been office-holders or had been qualified to become office-holders. Individual Florentines often kept private registers called *prioristi* in which they recorded members of their families who had held the highest communal offices.[18] It has been pointed out that there was an earlier Florentine family called Accolti who were prominent public figures in Florence during the thirteenth and early fourteenth centuries; although there is no conclusive genealogical evidence to connect these Florentine Accolti with the Aretine family to which Benedetto Accolti belonged, nevertheless in several *prioristi* of the sixteenth century the early Florentine Accolti were associated with the later Aretine family. Indeed, in several *prioristi* the Aretine and Florentine families were directly linked: 'Accolti, o Colti sono spenti et succedono con questo cognome li Accolti di Arezzo.'[19] It is possible that the Federighi and other Florentine patrician families were aware of this earlier Florentine family called Accolti and consequently were more willing to accept Benedetto Accolti into their ranks than if his family had had no previous connection with Florence. Indeed, the thirteenth and early fourteenth centuries, when the Florentine Accolti had been prominent in communal political life, was the period in which many of the families who ruled Florence in the fifteenth century had first gained an important position in public life; in one sense, therefore, Benedetto Accolti's family might have been able to claim a lineage in the fifteenth century of equal

---

[18] On the significance of *prioristi*, cf. *ibid.*, 114–15; Martines, *Social World*, 47; Kent, *Household and Lineage*, 198–9, for their wide circulation.

[19] ASF, MSS. 240, fol. 6r; *ibid.*, 244, not foliated: 'Accolti, o Colti hoggi sono spenti et succedono gl'Accolti d'Arezo'; Bodleian Library, 1024 (Priorista of Antonio Quaratesi), fol. 2v. In another sixteenth-century *priorista*, beside the name Caraccio d'Ugo Buonaccolti as well as those of other Buonaccolti, the author wrote 'agli Accolti'; cf. BMF, C 1, fol. 213v, 218v, 228v, 229v, 230v, 232r, 233r, 234r.

prestige to that of families such as the Guicciardini, Capponi or Strozzi. The Federighi family first enjoyed the priorate only in 1325, by which time the Accolti of Florence could claim two Gonfaloniers of Justice and seven priors, so that in this sense Benedetto Accolti may perhaps have been able to claim a lineage of even greater antiquity in Florence than Laura Federighi.

There must have been some quality which made Benedetto Accolti an attractive husband for Laura Federighi in the eyes of an eminent Florentine such as her father Carlo. In other cases of marriage between Florentine patricians and families either newly arrived or risen in Florence, the attraction was usually money. For example, Donato di Leonardo Bruni married Alessandra di Messer Michele Castellani; the Castellani were a distinguished Florentine family, whereas Donato Bruni was the grandson of a grain merchant, but his father, the humanist and chancellor Leonardo Bruni, was a very rich man.[20] Similarly, members of the Pucci and Cocchi-Donati families, who entered the upper ranks of Florentine society only in the fifteenth century, married well because they could offer riches to older patrician families.[21] Carlo Marsuppini, who married into the Corsini, an old patrician family whose economic fortunes were on the decline in the early fifteenth century, could offer not only riches from his father, but also contacts with the Medici family, with whom he was closely associated in the 1420s.[22] Benedetto Accolti, on the other hand, had none of these attractions, but, in addition to whatever personal charms he possessed, he could offer the Federighi the prestige and antiquity of the Aretine and perhaps Florentine Accolti name.

In 1446 Benedetto Accolti seemed to be committing himself to a home and a legal career in Florence, but only a few months after his marriage in the spring of 1447 he suddenly contemplated a radical change in his way of life. What precipitated this new attitude on Accolti's part was the death of Pope Eugenius IV and the elevation to the pontificate of Tommaso Parentucelli on 6 March 1447 as Pope Nicholas V. Parentucelli had been intimately involved with Florentine humanist circles since the 1420s when he was employed as tutor in the households of Rinaldo degli Albizzi and Palla Strozzi; after 1434 he lived in Florence with the curia as secretary to Cardinal Niccolò Albergati and he was closely connected with Accolti's humanist mentors Poggio and Bruni.[23] It is probable that he knew Accolti, which would explain why Accolti seized upon the idea immediately after Nicholas V's election in 1447 of abandoning his legal career in Florence

[20] Cf. Martines, *Social World*, 117–23, 201–10.
[21] *Ibid.*, 71–4.    [22] *Ibid.*, 127–31, 221–9.
[23] On his life before becoming pope, cf. Vespasiano, *Vite*, i, 35–55; G. Sforza, 'La patria, la famiglia et la giovinezza di Papa Niccolò V', *Atti della R. Accademia lucchese di scienze, lettere ed arti*, xxiii (1884), 1–400.

and seeking a position as a humanist in the papal curia. He turned for assistance to Poggio, who, as a humanist secretary in the curia of forty years' standing and lifelong friend of the new pope, must have seemed to offer his best hope of success. Writing to Poggio in late March or early April,[24] Accolti evidently complained of the distractions in Florence which were keeping him from his humanist studies, thus confirming that he had given little attention to anything but law since the Certame Coronario of 1441: Accolti was already yearning for the days of the late 1430s when, not yet oppressed by the burdens of family and career, he had taken an active part in the stimulating intellectual life of Florence during the residence there of the curia. He could watch too the rapidly advancing career in North Italy of his brother, Francesco, whose success was certainly due in part to his freedom from permanent commitments, enabling him to offer his services as a lawyer to the highest bidder anywhere in Italy. When he wrote to Poggio in 1447 he had just begun married life and perhaps he felt that if he did not make a move then, he would end up permanently committed to a legal career in Florence and forced to give up all hope of ever returning to humanist scholarship.

Poggio, however, gave Accolti little encouragement. Having failed to answer Accolti's letter for some time, on 6 May 1447 he wrote, emphasizing how arduous it was to be a papal secretary; 'all my energies', he declared, 'have been devoted to the duty of writing official letters, which is often so distasteful that I sometimes should have preferred to have been illiterate'. Poggio admitted that the new pope was 'the most learned and best of men', but stressed that the task which Nicholas V was undertaking was formidable, especially since the papal treasury was impoverished; the pope was therefore distraught within such a whirlwind of cares that he had time neither for himself nor for his friends. Poggio's vanity, nevertheless, made him quick to point out that he himself was valued by the pope and held in the highest honour and affection, but he had to be careful not to abuse his influence. These were all hints to dampen Accolti's expectations in the curia, and Poggio did not hesitate to declare outright that in his view Accolti was misguided to seek an appointment in Rome. 'As far as you yourself are concerned,' he wrote, 'I am astonished that, as a man of learning, you seek the kind of peace that is found in Rome; if you were offered this tranquillity as a gift, you would reject it, for what you seek will not herald any kind of repose but rather will mean hard work.' Distinguishing between the kind of work which Accolti knew in Florence and what he would come to experience in Rome, Poggio pointed out that 'there is work and work', the difference being that 'some is better paid and carries with it greater dignity'. Poggio warned Accolti that although the pope would be

---

[24] Poggio, *Epistolae*, ii, 340–1.

making many appointments, 'there will be more workers than the size of
the harvest warrants. I shall try to do what you ask, but I am doubtful of
the outcome. I am certain you will change your mind about moving',
Poggio concluded; 'I have heard that you have just been married. Tell your
wife, I implore you, of your plans, and write back to me whether you still
persist in your intentions. I know she will dissuade you from all thoughts
of moving; when you have considered her, you will understand that the
duties of the home must come first.'[25] It is interesting that Poggio fixed on
Laura Federighi as the one to put an end to thoughts of moving to Rome,
for this highlights the important role that Accolti's marriage would have in
confirming his ties with Florence.

This discouraging and condescending reply to Accolti from Poggio
suggests that their friendship had cooled since 1440 when Poggio had so
ardently campaigned to secure a teaching post in Siena for Accolti; Poggio
had always regarded Accolti's legal career as only a means of earning a
living and perhaps he felt that, with his single-minded dedication to law
since 1441, Accolti had failed to fulfil his promise as a humanist scholar.
There is a hint a few years earlier that Accolti may himself have been drawing away from Poggio. Girolamo Aliotti, the Aretine humanist and friend
of Accolti's[26] and Poggio's, was visiting Rome in 1444 at the time of
Leonardo Bruni's death; Poggio composed a funeral oration on Bruni and
gave a copy of Aliotti, who then forwarded it to Accolti in Florence.
Aliotti's letter accompanying the oration suggests that recently Accolti and
Poggio had not been in particularly close touch; Aliotti felt the need to ask
Accolti to write something, preferably flattering, to Poggio, whose vanity,
he pointed out, had been nurtured by old age.[27] Aliotti's letter gives the
impression that he was taking the opportunity of the death of Bruni,
Poggio's and Accolti's mutual friend, to reestablish closer contact between
them. It is possible that Accolti was disinclined to regard Poggio with the
same warmth after the Certame Coronario, in which Poggio had been one
of the adjudicators who insulted the competitors by refusing to award the
laurel crown. Certainly Poggio's letter of 1447 also indicates that, before
the election of Nicholas V, they had not been in particularly frequent contact, making it clear that Poggio had not learnt of Accolti's marriage
directly from Accolti himself. At any rate, Poggio was mainly concerned to
establish his own position at the curia in the early months of Nicholas V's
pontificate; his remarks to the effect that he enjoyed the particular confidence of the new pope sound defensive, as though he were attempting to
persuade himself as much as Accolti of his continuing importance in the

[25]  *Ibid.*
[26]  Accolti was probably a friend of Aliotti's by 1436 at the latest, when he acted as a witness
for Aliotti in Arezzo: cf. ASF, Not.A. A 47, fol. 27v.
[27]  Aliotti, *Epistolae*, i, 91.

curia. At about the same time as writing to Accolti, Poggio directed an oration to the new pope which betrayed considerable insecurity; indeed, Poggio was well aware that Rome under Nicholas V was quickly becoming the centre of humanist scholarship and was attracting leading humanists of the younger generation from all over Italy.[28] In 1447 Poggio was nearly seventy, and he may have felt that he did not need to add Benedetto Accolti to the mass of new competitors for the pope's favour.

After this rebuff, Accolti must have been more disposed to regard Florence as his home. He established his family residence at Por' San Piero, which was at the intersection of Via del Proconsolo and Via del Corso, in the parish of Santa Margherita and the quarter of San Giovanni;[29] this was very near to the parish of Sant'Apollinare where Michele Accolti had lived in Florence and Benedetto had spent much of his youth and, indeed, where a branch of the Aretine Accolti family had lived since the first half of the fourteenth century. In April 1448, just a year after his unsuccessful attempt to gain an appointment in Rome, Accolti submitted a petition to the Florentine government in which he expressly declared his intention of making Florence his permanent home. 'Benedetto Accolti', it was stated, 'now a lecturer in the Florentine Studio, has lived in this city for a not inconsiderable time, not to mention his tenure in the Studio for many years; he intends to establish permanent residence here, and he has taken a Florentine citizen for a wife. As a sign that he was beginning to assume Florentine citizenship and as a token of the trust and affection which had grown in him', Accolti wished to become eligible for two offices in the government which were ordinarily limited to Florentine citizens, those of *sapientes communis* and *assessor sindicorum rectorum forensium*.[30] The *sapientes communis* were two lawyers chosen by the Signoria for a term of four months to act as general legal advisers to all communal officials; the assessor of the foreign judges was a lawyer chosen by lot every six months to act as legal adviser to the committee of Florentine citizens elected to review the conduct of outgoing foreign judges who presided over most legal cases in Florence.[31] Both these were important communal legal offices, particularly that of *sapiens communis*, which was usually held by prominent Florentine lawyers and citizens; when Accolti's petition was

[28] Walser, 266–81; R. Cessi, 'La contesa fra Giorgio da Trebisonda, Poggio Bracciolini e Giovanni Aurispa', in his *Saggi romani* (Rome, 1956), 129ff.; Holmes, *Florentine Enlightenment*, 252ff.

[29] In 1446, Accolti's house was said to be in the parish of the Badia Fiorentia (ASF, Dip., Famiglia Baldovinetti, 3 October 1446); in 1455 and 1457 it was said to be in the parish of Santa Margherita (ASF, Not.A. L 189 (1451–66), fol. 111r, 142r); and in 1469 his heirs were said to be living at Por' San Piero in the parish of Santa Margherita (ASF, Cat. 929, fol. 610v). It is probable that Accolti always lived at Por' San Piero, which is just a few hundred yards from the Badia.

[30] Ed. Gherardi, in *Statuti*, 455–6.  [31] Cf. Martines, *Lawyers*, 144–7.

approved by the legislative councils on the first reading, therefore, he had taken an important step to establishing himself permanently in Florence.[32]

By the late 1440s Benedetto Accolti had achieved considerable success in the university, in legal practice and in society; that he had risen to this position in the exclusive and snobbish world of Renaissance Florence must have made him, as a foreigner, feel all the more conscious of the good fortune with which he had been favoured. However, there is evidence that Accolti was a deeply religious man, and it seems that his worldly success had, by about 1450, begun to trouble him. Much of his early poetry had had religious overtones: he concluded his *capitolo*, 'Quell' antico disio', by imploring everyone to avoid the agonies of love and,

> Uplift his soul to the divine
> Things of God, and seek that eternal place
> Where souls are never wretched
> And live always in that benign fire
> Of just love, of perfect kindness,
> Deserving to rise there little by little
> By the grace of Him who awaits everyone.[33]

In his poem, 'Quando el foco d'amor', before beginning to paraphrase Cicero's *Disputationes tusculanae*, he describes his misery after being abandoned by his love, and then declares,

> But by a holy thought, which excites me
> To divine virtues, I was moved and spurred
> To make my heart, in a different manner, more pure,
> And I began again: Why do you, conquered by so much error,
> Yearn in vain for this miserable life
> And fear dying before your time?
> Why do you not call God and life
> In that celestial place blessed, eternal, free
> Of love and earthly ties?[34]

Further along in this poem, he interrupts his adaptation of Cicero to exclaim:

> If in the highest heaven God offers you
> Blessed, eternal and true glory
> Which is merited through the highest virtues,
> Raise your soul which is brutish and black
> To desire that condition so felicitous
> In which torment and every pain perishes.[35]

In his *capitolo* on friendship he states that both friendship and its cause, are gifts of God,[36] who, he also declares, does not deny man grace despite his

[32] ASF, LF, 61, fol. 113r–v.
[33] Jacoboni, 'Rime', 269.    [34] *Ibid.*, 270.    [35] *Ibid.*, 272.    [36] *Ibid.*, 286.

transgressions;[37] moreover, he concludes this poem by exclaiming that through the union of true friendship men are made almost divine,

> Because the being of God, which is so profound,
> Is joined and united in the three persons
> Of power, knowledge and joyous love,
> As our faith openly states.[38]

These poems date from 1441 or before, and his religious inclinations had if anything become stronger by the late 1440s, when he is known to have been an active member of the Aretine lay confraternity.[39] It was common for members of confraternities to compose vernacular religious poetry for use in their societies; called *laudi*, these poems were usually simple lyrics, often accompanied by music, which expressed the humble and pious sentiments of the author.[40] Accolti composed one such *laude*, the 'capitolo in lode di Nostra Donna Gloriosissima', which was probably intended for use in his confraternity of Santa Maria della Misericordia, and this poem provides an insight into Accolti's religious sentiments in about 1450, the probable date of its composition.[41] The opening of the poem is conventional, restating orthodox theological points such as the virgin birth and immaculate conception and attributing to the Virgin vast powers of intercession on behalf of man with the Son and the Father;[42] however, this is only a general introduction to the heart of the poem, which is in fact a personal prayer to the Virgin by Accolti himself:

> Now sacred, benign, blessed Virgin,
>     Listen to me, your devoted servant,
>     Know and behold my dangers.
> I feel my breast weighed down by a mass
>     Of worldly desires, which I am still
>     Most obstinate in wanting to pursue.
> My soul feels almost estranged from
>     The love of Him who created me,
>     So much is it enamoured of the false world.
> Glory, position, riches have led me astray,
>     A miserable one, from true salvation,
>     Abandoned in yearning for such things.

Accolti thus explicitly states that worldly success, achieved as it had been over the previous decade, made him feel spiritually empty, and, he continues,

---

[37] *Ibid.*, 292.     [38] *Ibid.*, 297.     [39] Cf. Aliotti, *Epistolae*, i, 260–1.
[40] Cf. Kristeller, *Studies*, 102; V. Rossi, *Il Quattrocento* (Milan, 1933), 287–90, and his *Storia della letteratura italiana*[3] (Milan, 1905), i, 55–60.
[41] Jacoboni, 'Rime', 297.     [42] *Ibid.*, 297–300.

> False pleasures of love have blackened
> My mind so much that they have surely
> Become causes for me to perish.

He goes on with a scathing confession of his own envy, and then makes an emotional supplication:

> Virgin, these evils have confined
> My soul to such a dubious place
> That, in confusion, I await death from them,
> If you do not beseech your sacred Son a little,
> In his greatest pity, to defend me
> And renew in my heart a sweet fire
> Which will light within me the fervour of God
> So that I shall love Him over all honours
> And not be seized by the love of false pleasures,
> And, if honours and riches come, that I should desire them
> To do good and help others.
> And let me be lured by virtue, not error.[43]

Accolti's strong religious feelings were not only important in his private life but, in fact, had a profound effect on his development as a humanist. Indeed, his two principal humanist compositions were, it will be seen, stamped by his concern with the state of the contemporary church; this is especially true of his history of the first crusade, which was written to stimulate a revival of the religious fervour that had led to the crusades of the earlier middle ages.[44]

However, it was not only Accolti's spiritual tranquillity which was disturbed by success in Florence; his heavy commitments there also kept him away from his native city of Arezzo, where, as a result, practical difficulties ensued for his family. Accolti's responsibilities in Florence during the 1440s were a heavy burden, and it is not surprising that he had little time to give his native city of Arezzo. This was certainly true of his duty as an Aretine citizen to hold office in communal government: in 1440 and 1442 he was drawn to be a prior, in 1444 and 1445 to serve on the general council, in 1445 to be a captain of the Guelf party and in 1446 to be *caput scripte* and Gonfalonier of Justice, but on each occasion he was unable to take office because he was living and working in Florence.[45] He evidently spent considerably less time in Arezzo than his father Michele, who, although sometimes unable to serve as a communal magistrate because of commitments in Florence, nevertheless had been frequently enough resident in Arezzo to fulfil many of his civic obligations; similarly, Benedetto's

---

[43] *Ibid.*, 301–2.    [44] Cf. *infra*, pp. 204–8, 216–23, Ch. 9 *passim.*
[45] ASA, Estr. 9, fol. 113v, 117r–v, 144r–v, 190v, 191v; 10, fol. 20r–v, 26v, 57r.

brother Francesco was repeatedly drawn as a communal magistrate in the early 1440s but like Benedetto he was never in Arezzo to assume office.[46]

Aretines at first adopted a tolerant attitude to the failure of the Accolti brothers to perform their civic duties. Scrutinies (called *reforme* in Arezzo) to select citizens eligible for office were, it has been pointed out,[47] held in Arezzo every five years, and in 1437 Francesco was declared eligible for the priorate and, together with Benedetto, for the general council, while in 1442 they were both declared eligible for the priorate and captainship of the Guelf party as well as for several other minor communal offices.[48] However, in the *reforma* of 1447 neither Benedetto nor Francesco Accolti was declared eligible for communal office,[49] despite the fact that their cousin Agnolo di Grazia Accolti was a member of the commission which drew up the reform,[50] suggesting that some Aretines saw little point in qualifying them for offices which they would never hold. Another indication that Benedetto Accolti perhaps enjoyed less than universal favour in Arezzo in the late 1440s can be found in a letter of Aliotti to Accolti in October 1449. Aliotti referred to the mercurial temperament of his and Accolti's compatriots, who were 'in the habit of saying one thing and thinking another'; Accolti was well aware of 'who was to be trusted and who could safely be confided in'. All this of course implies that there were a number of Aretines who were less than well disposed to Accolti, and this is confirmed by Aliotti's direct reference to one of Accolti's relatives, to whom Aliotti had recently attempted to give assistance; 'in that case,' remarked Aliotti, 'although we thought we had many patrons and champions, in the end it turned out that we had none'.[51] In these years Accolti felt himself to be the victim of envy; his poem 'O tu che se' ', written probably in the 1440s, is directed against a slanderer whom Accolti, going beyond his classical source, Ovid's *In Ibin*, portrays as treacherous, cruel, scheming, perfidious and above all envious.[52] Envy has an important place too at the end of his poem to the Virgin, who is beseeched to intercede with her Son to act as the poet's shield against the blows of envy, which have furiously smitten his soul and reduced him to despair.[53]

[46] *Ibid.*, 9, fol. 124r, 127v, 170r, 172r; 10, fol. 9v, 15r, 41r–v, 81r–v.

[47] Cf. p. 29, *supra*.

[48] ASF, Tratte, 870, Registrum officiorum civitatis Aretii anno MCCCCXXVII, fol. 3v, 13v; *ibid.*, Registrum officiorum Aretii anni 1442, fol. 1v, 6r, 7r, 10v, 11r, 12v, 25v, 26r.

[49] The scrutiny list for 1447 does not seem to have survived: cf. ASF, Tratte, 870, which contains scrutinies for 1442 and 1452; however, it is clear that the Accolti brothers were disqualified for office in 1447, since they were drawn for no offices between September 1447 and October 1452: cf. ASA, Estr. 10, fol. 81r ff. and *ibid.*, 11, fol. 1r–50v. ASA, Camerlingo comunitativo, 84 (Libri dei non paghi, 1443–8), fol. 7r, 71v, 79v, 126r, 316r, 356v) shows that Accolti was not disqualified for office in this period because of tax debts, as happened to him between 1452 and 1456 (cf. p. 76, n. 78, *infra*).

[50] ASA, Provv. 8, fol. 149r.    [51] Aliotti, *Epistolae*, i, 260–61.

[52] Jacoboni, 'Rime', 282–5.    [53] *Ibid.*, 302.

It is not difficult to see why Accolti and his family did not enjoy universal favour in Arezzo during the 1440s, for his association with Florence, which was growing closer throughout these years, could not have been to the liking of everyone in Arezzo. A number of Aretines bitterly resented the rule of Florence, with its policy of exiling potentially subversive Aretines; moreover, the higher rate of taxation imposed on Aretines in contrast with taxes paid by Florentine citizens must have made Florentine rule seem to many Aretines no better than exploitation.[54] Families such as the Bostoli, Albergotti and Griffolini who had ruled Arezzo before 1384 had lost much more than lesser families who had simply exchanged Florentine masters for their former Aretine oligarchs. The vast majority of Aretines, however, suffered equally under the prolonged and severe economic depression as well as harsh taxation which accompanied Florentine rule, and so it would hardly be surprising if the few Aretines who actually prospered under the Florentine regime did not incur the envy and resentment of at least some of their compatriots. The Accolti by living in Florence had achieved considerably greater wealth and professional eminence than many of their compatriots who remained in Arezzo; indeed, they had done particularly well out of Florentine rule, for in the years before 1384 they had suffered exile in the Casentino whereas the coming of Florentine dominion brought the Accolti back to prominence in Aretine public life. The Accolti, moreover, had for two generations been connected by marriage with Florentine citizens: Michele Accolti's wife Margherita Roselli was the daughter of an Aretine who had taken Florentine citizenship, and now Benedetto Accolti was married to the daughter of a Florentine oligarch. Moreover, Accolti received direct financial benefit from his connections with the Florentines, who interceded on his behalf in 1443 to secure a reduction of tax arrears owed to the commune of Arezzo by himself and his brothers.[55]

All this was probably enough to earn Benedetto Accolti odium in the eyes of those Aretine patriots who loathed the very name of Florence. But Benedetto Accolti was also closely associated with the Marsuppini family, who were perhaps the Aretines most intimately connected with Florence in the 1420s, 1430s and 1440s. Gregorio Marsuppini was involved in large-scale commercial ventures in Florence with many leading Florentine patricians.[56] His son Carlo, who was tutor to Lorenzo di Giovanni de' Medici in the 1420s, always remained in close association with the Medici; he also had business dealings with the Lenzi, Martelli and Rucellai families.[57] Benedetto Accolti and Carlo Marsuppini were colleagues in the Florentine university for many years,[58] and they served together on two

---

[54] Cf. p. 12, *supra*.     [55] ASA, Provv. 7, fol. 163r, 166r.

[56] ASF, Cat. 203, fol. 644v–647r; cf. Martines, *Social World*, 127–31.

[57] *Ibid.*; cf. Zippel, 'Carlo Marsuppini', 202ff.     [58] Cf. Park, 'Readers', 288–302.

diplomatic missions for the commune of Arezzo in Florence, first in January and February 1440,[59] and, more importantly, in July and August 1443, when they represented Arezzo at the funeral in Florence of the condottiere Pier Gianpaolo Orsini.[60] Their friendship was encouraged by a mutual love of the humanities, and Marsuppini, it has been seen, dedicated to Accolti his elegy on the death of Bruni, in which he addressed the twenty-nine year old Accolti with the flattering epithet 'iurisconsultissimus'.[61] In the poem, Marsuppini emphasized the immortality of letters not only, as has been indicated, to console Accolti for the loss of his mentor Bruni, but also perhaps to encourage him to further study of the humanities at a time when, it has been pointed out, he was able to give them little of his attention. Moreover, Marsuppini concluded the poem with a general encomium of Florence, which may shed light on the kind of relationship shared by Marsuppini and Accolti:

> You, o Florence, rejoice,
> Rejoice again, having accumulated so many good things.
> Because of your waters you were given before the name Fluventia,
> But now, because you flourish, this is your name.
> The city of Rome happily sent its colonists then.
> With happy auspices your walls were erected.
> All admire your palaces reaching to the sky,
> Your displays of marble and holy temples of the gods.
> And they admire your houses and walls armed with high
> Towers: how well the roads are paved with stone.
> The mountains look down on you and in the middle flows the river
> Arno, about to give waters to the Pisan sea.
> Enormous riches, a great throng of men are present.
> There is no good art in which you are lacking . . .
> Here Cosimo founded the Laurentian temple
> And a temple was founded by him for you, Mark . . .
> Here sculpture flourishes: now the ancient Apelles lives
> And his hand creates live statues from air . . .
> This city certainly looks in its studies to ancient Athens,
> And Greek doctrines are read in its schools . . .
> All praise you more
> Because you give such rewards to learned men.
> Honour nourishes the arts; it goads competitors.
> Great glory also sparks off worthy men.
> You give birth therefore to philosophers, and holy poets.
> You give birth to orators and historians.
> Therefore all call you worthy, and praise you with verse,
> The one remaining certain hope for good studies.[62]

[59] ASA, Provv. 7, fol. 24v.    [60] *Ibid.*, fol. 149v–150v.    [61] BAM, Trotti, 373, fol. 41v.
[62] *Ibid.*, fol. 44v–45r: tuque o Florentia gaude,/ Gaude iterum tantis accumulata bonis./ Propter aquas positum [ms: posite] fuit ante Fluventia nomen,/ At nunc, quod flores, hoc tibi nomen inest./ Urbs Romana suos misit tunc leta colonos./ Felici auspitio menia iacta tua./ Suspitiunt omnes educta palatia coelo,/ Signaque marmoribus templaque sacra

Carlo Marsuppini had every reason to praise Florence, which had given
him by 1444 high public office, honour and riches, and these lines suggest
that he too was a mentor to Accolti, making it his particular mission to
encourage his younger compatriot to adopt the same favourable attitude
to life in Florence as he himself enjoyed. Moreover, these verses would
have been of direct personal concern to Accolti in the 1440s, which, it has
been seen, were a period of not inconsiderable anxiety for him; he had
religious and intellectual doubts about the course his life was then
assuming in Florence, and the concluding lines of the elegy, depicting as
they do so vividly the attractions and splendours of Renaissance Florence,
may have been penned by the older Aretine Marsuppini to dispel any second thoughts his younger fellow countryman may have had about
Florence as a proper home for himself and his family. For the rest of his life,
Marsuppini remained Accolti's friend, portrayed as such, for example, in
Poggio's *Historia tripartita* of 1450,[63] and on Marsuppini's death in 1453,
Accolti was fittingly chosen by the Aretine commune as one of their rep-
resentatives at his public funeral in Florence.[64]

Among Accolti's friends was another philo-Florentine, Michele di
Conte Marsuppini, who was Carlo Marsuppini's cousin. Michele di Conte
belonged to a branch of the family which had remained in Arezzo, where
he owned a clothing business and an apothecary's shop; he achieved considerable prosperity during the early fifteenth century as Arezzo's third
richest citizen,[65] and he was sufficiently appreciative of the advantages that
his family had enjoyed under Florentine rule to betray Mariotto
Griffolini's conspiracy in 1431 to the Florentine authorities, who in
gratitude to the Marsuppini family conferred Florentine citizenship not
only on Michele di Conte and his descendants but also on Gregorio
Marsuppini and his male issue including Carlo.[66] Benedetto Accolti stood

Deûm./ Suspitiuntque domos armataque turribus altis/ Menia; tum saxis quam bene
strata via est./ Despectant montes, mediusque interfluit amnis/ Arnus, Pisano flumina
danda mari./ Divitie ingentes, hominum vis magna frequentat./ Ars bona non ulla est quae
tibi defitiat./ Hic patribus nati similes, letusque parentum/ Os nati quisque spectat in ore
suum./ Hic decus, hic Cosmus condidit Laurentia templa/ Templaque sunt illi condita
Marce tibi./ Qui genere est clarus summa probitate verendus,/ Qui lumen patrie,
presidiumque bonis/ Qui favet ingeniis; faveant sibi numina cuncta/ Deprecor, atque
annis mollia facta suis./ Hic sculptura viget; priscus tum vivit Apelles,/ Et statuas vivas
ducit ab ere manus./ Hec iusta, hec sapiens, hec est moderata, nec altos/ Deicit hec
animos, dum bene bella gerit./ Hec certe antiquas studiis miratur Athenas,/ Graiaque
gymnasiis dogmata cuncta legit./ Hec omnes laudant merito mage, sed mage laudant/
Quot ponis doctis premia tanta viris./ Nutrit honos [ms: bonos] artes; stimulos
currentibus addit./ Addit et igniculos gloria magna probis./ Philosophos igitur gignis,
sanctosque poetas,/ Gignis et orantes, gignis et historicos./ Ergo omnes dicant meritam te,
et carmine laudent,/ Spes certa studiis una relicta bonis. Cf. *Carmina illustrium poetarum
italorum*, vi, 271.
[63] Cf. pp. 76ff, *infra*.     [64] Cf. p. 76, *infra*.     [65] Cf. p. 8, n. 45, *supra*.
[66] Cf. Zippel, 'Marsuppini', 199–200.

surety for Michele di Conte when he became Arezzo's chief magistrate, *caput scripte*, in 1439; Michele di Conte acted on Accolti's behalf in 1445 swearing to Accolti's absence from Arezzo when he was drawn to be Captain of the Guelf party;[67] and in 1451 Accolti declared the dowry of Michele's daughter, Frosina:[68] in the eyes of Aretine patrician extremists, therefore, Accolti could hardly have failed to be identified with the Florentine regime.

Accolti may have regarded his own disqualification from office in 1447 as a relief from unwelcome burdens, but failure in the Aretine *reforma* of 1447 extended to all members of his immediate family, including his younger brother Donato, who, unlike his older brothers, continued to live in Arezzo.[69] Donato Accolti had been successful in the 1442 *reforma* for the priorate,[70] and his failure to be qualified for any communal office in 1447 may have been an unwelcome experience for him as a resident of Arezzo, especially since it was the first time for thirty-five years that a member of the immediate family had not been successful in an Aretine scrutiny. Accolti's position as Michele's eldest surviving son meant that, regardless of the demands made upon him in Florence, he could not neglect his family obligations in Arezzo. Perhaps the failure of his family in the scrutiny of 1447 made him realize the difficulties which might ensue from his continued absence from Arezzo, for in the late 1440s and early 1450s Accolti appears to have spent more time in Arezzo and devoted more energy to communal affairs. Between 1439 and 1445, Accolti had sworn surety on only two occasions for other Aretines entering public office,[71] but between July 1449 and May 1451 he swore surety six times on behalf of his compatriots.[72] In the same period he was active in the Aretine lay confraternity of Santa Maria della Misericordia as a rector[73] and he was asked to use his influence in providing benefices under the fraternity's patronage;[74] at about the same time he seems to have maintained some professional ties with Arezzo, appearing together with his brother

---

[67] ASA, Estr. 9, fol. 79r; 10, fol. 20r–v.
[68] ASF. Not.A. A 50, fol. 76r (9 March 1450 (ab inc.)). I am grateful to Mr Frank Dabell for this reference.
[69] ASA, Cat. 7, fol. 227v.
[70] ASF, Tratte, 870, Registrum officiorum Aretii anno 1442, fol. 5r.
[71] ASA, Estr. 9, fol. 79r; 10, fol. 22v.
[72] *Ibid.*, vol. 137r, 142r, 145r, 149r, 155v, 197r.
[73] Accolti is recorded as a rector of the fraternity for four months from July to October 1449 (AFL, 220, unfoliated; I am grateful to Mr Frank Dabell for this reference) but no record of his holding this office at this time is found in the records of *estrazioni* in Arezzo: cf. ASA, Estr. 10, *passim.*
[74] Aliotti, *Epistolae*, i, 260–1. Accolti had acted as an arbiter of a dispute regarding the fraternity on 29 January 1442: cf. ASF, Not.A. A 50, fol. 1r; I am grateful to Mr Frank Dabell for this reference.

Francesco on a matriculation list of the Aretine guild of lawyers and notaries.[75]

Accolti's efforts to take a greater part in Aretine communal life were not in vain, for both he and his brother Francesco were successful in the *reforma* of October 1452, becoming eligible for the priorate, the captainship of the Guelf party and the rectorship of the fraternity of Santa Maria della Misericordia,[76] while his brother Donato was qualified for the priorate, the captainship of the Guelf party and other offices, in a special scrutiny held seven months later in April 1453.[77] Accolti took care not to offend Aretine opinion after the scrutiny, for when his name was drawn in 1453 first to serve on the general council and then to become a captain of the Guelf party he actually took office on both occasions.[78] Although Accolti had served in 1438 as an *ad hoc* supervisor of the *imborsazioni* of notaries for the Aretine *catasto*,[79] his tenure on the Aretine general council from September 1453 to 28 February 1454 was the first time that he held a fully fledged magistracy in Arezzo since he had first been qualified to hold office in 1437.

The years from 1449 to 1453 were the period in which Accolti was most fully involved in the life of his native city, and the Aretine commune on several occasions at this time made use of his connections with Florence, where he had previously served as their legal adviser[80] and where he now served repeatedly as their ambassador;[81] a particularly important legation took place on 27 April 1453 when Carlo Marsuppini was given a public funeral in Florence, and the Aretine government appointed Accolti to act as one of its official representatives at the ceremonies.[82] Accolti was probably selected because he was Marsuppini's personal friend, but the Aretine government may also have felt that Accolti had now replaced Marsuppini as the preeminent Aretine living in Florence and was therefore particularly suited to represent Arezzo in Florence on this occasion. However, Accolti's greatest service to Arezzo in these years was to foster the Aretine educational tradition of which he himself was so notable a beneficiary. In July 1454 when it was necessary to replace the public grammar teacher, the commune asked Accolti to help to find the new master,[83] and the result was

---

[75] ASA, Dott.Not. fol. 35v (1447).
[76] ASF, Tratte, 870, Registrum reforme civitatis Aretii facte de mense octobris anni 1452, fol. 9r, 13v, 15v, 23r.
[77] ASA, Estr. 11, fol. 68v.
[78] *Ibid.*, fol. 81v, 87r. Accolti had been drawn as *caput scripte* for November–December 1452, but he was disqualified to hold office on that occasion because his name was on the *specchio*, the list of citizens temporarily disqualified from office for tax arrears. Cf. *ibid.*, fol. 50v–51r. He was still on the *specchio* in October 1456: cf. *ibid.*, fol. 177r.
[79] *Ibid.*, 9, fol. 53v.      [80] ASA, Provv. 7, fol. 166r; 10, fol. 83r, 101r, 102r.
[81] ASA, QCanc. 3, fol. 44v (2 September 1453); *ibid.*, Provv. 10, fol. 8v (28 February 1455).
[82] *Ibid.*, 9, fol. 174v; *ibid.*, QCanc. 3, fol. 7r–v.
[83] *Ibid.*, Provv. 9, fol. 222r, 223r (8 July 1454).

that they were soon able to appoint Rinaldo Bettini of Città di Castello to the vacancy.[84] An even greater service rendered by Accolti had been his support for Aretine efforts to resurrect their university. Before approaching Emperor Frederick III for a renewal of their imperial privilege, it had been necessary for Aretines to secure the approval of their Florentine rulers,[85] and one of the ambassadors they chose for this embassy was Benedetto Accolti.[86] In securing Florentine favour, his efforts may have been decisive, as is suggested by the leading role played by Accolti's closest friend Otto Niccolini in these negotiations. A few months after the renewal of the imperial privilege, the first man to be granted a doctorate by the Aretine university was Niccolini's nephew Bartolomeo,[87] and this was done at the specific request of Otto Niccolini;[88] moreover, at about the same time Niccolini became the official advocate of the Aretine commune, in recognition, so it was stated, of the favour and advice that he had recently lent to Arezzo.[89] All this suggests that, instigated by his friend Accolti, Niccolini, who at this time enjoyed great authority in Florence as one of the Dieci di Balìa in charge of the war effort against Naples and Venice,[90] intervened to secure Florentine approval for the revival of Arezzo's university, and his *quid pro quo* was a doctorate for his nephew and the position of official communal advocate for himself.[91]

Accolti was much too occupied in Florence to continue to take an active part in Aretine communal life, so that, when in October 1456 he was drawn for the priorate and in August 1457 for the general council, once again he did not take office.[92] However, he now made an effort not only to save his family from embarrassment as a result of his absence from Arezzo but actually to let them profit from his failure to accept communal office. In January 1458 another *reforma* was held in Arezzo, and Accolti was successful in the scrutinies to become a prior, a captain of the Guelf party, an official of custody, a rector of the fraternity of Santa Maria della Misericordia and a syndic of communal notaries and rectors;[93] however, when news of his success reached him in Florence, realizing that he would be unable to assume office, he endeavoured to arrange for his cousin, Agnolo di Grazia Accolti, to serve in his place. 'I have understood', he

---

[84] *Ibid.*, fol. 225r–v (23 July 1454).     [85] *Ibid.*, fol. 138r (5 May 1452).
[86] *Ibid.*, fol. 139r (5 May 1452).     [87] *Ibid.*, fol. 150r–v (26 August 1452).
[88] *Ibid.*, fol. 150r (26 August 1452).     [89] *Ibid.*, fol. 153r–v (21 September 1452).
[90] As was recognized by the Aretines: cf. *ibid.*, fol. 150r.
[91] Accolti continued to be involved in negotiations over the Aretine Studio in the decade between the renewal of the imperial privilege and the appointment of the first roll of teaching staff (cf. p. 20, *supra*); during an attempt in 1460 to have the Florentine Studio transferred to Arezzo rather than to Pisa, Accolti's assistance was sought by the Aretines: cf. ASA, Provv. 10, fol. 217r.
[92] ASA, Estr. 11, fol. 177r; 12, fol. 11r.
[93] ASF, Tratte, 870, Registrum officiorum reforme civitatis Aretii facte de mense Januarii anni MCCCLVII (ab inc.), fol. 1r, 4v, 7r, 8v, 10v, 15v, 16r, 19v.

wrote to the Aretine priors on 25 February 1450, 'that the officials in
charge of the *reforma* of the city have voted that, should I be drawn as *capo
di scripta* of the priors and did not accept, ser Agnolo di Grazia would be
able to hold office in my place.' Perhaps remembering how his failure to
serve in the 1440s might have prejudiced the chances of the rest of his
family, however, Accolti was careful not to injure the pride of his compatriots on this occasion. 'And therefore I am advising you', he continued
in his letter to the Aretine priors, 'that it is my intention, should I be drawn,
not to accept, not because the office is not much more worthy than my
merits deserve but rather because of my many preoccupations and my
absence, which legitimately excuses me.' Concluding his letter, Accolti
again referred in deferential terms to the office that he was declining: 'And
I beseech you,' he declared, 'if, when the sortition is carried out, I am
drawn by chance, to give that honour to ser Agnolo, who I know will be
most pleased with it.'[94]

Accolti's Florentine connections may have alienated many in Arezzo,
but some of his compatriots did not hesitate to ingratiate themselves with
him. Perhaps the hope that Accolti would use his influence in Florence to
benefit Arezzo encouraged Aliotti to flatter Accolti in 1444, referring to
him as 'a patron and principal citizen' of Arezzo even before he had
reached the age of thirty;[95] indeed, in a letter written to Accolti five years
later Aliotti states, 'You have done so much for your native city that I think
not only its citizens are in your debt but even the stones and walls.'[96] Aliotti
clearly hoped that Accolti would direct his good offices in Florence not
merely towards Arezzo in general but more directly on behalf of the
monastery of Santa Fiora in Arezzo, of which he was himself abbot, and
other Aretines shared his pragmatic view that Accolti's Florentine connections were not a liability. One of these was Martino di fu Bernardo Grifoni,
a member of an old family,[97] who employed Accolti as a procurator in
1442.[98] Another was Francesco di Lippo Lippi, who married Accolti's
sister Tommasa in 1445.[99] It was another professional alliance, for both
Francesco and his brother Bernardo were lawyers;[100] it was also an
alliance of two rich families, for Francesco's father Lippo di ser Niccolò,

---

[94] Cf. Appendix I.     [95] Aliotti, *Epistolae*, i, 91.     [96] *Ibid.*, 261.
[97] Cf. Pasqui, *Documenti*, i, 70, 100, 102, 121, 139, 143, 152, 177, 197, 200, 208, 216,
228, 234, 239, 242, 245, 325, 549; Lazzeri, *Ubertini*, 271. In the fifteenth century, they
were moderately prosperous, the heirs of Bernardo Grifoni having a *valsente* of 483 florins in 1429: cf. ASF, Cat. 273, fol. 50v, for which I am grateful to Mr Frank Dabell.
[98] ASF, Not.A. P 290, ii, 4 April 1442 (unfoliated). I am grateful to Mr Frank Dabell for this
reference.
[99] ASF, Not.A. P 290 (1441–6), not foliated, 19 November 1445.
[100] *Ibid.*, P 289 (1437–55), n. 127, testament of Lippo di fu ser Niccolò di ser Lippo
Ritagliatore, 28 April 1452.

a retail cloth merchant, was one of the richest Aretines in 1427.[101] Moreover, both families belonged to the Aretine patriciate, as is shown by the marriages made by Lippo Lippi's children into such prominent Aretine families as the Bacci and Paganelli.[102] Francesco Lippi was doubtless also attracted to Tommasa Accolti by the large dowry of 450 florins which her brothers were willing to provide for her,[103] but it is probable that the Lippi family shared Accolti's attitude to the Florentine regime in Arezzo, for another of the key figures in thwarting the conspiracy of 1431 was Michele di Luca di Chele Lippi, who was given as a reward by the Florentine government an annual pension of 75 florins.[104] Another Aretine family who sought to ally themselves with the Accolti were the Taviani, one of whose members, Bartolomeo di Nanni, married Accolti's other sister Nanna in 1450.[105] The Taviani were an old Aretine family, although not so prominent as the Lippi;[106] perhaps it was for this reason that Accolti would not agree to give as large a dowry to Nanna as Tommasa had received, for at first the parties could not agree to a dowry. Eventually the Accolti and the Taviani had to appoint as arbiter the bishop of Arezzo, who fixed the dowry at 300 florins.

It was as an Aretine living in Florence that Benedetto Accolti appeared as one of the interlocutors in Poggio's *Historia tripartita*, consisting of *Disceptiones conviviales tres* or three after-dinner conversations among guests in the summer of 1449 at Poggio's villa near Terranuova.[107] Besides Accolti, the other participants in Poggio's work were Accolti's fellow expatriate Carlo Marsuppini and the physician Niccolò Tignosi da Foligno, who had been granted Aretine citizenship because of his successful practice of medicine there in the 1430s and 1440s and who also worked in Florence during the same period.[108] In the fifteenth century Aretines often were regarded as intellectuals and Poggio was perhaps flaunting his high-brow house parties in the curia, where the *Historia tripartita* was presented in 1450 with a dedication to Cardinal Prospero Colonna.[109] Another thing which Accolti, Marsuppini and Tignosi had in common was that they all taught in the Florentine university in the 1430s and 1440s;[110] moreover, Terranuova, where the conversations were said to have taken

[101] Cf. p. 8, n. 45, *supra*.
[102] ASF, Not.A. P 289 (1437–55), n. 127. On the Lippi family, cf. Lazzeri, *Ubertini*, 260; on the Paganelli, cf. *ibid.*, 255, and Bartolomeo di Gorello, *Cronica*, RIS², xv, pt 1, 16; on the Bacci, cf. p. 8, n. 44, *supra*.
[103] ASF, Not.A. P 290 (1441–6), 19 November 1445.
[104] Cf. Pasqui, 'Una congiura', 11.
[105] ASF, Not.A. P 289 (1437–55), n. 90 (6 April 1450), 110 (4 November 1450).
[106] Cf. Pasqui, *Documenti*, ii, 236, 319; Lazzeri, *Ubertini*, 258.
[107] Partly ed. in *La disputa*, ed. Garin, 15–33; for the entire text, cf. Poggio, *Opera*, 32ff.
[108] Cf. pp. 14–15, *supra*.
[109] Cf. Poggio, *Opera*, 32.
[110] Cf. Park, 'Readers', 295, 297, 302–3; *Statuti*, ed. Gherardi, 444.

place, would have been a convenient meeting place for all the speakers, located as it is about halfway between Florence and Arezzo. All this gives the conversations an air of verisimilitude, just as the arguments of the speakers are in harmony with their professional interests and sympathies. Accolti's main part is in the second of the three debates, in which the superiority of medicine or law is discussed, Accolti taking the side of law, whereas the physician Niccolò Tignosi defends medicine.[111]

Tignosi opens the debate maintaining that medicine is older than law; he goes on to cite various infamous laws of antiquity to show that they were alien to all reason. In contrast, he argues that medicine is founded on the immutable laws of nature, whereas law is based only on the will of the majority, so that laws vary according to time and place. He concludes that natural philosophy, which includes medicine, is superior to law, which is a branch of moral philosophy, for nature never changes, in contrast to *mores*, which are seldom the same. Accolti then rejoins that law is in fact older than medicine since men lived in society for many years without medicine and were probably better for it; law, he continues, is necessary to protect the weak, whereas medicine originated only in idle curiosity. His main point, taken from Cicero's *De legibus*, is that law is in fact natural and immutable;[112] it is right reason, emanating from the divine mind, which exhorts good and forbids evil. Niccolò retorts with Cicero's denunciation of law as a science for petty minds in his oration *Pro L. Murena*;[113] he clarifies his position, saying that he is not criticizing laws in general which are necessary for society, but Roman law as practised by civil lawyers such as Accolti, jurisdiction of which is limited to the almost totally defunct Roman Empire; indeed, each city within the Empire prefers its own laws, so that no subject as limited in scope as Roman law can be necessary or useful. Moreover, even if law were necessary, it would not follow that lawyers deserve honour and respect, for menial artisans such as cooks and tailors provide necessary services but are not accorded dignity. Niccolò goes on to say that lawyers are not worthy of honour since their only aim is to acquire wealth, and he concludes with the argument that, just as substance is superior to accident, so medicine, which protects man's very existence, is superior to law, which merely provides for a civilized life in society. By now the argument has become heated, and Accolti points out that citing a few corrupt lawyers does not condemn the entire profession; he argues that lawyers can only cause harm by taking money whereas an

---

[111] *La disputa*, ed. Garin, 15–33. For the dispute between medicine and law, cf. E. Garin, *L'umanesimo italiano* (Bari, 1952), 34–50; Thorndike, *Science and Thought*, 24–58; Walser, *Poggius*, 249ff.; *La disputa*, ed. Garin, *passim*; C. Salutati, *De nobilitate legum et medicinae*, ed. E. Garin (Florence, 1947).

[112] *De Legibus*, I,xii,33; II,iv,8. Cf. *La disputa*, ed. Garin, 20.

[113] *Pro L. Murena*, 23; cf. *La disputa*, ed. Garin, 23.

error by a doctor can mean loss of life. Accolti ridicules the lack of qualifi-
cations among the medical profession and the vile subject matter that
physicians have to deal with, and points out that they can never agree as to
medicine or treatment. The main point of Accolti's argument in this part
of the dialogue is that just as mind is superior to body so law is superior to
medicine, for medicine cares for man's carnal being in contrast to law
which as a civilizing influence provides for his mental and spiritual welfare; indeed, without law man would be only a beast. Niccolò then concludes the debate with a number of strikingly original arguments. He
maintains that laws are not necessary or useful because they are never
introduced spontaneously but are imposed on unwilling subjects; indeed,
it was for this reason that legislators in antiquity had to adopt the fiction
of divine sanction for their laws. Niccolò then goes on to state that laws are
for only the weak; whoever attains supreme power in a republic or principate does so not by law but by force and violence prohibited by law; if laws
were obeyed, there would be no great feats of arms, no empires. Indeed,
Niccolò maintains that there would have been no advances of civilization
if laws had been observed; without their empire built up by violence, for
example, the Athenians would never have been able to support the arts as
they did. All things worthy and excellent have been achieved by injury and
injustice in contempt of the laws. Today when the Florentines or Venetians
embark on a war, they do not summon lawyers to advise them on the
legality of their actions; great men establish their own laws, and even the
weak submit to the rule of law only from fear of punishment. After all this
Tignosi concludes by repeating several more conventional arguments and
Accolti, who is about to attempt a reply, is cut short by Marsuppini, who
asks what Tignosi thinks of canon law and lawyers.

Tignosi gets the better of Accolti in the debate, but there are a number
of reasons to doubt whether the conversations in the form reported by
Poggio actually took place. Verisimilitude – created in this instance by the
plausible friendship among the speakers as Aretines living in Florence and
as colleagues in the university, by their reputation as Aretine intellectuals,
by the convenient location of Terranuova between Florence and Arezzo
and by the defence of law undertaken by a prominent lawyer in contrast to
the advocacy of medicine by a leading physician – was one of the aims of
rhetoric.[114] In 1450 Poggio's standing in the curia was under threat from
a number of Greek scholars such as Valla, George of Trebizond, Theodore
Gaza, Niccolò Perotti and Giovanni Tortelli, who were in the height of
papal favour for their knowledge of Greek, of which Poggio was himself
almost ignorant.[115] In his *Historia tripartita* Poggio clearly was pulling out

[114] Cf. *Rhet. ad Her.* I, ix, 14, 16; *De inven.* I,xx,28; Quintilian, IV,ii,31–3; George of
Trebizond, *Rhet.*, fol. 5r.
[115] Cf. Holmes, *Florentine Enlightenment*, 252ff.

all stops to prove his virtuosity as a rhetorician; it was as though he were proving to the curia that, although not a Greek scholar, he was unequalled as a Ciceronian Latinist. In imitation of Cicero's philosophical and rhetorical dialogues, Poggio created a plausible setting for the conversations, which always maintain an informal, casual structure similar to that found in Cicero. Moreover, the two main points of Accolti's argument in favour of the superiority of law – that law is right reason and that law which cares for the soul is superior to medicine which looks after the body – are important arguments in Salutati's treatise *De nobilitate legum et medicinae*,[116] but Poggio is careful to disguise any resemblance between his work and Salutati's, which was a defence of law in the form of a scholastic disputation. The last thing that Poggio wanted was to give the impression that he was dabbling in scholasticism; indeed, he was already under attack for being behind the times because of his ignorance of Greek. There are a number of other arguments shared by Salutati's *De nobilitate* and Accolti's speeches in the *Historia tripartita*, such as the disgusting subject matter of medicine or legal abuses deriving not from the laws themselves but from corrupt lawyers,[117] and there can be no doubt that the anecdote related by Accolti about the bishop of Arezzo, Angelo Ricasoli, who hid medicines prescribed for him under the bed in order to embarrass his physicians when they claimed credit for his cure, is derived from Salutati's similar story about the Florentine Andrea da Luco.[118] What is significant is that Poggio has changed the Florentine citizen into an Aretine bishop to give the tale more local colour, enhance its verisimilitude and disguise the fact that it is derived from Salutati; Poggio here is clearly revealed as going to great lengths to give his work the appearance of spontaneity rather than reporting conversations as they actually took place.

It has been pointed out that in his later works Tignosi also attacked legal sophistry and that, as in the *Historia tripartita*, he tended to emphasize medicine's place among the liberal arts;[119] however, it is difficult to find more specific parallels between Tignosi's arguments *apud Poggium* and his own writings, just as Accolti's discussion of law in his own dialogue has only the most general resemblance to the words put in his mouth by Poggio.[120] But what is not in doubt is that Poggio in this section of the *Historia tripartita* was showing off his own skill as a rhetorician, one of whose accomplishments was meant to be the ability to defend a weak or impossible cause.[121] After Salutati's exhaustive proof of the superiority of

---

[116]   Ed. Garin, 50, 240, 254, 264.      [117]   *Ibid.*, 64, 264; cf. *La disputa*, ed Garin, 25–6.
[118]   Cf. Salutati, *De nobilitate*, 156–8, and *La disputa*, ed. Garin, 26.
[119]   Cf. A. Rotondo, 'Niccolò Tignosi', Rin. ix (1958), 227–8.
[120]   Cf. pp. 210–11, *infra*.
[121]   Cf. Plato, *Phaedrus*, 267 A; Aristotle, *Rhetoric*, II, xxiv, 11; Diogenes Laertius, IX, 53; Cicero, *Brutus*, 47.

law to medicine, Poggio was taking on what must have generally been regarded as a difficult cause; when Poggio had Tignosi argue the thesis that all great things have been accomplished by injury and injustice in contempt of the law, he was clearly attempting to uphold the impossible. The brilliance with which he has Tignosi argue his case has led one modern commentator to compare Poggio – with considerable justification – to Machiavelli;[122] however, it is unmistakably the work of a great rhetorician such as Poggio, who puts the traditional defence of law into the mouth of Accolti to give himself the opportunity of refuting it in the guise of Tignosi.

The *Historia tripartita* may not reveal Accolti's actual thoughts on the relative merits of law and medicine, but it certainly gives further proof of the deteriorating relationship between Poggio and Accolti by 1450, for it was hardly an act of friendship to make Accolti the butt of Tignosi's abuse and the victim of his superior rhetoric. In fact, some of Tignosi's arguments recall Poggio's letter of 1436 to Accolti, in particular, his contentions that lawyers' fees determine their opinions, that legal writings lose sight of truth in a maze of contradictions and that lawyers are strangers to the refinements of eloquence;[123] in 1450, however, Poggio's abuse of Accolti's profession is not mitigated by praise of Accolti's accomplishments as a humanist. Reference to Accolti's classical learning is rather by way of reproach, when Tignosi says that he will quote Cicero's words in *Pro Murena*, 'known to you I think but not to others'; it was if Poggio were saying to Accolti that, because of his humanist education, he ought to have known better than to waste his time as a lawyer.[124] Otherwise, Poggio has Tignosi make a number of jibes at Accolti for devoting himself to civil law, such as when he declares, 'You who are extremely learned in Roman law will be an ignoramus among people who do not obey these laws or need your skills; you will either have to learn other laws or emigrate to where you can sell this learning of yours.'[125] The implication is obvious: Poggio believed that Accolti had been devoting himself to law for the past ten years to the detriment of humanist studies, whose application, unlike that of Roman law, was universal; he clearly felt that Accolti had been neglecting the refinements of life in order to advance his career and make money.[126] The debate in the *Historia tripartita* was much more an explicit attack on the legal profession and an implied criticism of Accolti's conduct in the recent past than a defence of the medical profession, which suffers a vituperative denunciation from Poggio via Accolti; indeed, the only pro-

---

[122] Walser, *Poggius*, 258.    [123] Cf. pp. 54ff, *supra*.    [124] *La disputa*, ed. Garin, 22.
[125] *Ibid.*, 30.
[126] Cf. *ibid.*, 28. There may also be a touch of irony in Poggio's use of the pluperfect tense to describe Accolti's accomplishments as a humanist: 'Tum Benedictus qui ad legum scientiam etiam studia humanitatis adiunxerat . . . inquit . . .': cf. Poggio, *Opera*, 52.

fession which emerges unscathed is Poggio's own – rhetoric – which he evidently felt Accolti had forsaken.

The *Historia tripartita*, although not much of a source for Accolti's own ideas, reveals the image he presented in 1450. He is portrayed as a learned scholar of Roman law, to the study of which he had devoted himself for many years. He is seen as the representative of a profession which he is ready to defend against denigration at the hands of practitioners of rival professions. Most telling is the picture of Accolti as someone who had once gained knowledge of the classics and skill as a rhetorician, but who for a considerable time had devoted himself almost single-mindedly to law to the neglect of the humanities. What Poggio exaggerated, however, was Accolti's commitment to law; indeed, it has been seen that only three years before in 1447 Accolti had contemplated for himself a complete change of career as a humanist in the papal curia. Once again Accolti would attempt such a radical change of direction, but this time he would not be thwarted, for he was to succeed the great Poggio himself as humanist chancellor of Florence.

# 5

# Accolti's election as chancellor
# of Florence

In the 1450s Benedetto Accolti became more closely associated with
Florence while loosening his remaining ties with Arezzo. Accolti had been
bound to Arezzo and his family there by his father's estate, which had been
left undivided to the four surviving brothers, Benedetto, Francesco,
Donato and Giovanni. In 1445 the brothers had given a dowry of 450
florins to their sister Tommasa, 200 florins of which consisted of a farm
inherited from their father at Milisciano in the *cortine* of Arezzo and the
vineyards at San Giovanni in the Aretine countryside.[1] Otherwise, when
the Accolti brothers submitted their report for the Aretine *catasto* of 1454,
they had neither added to nor taken away from their patrimony, which had
itself remained almost unchanged since 1427.[2] Maintaining joint ownership of this property, which was all located in Arezzo, the Aretine countryside and the Casentino, was a considerable responsibility for Benedetto
Accolti as the eldest surviving son.[3] It would obviously have been less
burdensome for him if the estate were divided, which is what the three surviving Accolti brothers – Benedetto, Francesco and Donato – did in 1456,
fifteen years after their father's death. Benedetto took all the property at
Bagnena, while his brothers retained in common the property at
Poggibaldi and Salutio; all three continued to own jointly their house and
garden in Arezzo.[4] The terms of the division reflect the differing life styles
of the three Accolti brothers in the 1450s: Francesco, the successful itinerant lawyer, still had only Arezzo for his permanent home, and it suited him
to share his property there with his brother Donato, a permanent resident
who could attend to the day-to-day management of their affairs; Donato
was perhaps able to enjoy some of Francesco's growing wealth, particularly since Francesco was making investments in Aretine property with the

---

[1] ASF, Not.A., P 292 (1459), 5 July 1459.
[2] Cf. ASF, Cat. 201, fol. 351r–358v with ASA, Cat. 7, fol. 212v–221r.
[3] Cf. Poggio's portrait of Accolti stopping to see him in Terranuova on his way from
Florence to Arezzo in his *Opera*, 33.
[4] ASF, Not.A., S 1190 (not foliated), 25 April 1456.

profits of his legal career in North Italy.[5] Benedetto's principal home, on
the other hand, was now Florence and it was probably his wish to shed as
many of his Aretine responsibilities as possible. Although Accolti's ties
with his Aretine family were relaxed after the division with his brothers, he
still continued to take an interest in his Aretine relatives throughout the
1450s. It has already been seen how he attempted to resign his communal
offices in Arezzo in 1458 in favour of his cousin Agnolo di Grazia Accolti,[6]
whom he also employed at that time as his procurator,[7] and, as his father
Michele had done in the 1430s, Benedetto during his absence in Florence
lent Agnolo his house in Arezzo for notarial business;[8] moreover, in 1457
his sister Tommasa named Benedetto as one of her heirs in the event of her
own children's death.[9]

Nevertheless, by now Arezzo had become a peripheral concern for
Benedetto Accolti with his successful legal practice in Florence.[10] In the
1450s he worked as a legal consultant for members of the Florentine
patriciate, for the archdiocese of Florence and for the communal government.[11] Law also provided Accolti with his first opportunity to hold communal office in Florence. He had been made eligible for two legal offices in
government in 1448;[12] he was unable to serve as *sapiens communis*
because this office was abolished by the Balìa of 1449,[13] but in November
1456 he was selected to become the assessor of the syndics of the *podestà*,
one of the foreign rectors or judges in Florence.[14] This was the first time
that a member of the Accolti family had held public office in Florence since
the first half of the fourteenth century, and it is interesting to observe what
a slow process it was for the Aretine Accolti family to gain admittance to
public office in Florence during the fifteenth century. Accolti's father had

---

[5]  Cf. ASA, Cat. 7, fol. 221v–222r          [6]  Cf. pp. 77–8, *supra*.

[7]  ASF, Not.A., L 189 (1451–66), fol. 111r; *ibid.*, S 1190 (not foliated).

[8]  ASF, Not.A., A 50, fol. 62r (1 September 1450); I am grateful to Mr Frank Dabell for this
    reference.

[9]  ASF, Not.A. P 294 (1455–77), no. 7.

[10] His work as an advocate is documented by his *consilia*, some of which are found in the
    following manuscripts: ASF, C.Str., iii, 41; BNF, Magl. (Strozz.), xxix, 173, fol. 219r–
    220v, 337r ff.; *ibid.*, xxix, 193, fol. 177r–178r; *ibid.*, Panc. 139, fol. 138v–139v; BV,
    Vat. Lat. 8067; *ibid.*, Ott. Lat. 1726; *ibid.*, Urb. Lat. 1132; Forlì, Biblioteca Comunale,
    Autografi Piancastelli, 12; Isola Bella, Stresa, Archivio Borromeo, Fondo Autografi, A 11
    (I am grateful to Prof. P. O. Kristeller for this reference); Valenciennes, Bibliothèque
    Valenciennes, 261 [formerly 251] (D.5.8). A collection of *consilia* by other lawyers said
    to have been compiled by Accolti himself is BNF, Landau Finaly, 98, but there are no
    marginalia in Accolti's hand.

[11] ASF, Not.A., L 189 (1451–66), fol. 142r–v; Martines, *Lawyers*, 169; ASF, Not.A. D 86
    (1446–54), fol. 92v–93v; *ibid.* (1459–55), fol. 146v; *ibid.*, D 87 (1458–62), 15v–16r. I
    am grateful to Mr C. Fuller for the last three references.

[12] Cf. p. 67, *supra*.          [13] Cf. Martines, *Lawyers*, 147.

[14] ASF, Tratte, 81, fol. 57r. Accolti was drawn for this office again for six months on 11
    November 1460: *ibid.*, fol. 58r.

first worked as a lawyer in Florence more than forty years before in 1414
and it was only in 1456 that Benedetto Accolti finally attained office; this
is in sharp contrast to the career of the fourteenth-century Aretine Accolti,
Maestro Gregorio, who in 1324, within perhaps fifteen years of his own
arrival in Florence, was a captain of Orsanmichele. Benedetto and Michele
Accolti had to work within the evidently less flexible society of fifteenth-
century Florence and it is a tribute to Benedetto Accolti's eminence as a
lawyer that he was able to attain office at all. The picture of Accolti's
standing in Florence as a lawyer given by Vespasiano da Bisticci is
impressive:

> He had the greatest skill in civil and canon law . . . He was so excellent at giving
> legal counsel that a great many people came to him for advice from outside
> Florence . . . Regarding the laws and knowing how to interpret them, whenever
> there was a legal question in a case and Messer Benedetto was present, all others
> stood silent before his authority.[15]

Vespasiano also praised Accolti's work in the University of Florence,
pointing out that 'he lectured in Florence to a very wide audience and
acquired throughout all Italy the greatest reputation because he had a great
many pupils from various places'.[16] Vespasiano may not have exaggerated
this account of Accolti's success as a teacher of law, his long tenure of
more than twenty years in the university demonstrating the high reputation which he enjoyed. His salary in Florence in the 1450s is not known,
but some indication of it can be ascertained from negotiations in which he
was involved at that time with the University of Siena. In October 1451 he
was appointed to lecture in Siena for a salary of 300 florins,[17] but he preferred to remain in Florence where he was listed as a member of the teaching staff at the university that year.[18] He was again involved in negotiations
with Siena in 1456, when he instructed his agents not to accept any
appointment on his behalf for less than a salary of 500 florins, but once
more negotiations fell through.[19] In fact, the salaries mentioned would
have been very high in Florence, placing Accolti in the class of national
figures in the legal world who were occasionally attracted there.[20] In the
1450s Accolti had reached such a position of eminence in Florence that it
would have been difficult to persuade him to accept an appointment elsewhere. When he entered into negotiations with Siena in 1456, it is unlikely
that he was considering leaving Florence for good; lawyers frequently took
temporary posts in foreign cities such as Accolti's father had done in
Perugia in 1429 and his brother Francesco had been doing in Ferrara and

[15] Vespasiano, *Vite*, i, 595–7.   [16] *Ibid.*, 595.
[17] Cf. Corso, 'Francesco Accolti', BSenSP, lxii–lxiii (1955–6), 26–7.
[18] Cf. *Statuti*, ed. Gherardi, 461–2.
[19] ASF, Not.A., L 189 (1451–66), fol. 125r.   [20] Cf. Park, 'Readers', 272ff.

Siena since 1445. By 1456, moreover, it is possible that Accolti was already being considered as successor to the aged Poggio as chancellor of Florence.

Poggio had come to Florence as chancellor in 1453 after almost fifty years in the curia.[21] He was given a rapturous welcome by his fellow citizens, but at seventy-three it was, to say the least, late in life to begin a new career. Before leaving Rome his old friend Pope Nicholas V predicted that in less than a year he would become disillusioned with his compatriots,[22] and indeed it was just thirteen months after his arrival in Florence that he began to show signs of discontent. In July 1454 he had an attack of gout and retreated with his family to his country house at San Lorenzo in Collina near Grassina, four miles from Florence;[23] a few days after his arrival there he wrote to let the pope know of his illness, declaring that one consolation for his suffering was that he was avoiding the summer's heat in Florence and the many tedious official meetings.[24] His absence from Florence on this occasion lasted three months,[25] and by 1455 he was already discussing the possibility of returning to Rome.[26] He was apparently again absent from duty in Florence from January to April 1455, and again from the end of June 1455 to the beginning of November 1455.[27] Some of his absence from the chancery during 1455 was due to demands of other official duties which he was given that year. In January he became the first of the eight consuls of the Florentine guild of lawyers and notaries for four months, which coincides with his absence from the chancery during that time;[28] and in July he became one of the priors in the Florentine Signoria for two months, again at the same time as one of his absences from the chancery.[29] Poggio was delighted to receive these honours, not least because they freed him from the tedious routine of the chancery; his compatriots bestowed these offices upon him, in the words of Vespasiano, 'to honour him with the honours of the city',[30] certainly not thinking that he would use them as an excuse to neglect his duties in the chancery. Leonardo Bruni like Poggio had become chancellor at the apogee of his fame as a humanist, and the Florentines had honoured him with various high political offices including the priorate.[31] Bruni had carried out these additional duties seemingly without any detriment to the chancery; following his first year in office, however, Poggio lost interest in the chancery, which went to pieces after the summer of 1454. After an initial two-month period of adjustment in June and July 1453 when the

[21] Marzi, *La cancelleria*, 220–1.
[22] Poggio, *Epistolae*, iii, 63. Cf. Walser, *Poggius*, 282.
[23] *Ibid.*, 286, 522–3.   [24] Poggio, *Epistolae*, iii, 56–7.
[25] Cf. Walser, *Poggius*, 286, n. 2.   [26] Poggio, *Epistolae*, iii, 216–17.
[27] Walser, *Poggius*, 286, n. 2.   [28] *Ibid.*, 285.   [29] *Ibid.*
[30] Vespasiano, *Vite*, i, 547. For Poggio's reaction, cf. *Epistolae*, iii, 195ff.
[31] Cf. *infra*, p. 129.

chancery staff seem to have been getting used to their new head,[32] the chancery settled down to a more or less orderly routine of work, and for the first year of Poggio's chancellorship, from about August 1453 to July 1454, a division of responsibilities was achieved among the assistants and there may even have been a brief return to the ideal of two chanceries, one for foreign relations and the other for domestic business, which had come into effect under Bruni in 1437 but had been allowed to lapse at the end of Marsuppini's term in 1453. The principal coadjutor and vice-chancellor, Antonio di Mariano Muzi,[33] was charged by Poggio with minuting the meetings of the important advisory assembly, the *pratica*,[34] as well as with administering ambassadorial missions.[35] Foreign state letters, as well as letters and commissions to ambassadors, were copied by Bastiano di Antonio di Zanobi Foresi;[36] it is probable that second chancery business was delegated to Niccolò di Pardo di Antonio Pardi[37] and Jacopo di ser

[32] The conclusions reached here and subsequently regarding the organization of work in the Florentine chancery between 1444 and 1464 are based primarily on a study of the hands of the notaries working in the chancery during this period. It has been possible to name four of these scribes; there are four other hands which appear but which I have not been so far able to name. It is not possible in this book to offer the fullest documentation of these findings, which would require extensive photographic reproductions; I hope to publish this material in a study of scribes and reform in the Florentine chancery between 1444 and 1464.
   The period of adjustment to Poggio's arrival in the chancery can be seen in ASF, Miss. 40 for the period 12 June 1453 to 90 August 1453 (fol. 1r–11r) where three different scribes collaborated on the foreign state letters of the chancery: Antonio Muzi (fol. 1r–2r, 10r–11r; for the identification of his hand, cf. p. 89, n. 33, *infra*); Jacopo di ser Paolo (fol. 2v–3v, 4r–v; for the identification of his hand, cf. p. 90, n. 38, *infra*); and Bastiano Foresi (fol. 3v–4r, 4v–10r; for the identification of his hand, cf. p. 89, n. 36, *infra*).

[33] The hand of ser Antonio di Mariano Muzi can be identified by referring to ASF, Tratte, 95, which records elections to the chancery as well as other offices beginning in the mid-fifteenth century; this volume was written by the notary of the Tratte himself, since the hand changed whenever a new notary of the Tratte was appointed (cf. *ibid.*, fol. 75r–v), and Muzi, who was notary of the Tratte from 1475 to 1483, made his entries in this register in his own hand, which is recognizable as one of the hands found in chancery records in the 1450s and 1460s. It is also a hand frequently encountered in ASF, Miss. 2a, 3 (fol. 22v, 33v, 54r, 55r, 56v–57r, 66r etc.), dating from the period when Muzi was second chancellor.

[34] Cf. ASF, CP, 53, fol. 1r–184v (14 February 1453–17 October 1455), written entirely by Muzi.

[35] Cf. ASF, CdC, 51, fol. 125r–152r (10 February 1452–8 May 1456), written entirely by Muzi.

[36] The hand of ser Bastiano di Antonio di Zanobi di ser Forese is identifiable from ASF, CdC, 64, fol. 1r, where he identifies himself as the scribe, as well as from ASF, Not.A., S 499–503, which are his extant protocols as a practising Florentine notary. Foresi alone was responsible for ASF, LC, 13, fol. 41r–51v (23 February 1453–28 May 1454) and for ASF, Miss. 40, fol. 11r–54r (9 August 1453–6 July 1454).

[37] Ser Niccolò di Pardo di Antonio Pardi da Volterra is documented as working in the chancery on 29 May 1453 (cf. Luiso, 'Riforma', 140–1) and on 14 May 1455 (ASF, LC, 13, fol. 141r), between 28 June and 1 September 1455 (ASF, Tratte, 95, fol. 72v) and on 5 May 1458, 4 April 1460, 10 June 1460 and 23 August 1461 (ASF, Not.A., S 500, fol. 21r, 23r, 23v, 24r). The only hand which consistently appeared in chancery records over this

Paolo.[38] However, beginning in the summer of 1454, when Poggio's first prolonged absence from the chancery occurred, this organization began to collapse. In June 1454, Jacopo di ser Paolo began working, with Foresi, on ambassadorial letters,[39] and in August they were joined by Muzi[40] and Pardi,[41] so that by the autumn all four assistants were working on what had been the specialized responsibility of one of them. Similarly in July, Jacopo di ser Paolo began to share with Foresi responsibility for foreign letters,[42] and after August they were joined by Pardi,[43] with a very occasional appearance by Muzi.[44] The *pratica* remained in Muzi's sole charge for another year until October 1455,[45] when he was joined by Foresi[46] and then Pardi in February[47] and Jacopo di Paolo in March 1456.[48] By 1456, the only remnant of an organized division of labour was the administration of ambassadorial missions, which remained solely in the hands of Muzi, except for one appearance of Jacopo di Paolo on 8 June

period was that of Marsuppini's coadjutor, who continued to work in the chancery under Poggio and then in the second chancery after 1458; therefore, this is the hand of Pardi, and his long service would explain why he had a senior position among the coadjutors of Marsuppini (cf. Luiso, 'Riforma', 140–1) and why he temporarily replaced Poggio as chancellor in July and August 1455 during Poggio's service as a prior (ASF, Tratte, 95, fol. 72v). During his long service in the chancery between 1444 and the early 1460s, Pardi's hand underwent some changes of style. The volume of the *missive* written by him for Marsuppini (ASF, Miss. 36) is less cursive than his later work, but his cursive inclinations are already apparent in ASF, CP, 52; his growing tendency to a more cursive script, which became his normal hand in the 1450s, can be seen in ASF, CdC, 51, fol. 49v–100r (8 April 1444–20 June 1450). Pardi's hand does not appear in ASF, Miss. 40 before 15 August 1454 (fol. 63r–v), nor in any other first chancery volume, indicating that he was working on second chancery business during this period.

[38] The fourth scribe working under Poggio can be identified as ser Jacopo di ser Paolo from ASF, LC, 13, fol. 141r, which is a request on 14 May 1455 to the Florentine ambassador to Rome to seek indulgences for the current Signoria, the notary of the Signoria and the four coadjutors of the chancery. Besides those of Muzi, Foresi and Pardi, there is one further hand in the volumes of the chancery from this period (cf. ASF, CdC, 51, fol. 124r–125r; LC, 13, fol. 51v–52v, 54r–v; Miss. 40, fol. 2v, 4r–v, 54r–57r, 57v–59r), which therefore belongs to Jacopo di Paolo. Jacopo di Paolo did not work on first chancery volumes between 29 June 1453 (ASF, Miss. 40, fol. 4v) and 4 June 1454 (ASF, LC, 13, fol. 51v–52v), indicating that he was then confined to second chancery business only.

[39] ASF, LC, 13, fol. 51v–52v, 54r–v, 81r–v, 85v–88r, 89v, 106r–v, 168r–v, 177v–178r.
[40] *Ibid.*, fol. 67r–v, 67 bis r, 70r, 70v, 95r.
[41] *Ibid.*, fol. 71r–72v, 75r–81r, 81v–83r, 85v, 90v–95r, 96r–98r, 98v–99r, 99v–106r, 107r, 108r–110v, 113v–117r, 119v–121v, 124r–126r, 129r–v, 130v–131r, 136r, 141v, 145r, 145v–147r, 147v–152r, 154v–155r, 156v–157v, 160r, 163r–164r, 165v–166r, 167v.
[42] ASF, Miss. 40. fol. 54r–57r, 57v–59r, 60r, 61v–62r, 73r–v, 117r.
[43] *Ibid.*, fol. 63r, 63v–69v, 70v–72v, 74r, 77v, 78r–80v, 82v–87r, 91r–94v, 96r–98r, 102r–103v, 104r–105r, 106r–v, 107v, 108v–110v, 112r, 113v–114r, 116r, 117r–126v, 133r–134v, 136r, 137r, 143r–146r, 148v–149v, 153v–154r, 163r–164r, 164v–180v, 183v–188v, 190r–193r, 202r–v, 209r, 210v–212r, 213r–214r, 215r–217v, 220r, 223r–226v, 230r–231r.
[44] *Ibid.*, fol. 70v, 71r, 192v.      [45] ASF, CP, 53, fol. 1r–184v.
[46] *Ibid.*, fol. 185r–186r, 233r–v.
[47] *Ibid.*, fol. 223r–v.      [48] *Ibid.*, fol. 232r–v, 234r–v.

1456.[49] Indeed, such was the disorder that beginning in the second half of 1454 one notary frequently did not even complete his letter or entry, which was taken over by one of his colleagues,[50] sometimes in the middle of a line.[51] Another sign of deterioration was the state of the minutes of the *pratica*. While Poggio's predecessor, Marsuppini, was in office, notes were made at the meetings and then were written up as summaries in the permanent registers in a neat, semi-cursive script; under Poggio, however, Muzi's hand became almost illegible, and, to judge from their bad grammar and careless script, the summaries may have been copied into the permanent registers during the meetings themselves. At the beginning of November 1455, after a four months' absence from the chancery, Poggio finally returned to his duties, only to be selected a few days later as assessor of the syndics of the *podestà*, whose duties again led him to be absent from the chancery.[52] This time the Signoria had had enough and they ordered Poggio to be brought back forcibly to the chancery by their steward who, accordingly, 'took Messer Poggio, the assessor of the *podestà*, and dragged him struggling and protesting to the palace of the Signoria'.[53] After this episode Poggio made only desultory appearances in the chancery, and he seems to have carried out his official duties with the petulance of a spoilt child.[54]

Poggio's outrageous behaviour and dereliction of duty alienated Florentine public opinion, and his position was further undermined by his long-standing and intimate friendship with Cosimo de' Medici.[55] This might have been an advantage at the time of his election to the chancellorship in April 1453, but the virtual collapse of Medicean political controls by the summer of 1455[56] gave anti-Mediceans more scope for obstructing the regime, and one sphere into which they brought their opposition was the chancery. The notariate of the Riformagioni, one of the leading posts in the chancery, fell vacant after 30 May 1456,[57] and on 29 July 1456 the Medicean regime attempted to install one of its loyal adherents, ser Bartolomeo Guidi, in this office for the unusually long term of three years;

---

[49] ASF, CdC, 51, fol. 152r–v.
[50] Cf. ASF, LC, 13, fol. 90v, 108r, 121v, 145v; Miss. 40, fol. 96r, 104r, 110v, 149v, 154r, 183r–v, 188v, 193r, 209r, 213r.
[51] Cfr. ASF, LC, 13, fol. 152r, 157v, 160r; Miss. 40, fol. 143r, 190r, 202v, 214r.
[52] Walser (*Poggius*, 285) mentions that Poggio became assessor of the syndics of the *podestà*, but does not give the reference to his election to this office, which is ASF, Tratte, 80, fol. 218r; the term of office was six months and it began on 10 November 1455. Poggio had come back to the chancery on 5 November: cf. Walser, *Poggius*, 286, n. 2.
[53] Cf. *ibid.*, 397–7.
[54] Cf. e.g. the episode of Poggio's supper and the Dieci di Balìa, *ibid.*, 285–6, n. 6.
[55] Vespasiano, *Vite*, i, 548.
[56] Cf. Rubinstein, *Government*, 22, 28, 52, 79, 88ff.
[57] Cf. ASF, Tratte, 95, fol. 71r, for the last annual renewal of Filippo Balducci from 30 May 1455.

however, the proposal was rejected by the council of the people and had to be abandoned.[58] The notariate of the Riformagioni thus remained vacant, with the principal assistant, ser Alberto di Donnino di Luca, acting as a temporary substitute.[59] Next, the opponents of the regime struck at the chancellorship. Constitutionally, this was a temporary post, requiring renewal at regular intervals, but *de facto* the chancellor held office for life, Poggio's famous predecessors, Salutati, Bruni and Marsuppini, all having died in office. Poggio's term of office expired on 31 August 1456,[60] but he failed to obtain a renewal from the Signoria and colleges;[61] indeed, with the ending of electoral manipulations in June 1455, members of the Signoria and colleges were no longer necessarily hand-picked Mediceans, and the regime and Poggio himself were unfortunate in having none-too-pliant incumbents in the Tre Maggiori for the rest of 1456. After the chancellorship had been vacant for almost two months, the regime's inability to secure a renewal for Poggio was becoming a source of acute embarrassment. It was customary for the leading citizens to discuss problems in governing Florence at a meeting of the *pratica*, which was duly summoned for advice on 27 October 1456. 'We have understood that Messer Poggio has not been reelected', said Alessandro degli Alessandri and Luca Pitti, two leading members of the regime who were speaking for the entire *pratica*; 'we are of the opinion . . . that Messer Poggio must again be appointed, for no one else can be better in that job nor can the chancellorship be better filled than by his person, because of his knowledge, his practical skill, his experience and his great fame. And let this reappointment be considered and examined well with the colleges, and in such a way that it is obtained, for the sake of the honour of the Signoria as well as of Messer Poggio himself.'[62] It seems thus that the Signoria at last were willing to reappoint Poggio, but that the two colleges of the twelve good men and sixteen gonfaloniers were proving obstinate; although Poggio had been

---

[58]   Cf. Marzi, *La cancelleria*, 225.      [59]   *Ibid.*, 226; cf. ASF, Tratte, 95, fol. 71r.

[60]   Cf. *ibid.*, fol. 72v: Dominus Poggius fuit de novo electus per dominos et collegia die 30 Augusti 1455 pro uno anno initiato die prima mensis Septembris 1455 cum officio, salario et aliis ordinatis. I am deeply grateful to Dott. Daniela De Rosa for pointing out this important and hitherto unknown volume of the Tratte to me.

[61]   ASF, CP, 54, fol. 49v–50r.

[62]   This important passage was omitted by Walser in his unfortunately inaccurate edition of these debates (*Poggius*, 404–6): [ASF, CP, 54, fol. 49v–50r]
                              die xxvi [*sic* for 27] Octobris 1456
In saletta per infrascriptos de prattica . . .
Dominus Alexander [Alessandri]
Luca Pitti . . . et super cancelleria . . .
Che inteso non avere avuto la riforma Messer Poggio, siamo di parere tutti noi della praticha et anchora di quelli che non ci sono per essere impediti, che in quello luogho si debbi ricondurre Messer Poggio predetto, perché niuno altro può esser meglo in quello luogho né meglo può essere riformata la cancelleria che della persona sua, sì per la scientia et per la pratica et per la experientia et per la fama sua grande. Et questa

an incompetent chancellor, the leaders of the regime, whose views were expressed in this *pratica*, felt that they could not simply dismiss someone of Poggio's enormous stature. Moreover, they were apparently confirmed in their resolve to support Poggio by Cosimo de' Medici, who, according to Vespasiano da Bisticci, was unwilling to contemplate anyone but his old friend as chancellor.[63]

This stalemate over the future of the chancery dragged on throughout the autumn of 1456 but by the end of November the situation in the chancery had reached a point of crisis with both the chancellorship and the notariate of the Riformagioni still vacant, and so once again a *pratica* was summoned. 'The chancery and the office of the Riformagioni are in confusion to the detriment of public honour and welfare', said Alessandro degli Alessandri, speaking again for the entire meeting. 'A reappointment to the chancery must be made, though I do not know how. But I do know nevertheless that the old chancellor was called here from Rome and he is a most learned man and a very great ornament for our republic.'[64] Since the summer, three successive Signorie had failed to secure his renewal, and the leaders of the regime were beginning to despair of ever securing reappointment for Poggio, to whom, however, they still felt committed because he had been called from Rome to Florence especially to become chancellor, because he was such a famous scholar, and clearly also because he had the unflinching support of Cosimo de' Medici. It was not only Poggio's personal shortcomings that were preventing his reappointment; animosity to the regime is also clear from the failure of successive Signorie to make an appointment to the notariate of the Riformagioni. The entire chancery had become embroiled in the conflicts between Mediceans and their opponents, as is shown by debates in the *pratica* concerning the future of Bartolomeo Guidi, who at the end of 1456 was still the regime's candidate for notary of the Riformagioni. On 8 December 1456 another *pratica* was summoned to discuss the impasse reached over the chancery, Alessandro Alessandri declaring again that they 'must make provision for

---

ricondotta s'intenda et examinisi bene con li collegi, et in modo che quella si obtengha, sì per honore della signoria, sì anchora dela persona di Messer Poggio.

. . .

| | |
|---|---|
| Dominus Alexander de Alexandris | Dominus Thomasus Deti |
| Dominus Mannus Tenperani | Lucas de Pittis |
| Dominus Carolus de Pandolfinis | Dietisalvi Neronis |
| Dominus Octo de Nicholinis | Julianus Portinari |
| Dominus Jeronimus de Machiavellis | |

[63] Vespasiano, *Vite*, i, 548.
[64] Walser, *Poggius*, 404–6, in his edition of these debates, had difficulty reading the hand of Antonio Muzi, who made the minutes; he therefore omitted and mistranscribed a number of passages, especially those concerning the notary of the Riformagioni. I shall include the text when Walser made an omission or an error in transcription; otherwise, I shall simply cite Walser's edition.

the chancery and the Riformagioni since these offices are in a poor state
and in disorder'; what particularly mattered was finding someone for the
Riformagioni who was politically suitable, 'affectionatus regimini'.[65]
Other speakers agreed that the notariate of the Riformagioni was an office
of 'great weight', that it was of the utmost importance to appoint someone
'safe', and that Bartolomeo Guidi, a Medicean of long standing, was particularly suitable because of his 'fidelity', obviously, that is, to the regime.[66]
The great emphasis placed here by leading members of the regime on
Bartolomeo Guidi's political suitability demonstrates the extent to which
the future of the chancery had become a political issue in the mid-1450s;
like Poggio, Guidi was encountering opposition in his bid to become
notary of the Riformagioni because of his Medicean connections.

It is clear that by this time the regime was beginning to face the possibility that it might not be able to have its own way over the chancery.
'Regarding the Riformagioni', said Otto Niccolini at the *pratica* of 8
December, 'one or more names should be sent to the councils' for
approval; ser Bartolomeo is suitable, he continued, but, 'whoever is
chosen for that post, it is not safe to submit many names'.[67] Similarly, the
regime was beginning to be reconciled to finding a different chancellor.
Carlo Pandolfini, declaring that the chancery was in a bad state, said, 'the
old chancellor is best and ought to be reappointed, and if that cannot be
done, let another famous man be found'.[68] However, the regime was not
yet prepared to give up the fight for either Poggio or Guidi. The remaining
speakers agreed with Dietisalvi Neroni that Guidi 'was suitable in every
respect',[69] and similarly they were determined to keep Poggio, whom,
according to Alessandro Alessandri, 'we approved of' in the past,
emphasizing that Poggio, who 'is useful for our commune', had come
specially from Rome to take up this post.[70] Otto Niccolini, who realized
that Poggio's ineptitude and decrepitude were strong weapons in the hands
of the regime's opponents, suggested that 'help must be given to Poggio,

---

[65] ASF, CP, 54, fol. 61v (cf. Walser, *Poggius*, 404): Dominus Alexander de Alexandris . . .
Reformationum locus reformetur ut videbitur cunctis sapientioribus et presertim
dominis. fol. 67v (cf. Walser, *Poggius* 404): Dominus Alexander de Alexandris . . . et est
utilis pro communi nostro et refornatio dirigenda est notario affectionato regimini et est
qui est expertus.

[66] ASF, CP, 54, fol. 68r (cf. Walser, *Poggius*, 404–5): Dominus Carolus de Pandolfinis . . .
Eandem viam sequi reor de notario reformationum. [fol. 68v] Bernardus de Gherardis
. . . Locus reformationum aptandus est etiam de persona optima et prattica et fideli nec
sit opus mutare illam . . . [fol. 69v] Bernardus domini Laurentii [Ridolfi, not Walser's
Dini Laurentii].

[67] ASF, CP, 54, fol. 68v (cf. Walser, *Poggius*, 405): Dominus Octo de Nicolinis. Pro
reformationibus aut unus aut plures mittendi sunt ad consilia. Ser Bartolomeus pratticus
est. Quilibet percutietur in loco illo, mittere multos non est tutum quia populus potest
seduci.

[68] Walser, *Poggius*, 404.        [69] *Ibid.*, 405.        [70] *Ibid.*, 404.

who was an ornament to the chancery with his great fame; young men could be added who would give the best service'.[71] Niccolini was suggesting that Poggio be reappointed as a figurehead to keep up appearances with his great reputation and, obviously, moreover, to satisfy the wishes of Cosimo de' Medici and the rest of the regime, and that the actual work be done by new assistants. This was not very different from the status quo in the chancery, as Niccolini made clear when he closed his remarks with the statement 'et habemus qui servit',[72] that is, we have someone who is serving already. This possibly referred to the chancellor's principal assistant, Antonio Muzi, who, as vice-chancellor,[73] assumed the role of supervisor over chancery business in the interregnum after Poggio's retirement. Niccolini was therefore willing to put up with the far-from-perfect conditions then prevailing in the chancery, offering a few half measures to satisfy the regime's opponents; his remarks demonstrate the tenacity with which the regime was clinging to Poggio, as does the speech delivered by Bernardo Gherardi, who suggested that four citizens be delegated to examine how Poggio's reelection could be secured, and with the support of the remaining speakers, Gherardi's recommendation was followed.[74]

The committee of four were Otto Niccolini, Dietisalvi Neroni, Matteo Palmieri and Franco Sachetti, who submitted their report to the full *pratica* on 27 December.[75] They stated that the chancery was not functioning properly, especially because there had not been any changes for some time and because more help was needed; the reference to changes which had to be made in the chancery shows that the regime was now willing to accept some of the criticisms of the chancery made by their opponents, but they remained adamant in their support of Poggio, declaring that it was necessary to have a respected and famous chancellor to bring distinction to the city. They recognized, obviously like their opponents, that Poggio's age meant that he could not continue to serve for very much longer, but they

---

[71] *Ibid.*, 405.    [72] *Ibid.*

[73] Muzi appeared with the unusual title 'vicecancellarius' in an instrument ratifying the league 'cum Venetis et Duce' [of Milan] on 5 September 1454: cf. ASF, DelSA, 30, fol. 122r; Brown, *Scala*, 138. Muzi was accorded this title probably because he had been principal coadjutor of the reunited chancery under Marsuppini (cf. Luiso, 'Riforma', 141) and continued in this post under Poggio. Niccolini could possibly also be referring here to Pardi who had substituted for Poggio as chancellor in July and August 1455: cf. ASF, Tratte, 95, fol. 72v: Dominus Poggius suprascriptus fuit refirmatus per dominos et collegia die xviiiᵃ Aprilis 1455 in cancellarium predictum pro uno anno initiato die viiiᵃ Junii 1455 cum salario, officio et aliis ordinatis. Dominus Poggius predictus fuit extractus de dominis die 28 Junii 1455 et amisit officium cancellarie predicte. Quare petiit quod sui loco eligeretur in cancellarium predictum ser Nicolaus Pardi de Vulterris, et sic electus fuit dictus ser Nicolaus per dominos et collegia die secunda Julii 1455 pro tempore initiato die 28 Junii et duraturo usque ad per totum mensem Augusti dicti anni 1455 cum officio et aliis ordinatis. Deinde ipse dominus Poggius fuit de novo electus . . .

[74] Walser, *Poggius*, 405.    [75] Published *ibid.*, 405–6.

clearly felt that this was no reason to dismiss him, insisting that having a distinguished chancellor would provide a good example for someone else in the future who might be called from a long distance, like Poggio, to serve the Signoria. The committee were evidently attempting to work out a compromise which would be acceptable to their opponents, accepting the point that Poggio would soon have to be replaced but attempting to keep him in office for the time being on the grounds that if Poggio were dismissed they might have difficulty in persuading a suitable candidate to accept service under the Florentine government in the near future. They accepted that the demands of the chancellorship were too much for Poggio, offering as a compromise to make Poggio first chancellor alone while resurrecting the second chancellorship for Muzi, the vice-chancellor, so that the chancery would be formally divided into the same two sections as had existed until January 1453, when the second chancery had been reunited with the first chancery for the last few months of Marsuppini's life.[76] They also went some way to meeting their opponents' objections to Poggio's incapacity by recommending that four coadjutors should be appointed to assist the first chancellor and, to help pay their salaries, funds should be appropriated from the university where two of them should also be employed to lecture, thus at the same time filling a shortage of teaching staff in the faculty of rhetoric and moral philosophy. The final recommendation, that the first chancellor as the servant of the Signoria should be ineligible for other communal offices, was perhaps even more specifically directed to satisfy the regime's and Poggio's opponents who, it has been seen, had had him dragged back forcibly to the chancery when he was being distracted from his duties as chancellor by the demands of other communal offices to which he had been elected.[77]

Matters had reached such a pitch of tension between the regime and its opponents, however, that even these compromises could not be implemented; at the beginning of January 1457 the government was involved in delicate negotiations to secure the passage of adequate financial provisions and it was felt that, lest the negotiations over the Riformagioni and the chancery should tie up the councils, the financial legislation ought to be given priority and, once that was secured, the question of the chancery and the Riformagioni could be considered again.[78] This recommendation, which received the support of a large number of

---

[76] Cf. Luiso, 'Riforma', 139–41.

[77] Cf. Walser, *Poggius*, 396–7.

[78] ASF, CP, 54, fol. 79r (10 January 1457): Et alla parte delle riformationi et alla cancelleria, accioché quello non avesse ad annodare il fatto della proposta del provedimento et del monte, che e' s'attenda prima a quello provedimento et a' fatti del monte, et fatto questo, quando paresse alla magnifici signori, s'attenda alla riforma del luogo delle rinformagioni et della cancelleria.

leading figures in a *pratica* on 10 January,[79] was almost certainly put forward in order to postpone moves then being made by opponents of the regime to end the crisis in the Riformagioni. These delaying tactics, however, were notably unsuccessful with the new Signoria who had come into office at the beginning of the month; only four days later, on 14 January, the Signoria and colleges submitted legislation to the councils providing for an entirely new method of electing the notary of the Riformagioni.[80] This provision makes it clear why the regime had wanted to prolong the vacancy in the Riformagioni four days before: whereas the aim of the regime had been to secure the election of a politically suitable candidate by offering only one name to the councils as had happened the previous July with Bartolomeo Guidi,[81] or, if that was not possible, then to put forward only a few names, as had been suggested in the *pratica* of 8 December by Otto Niccolini,[82] now it was being proposed that more than a hundred names be placed before the Signoria, colleges and councils and whoever first received a two-thirds majority would become the new notary of the Riformagioni. This measure was immediately successful in the councils, where it was carried by large majorities,[83] and on 17 January 1457, the day after the new provision had become law, a new notary of the Riformagioni was elected: not the Medicean Bartolomeo Guidi but an opponent of the regime, Leone di Francesco Leoni, a lawyer from Prato who had been practising in Florence since 1425.[84]

In these circumstances, it is not surprising that no further attempt was made to secure the reelection of Poggio. A newly discovered register in the Florentine archives in which all elections to the chancellorship beginning with Marsuppini's are recorded does not contain any reference to Poggio's reappointment after his official term came to an end on 31 August 1456;[85] moreover, after this time he no longer was called or referred to himself as

[79] These were Carlo Pandolfini, Giovannozzo Pitti, Otto Niccolini, Bernardo de' Medici, Mariotto Lippi, Bartolo Lenzi, Bernardo Ridolfi, Dietisalvi Neroni, Antonio Martelli, Agnolo della Stufa, Alessandro del Vigna, Giovannozzo Biliotti, Piero de' Pazzi, Antonio Pucci, Guglielmo Cardinali, Piero Minerbetti, Niccolò Soderini, Matteo Palmieri, Bernardo Giugni, Domenico Ginori, Giuliano Portinari, Bencio Benci, Bernardo Gherardi and Giovanni Lorini: cf. *ibid.*

[80] Marzi, *La cancelleria*, 225–6, 592–4.   [81] Cf. *ibid.*, 225.

[82] Cf. p. 94, *supra*.   [83] Marzi, *La cancelleria*, 594.

[84] ASF, Tratte, 95, fol. 71r: Dominus Leo Francisci Leonis legum doctor civis florentinus fuit electus per consilia populi et communis simul in sufficientibus numeris congregata die xviia Januarii 1456 in officialem reformationum predictarum pro uno anno initiato die xviiia [Januarii] dicti anni 1456 cum salario fl. 315, pro persona sua pro dicto tempore et officio et aliis ordinatis maxime vigore provisionis obtente in consilio communis die xvia dicti mensis Januarii 1456 . . . Dominus Leo Francisci suprascriptus fuit refirmatus per dominos et collegia die xxviiiia Decembris 1457 pro uno anno initiando die xviiia Januarii dicti anni 1457 cum salario officio et aliis ordinatis. On Leo di Francesco Leoni, cf. Martines, *Lawyers*, 502; Buoninsegni, *Istorie*, 118–20.

[85] Cf. p. 92, n. 60, *supra*.

chancellor of Florence, a title which, on the other hand, he had frequently used before that time.[86] Finally, according to Vespasiano da Bisticci, it was after Poggio's departure from the chancery that he was forced to pay the extraordinary tax of 200 florins (*balzello*), which violated his tax privilege and inspired him to write his invective against the Florentines, *Contra fidei violatores*;[87] the *balzello* was levied in 1457[88] and so Vespasiano's account therefore verifies the other evidence that Poggio definitively ceased to be chancellor on 1 September 1456. Throughout these struggles Poggio retained the goodwill of Cosimo de' Medici, who had been his friend for many years and who, together with his sons, was actively assisting Poggio in his private affairs at this very time.[89] Vespasiano wrote of calumnies and vituperation against Poggio, which indicated that a concerted effort was being made to keep him out of office, but that Cosimo, out of devotion to his old friend, would not give up the contest. 'Having seen that he could not please the Florentine people since they were divided amongst themselves,' wrote Vespasiano, referring thus to the divisions between the regime and its opponents over the chancery, 'Poggio, already an old man, was content to resign in order to rest and devote more of himself to his studies.' Cosimo, continued Vespasiano, when he realized that Poggio did not care about the chancery, let him go; 'otherwise, he would not have given way'.[90]

In 1457, therefore, the chancery was left without a head, and the Signoria had no one on whom they could rely to compose important state letters to foreign governments or instructions to ambassadors on important missions. This situation gave Benedetto Accolti his first certain opportunity to work in the chancery, for on 16 February 1457, the *pratica* advised that the instructions for Guglielmo de' Benci, the ambassador about to leave for Rome, should be drafted not by the coadjutors but by Otto Niccolini and Benedetto Accolti.[91] Accolti, as a foreigner, could not

---

[86]  Cf. Walser, *Poggius*, 384ff. I am deeply grateful to Dott. De Rosa, not only for pointing me to Tratte 95, but for her generosity in letting me know some of the conclusions of her research on Poggio's chancellorship before it was published, in particular, her discovery that Poggio ceased to hold office after 1456.

[87]  Vespasiano, *Vite*, i, 548. The invective is published in *Opera omnia*, ed. Fubini, iv, 891–902. Dott. De Rosa will argue that the invective was directed not against Cosimo but rather against a faction of the Florentine people who were guilty, in Poggio's view, of acting tyrannically, and that Poggio was in fact not an anti-Medicean, as seems to be suggested by Fubini, *ibid.*, 889–90. It seems likely that the *balzello* was imposed on Poggio, at least in part, to humiliate Cosimo by attacking his close friend, Poggio.

[88]  Poggio received his demand at about the same time his eldest son, Pietro Paolo, entered the convent of San Marco (6 April 1457): cf. *Epistolae*, iii, 252–3 and Walser, *Poggius*, 300, 408 and 412.

[89]  Walser, *Poggius*, 408, 413. Cf. Poggio's own account of his intimacy with the Medici at this time at the beginning of *De miseria humanae conditionis*, in *Opera*, 88.

[90]  Vespasiano, *Vite*, i, 548.

[91]  ASF, CP, 54, fol. 90v: die xvi Februarii 1456 . . . super commisione danda Magistro

have been admitted to the *pratica* as an adviser, and so this was not simply a case of delegating a task to a small committee of *pratica* members. The only possible role for Accolti was an unofficial chancellor, composing these instructions for the ambassador, with Otto Niccolini representing the *pratica* to instruct Accolti regarding the contents of the mandate. The matter-of-fact tone in which Accolti is mentioned in the minutes of the meeting suggests that this was not the only occasion on which the government made use of Accolti's services as *ad hoc* chancellor; indeed, his service in 1457 shows that Muzi's supervision could be only a stop-gap and that a permanent and effective chancellor had to be found. Some attempt at a more permanent solution was made on 28 April 1457, when Antonio Muzi was elected second chancellor,[92] thus fulfilling at least one of the recommendations concerning the chancery put forward by four of the leading figures in the regime at the end of the previous December; however, even this proved to be only a stop-gap, as is clear from the state of the chancery records which showed little improvement after Muzi's promotion to the second chancellorship on 1 May 1457, after which time there may even have been further deterioration. The *pratica*, ambassadorial correspondence and administration of embassies continued to be the responsibility of the various assistants in the chancery;[93] a possible sign of recovery was that foreign letters were delegated to one notary after July 1457,[94] but the benefits of this step were wiped out by a new problem. There had been notable continuity among chancery staff in the earlier 1450s, and doubtless their experience had helped the chancery to weather the effects of the second chancellor Guiducci's death in January 1453, followed by Marsuppini's the next April, and Poggio's incompetence after the summer of 1454. Niccolò Pardi had served in the chancery since

---

Giuglelmo de Benchis ituro oratori ad papam, dominus Octo et dominus Benedictus illam componant.

[92] ASF, Tratte, 95, fol. 72v: Ser Antonius Mariani Mutii civis et notarius florentinus fuit electus per dominos et collegia die xxviii[a] mensis Aprilis 1457 in secundum cancellarium cancellarie suprascripte pro uno anno initiato die prima mensis Maii 1457 cum salario fl. trecentorum pro dicto tempore dicti anni pro se et duobus notariis quos secum tenere continue debet ad servitium cancellarie predicte et cum officio et allis ordinatis.

[93] After September 1456 four new hands appear in chancery records: Hand Y, which first appears on 5 December 1456 (ASF, CdC, 51, fol. 156r) and then regularly until Accolti's election in April 1458 (cf. *ibid.*, 156v, 157r, 157v, 158v, 160r); Hand B, which first appears for certain on 12 March 1457 (ASF, Miss. 41, fol. 15v) and then regularly appears until Accolti's election (cf. *ibid.*, fol. 15v–18r, 19r–20r, 21r–22v, 44v–102r; LC, 14, fol. 40r, 52v–53v, 54r–63v; CP, 54, fol. 112r–114r, 115r–v, 119v–120r, 122r–127r, 136r–v, 165r–166r, 180r–v); Hand G, a fine humanist cursive which appears briefly between 27 May and 8 June 1457 (CdC, 51, fol. 103v, 158v; LC, 14, fol. 42r–43v); and Hand D, which first appears for certain on 5 August 1457 (CP, 54, fol. 147r) and then regularly until Accolti's election (cf. *ibid.*, fol. 147r–151v, 157r, 164v–165r, 174r; LC, 14, fol. 53v; CdC, 51, fol. 156v).

[94] To Hand B: cf. ASF, Miss. 41, fol. 44v–102r (2 July 1457–16 April 1458).

1444,[95] Jacopo di Paolo since at latest 28 September 1452,[96] Muzi since at latest 10 February 1453,[97] and Foresi since at latest 24 September 1452,[98] but beginning at the end of 1456 a considerable number of new staff joined the chancery. First a new coadjutor was taken on in the winter of 1456,[99] possibly as a temporary replacement for Poggio, and then Foresi left in March 1457.[100] Foresi was replaced by a notary who had worked in the second chancery in the 1440s,[101] but the new assistants who joined the chancery in late May[102] and August 1457[103] may not have had any previous chancery experience, so that by the autumn of 1457 the chancery seems to have had two and possibly three novice assistants.[104]

It was not until the spring of 1458 that the regime were able or willing to tackle the problem of the chancery as a whole. On 1 March 1458 a new Signoria came to office, headed by Gonfalonier Matteo di Marco di Tommaso Bartoli.[105] The regime would have been able to exercise some influence on this new Signoria, which included at least one loyal Medicean, Orlando di Bartolomeo di Gherardo Gherardi.[106] What particularly characterized this Signoria, however, was a penchant for radical action. Sometimes this was taken in matters favourable to the regime's wishes; thus the Signoria took the bold step of sacking the anti-Medicean notary of the Riformagioni, Leone Leoni, on 2 March,[107] only the second day of its term of office. This action was undertaken for political, not administrative reasons, as is clear from the fact that Leoni had been reconfirmed in office by a previous Signoria at the end of the preceding December;[108] moreover, the March–April Signoria now attempted to side-step the recently revised procedure for electing the notary of the Riformagioni by which Leoni had been chosen and which had met with objection from leading members of the regime.[109] They dispensed with the new complex nomination procedures and submitted their new candidate directly to the

---

[95] Cf. pp. 119–20, n. 32, *infra.*    [96] ASF, CdC, 51, fol. 124r.    [97] *Ibid.*, fol. 125r.
[98] BRF, Big. 193, fol. 62r.    [99] Hand Y: cf. p. 99, n. 93, *supra.*
[100] Foresi's last appearance before Accolti's election was on 9 March 1457 (ASF, LC, 14, fol. 38r–39v).
[101] Hand B: cf. p. 99, n. 93, *supra*; for this scribe's work in the second chancery during the 1440s, cf. ASF, MissOr, 3, fol. 28r–31v (6 February–5 May 1447).
[102] Hand G: cf. p. 99, n. 93, *supra.*    [103] Hand D: cf. *ibid.*, *supra.*
[104] Scribe D probably replaced scribe G, since the period of activity of D follows so soon after that of G: cf. *ibid.*, *supra.*
[105] The other members were Giovanni di Piero Strada, Francesco di Bernardo di Uguccione Lippi, Orlando di Bartolomeo di Gherardo Gherardi, Ceffo di Lorenzo di Ceffo Masini, Antonio di Biagio di Lorenzo (Pezzaio), Jacopo di Pagolo di Jacopo (Linaiuolo), Matteo di Zanobi di Berto Carnesecchi, Tedice di Giovanni di Tedice degli Albizzi: cf. Cambi, *Istorie*, in *Delizie*, xx, 356–7.
[106] He became one of the *arroti* of the Balìa of 1458: cf. Rubinstein, *Government*, 288.
[107] ASF, Tratte, 95, fol. 71r: Cassatus fuit dominus Leo per dominos die secunda Martii 1457 (ab inc.).
[108] Cf. p. 97, n. 84, *supra.*    [109] Cf. p. 97, *supra.*

councils. In fact, he was Bartolomeo Guidi, the Medicean candidate rejected in July 1456,[110] which is further proof that Leoni had been dismissed for political reasons. When the Signoria failed to win the approval of the councils for Guidi's appointment on two occasions on 13 and 18 March 1458,[111] they still did not give up the fight.[112] They now proposed to amend the new method for electing the notary of the Riformagioni, submitting a bill eight times to the councils up to the very end of their term of office.[113] They were unsuccessful in their attempt to deal with the crisis in the Riformagioni, but what is particularly curious about this Signoria is that they were not only willing to take radical action in favour of the regime but also against its interests. Two members of the Signoria, the Gonfalonier Matteo Bartoli and Matteo di Zanobi Carnesecchi, had apparently been Medicean sympathizers in the past,[114] but there is some evidence to suggest that they may have been wavering at this time.[115] What is clear is that there must have been strong anti-Medicean sentiments as well among this Signoria, which proceeded to pass a radical bill rendering extremely difficult the kinds of constitutional manipulations by which the Medici regime had controlled Florence since 1434.[116] This Signoria also decided to take fundamental action not only over the Riformagioni and the constitution but also regarding the chancellorship. They decided to end the interregnum prevailing since Poggio's retirement, and so on 17 April 1458 they elected a new chancellor, Benedetto Accolti.[117]

Accolti was to become one of the major reformers in the history of the

---

[110] ASF, LF, 65, fol. 96r (13 March 1457 (ab inc.)): Provisionem continentem quod ser Bartolomeus ser Guidonis Jacobi sit electus in notarium reformationum comunis Florentini cum salario et numero notariorum cum quo electus fuit ultimus notarius reformationum.

[111] *Ibid.*, fol. 96r, 98r.

[112] *Ibid.*, fol. 100v (24 March 1457 (ab inc.)): Provisionem continentem formam electionis scribe reformationum modo et forma in provisione insertis.

[113] The bill was submitted four times to the council of the people on 24 March, 27 March, 8 April and 22 April 1458, when finally it was passed by a ⅔ majority of 1 vote (139 to 68); it then failed to pass the council of the commune on 24, 25, 26 and 29 April (cf. *ibid.*, fol. 100v, 101r, 103v, 107v, 108v, 109v, 110r, 112r). There was a brief debate in the council of the people on 8 April before voting took place which reveals that some Florentines felt that the notary of the Riformagioni should have a lower salary and that he and his assistants should not be eligible for other communal offices: cf. *ibid.*, fol. 103v.

[114] Bartoli had been a member of the Balìe of 1444 and 1452 (cf. Rubinstein, *Government*, 268, 279) and Carnesecchi, of the Balìa of 1452 (*ibid.*, 276).

[115] Neither was included in the Balìa of 1458.　　[116] *Ibid.*, 90–1.

[117] ASF, Tratte, 95, fol. 72v: Dominus Benedictus domini Michaelis de Accoltis de Aretio electus fuit die xvii[a] Aprilis 1458 per dominos et collegia in primum et pro primo cancellario cancellarie dominorum suprascripte pro tempore unius anni dicta die xvii[a] Aprilis initiati cum salario fl. trecentorum pro dicto tempore dicti anni pro se et uno notario quem secum tenere debet ad servitium dicte cancellarie et cum officio et aliis pro dicto primo cancellario ordinatis et quibus et prout electus fuit dominus Carolus de Aretio prima vice, videlicet de mense Aprilis 1443.

Florentine chancery, and one possible appeal which he may have had to the March–April Signoria was the prospect of achieving a radical reform after the period of neglect and decline under Poggio. However, there were probably also political undercurrents which swept him to success. The actions of the March–April Signoria regarding the Riformagioni show that it was not necessarily as an anti-Medicean that Accolti was appointed; on the contrary, Accolti was given a rise in salary by the Medicean Balìa of 1458,[118] which also was finally able to appoint Bartolomeo Guidi as notary of the Riformagioni,[119] showing that Accolti's election must have enjoyed the support of the regime. However, Vespasiano stated that Accolti was elected 'with the consent of all members of the governing classes', a point which he seems to have wished to emphasize about Accolti, in whose biography he later wrote again that Accolti was friendly with 'all the patricians in Florence'.[120] This may suggest that Accolti's appeal was wider than the narrow inner circle round the Medici, and it may be that he succeeded as a compromise candidate who would appeal to ardent Mediceans as well as to waverers among the ruling class of Florence. There were particular leading figures in Florence with whom Accolti, it can be shown, enjoyed close relations in the period leading up to his election as chancellor. One was perhaps his wife's cousin, Federigo di Jacopo Federighi, who, after Carlo Federighi's death in 1449, became the leading representative of the family in public life, serving as Gonfalonier of Justice in 1452 and as a member of the Balìe of 1452 and 1458.[121] After Carlo's death, however, no member of the Federighi family was in the front ranks of the regime, but one friend of Accolti's who enjoyed considerable influence in Florence at the time of his election as chancellor was Bernardo Giugni. Giugni was a member of the inner circle of the regime: during the 1450s, he was one of the most frequent speakers in the *pratica*; he was an *accoppiatore* in 1443, a member of all Medicean Balìe from 1434 to 1458 and was Florentine ambassador to Siena, Venice, Ferrara and Milan; he represented Florence at the peace negotiations at Rome in 1453, as well as at the coronation of Emperor Frederick III there in 1452. He had a knowledge of Latin literature, which may have been the common interest that he shared with Accolti, for they were later to join together in encouraging Marsilio Ficino to translate the pseudo-Platonic dialogue

[118] ASF, Balìe, 29, fol. 60r.
[119] Marzi, *La cancelleria*, 228. Marzi (226 and 514) incorrectly stated that Alberto di Donnino became notary of the Riformagioni beginning 13 March 1458: cf. ASF, DelSA, 31, fol. 76r (2 March 1458): Hic incipiunt deliberationes rogate per notarios coadiutores officii reformationum vacante officiali reformationum qui fuit cass[at]us die secunda Martii 1457 per dominos. Alberto di Donnino was at this time principal coadjutor in the Riformagioni: cf. ASF, Tratte, 95, fol. 71r.
[120] Vespasiano, *Vite*, i, 596–7.
[121] BNF, CPass, 8, fol. 95r; *ibid.*, 187, pp. 25–7; Rubinstein, *Government*, 279, 282.

*Minos* into Latin.[122] Piero de' Pazzi, another friend who was to join Accolti and Giugni in encouraging Ficino, was also a major figure in Florence during the 1440s and 1450s. A rich and generous man, Piero was the first member of his family to enjoy political prominence, and according to Vespasiano he was personally responsible for winning his family's entry into the oligarchy. He was Gonfalonier of Justice and a member of the Balìe of 1452 and 1458; he enjoyed a particularly close friendship with Piero de' Medici and he was personally responsible, according to Vespasiano, for arranging the marriage between Piero's daughter Bianca and his nephew Guglielmo Pazzi. Piero de' Pazzi was a classical scholar of some accomplishment, and his friendship with Piero de' Medici was due, at least in part, to their common interest in the classics; that may also have been the origin of Pazzi's friendship with Accolti.[123]

Accolti's closest and probably most influential friend, however, was Otto Niccolini. Niccolini was a lawyer who worked as a legal adviser to the Florentine government throughout the 1440s and 1450s, when he was also several times a member of the teaching staff of the University of Florence.[124] His real prominence in Florence, however, was as a political figure and one of the leading members of the inner circle of the regime, in which he was surpassed in importance only by Luca Pitti, Neri di Gino Capponi, Agnolo Acciaiuoli, Dietisalvi Neroni and the Medici themselves. An *accoppiatore*, Gonfalonier of Justice, member of the Balìe of 1444, 1452 and 1458, and an almost continual speaker in the *pratica*, Otto Niccolini also served on important diplomatic missions for Florence to the Emperor, to Naples, to Venice and several times to Rome.[125] Accolti and Niccolini were colleagues in the University of Florence and worked together frequently on private cases and as legal advisers to the Florentine government, which suggests that their friendship originated as a professional acquaintance.[126] In the end, however, it became much more than that. Niccolini involved Accolti in the private affairs of his family, such as the marriage of his niece to a member of the Federighi family and a dispute

[122] On Bernardo Giugni, cf. Vespasiano, *Vite*, ii, 321–9; Rubinstein, *Government*, 237, 248, 256, 267, 276, 284; Della Torre, *Storia*, 545ff.; Marcel, *Ficin*, 216.

[123] On Piero de' Pazzi, cf. Vespasiano, *Vite*, ii, 309–20; Rubinstein, *Government*, 280, 291; Della Torre, *Storia*, 545ff.; Marcel, *Ficin*, 216, 223ff., 290, 300, 565, 719.

[124] Martines, *Lawyers*, 169, 196, 351, 493; Brown, *Scala*, 10. On his life, cf. Niccolini di Camugliano, *Chronicles*, 179–355; L. Passerini, *Genealogia e storia della famiglia Niccolini* (Florence, 1870), 37–40.

[125] Rubinstein, *Government*, 19, 22, 24, 25–7, 76, 93, 94, 97, 99, 101, 113, 126, 127, 132, 134, 239, 268, 273, 284.

[126] Cf. Gherardi, *Statuti*, 462; Park, 'Readers', 296–7; Brown, *Scala*, 10; Martines, *Lawyers*, 169; BNF, Panc. 139, fol. 138v, 139v; *ibid.*, Magl. XXIX, 173, fol. 220v, 222r; ASF, Not.A., A 50, fol. 143r (9 April 1451). I am grateful for the last reference to Mr Frank Dabell.

over his brother's will;[127] they also shared intellectual interests, for
example, in the teachings of Argyropulos in Florence, and both men
promoted the early studies of Ficino.[128] Niccolini had great respect for
Accolti as an intellectual and scholar, describing him as a 'dottore
eccellentissimo, famosissimo ed eloquentissimo'; Accolti probably gave
help on legal questions to Niccolini, who once described Accolti as 'padre'
to him.[129] Accolti recommended Niccolini to the Aretines when he was
first appointed their communal advocate in 1452,[130] and he more than
repaid Accolti, for it was probably through Niccolini's influence more
than anything else that Accolti became Florentine chancellor. Niccolini
took a particular interest in the affairs of the chancery during 1456, playing a major role in the debates of the *pratica* over Poggio's renewal and
serving on the committee of four delegated to report on the reform of the
chancery in December of that year. He is known to have brought Accolti
into the work of the chancery in February 1457 and he was doubtless one
of Accolti's strongest backers when in March 1458 a more pliant Signoria
opened the door to the chancery for a candidate endorsed by the regime.
After he became chancellor, moreover, Accolti is known to have continued
to work in close contact on government business with Niccolini.[131]

Accolti came to office therefore with the support of the regime as a
whole, but it does not seem that he received any particular help from the
Medici family. He certainly knew Giovanni di Cosimo, with whom he
acted as arbiter of a dispute in 1457,[132] as well as Piero di Cosimo, who
sponsored the Certame Coronario of 1441, in which Accolti had participated,[133] and doubtless Cosimo himself, who had been an intimate friend
of Accolti's fellow Aretine and mentor, Carlo Marsuppini,[134] besides being
an associate of Accolti's closest friend, Otto Niccolini.[135] However, it
seems that Accolti had no particularly close personal relations with the
Medici before his election as chancellor. His first introduction to the lead-

[127] Niccolini, *Chronicles*, 138–9, 144.
[128] Vespasiano, *Vite*, ii, 203; Della Torre, *Storia*, 397–8, 545ff.; Marcel, *Ficin*, 203, 216, 264, 709, 731.
[129] BCA, 55, fol. 32v. This manuscript (*Vite di uomini illustri di Arezzo*, by the Aretine antiquary, F. Colleschi) refers to letters of Otto Niccolini written from Rome when he was ambassador to Pope Pius II in 1463 which according to Colleschi were in the possession of the Niccolini family. In the Archivio Niccolini which is in the possession of the Niccolini family in Florence, there are still a large number of Otto Niccolini's papers, which are contained in Filza E.1ª1 (modern number 13). The letter referred to by Colleschi, however, is no longer found among these papers; I made an examination of the Niccolini Archive in Florence and apparently the letter has been lost. A number of other manuscripts have also disappeared from this archive: cf. Lorenzo de' Medici, *Lettere*, i (1460–74), ed. R. Fubini (Florence, 1977), 58.
[130] ASA, Provv. 9, fol. 153r–154v (21–6 September 1453).   [131] Cf. pp. 175–6, *infra*.
[132] ASF, Cat., 818, fol. 603r; I am grateful to Prof. A. Molho for this reference.
[133] Cf. p. 51, *supra*.   [134] Cf. pp. 72–4, *supra*.
[135] Cf. Rubinstein, *Government*, 134; Vespasiano, *Vite*, ii, 203.

ing political figures of Florence had probably come through his father-in-law, Carlo Federighi, who had not been a Medici partisan before 1434[136] and who, like a number of other leading figures after 1434, managed to maintain an eminent position without close personal ties with the Medici.[137] Moreover, Vespasiano makes no mention of any particular favour enjoyed by Accolti with the Medici family, although he was usually quite specific about such Medicean contacts in the biographies of other humanists such as Traversari, Niccoli, Marsuppini and Poggio.[138] The clearest evidence of Accolti's distance from the Medici in the years before his election to the chancellorship is provided by a letter of the subsequently renowned humanist, Cristoforo Landino, to Piero de' Medici on 7 May 1458.[139] Landino had been an intimate of the Medici for a number of years and as such his name was put forward, together with other Mediceans,[140] as a possible assistant to Poggio in the chancery by the committee of the *pratica* in December 1456. He may have taught the humanities in the university intermittently in the years immediately following Marsuppini's death,[141] but his first certain appointment there was made in January 1458[142] and was secured through the support of Piero de' Medici, as he makes clear in his letter ('tua opera ea mihi provincia delegata sit'), where he also states that he had no fear that his appointment would be snatched from him 'as long as the great house of Medici remains such a powerful rock'. This letter, written less than three weeks after the fate of the chancellorship had been settled on 17 April 1458, strongly suggests that Landino had hoped to become chancellor himself. Having thus consoled himself with the fact that he had an honourable and well-paid position whose permanence was guaranteed by the Medici, he went on to declare, 'I had moreover not yet been a secretary, nor do I have such a high opinion of myself that I should dare to hope to be the next one.' All this of course implies the very opposite – that in fact he had very much hoped to become Poggio's successor in the chancery. He had been given hopes by his nomination as a possible assistant in December 1456: he would not entertain any such expectations unless, he continued, it were 'to serve as assistant (*minister*) to such a man as Poggio in order to maintain his dignity unimpaired'. Again he went on to cloak his true feelings, saying, 'be things as they may', this turn of events 'does not stir me very much'; then, however, he suggests that his hopes of the chancellorship itself had been fanned by none other than Piero, who in the end apparently had had to compromise and relinquish Landino's candidature in order not to weaken his own

[136] Cf. Kent, *Rise of the Medici*, 206, 231.    [137] Cf. p. 61, *supra*.
[138] Vespasiano, *Vite*, i, 450–6, 548, 592–3; ii, 228–38.
[139] Ed. Perosa, 187–90.
[140] Cf. Walser, *Poggius*, 406; Brown, *Scala*, 21; Marzi, *La cancelleria*, 251ff., 603ff.
[141] Cf. Brown, *Scala*, 263.    [142] *Statuti*, ed. Gherardi, 467.

political position: 'You go on and act in such a way as only to preserve yourself unharmed for the benefit of your own [family]; as far as we are concerned, whatever remains will ensue through prayer.' It sounds very much, therefore, as though Landino had been the Medici's own favourite for the chancellorship in March and April 1458; indeed, they had prepared the way by securing a lectureship in the humanities for him in the university, just as they had done earlier for Marsuppini. However, the regime's position was by no means secure in early 1458 and the Medici had not perhaps been willing to press Landino's candidacy against the wishes of other members of the regime, who had their own favourite, Benedetto Accolti. Landino devotes the rest of his letter to arguing why it was totally unsuitable for Accolti, a lawyer, to be appointed to such an office as the Florentine chancellorship:

It is true that I do not have the learning to deserve nor the temerity to expect for myself what is due to learned and eloquent men by right; nevertheless, when I see such damage as has recently been done to my profession [sc. the humanities], with the result that the highest of all dignities has been lost to it (through ill fortune, for I do not wish to accuse anyone of shamelessness or stupidity), I, in extreme despondency, cannot look upon this but as a general calamity for all the Muses. With the champions of the Muses, so to speak, thus spurned and insulted, it is now especially to be feared that those who have been ardently running the race and enduring the struggle in the hope of the rewards offered will now, in extreme despair, either slacken their efforts midway or give up entirely from the start. Once, this state of affairs often caused cities, flourishing in wealth and power, to suffer a dearth of learned as well as eloquent men. For no one, as you yourself know best, will submit to a task from which he has no apparent hope of reward. Indeed, even if virtue should be sought for its own sake, nevertheless can anyone amongst the great throng of humanity be found today or has anyone ever been found who, without hope of glory, will seek virtue as its own reward? Indeed, the severest philosophers, who in their writings have copiously and gravely held glory in contempt, have carefully written their books under their own names lest they be deprived of glory by later generations . . .
      Honour is the reward of virtue, and it is due only to him who has merited distinction in that particular virtue; it is not proper to jumble them together, nor do all rewards suit all virtues. For would anyone be considered a fair judge who gave the rewards suitable for a general to a philosopher or vice versa? It is not fitting for either to forego the fruits of his labours, but these rewards are distinct and the wisest men at one time distributed particular marks of honour to particular professions. Indeed, enjoying the keenest intelligence, they say above all that the desire for glory inspires ordinary men to pursue their studies and only as a result of honour do the fine arts flourish in cities. And certainly, unless I am mistaken, lawyers have no reason to complain of meanness or unfairness in the distribution of rewards by the rulers of states, especially since their achievements are not so distinguished by genius or learning as to be ranked with the greatest and most beautiful creations of poets and orators. But all the more learned men will understand these points, and you especially.

Landino's last remarks suggest that Piero de' Medici shared his view that

Accolti, as a professional lawyer, would not make an ideal chancellor. Moreover, the circumstances of the actual election substantiate the view that Accolti's success was not a foregone conclusion, in contrast to the dismissal of Leoni, the notary of the Riformagioni: the often-favourable Signoria came to power on 1 March 1458 and dismissed Leoni on 2 March but it was only in the last fortnight of its term of office that Accolti was elected.

One difficulty with Landino's candidature may have been his well-known intimacy with the Medici, whose patronage, it has been seen, had certainly contributed to the recent failure of both Bartolomeo Guidi and Poggio. In fact, Landino's remarks to the effect that Accolti enjoyed great authority and a wide following ('et auctoritate et clientelis hunc . . . pollere') suggest that he had achieved considerable popularity beyond the ruling group in Florence, which actually echoes Vespasiano's description of Accolti's popularity on the eve of his election to the chancellorship.[143] The Medici may not actually have opposed Accolti as openly as Landino would have liked to imagine, and, as Landino suggests, they apparently ceased to contest the election when they realized that Accolti's candidacy was more expedient than Landino's. It is interesting that Vespasiano made a particular point of Accolti's ability to get on with people as a qualification for the chancellorship: 'being by nature especially genial with everyone, with a vacancy for chancellor now in the palace, Messer Benedetto was elected'.[144] Landino, as a humanist by profession, may have been better qualified in the eyes of the Medici, but they probably felt that, in this period of political uncertainty, it was better to keep the regime united and win popular approval rather than press the candidature of one of their favourites; indeed, Vespasiano stressed the popularity of Accolti's election, saying that 'the entire city' of Florence was pleased by his success.[145] Moreover, the Medici, like other Florentines, must have keenly wished to end this period of factional conflict over the chancery; indeed, it was considered undesirable for the chancery in Florence to be the subject of overt party dissension, as had been demonstrated in the 1420s too when strife between the Medici and their opponents had engulfed the chancery.[146] When the chancellor, Paolo Fortini, an opponent of the Medici, was dismissed through efforts of Mediceans in 1427, it is significant that members of the Medici family themselves were reluctant to admit to each other that they had a direct role in the affair or that the chancery had become the subject of factional conflict through the machinations of their party; assuming an air of egregious innocence, they maintained instead that Fortini's dismissal had been instigated by Luigi Vechietti, a

---

[143] Vespasiano, *Vite*, i, 596–97.  [144] *Ibid.*, 596.  [145] *Ibid.*
[146] Marzi, *La cancelleria*, 184–6; Kent, *Rise of the Medici*, 224–8.

Medicean on the Signoria, for personal reasons: thus Giuliano de' Medici
wrote to Averardo, his father, that 'yesterday morning, when Luigi
Vechietti was making proposals for the Signoria, the chancellor was dismissed, for he had hated him for a long time, and it turns out, as with other
matters, that some like it, others not';[147] similarly Cosimo himself had
written to Averardo on the previous day, 'This morning the Signoria dismissed the chancellor, Luigi Vechietti making the proposal. Many reasons
have been alleged; I believe it was hatred and enmity rather than anything
else.'[148] But when Fortini's successor, Leonardo Bruni, was appointed on
2 December 1427, Giuliano showed considerable relief in writing to his
father Averardo, that Bruni's election was liked by all. 'Yesterday morning', he declared, 'Messer Leonardo d'Arezzo was elected chancellor . . .
The Signoria and the colleges made the appointment and it still has to be
confirmed by the councils, but everyone is pleased with it.'[149] It is particularly interesting that Giuliano de' Medici expressed exactly the same sentiments to describe the reactions to Bruni's election as Vespasiano subsequently would do regarding Accolti's thirty years later: 'this election
satisfied the entire city universally';[150] in both cases it was felt that a period
of irregularity had at last ended and that normal administration could once
more resume.

Political compromise and expediency, therefore, may have been
immediate causes of Accolti's success, but it was doubtless realized by his
close friends as well as by the Medici that, although not a humanist by profession like his rival Landino, he would nevertheless be able to maintain
the learned traditions of the Florentine chancery. The erudition of the
chancellor was considered one of Florence's greatest marks of distinction,

[147] ASF, MAP, 2, 63: [28 November 1427]: Iermattina, trovandosi proposto Luigi Vechietti,
rimossono el cancelliere, dicesi, per cierta gozaia avea col lui. Aviene di questo, come
del'altre cose, che a chi dispiace, a chi l'oposito. Cf. Kent, *Rise of the Medici*, 227, where
the text is not published.
[148] ASF, MAP, 2, 62: [27 November 1427]: Questa mattina e signori chassorono el
chancellere. Era proposto Luigi Vecchieti. Dicesi molte cagione. Credo sia più tosto
odio e nimicizia che altra. Cf. Kent, *Rise of the Medici*, 227, where the text is not published.
[149] ASF, MAP, 2, 65: [To Averardo de' Medici] Al nome di dio e dì iii di dicembre 1427 . . .
Ieri mattina fu eletto Messer Lionardo d'Arezo cancielliere con fiorini 600 l'ano. E' 'a a
tenere 2 chuitatori et ser Filippo di ser Ugolino alle tratte con 300 fiorini con 2 chuitatori.
'Anno lo fatto i signori e collegi. 'A anchora andare pe' consigli, ma chiaschumno piacie
tale electione . . . Giuliano. The passage has been published inaccurately and only in part
by G. Mancini, in his edition of Bruni's history (Florence, 1855–60), i, 32; it has also been
published in part by Kent, *Rise of the Medici*, 227. Bruni's election met resistance in the
councils from supporters of the deposed chancellor, Fortini: cf. ASF, MAP, 2, 69, Puccio
di Antonio Pucci to Averardo de' Medici: Arete sentito del chaso del chanceliere, e de'
suoi sucesori, i [ms: in] quali insino a qui no' si sono obtenuti nel chosiglio del popolo,
mediante l'opere degli amici suoi; pure, si crede, rispeto agli uomini singulari 'ano tolti,
il fine sarà l'oterano. (Referred to but not published by Kent, *Rise of the Medici*, 227.)
[150] Vespasiano, *Vite*, i, 596.

and it was for that reason that it had been so painful to accept Poggio's dismissal, despite the fact that the chancery had virtually disintegrated under his direction. Indeed, the last pages of Vespasiano's life of Poggio are a reproach to the Florentines for their ingratitude to Poggio, who had rendered, in Vespasiano's view, so great a service to the renaissance of classical letters.[151] Accolti had had little opportunity for literary composition since publishing his Italian poetry in the late 1430s and early 1440s, but he always had a profound interest in classical learning and enjoyed a considerable reputation for erudition at the time of his election as chancellor. One source of his reputation was his Italian poetry, which was widely circulated during the mid-fifteenth century and which was praised for its grace and skill.[152] But Accolti's main forum must have been the informal discussions on learned topics in which he took part with such amateurs of the classics as Bernardo Giugni, Piero de' Pazzi and Otto Niccolini. In these conversations, as described by Vespasiano da Bisticci, he impressed the Florentine patriciate with his quick and penetrating intelligence, his wide knowledge of classical poetry, moral philosophy and rhetoric and particularly his familiarity with sacred literature and history. It seemed that there were few Latin works which Accolti had not read, but what seems particularly to have impressed the Florentines was his astounding memory. He was able to discuss almost anything, because he remembered everything he read.[153] The chancellor was regarded as an official ornament of the city and the Florentine patriciate must have felt that Accolti would live up to their expectations, having seen for themselves that 'whenever he found himself in the company of learned men, he won honour for himself with his memory'.[154] Time and again in the debates of the *pratica* of 1456 the importance of the chancellor's reputation was stressed, and Vespasiano attributed Accolti's election to his 'reputation, which was growing greater every day among learned as well as unlearned men'.[155]

Several speakers in the *pratiche* of 1456 had mentioned the importance of the chancellor's practical knowledge,[156] and the main practical use to which the chancellor's classical learning was put was composing Latin letters for foreign governments on behalf of the Signoria. In fifteenth-century Italy the Latin style in which official letters were composed was a matter of pride, and in Florence especially a tradition of maintaining the highest standards of classical Latin in official letters had to be upheld. Leonardo Bruni was regarded by his contemporaries as one of the most eloquent men of his age and as one of the restorers of the Latin language;[157]

[151] *Ibid.*, i, 548ff.   [152] *Ibid.*, 596; cf. p. 45, *supra*.   [153] Vespasiano, *Vite*, i, 596.
[154] *Ibid.*   [155] *Ibid.*   [156] Cf. pp. 92ff, *supra*.
[157] Cf. G. Manetti, 'Oratio funebris', in Bruni, *Epistolae*, i, pp. xciii–xciv, xcvi–xcvii, c–cv,

for the most part he wrote in the best humanist Latin of his day. In both his
public and private writings he substituted classical for medieval Latin
words, such as *bellum* for *guerra*, and he did not use medieval construc-
tions, such as *quod* for *ut*, as Salutati had done.[158] But he still preferred
*nichil* and *michi* to *nihil* and *mihi*.[159] Carlo Marsuppini, like Bruni, was
considered a man of great eloquence, and in some respects he wrote more
rigorously classical Latin than Bruni, substituting *nihil*, for example, for
*nichil*.[160] Poggio admired only the classical languages, deprecating the
vernacular,[161] and was more fastidious in imitating classical Latin than
Bruni. The narrative style of his *Historia florentina*, for example, is more
closely modelled on Sallust and Livy than Bruni's,[162] and as early as 1406
he had advocated the use of *nihil* as opposed to *nichil*.[163] None of Accolti's
Latin writings from the period before he was chancellor have survived, but
it has been seen that Poggio himself in 1436 praised Accolti's Latin style,[164]
indicating that Accolti must have used the best classical style then known.
Indeed, Accolti's very first letters as chancellor show his command of
humanist Latin style; he used *nihil* rather than *nichil*, used *quod* and *ut*
correctly, did not omit connectives between sentences and substituted
classical for medieval Latin words.[165]

cx, cxii–cxiv; P. Bracciolini, 'Oratio funebris', *ibid.* cxx, cxxiv; 'Laudatio Leonardi', ed.
Santini, in his 'Leonardo Bruni Aretino', 151–5; Vespasiano, *Vite*, i, 464; B. Fazio, *De
viris illustribus*, ed. L. Mehus (Florence, 1745), 9–10; G. Mancini, in his edition of
Bruni's history (Florence, 1855–60), i, 21–8.

158  Bruni introduced standards of Latinity influenced by the new learning into the chancery
during his brief first term as chancellor in 1410, as is clear from the fragment of the register of *missive* in ASF, MRep. III, n. 88 (Frammento di un registro di lettere della Signoria
dal 10 gennaio 1410 al 24 marzo 1410) where, although he does not use diphthongs
and continues to use *nichil* (cf. fol. 9r: nichil esse tam arduum, nichil tam grande, nichil
tam difficile), nevertheless he does use *quod* and *ut* correctly, unlike Salutati: cf. *ibid.*:
speramus enim oratores nostros ad Regem Ladislaum transmissos sic operaturos ut infra
brevissimum tempus firma ac laudabilis conclusio circa huiusmodi lanas habeatur.

159  Cf. e.g. ASF, Miss. 33, fol. 80r: nichil aliud importat. Cf. H. Baron, *From Petrarch to
Leonardo Bruni* (Chicago, 1968), 221–2.

160  For Marsuppini's reputation, cf. M. Palmieri's oration in S. Salvini, *Fasti consolari
dell'Accademia fiorentina* (Florence, 1717), 525–7; Lapo da Castiglionchio the
Younger's proemium to his translation of Plutarch's life of Themistocles, in F. P. Luiso,
'Studi su l'epistolario e le traduzioni di Lapo da Castiglionchio Juniore', *Studi italiani di
filologia classica*, vii (1899), 266. For examples of Marsuppini's epistolary style, cf.
*Miscellanea ex MSS. Libris Bibliothecae Collegii Romani Societatis Jesus*, i (Rome,
1754), ed. P. Lazzeri, 160–3; R. Sabbadini, 'Briciole umanistiche. Carlo Marsuppini',
GStLI, xvii (1891), 212–17; A. Moschetti, 'Una lettera inedita di Carlo Marsuppini',
*ibid.*, xxvi (1895), 377–83. For Marsuppini's use of *nihil*, cf. e.g. ASF, Miss. 36, fol.
102v: nihil est gratius.

161  Cf. Poggio, *Opera*, 52ff.

162  N. Rubinstein, 'Poggio Bracciolini cancelliere e storico di Firenze', AMAPet, n.s. xxxvii
(1958–64), 226–8.

163  Salutati, *Epistolario*, ed. Novati, iv, 162–3. Examples of *nihil* in Poggio's *missive*: ASF,
Miss. 40, fol. 4r, 9r, 18r etc.

164  Cf. p. 48, *supra*.        165  ASF, Miss. 42, fol. 1r ff.

Another field in which the chancellor was expected to display his classical erudition and make use of his rhetorical skill was public oratory. When foreign dignitaries were received in Florence, the chancellor might be expected not only to recite a prepared speech, but to make a spontaneous reply to the ambassador's or spokesman's oration. When Emperor Frederick III passed through Florence in 1453, for example, the Signoria visited him at the convent of Santa Maria Novella, where he was staying, and in their name Carlo Marsuppini delivered a Latin oration. Aeneas Silvius Piccolomini replied on behalf of the emperor, asking some questions which called for an extempore response. The Signoria turned to Marsuppini, who, however, would not speak without preparation. Embarrassed, they had to call on Giannozzo Manetti, who delivered a spontaneous oration.[166] Clearly it was hoped that such an incident would not recur, and the Florentines must have felt that Accolti, with his remarkable memory, would never disappoint them; indeed, Vespasiano wrote that Accolti 'was the greatest ornament to the palace during his time there particularly for the great memory that he had'.[167] Memory, of course, was absolutely essential in mastering the art of oratory, and not only for memorizing prepared speeches. Rhetoric was based on a formal system of composition, the most important feature of which were *topoi* or commonplaces; these were standard arguments which could apply to many different situations.[168] Accolti's memory clearly enabled him to have ready a vast range of *topoi*, so that the Florentines clearly felt secure that he would be able to speak on their behalf either from a prepared text or extempore.

Practical experience was mentioned in the *pratica* of 1456 as a qualification for the chancellorship, and it is true that many former chancellors, as notaries, had been experienced in drawing up public documents and had served as chancellors or in the chanceries of other government offices or communes. Salutati was a notary and had been chancellor of several communes including Lucca;[169] Benedetto Fortini had worked with Salutati in the Florentine chancery and for many years had been chancellor of the Dieci di Balìa;[170] Pietro di Mino had been chancellor of the Guelf party;[171] Paolo Fortini had served as coadjutor to Benedetto Fortini in the Florentine chancery and had himself been chancellor of the Dieci di Balìa.[172] Leonardo Bruni was the first Florentine chancellor not to have been a notary, but as a former papal secretary he had a great deal of experience in writing state letters. Carlo Marsuppini was also not a notary, but he had

[166] Vespasiano, *Vite*, i, 518–20. [167] *Ibid.*, 596.
[168] Cf. Curtius, *European Literature*, 70.
[169] Marzi, *La cancelleria*, 114–15; cf. R. Witt, 'Coluccio Salutati, chancellor and citizen of Lucca (1370–1372', *Traditio*, xxv (1969), 191–216.
[170] Marzi, *La cancelleria*, 154–5. [171] *Ibid.*, 157. [172] *Ibid.*, 160.

served as a secretary to Eugenius IV during his residence in Florence;[173] moreover, Vespasiano made a particular point of Carlo's 'great and universal experience' as a preparation for the Florentine chancellorship.[174] Poggio was a notary and had spent nearly fifty years writing letters as a papal secretary before becoming Florentine chancellor; indeed, the fact that Poggio 'had satisfied the papacy with his letters throughout the world' was one more proof, to Vespasiano's mind, of the ingratitude and injustice that he had suffered at the hands of the Florentines.[175] Accolti's experience was obviously nothing like Poggio's, but it was perhaps more reliable as far as the Florentines were concerned. Poggio had been elected chancellor solely by virtue of his enormous reputation; he had never before worked for the Florentine government and the Florentines had no first-hand knowledge of what he would be like on the job. In the event, he proved to be a disaster. Accolti, on the other hand, had been helping in the chancery for perhaps just over a year before his election, but the Florentines had actually seen him working themselves and may have felt that the experience which he had to offer more than equalled Poggio's fifty years in the curia.

Indeed, too much experience would have been a disqualification, for the last thing the Florentines wanted was to appoint another old man. Vespasiano, Carlo Pandolfini and Alessandro Alessandri had all spoken of Poggio's old age,[176] and he was in fact the oldest chancellor ever elected. Salutati had been forty-four; Paolo Fortini, thirty; Bruni, forty-one and at his second election, fifty-eight; Marsuppini, forty-five; but Poggio had been seventy-three when he became chancellor.[177] After Poggio the Florentines returned to electing younger men: Accolti was forty-three in 1458 and his successor Bartolomeo Scala was thirty-seven when elected in 1465.[178] Poggio's age was probably responsible for much of his inept, indifferent and eccentric behaviour, and it had been to lighten his burden that the committee of four had recommended the appointment of four coadjutors as well as a second chancellor. Poggio was not the first chancellor for whom, having reached old age, it had been necessary to provide additional assistance. Except between 1375 and 1377, Salutati had served as notary of the Tratte as well as chancellor, the offices having become virtually united after 1378; in 1405, however, at the age of seventy-three, he relinquished the Tratte to his son Bonifazio.[179] In 1437, moreover, the office of second chancellor was created to deal with correspondence and

[173] Vespasiano, *Vite*, i, 593; G. Zippel, *Storia e cultura del rinascimento italiano* (Padua, 1979), 147.
[174] Vespasiano, *Vite*, i, 593.   [175] *Ibid.*, 548.   [176] *Ibid.* Cf. pp. 92ff, *supra*.
[177] Cf. Marzi, *La cancelleria*, 113, 117, 160, 188, 211, 212, 219–21.
[178] *Ibid.*, 236, 239.   [179] *Ibid.*, 112, 117–18, 134, 148.

administration within Florentine dominions. That reform has been regarded as a stage in the development of a more highly specialized chancery,[180] but it should be noted that Bruni was already sixty-seven when the second chancery was created. There were precedents for providing the chancellor with assistance in old age, therefore, but it was expensive to appoint additional coadjutors. Two of the coadjutors recommended by the committee of the *pratica* in 1456 were in fact to lecture in the university and were to be paid in part from funds allocated to the university, so that there must have been some relief when, in 1458, a younger chancellor could be appointed. Accolti, indeed, was elected with provision for only one coadjutor.[181]

Becoming chancellor of Florence meant an almost complete change in Accolti's career and way of life. Until 1458 he had been a successful practising lawyer and professor of law, but now he would have to abandon his legal practice and restrict his activities as a university teacher. Indeed, the much lower salary of 100 florins that he was paid for teaching after his election to the chancellorship[182] makes it clear that he was working much less in the university after 1458. He would have to devote himself now to composing state letters for the Florentine Signoria, administering ambassadorial missions and composing mandates for ambassadors, receiving foreign ambassadors in Florence and taking the minutes of the almost daily meetings of the *pratica*. Accolti was exchanging a career as a lawyer for one as Florence's senior civil servant. This was a far greater change than any previous chancellor had made in taking office. Former chancellors had been papal secretaries or chancellors of other communes or magistracies, whose work was very similar to that of the Florentine chancellor. Moreover, Accolti almost certainly would suffer financial loss by becoming chancellor. His income in Florence before becoming chancellor was probably considerably more than 500 florins a year, as is suggested by the negotiations he had had in 1456 with the University of Siena; on the other hand, his starting salary as chancellor was only 300 florins a year, out of which he had to pay the salary of his coadjutor.[183] One explanation of Accolti's action in 1458 is that he was tired of law, to which he had devoted himself for almost twenty years. It was a subject in which he obviously found, with his brilliant mind, few difficulties, especially considering the traditions and background of which he had the benefit on both sides of his family. But in the twenty years he spent as a lawyer, Accolti made no original theoretical contributions to the subject, unlike his uncle Antonio Roselli[184] or his brother Francesco, both of whom

---

[180]  *Ibid.*, 196–7.   [181]  ASF, Balìe, 29, fol, 60r.   [182]  *Statuti*, ed. Gherardi, 469.
[183]  ASF, Tratte, 95, fol. 72v; Balìe, 29, fol. 60r.
[184]  For a list of Antonio Roselli's legal works, cf. *Enciclopedia italiana*, xxx (Rome, 1936), 118.

composed important legal treatises and commentaries.[185] It was obviously
not that Benedetto Accolti lacked their aptitude; rather it was clearly that
law was only a means of earning a living, making a career and establishing
himself in Florence. All this clarifies Vespasiano's statement that Accolti
'withdrew from law willingly, because he said it was nothing but quib-
bling'.[186] What this means is that Accolti became chancellor, at considerable financial loss to himself, because his true interests were not in law.
This also explains why Accolti had jumped at the opportunity in 1447 to
establish himself in Rome with the election of Pope Nicholas V. Accolti's
real interest lay in the humanities, and by becoming chancellor he hoped to
return to the way of life which he had enjoyed as a young man in the years
before 1441, when he had been able to devote himself above all to the
*studia humanitatis*. During their terms of office, previous Florentine chancellors had made great contributions to humanist scholarship, and Accolti
was determined to follow their example.

[185] For a list of Francesco Accolti's legal works, cf. DBI, i, 105.
[186] Vespasiano, *Vite*, i, 597.

# 6

# *The Florentine chancellorship*

The chancery of the Florentine commune was divided into a number of sections. One of these was headed by the notary of the Riformagioni, who was in charge of recording the results of meetings of the ancient legislative assemblies and of drafting the legislation approved by these assemblies.[1] Another section was headed by the chancellor himself, whose functions were quite distinct from those of the notary of the Riformagioni; indeed, the chancellor was never head of the entire chancery, the section headed by the notary of the Riformagioni remaining autonomous throughout the life of the Florentine republic. The traditional duty of the chancellor was to compose letters on behalf of the commune and to write the commissions and instructions of communal ambassadors. In a rubric of the earliest extant compilation of Florentine statutes, the Statutes of the Podestà of 1325, it was required that each year an experienced notary from the Florentine guild of lawyers and notaries should be elected chancellor of the commune by the Signoria and colleges; he was to serve as '*dictator* of letters and embassies' for the commune and the Signoria, and perform all the duties of the chancellor.[2] The chancellor, however, was never in charge of all the business and correspondence of the Signoria. Frequently orders, warrants or announcements were despatched in the name of the Signoria itself rather than of the commune as a whole and were therefore drawn up by the Signoria's own notary, the notary of the Signoria, who, as head of a third autonomous section of the chancery, was responsible for the day-to-day deliberations and business of the Signoria. It was the chancellor's job, on the other hand, to write the letters of the Signoria in their capacity as representatives and highest magistrates of the commune; he was in charge of state letters, which were usually apologetic in nature.[3]

---

[1] On the notary of the Riformagioni before 1458, cf. Marzi, *La cancelleria*, 17–19, 29–34, 52–6, 74–7, 82–3, 85–91, 106–13, 120–5, 161–6, 180–2, 202–11, 217–19, 224–6, 335–53, 372–5, 441–2, 455–6; Brown, *Scala*, 136–7.
[2] Marzi, *La cancelleria*, 544. Cf. Luiso, 'Riforma', 132–3; *Statuta . . . Florentie*, ii, 704.
[3] Marzi, *La cancelleria*, 354–66, 396–431. Cf. Witt, *Salutati and his Public Letters*, 1–41; De Rosa, *Salutati*, 1–30; Brown, *Scala*, 138–43. On the notary of the Signoria before

Traditionally the chancellor had not been responsible for administering all details of ambassadorial missions, but only for composing instructions given to ambassadors about to depart and for corresponding with them in the name of the Signoria during their missions. According to the earliest statutes it was the notary of the Signoria's job to record the days on which ambassadors left and returned to Florence in a book to be kept in his office,[4] and this statute was confirmed by a provision of July 1361.[5] By the beginning of the fifteenth century, however, it had become the chancellor's responsibility to keep the register of ambassadors and record in it the dates of their embassies,[6] and it seems that he had been put in charge of administering all other details of ambassadorial missions as well. In the statutes of 1415, the rubric concerning the chancellorship copied from the statutes of 1325 and 1355 was amended, appending to the last sentence the instruction that the chancellor 'should record everything concerning ambassadors'.[7] Besides noting the dates of their missions, the chancellor alone was required to keep a record of the elections of ambassadors, of payments made to them and of all other actions concerning them which had been approved by the Signoria and colleges.[8] The chancellor was to be given a book by the chamberlains of the chamber of arms in which he was to keep a copy of this information and which was to be kept in the chamber of arms.[9] On the Signoria's instructions, moreover, the chancellor was to record the mandates given to ambassadors and their reports during the course of their missions,[10] and it was presumably in compliance with this statute that the series of records in the Florentine archives now called 'Legazioni e commissarie, elezioni ed istruzioni ad oratori' began to be kept, in which were recorded not only the initial instructions given to

---

1458, cf. Marzi, *La cancelleria*, 15–17, 26–9, 49–52, 59–62, 74–5, 84–5, 125–32, 164–8, 178–81, 198–202, 217, 224, 335–41.

[4] *Ibid.*, 364–5.

[5] *Ibid.*, 87. Cf. ASF, CdC, 49, fol. 17v: 1361 de mense Julii. Quod pene scribam dominorum sit liber unus in quo per eum vel suum coadiutorem scribantur nomina et prenomina ambaxiatorum et dies electionis et tempus quo steterint in ipsis ambaxiatibus . . . Et ambaxiator rediens videlicet a die reditus Florentiam inter triduum iurare coram dicto scriba quo die iverit in ipsam talem ambaxiatam et quo die rediverit.

[6] *Statuta*, ii, 705.     [7] *Ibid.*     [8] *Ibid.*, 707.

[9] *Ibid.* One such book is ASF, CdC, 51: [fol. 1r] Liber pertinens ad oratores tempore domini Leonardi inceptus de mense Januarii MCCCCXXXVI. Electiones et remotiones incipiunt a 2 usque ad 100. Stantiamenta incipiunt a 101 usque ad 200. Condemnationes et absolutiones incipiunt a 201 usque ad 220. Renuntationes et approbationes earum incipiunt a 221 usque ad 240. Nomina oratorum qui eligentur pro cognoscendis devetis et nonnulla alia ad legationem pertinentia incipiunt a 241 usque ad finem libri. This register of ambassadors continued to be used throughout Marsuppini's and Poggio's chancellorships and was abandoned during Accolti's term of office, the last entry being made on 2 April 1460 (fol. 169r); it was replaced by Accolti's *Protocollo*, ed. Del Piazzo (ASF, CdC, 64): cf. pp. 152–5, *infra*.

[10] *Statuta*, ii, 711.

ambassadors but also letters sent to them during their embassies. At the same time another series of records was begun, now called 'Rapporti e relazioni d'oratori', which consisted of reports made by ambassadors on their return to Florence. This series ends in November 1429,[11] probably because at that time it was enacted that the reports of ambassadors were to be included in a new series consisting of all instructions, letters and reports between ambassadors and the Signoria.[12] That series, however, was either subsequently destroyed or was never actually begun.

By the end of the fourteenth century, therefore, the chancellor was responsible for administering all the diplomatic business of the Signoria, and it may have reflected his enhanced competence in diplomacy that at this time he is first known to have been put in charge of recording the debates of the consultative meetings called the *pratiche* or *richiesti*. Diplomacy played only a small part in the work of the legislative councils of Florence, and apart from the Dieci di Balìa (Ten of War), which was not a permanent magistracy, it was mainly in the *pratiche* and the meetings of the Signoria and colleges that foreign affairs were discussed. It is not known who was responsible for the earliest surviving volumes of the series of records now known as the 'Consulte e pratiche'; Coluccio Salutati was the first chancellor known to have recorded those debates and henceforth the chancellor or one of his assistants was responsible for keeping records of them.[13]

By the fifteenth century, therefore, the chancellor was not only *dictator literarum et ambasciatarum* but was in charge of administering most diplomatic business of the commune, as well as of recording the debates of the *pratiche*. At the end of the fourteenth century, moreover, the chancellor began regularly to hold other important administrative posts along with the chancellorship. The most notable of these was the office of notary of the Tratte. Before 1374, the notary of the Riformagioni, whose principal duty was drawing up communal legislation, had been responsible for supervising Tratte or extractions[14] for communal offices which were drawn by lot, but on 21 February 1374 he was provided with a coadjutor, in the person of Coluccio Salutati, to be in charge of the Tratte.[15] After Salutati was elected chancellor on 21 May 1375, both he and Pietro di Grifo, the notary of the Riformagioni, carried out the duties of the notary of the Tratte;[16] but on 28 July 1378 the responsibility for the Tratte was formally taken from the notary of the Riformagioni and given to Salutati.[17] As notary of the Tratte, Salutati was also notary in charge of drawing up statutes for Florence's subject communities (Notaro delle approvazioni degli statuti delle terre del contado e distretto),[18] and he continued to hold

[11] Marzi, *La cancelleria*, 531.    [12] *Ibid.*, 589–90.    [13] *Ibid.*, 135, 343–6.
[14] *Ibid.*, 111–12.    [15] *Ibid.*, 112.    [16] *Ibid.*, 117–18.    [17] *Ibid.*, 118.    [18] *Ibid.*

both those offices until 1405, when his son, Bonifazio, was elected to them in his place.[19] Bonifazio continued to serve as notary of the Tratte and notary of the Approvazioni degli Statuti after his father's death.[20] Salutati's three successors in the chancellorship, Benedetto Fortini, Pietro di Mino and Leonardo Bruni (in his first term as chancellor from 1410 to 1411), all had no direct connection with the Tratte, but Paolo Fortini, who succeeded Bruni as chancellor in 1411, once again became notary of the Tratte and of the Approvazioni degli Statuti.[21] It was perhaps because of Salutati's and Fortini's association with the Tratte that, when the Florentine statutes of 1415 were compiled, the chancellor was given the duty, with the notary of the Riformagioni and the two friars of the chamber of arms (who were the keepers of the communal seals), of attending the scrutiny councils, in which citizens were periodically qualified for communal office. Eventually the offices of chancellor and notary of the Tratte were permanently separated; nevertheless, the chancellor continued to attend scrutiny councils throughout the life of the Florentine republic.[22]

Paolo Fortini was certainly the chancellor who had the widest range of chancery duties before the time of Bartolomeo Scala. Before his election as chancellor in 1411, Fortini had been chancellor of the Dieci di Balìa, and he continued to hold that office after becoming chancellor of the commune;[23] moreover, he became notary of the Tratte and of the Approvazioni degli Statuti in 1411 as well, so that he had even more duties than Salutati. As chancellor of the commune he was in charge of administering all the diplomatic business of the Signoria, writing state letters and recording the debates of the *pratiche*; as notary of the Tratte he was responsible for administering extractions and scrutinies for communal offices; as chancellor of the Dieci, he had to administer the conduct of Florence's foreign wars and the diplomacy connected with them. It is not surprising therefore that Fortini's term of office saw a reaction against the tendency to increase the chancellor's burdens and the beginning of a phase of increasing specialization in the Florentine chancery. The reform of the chancery and a growth in its specialization are usually associated with Leonardo Bruni, Fortini's successor;[24] however, under Fortini an attempt was made at first to give the chancellor a wider range of duties than he had ever before enjoyed, but it was quickly realized that one man could not perform so many different functions. Fortini in fact soon began to divest himself of a number of his auxiliary duties, a process which reached its conclusion in Bruni's reform of the chancery in 1437.

The first step towards specialization was taken in 1412, when Fortini

[19] *Ibid.*, 134, 148.    [20] *Ibid.*, 150, 183.    [21] *Ibid.*, 160–1.
[22] *Statuta*, ii, 468; cf. Brown, *Scala*, 152, n. 45.
[23] Marzi, *La cancelleria*, 160–1, 183.    [24] *Ibid.*, 196; De Rosa, *Salutati*, xi.

was given exemption from any communal office whose honours might conflict with those of the chancery;[25] then in 1415 the office of notary of the Approvazioni degli Statuti was formally taken from Fortini as notary of the Tratte and given to the notary of the Riformagioni;[26] finally in 1423 Fortini gave up the chancellorship of the Dieci,[27] which was given alternately to Domenico Mucini and Filippo Pieruzzi.[28] The chancellor, therefore, was once again required to carry out only those duties which had been entrusted to him explicitly by the statutes of 1415, but in 1437 his duties were even further restricted. In that year a fundamental reform of the chancery was enacted whereby there were henceforth to be two chancellors instead of one. Bruni, was was to be first chancellor, would remain in charge of administering the diplomatic affairs of the commune, writing letters and supervising ambassadorial missions to foreign states, as well as recording the debates of the *pratiche* and attending scrutiny councils; the second chancellor, who was to be Giovanni di Guiduccio di Riccio, would be responsible for administering Florence's relations with its subject territories, writing letters sent within Florentine territory and issuing safe-conducts.[29] This division of work between the two chanceries was an ideal, which, however, was only briefly realized in the period 1437 to 1458. During Bruni's chancellorship the second chancery continued to deal with a considerable amount of foreign business, including both foreign letters and instructions to Florentine ambassadors,[30] and it was only with the advent of Marsuppini[31] that a stricter division of work between the two chanceries was eventually realized in the years 1445 to 1451.[32] However,

---

[25] Marzi, *La cancelleria*, 161.    [26] *Ibid.*, 163–4, 180.    [27] *Ibid.*, 206.

[28] Cf. Luiso, 'Riforma', 134; Marzi, *La cancelleria*, 190, 206; G. Shepherd and T. Tonelli, *Vita di Poggio Bracciolini* (Florence, 1825), i, 148.

[29] Luiso, 'Riforma', 136–8; Marzi, *La cancelleria*, 196–7.

[30] Cf. e.g. ASF, Miss. 2ᵃ, 1, fol. 19r, 19v, 21r, 23r, 28v, 32r, 33v, 35r, 36r, 40v, 45r, 46r, 53v, 54v, 55v, 61v, 62v, 63v, 64r, 64v, 65r etc.; *ibid.*, 2, fol. 3r, 7v, 8v, 9v–10r, 12r, 13r–v, 17v, 22r–23v, 24v, 27r–v, 30v, 34v, 37r, 39v, 40v–41r, 42v–43r, 44r–v, 47r, 49v–50r, 51r, 52r, 53r–v, 54v, 57r, 59v–60r, 62r–v, 64v–65r, 66r, 68r, 69v, 71r–72r, 73r.Cf. Luiso, 'Riforma', 138.

[31] The same lack of specialization continued in the interregnum between Marsuppini and Bruni: cf. *ibid.*, 74v–75r, 78r, 79v, 81r, 82r. The exact date of Marsuppini's election, about which Marzi (*La cancelleria*, 213) was uncertain, was 5 April 1444, which was also the date from which his term began: cf. ASF, Tratte, 95, fol. 72r. For foreign and ambassadorial letters written during Marsuppini's term by the second chancery, which soon became less frequent than under Bruni, cf. ASF, Miss. 2ᵃ, 2, fol. 82r, 83v–84r, 87r, 88r, 99r, 107v, 109r, 116v, 117r, 118v, 124r, 126r, 132v–133r, 141r,144r, 153r, 205v, 210v, 224v, 241r.

[32] Apart from the above occasional role of the second chancery in the first chancery under Marsuppini, Niccolò Pardi was responsible for all first chancery business under Marsuppini, having been the scribe of ASF, Miss. 36, CP 52, and LC 11 and 12; he first appeared in chancery records in CdC, 51, fol. 49r on 6 April 1444, the day after Marsuppini's election, working together with Bruni's coadjutor for three days until 8 April 1444 (fol. 48v) when Bruni's notary made his last appearance, and thereafter Pardi

in the first half of 1451 it seems that second chancery staff may again have
been working in the first chancery,[33] and this occurred again in the autumn
and winter of 1452.[34] Giovanni di Guiduccio remained second chancellor
until his death in January 1453; at that time, it was decided not to replace
him but to reunite the two sections of the chancery under the first chancellor, Marsuppini.[35] This reunification did not change some chancery
procedures: separate registers of the second chancery are no longer extant
for the period between 1445 and 1470 but they apparently continued to be
compiled as before, since the *missive* of the first chancellor during those
years do not include letters sent within Florentine territory or safe-
conducts.[36] On the other hand, it has been seen that second chancery staff
had already begun to deal again with first chancery business in 1451 and
1452, and now the allocation of responsibilities among chancery assistants
became even less precise after the chancery was formally reunited in
31 January 1453. The principal coadjutor, Antonio Muzi, who had taken
the place of the second chancellor with the title of vice-chancellor, now
worked on first chancery business,[37] as did other coadjutors of the
chancery, Bastiano Foresi and Jacopo di ser Paolo.[38] During the first
year of his chancellorship, Poggio attempted with some success to achieve
specialization in the chancery, delegating first chancery business to two
particular notaries[39] and second chancery business to two others,[40] but

assumed complete responsibility for this volume until 25 September 1452 (fol. 49v–100r,
109r–124r).
   The volumes Miss. 37, 38 and 39 (26 October 1447–5 December 1453) are not in fact
letters of the Signoria written by the first chancery but rather those of the Dieci di Balìa.
Their format is different from that of the true *missive* volumes: the *missive* of the chancery are written only in the middle of the paper with two wide margins on the left and
right, whereas in these volumes the writing often extends to the very right hand edge of
the paper. They are composed by several different hands, and are not usually fair copies
of the quality contained in the true chancery *missive*. Cf. 39, fol. 2r: 'Noi abbiamo
veduto la lettera de dì 2 del presente scripta all'ufficio de' dieci'; fol. 2v: 'Noi abbiamo
vedute le lettere che avete scripto all'ufficio de' dieci della balia'; fol. 4v: 'Essendo intrati
di nuovo in questo officio della balìa', etc.
33  Marsuppini was elected with provision for only one notary (cf. ASF, Tratte, 95, fol. 72r),
and yet beginning on 25 February 1451 a hand other than Pardi's appears in a first chancery volume (BRF, Big. 193, fol. 1r) and continues from that date until 24 July 1451
(*ibid.*, fol. 26v), which is the same period as Pardi was in charge of CdC, 51 (cf. pp. 119–
20, n. 32, *supra*). Therefore this new hand is either that of Marsuppini himself, or of
another assistant who may have been seconded from the second chancery.
34  Between September 1452 and January 1453 there were three scribes working in the first
chancery: Pardi, who wrote BRF, Big. 193, fol. 52v–62r (31 July 1451–7 September
1452) as well as CdC 51, fol. 109r–124r (6 June 1450–25 September 1452); Jacopo di
Paolo, who wrote CdC 51, fol. 124r–125r (28 September 1452–10 February 1453); and
Bastiano Foresi, who wrote Big. 193, fol. 62r–63v (24 September–16 October 1452).
35  Luiso,'Riforma', 138–40; Marzi, *La cancelleria*, 214; ASF, Tratte, 95, fol. 72r.
36  Cf. ASF, Miss. 40, *passim*.
37  ASF, CdC, 51, fol. 125r–152r (10 February 1453–8 May 1456).
38  Cf. pp. 89, n. 36 and 120, n. 34, *supra*.     39  To Muzi and Foresi: cf. p. 89, *supra*.
40  To Pardi and Jacopo di Paolo: cf. pp. 89–90, *supra*.

after the summer of 1454 this attempt was abandoned and the first and second chanceries became even less separate than before his term of office.[41] It was during the discussions regarding Poggio's reappointment in 1456, as has been seen, that the idea of again dividing the chancery was aired as a way of lightening Poggio's burdens,[42] but it was put into effect only at the end of April 1457,[43] probably after Poggio's retirement had been accepted by the regime. Antonio Muzi was appointed second chancellor with effect from 1 May 1457 at a salary of 300 florins for himself and two assistants,[44] and the second chancellorship thereafter remained a permanent feature of the Florentine administration,[45] but still there was no effective division of the chancery, as Muzi himself and other chancery assistants continued to work on both first and second chancery business.[46]

In Accolti's time, despite the specialization that had taken place since the days of Fortini, the responsibilities of the first chancellor remained considerable. He composed all state letters to foreign governments; he was in charge of administering all the Signoria's diplomatic business; he or one of his assistants attended and minuted the meetings of the *pratiche*; and he also was privy to the secret results of the scrutiny councils for the highest communal offices. One historian has been led to compare the chancellor to a permanent secretary of state for external affairs;[47] another has written that 'the chancellorship of Florence became an important position during Salutati's incumbency, partly because he had the qualities to make it such and partly because the permanence of his tenure gave him the opportunity to develop his talents. As official letter writer he became essentially the foreign minister of Florence.'[48] 'The real importance of Salutati's office lay . . . in the powers attached to it', a third scholar has written:

through these he could influence decisions of state. This is why on one occasion the Signoria, concealing one of its diplomatic moves from the Ten of War, also withheld it from the chancellery head. He was evidently too close to certain members of the Ten or thoroughly shared their outlook . . . The first secretary also dictated the Signoria correspondence to Florentine ambassadors; he was present (except on very rare occasions) at all the meetings of the executive councils, and the discussions were recorded under his supervision. Consequently, because of his long and intimate association with the Signoria, whose personnel changed six times yearly, his advice on special questions was often solicited.[49]

---

[41] Cf. pp. 90–1, *supra*.  [42] Cf. p. 96, *supra*.  [43] Cf. p. 99, *supra*.
[44] Cf. p. 99, n. 92, *supra*.  [45] Cf. ASF, Tratte, 95, fol. 72v.  [46] Cf. pp. 99–100, *supra*.
[47] Garin, 'Cancellieri umanisti', in *La cultura filosofica*, 5.
[48] B. L. Ullman, *The humanism of Coluccio Salutati* (Padua, 1963), 11.
[49] Martines, *Social World*, 148. Cf. the reservations of N. Rubinstein, 'Machiavelli and the world of Florentine politics', *Studies on Machiavelli*, ed. M. Gilmore (Florence, 1972), 7ff., regarding the chancellor's political influence and R. Fubini's implications to the contrary, *ibid.*, 373ff.; cf. the detailed critique of Salutati's political influence in De Rosa, *Salutati*, ix–x, 59–73.

Such views, however, oversimplify the chancellor's position; moreover, anachronistic comparison, of the chancellor to a foreign minister, for example, obscures rather than elucidates the facts of Florentine political life. Indeed, there was an established tradition in Florence that the chancery was outside the arena of politics and that the chancellor and other chancery staff were meant to be politically neutral. This political tradition in the chancery has often been misunderstood, in part because many members of the Florentine chancery were distinguished humanists and it has been assumed that they must have had some significant role as statesmen; it has also been taken for granted that the wide range of administrative responsibilities entrusted to the chancellor provided him with political power. It must be pointed out, however, that communal laws never gave the chancellor authority to advise on, much less decide, political questions. His statutory and constitutional powers were entirely administrative: writing state letters for the Signoria, supervising ambassadorial missions, recording debates of the *pratiche* and attending scrutiny councils. The chancellor's principal duty was writing state letters, which he did on the instructions of the government, not according to his own discretion or on his own initiative. The Florentine statutes laid down that when letters were sent to the pope, the emperor, a cardinal or a king, the final version had to have the approval of the Signoria and the two colleges of twelve good men and sixteen gonfaloniers.[50] In fact, the practice of *lectio* or reading a letter to the government before despatch extended to all letters of any political importance and probably to all letters written by the chancery. There were apparently two occasions on which chancery letters were read to the Signoria: the first occurred after the first draft of the letter was written, and evidently all letters were read to the Signoria at this stage; the second occasion took place after the letter had been copied and was ready to be sealed. It was on this second occasion that the chancery staff were required to reread to the Signoria any letter of political importance;[51] moreover, any letter of importance was read not only to the Signoria but also to the two advisory colleges.[52] It is interesting that the great fame enjoyed by Salutati sometimes led foreign governments to misinterpret the position of the chancellor, attributing to him discretionary powers in com-

---

[50] *Statuta*, ii, 530. Cf. Witt, *Salutati and his Public Letters*, 11.
[51] Cf. the fifteenth-century instructions to incoming Signorie, probably prepared by the chancery staff, ASF, MRep. IV, n. 135: 'Ricordi di quello 'anno a fare i signori nel loro uficio et maxime il proposto et il ghonfaloniere: . . . Tutte le lettere o piccole o grandi o donde che si venghano, fa che le legha o facci leggere. Le lettere che vanno le quali importano pondo tutte le ti facci leggere inanzi si suggellino.' This seems to be the manuscript of the *Ordini di ciò s'a a fare in Palagio* (Florence, 1889), of which the only copy known to me, in BNF, was lost in the 1966 flood.
[52] ASF, M.Rep. IV, n. 135: Ogni lettera che porti niente fatela ogni volta leggere dinanzi a' collegi.

posing letters, but the Florentine government was ready to point out that they alone were responsible for the contents of state letters. Writing to the Bolognese during the War of the Eight Saints, the Signoria pointed out that 'it seems that you want to attribute the harsh tone of the language to the chancellor; but do not think that among us letters are written without our approval'.[53] Again writing to the Bolognese in 1393, almost twenty years later, the Signoria repeated, 'Do not think that our chancellor is allowed to insert anything in a letter of which we are unaware.' The Florentines prided themselves, as is revealed in another letter from Salutati's term of office, that 'just a few men are not, according to our customs, permitted to authorize letters or to instruct ambassadors',[54] and it is clear from another passage in Salutati's state correspondence that the chancellor was not one of those officials whose approval was required in order to despatch a letter. 'Do not believe', he wrote to the pope in 1401,

that what we write to your holiness depends solely on the office of the priors and the author of this letter. Indeed, according to the statutes of our commune, letters to popes, to the emperor or to kings cannot be sent without first summoning a meeting of our colleges and gaining their approval in a secret ballot of what has been read to them; you must realize that, although in public letters only our office is named, all that we write to your holiness or that has been written by our predecessors depends on the deliberation of thirty-seven citizens who at any one time preside over the republic.[55]

The thirty-seven citizens referred to by Salutati were the nine members of the Signoria, the sixteen gonfaloniers and the twelve good men, so that, by his own admission, Salutati excluded himself from having discretionary authority over the contents of state letters.

The debates of the *pratiche*, in which the leading citizens of Florence were often asked to express their views on the drafting of state letters, suggest that it was not the chancellor's job to participate in making decisions of policy; they highlight the chancellor's role, not as a member *ex officio* of the Florentine oligarchy, but rather as the spokesman for the views of the Florentine governing classes. For example, in 1401 when Perugia complained to Florence that some Perugian merchants had been arrested by Florence's subject city of Pistoia, Angelo degli Spini, speaking in the *pratica* for the twelve good men, advised that 'the commune of Pistoia can make its own reprisals since it is free';[56] in his formal reply to Perugia, therefore, Salutati stated that Florence could not intervene in the dispute since 'the city of Pistoia is free and lives by its own laws and statutes'.[57] Similarly, in 1389 when Giangaleazzo Visconti complained to Florence that a number of influential Florentines had plotted to have him

[53] De Rosa, *Salutati*, 60, n. 12.
[54] *Ibid.*, 61, n. 13    [55] *Ibid.*, n. 15.    [56] *Ibid.*, 63.    [57] *Ibid.*

poisoned, a meeting of the *pratica* was summoned to advise on the government's response to this accusation; the advice of several speakers in the
*pratica* was to reply that the Florentine commune was 'not accustomed to
use poison against its enemies but arms', and this became the principal
theme of Salutati's reply to Giangaleazzo.[58] During the fifteenth century,
it remained chancery procedure in drafting state letters to adhere closely to
the guidelines set out during the debates of the *pratica*. For example, on
12 September 1456 a *pratica* was summoned to discuss a reply to the king
of Portugal, who had requested safe passage and provisions for Portuguese
ships in Florentine territory on their way to take part in a crusading
expedition against the Turks. The members of the *pratica* advised that the
Signoria should praise the king's understanding, indicating that he would
thereby gain 'salvation of his soul and perpetual fame and that all
Christendom would be obliged to him';[59] in the letter despatched by the
chancery the same day, it was stated that 'he would gain splendour and
eternal glory' in this enterprise, which 'concerned faith, religion, the salvation of souls and divine glory', and that this 'pious, magnanimous and
most Christian undertaking must win for him immortal praise from all of
us and from all Christians'.[60] The *pratica* suggested regarding 'the request
for passage and provisions' that he should be allowed 'to treat everything
of ours as his very own on account of the ancient friendship and devotion
between our city and his royal house and the love which he has always
borne to our city, its citizens and its merchants';[61] in the letter the chancery
stated, regarding the passage and provisioning of the king's forces, that
they would act in such a way that 'the king would in fact consider everything' of their 'as his very own', for this was required by their 'devotion
towards him and his munificence towards' them and their 'citizens and
merchants'.[62] Regarding the Florentines' own contribution to this crusading expedition, the *pratica* advised informing the king, 'We are prepared to
contribute as much as the pope considers fit, according to the contribution
made by other Christians and to the pope's judgement of our means',[63] and

---

[58]  *Ibid.*, 63–5.
[59]  ASF, CP, 54, fol. 39v: Inteso la lettera che scrive la maiestà del Re di Portegallo, diciamo
      che all'ambasciadore si risponda in questo effecto: che c'è stato di grandissimo piacere
      che la sua maiestà pigli tanto honorabile impresa, perché gli fia salute dell'anima et
      perpetua fama et tutta la christianità glene sarà obligata.
[60]  The letter is published by Müller, *Documenti*, 183.
[61]  ASF, CP, 54, fol. 39v: et di richiederci di passo o vettuvaglia, perché ogni nostra cosa egli
      può usare come sua propria, per l'antica amicitia et devotione che ha havuto et ha la città
      nostra alla sua casa reale, et per l'amore che ha sempre portato la sua persona alla nostra
      città et a' cittadini et mercatanti di quella.
[62]  Müller, *Documenti*, 183.
[63]  ASF, CP, 54, fol. 39v: Che noi saremo presti a seguitare quello che paresse alla sua
      beatitudine secondo che si vedesse far gli altri christiani et secondo che giudicasse essere
      la nostra possa.

in the letter it was stated, 'What we are able to offer, in comparison with other Italian powers, we are leaving to the discretion of the pope, who is well acquainted with our means.'[64] In fact, the few instances when the procedure of *lectio* to the Signoria and colleges was suspended apparently did not increase the discretionary powers of the chancellor, who was still required to follow the instructions of the *pratica*, as for example on 18 May 1450, when the chancellor, Carlo Marsuppini, was exempted from reading certain letters to the Signoria and colleges and placed under the direct authority of the *pratica*.[65]

With the exception of the notary of the Signoria, who was elected by scrutiny and sortition like the Signoria that he served, officials of the chancery had *de facto* permanent tenure of appointment and it was customary for the chancellor and the notary of the Riformagioni to hold office for life. This of course gave the chancellor unique practical experience and technical knowledge which proved invaluable to the government of the day. Salutati, for example, is known to have been consulted by members of the *pratica* on technical questions such as the exact nature of treaties contracted by Florence with the communes of the Romagna in 1383 or on Florentine rights to various fortified places in the countryside of Arezzo which were being contested by the Sienese in 1385.[66] Salutati's practical experience was useful to the government too, for example, when he was able to confirm for the benefit of the *pratica* in 1385 what a previous Signoria had promised to Queen Margaret of Naples in the way of payments to the Count of Nola.[67] When Salutati mentioned in his private correspondence the advice that he gave the government,[68] he would have been referring to the kind of practical advice which his technical knowledge as a notary and his long experience in the chancery made him particularly qualified to offer.

However, the chancellor and other members of the chancery were excluded from the principal forum where political advice was officially solicited and expressed in Florence. This was the *pratica*, which was summoned to discuss important political questions by the government of the day, who were constitutionally as good as bound to follow the advice that they had received.[69] The chancellor attended the meetings of the

---

[64] Müller, *Documenti*, 183.
[65] Cf. ASF, CdC, 51, fol. 108r: Die xviii Maii 1450. Deliberatum fuit solemniter per dominos et collegia quod omnes littere scribende hinc ad per totum presentem mensem circa negotia pacis libere et impune scribi possit ut per eorum cancellarium prout et sicut videbitur illis de pratica.
[66] De Rosa, *Salutati*, 71.    [67] *Ibid.*    [68] *Epistolario*, ed. Novati, ii, 133.
[69] On the authority of the *pratica*, cf. ASF, MRep. IV, n. 135: se lla cosa portasse assai, in questo caso sempre ricorrete al consiglio de' richiesti o di pochi o d'assai come la materia richiede, il quale consiglio poi seghuite e non le voglie o appetiti d'alchuno di collegio o d'altri. On the political importance of membership in the *pratiche*, cf. D. Kent, 'The

*pratica* in order to minute the debates, but in the records of the 'Consulte e pratiche' preserved in the Florentine archives, the chancellor is not recorded as having offered advice in his capacity as chancellor, nor did the other chancery staff. They acted as permanent administrative officials and it was felt that this debarred them from taking part in official political debates. There can be no doubt that this was an established feature of the Florentine constitution, as is made clear by the career of Paolo Fortini, who served as chancellor from 1411 to 1427. Before his election as chancellor, Fortini was an occasional speaker in the *pratiche*, for example, between September and December 1407, when in his capacity as one of the sixteen Gonfaloniers he spoke on nine different occasions.[70] During his chancellorship, Fortini never spoke in the *pratica*, but less than two months after his dismissal from office on 27 November 1427, Fortini appeared as a speaker in the *pratica* and thereafter he was a regular contributor to the debates along with other leading members of the regime.[71] It was certainly Fortini's job in the chancery that excluded him from the *pratiche*, for his colleague, Martino di Luca Martini, the notary of the Riformagioni, did not, like Fortini, contribute to the *pratiche* while working in the chancery, but after his dismissal in January 1429, he too became a regular contributor to the debates.[72] Far from giving the chancellor political power, therefore, his permanent tenure of office rendered him ineligible to take part in the most important political forum in Florence.

In fact, their permanent tenure not only debarred chancery staff from the *pratica* but also usually prevented them from entering the Florentine *cursus honorum*, the series of high magistracies which Florentine statesmen held in the course of their political careers. This was for example true of Chello and Naddo Baldovini, who between them held the chancellorship from 1295 to 1340,[73] and of Salutati and Pietro di Mino da Montevarchi (chancellor from 1406 to 1410), who as foreigners, did not hold political office before or during their terms as chancellor.[74] But it was not only foreigners who as chancellors were excluded from office. This is shown by the fortunes of the Fortini family, who had been well established

---

Florentine *reggimento* in the fifteenth century', RQ, xxxviii (1975), 601ff.; P. Herde, 'Politische Verhaltensweisen der Florentiner Oligarchie 1382–1402', in *Geschichte und Verfassungsgefüge* [Frankfurter Festgabe für Walter Schlesinger] (Wiesbaden, 1973), 175ff.; N. Rubinstein, 'Oligarchy and democracy in fifteenth-century Florence', in *Florence and Venice: Comparisons and Relations*, ed. S. Bertelli, N. Rubinstein and C. H. Smyth (Florence, 1979), 105; Brucker, *Civic World*, 264ff.

[70] ASF, CP, 38, fol. 87r, 87v, 88v, 90v, 94v, 96r, 98v, 100v, 109v.

[71] *Ibid.*, 48, fol. 5r (21 January 1427 (ab inc.)), 9r, 25r, 29r, 32r, 49v, 50v, 53r, 61r, 62r, 63v, 65v, 67r, 67v, 71r, 73v, 74r, 77v, 81v, 134v.

[72] *Ibid.*, fol. 74r (1 and 2 June 1429), 75v, 118r, 125r, 126v, 131r. For the date of Martini's dismissal, cf. Marzi, *La cancelleria*, 202–3, n. 4.

[73] *Ibid.*, 56–60, 68–9, 71–3.

[74] *Ibid.*, 113–20, 124–5, 132–42, 148, 156–8.

in Florentine public life since the mid-fourteenth century. Benedetto Fortini, who served as co-chancellor with Salutati for a year between 1376 and 1377 and then succeeded to the chancellorship after Salutati's death for seven months until his own death in December 1406, never held high political office.[75] Similarly his brother Paolo, who had been one of the twelve good men in 1402 and one of the sixteen gonfaloniers in 1407,[76] held no more political offices from 1411 until the end of his chancellorship in 1427. During his time as chancellor, in fact, Fortini continued to develop his personal political ties with Rinaldo degli Albizzi and other leading Florentines, and immediately after his dismissal from the chancery in 1427 he made up for lost time in the Florentine political circuit by becoming a prior, a member of the Dieci di Balìa and Otto di Guardia and one of the sixteen gonfaloniers in the five years before his death in 1433.[77] Carlo Marsuppini, although a Florentine citizen after 1431, held no political offices,[78] and Poggio Bracciolini's term as prior in 1455 was honorific, as is made clear by Vespasiano da Bisticci.[79]

Qualification for political office and membership of the *pratica* were two of the most important indications that a Florentine belonged to the ruling group; the Florentines themselves referred to this oligarchy as *lo stato* or *il reggimento*[80] and it is clear that constitutionally the chancellor had no official position in the regime. This is evident not only from the career of Paolo Fortini, but also from that of Niccolò Monachi, who served as chancellor from 1348 until 1375. Monachi's father had had a political career,[81] but this precedent was not taken advantage of by his son, who held numerous minor communal offices such as one of the Sopprastanti delle Stinche or the Ufficiali di Torre during his chancellorship, but unlike

---

[75] *Ibid.*, 119, 153–6.

[76] *Ibid.*, 160–1; for the Fortini family, cf. *ibid.*, 153–4, n. 1–3 and Brucker, *Civic World*, 256.

[77] Marzi, *La cancelleria*, 186–7, n. 2. On Fortini's relations with anti-Mediceans, cf. Kent, *Rise of Medici*, 170, 178; on his dismissal, cf. *ibid.*, 224–8 and Marzi, *La cancelleria*, 182–6.

[78] Cf. Zippel, 'Marsuppini'; Martines, *Social World*, 127–31; Marzi, *La cancelleria*, 210–16; Vespasiano, *Vite*, i, 591–4.

[79] *Ibid.*, 547.

[80] Cf. N. Rubinstein, 'Notes on the word *stato* in Florence before Machiavelli', *Florilegium historiale. Essays presented to W. K. Ferguson*, ed. J. G. Rowe and W. H. Stockdale (Toronto, 1971), 314–26; *idem*, 'Oligarchy and democracy', 99–112; *idem*, 'Florentine constitutionalism and Medici ascendancy', *Florentine Studies*, ed. *idem* (London, 1968), 442–62; Kent, 'Reggimento', 575–638; A. Molho, 'Politics and the ruling class in early Renaissance Florence', NRivSt, lii (1968), 401–20; *idem*, 'The Florentine oligarchy and the Balìe of the late Trecento', *Speculum*, xliii (1968), 23–51; P. Herde, 'Politik und Rhetorik in Florenz am Vorabend der Renaissance', *Archiv für Kulturgeschichte*, xlvii (1965), 141–220; *idem*, 'Politische Verhaltensweisen', 156–249; R. Witt, 'Florentine politics and the ruling class, 1382–1407', *Journal of Medieval and Renaissance Studies*, vi (1976), 243–67; Brucker, *Civic World*, 248–318.

[81] Marzi, *La cancelleria*, 79–81.

his father never entered the Tre Maggiori.[82] This was despite the fact that he had powerful political connections with the opponents of the Guelf party such as Uguccione de' Ricci, Jacopo Alberti and Andrea de' Bardi and had become extremely rich while chancellor.[83] Moreover, Niccolò Monachi was such a notable personage that on two occasions his political enemies attempted to bring about his ruin. The first time, in 1366, they failed, thanks to the efforts of his powerful friends, but in 1375 Buonaiuto Serragli, one of the most extreme leaders of the Guelf party hierarchy, succeeded while Gonfalonier of Justice in having Monachi dismissed from the chancellorship.[84] Monachi certainly had the prominence, the family traditions and the political connections to give him an important place in the ruling group, but it seems that he was *de facto* ineligible as chancellor to enjoy a constitutional position in the *stato* such as his associates in the Ricci faction possessed. It is significant that after his dismissal from the chancellorship he finally attained a constitutional place in the ruling group as one of the most frequent speakers in the *pratiche* until he fell from power in 1382.[85]

There were exceptions to this pattern, but these seem to have occurred during periods of considerable constitutional innovation in Florence. The first known Florentine chancellor, Brunetto Latini, played an active role in Florentine political life at the end of the thirteenth century, serving as a prior in 1287 and speaking in debates of the councils of the people and commune on at least thirty-five occasions between 1282 and 1292.[86] This was when the Florentine constitution was still in its infancy, and none of Latini's immediate successors matched his importance, including for example Chello Baldovini, chancellor from 1295 until 1335, who spoke twice in the councils early in 1294 before becoming chancellor but after taking office appeared in the councils only as a notary, not as a councillor.[87] Ventura Monachi served as a second-rank political official during his chancellorship from 1340 to 1348, his offices including membership of the sixteen gonfaloniers and twelve good men,[88] but once again it is significant that the 1340s were a period of political instability and constitutional experimentation in Florence.[89] To find another example of a Florentine chancellor enjoying numerous high political offices, one has to

[82] For Monachi's life, cf. *ibid.*, 91–105; cf. also P. J. Jones, 'Florentine families and Florentine diaries in the fourteenth century', *Papers of the British School at Rome*, xxiv (1956), 192.

[83] Cf. Marzi, *La cancelleria*, 96–9; Jones, 'Florentine families', 192; Brucker, *Florentine Politics*, 207–8, 316.

[84] Cf. Marzi, *La cancelleria*, 99–103; Brucker, *Florentine Politics*, 207–8, 246.

[85] Cf. Marzi, *La cancelleria*, 103, n. 6. For his fall from power, cf. *ibid.*, 103–4.

[86] Cf. *ibid.*, 35–8, 42–7; B. Ceva, *Brunetto Latini* (Milan and Naples, 1965), 29–58.

[87] Marzi, *La cancelleria*, 56–60, 68–9.

[88] *Ibid.*, 79–81.     [89] Cf. Brucker, *Florentine Politics*, 3–9, 105–22.

wait for almost a century until the last years of the chancellorship of Leonardo Bruni, who served briefly as chancellor in 1410 and then again from 1427 until his death in 1444. Bruni, an Aretine by birth, was given Florentine citizenship in 1416,[90] but for more than another twenty years he took no regularly active part in Florentine political life. Then in the last seven years of his life, beginning in June 1437, he embarked upon the Florentine *cursus honorum*, so joining the *stato* or ruling group of Florence; during this period he was once a member of the twelve good men, three times a member of the Dieci di Balìa, once a member of the Otto di Guardia, a coopted member of the Balìa of 1438, and just before he died, a prior.[91] Vespasiano da Bisticci makes it clear that Bruni's service in Florence was given in two distinct areas of public life. 'On his return Messer Lionardo came to Florence', wrote Vespasiano in the first place, 'and he resigned his [papal] secretariat and writing office and he was given the chancellorship.' Then in a sentence whose meaning is quite distinct, Vespasiano continues, 'And having got to know his prudence and his universal practical experience, which he gained during his long stay at the Roman curia, they made him a member of the ruling group, as a result of which he was one of the priors and several times one of the Dieci.'[92] Vespasiano makes a particular point of saying that membership of the ruling group (*lo stato*) was given to Bruni as something additional to the chancellorship; he makes it clear that the chancellorship and *lo stato* did not automatically go hand in hand.

In the ten years between his election as chancellor in 1427 and his admission to the *stato* in 1437, Bruni like previous chancellors never spoke in the *pratiche*, but after June 1437, when he became one of the twelve good men, he participated in the *pratiche* on three occasions as spokesman for the twelve.[93] Unfortunately, less than a month after Bruni's last documented appearance in the *pratiche*, the records of the 'Consulte e pratiche' break off and do not resume again until 1446, two years after Bruni's death. Vespasiano, however, writing of the time in which Bruni was a member of the *stato*, stated that Bruni 'was called to all the *pratiche*' along with 'all the other principal citizens of the city', and that at these meetings, 'as chancellor and minister of the Signoria, it was his turn to speak last'.[94] This constitutional innovation cannot be confirmed by official records, but, in view of Bruni's numerous political offices in this period, Vespasiano's evidence cannot be discounted. Moreover, Vespasiano's account of Bruni's role in one of the debates of the *pratica* in

[90] Cf. A. Gherardi, 'Alcune notizie intorno a Leonardo Aretino', ASI, 4ª ser. xv (1885), 416.
[91] Cf. Martines, *Social World*, 170–5; Rubinstein, *Government*, 260.
[92] Vespasiano, *Vite*, i, 473.
[93] ASF, CP, 51, fol. 111r (15 July 1437), 112v (7 August 1437), 116r (16 August 1437).
[94] Vespasiano, *Vite*, i, 473–4.

March or April 1443 is extremely detailed. On this occasion, the Signoria had received a request from the Venetian government to detain in Florence Pope Eugenius IV, who had just formed an alliance with Milan and Naples, the enemies of Venice and Florence, and who wished to return to Rome. The Gonfalonier summoned a meeting of the *pratica*, in which all speakers were in favour of detaining the pope except for Bruni, who spoke last and who was able to convince all but one of his colleagues to change their opinions. Because of the late hour, Bruni left the debate after speaking, and his one remaining adversary attempted once again to persuade the Florentines to detain the pope, but Bruni's speech carried such weight that the *pratica* advised allowing the pope to depart. The next day, when the Signoria and colleges together with the *pratica* were meeting to put into effect the recommendations of the previous evening, Bruni once more spoke, justifying himself against the accusations of his adversary, who was so mortified that he never again dared to speak in Bruni's presence.[95] During these last seven years of his life, moreover, there is evidence that Bruni was consulted on important political, military and diplomatic questions by other leading members of the regime such as Agnolo Acciaiuoli.[96]

As when earlier chancellors had taken an official part in Florentine political life, the years after 1434 were a trial period in establishing the Medici regime in Florence, and Bruni's membership of the *stato* was a constitutional innovation similar to many others which were attempted at that time.[97] Indeed, Bruni's joining the *reggimento* exactly coincides with the reform of the chancery in 1437, and both these innovations were probably experiments with the constitution of the chancery which paralleled others in the rest of Florentine government. Moreover, there were a number of other reasons why Bruni was given the privilege of *lo stato* at this particular moment in 1437, nearly ten years after he had become chancellor. In the first place, Vespasiano mentions his long service in Rome as a qualification for membership in the *stato*, and this experience was particularly relevant in the years after 1434, when the papacy and Florence were enjoying a uniquely close relationship with Eugenius IV's residence in Florence, the Florentine–papal–Venetian alliance against Filippo Maria Visconti of Milan, and the Ecumenical Council of the church at Florence. It was obviously of particular importance to the Florentine government to maintain close relations with the papacy at this time, and the ruling group almost certainly brought Bruni into the inner circles of the regime as a liaison between Florence and the curia, in which Bruni had served for more

---

[95]  *Ibid.*, 473–7.
[96]  Cf. *Praefatio in Commentaria rerum Graecarum ad splendidissimum equitem Angelum Azarolum* (1439), in Bruni, *Schriften*, 146–7.
[97]  Cf. Rubinstein, *Government*, 14.

than twenty years. Indeed, Bruni had once before served Florence in a political capacity and this was also to make use of his special connections with the curia. At the end of May 1426, while Bruni was a papal secretary in Rome, he was appointed Florentine ambassador along with Francesco di Messer Simone Tornabuoni to Pope Martin V. The embassy had a dual purpose: first, to negotiate a peace with the ambassadors of the duke of Milan with the pope as intermediary and, second, to secure from the pope certain Florentine possessions in the Romagna seized by the papal governor of Bologna. The two ambassadors failed to make peace with Milan, but after Tornabuoni had returned to Florence Bruni succeeded in persuading the pope to return their possessions in the Romagna.[98] Bruni's success in negotiating with the curia in 1426 was probably an argument in favour of admitting him to the *stato* in the late 1430s when Florence was involved in relations of unprecedented intimacy with the curia. Moreover, in the anecdote related by Vespasiano da Bisticci regarding Bruni's role in the *pratiche*, it is interesting that Bruni's authority carried great weight on an occasion when the debate concerned relations between Florence and the papacy, a topic on which he seems to have been regarded as an expert.[99]

Nevertheless, the political influence and constitutional position which Bruni commanded during the last seven years of his life were unusual in the history of the Florentine chancery, perhaps only to be repeated during the period of Lorenzo di Piero de' Medici's predominance from 1469 until 1492 followed by that of his son Piero until 1494. This was the time of the most extreme constitutional and political manipulation and innovation yet practised by a dominant regime in Florence,[100] and during this period some members of the chancery enjoyed an official prominence perhaps equalling Bruni's position. One such figure was the chancellor, Bartolomeo Scala, who, after receiving Florentine citizenship in 1471, became a prior in 1473, a member of the Otto di Guardia in 1479 and Gonfalonier of Justice in 1486, when he also was made a life member of the council of seventy.[101] Others were Giovanni Guidi, notary of the Riformagioni after 1478, and Simone Grazzini, notary of the Tratte after 1483, both of whom served, for example, on the Dieci di Balìa in 1493.[102]

Nevertheless, a chancery standing above politics was always an ideal in Florence, and it would be wrong to argue that chancellors and other members of the chancery never had a role in Florentine politics. They could enjoy an unofficial political influence amounting to *de facto* membership of the ruling group, although it must be remembered that, unlike other

[98] Cf. C. Monzani, 'Di Leonardo Bruni Aretino discorso', ASI, n.s. v, pt 1 (1857), 47 and v, pt 2 (1857), 25–34; Martines, *Social World*, 168–9.
[99] Cf. p. 130, *supra*.     [100] Cf. Rubinstein, *Government*, 174ff.
[101] Cf. Brown, *Scala*, 46, 66–7, 75, 87–90, 99–101     [102] Cf. Marzi, *La cancelleria*, 261.

oligarchs, their political activity usually had to take place behind the scenes; their influence had most of the time to be exercised indirectly and they were usually denied a direct share in political power as magistrates. In the cases of Niccolò Monachi and Paolo Fortini, this indirect claim on political authority derived from a position in the Florentine political world built up by their families in previous generations; during their chancellorships they continued to exercise political influence through personal connections with important families in the ruling group such as the Ricci and Albizzi. The unofficial political activity of chancery figures in the later fifteenth century had perhaps a somewhat different origin, deriving from the personal predominance of the Medici family, who gave political favour to a number of chancery officials without any previous tradition of political activity or influence in their families. Men such as Giovanni Guidi and Simone Grazzini, who were permanent chancery officials, as well as occasional employees of the chancery such as Piero Bibbiena and Niccolò Michelozzi, enjoyed a kind of political influence and power extending far beyond what could have been provided by their modest official political careers.[103]

However, there were always present in Florence strong undercurrents which made this kind of unofficial political involvement hazardous for members of the chancery, who in theory were meant to remain aloof from politics. In periods of intense factional conflict, such as the 1370s or 1420s, chancery officials who engaged in politics behind the scenes were risking dismissal at the hands of their opponents, as was learnt by Niccolò Monachi, Paolo Fortini and Martino Martini.[104] Even a chancellor who was hardly a political activist, such as Poggio, suffered for his close personal association with Cosimo de' Medici during the mid-1450s, which were another period of increased factionalism.[105] Moreover, chancery figures who were involved in politics could pay very heavy penalties indeed in periods of revolutionary upheaval. In 1494, after the collapse of Piero de' Medici's regime, the mob burnt the houses of Michelozzi, Piero Bibbiena, Guidi and Grazzini; Bibbiena apparently was able to flee the city but Michelozzi was imprisoned and Grazzini was exiled from Florence and fined.[106] The greatest vengeance was taken on Giovanni Guidi, who seems to have been the most powerful and most hated of all chancery officials at the centre of the old regime. He had taken refuge in the convent of San Marco under the protection of Savonarola, who used his influence to save Guidi's life, according to one source, because he had consigned to Savonarola his reputedly vast hoard of jewels and money. Nevertheless,

[103] Cf. *ibid.*, 261–4, citing as evidence the accounts of Cerretani, Parenti and Nardi; Rubinstein, *Government*, 212, 216, 231 n. 2, 318, 321.
[104] Cf. pp. 107–8, 127–8, *supra.*
[105] Cf. pp. 91ff, *supra.*     [106] Marzi, *La cancelleria*, 261–3.

Guidi was tortured and then imprisoned for four years in the dungeons of the old fortress at Volterra; at first he was fined 10,000 florins, then sentenced to have all his goods confiscated. His sons too were condemned along with him; he suffered dreadfully and unremittingly during his imprisonment, which, however, was considered inadequate by some anti-Mediceans, one of whom, the historian Piero Parenti, considered him 'as the most scandalous and pernicious man' ever to live in Florence.[107] Parenti's attitude was not untypical of many Florentines, who regarded the political prominence enjoyed by chancery figures such as Guidi as a violation of their constitutional traditions.[108]

Moreover, the Medici in the fifteenth century seems to have moved cautiously in bringing the chancery into politics, just as they only gradually introduced their various electoral and constitutional manipulations.[109] The experiment of allowing the chancellor to embark upon a political career was not repeated for many years after Bruni despite the fact that Marsuppini[110] and Poggio were close personal friends of the Medici. For Cosimo and his allies, it may have been enough to ensure that there were no chancery officials forced upon them by their enemies, as Leone Leoni, the notary of the Riformagioni, had been in 1457,[111] and that chancery officials were tractable to their wishes, as Filippo Pieruzzi, the notary of the Riformagioni, had not been before his dismissal from office and exile in 1444.[112] The advantages of bringing the chancery into the political arena were not fully appreciated until the Laurentian period, and even then there was a certain amount of experimenting as to which chancery figures would be admitted to the heart of the regime. Lorenzo's father Piero is known to have interfered in certain lesser chancery appointments[113] and planned Bartolomeo Scala's election to the chancellorship in 1465;[114] however, it was not until the very end of Piero's life in 1469 that evidence exists to confirm that Scala had been brought into the centre of the regime.[115] At the beginning of his period of predominance, Lorenzo, fol-

---

[107] Cited *ibid.*, 261. Cf. *ibid.*, 261–3.

[108] Cf. Brown, *Scala*, 43, n. 6, and 199, n. 20, for the views of Alamanno Rinuccini and Francesco Guicciardini; cf. also F. Guicciardini, *Storie Fiorentine*, ed. R. Palmerocchi (Bari, 1931), 79, 107.

[109] Cf. Rubinstein, *Government, passim.*

[110] No evidence has yet emerged to demonstrate that Marsuppini's relationship with the Medici extended beyond personal, business and intellectual interests to politics: cf. Brown, *Scala*, 39–40, 43, 56; Vespasiano, *Vite*, i, 591–2.

[111] Cf. p. 97, *supra.*      [112] Cf. Vespasiano, *Vite*, ii, 244–54.

[113] Cf. ASF, Aquisti e doni, 11, n. 1 (Ricordanza of Antonio di ser Batista d'Antonio Bartolomei, notary of the Tratte, 1462–6 (cf. ASF, Tratte, 95, fol. 75r)): fol. 2v: Ricordo chome lunedì a dì 20 d'ottobre MCCCCLXVI per piacere a Piero di Cosimo et inteso l'opynioni di molti a fine di bene, rinunptai l'uficio del notaio delle tracte.

[114] Cf. Brown, *Scala*, 42–3.

[115] *Ibid.*, 48, 52, 224 (n. 12); cf. *ibid.*, 59, for a possible cooling in their relationship in the late summer of 1469.

lowing his father's lead, continued to place great confidence in Scala, but his position had been eclipsed, possibly by the 1480s[116] and certainly by the 1490s, when Scala managed to survive the fall of the regime relatively unscathed;[117] another earlier figure to enter the regime was the second chancellor Niccolò di Michele di Feo di Dino,[118] but it was not until the 1480s that Lorenzo fixed upon his permanent chancery team, Bibbiena, Michelozzi, Grazzini and Guidi, who were bequeathed unchanged to his son Piero and who remained at the heart of the regime until its fall in 1494.[119]

Before the Laurentian period it was not always easy for chancery figures to render services to a political faction in areas of administration over which they had charge. It has been pointed out that the correspondence with ambassadors and foreign governments, which was the chancellor's most important responsibility, was monitored both before and after final drafts of letters were made, thus preventing the chancellor from inserting his own or his faction's views in such letters contrary to the wishes of the government.[120] Of course, the chancellor was privy to government secrets, for example, in the scrutiny councils which declared eligibility for public office. Chancery officials could disclose such secrets to a political faction, but this kind of conduct in office was extremely dangerous, as was learnt by Martino Martini, notary of the Riformagioni and Medici partisan, who was dismissed from office in 1429 on charges of revealing the secret of the scrutiny and falsifying documents.[121] Sometimes the limitations on the chancellor's powers were misunderstood, particularly by outsiders unfamiliar with the workings of the Florentine constitution.[122] Poggio, who returned to Florence in 1453 after almost fifty years in the curia, apparently believed that as chancellor he could influence decisions of the scrutiny. During one such scrutiny, according to Vespasiano, Poggio spoke on behalf of a friend to members of the scrutiny council, one of whom promised to vote for him, but when the actual count took place Poggio's friend failed to receive one favourable vote.[123] This episode highlights the limits on the chancellor's role during the scrutiny: constitutionally, he was

---

[116] There appears to be no clear evidence that Scala was part of Lorenzo's innermost circle except in the early 1470s: cf. Brown, *Scala*, 61ff.

[117] *Ibid.*, 115ff.

[118] Cf. Marzi, *La cancelleria*, 249; Rubinstein, *Government*, 303, 310.

[119] Cf. p. 132, *supra*.      [120] Cf. pp. 122–3, *supra*.

[121] Cf. Marzi, *La cancelleria*, 202–4; Kent, *Rise of the Medici*, 225.

[122] The important evidence of the Milanese ambassadors in Florence discovered in Brown, *Scala*, 47ff., 61ff., regarding Scala's position in Florence may exaggerate his political influence, just as they exaggerated the power of Lorenzo in Florence (cf. Rubinstein, *Government*, 221–4); it is possible that they may have made too much of the analogy between the chancellorship in Florence and that in Milan, where Cicco Simonetta commanded vast political power before his fall in 1479.

[123] Vespasiano, *Vite*, i, 547.

there as an administrator without a vote on the scrutiny council, the members of which, moreover, he was unable to influence.

The chancellor occupied one among several autonomous offices in the chancery and of these it was not always the chancellorship which was felt by the regime to be most central to its political interests. This was demonstrated, for example, by the vicissitudes which the chancery underwent in the mid-1450s. In the *pratica* debates of late 1456, the regime, it has been seen, wanted to secure the appointment of Bartolomeo Guidi as notary of the Riformagioni and the reappointment of Poggio as chancellor;[124] what is interesting are the different justifications put forward in support of these two favoured candidates. In the case of the chancellor, it was argued primarily that Poggio's fame as a humanist made it necessary to secure his reelection, whereas the *pratica* wanted Bartolomeo Guidi as notary of the Riformagioni above all else because he was a loyal and trustworthy supporter of the regime;[125] indeed, ultimately Poggio's reappointment was allowed to lapse, but the regime never gave up its fight for Guidi, who was eventually appointed by the Balìa of 1458 and held office for twenty years.[126] The notary of the Riformagioni was in charge of administering the passage of bills through the legislative councils and if he were a man of considerable authority, such as Filippo Pieruzzi, it seems that he could influence in subtle ways the success or failure of important legislation;[127] moreover, he sometimes acted as an adviser on the enforcement of laws to various magistracies such as the conservators of the laws.[128] These could be delicate and even crucial functions for a regime whose power could sometimes depend on controlling or restraining the legislative councils[129] or whose position could be affected by the way in which the law was enforced.[130] It was obviously useful and perhaps even essential for the regime to have a tractable notary of the Riformagioni, and after their experiences with Filippo Pieruzzi, who seems to have regarded himself as the bulwark of justice rather than of the interests of the regime,[131] it became one of their priorities to secure a notary of the Riformagioni who would prove, in Alessandro Alessandri's words, 'affectionatus regimini',[132] as Bartolomeo and his son Giovanni Guidi showed themselves to be over a period of thirty-six years.[133]

Unlike the notary of the Riformagioni, the chancellor himself in the fifteenth century may not have performed such crucial political functions, but that does not mean that the chancellorship carried little importance or

[124] Cf. pp. 91ff, *supra.*   [125] Cf. p. 94, *supra.*
[126] Cf. Marzi, *La cancelleria*, 228–9, 245–6.   [127] Vespasiano, *Vite*, ii, 244–5.
[128] *Ibid.*, 252.   [129] Cf. Rubinstein, *Government, passim.*
[130] Cf. Vespasiano, *Vite*, ii, 252.   [131] *Ibid.*, 244, 252.   [132] Cf. p. 94, *supra.*
[133] Vespasiano was obviously referring to the contrast between the Guidi and Filippo Pieruzzi in the proemium to his life of Pieruzzi, written after the fall of Piero de' Medici, cf. *Vite*, ii, 459–60.

prestige in Florence. Accolti's predecessors, Coluccio Salutati, Leonardo Bruni, Carlo Marsuppini and Poggio Bracciolini, had been scholars of international reputation who had given the office a distinction which the Florentines themselves recognized. It was because the chancellor had for so long been a preeminent humanist that in the crisis of 1456 the regime attempted to keep Poggio in office despite the virtual collapse of the chancery. Indeed, chancellors were often accorded public funerals, the expense of which often far exceeded the cost of other funerals for public officials. Salutati was given a public funeral in 1406 costing 973 *lire* 10 *soldi*,[134] and Benedetto Fortini had a public funeral in 1407 as did Leonardo Bruni in 1444;[135] the vast sums spent on funerals for chancellors in fifteenth-century Florence are illustrated by Carlo Marsuppini's in 1453 which cost the Florentine commune 1500 florins.[136]

The Florentine chancellors were symbols of civic pride, no less than the great public buildings and churches erected by the commune. It was with true patriotism that Giovanni Villani described Florence's first chancellor, Brunetto Latini, as 'the supreme master of rhetoric, both in speaking and writing',[137] and this pride in their chancellor was enhanced during the fourteenth and fifteenth centuries by the series of great humanist chancellors. Other cities emulated Florence; for example, Perugia in 1440 wanted to elect a chancellor who was 'scientificus et in arte oratoria doctissimus'. It was realized that a large salary would be needed to attract such a scholar, and in the end the Perugians had to pay the famous Greek translator Rinuccio da Castiglion-Aretino 250 florins a year, only fifty florins less than Leonardo Bruni's salary in Florence. They were clearly looking for a Greek scholar since the other candidates mentioned, Filelfo, Aurispa and a Sicilian called Marrasius, were all Greek specialists;[138] they wanted to keep up with the Florentines, whose chancellor, Leonardo Bruni, was winning distinction for Florence with his knowledge of Greek, particularly during the Ecumenical Council of the Latin and Greek churches which had begun in Florence in 1439.

The glory rendered to Florence by the chancellor's fame was matched by an almost unbounded faith in the power of the chancellor's written words and of the oratory which he prepared for Florentine ambassadors abroad. As in other Italian cities, the tradition of rhetorical writing had long been associated with the office of chancellor, the earliest surviving letters of the Florentine commune having been the work of rhetoricians or *dictatores*, trained in the *ars dictaminis*.[139] In the Florentine statutes of

---

[134]  Marzi, *La cancelleria*, 68, 81, 149.
[135]  *Ibid.*, 156, 197–8.     [136]  *Ibid.*, 215.
[137]  *Cronica*, VIII, x; cf. Goro Dati's description, quoted by Brown, *Scala*, 135.
[138]  G. B. Vermiglioli, *Memorie di Jacopo Antiquari* (Perugia, 1813), 160–1.
[139]  Cf. Witt, *Salutati and his Public Letters*, 23–41; the first extant missive of the Florentine

1325, it was explicitly stated that the chancellor should be an 'expert in *ars dictaminis*',[140] which was repeated in the statutes of 1355 and 1415.[141] The chancellor supplied the eloquence which was regarded as an essential ingredient in successful diplomacy, as conducted by letters to foreign governments written by the chancellor or by ambassadors who received detailed instructions from him of what to say during their embassies. Even before Salutati's chancellorship, the chronicler Matteo Villani declared that 'eloquence prevails over force' and 'eloquence . . . is more useful than arms',[142] and Salutati's rhetoric confirmed the Florentines, not to mention other Italians and even foreigners, in their belief in the overwhelming power of eloquence. During Salutati's term of office, one speaker in a *pratica* of 1380 declared, 'And let provision be made for the security of the city, with pen, with words and with the sword, if necessary';[143] even the duke of Milan's chancellor, Umberto Decembrio, acknowledged the force of Salutati's eloquence when he wrote to him, 'You wanted to show all people how much power there is in eloquence.'[144] Giangaleazzo Visconti's famous remark that Salutati's letters were more damaging than thousands of soldiers may not be genuine, but it is significant that it became a standard feature of panegyric on Salutati, beginning with Vergerio shortly after his death and then repeated by Bruni, Landino and Ugolino Verino in the course of the fifteenth century.[145] Celebrating the legendary power of Salutati's words was a form of self-advertisement for such humanists, the successors to Salutati's art whose own importance would be enhanced by stressing the power of rhetoric; however, not just humanists but members of the Florentine patriciate such as Piero di Luigi Guicciardini perpetuated this legend, showing that the humanists had succeeded in persuading the Florentine regime of the power of eloquence and of the importance of employing a humanist chancellor.[146] In the fifteenth century the Florentines continued to earn praise for their practical good sense in appointing rhetoricians and humanists as their chancellors: as Pius II wrote, 'the prudence of the Florentines is commendable in many things, especially because in electing their chancellors they look . . . for rhetorical skill and knowledge of the humanities'.[147]

commune, sent to Pavia to justify the death in 1258 of the abbot of Vallombrosa, was the work of a trained *dictator*: it is published by G. C. Gebauer, in *Leben und denckwürdige Thate Hern Richards erwählten Romischen Kaysers* (Leipzig, 1744), 571–5.

140 Marzi, *La cancelleria*, 544.
141 Luiso, 'Riforma', 133; *Statuta*, ii, 704.
142 Cf. De Rosa, *Salutati*, 81.
143 *Ibid.*, 80.
144 *Ibid.*, 85.
145 *Ibid.*, 81–2, n. 30.
146 Cf. Brucker, *Civic World*, 292.
147 Cited by Brown, *Scala*, 135, n. 2.

# 7

# The Florentine chancery under Accolti

In view of Accolti's growing dislike of legal practice, it is not surprising that, immediately after his election, he threw himself entirely into the work of the chancery; it has been seen that the Florentine chancellorship was essentially the office of a professional humanist and so in his work as chancellor Accolti was finally able to devote himself to the field of study and activity for which he had hitherto been able to find little time because of the demands of his legal career. After Poggio's disastrous term of office and the interregnum between September 1456 and April 1458, the chancery was in dire need of an effective head, and Accolti was to prove himself more than able to meet the challenge. In his work of renewal and reform, Accolti had two eminently successful predecessors upon whom he could model himself. Indeed, both Leonardo Bruni and Carlo Marsuppini had been not only his compatriots from Arezzo but also his personal friends and mentors, which made it almost inevitable that Accolti would attempt to carry on the methods and practices which they had established in the chancery. In fact, the striking similarities between Accolti's reforms and those introduced by Bruni and Marsuppini suggest that Accolti not only looked to them as models but also had an ambition to join them in the annals of Florentine history, so creating a third Aretine crown among fifteenth-century chancellors to match the three crowns of fourteenth-century Florence, Dante, Petrarch and Boccaccio.

Bruni's ideal of a specialized chancery, it has been seen, had never been realized in his lifetime;[1] only his friend and fellow Aretine, Marsuppini, had achieved an effective separation in the first years of his chancellorship.[2] Even Marsuppini, however, at the end of his life had relinquished Bruni's vision,[3] and, although Poggio had achieved some specialization during the first year of his term,[4] this achievement soon fell victim to his boredom and indifference, so that by the time Accolti came to office the chancery had moved further than ever from Bruni's hope.[5] Accolti

---

[1] Cf. p. 119, *supra.*   [2] Cf. pp. 119–20, *supra.*
[3] Cf. p. 120, *supra.*   [4] Cf. pp. 89–90, 120, *supra.*   [5] Cf. pp. 90–1, 121, *supra.*

immediately put an end to this deterioration after assuming the chancellor-ship. Second chancery staff, including Muzi, Pardi and Jacopo di Paolo, who had continued to work in the first chancery even after the resurrection of the second chancery in May 1457, now had no further role in the first chancery.[6] Accolti put one notary, Bastiano di Antonio di Zanobi Foresi, who had worked in the chancery under Marsuppini and then Poggio but who had left six months after Poggio's retirement,[7] in charge of copying all letters abroad into the registers of *missive*[8] and all communications with ambassadors into the registers of *legazioni e commissarie*[9] as well as of copying the minutes of the *pratica* into the permanent registers.[10] Similarly, Foresi was in charge of writing originals of letters sent to foreign powers,[11] just as Pardi[12] and other second chancery staff were now con-fined to writing the originals of second chancery letters. During Accolti's term of office Foresi's hand alone (apart from occasional autograph cor-rections by Accolti himself[13] and five entries in the ambassadors' register on 4 and 5 October 1458)[14] appears in the records of the first chancery.

Bruni's reform of the chancery, as implemented by Marsuppini, had had the advantage of making the chancellor and his assistant specialists in the diplomatic business of the government, enabling them to reach a level of expert skill less attainable in an undivided chancery. The kind of specialization introduced by Poggio in 1453–4[15] had gone some way to reordering the chancery after the decline apparent in Marsuppini's last years,[16] which had been compounded by the death of the second chan-cellor Guiducci and the reunification of the chancery in January 1453,[17] but Poggio had not gone all the way to reviving Marsuppini's original practice of one assistant with overall competence in all areas of first chan-

---

[6] Pardi continued to work in the second chancery under Muzi after Accolti became first chancellor: cf. ASF, Not.A., S 500, fol. 21r (5 May 1458): Actum in cancelleria dominorum presentibus testibus ser Nicolao Pardi Antonii Pardi et ser Francesco Sini; *ibid.*, fol. 23r (4 April 1460): Actum in cancelleria dominorum priorum presentibus tes-tibus ser Antonio Mariani [Muzi] et ser Nicolao Pardi de Vulteribus; *ibid.*, fol. 23v (10 June 1460): presentibus testibus ser Nicolao Pardi Antonii Pardi notario cancellerie. Ser Francesco Sini, mentioned above, may have been the second coadjutor in the second chancery under Muzi.

[7] Cf. p. 100, *supra*.　　[8] ASF, Miss. 42, 43, 44.　　[9] ASF, LC, 15.

[10] ASF, CP, 55, 56.

[11] Cf. e.g. ASM, SPEFi, 269, n. 185 (20 May 1458), and then 22, 23,35, 37, 50, 106; *ibid.*, 270 n. 119, 120, 113 (24 November 1461), 79 (7 November 1462), 80; *ibid.*, 271 n. 108, 115, 125, 155, 170, 174, 180, 206, 240, 1 (24 December 1463), 11, 15, 30, 69, 89, 125, 172, 173. The only exception was 270, n. 79 (7 January 1462), an ambassadorial com-mission, whose text was written by Pardi but addressed by Foresi.

[12] Cf. e.g. *ibid.*, 270, n. 60 (12 May 1459), a copy of an original *missive* sent by the Florentine second chancery to the governors of Pisa, written by Pardi.

[13] For Accolti's autograph corrections, cf. ASF, Miss. 42, fol. 69v, 146v, 183r; 43, fol. 38r, 40v, 139r; 44, fol. 71r, 135r.

[14] ASF, CdC, 51, fol. 161r–162r, written by hands Y and D: cf. p. 99, *supra*.

[15] Cf. pp. 89–90, 120, *supra*.　　[16] Cf. p. 120, *supra*.　　[17] Cf. pp. 89, 120, *supra*.

cery business. Under Poggio's system only the chancellor himself as overall supervisor had continuous responsibility for all types of business in the first chancery, and it is significant that Accolti went back to Marsuppini's original practice as the best method of achieving the ideal of a specialized chancery first envisaged by Bruni.

Accolti was also able to reduce the number of assistants employed in the chancery and so restore productivity to what it had been under Marsuppini and Bruni. During the first half of the fifteenth century assistants in the chancery had been becoming more numerous at increased expense to the commune. Throughout the fourteenth century the chancellor had always had only one coadjutor, even during the period when Salutati was notary of the Tratte as well as chancellor.[18] Salutati's successors continued to have one coadjutor until the chancellorship of Paolo Fortini.[19] At first he was provided with only one coadjutor,[20] but because of the numerous additional offices he had assumed Fortini came to have five coadjutors to assist in all his duties.[21] In 1427 Leonardo Bruni was elected chancellor without Fortini's additional offices, but nevertheless provision was made to give him two coadjutors instead of one.[22] That was the first indication that the chancellor was being given additional assistance in his capacity as chancellor alone and it was carried further in 1437 with the division of the chancery. For now the first chancellor was provided with one coadjutor and the second chancellor with two, so that five officials were now doing what had been the work of three.[23] This arrangement was continued after the chancellorship was reunited in 1453, for now there was one principal coadjutor or vice-chancellor taking the place of the second chancellor in addition to three other coadjutors, so that there was no difference in the number of staff in the chancery.[24] However, after the chancery was again divided formally in 1457, the number of coadjutors apparently increased. After December 1456, the number of assistants working in the chancery increased to five,[25] and the following spring to six;[26] after Muzi became second chancellor in May 1457, he seems to have kept five assistants,[27] which suggests that the proposal of the *pratica* of December 1456 to provide two further coadjutors was implemented, as had been their proposal to appoint Muzi as second chancellor. The growing number of coadjutors was evidently felt to be a strain on communal

[18]  Cf. Marzi, *La cancelleria*, 62, 68, 71, 80, 86–7, 93, 119, 125, 132, 134, 139.
[19]  *Ibid.*, 155, 159.      [20]  *Ibid.*, 160–1.      [21]  *Ibid.*, 183.
[22]  Cf. p. 108, *supra*. It has not previously been known how many coadjutors were provided when Bruni was elected in 1427.
[23]  Luiso, 'Riforma', 136–8.      [24]  *Ibid.*, 139–41.
[25]  I.e. Foresi, Muzi, Pardi, Jacopo di Paolo and Scribe Y (cf. pp. 99–100 *supra*).
[26]  I.e. Muzi, Pardi, Jacopo di Paolo, Scribe Y, Scribe B, Scribe G (cf. pp. 99–100, *supra*).
[27]  I.e. Pardi, Jacopo di Paolo, Scribe B, Scribe Y, Scribe D (replacing Scribe G): cf. pp. 99–100, *supra*.

finances, since it was recommended during the *pratica* debates of late 1456
that two of the assistants proposed to assist Poggio should be paid from
funds set aside for the university.[28] This gradual increase in chancery staff,
however, was halted by the election of Accolti, who took only one
coadjutor, thus reducing the chancery staff as a whole to what it had been
under Bruni and Marsuppini.

Accolti's reform of chancery staffing, like his definitive separation of
the first and second chanceries, shows him following the lead of both Bruni
and Marsuppini; the important changes he introduced into the style of
public letter writing in the chancery reveal him as imitating Marsuppini in
particular. It has been observed that there was a tendency to descend from
the *stilus altus* achieved by Salutati in his public letters to a *stilus humilis*
in the fifteenth century;[29] whether this contrast between the public epistolography of Salutati and his successors in Florence holds true for the
period between 1406 and 1444 and in particular for the second chancellorship of Bruni remains to be demonstrated, but it is certainly true that
Poggio's public letters are far less lofty in style and content than those of
Salutati. Salutati's letters are filled with many weighty *sententiae* and
*exempla*, often drawn from classical sources not to mention medieval
history;[30] moreover, Salutati's letters are not confined to the immediate
circumstances but often contain elaborate generalized *exordia* or intro-
ductions.[31] Poggio himself did not write all the state letters produced by the
chancery during his term of office; those which he did write are signed with
a 'P' or 'Pog' at the end,[32] and of these letters, only one has an *exordium*
with some kind of generalized content.[33] Not untypically, this one

---

[28] Cf. p. 96, *supra*.
[29] Cf. Herde, 'Politik und Rhetoric', *Archiv für Kulturgeschichte*, xlvii (1965), 209, who
bases this conclusion on an impression gained from a rapid examination of ASF, Miss. 28
to 40, as he himself admits. Witt, *Salutati and his Public Letters*, 40–1, accepts this view
without offering any evidence of his own. De Rosa also accepts this view (*Salutati*, x–xi)
without any documentation, but her study of the *missive* of Bruni and Poggio, so she has
told me, has confirmed this conclusion. I can confirm that Bruni's letters from his first
brief period as chancellor in 1410 are written in a *stilus humilis*; in the fragment of a register of *missive* in ASF, MRep. III, n. 88 (Frammento di un registro di lettere della Signoria
dal 10 gennaio 1410 al 24 marzo 1410), there are no *exempla*, few *exordia* and only this
one simple *sententia*: (fol. 1v) Ipsa communis humane societatis ratio exigit ut bonis
atque fidelibus viris fraudem aliquam perpessis, quantum fieri potest, opportunis auxiliis
faveamus, ne, quod iniustissimum est, ipsi damnum ex bonitate et improbi lucrum ex
malitia sua reportare sinantur. However, this conclusion does not hold true for
Marsuppini or Accolti: cf. pp. 142ff, *infra*.
[30] Cf. De Rosa, *Salutati*, 13–30; Witt, *Salutati and his Public Letters*, 23–41.
[31] Cf. De Rosa, *Salutati*, 14.    [32] Cf. Walser, *Poggius*, 286, n. 2.
[33] There are also brief and insignificant *exordia* in letters countersigned P. or Pog. in Miss.
40, fol. 14r, 152v–153r and 170r. It seems very unlikely from the Latin style of fol. 170r
that Poggio himself composed this letter: fiducialiter recurramus ad certo tenentes
quod vestra beneficentia . . . ; it was written by Pardi, who perhaps showed it to Poggio
for approval.

generalized *exordium* written by Poggio is an attack on absentee abbots, resembling the dialogue *Contra hypocritas* which he had composed in 1449:

It is not unknown . . . what use is commonly made of benefices and monasteries which are given *in commendam*. For rarely does reason prevail in them or divine worship or the benefits of religion or usefulness but only care for private interest, so that it happens that many monasteries fall to ruin, just as we see also sometimes occur among us. For just as a wife requires the presence of her husband, so also a monastery needs its bridegroom by whose help and diligence it is governed.[34]

The rest of Poggio's state letters have no such notable passages, and usually the letters written by his coadjutors without his supervision are similarly mundane in content.[35]

The use of *stilus humilis* by Poggio and his assistants stands in direct contrast to the aulic style which characterized the public letters composed by Marsuppini. Marsuppini often used elaborate figures of speech such as metaphor:

It is often necessary for the governors of republics to act like the pilots of ships. For however much they determine on a port for which they have set their course, nevertheless often perforce stormy winds oblige them to divert their ship to another port.[36]

*epanaphora* (repeating the same word at the beginning of successive phrases):

if sometimes men are to be elected to give judgement and to have charge of justice, in that matter indeed no effort, no care, no diligence finally must be omitted.[37]

or *rogatio* (rhetorical question):

If these things are true, what first do we complain of? His iniquity and impropriety,

---

[34] *Ibid.*, fol. 18v: Non est ignotum . . . quo pacto tractentur communi usu beneficia et monasteria que in commendam conceduntur. Raro enim habetur ratio in illis aut cultus dei aut religionis aut utilitatis beneficiorum sed solum privati commodi cura, quo accidit ut multa monasteria collabantur prout in nostris quoque videmus aliquando contigere. Nam sicut uxor viri presentiam requirit, ita et monasteria suum sponsum exposcunt cuius ope et diligentia gubernentur.

[35] Letters with *exordia* in Miss. 40 written by Muzi: fol. 1v; by Pardi: fol. 64v, 65r, 70v, 92r, 97r, 102v, 106r, 119r, 122v, 146r, 168r, 169v, 170r, 173v, 175v, 186v, 191v, 202r, 216r, 223r, 225r, 230r, 231r; by Foresi, fol. 11r, 13r, 14r, 17r, 19v–20r, 24r, 81r, 90v, 126v, 130v, 138v, 152v–153r, 155r, 155v, 155v–156r, 156r–v, 219r, 222v.

[36] ASF, Miss. 36, fol. 19v: His qui rei publice gubernacula tractant aliquando id quod navim gubernatoribus agere necesse est. Illi et enim quamvis aliquem portum ad quem suum cursum dirigant proposuerint, vi tamen sepe ac ventorum tempestate alio suam navigationem flectere coguntur. Cf. *ibid.*, fol. 169v for an elaborate medical metaphor, and fol. 23r for another metaphor.

[37] *Ibid.*, fol. 64r: Si quando viri sint eligendi qui iuridicendo tuendeque iustitie preesse debeant, in eo profecto nullum studium, nulla cura, nulla denique diligentia est pretermittenda. For further examples, cf. *ibid.*, fol. 15v, 20v, 72v, 102v. Cf. also BRF, Big. 193, fol. 41v: Tacemus . . . tacemus . . .

or stupidity, or malevolence, or singular audacity? 'You, however, foolish man, no, iniquitous man, do you think the words which you use will command any trust with your most wise lord, a man benevolent to us? Do you hope that you will show how contemptible is the name of a prince, who among all is considered honourable and glorious, in our republic where he is not only loved but also both cherished and worshipped? And what was it that led us to this petulant language? Surely not hatred of that lord? No, on the contrary, the best intentions. Surely not his injuries against us? He, who always has regarded our republic, our merchants with as much favour and honour as has befitted our love and benevolence towards him.'[38]

Lofty themes abound in Marsuppini's letters, such as justice:

Although all laudable and worthy virtues have always been honoured in your republic, he wrote to the Venetians, nevertheless in our opinion as well as in that of everyone, justice has hitherto been cultivated and cherished over other virtues . . . Since that virtue is the soul of a city, and not only of a city but also of any kingdom or empire, if it were to lapse, no city, no kingdom, finally no empire could live or thrive or remain stable for long.[39]

or the rule of wisdom:

Although those in charge of governing a republic must show great care over anything pertaining to the dignity of the city, nevertheless if sometimes men must be elected to administer and protect justice, in that task indeed no effort, no care, finally no diligence must be omitted . . . Indeed, it has been wisely said that those republics are blessed which are governed by wise men or by those who are devoted to wisdom; for cities are usually only as great as their princes and leaders.[40]

---

[38] ASF, Miss. 36, fol. 69v–70r: Que si vera sunt, quid primum queremur? Illiusne nequitiam et improbitatem an stultitiam an malivolentiam an audaciam singularem? Tu vero, homo stultissime, ne diciamus flagiotisissime, apud dominum et benivolum nobis et sapientissimum cum talia referres tua verba fidem habitura putasti? Tu nomen illius principis qui apud omnes honori et glorie habetur, in nostra re publica in qua non solum amatur sed etiam et observatur et colitur, contemptui esse te fore probaturum sperasti?Et quid erat quod nos ad eam linguam petulantem impelleret? Num illius domini odium? At contra summa est benivolentia. Num iniurie illius erga nos? qui semper nostram rem publicam, nostros mercatores tanto favore honoreque prosecutus est, quantum noster erga eum et amor et benivolentia postulat. Cf. also *ibid.*, fol. 233v.

[39] *Ibid.*, fol. 79r: Quamquam . . . omnes virtutes que ad laudem et dignitatem pertinent in vestra re publica semper celebrate fuerint, tamen nostra atque omnium opinione in ea iustitia pre ceteris hactenus et culta et honori habita est, siquidem non solum civibus suis atque suo imperio subditis verum etiam peregrinis atque alienigenis sine aliquo discrimine ut leges moresque laudandi postulant ius suum unicuique reddidit. Quod nostro iudicio summopere laudandum est. Nam cum ea virtus anima civitatis sit, nec solum civitatis verum etiam regni cuiusquam et imperii, ea sublata nec civitas nec regnum nec ullum denique imperium vivere aut vigere aut stabile diuturnumve esse potest.

[40] *Ibid.*, fol. 64r: Quamquam ab his qui rei publice gubernande curam habent omnibus in rebus que spectant ad amplitudinem civitatis magna cura sit adhibenda, tamen . . . si quando viri sint eligendi qui iuridicendo tuendeque iustitie preesse debeant, in eo profecto nullum studium, nulla cura, nulla denique diligentia est pretermittenda, siquidem illud sapientissime dictum est beatas fore res publicas si aut a sapientibus viris gubernarentur aut qui eas regerent sapientie operam darent. Quales et enim sunt principes et rectores, tales civitates esse solent.

Marsuppini also sometimes appeals to distant history as in this letter to
Lucca:

If we should care to look back over annals since ancient times, we would indeed
always find that your city in both peace and war has always been joined to our
republic by the highest benevolence and charity.[41]

or to the recent past as in this letter to Pope Eugenius IV:

It is known to the entire Christian people and especially to us, with whom your
holiness dwelled for many years, that you, although occupied by many and various
matters, have devoted such attention and care to all monasteries, churches, convents, finally to all offices of the church that justifiably all priests must count themselves blessed and happy under your pontificate.[42]

The most characteristic feature of Marsuppini's public letters is the
elaborate *exordium*, which, it has been noted, was almost completely
absent from Poggio's missives; the most beautiful of Marsuppini's
*exordia*, in which he praises the art of music by reference to Plato,
Pythagoras and other Greek philosophers, has already been published,[43]
but another example is Marsuppini's panegyric of medicine:

Although all arts which concern a free man should rightly be praised, nevertheless
medicine is worthy of the highest commendation. For it cures diseases, heals
wounds, enhances and preserves good health and administers medicaments to the
infirm. Therefore among the ancients the founders of this art were blessed with
immortality; for indeed they saw that virtues and talents of the mind are to some
degree weakened and debilitated if the body languishes in sickness and disease.[44]

[41] *Ibid.*, fol. 27v: Et enim si annales ab antiquis temporibus repetere voluerimus,
inveniemus profecto semper vestram civitatem et pace et bello summa benevolentia et
caritate cum nostra re publica fuisse coniunctam. Itaque cum a nostris maioribus hoc
nomen benivolentie quodammodo hereditarium nobis relictum sit, nos id non solum
conservare et tueri verum etiam augere pro viribus parati sumus.
[42] *Ibid.*, fol. 32v: Notum est universo populo christiano, tum precipue nobis apud quos
vestra sanctitas multos per annos morata est, eam quamvis multis variisque rebus
occupatam, ita omnia monasteria, templa, conventus, omnes denique ecclesie dignitates
prospicere ac cure habere ut merito omnes sacerdotes vestro pontificatu se beatos esse ac
felices existimare debeant.
[43] Garin, 'Cancellieri umanisti', in his *La cultura filosofica*, 25.
[44] *Ibid.*, fol. 109v: Quamquam omnes artesque ad liberum hominem pertinent merito
laudari debeant, tamen imprimis medicina omnium commendatione digna est. Hec et
enim morbos curat, hec vulnera ad cicatricem deducit, hec bonam valitudinem auget et
conservat, malam vero medicamentis amoniet. Itaque inventores apud antiquos
immortalitati fuerunt consecrati. Videbant et enim virtutes dotesque animi
quodammodo mancas debilesque esse si corpora morbo aut egrotatione languescerent.
   Other notable *exordia* by Marsuppini are *ibid.*, fol. 36v, 41r, 72v, 102 (published by
Garin, 'Canc. umanis.' 25), 171v, 178v, 201v–202r. Marsuppini's letters in general
became less lofty in tone later in his chancellorship.
   The following letters by Marsuppini have *exordia*, albeit not as interesting or
elaborate as those mentioned above: *ibid.*, 36,fol. 2r, 2v–3r, 3v, 7r, 10v, 12r, 15r, 15v,
16v, 17v, 18v–19r, 21r, 25v, 26r, 33r, 37r, 41r, 42v, 50v, 51v, 53v, 54r, 57v, 66r–v, 66v,
67r, 68v, 71v, 73r, 78v, 81v, 84r, 84r–v, 84v, 86r, 87r, 87v, 88v–89r, 90v, 94r, 97v–98r,

On becoming chancellor, Accolti immediately rejected the *stilus humilis* used by Poggio in favour of the *stilus altus* preferred by Marsuppini. Thus, Accolti's letters are rich in *exempla* drawn from classical antiquity, as for instance when he cites Roman history to show the benefits accruing from nurturing learned and virtuous men in a republic:

Through the efforts of men who, drawn from everywhere, were given Roman citizenship, the Romans subdued the world, maintaining their liberty and empire as long as virtue prevailed over vice.[45]

Christian *exempla* are also not lacking in Accolti's missives, as in this passage celebrating Christ the peace-maker:

Peace was announced to mankind at the birth of Him who always greeted his disciples in the name of peace . . . who ordered them to wish for peace in every house they entered, who, we read, frequently enjoined all men to embrace in mutual charity and to cast aside all things which would destroy love and benevolence.[46]

or where he recalls the Christian prowess of the Hungarian crusader, John Hunyadi,

who waged so many wars, vanquished and put to flight so many enemies of Christ, destroyed so many armies that he seemed endowed with superhuman strength to accomplish deeds which have earned him the title of defender of Christians but scourge of the infidel.[47]

Classical wisdom in the form of *sententiae* abound in Accolti's letters, such as the Platonic maxim of the philosopher-ruler:

98v, 105r, 105v, 110r, 111r, 111v, 114r, 115r, 118r (2 letters), 119v, 120r–v, 122, 125v, 126r, 126v–127r, 129r, 130r, 134r, 134v, 135v, 137r, 137v, 138r, 139r, 142r, 146r, 146r–v, 149r, 149v, 150v, 151v, 152r, 154r, 155v, 156r, 156v, 157v, 159r, 160v, 161r, 162r, 163r (2 letters), 164v, 166v, 167r, 170v, 174r, 174v, 177r, 179v, 180v, 181r, 181v, 183v (2 letters), 185v, 187r, 188r, 189v, 191r, 194v, 195r–v, 196r, 196v, 198v, 200r–v, 200v, 201r, 201v–202r, 205v, 206v, 207v, 209v, 211v, 213r, 213v, 214r, 214v, 220r, 220v, 221r, 222v, 223r, 226v, 227v (2 letters), 228r–v, 231r, 234r, 235r; BRF, Big. 193. fol. 1v, 5v–6r, 8r, 9r, 10r–v, 12r–v, 12v, 16r, 16r–v, 17r, 17v, 19v, 28v, 32r, 32r–v, 32v, 33r, 34r, 35r, 35v, 36r, 36v (2 letters), 38v (2 letters), 39v, 41r, 43r (2 letters), 46r, 47r, 48r, 49r, 49v, 50r, 50v, 51r, 52r (2 letters), 53r, 53v, 54r (2 letters), 54v, 56r, 59r, 60r, 60v, 62r (2 letters), 62v, 63r

45 ASF, Miss. 42, fol. 6v: Sic Romani claros undique allicientes viros et civitate illos donantes cum eorum industria terrarum orbem subegerunt. Et tam diu apud illos libertas et imperium fuerunt quam diu vitiis virtus prevaluit et dominata est.

46 *Ibid.*, fol. 8v–9r: Eius enim in terris vices geritis [the pope] in cuius ortu pax hominibus nuntiata est, qui semper sub pacis nomine discipulos suos salutavit, qui eis pacem suam relinquere professus est, qui eisdem precepit ut quamcumque intrarent domum pacem illi exoptarent, a quo frequenter mandatum legimus ut homines cuncti caritate mutua se diligerent eaque abicerent omnia quibus amor et benivolentia dissolvuntur.

47 *Ibid.*, fol. 12v: . . . ipsum tot confecisse bella, tam multos Christi hostes sepe fudisse ac fugasse, tam magnos exercitus ab eodem esse deletos ut vix ea humanis viribus fieri potuisse videantur. Ob que quidem gesta Christianorum defensor infidelium, vero ingens terror est habitus.

Some have written that those republics are blessed which are ruled and administered by wise and erudite men.[48]

or the Ciceronian emphasis on the union of wisdom and eloquence:

Wisdom without eloquence is seldom useful in any way.[49]

or the Stoic idea, perhaps derived from Cicero's *Tusculan Disputations*,
which he had used as a source in his Italian poetry many years before,[50]
that death is not an unmitigated evil:

It is fitting to remember that we men are born subject to the law that one day we
must die, nor does death itself bring misfortune or misery but rather immortality
and felicity to those who have lived in such a way that they deserve to have a share
in divinity;[51]

or the Vergilian denunciation of Rumour:

Suddenly Rumour arises mixing truth with falsehood, more often even professing
many things entirely untruthful, so that not without cause did our ancestors
judge rumour worthy of little credence and poets themselves describe it as
mendacious and worthless.[52]

More specifically Christian themes are also frequently encountered in
Accolti's *missive*, such as the idea that the body is a prison upon release
from which the soul will ascend to the blessed life,[53] or the orthodox
theological doctrine rejecting absolute monastic poverty:

Even if it is fitting for those monks to leave the world in order to follow God and
to contemplate his majesty by rejecting worldly squalor and spurning riches, leading their lives in poverty, naked and unfettered, pursuing only pure virtue, nevertheless it is unjust for them to be so weighed down by destitution and care for
life's necessities that they are forced to neglect or desert entirely divine worship and
religious practices.[54]

[48] *Ibid.*, fol. 6v: litteris quidam tradiderunt beatas fore res publicas si eas a sapientibus et
eruditis viris regi administrarique contingeret.
[49] *Ibid.*, fol. 3r: sapientia sine eloquentia minus prodesse solet. For other Ciceronian
quotations, cf. ASF, Miss. 43, fol. 71v, 171v.
[50] Cf. p. 46, *supra*.
[51] ASF, Miss. 42, fol. 28r–v: Meminisse enim oportet nos homines esse ea lege natos ut
aliquando moreremur, nec mortem ipsam mali aliquid aut miserie afferre sed
immortalitatem potius ac felicitatem his qui ita vixerunt ut divinitatis participes fieri
mererentur.
[52] *Ibid.*, fol. 38r: Repente veris falsa immiscens fama exoriatur, plerunque etiam multa
ferens a veritate prorsus aliena, unde non absque causa maiores nostri parvam illi fidem
adhibendam censuerunt et poete ipsi eam velut mendacem et inanem descripsisse. Cf.
*Aeneid*, iv, 173ff.
[53] ASF, Miss. 42, fol. 28v: cum satis diu nature et glorie vixisset e carnis ergastulo solutum
beatam prorsus vitam assumpsisse.
[54] *Ibid.*, fol. 41r: Etsi monacis illis qui ideo mundum reliquerunt ut deum sequi et eius
numen liceret contemplari abiectis terrenis sordibus maxime convenit spretis divitiis
inopes etatem agere, ut nudam solamque virtutem nudi expeditique sequantur, nil aliud
quam deum ipsum intuentes, tamen equum est eos non ita urgeri ut necessariis ad vitam

High-flown humanist apologetics too are not absent from Accolti's letters, such as when he declares that Florence 'was never accustomed to wage wars unless it was to protect liberty or repel injuries inflicted by others'[55] or when he protests,

We are dearer to our subjects because the outstanding men among them realize that they are loved and cherished by us and that we do not act towards them differently than towards our own citizens, for we regard them not as slaves but as sons whom, like members of our city, we warmly esteem.[56]

Accolti's letters are usually written in a lofty Ciceronian style, rich in copious phrases such as this description of the horrors of wars,

from which usually result the slaughter of infants, the rape of wives, the devastations of fields, the sack of towns, the captivity of peoples, the high price of grain; as a result of wars too agriculture is deserted, trade and navigation cease, finally every kind of calamity is multiplied.[57]

Figures of speech are frequently found, such as *epanaphora*:

For the glory of the city our ancestors refused no expense, no danger, no labour.[58]

Accolti's favourite figure is *rogatio*, as for example:

What is more fitting to your office? What is more suitable to such majesty? What is better for the salvation of mankind?[59]

Especially noteworthy was Accolti's determination to reintroduce the *exordium* into the *missive* of the Florentine republic, a feature which had been usually absent from Poggio's public letters;[60] indeed, elaborate *exordia* are the hallmark of Accolti's public epistolography. A typical example is the beginning of this letter of recommendation to a cardinal:

rebus destituantur quarum defectu divinum cultum et religiosos mores aut remittere aut omnino deserere cogerentur . . .

55  *Ibid.*, fol. 9r: numquam hec civitas bella gerere solita est nisi ut libertatem tueretur vel ut illatas ab allis iniurias propulsaret.

56  *Ibid.*, fol. 6v: Et eo etiam subditis nobis cariores sumus quo intelligunt prestantes ex illis homines a nobis amari et foveri et non secus pro illis agere quam pro carissimis civibus ageremus. Eos enim non servorum loco sed filiorum ducimus et velut civitatis nostre membra vehementer a nobis diliguntur.

57  *Ibid.*, fol. 9r: Quis enim ex bellis gaudeat? aut quis ea cupiat bonus, ex quibus multorum neces infantium et mulierum raptus, agrorum populationes, expugnationes opidorum, captivitates gentium, annone caritas evenire solent? Ob illa etiam agricultura deseritur, mercatorum exercitia et navigatio conquiescunt, calamitas denique omnis accumulatur.

58  *Ibid.*, fol. 19v: Cum enim maiores nostri pro civitatis gloria nullam impensam, nullum periculum, nullum laborem recusarint ut ex parva re publica magnam facerent. Cf. also fol. 38r: Nulla enim dissensio civium, nullus asperior solito casus urbem nostram invasit, nulli denique hic sunt cives quos respectus aliquis rei publice possit tangere.

59  *Ibid.*, fol. 8v: Nam quid est officio vestro decentius? quid tante maiestati accomodatius? quid pro salute hominum melius?

60  I am very grateful to Dott. De Rosa for pointing me first to this feature of Poggio's official letters: cf. pp. 141–2, *supra*.

If we consider spiritual or secular life, Reverend father, it is fitting for those to be in positions of responsibility and authority, as you well know, who are distinguished not only by the integrity of their lives but by outstanding learning, eminent wisdom, splendid eloquence, wide and thorough experience of many things; and in two different skills, namely, obeying and commanding, they must be considered so proficient that they deserve in no way censure. Indeed, there are many who, although worthy and innocent, nevertheless are so inexperienced and ignorant that they are not even able to look after themselves, much less rule others; for them, because of the limitations of their characters or because of their inexperience, it is more fitting to be ruled than to rule. Hence it often happens that such men, celebrated for their preeminent integrity, gain offices for which, in the course of performing their duties, they later appear unsuited and unworthy.[61]

Even when the purpose of the letter was to regain possession of horses stolen from a rustic living in the Florentine countryside, Accolti did not neglect the *exordium*:

Since we are neighbours, he wrote to the Sienese, it is inevitable that many matters will arise which will necessitate exchanging letters to our mutual benefit, on the one hand, for the welfare of our republic, on the other, to support the interests of our citizens or subjects, whom it would be entirely wrong not to assist at least by letter. Therefore, we should not want you to take it amiss if we venture to intercede with you frequently on behalf of our people. Indeed, there are many things which persuade us that this is by no means annoying to you. First, our friendship; then, the fact that in our experience we have seen that nothing is dearer to you than to oblige us if the possibility arises; moreover, we ourselves regard your frequent letters to us by no means as irritating.[62]

Indeed, when Accolti declares that the formalities of rhetoric are inappropriate, his very protestations become an *exordium* in themselves:

It seems superfluous for us, he wrote in the college of cardinals, undertaking to

[61] *Ibid.*, fol. 2v: Cardinali Firmano. Illos ut probe noscis, reverendissime in Christo pater et domine, curam ac regimen habere decet, seu secularem sive spiritualem inspicimus vitam, qui non solum vite integritate sed egregia doctrina, sapienta insigni, splendido eloquio, multarum rerum usu et experientia claruerunt, et qui duabus in diversis rebus, parendo scilicet atque imperando, tales sunt habiti ut minimum sit quod in eis reprehensione dignum esse videretur. Sunt enim plerique, licet boni et innocentes, tamen usque adeo sepe inexperti et rudes ut nedum regendis aliis sed vix sibi ipsis queant sufficere quibus conducit, vel ob nature difficultatem vel ob minimum in rebus usum, subesse alteri potiusquam preesse. Unde accidit sepius eiusmodi homines bonitatis fama celebres ea officia eos magistratus esse assecutos in quibus gerendis postea inepti et vanissimi apparuerunt.
[62] *Ibid.*, fol. 20r: Cum finitima nobis vestra regio sit, magni viri fratres carissimi, necesse est multa crebro accidere quibus nos invicem litteris ad obsequia mutua provocemus, cum pro rei publice commodis, tum etiam pro eorum sepenumero causis quibuscum aut cives sint aut etiam subditi ipsorum viri litteris saltem deesse nefas omnino duceretur. Quocirca nequaquam graviter vos ferre volumus si pro nostris hominibus frequenter apud vos ipsos intercedere audemus. Id enim nobis haud molestum esse plura suadent. In primis amicitia nostra; deinde quod sepius experti facile intelleximus nil magis cordi vobis esse quam ut grata nobis facere aliquando facultas offeratur; ac etiam quia et ipsi vestras ad nos litteras continuo minime irritas esse volumus.

write on behalf of someone intimately known to you fathers, to use that style of writing often used by someone who wants to recommend his own friend to someone else. For they describe the habits and entire life of the man, and in praising and explaining individual points they go into such detail that the letters themselves do not differ very much from an elaborate oration.[63]

Accolti's missives are sometimes stamped by his own personal knowledge and experience, as in this letter to the pope in defence of Florentine legislation against rebellion and treason:

Nothing is more foreign to our customs, nothing more entirely contrary to our nature than cruelty and savagery, nor do we believe there ever were nor even are now any people who have determined penalties more lenient for punishing crimes or who have more frequently used clemency against enemies and all kinds of men. Although clemency is very often useful and worthy of praise, it can also provide a bad example and be the cause of many crimes. For the opportunity of mercy is an incentive to transgression for incorrigible and rash men who, with the hope of impunity before them, are excited to wickedness. Nor did Roman laws impose grave penalties on great crimes for any other reason than to intimidate criminals by fear, considering men worthy of no mercy who, having cast aside patriotism, made themselves enemies of their country. Therefore, although it is wrong to kill or contrive the death of anyone without legitimate cause, nevertheless we see that sometimes the laws themselves prescribe the sword against a man, especially someone whose crime of waging nefarious war against his own country has cut him off from natural society. Therefore our ancestors, although the most lenient and mild of men, having considered nothing more dear or holy to mortals than the welfare of the republic, believed that respect for virtue and honesty did not suffice to teach those citizens their duty whom ambition, indulgence, hatred and avarice often led astray, and so they promulgated now long ago this law against the enemies of the republic.[64]

---

[63] *Ibid.*, fol. 7v: Supervacuum nobis videtur esse cum pro viro patribus vestris notissimo scribere aggrediamur illo uti scribendi genere quo plerique dum alteri suum amicum commendatum volunt sepenumero uti consueverunt. Referunt enim mores vitamque hominis totam et in laudandis singulis explicandisque ita inmorantur ut epistole ipse non multum ab accurata oratione differant.

[64] ASF, Miss. 43, fol. 131v: Nil est alienius a moribus nostris, nil omnino nature nostre magis adversum quam sevitia et immanitas. Neque aliquos unquam fuisse credimus aut nunc etiam esse qui pro vinidicandis criminibus mitiores quam nos decreverint penas. Quive frequentius in hostes in omnium hominum genus clementia uti consueverunt. Que ut plerunque utilis est laude plurimum digna, ita etiam sepe mali exempli et causa est multorum scelerum. Nam facilitas venie incentivum est delinquendi perditis et temerariis viris qui spe impunitatis proposita magis ad malum accenduntur, nec ob aliam causam leges Romane magnis flagitiis graves irrogant penas quam et earum formidine cuncti a criminibus revocentur, et eos homines venia nulla dignos existimant qui abiecta patrie caritate illi hostes efficiuntur. Unde quamquam sit nefas absque legitima causa quemquam occidere aut illius vite insidias tendere, tamen videmus quandoque gladium ad occidendum hominem ab ipsis porrigi legibus, presertim eum qui patrie inferens nefarium bellum nature societatem suo scelere diremisset. Ideoque maiores nostri quamquam lenissimi et mitissimi homines rati nil debere mortalibus esse carius aut sanctius quam rei publice salutem nec sufficere ad continendos in officio cives virtutis atque honestatis respectum, quos sepenumero ambitio, luxus, hodium et avaritia transversos agunt, iam diu eam tulerunt legem in hostes rei publice cives ...

Accolti was thus impressive when able to draw on his legal knowledge, but, as in his vernacular poetry and in his later humanist writings, he was at his best when given a religious theme to embellish in his missives, as in this plea to canonize the Franciscan preacher, Giovanni da Capistrano:

It has indeed been rightly instituted that some men, having rejected the squalor of the world, have kept themselves pure and celibate, and, burning with the love of Christ, have refused no labour in protecting his teachings, no danger, no insults, finally not even death. Their learning and holy life and pious prayers for all have very often benefited the human race, in pursuit either of well-being on earth or of eternal felicity. After they have returned to Him from whom they issued, having been divested of their earthly bodies, they are celebrated as beneficiaries of heavenly gifts and their name is celebrated in eternal memory through holy rites. For thus esteem is shown to be the prize of virtue, and remaining mortals, moved by their example, more ardently strive for God. Moreover, the church of Christ, buttressed by such witnesses, emerges each day more illustrious and distinguished, showing its gratitude towards those by those support and merits it has been very much enhanced and strengthened. Therefore it behoves all Christians, especially those elevated in authority, not to allow the memory of such men to perish but, according to their ability, to strive vehemently for their glory to be preserved for posterity in perpetuity. For if the ancients cherished many men as gods on account of their empty reputation for virtue, how much more just is it for us to venerate and cherish those who truly appear as holy and incorruptible, without doubt the cornerstones of the church? Since God on account of their prodigious merits has bestowed on them immortal felicity, it would be impious indeed and contrary to His judgement if men neglected the glorification, praise and veneration of such holy men. Since therefore in our time almost all have seen or heard that Giovanni da Capistrano, of the minorite order, has led a celestial life on earth, and, following the footsteps of holy Francis, showed signs of the highest humility, patience and charity, and also added to the purest morals extraordinary learning by which he subjected many mortals to the yoke of religion and led them to reform their lives by his preaching of the evangelical doctrine throughout the Christian world. On behalf of the Christian faith he showed himself to be a sturdy champion who moved many Christians to protect the Catholic faith against the barbarians. Finally he had such a reputation by nature that all confessed him to be a holy and innocent man, and so it must be the duty of all . . . to protect the memory of such a man and to endeavour to honour him worthily with every kind of effort, zeal and esteem so that this ornament of our age is placed in the catalogue of saints in the usual manner, thus receiving the fullest reward for his virtue not only in heaven but also on earth; indeed, we think that his prayers to God will be of great benefit to the human race and especially to those who, with grateful and pious devotion, will venerate his name.[65]

[65]  ASF, Miss. 42, fol. 135v–136v: Recte quidem institutum est ut qui abiectis mundi ordibus integros se castosque servarunt, et amore Christi flagrantes nullum pro eius tuendis preceptis laborem, nullum periculum, nullas contumelias, non denique mortem recusarunt, quorum doctrina vel vite sanctitas et pie pro cunctis preces plurimum humano genero profuerunt, vel ad terrenam salutem vel ad divinam felicitatem postquam ad eum a quo profecti erant redierunt, terrenos exuti artus, velut sancti celestis participes numeris celebrentur, eorumque nomen inter solemnia sacra sempiterna memoria referatur. Sic enim dignus virtuti habetur honos et mortales reliqui eorum permoti exemplis ardentius in deum rapiuntur, necnon Christi ecclesia talibus subnixa

Accolti, however, was not content only to restore the chancery to the standards which had been reached before Poggio's term; he initiated extensive reforms which earn for him a place besides his predecessors Salutati, Bruni and Marsuppini and his successor Scala as one of the principal reformers in the history of the Florentine chancery. As a result of one of his reforms, both the chancellor and his assistant were placed in a better position to form an overview of Florentine diplomacy and its development. A disadvantage of increasingly specialized chancery procedures during the fourteenth and fifteenth centuries had been the trend for the different areas of diplomacy to become separated; instead of one overall

testibus clarior evadit quotidie atque illustrior, gratum erga illos exercens opus, quorum suffragiis ac meritis plurimum aucta roborata est. Itaque ad omnes christianos pertinet presertim illos quorum auctoritas eminet eiusmodi memoriam hominum non deleri sinere, sed pro viribus vehementer niti quod ea perpetua gloria posteritati consecretur. Nam si veteres illi homines multos ob virtutis inanem famam velut deos coluerunt, quanto equius est nos illos venerari et colere qui vere sancti et incorrupti apparuerunt, procul dubio ecclesie angulares lapides, quos cum deus ob ingentia merita sui participes fecerit immortali felicitate decoratos, impium profecto esset et eius adversum iudicio, si homines eiusmodi sanctorum laudem, gloriam, venerationem negligere non formidarent. Cum ergo etate nostra viderint pene omnes aut audiverunt Joannem Capestranum minorum ordinis celestem in terris egisse vitam, et divi Francisci vestigiis inherentem, summe humilitatis, patientie, caritatis signa ostendisse, adiecisse quoque castissimis moribus doctrinam eximiam, qua mortales multos vel religioni colla subdere vel meliorem vite frugem capere provocarit, vigiliis fletui orationibus incubuisse, totum peragrasse Christianum orbem evangelicam doctrinam predicantem, proque illa se athletam fortissimum prestitisse, commonuisse Christianos multos ut Catholicam fidem adversus barbaros tuerentur. Cum ea denique fama nature concessisset, ut omnes sanctum et innocentem hominem fuisse illum fateantur, omnium opus sed imprimis vestrum esse debet tanti viri memoriam tueri atque illam honoribus dignis afficere omni studio, industria, caritate niti ut hic etatis nostre decus in sanctorum cathologo solito more referatur, habiturus ex hoc sue virtutis nedum in celo sed in terris quoque amplissimum premium, cuius apud Deum preces multum humano generi profuturas arbitramur et presertim illis qui suum nomen grata et pia devotione prosequentur. Cf. also his letter of congratulations to Siena on the canonization of St Catherine: *ibid.*, 43, fol. 146r–v. For more letters with notable religious passages, cf. ASF, Miss. 42, fol. 76v–77r; *ibid.*, 43, fol. 141r (the contribution of the Guelf party to the religious life of Florence).

    Other letters by Accolti with notable *exordia* are: Miss. 42, fol. 95v (in praise of peace), 125v (against calumny), 128v (about adultery), fol. 160v (Florentine relations with France); Miss. 43, fol. 63r (church government), fol. 124r–v (about trade with infidels and excommunication of Florentine merchants by the Florentine archbishop), fol. 147r–v (liberal arts); Miss. 44, fol. 64r (concord and discord), fol. 84v (justice), fol. 108v (the Neapolitan wars in the 1460s), fol. 140v (crusade). As in Marsuppini's chancellorship, there was a decline in complexity and eloquence in Accolti's letters during the last two or three years of his chancellorship.

    Other letters by Accolti with *exordia*, albeit not so notable as those already mentioned: ASF, Miss. 42, fol. 50v, 51r, 52r–v, 56v, 59r–v, 62v, 65v, 66v–67r, 67v, 68r, 68v, 73v, 74r, 78v, 79r, 83v, 87r, 88r–v, 89v–90r, 93v, 101v, 108r, 111r, 118r, 120r, 122v, 123r, 123v, 129v–130r, 130v, 131v, 132v, 139v–140r, 147v, 166r–v, 172v, 177v, 178v, 181v–182r, 183r–v; Miss. 43, fol. 2r, 3r–v, 12v, 14v–15r, 15v, 16r, 18r, 26r–27r, 37r–v, 48r–49r, 51r, 66r–v, 67v, 71v, 75r, 76r, 82v–83r, 85r, 85v, 105v, 110r, 114r–v, 114v–115r, 126v, 130r, 131v, 140v, 146r, 148r, 149r–v, 157r, 161r–v, 171r–v, 180r–v, 180v–181r, 181v, 183r, 188r; Miss. 44, fol. 2v, 4r, 7v, 10v, 14v–15r, 18r, 20r, 22v, 31v, 46r, 53r–v, 55v, 58r, 64v, 66v, 71r, 87v, 116v, 149v, 150r, 161r.

administrative procedure for all diplomatic business, there was a tendency
for the Signoria's diplomacy to be conducted and administered in two
distinct areas – by letters to foreign governments on the one hand and by
ambassadors on the other. Each type of business had its own records and
the possibility of contradictions in policy or of failure to perceive the
general direction of diplomacy is obvious; this danger was even more pronounced when many different notaries were working in the chancery, as
for example under Poggio. Accolti went some way to remove the possibility of diplomatic blundering by placing the same notary, Bastiano
Foresi, in full charge of both ambassadorial business and foreign letters.
However, the system still depended for a safeguard on Accolti's and
Foresi's personal alertness and memory, and evidently this was not enough
for Accolti, who after nine months in office instructed Foresi to keep a new
kind of register coordinating all the Signoria's diplomatic business. This
was called a *quaternus*, containing 'all deliberations made by the priors
and colleges or by the priors alone'.[66] It did not correspond to the records
of the ordinary deliberations of the Signoria and colleges, which were kept
by the notary of the Signoria, nor to their special deliberations, which were
the responsibility of the notary of the Riformaigioni. Rather the *quaternus*
was a diary of all diplomatic business carried out by the chancellor, noting
the letters sent by the Signoria to foreign governments, foreigners and
Florentine ambassadors as well as indicating the deliberations whereby
ambassadors were elected by the Signoria, the colleges and the council of
one hundred. Entries were made according to the day on which the business was conducted and therefore it comprised a day-to-day account of
all the work of the first chancellor with the exception of minuting the
*pratiche*. The language used was notarial Latin, suggesting that it was
intended for chancery use, since records of the first chancery under Accolti
intended for use of the government as well as the chancery, such as the
'Consulte e pratiche', 'Legazioni e commissarie' and 'Missive', were composed in an elevated literary style. It often gives additional information,
such as the name of the person who carried a letter or the number of votes
by which a measure was approved by the Signoria.[67] It is a complete
record of all letters sent by the Signoria between 1 January 1459 and
28 June 1468, but a few elections of ambassadors were omitted.[68] Its value
as a work of quick reference to past Florentine diplomacy and as a guide
to diplomatic business in progress must have been considerable, and it is
not surprising that Accolti's successor, Bartolomeo Scala, continued to

---

[66] Published by Del Piazzo, *Il protocollo*. Cf. *ibid.*, 21, for the title.
[67] *Ibid.*, 25, 33, 35, 39 etc.
[68] E.g. the elections of Pietro Acciaiuoli on 7 March 1462 (ab inc.) and Otto Niccolini on
25 August 1463 were omitted; cf. ASF, LC, 15, fol. 81v, 92r.

have this diary kept, during the first years of his administration, by his own coadjutors in the first chancery.[69]

It has been stated that such a calendar of correspondence and business was a novel secretarial procedure in the fifteenth century,[70] and it is true that there was no other comprehensive guide to the diplomatic business of the Signoria before Accolti's *quaternus*. However, it is incorrect to say that there is no similar register among the records of the Florentine republic and that subsequently its nearest relative would be the protocol of letters kept in Lorenzo de' Medici's private secretariat.[71] In fact, the *quaternus* clearly was evolved from the series of registers now known as the *missive* of the second chancery.[72] Two volumes of this series exist for the years 1441 to 1445 and then there is a long lacuna until 1470, after which there is a regular series of registers until 1532.[73] It is actually a misnomer to refer to the first two volumes of this series as *missive* of the second chancery, as is clear from their title captions which, far from stating that these volumes record the work of the second chancery, instead refer to the chancery as a whole, declaring that they 'contain letters, injunctions, safe-conducts and many other writings pertaining to and regarding the office of the chancery' and that the chancellors then serving were Leonardo Bruni and Giovanni Guiducci, in other words, both the first and second chancellors;[74] in them, letters and mandates are not copied in full as in the volumes of the first chancellor's *missive* and *legazioni* but are only summarized.[75] These two volumes are in fact a full record of the business conducted by the second chancellor and his staff, who, it has been seen, still continued to do a great deal of work for the first chancellor, Leonardo Bruni.[76] These two volumes, therefore, constitute a calendar or diary of the work of the second

---

[69] The *quaternus* (ASF, CdC, 64) was written entirely by Foresi until fol. 45r (18 March 1464 (ab inc.)). Thereafter his hand alternates with a new hand until 23 April 1465 (fol. 46r) when it is replaced definitively by the new hand. On Scala's continued use of the *quaternus*, cf. Del Piazzo, 179ff.; Brown, *Scala*, 139ff.

[70] Del Piazzo, *Il protocollo*, 5.

[71] Cf. *Protocolli del carteggio di Lorenzo il Magnifico per gli anni 1473–4, 1477–92*, ed. M. Del Piazzo (Florence, 1956).

[72] I am very grateful to Dott. Daniela De Rosa for suggesting to me the resemblance between the *quaternus* and the volumes of the second chancery.

[73] Cf. Marzi, *La cancelleria*, 529–30.

[74] E.g. cf. ASF, Miss. 2a, 1, fol. 37r: In dei nomine amen. Hic est liber sive quaternus in se continens litteras, precepta, salvoconductus et quam pluras alias scripturas pertinentes et spectantes ad officium cancellarie factus, editus et compositus pro magnifico et victorioso populo et commune Florentie, existentibus magnificis et gloriosissimis dominis dominis prioribus artium et vexillifero iustitie . . . existentibus eorum cancellariis spectabilibus viris domino Leonardo Francisci Bruni et ser Johanne Guiduccii.

[75] E.g. [7 May 1442] fol. 86v: Duci Janue et domino Baptiste de Campofregoso, responsiva suis et quod de eorum amoris redintegratione dominatio gratulatur. Cf. Del Piazzo, *Il protocollo*, *passim*, for the similarity in the style of entries with Accolti's *quaternus*.

[76] Cf. p. 119, *supra*.

chancery, just as Accolti's *quaternus* was a calendar of the work of the first chancery. Another point of similarity is that these volumes are exactly the same long, rectangular shape as Accolti's *quaternus*, in contrast to the other volumes of the first chancery which are shorter and wider. Finally, it is clear that Accolti's *quaternus* evolved from these second chancery records from the fact that when foreign and ambassadorial letters in these second chancery volumes were copied out in full in the principal *missive* and *legazioni* of the first chancery a capital 'R' was written in the left-hand margin;[77] this practice of writing 'R' against registered letters was adopted on the first three folios of Accolti's *quaternus* but then gradually phased out,[78] evidently because the vast majority of letters in Accolti's *quaternus* were registered,[79] whereas in the earlier second chancery volumes only a relatively smaller proportion of the business transacted by the second chancery were important state letters of which it was necessary to preserve a full copy.[80]

Although Accolti's *quaternus* therefore had its forerunners in the chancery, nevertheless it did constitute an important innovation in procedures of the chancery. The second chancery volumes provided a record of the activities of the second chancery staff and a full summary to the Signoria's correspondence with its subject dominions but only a sporadic guide to the Signoria's foreign diplomacy. Accolti's *quaternus*, although composed in a form deriving from the second chancery volumes, served a new purpose: neither a summary of unregistered letters nor an index of letters registered elsewhere, it was instead a comprehensive guide to the Florentine Signoria's diplomacy as a whole. Accolti therefore created a new and important chancery procedure out of existing elements, just as other constitutional innovations in Florence at this time were being developed out of elements of previous institutions. In fact, this calendar of diplomacy was begun on 1 January 1459, the very day on which the new legislative council of one hundred was inaugurated.[81] This council's purpose in fact was an innovation: to give a permanent place in governmental office to members of the ruling group as well as to restrict the legislative initiative of the ancient councils; nevertheless, its structure clearly evolved from elements inherited from previous Balìe and *ad hoc* councils.[82] Indeed, it is likely that Accolti's new administrative procedure in the chancery was initiated in the

[77] Cf. ASF, Miss. 2a, 1, fol. 19v, 53v, 55v, 62v, 63v, 64r, 64v, 77r, 80r etc.; 2, fol. 3r, 7v, 8v, 13v, 27r, 27v etc. The 'R' was an abbreviation for 'reservata copia' or 'registrata': cf. ASF, Miss. 2a, 1, fol. 132v where these two abbreviations are spelled out.
[78] ASF, CdC, 64: 'R' appears regularly in the left margin for fol. 1r–3r, then not until 28v, 29r, 29v, 20r, 31r and then no longer.
[79] For the registration of Accolti's letters in the *quaternus*, cf. Del Piazzo, *Il protocollo*, passim.
[80] Cf. p. 119, *supra*.
[81] As is suggested by Del Piazzo, *Il protocollo*, 7. [82] Cf. Rubinstein, *Government*, 113ff.

general spirit of governmental reform following the Parlamento and Balìa of 1458, which also led to the creation of the council of one hundred.

Accolti's reforms were not limited to administrative procedures of the chancery; he also introduced innovations which continued to earn for the Florentine chancery a place in the front ranks of the humanist *avant garde* in the mid-fifteenth century. One of these concerned the script used in the chancery.[83] Humanist cursive script had been developed in Florence in the 1420s by Niccolò Niccoli, who wanted to find a substitute for Italian gothic cursive (*bastarda* or *rotunda*) which would incorporate some of the innovations introduced into book hand by Poggio at the beginning of the fifteenth century.[84] Niccoli replaced the gothic uncial 'd' with a straight 'd', the gothic round 's' with a long 's' and the gothic round 2-shaped 'r' with a half-uncial 'r'; he eliminated gothic fusion of letters, he substituted a uniformly thin stroke for gothic shading, he replaced angular letters with rounded ones and he introduced a distinctively uniform slope to the right in his script.[85] The influence of Niccoli's reform of cursive script was soon felt in the Florentine chancery, where elements taken from Niccoli's script are found as early as the late 1420s.[86] However, the development of a chancery italic incorporating a preponderant number of Niccoli's reforms occurred only very gradually in the middle decades of the fifteenth century, and many of the notaries employed in the chancery showed little inclination to adopt the innovations of humanist cursive.[87] This conservatism prevailed during Bruni's and Marsuppini's chancellorships, and even Poggio, who had himself been the great innovator in the development of humanist book hand, employed for the most part notaries who were but slightly influenced by reforms in humanist cursive. Indeed, the two principal notaries who served under Poggio used undistinguished, conservative hands: Antonio Muzi, the vice-chancellor, used extensively the gothic 's' in the shape of a '6', fused the 'e' with the preceding letter, and had a very prominent 'd' with an enlarged upper loop characteristic of Italian chancery *bastarda*. He showed a tendency, however, to avoid the thickening and thinning of the stroke typical of gothic, a characteristic which he shared with Poggio's other principal notary, Niccolò Pardi,[88] whose script was perhaps less conservative on the whole than Muzi's. Pardi showed a preference for the long 's' and avoided gothic fusions; however, he still had a penchant for the gothic round 'r' and almost invariably used the uncial 'd'. Moreover, neither Muzi nor Pardi showed any tendency to slope his script to the right. The least conservative scribe who regularly worked in

---

[83] Herde, 'Die Schrift' is the fundamental study.
[84] Cf. Ullman, *Humanistic Script*, 59–77.    [85] *Ibid.*; Herde, 'Die Schrift', 306–7.
[86] *Ibid.*, 317–20.    [87] *Ibid.*, 313–14, 317–23.
[88] Cf. *ibid.*, table III, n. 5, for an example of Pardi's hand, unidentified by Herde.

the chancery at the end of Marsuppini's tenure of office and throughout
Poggio's chancellorship was Bastiano Foresi, who occupied in that period
a position junior to those of Muzi and Pardi.[89] However, it was Foresi
whom Accolti appointed his coadjutor in the first chancery, bringing him
back from private notarial practice,[90] whereas he excluded the more traditional scribes Muzi and Pardi from a role in preparing first chancery
documents.[91] Foresi is really the first scribe in the Florentine chancery who
can be described as having a chancery italic hand.[92] He retained a number
of features from gothic chancery cursive, as of course did Niccoli himself,
who kept for example the gothic rounded 'a'; indeed, mature chancery
italic of the later fifteenth century was a hybrid derived from elements of
both gothic and humanist script.[93] However, Foresi's script, with its
uniform slope to the right, its preference for straight 'd', half-uncial 'r', and
long 's', its rounded letters, its even pen-stroke, and clear separation
between letters, is an excellent example of the humanist chancery italic
which became prevalent in Italian secretariats in the later fifteenth century.
Indeed, Bastiano Foresi seems to have been recognized as a scribe of
superior quality during the period that he worked in the Florentine chancery, as is clear from a formulary of sample letters, titles and salutations
which he prepared for chancery use.[94] An autograph manuscript of
Foresi's, this formulary is a finished book prepared in a form suitable for
publication and preservation like a high-quality literary work: it has a
hard, wooden cover found usually on expensive books; it is written on fine
vellum; and it has an illuminated initialled first page and coloured head-

[89]   Luiso, 'Riforma', 141.
[90]   Foresi's hand last appears in the registers of the chancery before Accolti's term of office
       in ASF, LC, 14, fol. 38r–39v (9 March 1456 (ab inc.)). After this he worked regularly as
       a private notary, sometimes completing as many as five different pieces of business in the
       same day: cf. ASF, Not.A., S 500, fol. 1r–21r (2 March 1456 (ab inc.) to April 1458). In
       none of the pieces of private business did he mention working in the Palazzo della
       Signoria, but almost immediately after he began working for Accolti, he began to conduct
       his private notarial business in the palace: cf. *ibid.*, fol. 21r (5 May 1458) Actum in
       cancelleria dominorum, fol. 21v: in cancelleria dominorum (7 June 1458), Actum in
       palatio populi florentinorum (17 July 1458); moreover, he did far less private business
       after this time: all his private business for the six years of Accolti's chancellorship
       occupies fol. 21r–27r.
[91]   Cf. p. 139, *supra*.
[92]   This is Herde's conclusion about Foresi's script ('Die Schrift', n. 92, p. 323), but he did
       not identify the writer as Foresi.
[93]   Cf. table VI, n. 11 in Herde, 'Die Schrift', for an example of Foresi's script. Herde (n. 91,
       pp. 322–3) points out that a scribe such as Antonio Sinibaldi continued to use the round
       's' at the end of a work, a characteristic of Gothic script: e.g. Ullman, *Humanistic Script*,
       plate 66, for this practice in Sinibaldi's humanist cursive.
[94]   ASF, CdC, 59: fol. 1r: Questo libreto et di Piero di Matteo di Cosimo Bartolli proprio
       [sixteenth-century hand]; fol. 2r–11r: formulary for titles of recipients of letters; fol.
       12r–39v: sample letters and orations; fol. 57v: Italian poem written in the hand of the
       sixteenth-century owner, Piero Bartoli.

ings and decorated initials throughout.[95] Moreover, it is written in a fine, cursive chancery italic script, not entirely dissimilar to that often used for literary manuscripts in the second half of the fifteenth century.[96] This book was clearly meant not only as an exemplar of chancery *formulae* and style but also to inspire future generations of chancery staff to strive for the highest possible standards of script in their everyday work; the fact that it was entrusted to Foresi suggests his preeminent position as a scribe in the chancery during the 1450s and early 1460s,[97] and it was to Benedetto Accolti's credit that he took the decisive step of employing Foresi as his only scribe in the first chancery, thus for the first time winning a preponderant place for chancery italic at the highest levels of the Florentine administration. Indeed, Accolti himself had a personal admiration for humanist script, as is shown by the scribes to whom he entrusted the two literary works which he completed as chancellor. The unidentified scribe of Vat. Ottob. Lat. 1291 (a Livy made for Antonello Petrucci),[98] who made the presentation copy of Accolti's *Dialogus* (Bibl. Laur. 54, 8)[99] 'wrote a fine humanist hand'[100] and received commissions for several important manuscripts in the mid-fifteenth century;[101] moreover, ser Gherardo del Ciriagio, who made the presentation copy of Accolti's history (Bibl. Laur. 54, 6)[102] was 'the dominant figure among the scribes of the third quarter of the century' in Florence.[103]

One of the most important reforms undertaken by Accolti concerned the minutes of the debates in the *pratiche*. While Bruni was chancellor the debates were recorded in much the same way as they had been during the fourteenth century. Notes were probably made by the chancellor or his assistant during the meetings, and these were subsequently copied into the registers that are extant today. There was probably no intermediate copy, because the minutes were not copied in book-hand or elegant cursive, but

---

[95] Cf. *ibid.*, fol. 2r, 12r, for the best examples of illumination.

[96] Cf. Ullman, *Humanistic Script*, 120, 124–5, for examples of humanist and classical authors copied by Antonio Sinibaldi and Pietro Cennini in italic cursive script in the second half of the fifteenth century.

[97] In fact, Foresi became an important humanist scribe in Florence in the later fifteenth century: Dr de la Mare has identified twenty or so manuscripts which can now be attributed to Foresi, and we plan to collaborate on a study of Foresi's work as a scribe of classical and humanist manuscripts as well as in the chancery.

[98] Cf. A. de la Mare, 'The book trade', in A. M. Brown and A. de la Mare, 'Bartolomeo Scala's dealings with booksellers, scribes and illuminators, 1459–63', JWCI, xxxix (1976), 243–44.

[99] I am extremely grateful to Dr de la Mare for identifying the scribe of this manuscript for me.

[100] *Ibid.*  [101] *Ibid.*

[102] I am again extremely grateful to Dr de laMare for identifying ser Gherardo as the scribe of this manuscript.

[103] Ullman, *Humanistic Script*, 111; cf. *ibid.*, 111ff., for further discussion of Gherardo and identifications of other manuscripts copied by him.

only in neat everyday chancery script. Moreover, their language was simple and direct; no attempt was made to rewrite the debates in a literary style. They were constructed in the third person, but not in true indirect discourse since frequently the first person plural was used. Moreover, clauses of indirect speech were introduced by *quod* instead of being constructed with the infinitive.[104] While Marsuppini was chancellor the debates continued to be translated in simple language and written in ordinary script; however, there was an attempt to purify the Latin style of the minutes, so that indirect discourse was sometimes constructed with the infinitive. Nevertheless, there were frequent lapses into indirect speech constructed with *quod*, not to mention many examples of incorrect grammar, suggesting that the minutes were still transcribed directly from notes made at the meetings and that the use of purer Latin in the *pratiche* minutes had not yet become official chancery procedure.[105] It has already been pointed out that under Poggio the condition of the records of the *pratiche* deteriorated drastically. They were written in extremely careless script and may not even have been a copy but the actual notes made at the meetings. The occasional improvement in Latin grammar that had occurred under Marsuppini was at first maintained, but by 1456 any attempt to introduce purer Latin seems to have been abandoned.[106] Accolti however instituted

---

[104] E.g. ASF, CP, 51, fol. 47r: Die iii iulii 1435. Dominus Angelus de Acciaiulis, dominus Petrus de Beccanigis retulerunt pro se et infrascriptis quod scriberetur Taliano Capitaneo in forma que lecta fuit per cancellerium, cuius erat effectus quod licet non venerit tota armata sed . . . For more examples, cf. *Appendice di documenti tratti dal R. Archivio di Stato di Firenze* (Pisa, 1891), ed. F. C. Pellegrini, xxxiii ff., xli ff., xlviii ff., etc.

[105] E.g. ASF, CP, 52, fol. 51r: Die v Junii 1448. Consultum est de tuenda re publica et precipue qua via pecunia parari possit.

Dominus Johannotius de Pittis dixit, cum ex presenti onerum distributione exigantur quinquaginta milia florenorum, est necesse quod provideatur de novo onere. Et quod fiat cum quanta equalitate fieri potest. Et quod dentur socii civibus vestris in supportandis oneribus et tandem conclusit quod fiat pratica cum paucis delectis civibus.

Dominus Carolus de Federighis dixit opus esse novo modo tributorum. Attamen, si fieri posset, esset providendum illis qui minus onerati sunt. Si hoc non fiat, cum paucis ut superior dixit de modo novi tributi esse consulendum.

Dominus Johannes Pieri de Bertaldis dixit materiam esse gravem magnique momenti, tributaque esse mutanda. Tempus tamen adversarii. Iccirco cum paucis quid agendum sit esse consulendum. Idque etiam aliis nonnullis placere dixit.

[106] Cf. ASF, e.g. CP, 53, fol. 86r–86v: Die iii° Julii 1454. Consilium agitatum per infrascriptos cives coram magnificis dominis, quorum nomine vexillifer iustitie proposuit . . . utrum reliquie quedam sancte et liber evangeliorum grece scriptus ac mirifice ornatus sint emende . . .

Dominus Orlandus de Medicis dixit se locuturum primum ut det allis viam loquendi. Dominos sumopere de eorum diligentia commendavit, et quod earum que veniebant in consultationem, erat faciendum principium a rebus religionis et ad cultum dei pertinentibus. Cum igitur Florentiam venerint reliquie de quibus loquatur et non attulisset illo grecus nisi casu Constantinopolis accedisset, hortatus est ut emantur, tum pro cultu religionis, tum pro honore civitatis nostre. Existimabat quod expeditissimum et aptissimum medium esset dare operam, ut ars lane emat, quia curam habeant maioris

a radical change in the minuting of the *pratiche*. In the first place, he rigorously adhered to correct Latin grammar in the text, going further even than Marsuppini in insisting on indirect discourse constructed at all times with the infinitive. Moreover, his assistant, Bastiano Foresi, now made a fair copy of the debates in a fine, calligraphic cursive script, the same as that used for the copies of the official *missive*. A fair copy compiled with such care would seem to presuppose an intermediate set of minutes existing between the notes and the finished copy, and that is further suggested by the language of the debates. For whereas under Marsuppini the debates had been transcribed in simple and often correct Latin, the fair copies of the debates made under Accolti were composed in indirect discourse of such complexity as to resemble the reported speeches of Roman historians. Thus in a speech given by Matteo Palmieri in 1449 while Marsuppini was chancellor, the grammar is correct but the style is simple.[107] On the other hand, the speeches made by Palmieri while Accolti was chancellor are more elaborate in style as well as more complex in argument: for example, in 1460 he began a speech on ecclesiastical taxation with an introduction on the different types of republic.[108]

Moreover, there is evidence that the differences of both content and form apparent in the speeches of the *pratiche* after 1458 did not result from changes in the manner in which the speeches were actually delivered but rather were the work of Accolti himself. For a page of what were the notes made at a meeting of the *pratiche* while Accolti was chancellor has survived, in addition to the finished copy of the same debate, which occurred on 24 February 1461.[109] The rough copy is an autograph of Foresi's and it was recorded at the meeting itself since each of the speakers signed in his own hand at the end of the debate, confirming that he agreed with what

---

ecclesie, que, ubi illa receperit, erit honoratior. Quod si alius modus melior reperietur ad eas comparandas, ille capiatur, ita ut omino remaneant Florentie . . . These debates from early in Poggio's chancellorship show that some effort was being made to purify the Latin, but that it was not entirely successful; they contrast markedly with the *pratiche* after 1456 when there was no attempt to use classical syntax for the debates: cf. e.g. Walser, *Poggius*, 404–5.

[107] ASF, CP, 52, fol. 76r: Nihil prudentius esse quam pericula rei publice eiusque status antea quam eveniat providere. Nec dubium esse securius fore marsupia esse aperta quam clausa. Et quamvis videatur magis populare ut claudantur, tamen illi popularitati securitatem anteponendam. Nec ad sex menses esse reducendum cum id magis ad albas quam ad nigras provocaret. Et tandem securitati dixit esse prospiciendum.

[108] ASF, CP, 56, fol. 60r–v: Si quis recte velit consulere, considerare ipsum debere duas esse republicas: unam particularem, id est, eam civitatem in qua quis origine vel constitutione sit civis et pro illa tuenda aut servanda quemquem civem debere fortunas, liberos et vitam denique suam exponere, quoniam a natura ipsa et a legibus decretum est ut ipsam rem publicam cunctis aliis rebus preferamur; alteram vero esse rem publicam universalem Christianorum omnium qui obligati sunt ad tuendam Christianam fidem adversus barbaros.

[109] *Ibid.*, fol. 140v–141v (finished version), fol. 160r–v (rough version).

had been advised by the *pratica*.[110] It appears to have been bound by accident in the register of fair copies, and is complete in itself with the date
written at the top of the page indicating the beginning of the debate. With
regard to content the two versions differ significantly. The first important
divergence between the versions is that the rough copy does not include the
speech with which the Gonfalonier of Justice introduced the subject to be
discussed.[111] This speech might have been omitted accidentally in the
minutes; on the other hand, on this occasion no introduction by the
Gonfalonier may have been given and in order to make the records appear
consistent a speech was invented. This explanation perhaps seems more
likely in view of other differences between the versions, for it was clearly
the chancellor's intention to convert rough and simple statements into
polished classical prose. Whereas according to the rough version Manno
Temperani said, 'Verba sua futura brevia', in the finished copy he more
eloquently states, 'Rem hanc longiorem orationem non poscere'; in the
rough copy he continues, saying, 'Posse ipsum adhibere remedia que nobis
obirentur et cogerent cives ad mutandam opinionem', whereas in the
finished version he says more elegantly, 'Satius esse libenter cives illi
obsequi quam coactos postea et invitos mutare voluntatem; habere enim
pontificem remedia plurima quibus cum ignominia et dedecore compeleret
civitatem ut sibi obtemperaret.'[112] Otto Niccolini similarly in the first

---

110  *Ibid.*, fol. 160v: Io Manno Temperani sono chontento a quanto di sopra è chonsigliato.
Io Octo di Lapo Nicholini doctor legum sono contento a quanto di sopra è consigliato.
Io Francesco Ventura sono contento a quanto di sopra è consiglato. Io Giovanni Bartoli
sono chontento chome di sopra. Io Franco di Niccol Sacchetti sono contento quanto di
sopra è consiglato. Io Dietisalvi di Nerone di Nigi sono contento di quanto di sopra è
consigliato. Io Luigi di Piero Ghuicardini sono cotento a quanto di sopra è stato consigliato. Io Lodovicho di Ciecie da Verazano son chontento a quanto di sopra è consigliato.
Io Bernardo de' Medici sono chontento chome di sopra. Io Luigi Ridolfi afermo come
sopra. Io Giovanni Chanigiani son chontetto chome di sopra. Io Antonio di Puccio son
chontento chome di sobra.

111  *Ibid.*, fol. 160v: Die xxiiii Februarii 1460. Proposuit magnificus dominus vexillifer
venisse ad dominos pontificis nuntium cum suis litteris petentem ut exactas decimas in
florentino agro a clericis pontifici dari permitterent. Ipsum enim habere in animo cogere
pecunias ex eiusmodi decimis ab omnibus clericis non ob aliam causam nisi ut
expeditionem in Teucros Mantue destinatam preparet pro salute Christiani nominis. Nec
debere sibi amico pontifici rem hanc negari que nulli alteri negata est, utpote pro comuni
causa nitenti et clericorum omnium legiptimo domino. Quamobrem convocasse
dominos ipsos cives ut ex eis intelligant quid respondendum videatur presertim cum alias
pontifici assensa civitas sit ut eiusmodi pecunias exigeret.

112  Cf. *ibid.*, fol. 160r and 140v:

| | |
|---|---|
| Dominus Mannus dixit verba sua futura brevia, quoniam materia requirit brevitatem sermonis, quoniam que petit pontifex denigari sibi non potest. Preterea posse ipsum adhibere remedia que nobis obirent et cogerent cives ad mutandam opinionem. Esse preterea civitatem in | Dominus Mannus dixit rem hanc longiorem orationem non poscere quoniam satis cuique patere potest petitionem pontificis adeo iustam et equam esse, ut honeste negari nullo modo queat. Omnes enim scire ac fateri pontificem potestatem habere de clericis |

version says, 'Nec esse parem conditionem Florentinorum et aliorum esse', but in the final copy he is made to say, 'Aliam enim esse cum pontifice Florentinorum conditionem, aliam aliorum esse'.[113] All the revisions made in the finished version involve improving the style of the rough copy, but

magna felicitate quam unquam fuerit, reputare presertim ex navigatione triremenium que cum magna reputatione reversure sunt. Procedere vero felicitatem ex pluribus, id est, ex bona ministaratione iustitie et gubernatione civitatum. Accedere preterea benevolentiam omnium principum qui circa sunt, que, si servabitur, continuo civitas in pace futura est. Ergo ad conservandam eam opus esse id agere ut illis non displiceatur et que sunt Cesaris Cesario et Domini Domino dentur. Itaque pertinentia ad pontificem illi non deniganda modo aliquo. (rough version)

quemadmodum velit statuendi. Unde non posse illi negari quin decimas ab illis exigat presertim ob causam tam honestam que ad omnes pertineat. Ac satius esse libenter cives illi obsequi quam coactos postea et invitos mutare voluntatem. Habere enim pontificem remedia plurima quibus cum ignominia et dedecore compelleret civitatem ut sibi obtemperaret. Que cum felix vehementer sit ob plurimas causas quoniam in pace est et iuste ac sapienter regitur quodque omnes finitimi domini et principes eidem amicitia deiuncti sunt, laborandum vehementer esse ne talis ac tanta felicitas aliqua ex parte auferatur. Id vero facile fieri posse, si pax et iustitia domi maneat, foris vero benivolentia conservetur. Non ergo irritari pontificem oportere ne hostis pro amico efficiatur. Et que pontificis sunt illi danda esse, que vero ad nos pertinent conservanda. (finished version)

[113] *Ibid.*, fol. 160r and 141r:

Dominus Otto dixit se concordem esse cum his que dixit dominus Mannus et cum eo bene agendum esse.Meminisse preterea anno preterito fuisse de hoc consultatum et promissum ut exigarentur decime. Nec esse parem conditionem Florentinorum et aliorum cum pontifice ob plures causas et pertinere ad eos consentire pontifici et honorem in eo versari. Et dedecus in contrarium et onus apud omnes Christianos hoc intelligentes. Itaque videri sibi omnino consentendum pontifici. (rough version)

Dominus Otto dixit se concordem esse in eandem sententiam, presertim quia preterito anno cum de huiusmodi re agitatum esset vehementer inter plurimos cives, tandem omnes assensi sunt ut pontifici exactio decimarum permitteretur, nec capiendum exemplum esse ab aliis plurimis qui hoc denegarunt. Aliam enim esse cum pontifice Florentinorum conditionem, aliam aliorum esse ob plurimas causas, quas exprimere non sit opus. Quod si illi pergant contradicere voluntati pontificis, scandalum et discordiam nasci posse, ex quibus nil aliud nisi pernities evenire posset civitati, duabus ergo rebus in consultatione propositis, quarum una detrimentum prope certum, altera vero pacem et benivolentiam atque honorem allatura sit. Nemo dubius esse debet quin utilis via capienda sit atque inutilis respuenda, presertim quia honor magnus erit Florentinis dominis liberaliter consensisse ut pro tam pia et honorabili causa decime a suis clericis exigerentur. Ideoque videri sibi omnino pontificis voluntati obtemperandum esse. (finished version)

sometimes this was taken to the point of changing details of what had actually been argued. Thus Manno Temperani never in fact stated that the pope's request was just and equitable and that it was well known that he had full jurisdiction over the clergy; nevertheless, in the finished copy he is reported to have said, 'Satis cuique patere potest petitionem pontificis adeo iustam et equam esse et honeste negari nullo modo queat. Omnes enim scire ac fateri pontificem potestatem habere de clericis quemadmodum velit statuendi.' Moreover, his statement in the rough copy that the city was enjoying prosperity 'ex navigatione triremenium que cum magna reputatione reverse sunt' is omitted in the finished version.[114] In Otto Niccolini's original statement, too, it was not pointed out explicitly that there were two alternatives facing Florence – certain detriment or goodwill and peace;[115] and whereas Franco Sachetti in his original speech said merely, 'Audisse se quoque papam fuisse in dispositione ut prohiberet navigationem in damnum civitatis', in the final version he was reported to have said that it was at the Congress of Mantua in 1459 that the pope had been on the point of banning all trade with the Turks and that only with great difficulty had he been dissuaded from that course of action.[116] This evidence shows that it was the chancery itself, not the actual speakers, which was the source of the newly embellished arguments and more elaborate prose style characteristic of the *pratiche* after 1458.[117]

---

[114] Cf. pp. 160–1, n. 112, *supra.*     [115] Cf. p. 161, n. 113, *supra.*

[116] *Ibid.,* fol. 160r and 141r–v:

| | |
|---|---|
| Franchus Sachettus dixit se esse eiusdem iudicii cuius alii locuti sunt. Qui certam ab aliis gratiam et obsequium petunt, debunt illa facere. Audisse se quoque papam fuisse in dispositione ut prohibeat mercaturam apud barbaros. Si ergo negaretur, prohiberet navigationem in damnum civitatis. Et se et consentiri. (rough version) | Franchus Sacchettus dixit consuesse hanc rem publicam sepenumero ab aliis dominis obsequia plurima petere atque optare, nec spem esse alios eidem placituros, nisi et ipsi domini in rebus honestis plerunque aliis morem gerant. Nec quenque refragari posse quoniam iusta et honesta pontifex petat ob ea que ab aliis discussa sunt. Et imminere periculum si pape domini non assentirentur. Agitatum enim semel Mantue apud illum fuisse ut mercatores omnes ad barbaros cum mercibus navigare prohiberentur, et vix pontificem ab eo proposito mutatum fuisse. Quod si nunc pergerent homini negare illi decimarum solutionem, facile ipse indignatione commotus ad prohibendam nobis navigationem incitaretur cum maximo danno ac dedecore civitatis, que ex eiusmodi exercitio plurimum fructum capit. Unde videri sibi omnino pontifici adsentiendum. (finished version) |

[117] The role of the chancery in elaborating the speeches in the *pratiche*, demonstrated here for the period after 1458, must cast doubt on G. Brucker's recent conclusions regarding the changes in the content of the *pratiche* after Salutati's death. (Cf. *Civic World*, 284–94; *idem*, 'Humanism, politics and the social order in early Renaissance Florence',

Accolti took great care in composing his version of the *pratiche* debates and in the interests of eloquence did not hesitate to alter details of what was said. His concern did not cease once the finished version had been handed to Foresi to be copied; for he went over the final copy after it had been written, and changes and corrections in his handwriting may still be seen in registers. At times he added only a word that had apparently been omitted by Foresi; thus 'civitatem' was omitted from the sentence 'ob defectum exercitiorum quibus civitas hec semper crevit et substantata est fere civitatem defecisse'. At other times he added entire phrases which give the impression of having been fitted into a sentence already composed in order to give the argument greater clarity.[118] Thus, whereas on one occasion it was simply stated, 'attenta varietate fortune in rebus cunctis et quantum longo iam tempore civitas ista procul ab ea gubernatione fuit que salutem et gloriam civitatis soleat parere', he added in the margin to be inserted after *parere*, 'censuit omnino providendum esse ut meliore in loco poneretur', completing the argument of the speaker and making it quite clear what his advice to the *pratica* was.[119]

It is possible that Accolti's attempt to elevate the level of discourse in the *pratiche* to classical standards of eloquence is derived from a renewed emphasis on public speaking in the fifteenth century, principally among professional humanists but also among lawyers, clerics, diplomats and political officials. The history of oratory in the middle ages and Renaissance is still largely unexplored; but from the later twelfth century secular oratory was widely practised in Italy and under the influence of the general classical revival it became highly fashionable in the fifteenth century. The number of speeches surviving from the fifteenth century is much greater than from earlier centuries, and the new interest in oratory was reflected both in sermons and in vernacular speeches.[120] Perhaps related to this

*Florence and Venice: Comparisons and Relations*, ed. S. Bertelli, N. Rubinstein and C. H. Smyth, (Florence, 1979), i, 3–11). Brucker has observed that these changes consisted of more elaborate speeches, more citations from classical authors and more references to history, and that the 'first signs of this new style appear after Salutati's death in 1406', and 'proliferate after Leonardo Bruni's brief tenure as chancellor in 1411' (*Civic World*, 290). Any final judgement on Brucker's hypothesis must await a detailed study of the *pratiche* and chancery procedures in the years immediately following Salutati's death; nevertheless, it must be pointed out that Pietro di Mino, Salutati's successor after the brief tenure of Benedetto Fortini in 1406, was a member of the humanist *avant garde* (cf. Marzi, *La cancelleria*, 156–8; Salutati, *Epistolario*, iii, 422–33, 523–7, 556–67; Bruni *Epistolae*, ed. Mehus, ii, 169–70; Bruni, *Dialogue*, in *Prosatori latini*, ed. Garin, 76ff.) as was of course Bruni. In view of the extensive rewriting of *pratiche* minutes which took place in the mid-fifteenth century, it is possible that the changes noted by Brucker were the work of the chancery and did not signify new attitudes among the patriciate.
[118] ASF, CP, 55, fol. 24r.   [119] *Ibid.*, fol. 30r.
[120] Kristeller, *Renaissance Thought and its Sources*, 248–9, 324–5; A. Galletti, *L'eloquenza dalle origini al xvi secolo* (Milan, 1904–38), 538–94; Müllner, *Reden und Briefe*, passim; J. W. O'Malley, *Praise and Blame in Renaissance Rome* (Durham, N.

fashion for oratory was the growing importance of ambassadors in fifteenth-century Italian diplomacy.[121] Accompanying the ever-increasing number of non-resident and resident ambassadors were more and more occasions for formal oratory, and often in Florence amateur humanists such as Piero de' Pazzi or Bernardo de' Giugni, not to mention renowned professional scholars such as Giannozzo Manetti and Donato Acciaiuoli, were chosen to represent Florence abroad.[122]

Evidence that Accolti's reforms in the chancery were influenced by the fashion for oratory particularly in diplomacy is provided by another of his innovations. The series now known as 'Legazioni e commissarie, risposte verbali di oratori', which begins three months after Accolti took office, consists of formal speeches delivered by foreign ambassadors in Florence and the replies made by the Gonfalonier of Justice. There is only one register of these speeches extant from Accolti's term of office, the other volumes having been lost, but they resume after 1465, continuing until 1495. The reports of the orations were copied by Foresi in the same calligraphic, cursive script used for the *pratiche*, *missive* and *legazioni*, and their style was complex indirect discourse similar to that used to minute the *pratiche*. Thus on 14 April 1459 the papal ambassador came to Florence to announce that the pope would shortly be arriving in the city. His opening speech was elaborately recorded by Accolti,[123] as were the reply made by the Gonfalonier of Justice, Agnolo Vettori,[124] and the ambassador's closing remarks.[125] Such formal diplomatic proceedings had never before

---

Car., 1979); E. Santini, *Firenze e i suoi 'oratori' nel Quattrocento* (Milan, 1922); *idem*, 'La *protestatio de iustitia* nella Firenze medicea del secolo xv', Rin. x (1959), 33–106.

[121] Cf. G. Mattingly, *Renaissance Diplomacy* (Boston, 1955), ch. 5 and ff.

[122] Cf. Santini, *Firenze e i suoi 'oratori'*, *passim*.

[123] ASF, RVdO, 1, fol. 32v: Venit ad magnificos dominos Magister Stefanus prothonotarius et referendarius apostolice sedis, summi pontificis orator et, presentatis credentie litteris, dixit se missum a pontifice ut illis imprimis significaret pontificem ipsum brevi ad civitatem hanc cum sua curia venturum. Et quamquam existimet florentinos dominos pro summa in eum benivolentia, pro veteri consuetudine proque suis egregiis virtutibus ipsi pontifici debitum honorem exhibituros et omnem commoditatem curie facturos sue, tamen ipsum cupere ut vel domini ipsi vel deputandi ad hanc rem cives una cum oratore ipso de ordine agende rei, cum tempus aderit, colloquantur. Et legatus ipse, que agenda intelliget, pontifici suis litteris significabit.

[124] *Ibid.*, fol. 32v–33r: Respondit Angelus Vettorius magnificus vexillifer iustitie, dicens pergratum fuisse oratoris adventum ipsis dominis, et letissimis animis audivisse illos summum pontificem Christianorum omnium patrem virtute prestantissimum ad hanc civitatem brevi perventurum, presertim quoniam pontifex ipse semper Florentine urbi magnam benivolentiam ostendisset. Et quamquam meritus eidem honor haberi nequaquam possit, tamen adnixuros dominos ne quid omissum sit quod ad honorandum eum et curiales omnes et ad quecumque eorum commoda pertinere videatur. Et ob hoc plurimos delegisse cives prestantissimos qui omnia que in rem fore videbuntur diligenter statuant. Daturos quoque operam dominos ut cives illi de his rebus omnibus una cum oratore ipso colloquantur.

[125] *Ibid.*, fol. 33r. Respondit iterum legatus pontificis gratias agere magnificis dominis pro his que benigne obtulerunt. Et optime ab illis provisum esse qui, quoniam multis negotiis

been minuted by the Florentine chancery, and Accolti's wish to preserve such records in pure classical Latin shows how much he was influenced by the vogue for classical oratory in the fifteenth century.[126]

The new emphasis on public speaking which characterized the chancery reforms after 1458 also reflected Accolti's personal talents as an orator. Leonardo Bruni had distinguished himself in oratory as chancellor, particularly during the Council of Florence;[127] Marsuppini, however, although renowned as a lecturer on rhetoric and poetry, lacked confidence as a diplomatic orator, particularly when it was necessary to extemporize.[128] A talent for spontaneous public speaking in Latin was highly desirable in a chancellor, who by the mid-fifteenth century was regularly asked to address ambassadors on behalf of the Signoria when Latin rather than Italian was the common language.[129] With his astounding memory and ability to extemporize in Latin, Accolti was the ideal chancellor, and when ambassadors from abroad came to Florence, Accolti was normally summoned to answer on behalf of the Signoria.[130] Once, according to Vespasiano,

the ambassador of the king of Hungary, a man of great eloquence, came and expounded his mission to the Signoria in Latin. Thereupon Messer Benedetto committed it to memory, wrote it out word for word in Latin, then translated it into the vernacular for the Signoria. Then having been called on by the Signoria to answer and having been instructed what to say, he composed his reply on the spot and delivered it in such a way that the ambassador, who was himself an extremely learned and eloquent man, was truly astonished. Messer Benedetto and the ambassador went out together, and when he praised Messer Benedetto for this feat, he repeated from memory the entire oration in Latin just as he had given it. According to what the ambassador himself told me, he was absolutely amazed that Accolti repeated it entirely without omitting a word, and he praised his intelligence and his memory, which he considered truly remarkable.[131]

In his efforts at reform, Accolti was given invaluable assistance by his coadjutor, Bastiano Foresi, a notary of very high calibre, who, despite his failure after Accolti's death in 1464 to advance further in the public

---

impliciti sunt, alios cives super hoc adventu pontificis celebrando delegerent. Et ipsum daturum operam ut cum illis adsit, et que honeste sciri potuerunt ab illis intelligat quisnam modus in pontifice honorando.

[126] One series in the Florentine archives containing entries from Accolti's chancellorship for which he was not responsible is Responsive, Copiari, consisting of copies of letters sent to the commune by foreign states, the first entry in which dates from 1453; this was begun by Scala in compliance with the orders of the Balìa of 1466: cf. Brown, *Scala*, 167.

[127] Cf. J. Gill, *The Council of Florence* (Cambridge, 1959), 183; E. Santini, 'La produzione volgare di L. Bruni Aretino', GStLI, lx (1912), 332–9.

[128] Cf. p. 111, *supra*.

[129] Cf. ASF, RVdO, 2, fol. 62r (11 January 1479): Quod oratio latina fuit, Magistratus iussu Cancellarius breviter respondit, as cited by Brown, *Scala*, 87, n. 71. Cf. also Marzi, *La cancelleria*, 293, quoting Parenti about Marcello Virgilio Adriani.

[130] Vespasiano, *Vite*, i, 596.    [131] *Ibid.*, 596–7.

service,[132] nevertheless made an important personal contribution to the history of the Florentine chancery during Accolti's term of office. Born on 1 January 1425, the son of Antonio di Zanobi di ser Forese, a Florentine money-changer,[133] Bastiano Foresi was practising as a notary in Florence by 1448,[134] and he was employed by Marsuppini as one of his coadjutors in the chancery not later than 24 September 1452, when his hand first appears in a register of *missive*.[135] This was the period in which the division between first and second chanceries was breaking down,[136] and it is possible that Foresi had been seconded from the second chancery, since in a poem he wrote many years later Foresi paid special tribute to the second chancellor, Giovanni Guiducci, calling him 'el mio Guiduccio' and including him in a list of the great humanist chancellors along with Bruni, Marsuppini, Poggio, Accolti and Scala;[137] Guiducci was obviously not in this league, and Foresi here gives the impression that he was paying tribute to a former benefactor. After Marsuppini's death in April 1453, Foresi continued to work as third coadjutor in the chancery at a salary of thirty-six florins a year,[138] and he continued to serve in the chancery under Poggio[139] but seems to have left between Poggio's retirement and Accolti's appointment.[140] Before the second half of the fifteenth century, there is little evidence to suggest that men employed in subordinate positions in the chancery were anything more than notaries and scribes,[141] but Foresi was

---

[132] Foresi continued to work in the chancery in the interregnum after Accolti's death on 26 September 1464 and Scala's appointment, of which the date is unknown for certain, although Brown (*Scala*, 44–5) offers evidence to suggest it was 24 April 1465. This is confirmed by the fact that Foresi's hand disappears definitively from the *quaternus* (ASF, CdC, 64) after 23 April 1465 (cf. fol. 46r), before which time he had shared duties with Alessandro Braccesi, who had begun work in the chancery on 18 March 1464 (ab. inc.): cf. *ibid.*, fol. 45r, for the first appearance of Braccesi's hand, and Brown, *Scala*, 45, n. 10. Thereafter Foresi became chancellor of the guild of builders (Ars magistrorum lapidis et lignanis), where he conducted much of his private notarial business (cf. ASF, Not.A., S 500, fol. 27v ff.) beginning on 6 June 1465, and where he continued to serve as late as 10 January 1488 (ab inc.): cf. *ibid.*, S 503, fol. 91v. Foresi, however, did make a brief reappearance in the chancery on 27 and 28 June 1468, when he made the last five entries in the *quaternus*: cf. ASF, CdC, 64, fol. 60r.

[133] Del Piazzo, *Il protocollo*, 8–9.     [134] Cf. ASF, Not.A., S 499, fol. 1r.

[135] BRF, Big. 193, fol. 62r–v.     [136] Cf. Luiso, 'Riforma', 138–40.

[137] BNF, Magl. VII, 816, fol. 52v: V'è L'Aretino, che col suo chiaro stile/ Risurger fa le già perdute carte/ Dell'eloquenzia, che cotanto avile/ Inanzi a llui per gran tempo si trouva/, Col Marsupino e nel medesimo ovile/ El mio Guiduccio et con sua degna pruova,/ Ma'l Bracciolin gli avanza di paraggio/ Per le sue opre ch'al futur gli giova./ L'Acolto in questo loco è dextro e saggio,/ Lo Scala monstra che virtù 'l conduce/ Far degne pruove nel suo fatal raggio. The lines on Scala have been published by Brown, *Scala*, 209.

[138] Cf. Luiso, 'Riforma', 141.     [139] Cf. pp. 89–90, *supra*.     [140] Cf. p. 100, *supra*.

[141] Before their appointments to the chancellorship, Salutati had been notary of the Tratte and Pietro di Mino had been chancellor to the Guelf party; ser Filippo Pieruzzi, notary of the Riformagioni from 1429 to 1444, had an interest in the humanities. However, these offices were not subordinate to the chancellor, and I know of no coadjutor to the chancellor with a humanist background before Foresi.

exceptional in having had the benefit of a good humanist education. His humanist interests are clear, in the first place, from the two long vernacular poems he composed later in life;[142] by no means popular lyrics, these are weighty compositions, revealing Foresi's wide knowledge of ancient and humanist literature, history and philosophy.[143] Moreover, Foresi prefaced to one of these poems a dedicatory letter to Lorenzo de' Medici which, composed in humanist Latin, shows that Foresi's own education in Latin letters went far beyond the level attained by most notaries in the fifteenth century.[144] Foresi enjoyed the close personal friendship of Ficino;[145] he

[142] They were *Trionfo delle virtù*, and a translation into Italian verse with a long introduction of Vergil's *Georgics*. The *Trionfo* is found in three manuscripts: Harvard College, Richardson 46, which is the dedication copy, written by Foresi himself (I am grateful to Dr A. de la Mare and Prof. P. O. Kristeller for bringing this manuscript to my attention); BNF, Magl. VII, 816, autograph; and BNF, Palat. 345, copied by Corso di Maso Corsi (cf. fol. 1r: Questo libro si è di Corso di Maso di Corso scrivano al Monte, scripto di mia mano) with autograph corrections and marginalia written by Foresi; it is still unedited but a few passages were published by P. Giorgi, F. Novati and G. A. Venturi, in *Il trionfo di Cosimo de' Medici. Frammento d'un poema inedito del secolo xv*, nozze Pellegrini-Marchesini (Ancona, 1883). Foresi's translation of the *Georgics* appeared as *Libro chiamato ambitione composto per ser Bastiano Foresi notajo fiorentino al Magnifico Lorenzo de' Medici nel quale si dichiarano e' precepti della agricoltura secondo la georgica di Virgilio* (Florence, 1490).

[143] Cf. BNF, Magl. VII, 816, fol. 2r for many *exempla* and *sententiae* from ancient and medieval history as well as the Old and New Testaments; cf. *Libro chiamato ambitione*, fol. 1r ff., for Foresi's interest in pagan mythology, astrology and the origins of Florence. For Foresi as an Italian poet, and especially the influence of Petrarch and Dante, cf. Giorgi *et al.*, *Il trionfo*, 9–10; Rossi, *Il Quattrocento* (Milan, 1933), 260.

[144] BNF, Magl. VII, 816, fol. 1r–v: Prestantissimo viro Laurenzio Medici Bastianus Foresius notarius salutem. Vellem, prestantissime Laurenti, hac nostra tempestate tantam mihi facultatem et dicendi copiam suppeditatam esse, ut singularissimas virtutes tuas et gloriam pro dignitate litteris mandare potuissem, quo et desiderio meo satisfacerem et non mediocre exemplum imitande virtutis tue posteris traderem. Verum cum ingenio et doctrina facile omnibus cedam, voluntate autem et perpetuo studio ornande dignitatis tue aut omnibus parem aut certe superiorem me esse profitear, nolui committere quin aliqua benivolentie mee in te signa obstendam. Quae nil aliud esse possunt quam gratus animus, fides et vigiliarum mearum lucubrationes hunc representantes libellum quem ad te nunc mitto, minime nescius te optime novisse tantum ab uno quoque exigendum esse quantum cuiusquam facultas et ingenium prestare potest, Artaxersem Persarum regem sapienter imitatum cui obsequitanti agricolam obviam factum aquam cavis manibus ex flumine haustam obtulisse ferunt, quam rex iocundo vultu suscipiens non quid daretur sed qua mente daretur metiendum esse arbitratus est. Liberalitatem quoque pariter in tenue ac divite esse posse metitus est. Ingenii igitur tui tueque nature prestantiam atque facilitatem multum diuque mecum ipse considerans minime veritus sum te hanc tantulam rem benigno vultu gratoque animo suceputrum ac prebentis potius voluntatem quam ipsum munus etiam si pergrande esset respecturum. Vale.

[145] Cf. his correspondence with Ficino in M. Ficino, *Opera omnia* (Basel, 1576), 725–6, 788, 822–3, which concerns their mutual enthusiasm for lute playing; Foresi apparently not only played the lute proficiently but also made lutes. Cf. Della Torre, *Storia*, 102, 792–3, Foresi frequently acted as notary for Ficino and his family: cf. ASF, Not.A., S 502, fol. 21r–v (12 September 1477), fol. 100r–114 bis r–v (4 January 1480 (ab inc.)); *ibid.*, S 503, fol. 46v (1 November 1485). Ficino recommended Foresi's *Trionfo delle virtù* to Lorenzo de' Medici: cf. Ficino, *Opera*, 643, and BNF, Palat. 345, fol. 1v for Ficino's letter to Lorenzo.

was the correspondent of a noted humanist such as Sabellico[146] and his poetic inclinations and intellectual interests suggest that he may possibly have been connected with Poliziano's circle as well.[147] Moreover, a curious list preserved in the first of the volumes of the 'Consulte e pratiche', from Poggio's chancellorship[148] shows that Foresi's humanist interests date from a period in his life before he became Accolti's coadjutor. This is a record of books borrowed, possibly from Poggio himself, by various figures associated with humanist circles such as Naldo Naldi, Bernardo Nuti and Vespasiano da Basticci;[149] among the borrowers was Bastiano Foresi, who is recorded in three separate entries as having taken Cicero's *De officiis*, part of Varro and the poetry of Horace.[150]

Foresi's personal contributions to the reforms of the chancery under Accolti may include the *quaternus*, which he himself wrote; it is possible that he made use of his experience in the second chancery, where, it has been seen, a similar administrative procedure was used, in his work for the first chancery under Accolti. Another contribution was the script that he used for all chancery records, which, it has been pointed out, finally established the predominance of italic in the Florentine chancery. One of Accolti's most significant reforms was to improve the Latinity of chancery records, and there is clear evidence that Bastiano Foresi had an important personal role in overcoming traditional chancery practices and establishing humanist standards of Latin style. An insight into the methods used by Accolti and Foresi to achieve this reform of chancery Latinity is provided by a draft of a letter to Borso d'Este. This is an autograph of Accolti's, bound by chance at the end of a volume of instructions and letters to ambassadors dating from Poggio's chancellorship; like many other such letters on behalf of private individuals, this letter was not copied into the registers of the *missive*.[151] It is written on thinner paper than that ordinarily used for final copies of letters in the registers of *missive*; it is clearly Accolti's own first draft, since a number of corrections which he himself made in the text indicate a change of mind about wording while he was in the course of composing the letter.[152] Accolti was writing on behalf of a

---

[146] Cf. Giorgi *et al.*, *Il trionfo*, 7, n. 5.     [147] Cf. *ibid.*, 9–10.

[148] ASF, CP, 53, fol. 240v. I am extremely grateful to Dott. Daniela De Rosa for pointing out this list to me.

[149] *Ibid.* Hi ex meo habent hec commodo. The works borrowed included Ezekiel, Cicero's *De amicitia* and *Paradoxa Stoicorum*, Alan of Lille's *Planctus naturae*, Aristotle's *Politics* and *Ethics*, and Seneca's letters.

[150] *Ibid.*, ser Bastianus – Partem Varronis . . . ser Bastianus Antonii – Poeticam Oratii . . . ser Bastianus – *De officiis*. The inventory of Poggio's library at the time of his death (cf. Walser, *Poggius*, 418–23) included all these works except for Alan's *Planctus*.

[151] ASF, LC 14, fol. 64r–v.

[152] E.g. Accolti changed 'qualibet in re summa iustitia' to 'summa qualibet in re iustitia', 'demictere' to 'remictere', 'commendaremus nostris licteris' to 'nostris licteris commendaremus', 'eiusmodi hereditatis bona tanquam ad fiscum pertinerent vestrum

Florentine citizen, Fastello di Matteo Petriboni, whose brother, Gherardo
Petriboni, had died intestate leaving property near Reggio Emilia, in
Modenese territory and Borso d'Este's officials were attempting to have
the property revert to his treasury. This was not an important state letter,
but Accolti made numerous corrections in the text to secure the most
felicitous wording. At one point Accolti changed a phrase containing a
medieval construction for more classical syntax,[153] which shows that even
in a letter on behalf of an unimportant private petitioner Accolti was determined to maintain a high standard of classical Latin. It emerges from this
same letter that classical purity did not come easily to Accolti, despite his
long association with the humanist movement; besides his lapse into
medieval syntax already mentioned (which he himself corrected), Accolti
used a number of medieval spellings such as 'hac' for 'ac', 'remictere' for
'remittere', 'circha' for 'circa' and 'holim' for 'olim'. Such orthography
was not characteristic of the finished copies of the *missive*, and at this early
stage of drafting, orthographical improvements were begun, not by
Accolti but by his assistant, Foresi. The manuscript contains a number of
Foresi's autograph emendations, some of which were intended to correct
mere slips of the pen such as putting the 'tu' in 'virtutes' or the 'u' in 'seu';
however, others such as striking out the 'h' from 'hac' (for 'ac'), 'circha'
and 'holim' were made to purify the Latin. Medieval chanceries, which
depended on formularies, standard procedures and time-honoured models
to produce letters and documents rapidly with a minimum of staff, were by
their very nature institutions which conserved traditions; even in the
Florentine chancery, the humanist *avant garde*, men such as Poggio and
Bruni who had rejected in their own work medieval standards of script,
Latinity and classical learning[154] made surprisingly limited attempts to
bring the new learning into the work of the chancery.[155] Accolti himself did
not find it easy to eliminate medievalism from the work he did for the chancery, as is shown by this autograph letter, but it is noteworthy that, in contrast to earlier chancellors, he made an enormous effort, together with
Bastiano Foresi, to bring the new learning into the Florentine chancery.

Of course, Accolti was not entirely successful in eliminating traditional
practices from the chancery. For example, he continued in state letters to
use the second person plural rather than the second person singular, which
had been the normal classical practice;[156] in this case, the dictates of
courtesy in diplomatic correspondence had to take precedence over the
requirements of good Latinity.[157] Occasionally Foresi failed to eliminate

---

presides vestri acceperunt' to 'eiusmodi hereditatis bona presides vestri tanquam ad
fiscum pertinerent vestrum acceperunt'.
[153] *Ibid.* In place of 'quam ob rem nichil est quod' Accolti wrote 'quam ob rem absit ut'.
[154] Cf. pp. 109–10 *supra*.      [155] Cf. pp. 141–2, 155–6, *supra*.
[156] Cf. B. L. Ullman, *The Humanism of Coluccio Salutati* (Padua, 1963), 106–8.
[157] Cf. e.g. p. 147, n. 59, *supra*.

the impure 'h', writing for example 'hodio' and 'hodisse' instead of 'odio' and 'odisse',[158] and there were occasional incorrect vowels such as 'y' in place of 'i' in 'sydus'.[159] The most persistent shortcoming of Accolti's reforms, however, was the almost complete failure to use diphthongs, which had been recognized as a sign of the best Latinity since the days of Niccoli.[160] Diphthongs occasionally appear in chancery records before Accolti's time,[161] and he and Foresi did not manage to secure any more regular use of them than before. This is primarily due to Accolti's own indifference to diphthongs, which is also clear in his two literary works; the earlier dialogue makes consistent use of diphthongs whereas in the later history they hardly appear at all. Evidently the use of diphthongs here was at the discretion of Accolti's scribes, of whom ser Gherardo del Ciriagio is notable for hardly ever writing a diphthong. Similarly in the preparation of chancery documents, Accolti gave free rein to Bastiano Foresi, whose own Latinity, although far superior to the usual notary's in the fifteenth century, was perhaps not quite of the highest quality; his apology later in life to Lorenzo de' Medici for the shortcomings of his learning[162] may be merely a standard *topos* of affected modesty,[163] but it is also true that in his sole surviving Latin literary composition he makes use of only one diphthong.[164]

Bastiano Foresi's service in the first chancery under Accolti marks the beginning of a new phase in the history of the Florentine chancery; by Accolti's time it had become an established feature of the Florentine constitution to employ a humanist as first chancellor, while leaving subordinate positions to ordinary notaries. Perhaps the first sign of a changing attitude was the suggestion of the *pratica* of 1456 to provide two additional assistants for Poggio from a shortlist of four, consisting of Cristoforo Landino, Bernardo Nuti, Bartolomeo Scala and Antonio Rossi,[165] who were all young men with humanist training; however, such candidates may have been put forward, not because of any particular wish to introduce more humanists into the chancery, but merely because it was hoped that they would teach as well in the faculty of rhetoric and moral philosophy in the university, out of whose funds they were to be paid.[166] At any rate, these proposals may not have been implemented,[167] and it was

[158] Cf. e.g. ASF, Miss. 42, fol. 23v.    [159] *Ibid.*, fol. 44r.
[160] Cf. Ullman, *Humanistic Script*, 70–1.    [161] Cf. Herde,'Die Schrift', 320–2.
[162] Cf. p. 167, n. 144, *supra*.    [163] Cf. Curtius, *European Literature*, 83–5.
[164] Cf. p. 167, n. 144, *supra*.
[165] Cf. ASM, SPEFi, 269, n. 17. (28 September 1457): Dicto Detesalvi nostro [Dietisalvi Neroni] . . . trovandossi in Valle de Serchio presso a Luca in lecto cum un suo figliolo et havendo ali pedi loro uno Antonio de' Rossi, preceptor de soy figlioli, docta persona . . .
[166] Cf. p. 96, *supra*.
[167] *Ibid.* Landino's letter to Piero de' Medici (ed. Perosa, 190) also suggests that the proposal to give Poggio assistance from one of the four young humanists may not have been implemented.

only with Accolti's appointment that the new learning embraced not only the first chancellorship but also the chancellor's staff. Indeed, Accolti's changes of staff seem to have been part of a deliberate plan, formed at the beginning of his chancellorship, to introduce the new learning into the chancery, as is clear from the fact that he relegated Muzi and Pardi, two notaries without any apparent humanist education, to the second chancery[168] and brought back from private notarial practice Foresi,[169] who had the humanist education necessary to implement his comprehensive scheme of reform. Because Accolti employed a humanist such as Foresi as his assistant, the character of chancery work changed and new standards, under the influence of the new learning, were expected of the chancery. It is no accident that after Accolti's death it became normal practice to employ noted humanists in subordinate chancery positions, such as Braccesi, Michelozzi, Nuti, Francesco Gaddi and Landino,[170] all of whom had the education appropriate to maintain the higher standards in the chancery originally set by Benedetto Accolti. The most famous appointment of this nature was that of Machiavelli in 1498,[171] and by the end of the century not only was the chancellor a distinguished humanist but the chancery as a whole was a centre for humanist studies,[172] a development which owed its origins to Benedetto Accolti's reforms.

Accolti undertook the reform of the Florentine chancery for a number of reasons. There was widespread dissatisfaction in Florence with the decline of the chancery under Poggio and a wish to restore the standards established by his mentors, Bruni and Marsuppini. Accolti instituted his reforms at a time when there was growing dissatisfaction with the inflexibility and inadequacy of certain features of the traditional Florentine constitution, a trend which culminated in the Parlamento and Balìa of 1458, and it is likely that the spirit of reform in Florence entered administrative as well as political centres of government, leading to such innovations as Accolti's *quaternus*. The fashion for humanist oratory and the growing importance of ambassadors in diplomacy led to greater interest in the records of meetings such as the *pratiche* and diplomatic audiences, occasions where public oratory was very much a reality in the fifteenth century. There were also the personal inclinations of Accolti and Foresi, both of whom wanted clearly to make the greatest possible use of their humanist training and erudition. In the case of Accolti, there was a strong desire to prove himself as a professional humanist, intensified by his growing frustration over many years with law, by his desire to return to the

---

[168] Cf. p. 139, *supra*.     [169] Cf. p. 156, *supra*.
[170] Cf. Marzi, *La cancelleria*, 236ff.; Brown, *Scala*, 203ff.
[171] Cf. M. Martelli, *L'altro Niccolò di Bernardo Machiavelli* (Florence, 1975), 13, 57–58.
[172] Cf. F. Gilbert, 'Humanism in Venice', in *Florence and Venice*, ed. S. Bertelli *et al.* (Florence, 1979), i, 14.

favoured studies of his youth, by his undoubted irritation at the condescending jibes and sniping of his humanist friends such as Poggio, and by
his determination to show up doubters such as Landino, proving that he
could not only equal but even surpass the achievements of Bruni and
Marsuppini as chancellors. Finally, it must be remembered that Accolti's
private scholarly work as chancellor was undertaken in the field of historiography,[173] and that he was therefore fully aware of the distinction
made in antiquity between the two genres of historical writing, annals and
history.[174] He certainly took anything but a utilitarian view of the records
which he kept for the Florentine government, as is clear from the high
degree of finish in style as well as physical appearance evident in the
volumes of his chancellorship. Leonardo Bruni actually used the records of
the Florentine government as the annals upon which he partly based his
Florentine history,[175] a work which Accolti greatly admired,[176] and it is
possible that Accolti felt that as chancellor he was preparing the annals of
the Florentine republic for some future historian,[177] just as annalists in
Rome did the preliminary work for Livy.[178] Annals themselves were a type
of historical literature, and Accolti seems to have been determined to prepare records which were worthy of Florence as the new Rome or the new
Athens.

The reform of the Florentine chancery through improving administrative efficiency and securing a firm place for the new learning was not
Accolti's only achievement as chancellor; like his predecessors, he had to
act as technical adviser to the government,[179] and in this capacity he was
eminently successful according to Vespasiano, who declared that in 'all the
differences which came before the Signoria, they sent for Messer Benedetto
and with his help the problem was quickly despatched'.[180] The chancellor
was frequently called upon to solve technical problems regarding eligibility for public office in his capacity as one of the palace officials,[181] who,
admitted to the secret of the scrutiny, had to ensure that those candidates
qualified for office were in fact eligible according to communal laws.[182] In
legal disputes Accolti's eminence as a lawyer had already given him such an
authoritative position that, in Vespasiano's words, 'wherever Messer
Benedetto was present, all others stood silent before his authority',[183] and

---

[173] Cf. Ch. 8 and 10, *infra*.
[174] E.g. *De oratore*, ii, 51–64; Aulus Gellius, V, xvii, 8–9. Cf. Black, 'B.A. and the begin-
      nings', 53–4.
[175] Cf. Santini, 'Leonardo Bruni Aretino', 50ff.
[176] Cf. p. 321, *supra*; Dialogue, fol. 18v–19r (Galletti, 112).
[177] As a result of the chancery reforms of 1483, one of the secretaries was given the formal
      duty of writing the annals of Florence: cf. Marzi, *La cancelleria*, 252ff., 606; Brown,
      *Scala*, 184.
[178] Cf. *De oratore*, ii, 51ff.    [179] Cf. p. 125, *supra*.
[180] Vespasiano, *Vite*, i, 596.    [181] Cf. Brown, *Scala*, 136–7, 151–3.
[182] *Ibid.*, 152–3.    [183] Vespasiano, *Vite*, i, 597.

similarly in electoral questions arising during his chancellorship Accolti
took precedence over the notary of the Riformagioni, the notary of the
Tratte and the second chancellor, the three other palace officials. One such
occasion occurred on 30 September 1458,

when it was discovered that Jacopo di Pagnogo Ridolfi, . . . elected for the quarter
of Santo Spirito [as one of the officials of the *catasto* for the *contado*], had not
reached the age of forty on the first day of his term of office, as is required according to the law concerning the election of such officials; I, Alberto di Donnino di
Luca, notary of the Tratte of the Florentine commune, held a consultation with the
illustrious doctor of laws Messer Benedetto di Messer Michele d'Arezzo, the very
worthy Florentine chancellor and the excellent men ser Bartolomeo di ser Guido di
Jacopo Guidi, the scribe of the Riformagioni, and ser Antonio di Mariano Muzi,
the second chancellor . . . to whom and to me . . . it pertained in this case and in
similar ones during our time [in office] to judge what was to be done . . . and since
Jacopo himself and Alessandro di Filippo Machiavelli . . . were the only ones
[qualified] for this office for the quarter of Santo Spirito [it was wondered] whether
there must be a new scrutiny for Santo Spirito or whether on the other hand the said
Alessandro should take office without another scrutiny . . . After a diligent
examination among us four of the relevant law . . . at length we concluded, on the
authority and decision principally, as is fitting, of the aforementioned Messer
Benedetto, that the said Jacopo by the law itself should give up the office and
Alessandro should take it up, not because a rigorous interpretation of the law
would dictate that he should assume office, but because of custom observed . . . in
many similar past cases . . . since it is asserted that custom has the force of law.[184]

Accolti's legal knowledge and standing as a lawyer, added to the dignity of
the first chancellorship, made him a figure of preeminent authority in the
palace during his term of office.

Accolti had come to office through the support of the Florentine oligarchy, with whom he had, of course, to maintain good relations throughout his chancellorship. Like previous chancellors, he was subject to the
discretion of the Florentine ruling group in composing state letters, which
primarily reflected their views, not necessarily his own.[185] This is clear
from the debates of the *pratica*, where the oligarchs expressed their views
on questions of policy and to which Accolti, like previous chancellors,
adhered closely in writing his *missive*. An example is the letter which
Accolti wrote to the Perugians on 5 January 1460,[186] which was preceded
by a debate in the *pratica* on 3 January.[187] The issue was whether or not
Florence should accede to a request of the Perugians and, in a time of
peace, replace Carlo di Guido degli Oddi, one of their mercenary captains
who had recently died, with his brother Sforza. The *pratica* was by no
means unanimous on this question, but the weight of opinion went against

---

[184] Cf. Appendix II.    [185] Cf. pp. 122–5, *supra*.
[186] ASF, Miss. 42, fol. 183r–v.    [187] ASF, CP, 56, fol. 21v–24r.

the wishes of the Perugians,[188] who were informed by Accolti in his letter
of Florence's refusal. Accolti's letter repeats many of the arguments of
those speakers in the *pratica* who had advised against replacing Carlo degli
Oddi. Thus Donato de' Cocchi had said that 'it has always been the custom
in time of peace to reduce expenditure',[189] and in his letter Accolti indicated that 'citizens are accustomed to seek any way of reducing expenditure after a peace'.[190] Manno Temperani stated that 'the Oddi family have
always been most beloved to the city [of Florence] and it has received many
benefits from them',[191] a view repeated by Otto Niccolini,[192] while Accolti
stated that 'the merits of Guido [degli Oddi] and his sons shall live in our
hearts and memory forever'.[193] Bernardo de' Medici declared, 'This city
was afflicted for a very long time by great wars and many burdens',[194] an
opinion which Accolti repeated stating that 'this city for a long time
endured the gravest war, undertaking enormous and exhausting expenditure which led to great inconveniences'.[195] The Gonfalonier of Justice said
that 'nothing was more necessary to the city, exhausted from wars, than to
reduce public expenditure',[196] a view repeated by Carlo Pandolfini, who
said that 'the policy of peace, namely, to reduce expenditure, must be pursued',[197] and reflected in Accolti's letter, where it was stated, 'peace finally
having been made, we judged that nothing would help recovery more than
removing all expenses other than those which were, nevertheless, necessary to the city'.[198] Bernardo de' Medici pointed out that 'after peace was
made Carlo was retained not out of necessity but for the honour of the city

[188] Opposed to the Perugians' request were Manno Temperani, Carlo Pandolfini, Donato
de' Cocchi, Otto Niccolini, Martino Scarfa, Francesco Ventura, Bernardo Gherardi,
Bernardo de' Medici, Dietisalvi Neroni, Guglielmo Rucellai, and Pietro del Benino; in
favour were Giovannozzo Pitti, Giovanni Bartoli, Matteo Palmieri, Luigi Guicciardini
and Antonio Lenzi; undecided were Bernardo de' Giugni and Mariotto Benvenuti.
[189] ASF, CP, 56, fol. 22v: semper consuetum fuit pacis tempore impensas minuere.
[190] ASF, Miss, 42, fol. 183v: cives . . . post pacem quamlibet causam minuende impense
querere consueverunt.
[191] ASF, CP, 56, fol. 22r: familiam de Oddis semper amantissimam fuisse civitati et multa
beneficia ab illa eadem recepta.
[192] *Ibid.*, fol. 22v: verissimum esse familiam de Oddis multa fecisse in utilitatem rei publice
plusquam quemlibet alium.
[193] ASF, Miss. 42, fol. 183v: Guidonis quoque ac filii merita herent animis nostris memoria
sempiterna.
[194] ASF, CP, 56, fol. 22v: civitas hec diutissime magnis bellis vexata fuit et oneribus multis.
[195] ASF, Miss. 42, fol. 183v: civitas hec diu gravissimum bellum passa sumptus immodicos
fecisset quibus pene exhausta magna incommoda susceperat.
[196] ASF, CP, 56, fol. 21v: civitas bellis fessa vix dum ab illis respirarit nec magis ei conducat
quam minuere impensas publicas.
[197] *Ibid.*, fol. 22r: consilia pacis agirentur, videlicet ut impensa minuantur.
[198] ASF, Miss. 42, fol. 183v: pace demum facta nil eidem recreande magis conducere
existimavimus quam removere impensas omnes preter eas tamen que civitati necessarie
essent.

of Perugia',[199] while Donato de' Cocchi pointed out that 'they had dismissed most remaining soldiers'[200] after peace was made, views which were repeated in Accolti's statement that, 'having dismissed almost all troops, we retained a few, among whom Carlo was himself kept, not because the city needed his services, but lest we should appear to have forgotten his excellence and his enormous merits'.[201] Finally, Manno Temperani suggested that if any other dangers should threaten, then he [Sforza degli Oddi] should be elected before any one else',[202] a view repeated by Bernardo de' Medici[203] and found in Accolti's letter, which concluded that 'if necessity requires the hiring of soldiers, we promise that the sons of Guido [degli Oddi] will be among the first whom we shall call to fight with us'.[204] Donato de' Cocchi, Manno Temperani, Carlo Pandolfini, Bernardo de' Medici and Otto Niccolini were leading figures in the regime, and it was incumbent on Accolti to take full heed of the view of such men in his work as chancellor.

One man whose wishes Accolti had to be particularly careful to respect was Cosimo de' Medici. An insight into the way in which official chancery business took into account the unofficial opinions of the Medici is provided by a surviving private letter of Accolti's to Cosimo.[205] Bernardo da Castiglionchio, a Florentine patrician, was the captain of a galley being used for a papal crusading expedition. He had left his galley in the care of Pietro di Raimondo Manelli and had accompanied the pope, Pius II, to the Congress of Mantua in 1459. In the meantime, Manelli allegedly began to commit acts of piracy with Bernardo's galley without his approval. Bernardo wanted to pursue Manelli to recover his galley and clear his name. There was a rumour that Manelli was approaching Provence with Bernardo's galley,[206] and therefore Bernardo asked Accolti as Florentine chancellor to write to King René of Anjou, the Provençal sovereign. Accolti wrote the letter on the advice of his friend Otto Niccolini, who told

---

[199] ASF, CP, 56, fol. 23r: cum pax constituta fuit non ob necessitatem sed in honorem civitatis Perusii retentum fuisse Carolum.

[200] *Ibid.*, fol. 22v: post pacem . . . reliquos vero milites cassasse.

[201] ASF, Miss. 42, fol. 183v: dismissis fere militibus cunctis paucos retinuimus quos inter Carolus ipse retentus est, non quia eius opera indigeret civitas sed ne sue virtutis et meritorum ingentium obliti videremur.

[202] ASF, CP, 56, fol. 22r: Si enim aliqua imminerent pericula tunc consuleret istum pre ceteris eligendum esse.

[203] *Ibid.*, fol. 23r: Quod si aliqua necessitas superveniret conducendi milites tunc ipsi potiusquam alii conducentur.

[204] ASF, Miss. 42, fol. 183v: Sed si, quod tamen absit, novi quicquid emergeret ex quo milites conducendi essent, pollicemur Guidonis filios ex primis futuros quos ad militandum nobiscum provocemur.

[205] Cf. Appendix I.

[206] Accolti's letter on behalf of Bernardo da Castiglionchio is ASF, Miss. 42, fol. 146r–147r (30 July 1459).

him that Cosimo de' Medici approved of the government's intervention on behalf of Bernardo. Accolti then sent his letter to Cosimo for approval, accompanied by this note:

Bernardo da Castiglionchio requested a letter to King René, and it was decided [to write one] because Messer Otto [Niccolini] told me that you thought it was a good idea, and he told me what the letter should say. In his view I wrote the letter well, and, as you will see, Bernardo is not declared to be entirely blameless, nor is he also accused. I am sending it to you, and if you think that nothing should be changed, let me know and it will be prepared. Bernardo is pressing for it very much and would like it today.

However, it was not always easy for Accolti to know the opinions of the Medici on all matters of state business, especially since he apparently never gained their intimate confidence during his term as chancellor. Accolti's independence of the Medici as well as the authority he commanded as chancellor in government circles are apparent in an episode regarding Florentine and Milanese relations with Caterina Campofregosi and Marchese Jacopo Malespini over the fortress of Ponzano in the summer of 1463.[207] Ponzano had belonged to Caterina Campofregosi but was seized by Jacopo Malespini in 1463; Caterina was a feudatory under the protection of the Florentine republic, to whom she appealed for assistance in regaining Ponzano. By the terms of their alliance, Florence was obligated to defend Caterina and so the Florentines appealed to the duke of Milan to intercede with Jacopo Malespini to restore Ponzano to Caterina. However, Jacopo was a feudatory under the protection of the duke of Milan, who replied to Florence, through his ambassador Nicodemo Tranchedini, that the alliance with Jacopo Malespini, having been formed before the alliance between Caterina and Florence, took precedence and therefore the duke could not intervene with Jacopo on behalf of Florence and Caterina. At this point, the Florentine Signoria, bewildered by the technicalities of the affair, asked for the advice of their chancellor, Accolti, whose legal authority, it has been seen, carried great weight in Florence and who gave them a characteristically clear and decisive answer. In his view, the fact that Jacopo's alliance with Milan preceded Caterina's with Florence was irrelevant, because Caterina was in possession of Ponzano and allied with Florence at the time of the general Italian league of 1454; as one term of the league of 1454 was that the possessions of all signatories of the league and those of their dependants were to be respected by all other signatories of the league, the duke of Milan, as a signatory, had guaranteed Caterina's possession of Ponzano, irrespective of any alliance he had with Jacopo Malespini. The Signoria accepted Accolti's advice and despatched a reply in those terms to Francesco Sforza.

---

[207] Cf. Appendix IV.

It is well known that Cosimo de' Medici conducted private diplomacy with other Italian powers, and especially Francesco Sforza of Milan, simultaneously with the official diplomacy carried on by the Signoria; it is often thought that Cosimo's voice in Florence was decisive, especially regarding foreign affairs, but in the case of Ponzano the Signoria and their chancellor, Accolti, did not consult the Medici but sent their reply direct to Francesco Sforza, who did not like what the Florentines had to say, as is clear from the despatches sent back to Milan by Tranchedini:

Yesterday evening, he wrote to Sforza on 14 August 1463, I had your letter of the 9th regarding the letter which this Signoria wrote to you concerning the question of Ponzano, which I showed to the magnificent Cosimo. At length I have found that this Signoria, without consulting Cosimo and without my knowledge, said to Messer Benedetto d'Arezzo, their secretary, that he should write you a justificatory letter, according to his own opinion. And [they did] this because it seemed to them that I was putting pressure on them, when you wrote me your other letter, to such an extent that they did not know what to say; so they had recourse to the Doctor [viz. Benedetto Accolti, doctor of laws]. Thus this letter came to be sent. I shall therefore go to the Signoria and, besides complaining as respectfully as I can, I shall tell them again what is going on.

Tranchedini's audience proved to be an embarrassment both for the Signoria and for Accolti:

When I complained to the Signoria for my part, he wrote to Sforza on 22 August, about the letter they sent you, I found that the Signoria, having promised to respond to me after they had consulted the citizens, became embarrassed and gave the blame to Messer Benedetto d'Arezzo, especially because he did not take the advice of either Cosimo or myself. Messer Benedetto blamed the Signoria, saying that they gave him the commission and said nothing else to him, nor did he think of it [*i.e.*, consulting Cosimo or Nicodemo]. The result is that everyone is embarrassed.

These letters not only give a fascinating picture of the limitations of Cosimo de' Medici's influence in government and in the formation of foreign policy but also confirm that Accolti was distant and even independent of the Medici in his work as chancellor. Moreover, Accolti continued to take an independent line contrary to the wishes and efforts of the Medici and Francesco Sforza as the affair developed at the end of August. Sforza sent to Florence the original of his treaty with Jacopo Malespini and wished to have in return the original of the Florentine treaty with Caterina; Cosimo de' Medici agreed to try and secure this document for Sforza but again they were frustrated and embarrassed by the Signoria's fastidious regard for legality:

With regard to sending to your highness the alliance of Madonna Caterina Campofregosi, Cosimo says that he will endeavour to have me given the original, as it appears in their records, which I have seen ... The Signoria promised to give me the copy, as I told your highness in my other letter. Then, having elected

Dietisalvi [Neroni as their ambassador to Milan], they had their chancellor, Messer
Benedetto d'Arezzo, reply to me that they could no longer give me the treaty
because they had instructed Dietisalvi. I protested strongly at this, although I do
not like to have to write this to your excellency, saying that you had sent your treaty
here and that you had proceeded with perfect frankness with them but that they
were not acting thus with your excellency. Then, I complained about this to
Cosimo, who said that when they promised it to me they did not know that they
could not give it without the approval of the colleges. Therefore, they were
embarrassed to tell me the truth, but it must suffice that I have seen it.

Accolti thus was the one who told Tranchedini that he could not have the
original, which, together with the legal justifications for denying the
Milanese request, suggests that it was Accolti who again intervened to
frustrate both Cosimo de' Medici and Francesco Sforza. In the end, the
Florentine government maintained the position originally counselled by
Accolti,[208] which shows the kind of influence Accolti could enjoy in
Florence as a result of his legal authority; indeed, in view of this evidence
of Accolti's independence of the Medici, it is perhaps less surprising that
they went to great lengths in the seven months after his death to secure the
appointment of a truly Medicean chancellor in the person of Bartolomeo
Scala.

Despite his personal difficulties with the Medici, Accolti maintained the
keen support of the regime as a whole, who were quick to show their
approval of his reforms and conduct in office. When he was first elected he
received a salary of 300 florins a year for himself and one coadjutor, which
was the salary that had been granted to the first chancellor since 1437.[209]
It had been customary to increase the first chancellor's salary only when he
was made responsible for other offices. When there were two chancellors,
the first chancellor had received 300 florins,[210] but when there was only
one chancellor he received 600 florins a year for himself and his entire staff
including the first and second chanceries.[211] Nevertheless, on 7 October
1458, only six months after assuming office, the Balìa ordered that
Accolti's salary be increased from 300 to 450 florins. For it was realized
that, in his eagerness to serve the commune, he had accepted office even
though he had earned far more as a lawyer and that he would look to the
goodwill of the government to prevent him from suffering any inconvenience. Therefore, the Balìa considered it befitted the dignity of the
Florentine people for Accolti to realize that his work in the chancery was

[208] ASF, Miss. 44, fol. 125r–128r.     [209] Cf. Luiso, 'Riforma', 137.
[210] Marsuppini before the chancellorship was reunited in 1453 received 300 florins: cf. ASF,
Tratte, 95, fol. 72r.
[211] Bruni was given a salary of 600 florins a year for himself and two coadjutors: cf. p. 108,
n. 149, *supra*. After 31 January when the chancellorship was reunited Marsuppini was
given 600 florins a year for himself and four coadjutors and the same was granted to
Poggio in April 1453 when he was first elected: cf. Luiso, 'Riforma', 139–41.

appreciated and that he should not suffer as a result of his duties.[212] Then five months later on 20 February 1459 the council of 100 voted by 119 to 14 to reelect Accolti for another three years at his present salary of 450 florins, 'in view of Accolti's virtues and desiring to retain him as chancellor'.[213]

Evidently, however, 450 florins was considered insufficient, for on 5 February 1461 a further rise was discussed in the *pratica*.[214] Introducing the subject, the Gonfalonier of Justice, Piero de' Medici, said, 'The Signoria believe that something must be done about increasing the salary of Messer Benedetto, the chancellor, but they did not wish to come to a decision without the consent and advice of the *pratica*.' Francesco Ventura then said that 'it would be a pleasure to increase the salary of someone who did such good work, and money well spent was never wasted'. Manno Temperani said that 'since Accolti had served devotedly he thought that he should be rewarded accordingly and that his salary should be increased'. The next speaker, Domenico Martelli, was extravagant in his praise of Accolti, saying, 'No one had ever been in that position who had . . . conducted himself more diligently; he left the practice of law which had been especially lucrative and therefore his salary ought to be increased.' Then Otto Niccolini agreed with the previous speakers, mentioning that Accolti had given up the practice of law and suggesting that his salary should be increased by 100 florins. Giovanni Bartoli said that 'since all citizens have equally praised the chancellor it was just that his salary should be increased; in that office he did the city more service than himself'. Declaring that 'it was not possible to speak fittingly of the chancellor's excellence', Franco Sachetti agreed that his salary should be raised. Then Dietisalvi Neroni said that 'the chancellor was a truly excellent man and that therefore his salary should be increased not only by 100 florins but by a far greater amount'. Luigi Guicciardini agreed with the others, 'affirming that it greatly enhanced the honour of the city to have such a man exercise this office, and therefore his salary should be increased'. Bartolomeo Lenzi exceeded all previous speakers in his praise of Accolti, saying that 'the office of chancellor has never been such as it is now and therefore it was very gratifying to increase his salary'. Vanni Rucellai said that 'each day his virtues became more apparent and, just as good princes rewarded learned men, so the commune must provide for Accolti and therefore his salary should be raised'. Nicola Capponi was the first to suggest that it should be increased by 150 florins, and Bernardo de' Medici agreed with the others saying that such 'virtue and fidelity could not be purchased'. Luigi Ridolfi spoke next, adding that 'his learning deserved every reward

[212] ASF, Balìe, 29, fol. 60r.
[213] ASF, Cento, 1, fol. 15r–v; *ibid.*, LF, 66, fol. 1r.      [214] Cf. Appendix III.

and that there was no satisfactory recompense for his merit'. Mariotto
Benvenuti agreed saying that 'each day the good offices of the chancellor
grew and therefore deserved reward'. Matteo Palmieri agreed with the
others, and Agnolo della Stufa said that 'a reward could not be found that
would befit the chancellor's virtues; it is customary to lead men to the pursuit of greater virtue by reward and therefore his salary should be increased
in order that he might be made better each day by the hope of reward'.
Leonardo Bartolini agreed, saying that 'Messer Benedetto deserved every
kind of salary', and Piero de' Pazzi said that 'it was not possible to praise
the chancellor and grant him rewards without his deserving even greater
ones'. Finally Antonio Pucci agreed, saying that 'never in the city had there
been a more illustrious chancellor than the present one and that therefore
his salary should be raised'. Considering the stature of previous Florentine
chancellors, this was certainly high praise and so the Signoria on
18 February 1461 took the step of doubling a chancellor's personal salary
within less than three years of his taking office; indeed, no previous chancellor had received anything approaching this scale of financial recognition. On 19 February the proposal to increase Accolti's salary by another
150 florins to 600 florins a year was submitted to the colleges, where it was
approved; then it was examined and approved by four conservators of the
laws. In the final provision submitted to the legislative councils, it was
stated that in view of Accolti's singular virtues and because he had earned
more as a lawyer than as chancellor, and in order for him to benefit, not
suffer, as a result of his work for the Signoria, his salary should be
increased by 150 florins a year.[215] On the first reading the bill was
approved by the council of the people on 23 February 1461 by 152 votes
to 63, on 25 February by the council of the commune by 126 votes to 33,
and on 27 February 1461 by 96 votes to 16 in the council of one
hundred.[216] Moreover, at the same time as his new salary was being
approved, the council of one hundred reelected him as chancellor for
three more years, although his previous term of office did not expire until
17 April 1462; it was from that date that his next term was to begin, and
the measure was approved by 97 votes to 15.[217] Clearly Accolti's reforms
met with the hearty approval of the entire ruling class of Florence, and so
it is hardly surprising that Vespasiano da Bisticci heard 'from many of
those members of the government who had frequented the palace during
Accolti's term that it had been a long time since there had been someone in
the palace who had conducted himself better than he or who had brought
greater honour' to Florence.[218]

---

[215] ASF, Provv. 151, fol. 367r–v.    [216] *Ibid.*, LF, 66, fol. 140v, 142r, 143v.
[217] *Ibid.*, Cento, 1, fol. 39v–40r; LF, 66, fol. 145r.    [218] Vespasiano, *Vite*, i, 597.

The eminence achieved by Accolti as chancellor was also recognized outside Florence, as is clear from a letter sent to him,[219] probably in September 1464,[220] by the well-known humanist, Antonio Ivani, who had served as chancellor to Lodovico Campofregosi, doge of Genoa, until his fall from power in January 1463.

Recognizing the singular distinction of your intellect, most illustrious man, he wrote to Accolti, I should hesitate to address this letter to you . . . if your distinguished reputation for kindness had not been known to me for some time. Therefore I am writing to you with less propriety than perhaps is fitting, persuaded above all by the confidence that, if I am in error, you will attribute it to our established intimacy rather than to my temerity. Indeed, I feel this way because of your incredible good nature and singular modesty. But, with such matters put to one side, I shall come to what leads me to write this letter to you. At various times and indeed on diverse journeys I have wandered through almost all Italy, at the mercy of my fate. This has allowed me to contemplate many cities and the customs of many nations. But, having looked very carefully at many cities and compared diligently ones that are similar, I have come to the conclusion that Florence is the only one which, as the brightest beacon of all Italy, not only illuminates Tuscany by its splendour, but is regarded as the most brilliant ornament of all Italy . . . You, therefore, rejoice, as one who has been accepted into [Florentine] citizenship and, having settled in that city, exercises so illustrious and lofty an office. I, however, having contemplated the special warmth of its citizens and the dignity of the city, desire nothing more than to be able for a time to live comfortably in such a city and among so many virtuous [men]. For even if I do not lack the comforts necessary to live, nevertheless I think another kind of nourishment is to be found in frequent civic intercourse . . . I want you to see if in any way you can satisfy the wishes of your friend, and just as I rejoice at your virtue and good fortune, I beseech and implore you to cherish me as your own.

---

[219] Published by P. L. Ruffo, 'L'epistolario di Antonio Ivani (1430–1482)', Rin., xvii (1966), 157–8. I am extremely grateful to Dott. Gabriella Bertone, the librarian of the Biblioteca Comunale of Sarzana, for providing me with a microfilm of Accolti's letter from the Archivio storico del comune di Sarzana, and for confirming that there are no further letters to Accolti in this archive.

[220] The date of September 1465 assigned to the letter by Ruffo (ibid., 158) is impossible as it is almost a year after Accolti's death. The letter refers to the fall from power in Genoa of Ivani's patron, Lodovico Campofregosi, which took place in January 1463 (cf. A. Ivaldi, 'La signoria dei Campofregoso a Sarzana (1421–1484)', Atti della società ligure di storia patria, n.s. vii (lxxxi), fasc. 1 (1967), 135) so that the letter must date from either September 1463 or September 1464. Ivani says in the letter that he had spent fourteen years in Lodovico's service, and since there is good evidence that he first entered his service in 1450 (cf. F. L. Manucci, 'L'operosità umanistica di Antonio Ivani', Giornale storico della Lunigiana, v (1913–14), 172), then the letter would date from 1464. This is supported by the fact that Ivani had been in Florence on 23 September 1463 (cf.R. Fubini, 'Antonio Ivani da Sarzana', in Egemonia fiorentina ed autonomie locali (Settimo convegno internazionale: Centro di studi di storia e d'arte Pistoia) (Pistoia, 1975), 133) and in the letter Ivani refers to an established friendship between himself and Accolti. In support of 1463 is the information communicated to Fubini privately (ibid., 135, n. 45) that Ivani was in Milan in September 1464, whereas the letter was sent to Accolti in Florence from Sarzana.

This letter suggests that the time had passed when it would have been necessary for Accolti to seek the support of leading figures of the Italian humanist community, as he had done earlier in life; indeed, his success in the Florentine chancellorship placed him in the front ranks of Italian humanists, a position which made aspiring scholars and even established humanists such as Ivani now look to him as a possible patron.

The impression that Accolti made during his chancellorship continued to influence his contemporaries even after his death; indeed, there seems to have been a strong feeling in Florence that a replacement of his stamp should be found. This was anathema to Accolti's old rival, Cristoforo Landino, who once more hoped to become chancellor through the support of the Medici; this time he wrote not to Piero, perhaps because he knew Piero supported Bartolomeo Scala's candidacy, but to Piero's son Lorenzo.[221] Recently a secretary of the chancery had died, he wrote in 1465, and he desired to succeed him. Frequently such offices were filled by lawyers or foreign humanists, but who does not see that in such an office there is little need for a lawyer but great need for a humanist? There are few eloquent lawyers, who do not therefore deserve blame, since rhetoric is not their subject. Foreigners moreover can only be trusted at great risk with state secrets. There are many eloquent Florentines, but few of them are suitable; some are ecclesiastics, others, as members of patrician families, would not want such an office as the chancellorship; still others are too young. Landino himself was not a priest, not of patrician descent, and not, at forty-one, too young; indeed, he said, distorting the facts slightly, the deceased chancellor had not been older when elected (in fact Accolti had been forty-three). Returning to a theme of his earlier letter to Piero de' Medici in 1458,[222] Landino concluded that lawyers, enjoying almost every kind of opportunity, can earn great sums, but the muses, on the other hand, pay nothing. This letter shows the legacy in Florence of Accolti, who had been, of course, a lawyer, a foreigner and not a Florentine patrician. Indeed, Bartolomeo Scala, Accolti's eventual successor, probably came to office, on the evidence presented here, not only as an intimate of the Medici who would show perhaps less independence in office than Accolti had done, but also because, as a lawyer, foreigner and outsider to the Florentine patriciate, he was regarded as a fitting replacement to the pre-eminently successful Benedetto Accolti.

Accolti's success as chancellor of Florence was due to many of the qualities of character and intellect which had given him success as a

[221] Published by A. M. Bandini in his *Collectio veterum aliquo monumentorum* (Arezzo, 1752), 1ff., with the date 1475. However, Marzi (*La cancelleria*, 240–1), must be correct in assigning it to 1465, as the contents of the letter fit the circumstances after Accolti's death perfectly but would make no sense in 1475.
[222] Cf. pp. 105–7, *supra*.

lawyer. He had great determination to succeed, which was characteristic of many members of his family including his father and his brother Francesco as well as his grandfather, uncles and cousins in the Roselli family. He had an ability to gain rapid mastery of new subjects, as demonstrated by his achievements in law and the humanities by the age of twenty, and in vernacular poetry by twenty-five; indeed, it is truly remarkable that Accolti, who had never before been a professional secretary or humanist, achieved a comprehensive reform of the chancery almost immediately after taking office. Accolti's abilities as a humanist, however, were not confined to the work of the chancery; during his term of office he turned to Latin literature, and the two important and original humanist works which he was able to complete during his six years' chancellorship show the same imaginative qualities which stamped his career as Florentine chancellor.

# 8

# *Accolti's 'Dialogus'*

It was while Accolti was chancellor that he published his first extended Latin composition, a dialogue.[1] It takes the form of two long speeches, one by an unidentified young man who attacks the merits of modern times in contrast to antiquity, the other by Accolti, who defends the moderns against the ancients. They examine ancient and modern warfare, morals, statesmanship, cities, poetry, rhetoric, philosophy, law and religion; although the young man offers a comprehensive defence of antiquity and condemnation of modern times, all his arguments are refuted by Accolti, who in an even more vigorous defence of moderns and censure of ancients, emerges victorious in the debate.

The origins of Accolti's dialogue can be traced to his cool relations with the Medici. Accolti dedicated the work to Cosimo, who also receives there an effusive panegyric; it has been observed that Accolti's is one of the most extravagant encomia among those written during Cosimo's lifetime,[2] and one reason for the dedication, as well as the particularly sycophantic tone of this panegyric, was Accolti's desire to achieve an intimacy with the Medici which had so far eluded him. In the preface Accolti makes no secret of his intention to win the friendship of Cosimo, to whom, he declares, he has dedicated the work, 'not because it is worthy of you but so that my love for you should become better known'.[3] Accolti believed flattery would gain Cosimo's favour:

According to everyone, he continued, you are endowed with such wisdom, such learning, such force of intellect that you are admired not as a human being but as a god descended from heaven ... And not without merit. For among all Italians you have given the most immense evidence of your virtue, the fame of which has spread through almost the entire world. And lacking no good fortune, you have begot for

---

[1] For the manuscripts of the dialogue, cf. p. 347, *infra*. In the presentation copy (BLF, 54, 8) the work is called simply 'Benedicti Arretini Dialogus' (fol. 3r); the title *Dialogus de praestantia virorum sui aevi* was given to the work by Benedetto Bacchini, the editor of the first edition (Parma, 1689).

[2] Cf. A. Brown, 'The humanist portrait of Cosimo de' Medici', JWCI, xxiv (1961), 194.

[3] Dialogue, fol. 2r: Quem ego tuo clarissimo nomini dedicavi, non quo te dignum opus sit, sed quo clarius amor in te meus innotescat. Cf. Galletti, 105.

the benefit of your native land the most excellent sons, who are like you, and who, following in your footsteps, will preserve the name and glory of your family and together will always love and protect this republic.[4]

In the body of the dialogue, Accolti includes another panegyric of Cosimo in the form of a short biography. Beginning with his scholarly attainments, Accolti declares that only the distractions of public life and private business prevented him from becoming a prince of eloquence, but whatever spare time remained he devoted to the patronage of scholars, especially Niccoli, Bruni, Marsuppini and Poggio. In public life Cosimo distinguished himself in numerous magistracies reserved for leading citizens, winning popularity with his humanity, generosity and clemency; his success, however, aroused great envy and he and his brother were banished to Venice, where he was received not as a miserable exile but as an aristocrat. Florence, however, could not long bear his absence, and he was brought back by the will of the people and some of the patriciate; although now first citizen of Florence, he was clement to his enemies, on whom banishment was the worst punishment inflicted. Accolti then narrates Florence's diplomatic triumphs under Cosimo's leadership against Filippo Maria Visconti, Giovanni Vitelli, the Venetians and Alfonso of Aragon, emphasizing his loyal support for Francesco Sforza, who gained the duchy of Milan with Cosimo's assistance; indeed, only cooperation between Cosimo and Sforza had stopped the Venetians from securing the mastery of all Italy. Finally Accolti praises Cosimo's magnificent endowment of churches, monasteries and chapels, his liberal charity to the poor, and his modest and unpretentious private life.[5]

A further incentive for Accolti's obsequious panegyric of Cosimo was his rivalry for the favour of the Medici with the Greek scholar, Francesco di Mariotto Griffolini.[6] Griffolini had translated Chrysostom's eighty-

---

[4] Dialogue, fol. 2r–v: Ea enim sapientia, ea doctrina, ea ingenii vi te praeditum omnes intelligunt, ut te non sicut humanum hominem sed tanquam divinum et ex caelo lapsum admirentur, et tantum tuo iudicio tribuunt, ut nullo modo illud falli posse arbitrentur. Nec immerito. Dedisti enim apud Italos omnes virtutis tuae documenta permaxima, quorum fama per universum pene orbem diffusa est. Et ne quid tibi aut tuae fortunae deesset, filios praestantissimos et tui simillimos patriae genuisti, qui tuis inherendo vestigiis, generis nomen et gloriam conservabunt, atque hanc rem publicam unice semper diligent et tuebuntur. Cf. Galletti, 105.

[5] Dialogue, fol. 32r–36r; Galletti, 118–19.

[6] The basic work on Griffolini is Mancini, *Francesco Griffolini*, many of whose findings were based on J. Vahlen, *Laurentii Vallae opuscula tria* (Vienna, 1869), 74–127; other important material has been published by A. Battaglini, 'Dissertazione sopra l'autore della prima traduzione latina delle lettere greche di Falaride e di altre traduzioni delle quali si attribuisce la gloria al famoso leggista Aretino Fr. Accolti', *Dissertazioni dell'Accademia romana di archeologia*, ii (1825), 369–400, by G. Mercati, *Scritti d'Isidoro il cardinale ruteno e codici a lui appartenuti* [*Studi e testi*, 46] (Rome, 1926), 128–32, by R. Sabbadini, 'Andrea Contrario', *Nuovo archivio veneto*, n.s. xxxi (1916), 409–13, and by Mancini, 'Giovanni Tortelli', ASI, lxxviii (1920), 191–8, 216–17.

eight homilies on the Gospel of St John with a dedication to Cosimo,[7] in which, like Accolti in the dialogue, he had argued that moderns were equal or superior to ancients.[8] Griffolini was a fellow citizen of Accolti's from Arezzo, but they had little reason for friendship; their families were bitterly opposed in Aretine politics and their rivalry seems to have inspired Accolti to outdo Griffolini's version of the ancients and moderns, especially in the number of examples and arguments, in order to demonstrate that he was the better rhetorician and humanist.

The enmity between Accolti and Griffolini had its roots in Arezzo's relations with Florence. Griffolini's father, Mariotto, had been the leader of the conspiracy of 1431 to overthrow Florentine rule in Arezzo.[9] He was a feudal noble, whose family had lands and jurisdiction in the countryside northeast of Arezzo,[10] and a leading merchant in the city.[11] Griffolini's interests were threatened by Florentine rule both in the countryside, where Florence's policy of limiting feudal jurisdictions interfered with his family's traditional prerogatives,[12] and in the city, where his business ventures were subjected to increasing taxation.[13] Besides feudal retainers in the countryside, Griffolini had a substantial following in the city of Arezzo,[14] all of whom he attempted to turn against Florence in the spring of 1431, when he conspired to betray Arezzo to the condottiere, Niccolò Piccinino.[15] The plot, however, was revealed to the Florentine authorities in Arezzo, Griffolini was apprehended and he was summarily tried on 18 May 1431 and executed on the following day. All his goods were confiscated, his family was expelled from Arezzo and his sons were declared rebels and banished from Florentine dominions for life.[16] Among them was the eleven-year-old Francesco, who went with his mother and sisters to Ferrara and then to Rome,[17] where, deprived of all their property, they lived in poverty and insecurity throughout the 1430s and 1440s.[18] The

---

[7] The presentation copy is BNF, CSopp. J. 6.7. (cf. fol. 1v: Iste liber est conventus sancti Marci de florentia ordinis predicatorum quem donavit dicto conventui vir clar. Cosmas Iohannis de Medicis civis nobilis florentinus . . . et est hec originalis traductio quam Cosmo emendatam misit dictus Franciscus). There are also numerous autograph corrections by Griffolini in the text: cf. e.g. fol. 130r, 156v, 188v, 215r–v etc. For Griffolini's autograph, cf. ASF, MAP, 14, 47 and 137, 115). Cf. Mancini, *Francesco Griffolini*, 27ff.
[8] BNF, CSopp. J. 6.7. fol. 2r–v.    [9] Cf. pp. 4–5, *supra*.
[10] ACA, 617, fol. 47r; ASF, Not.A., I 57, fol. 46r (I am very grateful to Dr J. Muendel for this reference). Cf. E. Gamurrini, *Istoria genealogica* (Florence, 1668–85), iv, 133; Repetti, *Dizionario*, v, 630; Lazzeri, *Ubertini*, 289–90; ASF, Cat. 201, fol. 334r, 427v.
[11] *Ibid.*, fol. 328r–334r bis, 424r–427v; cf. pp. 7–9, *supra*. The Griffolini had been a leading mercantile family in Arezzo since the early fourteenth century: cf. ACA, 609, p. 23; 610, fol. 74v; 617, fol. 7r. For other members of the Griffolini family settled in Arezzo during the fourteenth century, cf. *ibid.*, 597, fol. 69v; 605, fol. 65v; 606, pp. 26, 67; 607, fol. 79v; 608, fol. 77v–78v; 610, fol. 68r, 74v; 616, fol. 17v; 600, fol. 98v.
[12] Cf. p. 3, *supra*.    [13] Cf. p. 5, *supra*.    [14] Pasqui, 'Una congiura', 13.
[15] *Ibid.*, 3–19.    [16] *Ibid.*, 16–19.    [17] Mancini, *Griffolini*, 13–14.
[18] *Ibid.*, 13ff.

fortunes of the Griffolini thus offer a complete contrast to those of the Accolti, who, it has been seen, prospered as a result of Florentine rule in Arezzo. Benedetto Accolti, therefore, looked with suspicion upon Francesco Griffolini; added to this was the fact that Accolti was a friend of the man who had betrayed the Griffolini plot, Michele Marsuppini.[19]

Having attended Guarino's school at Ferrara and Valla's lectures in Rome and studied in Greece, Francesco Griffolini became a well-known Hellenist; in the 1450s he was seeking patronage and it began to seem that one possible source of support might be the Medici family. This had the added advantage that, through the Medici, Griffolini might be able to be readmitted to Florentine territory and regain some of his family's confiscated property. Griffolini's first contacts with the Medici were through Cosimo's illegitimate son, Carlo, who lived in Rome; Carlo's brother, Giovanni, was keen to have a copy of Griffolini's translation of the letters of the pseudo-Phalaris, so that in the spring of 1456 Carlo had it copied and then corrected by Griffolini himself.[20] The translation of the pseudo-Phalaris had given Griffolini national fame as a Greek scholar, and it was for this reason that he was attracting the attention of the Medici, who as a family had a deep interest in the Greek classics. This had been the foundation of their close association with Marsuppini, but since his death in 1453 Cosimo and his two sons Giovanni and Piero may have been attempting to find someone to fill the void. It is clear that they were considering Griffolini for this position, especially when he appeared briefly in Florence as part of the papal entourage on the way to the Congress of Mantua in 1459.[21] In his own words, he was received by Cosimo 'as a son' and treated by Piero and Giovanni with a humanity that he would remember for the rest of his life;[22] he made a great impression on the Medici and soon after his arrival in Mantua, despite the injury done to his family by the Marsuppini, he received a commission from the Medici to compose an epitaph for the tomb of Carlo Marsuppini in Santa Croce in Florence, which he fulfilled while still in Mantua.[23] The significance of this commission in the eyes of the Medici is obvious; moreover, Cosimo asked Griffolini to prepare a translation of the homilies of Chrysostom on St John the Evangelist, which Griffolini returned to Rome to complete two months after he sent the Medici the epitaph for Marsuppini.[24]

It must have appeared that the Medici were preparing the way to have

---

[19] Cf. pp. 74–5, *supra*.
[20] Cf. V. Rossi, 'L'indole e gli studi di Giovanni di Cosimo de' Medici', *Rendiconti dell'Accademia dei lincei, classe di scienze morali e storiche*, ser. 5, ii (1893), 131–3.
[21] Mancini, *Griffolini*, 27–8.
[22] BNF, CSopp. J. 6.7, fol. 2v; ASF, MAP, 14, 47, and 137, 115. Cf. Mancini, *Griffolini*, 27–9.
[23] ASF, MAP, 14, 47.    [24] *Ibid.*

Griffolini return from exile and take Marsuppini's place as the leading Greek scholar in Florence; indeed, during his visit to the Medici in 1459, Griffolini declared that Cosimo had given him 'good hope'.[25] These moves must have been disturbing for Benedetto Accolti, who would have recoiled at the idea of an Aretine enemy as the favoured protégé of the Medici. Accolti's opportunity to thwart Griffolini came in September 1461, when news reached Florence that Pope Pius II had granted Griffolini the living of a church in Castiglion-Fiorentino in Florentine territory.[26] As Florentine chancellor, Accolti had no direct power in making political decisions, but he did sometimes advise the Signoria on legal or technical questions,[27] on which, as one of the most eminent lawyers in Florence, he commanded considerable authority.[28] When information reached Florence that Griffolini, still a Florentine exile and rebel, had been granted a benefice in Florentine territory, the Signoria had to decide whether to allow him to reenter Florentine territory in order to take possession of the living or indeed whether it was possible for him, as a rebel, to hold the benefice at all. The Medici, who had been encouraging Griffolini over the previous two years,[29] may have preferred for him to have the benefice as a first step to being readmitted to Florence; however, this was already the period in which Cosimo's influence over some leading members of the Florentine ruling class was waning,[30] and the Signoria would not necessarily have been guided by the sentiments of the Medici. The head of the Signoria, the Gonfalonier of Justice, at this time was Carlo Pandolfini, who, neither a staunch Medicean nor anti-Medicean, seems to have favoured adhering to Florentine traditions in political matters.[31] He and his colleagues on the Signoria were sympathetic to a strict interpretation of Florentine law and custom, which seems to have been the advice that they were given by their chancellor, Benedetto Accolti, on this occasion. It was doubtless Accolti, the legal pundit, who made it clear to the Signoria that Florentine law forbade Griffolini as a rebel from taking the benefice.

Accolti himself composed the letter from the Signoria beseeching the pope to rescind the grant of the living to Griffolini.

We understand, begins the letter of 23 September 1461, that Francesco Aretino, who is living in the curia, has sought the benefice of St Michael the Archangel, a parish which is located in the town of Castiglion-Fiorentino, and we believe that your holiness, ignorant of what his father did against us, has been clement towards him, because you judge in your wisdom that men learned and distinguished in the arts are worthy of reward and are especially suited to holy orders. But we are astonished that he himself has dared to seek something which is not appropriate for him on account of the injury caused by his father and which is contrary to our

---

[25] *Ibid.*, 137, 115; BNF, CSopp. J. 6.7, fol. 2v.   [26] ASF,Miss. 43, fol. 165r–v.
[27] Cf. p. 125, *supra*.   [28] Cf. pp. 172–3, *supra*.   [29] Cf. p. 187, *supra*.
[30] Cf. Rubinstein, *Government*, 134–5.   [31] *Ibid.*, 147.

integrity and honour, and which our laws will not permit him to enjoy. For men should desire and seek those things which can be attained without injury or dishonour to others; from other things, however, they should abstain, lest they seem to be more concerned with their own self-interest than with honour. For his father Mariotto, who was for long a rich and honoured man in Arezzo, in the midst of the hardships of a long and grave war, conspired with desperate men to betray Arezzo to the enemy, although he had received no particular injury; and in the end he would have accomplished this deed with the help of armed men then present if the favour of God and our own vigilance had not uncovered his plot. At length he was executed, and in accordance with the law his children were exiled as rebels. In view of these facts, holy father, you are asked to consider whether it is just for us to allow someone to preside over our churches who, for such a grave cause, has been made an exile from his country, whose father plotted our ruin, and by whose actions we came very close to losing our dignity and our liberty. What kind of example would it be for our subjects to allow the sons of those who had committed such a crime to return from exile and be rewarded? How would the citizens of Castiglion-Fiorentino receive the news that in their church someone was being preferred over their unanimous candidate and that the church would always have an absentee vicar? Therefore it is contrary to the welfare of their souls and the good of religion, nor in our view is it suitable for Francesco to have this living when the people are unwilling, in the teeth of our protests and contrary to long-established laws; indeed, it is wrong for Francesco to want something which would lead to our dishonour. Therefore we humbly ask your holiness to revoke this decree and persuade Francesco to seek what is honest, and to award the benefice to the candidate chosen by the citizens of Castiglion-Fiorentino, lest something ensue which we cannot bear with honour. If your holiness does this, we shall be extremely grateful.[32]

---

[32]  ASF, Miss. 43, fol. 165r–v: Pape. Impetrasse accepimus Aretinum Franciscum, qui vestra in curia vitam ducit, Micaelis Arcangeli sacram edem quam in oppido Castilionis Florentini sitam plebem homines appellant. Credimusque sanctitatem vestram ignaram prorsus quod parens eius in nos admiserit, iccirco illi clementer fuisse, quod sapienter existimat eos premio dignos ac precipue sacris idoneos qui doctrina bonarum artium clari evaserunt. Sed satis miramur ipsum id appetere ausum esse quod sibi non convenit ob paternam iniuriam et honestati atque honori nostro est adversum, quodque illum consequi leges nostre non patiuntur. Debent enim homines ea cupere aut petere que sine altera iniuria vel dedecore consequi possunt; ab aliis vero abstinere ne magis proprii commodi rationem quam honesti habere videantur. Nam huius parens Mariottus nomine, qui in urbe Aretio diu locuples et honoratus fuerat, cum longo et gravi bello premeremur, coniurans cum perditis viris Aretium prodere hostibus instituerat, nulla iniuria lacessitus. Perfecissetque tandem facinus cum adessent armati hostes, nisi dei benignitas et nostra industria suum consilium detexissent. Quo tandem supplicio affecto, illius liberi, legibus ita iubentibus, velut rebelles exularunt. Que cum ita sint, beatissime pater, cogitet sanctitas vestra num equum sit nos eum pati preesse nostris ecclesiis qui ob causam adeo gravem extorris patria factus est, cuius pater ad nostram perniciem conspirarit, per cuius facinus parum abfuit quin nos dignitate simul ac libertate privaremur. Quod sit exemplum hominibus nostris, nos videlicet pati eorum filios reduces esse vel affici premio in agris nostris qui tantum flagitium commiserunt? Quo animo sint laturi Castilionenses in sua ecclesia hunc ei preferri quem omnibus votis cupierunt, eandemque ab illo regi qui semper absens sit futurus. Ideoque non recte animarum saluti aut sacris rebus consultum erit, neque, ut nobis videtur, conducit Francisco hanc ecclesiam regere, invito populo, repugnantibus nobis, atque ipsis iam diu statutis legibus, atque id protinus velle quod in dedecus nostrum redundaret. Itaque rogamus humiliter beatitudinem vestram ut in hac re decretum revocet suum, Francisco suadeat id appetere quod sit honestum atque illum huic preficiat edi quem Castilionenses desiderant, ne quicquam sequatur quod nos

Repeatedly in the letter it was stated that Florentine law prohibited
Griffolini from holding the benefice, and the influence of Accolti's legal
authority here is clear. Although written in the name of Florence, the letter
is filled with personal antipathy towards Griffolini and his family deriving
from deep-rooted local animosities so characteristic of Italian society.
Accolti felt that Griffolini's family had already brought Arezzo, including
the Accolti family, to the brink of ruin, and now it was only fair that he
should cause them no more trouble and keep away from Florence and
Arezzo.

It was in these circumstances that during the following summer of 1462
Griffolini's completed translation of Chrysostom's homilies on St John
arrived in Florence with a dedication to Cosimo de' Medici,[33] in which the
superiority of the moderns over the ancients was used by Griffolini to
praise Cosimo and other fifteenth-century figures. Accolti felt that the time
had come to show the Medici that, as a man of eloquence, he was the equal
of Griffolini. He was not a Greek scholar and so could not compete with
Griffolini as a translator of the Greek classics, but as chancellor he was a
proficient Latinist and rhetorician. Accolti made no secret of his concern
to display his skill in eloquence, admitting in the preface of the dialogue
that he was eager to show how 'copiously and ornately' he could write,[34]
and in fact there is internal evidence that Accolti's dialogue was written
about the time that Griffolini's translation reached Florence, which was
some time between May and November 1462.[35] A *terminus post quem* is
provided by a reference in the past tense to Guarino Veronese, who died on
4 December 1460;[36] a *terminus ante quem* may be inferred from Accolti's
mention of Cosimo de' Medici's 'sons', indicating that Giovanni, who died
in November 1463, was still alive when Accolti was writing.[37] Cosimo had
not kept his copy of Griffolini's translation as a private possession but had
personally donated it to the 'public library' in San Marco in Florence,[38]
where Accolti would have been able to gain access to it. Further evidence
that Accolti composed the dialogue in response to Griffolini's preface to
the translation of Chrysostom is the similarity in the encomia of Cosimo

honeste pati non possumus. Hoc, si fecerit sanctitas vestra, nos loco magne gratie
recipiemus. 23 Septembris 1461.

[33] For the date, cf. Mancini, *Griffolini*, 33–4.

[34] Dialogue, fol. 2v: Nec vereor abs te praesumptionis argui, quasi rem agressus, quam non
omnino ample, nec ornate satis explicare potuerim, in hoc scribendi genere minime
versatus. Cf. Galletti, 105.

[35] Cf. p. 190, n. 33, *supra*.

[36] Dialogue, fol. 41r (Galletti, 122); cf. R. Sabbadini, 'Guarino Veronese', *Enciclopedia
italiana*, xviii (Rome, 1933), 27.

[37] Dialogue, fol. 2v, 35v; Galletti, 105, 119.

[38] Cf. p. 186, n. 7, *supra* and B. L. Ullman and P. A. Stadter, *The Public Library of Renaissance Florence* (Padua, 1972), 141.

de' Medici, which occupy prominent places in both works. Both praise
Cosimo for his role in making Francesco Sforza duke of Milan; both
celebrate his great wealth, his liberality, his charity, his civic and religious
munificence and his devotion to scholarship; both refer to him as the 'first
citizen' (*princeps*) of Florence and emphasize his role as one of the arbiters
of Italian diplomacy.[39] Similarly, Accolti was particularly concerned to
display his knowledge of early Christian history and Latin patristic literature in the dialogue, in competition with Griffolini's erudition in the Greek
fathers; praise of the modern church also formed an important part of both
texts.[40] Moreover, Accolti's praise of Cosimo as more god than man,
which was unprecedented among encomia of Cosimo during his lifetime,[41]
was probably an attempt to outdo Griffolini's panegyric in which Cosimo
was compared to the most distinguished mortals including Pompey, Cato,
Lucullus, Crassus and Cicero.[42] Similarly, the greater detail and broader
scope of Accolti's dialogue would have demonstrated his superiority in
eloquence over Griffolini since abundant use of arguments and examples
(*copia*) was regarded in the Renaissance as a sign of rhetorical proficiency
and literary excellence.[43]

Accolti was anxious as to how his dialogue would be received by the
Medici, excusing it as the work, not of a master, but of a not entirely
ignorant pupil, and declaring to Cosimo at the end of his dedicatory
epistle, 'If in your view I am not judged to be inadequate, I shall devote
myself more boldly to study and letters in the future, confident above all in
the support of your name.'[44] Accolti's doubts about his work as a humanist
resulted not only from the coolness of his hoped for Medici patrons and
the open hostility of humanist intimates of the Medici such as Landino,[45]
but also from a real sense that his dialogue was the work of a novice not
entirely divested of his former professional habits. Although he had
received a humanist education, more than twenty years as a practising
lawyer still left its mark on Accolti's first composition, which in certain
ways resembles a legal disputation more than a Ciceronian dialogue.
Accolti's predecessors in the chancery, Bruni and Poggio, as well as other
humanists, had written a number of dialogues closely modelled on
Ciceronian works such as *De oratore*; in particular, they had achieved an

---

[39] Dialogue, fol. 32r–36r (Galletti, 118–19); BNF, CSopp. J. 6.7, fol. 2v.
[40] Dialogue, fol. 45v–55r (Galletti, 123–7); BNF, CSopp. J. 6.7, fol. 2r–v.
[41] Cf. Brown, 'Humanist portrait', JWCI, xxiv (1961), 186ff.
[42] BNF, CSopp. J. 6.7, fol. 2v.
[43] On *copia*, cf. Cicero, *Orator*, 97; Quintilian, VIII, iii, 86–7, X, i, 61, X, v, 9.
[44] Dialogue, fol. 2v: . . . pro tua sapientia opinabere me non ut magistrum sed ut non
ignarum discipulum quid in hac re possem experiri voluisse; quod si tuo iudicio non
ineptum me esse sensero, audacius posthac disciplinis et litteris incumbam, tuo nomine
atque auxilio inprimis fretus. Cf. Galletti, 105.
[45] Cf. pp. 105–7, *supra*.

informal atmosphere, an impression of actual conversation and a lively sense of repartee, and, like Cicero, they had used the dialogue form to express various shades of opinion and to retain a certain ambiguity as to their own personal opinions in controversial or complex questions.[46] Accolti's dialogue, on the other hand, does not have these Ciceronian qualities. There is some attempt to create the ambience of after-dinner conversation,[47] but the work is in fact two long uninterrupted speeches arguing two clearly defined, opposite positions, which is exactly the form of legal treatises composed by civil and canon lawyers. Moreover, Accolti could not free himself from the habit of reaching a clear conclusion at the end of his work such as always occurred in a legal disputation, in which after arguing for and against a certain proposition (*sic et non*) the counsel would declare which side he supported (*sententia*); in Accolti's dialogue, the *sententia* appears in the final sentence, where he states, 'And when at length everyone agreed with me, we departed.'[48] The only named participant in the dialogue is Accolti himself; unlike other humanist dialogues, his opponent is anonymous, so that in this way too Accolti's work resembles the abstract disputation of the legal treatise, not the discourse of genuine historical figures set in the contemporary world typical of the Ciceronian dialogue.[49]

Such vestiges of legal methods escaped the scrutiny of Accolti, who nevertheless was just as determined to raise his dialogue to the highest possible standards of humanist rhetoric as he had been to expurgate medieval practices from the chancery and introduce the new learning. Accolti did not completely succeed in the dialogue just as he fell short of the best Latinity in the chancery, but what is significant is the attitude he took to composition. Just as his sense of inexperience turned him into a comprehensive reformer of the chancery, so his lack of confidence as a humanist made him all the more determined to perform a rhetorical *tour de force* in his dialogue, where, it is no exaggeration to say, he followed the rules and methods of classical rhetoric with a vengeance. The dialogue belongs to the *genre* of *epideixis*, the rhetoric of praise and blame,[50] and,

---

[46]  Cf. D. Marsh, *The Quattrocento Dialogue* (Cambridge, Mass. 1980).

[47]  Dialogue, fol. 3r: Nuper cum apud amicum quendam plures convivio cives et ipse simul comiter recepti essemus, ac post epulas quaedam, ut solet, ioci gratia inter nos facete dicerentur, tandem in eum sermonem incidimus, ut quaererent quidam . . . (Galletti, 105).

[48]  Dialogue, fol. 57v: Et cum tandem omnes mihi assensi essent, discessimus (Galletti, 128).

[49]  Dialogue, fol. 3r: Cumque ego nonnulla protulissem . . . commotus meis verbis, adolescens quidam qui nobiscum aderat, litterarum eruditus, me compellans . . . inquit . . . (Galletti, 105–6).

[50]  For a survey of rhetoric from antiquity to the Renaissance, cf. Kristeller, 'Philosophy and rhetoric from antiquity to the Renaissance', *Renaissance Thought and its Sources*, 211–59, 312–27. On *epideixis*, cf. *Rhet. ad Her.*, III, 10–15; Cicero, *De inventione*, ii, 177–8; *idem, De part. orat.*, 70–82; *idem, De oratore*, ii, 341–9; Quintilian III, vii; T. Burgess,

as in the other branches of rhetoric, there were five stages in composing a panegyric: invention, disposition, diction, memory and delivery. Of these, invention, or thinking of what to say, was the most important,[51] and was based on a series of standard arguments or commonplaces called *loci communes* or *topoi koinoi*; these were intellectual themes, suitable for development or modification according to the circumstances, which could be used on the most diverse occasions.[52] For example, Accolti included biographies of three contemporaries, besides mentioning many others, and the arguments which he used to praise them were the *topoi* of panegyric. The commonplaces for praising an individual were based on character, physical endowments, and external circumstances.[53] Virtues of character are prudence, justice, temperance and courage,[54] all of which, especially prudence, Accolti puts to frequent use.[55] Other virtues such as liberality, eloquence, magnanimity and clemency are recommended[56] and used by Accolti.[57] One special feature of a good character is a worthy education,[58] for which Accolti praises Cosimo de' Medici.[59] Another is to have earned the praise of one's contemporaries:[60] Accolti observes that in their youth it was predicted that both Cosimo and Francesco Sforza would become great men,[61] and he declares that not only Florence but all Tuscany sings Cosimo's praises.[62] Good qualities that were the sole possession of the individual are considered especially praiseworthy:[63] thus Accolti praises Francesco Sforza for his 'rare virtue'[64] and Cosimo for having been the only Florentine to oppose the Venetian alliance in 1447 and support

---

'Epideictic literature', *Studies in Classical Philology*, iii (1902), 89–261; Curtius, *European Literature*, 69, 154ff.; J. W. O'Malley, *Praise and Blame in Renaissance Rome* (Durham, N. Car., 1979), 36ff.

[51] *Rhet. ad Her.*, II, i, 1.

[52] On the importance of commonplaces, cf. Curtius, *European Literature*, 70, 79ff. and *passim*.

[53] *Rhet. ad Her.*, III, 10; *De inven.*, ii, 177; *De part. orat.*, 74; Quintilian, III, vii, 12.

[54] *Rhet. ad Her.*, III, 10–11; *De inven.*, ii, 159; *De part. orat.*, 76–80; *De oratore*, ii, 343–5.

[55] Dialogue, fol. 19v–37r (Galletti, 112–20): *prudentia*: Niccolò Acciaiuoli, Francesco Sforza, Donato Acciaiuoli, Rinaldo Gianfigliazzi, Filippo Magalotti, Gino Capponi, Migliore Guadagni, Agnolo Pandolfini, Giannozzo Pandolfini, Cosimo de' Medici, Francesco Foscari; *iustitia*: Francesco Carmagnola, Francesco Sforza; *fortitudo*: Filippo Scolari, Braccio da Montone, Francesco Sforza; *temperentia*: Donato Acciaiuoli, Rinaldo Gianfigliazzi, Filippo Magalotti, Bartolomeo Valori, Niccolò da Uzzano, Guido del Palagio, Cosimo de' Medici.

[56] *De oratore*, ii, 343–45; *De part. orat.*, 76–80.

[57] Dialogue, fol. 19v–37v (Galletti, 112–20): *liberalitas*: Cosimo de' Medici; *eloquentia*: Rinaldo Gianfigliazzi, Filippo Magalotti, Cosimo de' Medici, Francesco Foscari; *magnitudo animi*: Francesco Sforza; *clementia*: Francesco Sforza, Cosimo de' Medici.

[58] *Rhet. ad Her.*, III, 10, 13; *De part. orat.*, 82; Quintilian III, vii, 15.

[59] Dialogue, fol. 32r; Galletti, 118.    [60] *De oratore*, ii, 347.

[61] Dialogue, fol. 21r, 32v; Galletti, 113, 118. For success to be predicted was considered praiseworthy: cf. *De part. orat.*, 73 and Quintilian III, vii, 11.

[62] Dialogue, fol. 32r; Galletti, 118.

[63] *De oratore*, ii, 347–8; Quintilian III, vii, 16.    [64] Dialogue, fol. 21v; Galletti, 113.

Francesco Sforza.[65] Another highly recommended *topos* is to argue that the individual's virtue worked not to his own but to the common advantage,[66] and so Accolti praises Cosimo for not having ceased to work while in exile for Florence's benefit[67] and Francesco Foscari for having continued to work in the public interest although persecuted by enemies.[68] Physical accomplishments and external circumstances are regarded as *topoi* of praise especially when providing the individual with scope for demonstrating his virtue;[69] thus Accolti praises Braccio and Sforza for the agility and quickness which made them good soldiers.[70] High birth is considered praiseworthy if the subject lived up to his promise,[71] as did Cosimo and Antonio, Niccolò and Benedetto Alberti;[72] low birth, on the other hand, can become a *topos* of praise by pointing to the obstacles overcome by the individual's virtue,[73] as in the case of Carmagnola.[74] Good fortune can be praised for the use to which it was put,[75] as in the instances of Braccio and Carmagnola,[76] but it is especially laudable to have borne adversity with nobility,[77] as did Cosimo during his exile and Foscari after his son's disgrace.[78] Wealth and public honour are praiseworthy if put to good use and borne without ostentation or arrogance.[79] Accolti says that Bartolomeo Valori, Niccolò da Uzzano and Guido del Palagio had reputations for integrity rather than riches,[80] and it is worth seeing Cosimo and his sons 'walking through the city, without pomp, without slaves, without ornate clothing; indeed, when visitors see them, they do not think they are the famous Medici but just ordinary men'.[81]

Epideictic rhetoric also provided Accolti with the theme of his dialogue, for one commonplace of panegyric was the contrast between ancients and moderns or between antiquity and modern times. A writer could censure contemporary individuals or institutions by declaring that they were inferior to their predecessors; on the other hand, he could praise them by showing that they were superior to their counterparts in the past. With its

---

[65] Dialogue, fol. 34v; Galletti, 119.
[66] *De oratore*, ii, 343–4, 346; Quintilian, III, vii, 16.
[67] Dialogue, fol. 33v; Galletti, 118.     [68] Dialogue, fol. 37r–v; Galletti, 120.
[69] Quintilian III, vii, 13–14.
[70] Dialogue, fol. 20v–21r; Galletti, 113. Cf. *Rhet. ad Her.*, III, 10; *De oratore*, ii, 342.
[71] *Rhet. ad Her.*, III, 13; Quintilian, III, vii, 10.
[72] Dialogue, fol. 30v, 32r; Galletti, 117, 118.
[73] *Rhet. ad Her.*, III, 13; Quintilian, III, vii, 10.
[74] Dialogue, fol. 19v; Galletti, 112.     [75] *De oratore*, ii, 342.
[76] Dialogue, fol. 19v–20r; Galletti, 112–13.     [77] *De oratore*, ii, 346.
[78] Dialogue, fol. 33v, 37r–v; Galletti, 118, 120.
[79] *Rhet. ad Her.*, III, 10; *De oratore*, ii, 342.     [80] Dialogue, fol. 30v; Galletti, 117.
[81] Dialogue, fol. 35v (Galletti, 119): Opere pretium est videre ipsum eius clarissimos et optimos filios sine pompa, sine servis, sine vestium ornatu per urbem incedere ut qui illos advenae conspiciunt non eos quorum adeo illustris fama est sed mediocres quosdam viros arbitrentur.

derivation from epideictic rhetoric, it is not surprising that the quarrel of
the ancients and moderns was one of the most prominent themes in
humanist literature,[82] and so Accolti could have little fear that the topic of
his dialogue would be criticized as unworthy of humanist study.
Moreover, he could have had no anxiety lest the particular position he
took in the quarrel – the defence of the moderns – should offend humanist
prejudices in favour of antiquity. Humanists, participating as they did in
the quarrel as practitioners of epideictic rhetoric, chose the side of the
argument which was appropriate to the particular panegyric which they
were composing, and so there was no unanimity of opinion on the question
of ancients and moderns in humanist literature: as in other major themes
of humanist thought such as the superiority of the active or contemplative
life, the merits of republics or monarchies, the worth of the vernacular
languages in comparison with the Latin and Greek or the dignity of man,
both sides of the quarrel had notable champions among the humanists.[83]
On the one hand, there were Petrarch's condemnations of his own age in
contrast to Roman antiquity,[84] which were echoed by his antiquarian
friend, Giovanni Dondi,[85] Salutati's denunciation of his contemporaries as
botchers who patch together the scraps of antiquity without inventing anything new themselves,[86] Niccolò Niccoli's attacks on the modern age in
contrast to classical antiquity in Bruni's *Dialogus*,[87] and Bruni's own view
of his contemporaries as dwarfs in comparison with the stature of the
ancients.[88] On the other hand, Petrarch also said that his law professors at
Bologna resembled ancient legislators and praised Cola di Rienzo for his
similarity to the two Bruti;[89] Giannozzo Manetti said that Brunelleschi's
dome rivalled the pyramids;[90] Poggio said that Alfonso of Aragon was a
greater prince than Augustus, Trajan, Marcus Aurelius or the Antonines;[91]
and Flavio Biondo likened the papal domains to the ancient Roman
Empire.[92]

Just as panegyric was not an invention of the Italian humanists, so its
hand-maiden, the quarrel of the ancients and moderns, had a long history
both preceding and following the Renaissance; the connection of the
quarrel with rhetoric always meant that, as in the Renaissance, a consensus

[82] On the quarrel in the early Renaissance, cf. Margiotta, *Origini italiane*; Buck, *Die 'Querelle'*; H. Baron, 'The *Querelle*'; Black, 'Ancients and moderns'.
[83] Cf. P. O. Kristeller, 'The moral thought of Renaissance humanism', in his *Renaissance Thought II* (New York, 1965), 53ff.
[84] Cf. A. Tripet, *Pétrarque ou la connaissance de soi* (Geneva, 1967), 117–25.
[85] Gilbert, 'A letter of Giovanni Dondi', 302, 307–14, 330–8.
[86] *Epistolario*, ii, 145.
[87] Ed. E. Garin, *Prosatori latini del Quattrocento* (Milan, n.d.), 52–74.
[88] *Epistolae*, ed. Mehus, i, 28; cf. also Bruni, *Schriften*, 123–5.
[89] Sen. x, 2; Var. 48.    [90] Cf. Baron, 'The *Querelle*', 18.
[91] *Epistolae*, ii, 305–6.    [92] *Scritti*, ed. Nogara, xcix–ci.

was never reached. On the one hand, Horace censured his contemporaries as impious, factious, and degenerate by contrasting them with the early Romans portrayed as paragons of gravity and severity;[93] similarly, Vergil condemned the corruption of modern Rome by citing the simplicity of old Rome,[94] as did Juvenal, who contrasted old Roman purity with contemporary gluttony, effeminacy, and Greek decadence.[95] This commonplace continued to be found useful in the middle ages, for example, by Charlemagne, who, when he wished to point out the shortcomings of his court scholars, is said to have declared, 'I wish I had twelve men with the wisdom of Jerome and Augustine.'[96] Similarly, Alan of Lille wrote of the crudity of modern poetics in contrast to the learning of ancient poets,[97] and a famous medieval example comes from *Carmina Burana*:

> Once learning flourished, but alas!
> 'Tis now become a weariness.
> Once it was good to understand,
> But play has now the upper hand . . . [98]

The idea of 'il buon tempo antico', the golden age of the Italian communes, was a version of this commonplace which became a favourite theme in the literature of the Italian city-states in the thirteenth and fourteenth centuries:[99] Dante referred to the age of his ancestor, Cacciaguida, to highlight the deficiencies of contemporary Florence,[100] whereas Filippo Villani, writing in the late fourteenth century, saw the time of Dante as a golden age in contrast to the contemporary world.[101] The commonplace continued to be useful after Accolti's time, as was shown by Machiavelli, who censured his contemporaries by making a detailed comparison between them and ancient Romans.[102] Similarly, Lazzaro Bonamico, one of the interlocutors in Speroni's *Dialogo delle lingue*, illustrated the deficiencies of contemporary Italian by declaring that, compared to the Latin language, which he likened to wine, the vernacular was like the dregs,[103] a view shared by Romolo Amaseo, who argued that Latin was superior to Italian because of its antiquity and universality.[104] Later in the sixteenth century, Trajano Boccalini condemned the contemporary world in which

[93] Ode iii, 6.     [94] *Georgics*, iii, 458–540.     [95] Satires, ii, vi and xi.
[96] Cf. Gössmann, *Antiqui und Moderni*, 52.
[97] Cf. Chenu, *Nature, Man and Society*, 318–19.
[98] Cf. Curtius, *European Literature*, 94–5.
[99] Cf. C. Davies, 'Il buon tempo antico', *Florentine Studies*, ed. N. Rubinstein (London, 1968), 45–69.
[100] Paradiso, xvi, 34ff. For the related theme of 'mundus senescens' in antiquity and the middle ages, cf. G. Miccoli, *Chiesa gregoriana* (Florence, 1966), 301–3.
[101] *Liber de civitatis Florentiae famosis civibus*, G. Galletti (Florence, 1847), 5.
[102] *Discorsi*, passim.
[103] Cf. Margiotta, *Origini italiane*, 102; Buck, *Die 'Querelle'*, 15–16.
[104] Margiotta, *Origini italiane*, 100.

there was no longer any love, even between father and son, viewing modern times as an age in which money had become man's only concern.[105] Marcantonio Zimara's view was that the contemporary world in contrast to antiquity had fewer great men because human nature had grown weaker,[106] an opinion somewhat more extreme than Doni's view in the *Marmi*, where modern times were censured in comparison to antiquity because 'whatever one writes has been said and whatever one imagines has been imagined'.[107] This was repeated at the end of the seventeenth century by La Bruyère, who wrote, 'All has been said', and it has been 'more than seven thousand years since there were men who thought',[108] which shows that demonstrating the superiority of the ancients over the moderns remained an effective *topos* of epideictic rhetoric after the end of the Renaissance.

Just as important in classical, medieval and Renaissance thought was the theme that moderns were superior or equal to ancients. Ovid praised the sophistication of contemporary Rome in contrast to the crude manners of early Rome,[109] and Statius said that Lucan was a greater poet than Ennius, Lucretius and Vergil; this commonplace remained a favourite in late antiquity, as is shown by many passages from authors such as Ausonius, Claudian, Sidonius Apollinaris and Fortunatus.[110] It was found particularly useful by Cassiodorus, who said that some of his contemporaries possessed the morals of the ancients and who praised Boethius as being the equal or superior of ancient authors in logic and mathematics.[111] In the early middle ages, Bede said that modern poetry was comparable to Vergil's since both followed the same rules,[112] and at the Carolingian court academy Charlemagne was praised as the new David and Aachen as the new Athens,[113] while Walafrid Strabo, another Carolingian, declared that someone called Probus wrote better poetry than Vergil, Horace and Ovid.[114] In the eleventh century, Pope Gregory VII praised the modern papacy by maintaining that the pope's jurisdiction was wider than the Roman Empire's,[115] and Wido of Amiens said that the battle of Hastings was the greatest since the time of Julius Caesar.[116] In the twelfth century typical examples are Abbot Suger's claim that King Louis VII's triumphs were more distinguished than many in antiquity,[117] John Cotton's statement that 'moderns had more subtlety and wisdom in understanding all

---

[105] Buck, *Die 'Querelle'*, 17.   [106] *Ibid.*   [107] Margiotta, *Origini italiane*, 131.
[108] Buck, *Die 'Querelle'*, 16.   [109] *Ars amatoria*, iii, 113.
[110] Curtius, *European Literature*, 162–3; another version was to ridicule the notion that age conferred value: cf. Horace, *Epist.* ii, 1, 18ff.; Curtius, 165–6, 253.
[111] Cf. Gössmann, *Antiqui und Moderni*, 25–9.
[112] *Ibid.*, 29–31.   [113] *Ibid.*, 39.
[114] Curtius, *European Literature*, 163.   [115] Gössmann, *Antiqui und Moderni*, 46.
[116] Curtius, *European Literature*, 164.   [117] Gössmann, *Antiqui und Moderni*, 38.

things'[118] and Abelard's view that it was his task to reveal and correct the imperfections of Aristotle and Boethius.[119] In the thirteenth century, Aubry of Trois-Fontaines declared that 'the ancients devoted themselves to many things which today are held in ridicule'[120] and the Paduan historian Rolandino scorned the crude works of his father, who in his view had written in the 'rude style of the ancients'.[121] The appeal of the commonplace did not wane after Accolti's day, as was shown in 1473 by Alamanno Rinuccini's prefatory epistle to his translation of Philostratus's *De vita Apollonii Tyanei* in which he praises moderns in comparison with ancients for their achievements in the visual arts, grammar, philosophy, eloquence, statesmanship and warfare,[122] and this theme remained in wide use in the later Renaissance, as is clear from authors such as Bembo, Speroni, Gelli and Varchi, each of whom justified and defended the vernacular by arguing that as a language it was equal or superior to classical Latin.[123] One of the most important versions of this theme in the Renaissance was praising the moderns by comparing them to the ancients in more general terms; indeed, the idea of the revival of the arts was a variation of this commonplace in which moderns were praised by showing that they had once more equalled or even surpassed the achievements of antiquity.[124] Moderns were praised in these terms by such authors as Filippo Villani,[125] Palmieri,[126] Biondo,[127] Valla,[128] Ficino,[129] Castiglione,[130] Reuchlin, Melanchthon and Le Roy,[131] and in the early seventeenth century by Lancillotti and Tassoni, both of whom wrote extensive works comparing ancients and moderns which were in fact encomia of modern times;[132] Tassoni's *Pensieri diversi*, the last book of which contains his comparison of ancients and moderns, was translated into French and served as the model for Perrault's *Parallel of the Ancients and Moderns*,[133] which too was a version of this traditional commonplace of epideictic rhetoric, as were other works in the well-known *querelle des anciens et modernes* of the seventeenth and eighteenth centuries.[134]

[118]  Cf. Silvestre, ' "Quanto iuniores, tanto perspicaciores" ', 235.
[119]  Gössmann, *Antiqui und Moderni*, 67.    [120]  Silvestre, ' "Quanto iuniores" ', 243.
[121]  Gössmann, *Antiqui und Moderni*, 39.
[122]  A. Rinuccini, *In libros Philostrati De vita Apollonii Tyanei ... praefatio*, ed. Giustiniani, *Lettere ed orazioni*, 104–13.
[123]  Margiotta, *Origini italiane*, 101–7, 138.
[124]  Weisinger, 'Renaissance accounts', 105–18.
[125]  Cf. Galletti, 8ff.    [126]  *Della vita civile*, ed. F. Battaglia (Bologna, 1944), 36–7.
[127]  Weisinger, 'Renaissance accounts', 110.    [128]  *Ibid.*
[129]  Cf. P. O. Kristeller, *The Philosophy of Marsilio Ficino* (New York, 1943), 22–3.
[130]  Margiotta, *Origini italiane*, 122.
[131]  Weisinger, 'Renaissance accounts', 111–12, 116–17.
[132]  Cf. Buck, *Die 'Querelle'*, 18–23; Margiotta, *Origini italiane*, 151–61.
[133]  *Ibid.*, 160–1.
[134]  On the quarrel, besides the works already cited, cf. A. Buck, 'Aus der Vorgeschichte der "Querelle des anciens et des modernes" in Mittelalter und Renaissance', in his *Die*

Much has been made of Renaissance texts such as Accolti's dialogue in the development of the quarrel of the ancients and moderns; it has been assumed that in the history of thought a progression occurred in which the first stage was characterized by deference to antiquity, the second by self-confident equality with the ancients, leading to the idea of progress and a sense of ever-growing superiority over the ancients. Sometimes the classicism of the Renaissance has been identified as the first stage and the development of modern science in the seventeenth century as the second;[135] recently this has been challenged by the view that Renaissance humanists, among whom Benedetto Accolti has been given a prominent place, developed a sense of equality with or superiority to the ancients which prepared the way for the emergence of the idea of progress in the late sixteenth and early seventeenth centuries.[136] However, these schemes skirt round the fact that the quarrel of the ancients and moderns was part of the rhetoric of praise and blame, and therefore not only in the Renaissance but throughout much of the history of western thought supporters of the moderns and denigrators of the ancients can be found and *vice versa*. It is difficult to detect progression or development because both sides of the argument were present from antiquity until the end of the eighteenth century – in other words, for as long as rhetoric remained a fundamental technique of composition. By attaching particular historical significance to the support of one side or the other, one can overlook the role of rhetoric, which always made both sides of the argument available to an author; when, for example, Griffolini, Accolti and Rinuccini chose to defend the moderns, they were not so much marching forward in the vanguard of an historical progression which would eventually lead to the overthrow of the authority of the ancients as choosing the side of the argument which was appropriate to the task with which they were faced as rhetoricians. Moreover, the attempt to see the history of the quarrel as the gradual triumph of modernity over classicism is bedevilled by the unnerving habit of the leading protagonists to argue on both sides of the question. The case of Leonardo Bruni is now famous,[137] and he is joined by Horace,[138] Einhard,[139] Otto of Freising,[140] Ermenrich,[141] John of Salisbury,[142]

---

*humanistische Tradition in der Romania* (Bad Homburg v.d.H. 1968), 75–91; *Antiqui und Moderni: Traditionsbewusstsein und Fortschrittsbewusstsein im späten Mittelalter*, ed. A. Zimmerman (*Miscellanea Mediaevalia*, 9) (Berlin, 1974).

[135] Cf. e.g. R. F. Jones, *Ancients and Moderns* (St Louis, 1936); J. P. Bury, *The Idea of Progress* (London, 1920).

[136] Cf. Baron, 'The *Querelle*'; Buck, *Die 'Querelle'*; Margiotta, *Origini italiane*.

[137] Cf. J. Seigel, ' "Civic Humanism" or Ciceronian rhetoric?', PP, xxxiv (1966), 3–48.

[138] Ode iii, 6 and Epist. ii, 1.

[139] Cf. Einhard, *Vita Karoli Magni*, ed. G. H. Perta, G. Waitz and O. Holder-Egger, in *Scriptores rerum germanicarum in usum scholarum* (Hannover and Leipzig, 1911), 1–2.

[140] Cf. Gössmann, *Antiqui und Moderni*, 57–8.

[141] *Ibid.*, 84.   [142] Curtius, *European Literature*, 163.

Petrarch,[143] Salutati,[144] Alberti[145] and Machiavelli.[146] Indeed, Accolti himself, in his poem on friendship, went beyond his paraphrase of Cicero's *De
amicitia* to give his own view of how the moral standards of his century
had declined since the days of his ancestors.[147] Such inconsistency, problematic though it may be for some modern scholars, is inherent in the
traditions of rhetoric, in which an orator proved his virtuosity by
demonstrating his ability to argue on both sides of a question.

　　In the history of the quarrel, it would be misguided to argue that Accolti
deserves prominence as a leader of the moderns in their assault on the
entrenched authority of antiquity. This is not to say that there were no
developments in the history of the quarrel during the Renaissance; on the
contrary, the idea of progress, for example, although present in medieval
authors such as Otto of Freising or Roger Bacon,[148] became one of the
major themes in the quarrel during the late Renaissance. Like other early
humanists, Accolti was not concerned with the concept of progress in his
dialogue, but, unlike his contemporaries, he did foreshadow the later
development of the quarrel in several important ways. In the history of this
theme Accolti's dialogue was a landmark as the first full-scale work
expressly devoted to the question of the ancients and moderns.[149] The
theme had previously been used in broader terms than merely to praise
individuals; indeed, it has been seen that the idea of the revival of the arts,
which was so significant for the humanists' own concept of the Renaissance, was a variation of the commonplace of ancients and moderns in
which moderns were praised by showing that they had once more equalled
or even surpassed the achievements of antiquity. Before Accolti moderns
had been praised in these broad terms by authors such as Palmieri, Biondo
and Valla, who, however, developed these general ideas about ancients
and moderns in works devoted to other subjects. Moreover, Accolti's
dialogue contains a far more extensive and detailed treatment of the question than any previous work; in Bruni's *Dialogus*, for example, two
aspects only of the question are discussed – the superiority of ancient or
modern philosophers and authors, whereas in a series of biographies such
as Filippo Villani's, the theme of ancients and moderns was one among
many ways of praising the author's fellow citizens. Indeed, Accolti's
dialogue is unique before the seventeenth century, for there is no sub-

143　Cf. p. 195, *supra.*
144　Cf. Margiotta, *Origini italiane,* 65–72 and p. 195, *supra.*
145　Cf. Margiotta, *Origini italiane.* 81–2.
146　Cf. the contrast between *Discorsi, passim* and his *Istorie fiorentine,* v, 1.
147　Ed. Jacoboni, 286, 294; cf. *De amicitia,* ix, 32.
148　Cf. esp. Silvestre, ' "Quanto iuniores" ', for a collection of ancient and medieval texts
　　implying an idea of progress.
149　This point is confirmed by Buck, *Die 'Querelle',* 12.

sequent work examining the question in such breadth and detail before the appearance of Tassoni's *Pensieri diversi* in 1620.

The originality of Accolti's dialogue in this sense resulted from his wish to excel in his new profession as a rhetorician; not only did he wish to prove his competence in Medicean humanist circles by composing a work far more copious and erudite than any previous treatment of the ancients and moderns, but he also wished to thwart any possible challenge from his Aretine rival Griffolini by composing a discussion of the ancients and moderns superior to Griffolini's version in his preface to the Chrysostom translation. Far from stifling originality, therefore, rhetoric spurred Accolti on to attempt new intellectual heights, and there were other ways in which his adherence to the precepts of rhetoric encouraged originality in Accolti's dialogue. Certainly the use of commonplaces could lead to unoriginal arguments in rhetorical works; nevertheless, no stigma was attached to commonplaces, which formed the basis of the rhetorical method. They were essential ingredients of eloquence and the more of them, the better. According to Quintilian they were the seats of argument (*sedes argumentorum*).[150] For the humanists a knowledge of commonplaces was a sign of erudition; originality was not always a virtue. Nevertheless, rhetoric could lead an author into untried and even adventurous territory. An orator, said Protagoras, can make the weaker cause seem the stronger,[151] and such power was attributed to rhetoric by later writers.[152] In his dialogue, Accolti wished to show that he was capable of defending the indefensible, for he chose to concentrate on a number of weak causes; in this way rhetoric influenced Accolti's choice of topics in his comparison of antiquity and modern times, leading him to select subjects in which he could defend unusual points of view and so stimulating his originality.

In the Renaissance it was, of course, unusual to criticize ancient rhetoric since it had been the admiration of Roman eloquence that had inspired the early humanists to launch their revival of classical learning; nevertheless Accolti maintains that modern oratory and eloquence compare favourably with ancient.[153] What is particularly interesting about this section of the dialogue is that, although he was defending an unusual position, Accolti constructed his argument entirely out of commonplaces; in this way he was able to demonstrate his skill as a rhetorician both through knowledge of commonplaces and by successfully defending a weak cause. He begins by stating that the ancients' proficiency was the result of fortunate circumstances. Here he uses an argument from Cicero: 'honos alit artes',[154] or an

---

[150] V, x, 20.    [151] Plato, *Phaedrus*, 267 A.
[152] Aristotle, *Rhet.*, II, xxiv, 11; Dioogenes Laertius ix, 53; Cicero, *Brutus*, 47.
[153] Dialogue, fol. 38r–41r; Galletti, 120–2.
[154] *Disp. tusc.*, I, 4, quoted by Accolti, Dialogue, fol. 38v (Galletti, 120); for this commonplace applied specifically to oratory, cf. Cicero, *Brutus*, 40, 51, 182.

art flourishes so long as it is held in esteem; since in antiquity oratory was honoured and in constant use, it is no wonder that it flourished. Hence the apology for modern times: since rhetoric is no longer put to practical use, modern orators cannot be expected to equal the ancients. He then goes on to point out the shortcomings of rhetoric in antiquity by showing that the Romans were inferior to the Greeks, because orators were less prominent in political life in Rome than in Athens.[155] Here Accolti is using two commonplaces of ancient rhetoric: that the Greeks, especially the Athenians, excelled in rhetoric and were ruled by orators,[156] and that in learning the Romans were inferior to the Greeks.[157] Accolti then goes on to say that in Rome rhetoric began to be practised only with Cato the Censor, who was frequently cited in Latin literature as an example of one of the first orators,[158] and that few great Latin orators came after him, also a commonplace in antiquity.[159] Accolti next says that oratory in Rome ceased to flourish under the Empire, for, with all power in the hands of one man, the art of persuasion was neither needed nor valued.[160] Here Accolti makes a specific reference to the elder Seneca,[161] and there were many others who also said that rhetoric was in decline during and after the collapse of the republic.[162] Accolti's argument that the decline was due to political conditions goes back to antiquity – Cicero says that monarchy is inimical to oratory[163] which generally flourishes among free nations.[164] But the point that the cultural decline of Rome was the result of the rise of the principate played an important role in humanist literature too; it was, for example, Leonardo Bruni's argument for condemning the Empire in his Florentine history.[165] Accolti concludes this section of the dialogue with an encomium of modern rhetoric by pointing to the eloquence of many of his contemporaries.[166] The revival of letters was one of the fundamental aspirations of the Renaissance, other humanists like Accolti finding it a useful way to praise their contemporaries.[167]

[155] Dialogue, fol. 38v; Galletti, 120–1.
[156] Cf. Cicero, *Brutus*, 26–9, 44; *De oratore*, i, 13; Quintilian X, i, 76–80.
[157] Cf. *Disp. tusc.* i, 1–6; ii, 1–9; iv, 1–7. Cf. also Horace, *Epist.* ii, 1, 90–117.
[158] *Brutus*, 61; *De oratore*, i, 171 and iii, 135; *Disp tusc.* i, 5; Quintilian, III, i, 19.
[159] *Brutus*, 137–8, 182, 333; *De oratore*, i, 6–18.
[160] Dialogue, fol. 39v–40r; Galletti, 121.
[161] Dialogue, fol. 40r; Galletti, 121. Cf. *Controversiae*, Praef. 7.
[162] Petronius, *Satyricon*, 1–4; Seneca, *Epist.*, 114; Pliny, *Epist.*, ii, 14; Quintilian II, x, 3–5; V, xii, 17–23; *Brutus*, 6–9, 22–3; *Disp. tusc.*, ii, 5. Cf. M. Clarke, *Rhetoric at Rome* (London, 1953), 100–8; H. Caplan, 'The decay of eloquence at Rome in the first century', in his *Eloquence: Studies in Ancient and Medieval Rhetoric*, ed. A. King and H. North (Ithaca and London, 1970), 160–95.
[163] *Brutus*, 45.   [164] *De oratore*, i, 30; cf. also *Brutus*, 6–9, 22–3, 46.
[165] Cf. Bruni, *Historiae*, 14–15.   [166] Dialogue, fol. 40v–41r; Galletti, 121–2.
[167] Cf. Weisinger, 'Renaissance accounts', 105–18; Palmieri, *Della vita civile*, ed. Battaglia, 36–7.

Another unpromising cause which Accolti chose to defend in the dialogue was contemporary military practice, and in particular the mercenary system. Most authorities in antiquity and the middle ages had said that a citizen militia was better than a mercenary army,[168] and for most humanists contemporary military institutions had become a subject of ridicule.[169] Nevertheless, there were occasions for humanists to praise contemporary practice: Stefano Porcari had once had the task of praising the Florentine Signoria for its military policy,[170] and Giannozzo Manetti had once had to give an oration after he had delivered a commission to a condottiere.[171] Accolti's arguments were much the same as those used by other humanists faced with the same task. Different customs, he said, might be equally praiseworthy, since the same practice was not suited to all times and places. All pursuits admitted of different types of excellence, not least the art of war; indeed, the ancients themselves used different forms of military organization.[172] Accolti took this argument from Cicero's *De oratore*, where it had been applied to sense perceptions, painting, sculpture, poetry and oratory.[173] It was used by other humanists in defence of mercenaries and is found in Manetti's speech, in Campano's life of Braccio and in Crivelli's life of Muzio Attendolo.[174] Accolti also claims that moderns excel in the subtler military arts, trickery and deceit, a claim based on a statement attributed to Hannibal by Livy that the Romans were unacquainted with the fine points of warfare;[175] like Accolti, Campano regarded his contemporaries' ability to deceive the enemy as a reason for their military superiority over the ancients.[176] Accolti, moreover, cited the support of ancient authority to demonstrate that ancient armies lacked discipline.[177] Campano made the same point,[178] and like Accolti[179] praised contemporary discipline by way of contrast.[180] Finally, Accolti in common with other humanists argued that contemporaries because of the invention

---

[168] Cf. C. Bayley, *War and Society in Renaissance Florence* (Toronto, 1961), 178–84.

[169] *Ibid.*, 184–231.

[170] Stefano Porcari, 'Orazione', in *Testi di lingua inediti tratti da' codici della Biblioteca Vaticana*, ed. G. Manzi (Rome, 1816), 23–7.

[171] G. Manetti and Bernardo de' Medici, '. . . Orazione . . . quando e' dierono . . . el bastone . . . a Gismonde . . . de' Malatesti', in *Commentario della vita di G. Manetti, scritto da Vespasiano da Bisticci*, ed. P. Fanfani (*Collezione di opere inedite o rare*, II (Turin, 1862)), 203ff.

[172] Dialogue, fol. 23r–24r; Galletti, 114.   [173] III, 25ff. Cf. *Brutus*, 204–5.

[174] Manetti and Medici, 'Orazione', 204ff.; G. A. Campano, *Braccii Perusini vita et gesta*, ed. R. Valentini, RIS², xix, pt 4, 168; L. Crivelli, *De vita et rebus gestis Sfortiae . . . historia*, RIS, xix (Milan, 1731), 635, 639.

[175] XXI, liv, 3, paraphrased by Accolti, Dialogue, fol. 25r (Galletti, 115).

[176] Campano, *Braccii vita*, 165–7.

[177] He quotes Lucan, x, 407–8: Dialogue, fol. 27v (Galletti, 116).

[178] Campano, *Braccii vita*, 166–8.

[179] Dialogue, fol. 26v–27v; Galletti, 115–16.   [180] Campano, *Braccii vita*, 166–8.

of the cannon were superior to the ancients in siege warfare,[181] and that modern cavalry was superior to ancient, especially because of advances in armour.[182]

Accolti entered a plea on behalf of scholastic philosophy, a favourite subject of ridicule by humanists,[183] as was another modern university subject, law, which Accolti also defended in the dialogue,[184] but the most original section of his work was his defence of the modern church, which was often compared unfavourably with the ancient or primitive church.[185] The idea of Christian antiquity, implying a division of religious history into an ancient and a modern period, goes back at least to the fifth century when it seems that the writings of the church fathers contain the first references to the primitive church and Christian antiquity. From its first appearances the idea of the early church implied that Christian antiquity was superior to the modern period in religious history. The primitive

[181] Dialogue, fol. 25r (Galletti, 115); Biondo, *Decades*, in his *Opera* (Basel, 1531), 394; Crivelli, *Historia*, 711; Campano, *Braccii vita*, 167.

[182] Dialogue, fol. 25r–v (Galletti, 115); Crivelli, *Historia*, 635; Campano, *Braccii vita*, 166, 168. Bayley, *War and Society*, 227–8 and Baron, *Crisis²*, 435–7, have assumed that Accolti's defence of mercenaries is connected with declining republicanism in Florence during the later fifteenth century. However, it was a commonplace to praise a citizen militia and criticize mercenaries, and such statements by humanists were not always taken literally, as was shown by Roberto Valturio, who dedicated his *De re militari*, which advocated a militia, to the condottiere Sigismondo Malatesta. Nor did all humanists assume that military excellence and republican liberty went hand in hand: Biondo, a critic of mercenaries, declared that the Roman Empire expanded under many of the emperors (*Decades*, 4). Baron's scheme that the defence of mercenaries signalled the decline of republicanism during the 'age of Lorenzo de' Medici' has to make allowance for too many exceptions. Porcari was part of Niccoli's and Bruni's circle (cf. Pastor, *Storia*, i, 568–9) and Manetti was, according to Baron, one of the principal continuators of civic humanism after Bruni, but the one in 1427 and the other in 1453 defended the mercenary system; Platina and Patrizi, who according to Baron were connected with Florence, attacked mercenaries as late as 1471 (*Crisis²*, 427–8). Even Bruni argued for and against mercenaries: in the early books of his Florentine history, Bruni consistently praised the militia, whereas in the later books he consistently praised mercenaries (cf. D. Wilcox, *Development of Florentine Humanist Historiography* (Cambridge, Mass. 1969) 96–8). Bruni here was applying the rhetorical commonplace used by Cicero and then later by Accolti, Campano, Crivelli and Manetti that the same practice is not suited to all times and places. Bruni's point is that in the early period of Florentine history, the militia system was adequate, whereas later, when warfare became more complex, professional mercenaries were needed. Bruni's point of view did not change in response to altering conditions in Florence; rather, as a rhetorician writing history, he adapted his ideas to the requirements of his subject, using the rhetorical method of arguing for and against to analyse developments in Florentine history.

[183] Cf. P. O. Kristeller, 'Humanism and scholasticism', reprinted with recent bibliographical editions in *Renaissance Thought and its Sources*, 85–105, 272–87; cf. Dialogue, fol. 42r–44v (Galletti, 122–3) and pp. 211–12, *infra*.

[184] Cf. Bruni's letter to Niccolò Strozzi, in *La disputa*, ed. Garin, 8; Lapo da Castiglionchio's letter to Roberto Strozzi, in *Reden und Briefe*, ed. Müllner, 258–9; Garin, *L'umanesimo italiano*, 46ff. and pp. 210–11, *infra*.

[185] Dialogue, fol. 45r–55r; Galletti, 123–7.

church continued to be cited as an ideal for reform throughout the early Middle Ages and provided a justification for the Hildebrandine reform after the middle of the eleventh century. In the writings of twelfth-century moralists such as St Bernard, the contrast between the ancient and modern churches was drawn even more sharply than before, and in the thirteenth century, with the appearance of the mendicant orders and their call for apostolic poverty, which was supported by heterodox movements such as the Cathars, Waldensians, Fraticelli, Beguines and Beghards, the superiority of the ancient church was an assumption so widely accepted that advocates of conciliarism as well as champions of papal supremacy supported their claims by reference to Christian antiquity; moreover the major heresies of the fourteenth and fifteenth centuries, such as Lollardy and the Hussite movement, were based on a call to return to the primitive church.[186]

In his panegyric of the modern church, therefore, Accolti could claim to be defending the indefensible; moreover, Accolti was going against the mainstream of humanist thought, in which the superiority of Christian antiquity was a commonplace.[187] Petrarch preached apostolic poverty and condemned the Donation of Constantine as a source of corruption in the modern church;[188] another example is the chapter on poverty in Salutati's treatise, *De seculo et religione*,[189] a widely read work in the fifteenth cen-

---

[186] On the primitive church and Christian antiquity, cf. Olsen, 'The idea of the *ecclesia primitiva*', 61–86; E. McDonnell, *The Beguines and Beghards in Medieval Culture* (New Brunswick, N.J., 1954), esp. 30ff., 56ff., 141ff.; idem, 'The Vita Apostolica', *Church History*, xxiv (1955), 15–31; G. Miccoli, *Chiesa gregoriana* (Florence, 1966), 75–167, 225–99; Chenu, *Nature, Man and Society*, 202–69; H. V. White, 'The Gregorian ideal and St Bernard of Clairvaux', JHI, xxi (1960), 321–48; P. De Vooght, 'Du *De consideratione* de saint Bernard au *De potestate papae* de Wyclif', *Irenikon*, xxvi (1953), 114–32; E. Kennan, 'The "De consideratione" of St Bernard of Clairvaux and the papacy in the mid-twelfth century', *Traditio*, xxiii (1967), 73–115; H. Kaminsky, *A History of the Hussite Revolution* (Berkeley and Los Angeles, 1967); idem et al. eds., *Master Nicholas of Dresden, The Old Color and the New* (*Transactions of the American Philosophical Society*, n.s. lv, pt 1) (Philadelphia, 1965); G. Leff, 'The making of the myth of a true church in the later Middle Ages', *Journal of Medieval and Renaissance Studies*, i (1971), 1–15; idem, 'The apostolic ideal in later medieval eccesiology', *Journal of Theological Studies*, n.s. xviii (1967), 58–82; L. B. Pascoe, 'Jean Geirson: the "Ecclesia Primitiva" and reform'; P. Stockmeier, 'Causa Reformationis und Alte Kirche', in *Von Konstanz nach Trient*, ed. R. Bäumer (Munich, 1972), 1–13; P. Stockmeir, 'Die alte Kirche – Leitbild der Erneuerung', *Theologische Quartalschrift* (Tübingen), clvi (1966), 385–408; J. Preus, 'Theological legitimation for innovation in the middle ages', *Viator*, iii (1972), 1–26; G. Ladner, 'Gregory the Great and Gregory VII: a comparison of the concepts of renewal', *Viator*, iv (1963), 1–31; S. Hendrix, 'In quest of the *Vera Ecclesia*: the crises of late medieval ecclesiology', *Viator*, vii (1976), 347–78.

[187] For a general account of ideas of church reform among humanists, cf. Garin, 'Desideri di riforma nell'oratoria del Quattrocento', in *La cultura filosofica*, 166–82.

[188] Cf. P. Piur, *Petrarcas 'Buch ohne Namen' und die Päpstliche Kurie* (Halle, 1925), 57–77; H. Baron, 'Franciscan poverty and civic wealth', *Speculum*, xiii (1938), 6–11.

[189] Ed. B. L. Ullman (Florence, 1957).

tury.[190] Salutati argues that although Christians for the first three hundred
years were poor, yet by virtue of their sanctity they spread the faith
throughout the world; on the other hand, since the Donation of
Constantine, although the church has become rich in temporal goods, it is
spiritually impoverished, too weak to combat Saracens and schismatic
Greeks, and even divided against itself.[191] The Great Schism, here referred
to by Salutati, inspired another humanist panegyric of the ancient church,
Pier Paolo Vergerio's oration for the reunification of the church, delivered
in the presence of the Roman cardinals in November 1406,[192] but a particularly famous instance of primitive Christianity idealized in humanist
thought is Lorenzo Valla's *De falso credita et ementita Constantini
donatione*, in which Pope Sylvester I is cited as an example of Christian
simplicity in contrast to Eugenius IV.[193] The theme of Christian antiquity
as an ideal for the reform of the modern church has an important place in
the thought of the Florentine humanist and Greek scholar, Ambrogio
Traversari, who contrasted the almost universal sway of Christianity in the
patristic age with shrinking Christendom in his own day; Traversari,
general of the Camaldulensian order, wanted to restore his order to the
sanctity of ancient cenobitic life, and in his active role at the Councils of
Basel and Florence he upheld the general councils of the primitive church
as models by which to judge modern councils.[194] Traversari's contemporary, the Milanese humanist and Augustinian canon Andrea Biglia, adopted
a similar perspective, seeing the rise of Islam and the decline of Christianity
in the East as symptoms of a 'universal Dark Age',[195] and the same assumption was implicit in comparisons made by the humanists between the bad
style of the scholastics and the eloquence of the church fathers.[196]

The defence of the modern church was a cause to tempt an aspiring
humanist such as Accolti, especially since his rival, Francesco Griffolini
had undertaken a brief panegyric of the contemporary church in his dedicatory letter to Cosimo by praising Pope Pius II, as well as his predecessors
Martin V and Nicholas V:

[190] Cf. *ibid.*, vi–xv for a list of many fifteenth-century manuscripts.
[191] *Ibid.*, 128–31.
[192] *Pro redintegranda uniendaque ecclesia ad Romanos cardinales oratio tempore schis-
matis in consistorio habita, a. 1406, novembri*, ed. C. A. Combi, *Archivio storico per
Trieste, l'Istria e il Trentino*, i (1881–2), 360–74.
[193] Ed. W. Setz, *Monumenta Germaniae Historica. Quellen zur Geistesgeschichte des
Mittelalters*, x (Weimar, 1976), 175. Cf. H. Gray, 'Valla's *Encomium* of St Thomas
Aquinas' and the humanist conception of Christian antiquity', *Essays . . . to Stanley
Pargellis*, ed. H. Bluhm (Chicago, 1965), 40–2.
[194] Cf. C. Stinger, *Humanism and the Church Fathers: Ambrogio Traversari* (Albany, N.Y.
1977), 137–8, 167–210, 283–6, 292–3.
[195] Cf. Webb, 'Decline and fall', 206–7.
[196] Cf. Gray, 'Valla's *Encomium*', 37ff.; Bruni, *De studiis et literis liber*, in *Schriften*, ed
Baron, 5–19.

What shall I say of Martin V, who on his accession to the pontificate found the condition of the church weakened and disturbed by various misfortunes? He settled the long-standing schism and reunited the church into one body, guiding the endangered ship of Peter into the most tranquil harbour out of the greatest disorders and tempests with the skill of a considerable pilot. What was lacking in Nicholas V in comparison with the most distinguished prince? Even though his pontificate was brief, nevertheless in Italy he reestablished the peace of Augustus, and under his auspices and through his leadership the city of Rome and the Roman language were renewed. Even if unwelcome death had not suddenly removed him in the midst of his work, one could boast that he, no less than Augustus, transformed the city from brick to marble. What is equal to the piety of Pius II? Truly I say pious of a man who has refused no labour with his infirm and weak body in order to care for the church and the Christian religion entrusted to him.[197]

Accolti may have seen that Griffolini had not taken full advantage of the opportunities for rhetorical display offered by a weak cause such as the modern church; certainly a number of arguments in Accolti's defence of modern Christianity show him at work mainly as a rhetorician. For example, Accolti censures ancient pagans who had the opportunity of witnessing many miracles and yet tenaciously clung to their false beliefs; on the other hand, he excuses modern clerics who sin on the grounds that they are only human and argues that in general wicked men would not become members of religious orders in which they would have little opportunity for indulging in vice.[198]

Especially topical was Accolti's defence of clerical wealth and of magnificence at the Roman curia. At the beginning of his pontificate, Pius II had established a commission to launch, among other things, a reform of the Roman curia; this resulted in two memoranda, one by Domenico de' Domenichi and the other by Cardinal Nicholas of Cusa, as well as in a draft of a reform bull by Pius II himself.[199] Particular features of the reform proposals were a condemnation of luxury at the curia and a ban on jewels and gold and silver plate, as well as on sumptuous banquets in the houses of cardinals and prelates.[200] The hand of papal reform

---

[197] BNF, CSopp. J. 6.7, fol. 2r–v: Quid nam de Martino quinto dicam qui cum primum ad summum est pontificatum assumptus imbellicum et variis casibus agitatum ecclesiae statum et diuturnum schisma ita sedavit, ita in unum corpus redegit, ut ex maximis perturbationibus et procellis in tranquillissimum portum tanti gubernatoris peritia periclitantem Petri naviculam appulerit? Quid ad clarissimum principem Nicolao quinto defuit? Cuius tempora etsi brevissima quantulacumque tamen in hac nostra inferiore Italia Augusti paci contulerim. Cuius ductu et auspicio ut urbs Roma ita et romana lingua renovata est. Quem nisi tam repente invida mors e medio substulisset, non minus quam Augustus urbem e lateritia marmoream reliquisse gloriari potuisset. Quid Pio secundo pietate par? Vere inquam pio qui ut commisse sibi ecclesiae et christianae relligioni [sic] consuleret invalido et imbecillo corpore nullum recusavit laborem.

[198] Dialogue, fol. 48r, 50r–v; Galletti, 124–5.

[199] Haubst, 'Der Reformentwurf Pius des Zweiten', 188–242; Pastor, *Storia*, ii, 176ff.; Hay, *Church in Italy*, 86, 151–52.

[200] *Ibid.*, 86; Haubst, 'Der Reformentwurf', 209ff.; Pastor, *Storia*, ii, 176ff.

touched the Florentine church when the pope summoned the archbishop
of Florence, Antonino, to join his commission,[201] and so Accolti had found
an ideal topic for proving his rhetorical prowess when he countered the
views of such princes of the church as Domenichi and Cusa, not to mention
the pope himself, by arguing in favour of curial wealth and pomp:

> Nor should [the cardinals of the church], although they proceed with an entourage
> of many servants and dependants, be accused of insolence or vanity. What indeed
> could be further from their [conduct]? But since cardinals, after the pope, are con-
> sidered princes of the church, I think the practice is correct whereby they make
> themselves conspicuous among men by such pomp in order to seem more august
> and authoritative among all men. Nor indeed do kings, dictators, consuls or other
> magistrates lead the lives of private men but one far more cultivated and splendid,
> making them seem of higher majesty so that men not only learn to revere but also
> to fear them. Indeed, often the office alone is not enough to make great men
> respected, but frequently we see that they are held in contempt unless a certain
> greater power and authority are present.[202]

It is worth noting that there was more than a hint of rhetorical display in
another early Renaissance defence of clerical wealth, Lapo da Castiglionchio's *Dialogus super excellentia curie Romane*, where it is argued, as in
Accolti's dialogue, that although poverty suited the early church, wealth
befits the modern church;[203] curial reform was also a topical issue when
Lapo composed his work in 1438 in the midst of the contest between
Eugenius IV and the Council of Basel,[204] and like Accolti Lapo could have
found no cause better suited to enhancing his reputation as a humanist
than the defence of curial magnificence.

Accolti made his debut as a humanist with a showpiece of rhetorical
virtuosity, but there were other levels to his dialogue. The substantial and
even profound contribution made by this work to Renaissance historical
thought will be considered in a later chapter,[205] but it is important to
realize that the dialogue did not exist alone on the lofty planes of classical
eloquence and historical speculation; indeed, much of what Accolti says

---

[201] *Ibid.*, 179.

[202] Dialogue, fol. 52v–53r: Neque hi, quamquam servis et familiaribus multis comitati
incederent, vel insolentiae vel vanitatis arguendi sunt. Quid enim ab illis fuit remotius?
Sed cum cardinales post pontificem ecclesiae principes habeantur, recte institutum
censeo tali eos pompa ab hominibus conspici, quo apud cunctos augustiores et maioris
auctoritatis viderentur. Neque enim reges, dictatores, consules aut magistratus alii
privatorum more vitam agebant, sed longe cultiorem ac splendidiorem, ut videlicet
eorum maiestas excelsior esset et homines venerabundi simul etiam timentes eos
intuerentur. Plerumque enim magnos homines nec satis verendos dignitas facit sed saepe
comtemni videmus si non maior quaedam accedat potentiae vis atque auctoritas
(Galletti, 126).

[203] Ed. R. Scholz, in *Quellen und Forschungen aus italienischen Archiven und Bibliotheken*,
xv (1914), 148–50; cf. H. Baron, 'Franciscan poverty and civic wealth', *Speculum*, xiii
(1938), 29–30.

[204] Cf. Hay, *Church in Italy*, 85.     [205] Cf. pp. 286–98, *infra*.

reflects his personal preoccupations as well as the intellectual, political and religious concerns of Renaissance Florence in the mid-fifteenth century. The growing strains within the Florentine ruling elite at the end of Cosimo de' Medici's life are apparent in the dialogue from a list of distinguished Florentine statesmen of the past[206] which includes a number of individuals and families who had been opposed to the Medici faction before 1434 and who had fallen from political power after the Medicean victory of that year.[207] It may seem odd at first that Accolti praises the statesmanship not only of members of the Medici family and their party but also of those who were most bitterly opposed to them. On the one hand, this was partly due to the conventions of epideictic rhetoric, which meant that Accolti had to praise all the modern statesmen he mentions; explicit criticism of modern political leaders was impossible at it would have contradicted Accolti's intention to write a work of panegyric about the modern age. On the other hand, this rhetorical convention could serve as a useful device to disguise political hostility when open criticism was imprudent or impossible: it is interesting that Alamanno Rinuccini, an ardent anti-Medicean, used it to cloak his opposition to the Medici in the preface to his translation of Philostratus's *De vita Apollonii*, a work of panegyric similar to Accolti's dialogue where he praises both the Medici and their opponents such as Rinaldo Gianfigliazzi and Niccolò da Uzzano.[208] Although there is no positive evidence to suggest that Accolti was a clandestine anti-Medicean like Rinuccini, nevertheless he had little reason to feel affection for the Medici; at the very least, this list reflects the predicament of many Florentines caught between rival factions in the 1460s. As chancellor, Accolti had to work with all members of the regime, Mediceans and anti-Mediceans alike, and he would hardly have wished to offend either camp. Moreover, in the 1460s, dissatisfaction with the Medici as leaders of the ruling group was often expressed by referring to a golden age in the past before the Medici had become predominant, particularly the period between 1382 and 1430,[209] and Accolti's list may well reflect this idea of a golden age. Of

[206] Dialogue, fol. 30r–31v (Galletti, 117–18): Donato Acciaiuoli, Lotto Castellani, Maso degli Albizzi, Neri Acciaiuoli, Antonio Alberti, Niccolò Alberti, Benedetto Alberti, Rinaldo Gianfigliazzi, Filippo Magalotti, Bartolomeo Valori, Niccolò da Uzzano, Guido del Palagio, Giovanni de' Medici, Gino Capponi, Migliore Guadagni, Vieri Guadagni, Agnolo Pandolfini, Giannozzo Pandolfini, Dino Gucci, Piero Baroncelli, Bartolomeo Corbinelli, Domenico Giugni, Francesco Federighi, Uguccione Ricci, Lapo da Castiglionchio, Giovanni Serristori, Filippo Corsini, Carlo Strozzi, Stoldo Altoviti, Tommaso Sachetti, Andrea Vettori, Tommaso Soderini, Ugo della Stufa, Vieri de' Medici, Salvestro de' Medici, Lorenzo Ridolfi, Alamanno Salviati, Neri Capponi.
[207] This list therefore includes members of the Castellani, Albizzi, Gianfigliazzi, da Uzzano, del Palagio, Guadagni and Altoviti families, who were prominent among opponents to the Medici in the years before 1434: cf. Kent, *Rise of the Medici*, 173, 209, 355–7.
[208] *Lettere ed orazioni*, 109.
[209] Cf. Rubinstein, *Government*, 144; *G. Rucellai ed il suo Zibaldone*, ed. A. Perosa, i

course, Accolti could have justified this kind of political ambivalence on the grounds that his office as chancellor placed him above politics; similarly, conventional political theory stressed unity and condemned faction,[210] enabling Accolti in the dialogue to avoid taking sides by arguing that statesmanship transcends party politics. 'Maso degli Albizzi, Neri Acciaiuoli, Antonio, Niccolò and Benedetto Alberti', he wrote, 'were noble and distinguished knights in their city, even though they belonged to opposing political factions',[211] but again this kind of commonplace could mask political hostility, as in the case of Rinuccini, who, reminiscent of Accolti, wrote that, although Rinaldo Gianfigliazzi, Bartolomeo Valori, Niccolò da Uzzano and Giovanni de' Medici 'had different opinions and sometimes seemed to contradict each other, nevertheless they intended and endeavoured to strive for the good of the republic'.[212] Whatever would ensue in Florence, Accolti wanted to remain chancellor; the traditional political stance of the chancellor was neutrality, and that suited Accolti's situation in the 1460s. He had some reason to resent the Medici, but the safest course was, if possible, to appeal to both sides, which is just what he managed to do in his dialogue.

Accolti's personal feelings emerge even more clearly in the section of his dialogue devoted to the defence of modern law and lawyers. As a lawyer he himself had been the butt of frequent abuse by Poggio, and his defence of law is very much aimed at humanists such as Poggio, who in his opinion had attacked the legal profession from the standpoint of anything but real knowledge.[213] Anyone, Accolti declares, who understands law would not question the erudition of contemporary lawyers: the humanists ought to respect the judgement of lawyers, for it does not follow that bad style means ignorance:

If you compare ancient lawyers with the most recent, those namely who have written commentaries on the *Digest* and *Codex*, they do not, in knowledge, in keenness of intellect, in diligent discussion of cases, seem at all inferior to early lawyers; it can scarcely be described with what amazing order, with what arguments, with what subtle investigations, to use poetic words, they solve the knots and enigmas, deciding cases, where the laws themselves are unclear, with the best proofs. This makes me wonder all the more that some people, ignorant of law, with a certain innane arrogance derived from knowledge of letters and the art of

(London, 1960), 46; Luca di Simone della Robbia, 'Vita di Bartolommeo di Niccolò di Taldo [Valori]', ASI, iv (1843), 239–40.

210  Cf. Warner, 'Palmieri', 33ff.; N. Rubinstein, 'Political ideas in Sienese art', JWCI, xxi (1958), 184ff.; *idem*, 'Marsilius of Padua', in *Europe in the Late Middle Ages*, ed. J. Hale, R. Highfield and B. Smalley (London, 1965), 61–2; *idem*, 'Beginnings of political thought in Florence', JWCI, v (1942), 218ff.

211  Dialogue, fol. 30v (Galletti, 117): Masius item Albizus, Nerius Acciaiuolus, Antonius, Nicolaus et Benedictus ex Albertorum familia nobiles equites, in civitate sua consiliis factisque clarissimi, licet diversas in republica partes secuti sint.

212  Rinuccini, *Lettere ed orazioni*, 109.     213  Cf. pp. 54ff., 80–1, *supra*.

rhetoric, in which they want to seem erudite, detract from the writings of lawyers, implying that they are not distinguished men but rude and entirely ignorant.[214]

Accolti seems to be taking his vengeance on Poggio for the rough treatment he had received in the *Historia tripartita*;[215] certainly his portrait of a humanist whose erudition in literature and skill in rhetoric had led to almost unbearable arrogance towards other professions fitted no one better than Poggio. As a humanist himself, however, Accolti of course had to agree that lawyers' Latin style left much to be desired:

I should agree with them, said Accolti referring to the humanists, if they were complaining only of such books having been written without the polish of eloquence; but it does not follow therefore that in interpreting and explaining the law they are not the greatest and most learned men. Since they [the humanists] are ignorant regarding jurisprudence, they would show greater modesty if they followed in this question not their own opinions but the judgement of learned men. Therefore it is fair to admit that earlier lawyers in elegance, eloquence and literary skill come before our own lawyers; but the books of modern lawyers are filled with greater knowledge and reveal sharper intellects, and legal skill has flourished more widely everywhere in the world in our own time than under the Roman Empire.[216]

In fact, one of Poggio's arguments in the *Historia tripartita* had been that Roman law was restricted to a smaller geographical area in the contemporary world than in antiquity,[217] which suggests again that Accolti's main purpose in this section of the dialogue was to settle an old score with Poggio.

A major concern in Florentine humanist circles in the 1450s and 1460s was the relative value of speculative and moral philosophy; this was the period in which the culture of Bruni's, Poggio's and Traversari's generation, preoccupied with eloquence, philology, moral philosophy, patris-

---

[214] Dialogue, fol. 44v–45r (Galletti, 123): Neque etiam si iurisconsultos veteres cum novissimis compares, illis videlicet qui super Digestis et Codice commentarios scripserunt, scientia, ingenii acumine, diligenti casuum discussione, nulla ex parte hi primis inferiores cuiquam videbuntur, qui, dici vix potest, quam miro ordine, quibus argumentis, quam subtili investigatione, ut poetae verbis utar, legum nodos et enigmata dissolverunt, casusque a legibus indecisos demonstratione optima deciserunt. Quo magis admirari soleo, quosdam iuris ignaros arrogantia quadam inani litterarum peritie seu rhetoricae artis, cuius eruditi videri volunt, illorum scriptis detrahere, velut si non insignes fuissent viri sed indocti penitus et rudes.

[215] Cf. pp. 80ff., *supra*.

[216] Dialogue, fol. 45 (Galletti, 123): Quibus ego assentirer, si duntaxat eiusmodi libros absque ornatu eloquentiae scriptos arguerent, nec propterea consequens est ut in iure interpretando declarandoque non summi et peritissimi fuerint. Cuius cum ignari ipsi sint, modestius agerent si doctorum in ea re, non suum, iudicium sequerentur. Igitur fateri aequum est priores quidem iurisconsultos elegantia, eloquio, litterarum peritia nostros anteisse; scientia vero et ingenii acumine recentiorum libros magis refertos esse, magisque ubique terrarum facultatem hanc aetate nostra quam vigente Romano imperio floruisse.

[217] Cf. p. 80, *supra*.

tics, history and archaeology, was encountering growing criticism from a new generation of humanists who, without necessarily rejecting the merits of these humanist studies, added a renewed interest in scholasticism and natural, speculative and metaphysical philosophy.[218] These new humanist preoccupations are reflected in the section of Accolti's dialogue devoted to philosophy, which, he points out, means *sapientiae studium* and requires sound arguments, not ornate language. He finds many modern philosophers to praise, while maintaining that in ancient Rome philosophers were for a long time unheard of, and later were accepted only with hostility.[219] Significantly, Accolti fails to mention Cicero among the few Roman philosophers, in contrast to other humanists such as Bruni, who assigned him the highest rank among philosophers.[220] Bruni and other humanists in fact condemned scholastics for their bad style and maintained that philosophy was inseparable from eloquence.[221] For the source of Accolti's arguments about the merits of scholasticism one has to consider the influence of Johannes Argyropulos, who began lecturing in Florence in 1457. From the beginning Argyropulos criticized humanists such as Bruni for their ignorance of philosophy, for their insistence that philosophy and eloquence were necessarily linked, and for their disdain of speculative philosophy. Some of Argyropulos's pupils, such as Alamanno Rinuccini, gained from him a respect for the scholastics[222] which resembles Accolti's views in the dialogue; as the dialogue appears to have been written between 1462 and 1463, the passage on philosophy probably shows the influence of Argyropulos's early lectures. There is evidence to suggest that Accolti was part of Argyropulos's circle in Florence, since in the 1450s and 1460s Accolti's closest friend was Otto Niccolini,[223] who is known to have had learned discussions with Argyropulos on such subjects as the relative merits of law and philosophy.[224]

Accolti may have had personal motives for associating himself with the group of Florentine humanists who favoured philosophical speculation. Accolti and Argyropulos shared a common rival during the 1450s in Cristoforo Landino, who not only put himself forward as a candidate for the chancellorship in 1458 against Accolti[225] but was Argyropulos's challenger in the contest for the chair of rhetoric in Florence after 1455.[226] It may be an exaggeration to speak of factions in the Florentine humanist world of the 1450s, but there do seem to have been two tendencies or groups at this time. On the one hand, there were the so-called 'Academy'

[218] Cf. Seigel, 'The teaching of Argyropulos', 237–60.
[219] Dialogue, fol. 42r–44v; Galletti, 122–3.
[220] *Prosatori latini*, ed. Garin, 54.       [221] Seigel, 'Argyropulos', 238–40.
[222] *Ibid.*, 240–56.       [223] Cf. pp. 103–4, *supra*.
[224] Cf. Vespasiano, *Vite*, ii, 203; Della Torre, *Storia*, 397–8.
[225] Cf. pp. 105–7, *supra*.       [226] Cf. Seigel, 'Argyropulos', 241–2.

of Donato Acciaiuoli, Almanno Rinuccini, Andrea Alamanni and Marco
Parenti who brought Argyropulos to Florence; they became sympathetic
to scholasticism and tended at times to be anti-Medicean in politics.[227] On
the other hand, there was Poggio's circle, who remained more firmly committed to the literary culture of earlier Florentine humanism of which
Poggio himself was the last great representative;[228] this group included
Landino[229] and possibly also Antonio Rossi, Bernardo Nuti and
Bartolomeo Scala.[230] This latter circle initially had closer connections to
the Medici than the Academy, but the Medici eventually assumed a place
between these two groups, each of which competed for their favour; this
was especially true after the arrival in Florence in 1456 of the Academy's
new mentor, Argyropulos, who, as a foreigner detached from Florentine
political alignments, immediately began to seek the favour of the
Medici.[234] There is no positive evidence of where Accolti stood in these
divisions, but his rivalry with Landino, his strained relations with Poggio
and his distance from the Medici, all suggest that he had been closer to the
orbit of the Academy. Accolti may have seen the advent of Argyropulos as
another path to greater favour with the Medici, who were strongly
attracted to Argyropulos's teaching. Cosimo, who himself found scholastic disputation intellectually stimulating and had a genuine interest in
scholastic philosophy and theology,[232] as is clear from the books he purchased for the libraries at San Marco and the Badia at Fiesole,[233] had frequent discussions with Argyropulos on philosophical and theological
questions such as the immortality of the soul;[234] Poggio and Landino had
attempted to close one door to Medicean favour on Accolti and so his
advocacy of scholasticism in the dialogue and his approach to
Argyropulos's circle may have been intended as another entrée to intimacy
with the Medici.[235]

---

[227] *Ibid.*    [228] Cf. Poggio, *Epistolae*, iii, 183–8.
[229] For Landino's close association with Poggio, cf. his *Carmina*, ed. Perosa, 123–29, 190.
[230] Poggio's letter opposing Argyropulos's candidacy (ii, 184) states that there were four
local candidates better suited for appointment to the Studio, and it may be more than
coincidence that in the autumn of 1456 the 'shortlist' of possible assistants to Poggio in
the chancery consisted of four names (Landino, Rossi, Nuti and Scala); since the proposed assistants were also to teach in the Studio, it seems reasonable to suggest that the
four proposed chancery assistants were the same as the four local candidates for the
Studio. It is likely that the four proposed candidates for the chancery were closely
associated with Poggio, especially since at least two of them, Landino and Scala, are
known to have been, like Poggio, intimately connected with Medicean circles. Cf. pp.
105–7, *supra*.
[231] Cf. Seigel, 'Argyropulos', 245–56, 256–60; Vespasiano, *Vite*, ii, 203, 205.
[232] *Ibid.*, 203–4.
[233] Ullman and Stadter, *Public Library*, 15, n. 2, 310–13.
[234] Vespasiano, *Vite*, ii, 205–6.
[235] J. Seigel, *Rhetoric and Philosophy in Renaissance Humanism* (Princeton, 1968), 233–6,
240–1, gives a sociological interpretation of Accolti's defence of scholasticism, maintain-

Similar motives may also have encouraged the support which Accolti gave at this time to Marsilio Ficino, whose ideas about philosophy and scholasticism, resembling as they did those of Argyropulos and Accolti,[236] helped him to become the Medici's protégé in the early 1460s;[237] moreover, Accolti probably had even deeper personal reasons for befriending Ficino in the 1460s. The decision of the Signoria to exclude Accolti's rival Griffolini from Florentine territory in September 1461 had placed the Medici in an uncomfortable position. They had given Griffolini every encouragement following their meeting in 1459, but now the Signoria, as they were perfectly entitled to do, had refused to allow Griffolini to assume his benefice. Cosimo's embarrassment became clear when Griffolini sent him the volume of eighty-eight homilies of Chrysostom which Cosimo himself had asked Griffolini to translate into Latin. Just before May 1462, Griffolini had consigned the text of his translation to Giovanni Tornabuoni, Cosimo's business associate in Rome, for delivery to Florence,[238] but by the beginning of November Griffolini had still had no reply or even acknowledgement from Cosimo, who was obviously too embarrassed by the turn of events in Florence to reply. Clearly hurt, especially since he had worked over two years on this translation, Griffolini wrote to Cosimo on 2 November 1462:

> Although I am certain that you have had my version of Chrysostom for quite some time now together with my letter, I did desire so much to have some kind of little note from you. Even if you had nothing new to say, I nevertheless would have rejoiced in one of your letters.[239]

Griffolini then asked Cosimo to aid him in recovering some property of his mother's which had been seized in Città di Castello so that he could provide his sister with a dowry. He had instituted legal proceedings which were going well, but once again he feared that the Florentines, whom he had hoped the Medici could mollify, were about to act against him, since ambassadors from Città di Castello had arrived in Florence complaining

---

ing that Accolti's higher social status made him more secure of his position in Florence than Bruni, whose insecurity led him to attack his scholastic rivals. However, this is an oversimplification of both Bruni's and Accolti's social position in Florence and Arezzo, a complex and ambiguous subject which Seigel has not investigated in any depth. By that argument, Accolti should have been the one to attack scholasticism, for when he wrote the dialogue, he admitted that he had had little experience as a humanist. Cf. pp. 191–2, *supra.*

[236]  Kristeller, *Studies*, 146.

[237]  *Ibid.* Cf. his 'Marsilio Ficino as a beginning student of Plato', *Scriptorium*, xx (1966), 42ff.

[238]  Mancini, *Griffolini*, 33.

[239]  ASF, MAP, 137, 115: Et si certo sciam reliquam Chrysostomi partem cum litteris meis iamdiu magnificentiae tuae redditam . . . cupiebam tamen vel breves ab humanitate tua litterulas; licet enim nihil novi mihi significaturus esses . . . delectassent tamen talis et tanti viri et domini mei litterae.

that the Florentine government was favouring exiles and rebels against their friends and allies. Again Griffolini reminded Cosimo of the now embarrassing encouragement which he had been given by the Medici:

In my innocence I have never harboured any evil designs against your city, especially since I was there more than two years ago, when you and your most excellent sons embraced me with the greatest kindness and gave me good hope for the future.[240]

Griffolini closed his letter by reminding Cosimo that he had already been disappointed by the Florentines, alluding to the loss of his benefice in Castiglion-Fiorentino in 1461:

I am forced to lead a life here without wealth, without income, and I am made to refuse all positions which are offered to me.[241]

Griffolini was an embarrassment now to the Medici, who would at this moment have been particularly willing to bestow their patronage without such awkward consequences. Indeed, at the very time that Griffolini's translation of Chrysostom arrived in Florence – namely the summer of 1462 – Cosimo de' Medici acquired a new Greek scholar as his protégé: Marsilio Ficino, to whom he gave a house in Careggi in September 1462.[242] It is possible in fact that Benedetto Accolti and his friends in Florence had some part in bringing Ficino and Cosimo together at this time, perhaps in order to help Cosimo to forget Griffolini. There is no positive evidence of this; nevertheless, Ficino wrote in later life that Accolti was one of his early benefactors.[243] Moreover, Accolti and three of his friends, Otto Niccolini, Bernardo Giugni and Piero de' Pazzi, encouraged Ficino to carry out his translation of the *Minos*[244] which was one of the ten Platonic dialogues which Ficino had translated by the time Cosimo died on 1 August 1464.[245] It was in Accolti's interest to encourage Ficino's Greek scholarship as a way of diverting the Medici's attention from Griffolini, and it is not surprising that in the course of his friendship with Ficino Accolti assimilated ideas on philosophy and scholasticism which were to appear in his own dialogue.

Another section of the dialogue included to gratify the Medici was Accolti's extravagant panegyric of Francesco Sforza, Cosimo de' Medici's

[240] *Ibid.* Ego, Cosme vir clarissime, pro innocentia mea numquam me isti civitati exosum duxi, maxime vero ex quo ante tertium annum istic fui, ubi me humanissime et tu et optimi filii tui complexi estis et spem bonam dedistis.
[241] *Ibid.* Cogorque hic vitam agere sine lucro, sine emolumento et omnes quae mihi proponuntur condiciones recusare.
[242] Cf. Kristeller, 'Ficino as a beginning student', 43.
[243] Cf. Della Torre, *Storia*, 29, 32, 550, 573; Marcel, *Ficin*, 300.
[244] *Ibid.*, 203, 216, 709, 731; Della Torre, *Storia*, 545ff.
[245] Kristeller, 'Ficino as a beginning student', 45.

closest ally,[246] and Cosimo exercised a more subtle but equally pervasive influence on the most original section of the dialogue, Accolti's defence of the modern church. A devout Christian, Cosimo was preoccupied with the condition of the church and was, of course, one of the preeminent ecclesiastical patrons of his day; he was deeply concerned to raise the quality of religious life, providing extensively for the liturgical, educational, spiritual and material needs of the clergy. He was highly critical of any sign of moral laxity among the clergy,[247] and he gave particular support to the Observant movements; indeed, the project of ecclesiastical patronage in which he had the greatest personal involvement, the convent of San Marco, was an establishment of the Observant Dominicans, while Cosimo also gave support to the Observant Franciscans with his patronage of San Francesco al Bosco in the Mugello.[248] To criticize the contemporary church was, in one sense, to demean the achievements of ecclesiastical patrons such as Cosimo, and clearly Accolti had Cosimo's contribution to the Observant reform in mind when he particularly emphasized the high religious standards reached by the Observants in his day:

Do you dare to say, declared Accolti to his anonymous adversary, that those clerics who are called Observants of their rule, are not and are not regarded almost all as holy and entirely pure in life, and do not so greatly abhor the attractions of the world that they do not allow them even to be spoken of? Who is so foolish as to think that such men, if they wanted to be evil, would choose a way of life which is the strictest and furthest removed from all the pleasures of the world, in which only bodily hardship and austerity are to be found, so that there can scarcely be a possibility for a person even so wishing to offend? We see that their special duty is devotion to prayer, lamentation, fasting, devout celebration of the mass, the praise of God with psalms, hymns and canticles, frequent intercession on behalf of all Christians; and many of them, erudite in sacred letters, deter men from sin and lead them to a more virtuous life.[249]

Cosimo's support for the Observants also provides an insight into Accolti's denunciation of absolute apostolic poverty as advocated by the few remaining Fraticelli in the fifteenth century. The Fraticelli were for the most part a spent force by mid-century, but there were a few last bursts

---

246 Dialogue, fol. 20v–23r; Galletti, 113–14.
247 Cf. Vespasiano, *Vite*, ii, 177–202.     248 *Ibid.*, 177–78, 180.
249 Dialogue, fol. 49v–50r: Audebisne dicere religiosos illos qui regulae suae observantes vocitantur non fere omnes sanctae atque integerrimae vitae esse et haberi, atque ita mundi illecebras horrere ut ne illas quidem audire patiantur? Quisquamne adeo demens est qui existimet eiusmodi homines si mali esse cuperent eam vitam eligere quae sit arctissima et a cunctis mundi delitiis procul remota, in qua nil nisi corpori durum et austerum reperitur, ut vix quidem volenti deliquendi facultas esse possit? Eorum praecipuum munus videmus esse orationibus, fletui, ieiuniis incumbere, missarum solemnia devotissime agere, pslamis, ymnis et canticis deum laudibus prosequi, pro christianis cunctis frequenter intercedere et ipsorum multos sacris eruditos litteris homines a flagitiis deterrere et ad meliorem vitae frugem deducere (Galletti, 125).

of this particular heresy in the 1450s and 1460s;[250] indeed, the most notorious heresy case in fifteenth-century Florence occurred in 1450 when the physician Giovanni Cani of Montecatini was executed for holding Fraticelli beliefs.[251] The Fraticelli heresy was still a topical issue when Accolti wrote his dialogue in the 1460s, inspiring Cardinal Jean Jouffroy to compose a dialogue between a cardinal and a *fraticello* and leading to a last wave of inquisitorial persecution under Paul II.[252] The Fraticelli's doctrine of absolute poverty was anathema to all orthodox religious persuasions, and Accolti's denunciation of it would have appealed to the Observant inclinations of Cosimo de' Medici.

Accolti's discussion of the ancient and modern church is noteworthy not only, as has been seen, for going against the mainstream of religious thought in the later middle ages but also because it anticipated the close alliance between humanism and church reform which became so powerful a force in the sixteenth century. Other humanists such as Petrarch, Salutati, Traversari, Vergerio, Valla, Lapo da Castiglionchio and Biglia had discussed the merits of the ancient and modern church, but they had not done so in the context of the general history of culture; some, such as Petrarch and Valla, had on different occasions compared the ancient and modern church on the one hand and ancient and modern culture in general on the other,[253] but Accolti's dialogue is unique among earlier humanist texts for discussing the history of the church in the context of the general history of culture, and this connection between the history of the church and the history of civilization as a whole[254] became a prominent feature of sixteenth-century humanism. Thus, whereas Vespasiano da Bisticci excluded religion in his account of the revival of the arts:

In this age all the seven liberal arts have been fruitful in men of excellence – not only in Latin but also in Hebrew and Greek, writers most learned and eloquent not inferior to those of the past. In painting, sculpture and architecture we find the arts at their highest level, as we may see from the works which have been wrought among us . . .[255]

---

[250] Hay, *Church in Italy*, 74, 148; J. Stephens, 'Heresy in medieval and Renaissance Florence', PP, liv (1972), 42–53.

[251] *Ibid.* 47–8.

[252] Hay, *Church in Italy*, 148; E. Dupré-Theseider, 'Sul "dialogo contro i fraticelli" di S. Giacomo della Marca', *Italia sacra*, xvi (1970) (*Miscellanea G.G. Meersseman*, ii), 577–611; M. Miglio, 'Vidi thiaram Pauli papae secundi', *Bulletino dell'Istituto storico italiano per il medio evo*, lxxxi (1969), 273–96, reprinted in his *Storiografia pontifica* (Bologna, 1975), 1–30, 175–85; Stephens, 'Heresy', 46–8.

[253] Cf. pp. 195, 198, 205–6, *supra*.

[254] The only other early humanist text which includes religion in a general discussion of the ancients and moderns is Dondi's letter (cf. Gilbert, 'Dondi', 331–2, 340), but he is not discussing the same question in contrasting ancient paganism with modern Christianity; his concern is with the history of religion, whereas Accolti and his Erasmian and Protestant successors are concerned with ecclesiology and the history of the church.

[255] Vespasiano, *Vite*, i, 32.

as did Ficino:

... this century, like a golden age, has restored to light the liberal arts, which were
almost extinct: grammar, poetry, rhetoric, painting, sculpture, architecture, music,
the ancient singing of songs to the Orphic lyre . . . Achieving what had been
honoured among the ancients, but almost forgotten since, the age has joined wisdom with eloquence, and prudence with the military art . . . this century appears
to have perfected astronomy, and in Florence it has recalled the Platonic teaching
from darkness into light . . .[256]

Erasmus in contrast highlighted theology among the arts reborn:

I am led to a confident hope that not only morality and Christian piety, but also a
genuine and purer literature, may come to renewed life or greater splendour . . .
Polite letters, which were almost extinct, are now cultivated and embraced . . .
Medicine has a host of champions . . . The Imperial Law is restored . . . and
mathematics . . . In the theological sphere there was no little to be done, because
this science has been hitherto mainly professed by those who are most pertinacious
in their abhorrence of the better literature . . . But even here I am confident of
success if the knowledge of the three languages continues to be received in schools,
as it has now begun. For the most learned and least churlish men of the profession
do in some measure assist and favour the new system; and in this matter we are
especially indebted to the vigorous exertions of James Lefèvre of Étaples . . .[257]

who himself gave the limelight to the revival of the early church:

Why may we not aspire to see our age restored to the likeness of the primitive
Church, when Christ received a purer veneration, and the splendour of His Name
shone forth more widely? . . . As the light of the Gospel returns, may He Who is
blessed above all grant also to us this increase of faith, this purity of worship: as the
light of the Gospel returns, I say, which at this time begins to shine again. By this
divine light many have been so greatly illuminated that, not to speak of other
benefits, from the time of Constantine, when the primitive Church, which had little
by little declined, came to an end, there has not been greater knowledge of
languages, more extensive discovery of new lands, or wider diffusion of the name
of Christ in the more distant parts of the earth than in these times.[258]

In the origin and development of the Reformation, it is now realized
that there was the closest possible bond between humanists and reformers;
not only for Melanchthon and Calvin but even for Luther, a distinction
between reforming and humanist activities has become more and more difficult to draw.[259] The renewal of the primitive church was a common goal

---

[256] Translated in *The Portable Renaissance Reader* (New York, 1953), ed. J. B. Ross and
M. M. McLaughlin, 79.
[257] *Ibid.*, 81–2.
[258] *Ibid.*, 85–6. For more examples, cf. Ferguson, *Renaissance in Historical Thought*, 39–
57.
[259] The close connection between reformers and humanists has recently been stressed by
many scholars; for a survey of current opinion, cf. L. Spitz, 'Humanism in the Reformation', in *Renaissance Studies in Honor of Hans Baron*, ed. A. Molho and J. Tedeschi
(Florence, 1971), 641–62, and his 'The course of German humanism', in *Itinerarium*

shared by a vast and increasing number of Christians in the course of the later middle ages, including many early humanists and proto-Reformers; in itself, there was nothing distinctive in this aim and it would be unconvincing to stress its role as a common bond between humanists and would-be protestants when so many other groups, movements and individuals also idealized the primitive church and yet felt no sympathy for humanism or reforming heterodoxy. A truly distinctive link between humanists and reformers in the sixteenth century, however, was the bond they forged between church history and the revival of the arts; in the union between ecclesiology and cultural rebirth, a common goal was created which could satisfy the deepest aspirations of both a humanist and a reformer. The Renaissance and the Reformation now had a common standard to which they could rally against the barbarian wreckers of the Christian church and classical civilization, and the idea that the general revival of culture during the Renaissance embraced religion made it possible for a figure to emerge such as Melanchthon, who, working equally as a humanist and reformer, was able without any conflict of loyalties to celebrate the great religious and cultural rebirth of his age:

But after the Florentines helped the liberal arts to revive, great benefit accrued to all peoples and the talents of many men everywhere were inspired to study the best subjects. Indeed, rivalry with the Greeks stimulated the Latins to restore their own language, which had almost completely fallen to ruin. In their cities public laws were emended, then religion was purified, lying as it was oppressed and torn asunder by the negligence of monks . . . There is no doubt therefore that Florence deserves the gratitude of all men for offering a port, so to speak, to the shipwreck of letters.[260]

Thus, Accolti's adversary in the dialogue could almost be an Erasmian or Protestant humanist when he reviles the modern church as the conclusion to his denunciation of modern culture as a whole:

[Modern clerics] have such a base way of life, are defiled and stained by so much sin that . . . it is to be feared that . . . they are the cause of our moral degeneracy. Who indeed thinks that prayers . . . help which do not help the clerics themselves, since it says in the scriptures that God does not listen to unrepentant sinners? . . . Thus it happens that by their bad example . . . they drag us with them over the precipice . . . It is possible to see that . . . the particular concern of cardinals, bishops and finally the whole curia . . . is to cling to avarice, cruelty, lust, luxury, to put churches, all benefices, indulgences, justice itself up for sale, to deceive miserable Christians, to entangle them in infinite litigations, to sew discords and scandals among men, to parade with a throng of retainers, to seek nothing, finally, unless it will make them feared and venerated as gods. But if among such evils they would at least themselves cultivate learning or give the highest esteem to learned men, they

---

*Italicum* [dedicated to P. O. Kristeller], ed. H. Oberman with T. Brady, Jr (Leiden, 1975), 371–436.
[260] For the text, cf. Weisinger, 'Renaissance accounts', 112.

would be worthy of less contempt . . . but since they themselves hate and ridicule good and learned men, who can bear such men? Who must not detest their manners, customs and pride? I have known many of the most learned men in our time who, although making the greatest possible attempt with any means except bribery, have found little or no success in the curia. On the other hand, if there were or are any adulators, mimics, procurers or ministers of vice, or men offering money, they are received greedily and are granted benefices, honours and offices . . . But this disease has spread not only among the princes of the clergy but also among almost all clerics. The day would run out if I should commence to refer to the adultery, outrages, pandering, avarice, treachery, discord and improprieties of priests, friars or monks.[261]

He then lights on the shortcomings of one particular Franciscan who recently in Florence

had so deceived the blind minds of men that all followed after him like a saint and miracle worker; indeed, there was a common rumour that he had cured many people stricken with various diseases, had returned sight to the blind, had made the deaf hear and the mute speak. He himself did not, as befits holy men, flee such glory but going further offered miracles themselves as merchandise for sale and not only the rabble but also friars followed him, doubtless in the hope of having more alms and pickings, and having taken them, they secretly ridiculed the people for their gullibility. It was amazing to see the sick who gathered from everywhere throng round him, the infinite crowd of people who followed him through villages and hamlets. And when he had done nothing truly admirable, when many knew finally that he was the subject of public infamy, nevertheless such was their keenness, such was the faith of all that they would admit nothing to their ears to shake their belief. The affair was indeed a bad example, calling into doubt among many the veritable deeds of saints . . . [262]

---

[261]  Dialogue, fol. 10v–12r: Immo vero ita turpiter vivunt, ita se scelerum maculis inquinant . . . ut magis timendum sit ne ipsorum luxuries . . . nobis . . . causa sit malorum omnium. Quis enim existimabit eorum preces . . . prodesse hominibus quae eosdem non iuvant quoniam in litteris refertur sacris quod non penitentes peccatores non exaudit Deus? . . . Quo fit ut hi . . . malis exemplis et contraria qua ducunt via nos una secum in praecipitium trahant . . . Intueri licet cardinales, episcopos, curiam denique totam . . . quod illorum vel praecipua cura est avaritiae, crudelitati, gulae, luxuriae inhaerere; ecclesias, beneficia omnia, indulgentias, iustitiam ipsam venalia habere; miseros Christianos fallere, litibus infinitis implicare, discordias et scandala inter homines serere; cum omni pompa, servis plurimis stipatos incedere, nihil denique aliud quaerere nisi quemadmodum cuncti eos timeant ac ut deos venerentur. Etsi saltem inter tot mala vel disciplinis ipsi incumberent vel earum peritos item viros optimos diligerent, essent quippe minore odio digni . . . Cum vero ipsi bonos omnes et litteratos oderint et ludibrio habeant, quivis posset tales homines ferre? quis non debet eorum ritus, mores et superbiam detestari? Novi ego plures nostra aetate viros doctissimos qui cum omni conatu, praeter quam pecuniis, niterentur; nullum aut exiguum in curia locum invenerunt. Contra vero si qui fuerunt vel sunt adulatores, mimi, lenones at scelerum ministri vel pecunias offerentes, hos cupidissime receperunt; illis beneficia, illis honores, illis officia concedunt . . . Atque morbus iste non solum apud ipsos cleri principes, verum etiam apud omnes fere religiosos increbuit. Dies certe me deficeret si pergam sigillatim sacerdotum fratrum aut monachorum, adulteria, stupra [ms: strupra], lenocinia, avaritiam, proditiones, discordias, improbitatesque referre. Cf. Galletti, 108–9.

[262]  Dialogue, fol. 12v–13r: Vidimus nuper quandam minorum ordinis fratrem, qui adeo caecas hominum mentes deceperat, ut omnes post illum abirent, velut sanctum et

He concludes with a direct comparison between the ancient and modern churches: the primitive church abounded in learned and holy clerics who endured the most abject conditions of hunger, cold, persecution, who were prepared to suffer martyrdom rather than apostatize, who strove to promote concord and harmony in society and who urged the laity to refrain from all types of immoral conduct; the modern church, on the other hand, has degenerated, despite the peace, leisure and riches that it enjoys, so that modern clerics are not true shepherds of their flocks but wolves, dedicated to hypocrisy, discord, adultery, robbery, rapine, fornication and sodomy, among whom there are neither saints nor scholars but rather purveyors of vice and teachers of impropriety.[263]

Although these claims are ultimately dismissed by Accolti in the dialogue, they are stated with such vigour and conviction as to suggest that they possibly represent, at least to some extent, Accolti's private views. Some weight is given to this interpretation by the pronouncements on the contemporary church by other members of Accolti's family. One such composition is the poem 'Quelli or' veggiam che si dirieno in sorte' by Accolti's uncle, Antonio Roselli, the famous canonist, who, after reaching high position in the curia, quarrelled with Eugenius IV and left papal service for a teaching post at the University of Padua in 1438.[264] In the wake of this dispute with the pope, he wrote a treatise, *Monarchia*, in which he attacked papal claims to temporal power as compared with the emperor's;[265] it was probably at the same time that he wrote his vehemently anti-clerical and anti-papal poem, 'Quelli or' veggiam', which has a noticeable resemblance to the denunciation of the modern church in Accolti's dialogue.[266] Both distinguish two periods in Christian history and see the dividing line not as the birth of Christ but rather the end of antiquity; both maintain that in the modern church appointments go to unworthy candidates, to the neglect of the virtuous; both argue that the

---

mirabilium factorem operum. Vulgo enim fama erat ipsum plures variis oppressos languoribus sanasse, caecis visum reddidisse, audire surdos et mutos loqui fecisse. Ipse vero non ut sanctos decet huiusmodi gloriam fugiebat sed ultro se offerens, miracula ipsa velut mercem aliquam pollicebatur et non solum vulgus sed etiam fratres illi astipulabantur, ad id nimirum intenti ut obsonia et elemosinas haberent crebriores atque illas nacti, populos clam suae temeritatis irriderent. Stupor erat cernere circa illum cathervas languentium qui undique confluebant, turbam gentium infinitam quae per oppida et vicos illus sequebatur et cum nihil penitus faceret quod esset admiratione dignum cum denique plures nossent ipsum publica infamia notatum, tamen is erat animorum ardor, ea cunctorum fides, ut nihil quo vanior eorum opinio fieret auribus admitterent. Res fuit profecto pessimi exempli, ut quae apud multos verissimas sanctorum res gestas in dubium revocaret . . . Cf. Galletti, 109–10.

[263] Dialogue, fol. 13r–14v; Galletti, 10.

[264] On Roselli's life, cf. BCA, 55, fol. 267r–v, as well as p. 42, n. 7, *supra*.

[265] *Tractatus de monarchia, sive tractatus de potestate imperatoris et papae* in M. Goldast, ed., *Monarchia* (Hanoviae, 1611), 252–556.

[266] Ed. A. Lumini, *Scritti letterari*, ser. 1ᵃ (Arezzo, 1884), 159–63.

modern clergy misgovern Christendom and lead the laity down the path of
sin; both contrast the princes of the modern church, attended by pomp and
luxury, with the saints of the primitive church, who suffered martyrdom
and persecution. The failings of the modern church were a family preoccupation, for Benedetto Accolti's brother, Francesco, was the author of
another vernacular verse invective, 'Tenebrosa, crudel, avara e lorda',
written 'in detestation and censure of the Roman court and of all
priests'.[267] Like Benedetto and Antonio Roselli, Francesco idealizes the
early church where 'prison, agonizing death, hunger and cold' were
suffered to overcome pagan error and establish the Christian religion,
whose 'holy, inviolable bark was steered on a straight course by the virtues
of the pilots through great storms', nor did the early church, 'poor and
naked', ever deviate from divine pleasure; the modern church, on the other
hand, 'a guilty synagogue', 'an obscene Sodom', a 'whore', and 'avaricious
Babylon', was not freed from its former travails and harsh sufferings to
become an 'ark for the damned', but now 'long peace and leisure have
turned' the church 'from a perfect beginning to an insane end'. There are
numerous specific points of similarity between the dialogue and
Francesco's poem. Both argue that virtue will find no reward in Rome,
where gold is all powerful; both argue that the prayers of the Roman
church have no power with God; both maintain that the bad example of
the Roman court has extinguished the true light in the minds of Christians;
both depict in detail the hedonism and depravity of modern curial life.
Given Accolti's deep personal piety, as manifested in his own vernacular
poetry, and the traditions of reformist criticism in his own family, it seems
plausible that the defence of the modern church in the dialogue was
mounted to gratify the Medici and to outdo Griffolini's panegyric of
modern popes, whereas Accolti's personal sympathies inclined, like those
of his uncle and his brother, more to his opponent's censure of the contemporary church. Accolti and his family were particularly concerned with
moral laxity and materialism at the heart of the church, the Roman court,
and it is arguable that Accolti's especially impassioned denunciation of
curial vice and worldliness was stimulated not only by his family's spirit of
religious criticism but also by the reform efforts of Pius II and his commission, which had given particular notoriety to the moral deficiencies of
the Roman court in the 1460s, when Accolti was composing his
dialogue.[268] Certainly Accolti's profound concern with religion, manifest
in the dialogue, provides a convincing explanation for the intellectual

[267] Ed. M. Messina, GStLI, cxxii (1955), 211–15.
[268] Haubst, 'Der Reformentwurf', 205–30; Pastor, *Storia*, ii, 177ff. Anti-clericalism in
Accolti's dialogue may have compelled Bacchini, its first editor, to seek a French printer:
cf. DBI, v, 23–4.

breakthrough he was able to achieve in the link forged between church history and cultural development in the dialogue; preoccupied as he was with the state of the church and religious reform, he was inspired to give the place of honour to religion in the general history of culture which he developed in the dialogue.

Comparing the ancient and modern churches and idealizing the primitive church were characteristic features of medieval thought and medieval religious reform; it was nothing novel or distinctive for the early humanists to appropriate these ideas in their discussions of religious history, in their apologetic religious works or in their critiques of the contemporary church. What distinguished Erasmian and Protestant religious thought from medieval reformist ideas was that the later humanists and Protestant reformers saw religion as part of a general cultural revival whereas their medieval forerunners were preoccupied with religious renewal alone. A fundamental and distinctive feature of Erasmian humanism and the Reformation was a comprehensive programme of general cultural renewal, including religion, which was born of a union between medieval ecclesiological thought about the early church and the Renaissance humanists' concept of cultural revival and the rebirth of the arts. What is clear from a study of Accolti's dialogue is that this programme was not created by Erasmus or his Protestant contemporaries but was anticipated by the Italian humanists of the earlier Renaissance. Such a programme may have been implicit in the patristic scholarship and interests of the early humanists and in particular in the contrast they drew between the church fathers and the medieval scholastics, but the link between religious and cultural history is explicit in Accolti's dialogue, which shows, as much as any other fifteenth-century text, how Erasmian humanism and the Reformation had their roots in the work of the Italian humanists of the earlier Renaissance.

# 9

# Accolti's history of the first crusade and the Turkish menace

Benedetto Accolti's second composition as chancellor and his longest work was *De bello a christianis contra barbaros gesto pro Christi sepulcro et Iudea recuperandis libri IV*, a history of the first crusade.[1] He begins the first book with an account of the rise of Islam and the loss to Christianity of the holy lands, and goes on to recount Peter the Hermit's and Pope Urban II's efforts to launch a crusade, including a version of Urban's famous oration at Clermont in 1095. He then describes the abortive expeditions of Peter the Hermit, Walter the Penniless and Gottschalk, and ends the first book with Bohemond, the Norman prince of Taranto, taking the cross and delivering a long oration to persuade his compatriots to follow his lead. In the second book, after describing the journey to the East of the main crusading armies under Bohemond and Godfrey of Bouillon, Accolti gives an account of the siege and capture of Nicea, whose Moslem governor is portrayed delivering an impassioned oration to rouse his subjects to withstand the Christian onslaught. There then follows a long digression on Baldwin of Bouillon's success in winning a principality in Armenia, and an account of the journey of the main crusading force to Antioch; the second book concludes with an oration by Godfrey to the crusading army before the walls of Antioch. The main event of the third book is the siege and capture of Antioch by the crusaders, after which Accolti describes the unsuccessful attempt by a large Muslim force to recapture the city. Then following a long oration of thanksgiving delivered to the crusaders by the papal legate, Adhemar of le Puy, the third book concludes with an account of the crusaders' efforts to consolidate their conquests round Antioch. The final book opens with the march of the crusading army to Jerusalem and includes a detailed description of Judaea and Jerusalem itself; with the successful outcome of the crusade and the election of Godfrey as the first Latin king of Jerusalem, Accolti points out the virtues of unity among political leaders in an oration by the count of Flanders. The fourth book closes with an account of Godfrey's premature

[1] For the manuscripts of *De bello*, cf. pp. 347–8, *infra*.

death and a summary of the history of the Latin kingdom of Jerusalem up to 1187, when Jerusalem was recaptured by Saladin.

## (i) The date of Accolti's history

The history was dedicated to Piero di Cosimo de' Medici,[2] and it is likely that it was completed some time between November 1463 and 1 August 1464. It was not presented to Piero before November 1463 when his brother Giovanni died, for in the preface Accolti refers to Cosimo and Piero without mentioning Giovanni.[3] In his dialogue, Accolti had praised all three Medici,[4] and it would have been inconsistent to single out Piero and Cosimo in the history if Giovanni had still been alive. On the other hand, if the history had been presented after Cosimo himself had died on 1 August 1464, some reference to his death would have been expected. There are indications of an even more precise dating in the preface. Addressing Piero, Accolti declares, 'For to whom else but to you or your father, who, according to everyone, are the adornments of our country, the greatest luminaries of our age, the almost unique protectors of scholarship, should I properly dedicate my labours?'[5] At first sight it would be supposed that while Accolti was writing both Cosimo and Piero were alive. In the next sentence, however, referring to Cosimo, Accolti uses the past tense: 'he lacked nothing which, in the view of any wise man, the greatest man should have'.[6] This gives the impression that Cosimo was dead, but in the following sentence Accolti once more uses the present: 'he has a prodigious memory, a divine intellect so versatile that he seems born for everything'.[7] Accolti then goes on to say, however, that Cosimo 'joined eloquence and learning to wisdom', and in speaking of his other qualities and accomplishments he continues to use the past.[8] But at the end of the

---

[2]  History, fol. 1r; *Recueil*, 529.     [3]  History, fol. 2r–v; *Recueil*, 530–1.

[4]  Cf. pp. 184–5, 194, *supra*.

[5]  History, fol. 2r: Nam ad quem alium quam ad te aut patrem tuum meos labores rectius destinarem, quos patrie decus, maxima lumina nostre etatis, unicum pene doctis presidium omnes esse confitentur? (*Recueil*, 530).

[6]  History, fol. 2r: Nihil ei defuit unquam quod in summo protinus viro sapiens quisque desideraret (*Recueil*, 530).

[7]  History, fol. 2r: Viget in eo ingens memoria, divinum ingenium atque ita versatile, ut ad omnia natus videatur (*Recueil*, 530).

[8]  History, fol. 2r–v: Eloquentiam sapientie ac doctrinam addidit litterarum; privatis in rebus libero quidem dignis homine quecumque tandem ille fuerint studio incredibili, summa industria est versatus; rem suam familiarem ita constituit ut, in maxima rerum copia nulla honestior, elegantior, castior, aut ditior bonis exemplis unquam fuerit. In omni vita gravitati comitatem, severitati clementiam, auctoritati humanitatem copulavit; rem vero publicam ita gessit, belli et pacis temporibus, ut maiorum virtutem et omnes alios nostre etatis haud dubie superarit. Quis etiam digne vel exprimat verbis vel recenseat litteris eius modestiam, religionem, pietatem, magnificentiam, liberalitatem, qui non ob aliud opes quesivit nisi ut multorum inopiam sublevaret, construeret templa

preface Accolti again implies that Cosimo is alive: 'all good men desire that, after Cosimo has paid his debt to nature', you will succeed to his position.[9] These changes of tense seem to indicate that, at the time Accolti was writing the preface, Cosimo's death was imminently expected. Accolti's mention of Cosimo's excellent memory and keen intellect sounds like an observation made at someone's deathbed, as though Accolti were exclaiming how remarkable it was that Cosimo still had full command of his mental faculties. Especially suggestive is Accolti's mention of Piero's succession after Cosimo's death. Cosimo in fact underwent a long illness before his death. In May 1464 he began to suffer from a urinary complaint, a severe rash and a fever; by the middle of July it had become clear that he was dying.[10] This evidence, therefore, suggests that Accolti presented his history to Piero between May and 1 August 1464, the date of Cosimo's death.

### (ii) Accolti's history and humanist literature on the crusade, the Near East and Eastern Europe

As in the dialogue, Accolti was again attempting with his history to demonstrate his competence as a humanist in Medicean circles, where, it has been seen, his appointment as chancellor had been questioned on the grounds that his profession was law, not the humanities.[1] Indeed, the topic for historical study that he chose – the struggle between Christianity and Islam in the Orient – had by Accolti's day become one of the great themes in humanist literature.[2] Even before the fall of Constantinople in 1453

---

in dei honorem, et eius cultum omni ex parte amplificaret amicis et rei publice cum expediret opitularetur? (*Recueil*, 530).

[9] History, fol. 2v: boni omnes esse desiderant, ut postquam Cosma quod nature debet exsolverit, tu patriam, amicos et omnem Etruriam tuearis (*Recueil*, 531).

[10] Cf. G. Pieraccini, *La stirpe de' Medici di Cafaggiolo* (Florence, 1924–5), i, 30–1.

[1] Cf. pp. 105–7, *supra*.

[2] On this humanist literature, cf. Pertusi, *La caduta di Constantinopoli*; *idem*, 'I primi studi in occidente sull'origine e la potenza dei Turchi'; *idem*, 'Giovan Battista Egnazio e Ludovico Tuberone tra i primi storici occidentali del popolo turco', in *Venezia e Ungheria nel Rinascimento*, ed. V. Branca (Florence, 1973), 479–87; *idem*, 'Le notizie sulla organizzazione amministrativa e militare dei Turchi nello "Strategicon adversum Turcos" di Lampo Birago (c. 1453–1455)', in *Studi sul medioevo cristiano offerti a Raffaello Morghen*, ii (Rome, 1974), 669–700; *idem*, 'La lettera di Filippo da Rimini, cancelliere di Corfù, a Francesco Barbaro sulla caduta di Costantinopoli (1453)', in *In memoria di Sofia Antoniadis* (Venice, 1974), 120–57; F. Babinger, 'Die Aufzeichnungen des genuensen Iacopo de Promontorio de Campis über den Osmanen Staat um 1475', *Sitzungsberichte des Bayerischen Akademie der Wissenschaften*, philos.-hist. Klasse (1956), Heft 8; Schwoebel, 'Coexistence, conversion and the crusade'; *idem*, *The Shadow of the Crescent*; L. Gualdo Rosa, 'Il Filelfo e i Turchi', 109ff.; E. Cochrane, *Historians and Historiography in the Italian Renaissance* (Chicago, 1980), 324–37; M. J. Heath, 'Renaissance scholars and the origins of the Turks', BHumRen, xli (1979), 453–71; T. Spencer, 'Turks and Trojans in the Renaissance', *Modern Language Review*,

brought Italian learned society to the point of near frenzy, humanists had composed a large quantity of orations, letters, histories, poems and treatises on the conflict between cross and crescent, and much of this literature, like Accolti's history,[3] was written with the intention, explicit or implicit, of inspiring contemporary Christians to join a crusade against the Turks. Petrarch had written the *canzone* 'O aspettata in ciel beata e bella' in 1333 to celebrate the decision to join a crusade by King Philip VI of France;[4] in his *Triumph of Fame* he rebuked Christians for 'caring not that the tomb of Christ be in the clutch of dogs'; he wrote letters to Venice and Genoa in support of the efforts of John V Paleologus and Innocent VI in 1356 to launch a crusade; in about 1358 he composed an *Itinerarium breve de Janua usque ad Jerusalem et Terram Sanctam* for the Milanese pilgrim, Giovanni di Mandello, in which, after declaring that he would have liked to join the pilgrimage, he gives a mythological and geographical account of the holy lands as well as a devotional description of their religious associations;[5] and his letter Sen. VIII 8 was a panegyric of King Peter I of Cyprus for his conquest of Alexandria from the Muslims in 1365.[6] In a letter of 1397 Salutati warned Christians, divided by schism and corrupted by luxury, of the imminent danger posed by the Turks who, confiding in their rigorous military discipline, threatened to lay Italy to waste and burn Rome itself to the ground.[7] In 1432 or 1433 the Milanese humanist Andrea Biglia composed his *Comentarii historici de defectu fidei in Oriente*, which in twelve books narrate the decline and fall of Eastern Christianity; until recently almost unknown, this important work contains the first substantial discussion of early Turkish history by an Italian humanist, as well as exhortations to join a crusade directed to the German chancellor, Kaspar Schlick, to Cardinal Giulio Cesarini and to Emperor Sigismund.[8] Another early fifteenth-century humanist text on the crusade

xlvii (1952), 330–3; A. Linder, ' . . . the Trojan ancestry of the kings of France . . . ', BHumRen, xl (1978), 497–512; C. Patrides, 'The Bloody and Cruell Turke: the background of a Renaissance commonplace', SR, x (1963), 126–35; L. Smith, 'Pope Pius II's use of Turkish atrocities', *The Southwestern Social Science Quarterly*, xlvi (1966), 407–15.

3 Cf. p. 237, *infra*.
4 Cf. F. Cardini, 'La crociata mito politico', *Il pensiero politico*, viii (1975), 31.
5 Cf. F. Cardini, 'Viaggiatori medioevali in terra santa', RSI, lxxx (1968), 336–7; *The Triumphs of Petrarch*, ed. and tr. by E. Wilkins (Chicago, 1962), 84;cf. Schwoebel, 'Coexistence', 182.
6 Setton, *Papacy and the Levant*, i, 278. For further references to Petrarch's crusading apologetics, cf. P. Piur, *Petrarcas 'Buch'* (Halle, 1925), 95–9.
7 *Epistolario*, iii, 207–11.
8 Cf. Webb, 'Decline and Fall', 198–216, where Biglia's *De defectu*, still unpublished, is summarized, dated and examined in terms of Biglia's biography (on which see also *idem*, 'Andrea Biglia at Bologna, 1424–7', BIHR, xlix (1975), 41–59), but not placed in the context of humanist studies on the rise of Islam and the Turks; this work, unknown to Pertusi ('I primi studi', *passim*), shows that humanist study of the rise of Islam and the

is the *Epistola de crudelitate Turcarum in Christianos*, sent from Constantinople on 12 December 1438 by Bartolomeo da Giano, a minorite friar to his fellow Franciscan, Alberto da Sarteano, in Venice; this letter, which contains information on the hardships endured by Christians under Turkish rule, includes a passionate exhortation, bolstered by humanist erudition, to bring aid to Eastern Christians.[9] Poggio composed a funeral oration for Cardinal Cesarini, whom he hails as a modern martyr for his death at the hands of the Turks at the battle of Varna in 1444,[10] and Cesarini's martyrdom was also celebrated in a Latin epigram by another Florentine humanist, Leonardo Dati,[11] who praised the crusading intentions of Alfonso of Aragon in a Latin verse epistle directed to the Florentines in 1447.[12] The Venetian humanist, Bernardo Giustiniani, delivered an oration on 5 January 1452 to Frederick III, on his way to the imperial coronation, urging him to lead a crusade,[13] while Flavio Biondo followed the imperial coronation with an oration at Naples exhorting both the emperor and Alfonso of Aragon to participate in a crusade,[14] but the leading humanist publicists of the holy war in the first half of the fifteenth century were men who enjoyed intimate personal connections with the Orient and Eastern Europe. Cyriac de' Pizzicoli of Ancona, the great antiquary, spent much of his time engaged in archaeological research in the Eastern Mediterranean, where he observed the plight of Eastern Christians at first hand, and his letters, especially from the 1440s, testify to his concern over the rise of Islam and to his efforts to win support for a crusade.[15] Aeneas Sylvius Piccolomini, who enjoyed close connections with the courts of Eastern Europe after his appointment to the imperial chancery in 1442, witnessed at first hand the advance of the Turks into Hungary and Hapsburg lands, and as early as 1436 in an oration to the Council of Basel he dwelled on the Turkish threat, a theme which frequently recurs in his

Turks antedated by almost two decades Filelfo's writings on the subject (cf. *ibid.*, 467ff. and Gualdo Rosa, 'Fielfo', 109–65), believed by Pertusi ('I primi studi', 467), to be 'uno dei primissimi tentativi umanistici di scrivere la storia del popolo turco'.

9  Ed. J. B. Mittarelli, *Bibliotheca codicum manuscriptorum Monasterii S. Michaelis Venetiarum* (Venice, 1779) 513–23, reprinted in PG, clviii, 1055–68; cf. Pertusi, 'I primi studi', 467, and Babinger, 'Die Aufzeichnungen', *Sitz. berichte Bayer. Akad.* viii (1956), 9–10.

10  Ed. Angelo Mai in *Spicilegium romanum*, x (Rome, 1844), 373ff.; a partial edition exists in N. Iorga, 'Notes et extraits pour servir à l'histoire des croisades au XVe siècle', *Revue de l'orient latin*, viii (1900–1), 268–72. Cf. Walser, *Poggius*, 206–7; Setton, *Papacy*, ii, 89, 91.

11  Cf. Flamini, 'Leonardo di Piero Dati', 57–8.

12  *Ibid.*, 58–60.

13  B. Giustiniani, *Orationes* (Venice, 1493), fol. A5v–B2v; cf. Labalme, *Bernardo Giustiniani*, 139–40.

14  Ed. Nogara, *Scritti inediti*, 107–14; cf. *ibid.*, cxxxi–cxxxiii.

15  Cf. F. Pall, 'Ciriaco d'Ancona e la crociata contro i Turchi', *Bulletin historique de l'Academie roumaine*, xx (1938); Setton, *Papacy*, ii, esp. 71ff.

correspondence[16] and which was the subject of an oration that he delivered to Pope Nicholas V on behalf of the emperor shortly after the imperial coronation at Rome in 1452.[17] Francesco Filelfo, among Latins perhaps the doyen of Greek scholars, had a Greek wife, had spent many years in Constantinople, and had played a role in Byzantine diplomacy against the Turks;[18] he was one of the pioneers of Turkish studies among the humanists,[19] and his recently discovered treatise on the history of Mohammed, the Arabs and the Seldjuk Turks testifies to a genuine historical interest in the Muslim world,[20] as does his well-known letter to King Charles VII of France of 17 February 1451, where, besides including a copious crusading exhortation inspired by the recent French victory over the English, he summarizes the history of the Seldjuk Turks up to the Mongol conquest of Damascus in 1299.[21] But the humanist with perhaps the most consuming interest in the eastern Mediterranean during the years before 1453 was the Cretan, George of Trebizond, who was obsessed by an apocalyptic vision in which the rise of the Ottoman Turks played a central role in the imminent final drama of human history.[22] This apocalyptic vision may yet have been unformed in his now lost Latin exhortation of 1427 calling for relief to beleaguered Constantinople which is mentioned in a letter by Filelfo in 1428;[23] this work dwelled on the danger of Turkish naval domination for the survival of Constantinople, the Venetian empire and Italy itself,[24] ideas which were repeated briefly in his *Rhetoricorum libri v* of 1433–4.[25] But his millenarianism is explicit in an oration composed in 1437 in praise of Eugenius IV, whom he saw as a saviour of Christendom threatened with imminent destruction at the hands of the Moslems.[26] Another saviour, in George's view, might be Alfonso of Aragon, to whom he directed a Latin oration in 1442; in his vision, he foresaw that the destroyers of Christianity would come out of Ethiopia, and Alfonso's conquest of Naples in 1442 inspired George to

---

[16] Cf. *Der Briefwechsel des E.S.P.*, ed. R. Wolkan, i [*Fontes rerum austriacarum*, lxi (1909)], 158–9, 165, 186, 203, 281–3, 321–2, 342, 487–90, 495–6, 506, 512–22, 550–8, 562–79, 585; ii [*ibid.* xlvii (1912)] 74–7, 110.

[17] Ed. J. Mansi, *Pii II . . . orationes* (Lucca, 1755–9), i, 163–81; cf. also *ibid.*, 11ff., and Setton, *Papacy*, ii, 201.

[18] Cf. Gualdo Rosa, 'Il Filelfo', 111–12.   [19] Cf. Pertusi, 'I primi studi', 467ff.

[20] *Ibid.* Ed. Gualdo Rosa, 'Filelfo', 131–65.

[21] Ed. in F. Philelphi, *Epistularum familiarum libri xxxvii* (Venice, 1502), fol. 55r–59v. Cf. Pertusi, 'I primi studi', 469–70; Schwoebel, 'Coexistence', 182–3, and *Shadow*, 150, 172. For a discussion of Filelfo's other writings on this theme, cf. Gualdo Rosa, 'Il Filelfo', 111–14.

[22] Cf. Monfasani, *George of Trebizond*.

[23] Ed. E. Legrand, *Cent-dix lettres grecques de F. Filelfe* (Paris, 1892), 5–6.

[24] Cf. Monfasani, *George of Trebizond*, 22; Pertusi, *Caduta*, i, p. xii; ii, 68–9.

[25] *Ibid.*, i, p. xii.

[26] Monfasani, *George of Trebizond*, 35; cf. Pertusi, *Caduta*, i, p. xii.

regard him as a conqueror who might forestall the destined march of the Ethiopians.[27] In 1452 George wrote two further works in this apocalyptic vein, one a crusading exhortation to Frederick III at the time of his coronation,[28] the other an appeal to Pope Nicholas V calling for the relief of Constantinople and the safeguarding of the Bosphorus as the bulwark of Western Christendom.[29]

The growing concern for the Orient in humanist circles, however, was given an unprecedented intensity after 1453 by the fall of Constantinople; the final collapse of the Roman Empire in the East, the growing plight of the Eastern Church, the dramatic and even cataclysmic circumstances in which Constantinople had been captured, the declining fortunes of the Venetian and Genoese empires in the East, and the spectacular rise of Muslim power under Mehmed II caused humanist interest in the Near East, already well nurtured in the course of the previous century, fully to burgeon. Humanist texts concerned with the Orient, which multiplied vastly in number after 1453, included several from participants in the final tragedy at Constantinople: Cardinal Isidore of Kiev, papal legate in Constantinople, before reaching Italy addressed a number of letters to rulers, states, dignitaries and Christians at large, narrating the Turkish victory and appealing for Christian retaliation;[30] Isidore knew little Latin,[31] but his letter to Cardinal Bessarion was translated by the Bolognese humanist, Lianoro de' Lianori,[32] and several of his other letters were composed in an elevated Latin style. One of his entourage, who may have been Francesco Griffolini,[33] contributed a Latin letter addressed to Cardinal Capranica narrating Isidore's part in the final siege,[34] while Leonardo, archbishop of Mytilene, who had also been part of the papal legation to Constantinople, contributed an eloquent account of the Turkish triumph in his letter to Pope Nicholas V, to whom he appealed to

[27] Monfasani, *George of Trebizond*, 51–2; cf. Pertusi, *Caduta*, i, p. xii.
[28] Monfasani, *George of Trebizond*, 52.
[29] *Ibid.*, 128–30; Pertusi, *Caduta*, i, p. xiii and ii, 69.
[30] For selections from these letters, usually in editions superior to those otherwise in print, cf. Pertusi, *Caduta*, i, 58–111; Pertusi discusses the texts, manuscripts, previous editions and bibliography regarding Isidore, *ibid.*, 54–7; three other letters by Isidore regarding the fall of Constantinople, to Cardinal Capranica, to the Florentines and to the Bolognese, are referred to by Pertusi, *ibid.*, ii, 498 and edited by Iorga, *Notes et extraits*, ii, 518–19 (extracts), G. Hofmann, 'Quellen zu Isidor von Kiev', *Orientalia christiana periodica*, xviii (1952), 146–8, and W. Röll, 'Ein zweiter Brief Isidors von Kiew', *Byzantinische Zeitschrift*, lxix (1976), 13–16.
[31] Pertusi, *Caduta*, i, 53.
[32] *Ibid.*, 53, 578. On Lianori, cf. L. Frati, 'Lianoro de' Lianori ellenista bolognese', *Studi e memorie per la storia dell'Università di Bologna*, x (1930), 165–77.
[33] Cf. G. Mercati, *Scritti d'Isidoro* (Rome, 1926), 131; Pertusi, *Caduta*, i, 112–13.
[34] Ed. *ibid.*, 114–19.

rouse Western Christendom.[35] The principal literary work composed by a participant at the siege of Constantinople was the Latin epic in four books, *Constantinopolis*, written between 1454 and 1457 by the Brescian humanist, Ugo Puscolo, who had gone to Constantinople shortly before 1453 to further his Greek studies; this detailed narrative poem was not limited to events actually witnessed by Puscolo but included a full account of events in the Near East from the battle of Varna in 1444 to the fall of Constantinople.[36] A number of accounts of the Christian disaster emerged from humanist circles in Italy, including the *Expugnatio Constantinopolitana*, addressed by Antonio Ivani of Sarzana to Federigo da Montefeltro between autumn 1453 and spring 1454,[37] the *De expugnatione Constantinopolitana* by Niccolò Tignosi,[38] the physician closely connected with Aretine and Florentine humanists, and the apologetic letters written by the Venetian humanist resident in Crete, Lauro Quirini, to Pope Nicholas V on 13 July 1453[39] and by Cardinal Bessarion to Francesco Foscari, doge of Venice, on the same day.[40] Many humanist texts in the wake of the fall of Constantinople were orations composed to inspire action against the Turks, such as Girolamo Guarini's *Ad papam Nicolaum V adversus Turcos cohortatio* of 1 August 1454,[41] the orations dating from 1455 and 1456 addressed to King Ladislas of Hungary and Emperor Frederick III by the Genoese bishop of Caffa, Giacomo Campora,[42] the oration directed to Alfonso of Aragon on 25 January 1454 by the Greek humanist, Nicholas Sagundinus,[43] who redirected the same work to Cardinal Aeneas Sylvius Piccolomini in 1456,[44] and the orations

[35] Ed. Pertusi, *ibid.*, 124–71 (excerpts); an inferior but complete edition in PG, clix, 923–41; other editions listed in Pertusi, *Caduta*, i, 121. Cf. *ibid.*, 120–3, 390–407; Setton, *Papacy*, ii, 111ff.

[36] Ed. A. S. Ellissen, *Analekten der mittel- und neugriechischen Literatur*, Anhang to vol. iii (Leipzig, 1857), 12–83; Pertusi, *Caduta*, i, 200–13 (brief excerpts). Cf. *ibid.*, 198–9 for further bibliography; Schwoebel, *Shadow*, 17–18, 28; L. Loomis, 'The fall of Constantinople symbolically considered', in *Essays . . . to James Harvey Robinson* (New York, 1929), 243–58.

[37] Cf. Pertusi, *Caduta*, ii, 502–3.

[38] Ed. Sensi, 'N. Tignosi', 423–31, an edition unknown to Pertusi, *Caduta*, ii, 501. On Tignosi, cf. pp. 14–15, *supra*.

[39] Ed. A. Pertusi, 'Le epistole storiche di Lauro Quirini sulla caduta di Costantinopoli e la potenza dei Turchi', in K. Krautter *et al.*, *Lauro Quirini umanista* (Florence, 1977), 223–33.

[40] Ed. L. Mohler, *Kardinal Bessarion*, iii (Paderborn, 1942), 475–7.

[41] Cf. Pertusi, *Caduta*, ii, 504.

[42] The former is partially edited by Pertusi, *Caduta*, i, 192–7, and more fully but less accurately by Iorga, *Notes et extraits*, iv, 57–63; the latter is unpublished: cf. Pertusi, *Caduta*, i, 190–1.

[43] Ed. V. Makusev, *Monumenta historica Slavorum meridionalium vicinorumque populorum*, i (Warsaw, 1874), 295–306; partially edited by Iorga, 'Notes et extraits', *Revue orient latin*, viii (1900–1), 280–8, and by Pertusi, *Caduta*, ii, 128–40 (a superior edition). For further bibliography, cf. *ibid.*, 126–7.

[44] *Ibid.*, 126.

delivered in the presence of Emperor Frederick III in 1455 by the founding
father of Hungarian humanism and close associate of Aeneas Sylvius,
Johannes Vitéz de Zredna, bishop of Grosswardein and chancellor of the
kingdom of Hungary;[45] other orations such as Bernardo Giustiniani's
*Oratio funebris* on behalf of Francesco Foscari of 1457[46] included the
crusade against the Turks among the themes discussed, while the Florentine humanist, Alamanno Rinuccini, in his practice oration of 1455
directed to Pope Callixtus III,[47] showed that the crusading exhortation had
become a standard topic for rhetorical exercise well before the later
fifteenth century, when the *Declamationes* of Benedetto Colucci represented Marsilio Ficino as giving a crusading oration for rhetorical practice to five of his pupils.[48] Examples of humanist Latin poetry soon following the fall of Constantinople were Publio Gregorio Tifernate's *Vaticinium
cladis Italiae* of 1453, in which the Turks are portrayed already having
landed in Italy,[49] and Leonardo Dati's *Carmen ad Pontificem Maximum
Dominum Nicolaum Papam V in Thurcum Mahomet*, composed in Rome
between 1453 and 1455, which, besides including a passionate crusading
appeal to the pope, is notable for a pair of dialogues, one between Satan
and Mehmed II, who are depicted sealing an infernal pact, followed by
another between the Virgin and Christ, who lament the weakness and
inaction of Christendom.[50] Several humanist treatises also date from these
years, including the *Strategicon adversum Turcos* composed between
1453 and 1455 by the Lombard humanist, Lampo Birago, an assessment
of the strategy best suited to combat the Turks probably composed for the
commission of cardinals created by Pope Nicholas to study this problem,[51]
Flavio Biondo's *Consultatio an bellum vel pax cum Turcis magis expediat
reipublicae Venetorum* (also entitled *De origine et gestis Venetorum*) of
July 1454 which contains an historical compendium of Venetian activities
against all barbarians and especially the Muslims,[52] and Nicholas
Sagundinus's *Liber de familia Autumanorum id est Turcorum* (also
entitled *De origine et gestic Turcarum liber*) dedicated in 1456 to Aeneas

---

[45] Johannes Vitez, *Orationes in causa expeditionis contra Turcos habitae* (Budapest, 1878),
ed. Fraknói, 13–33. On Vitez, cf. *ibid.*, 5–9; Setton, *Papacy*, ii, 151, 297, 579;
Schwoebel, *Shadow*, 50–1; Pertusi, *Caduta*, ii, 505; Vespasiano, *Vite*, i, 319–26.

[46] Cf. Labalme, *Giustiniani*, 124–5.

[47] *Oratio exercationis gratia . . . in creatione Calisti pontificis . . . de a.* MCCCCLV, in his
*Lettere ed orazioni*, ed. Giustiniani, 7.

[48] Cf. Kristeller, *Studies*, 112; Schwoebel, 'Coexistence', 165.

[49] Published in his *Opuscula* (Venice, 1498) not paginated; cf. Pertusi, *Caduta*, ii, 509.

[50] Cf. Flamini, 'L. Dati', 65–9; Pertusi, *Caduta*, ii, 509.

[51] Ed. Pertusi, 'Le notizie', in *Studi . . . a R. Morghen*, ii, 669–700, omitting the proemium,
which was edited by D. Giorgi in the appendix to his *Vita Nicolai quinti* (Rome, 1742),
214–15.

[52] Published in Biondo's *Opera* (Basel, 1531), 293–92; cf. *Scritti inediti*, ed. Nogara, cxli–
cxliv.

Sylvius,[53] which has been described as the first European attempt at an Ottoman history;[54] but the most important humanist treatises concerned with the Orient and Eastern Europe at this time came from Aeneas Sylvius himself, whose epistolary history of the Diet of Regensburg of 1454,[55] summoned to organize a crusade, was followed in the years between 1454 and 1458 by his commentaries on Panormita's *De dictis et factis Alphonsii Regis* (1456),[56] *De ritu, situ, moribus et conditione Germaniae descriptio* (1457),[57] *Historia rerum Friderici III Imperatoris* (before 1458),[58] *De Europa*[59] and *Historia Bohemica* (1458),[60] works which contain considerable passages on the crusade as well as on developments in Eastern Europe and the Near East. In the years immediately after the fall of Constantinople humanists were equally prolific in composing letters, often highly literary and erudite in character, concerning past and present developments in the Near East; typical examples of this epistolary literature are the letter addressed to all Christian princes by Timoteo Maffei of Verona from late 1453 or early 1454,[61] Poggio's two exhortatory epistles addressed to Frederick III and the king of Naples early in 1455,[62] and the dedicatory letter prefaced by George of Trebizond to his translation of Cyril of Alexandria's *Thesaurus de sancta et consubstantiali trinitate* sent to Alfonso of Aragon shortly after the fall of Constantinople.[63] Particularly rich in historical examples from classical antiquity and the middle ages are Flavio Biondo's two substantial letters written in the immediate aftermath of the disaster at Constantinople, one on 1 August 1453 addressed to Alfonso of Aragon,[64] the other dating from November 1453 and directed to Pietro Campofregosi, doge of Genoa,[65] but again the most notable humanist in this genre of apologetic literature was Aeneas Sylvius, who produced scores of letters on the crusade and related oriental and Eastern

---

[53] There are several fifteenth- and sixteenth-century editions; I used *Elegiarum lib. duo....De rebus turcicis libri tres ... partim a Secundino ... descripti* (Lovanii, 1553): 'Rerum turcicarum Liber primus Nicola Secundino Autore', fol. 24r–32v. Cf. Pertusi, 'I primi studi', 471–5; idem, *Caduta*, ii, 126–7, 506; Iorga, 'Notes et extraits', *Rev. orient lat.* viii (1900–1), 288–90; Schwoebel, 'Coexistence', 179.

[54] Pertusi, *Caduta*, ii, 127.

[55] Ed. R. Wolkan, *Der Briefwechsel des E.S.P.*, iii (*Fontes rerum austriacarum*, lxviii (1918)), 492–563.

[56] *Opera*, 478–83, 492–9.

[57] *Ibid.*, 1035, 1038–40, 1046–9, 1060, 1077–9.

[58] Published by A. F. Kollar, *Analecta monumentorum omnis aevi Vindobonensia* (Vienna, 1762), ii, 1–475.

[59] *Opera*, 387–411.   [60] *Ibid.*, 124–43.

[61] Ed. Iorga, *Notes et extraits*, iv, 74–5; cf. Schwoebel, *Shadow*, 31–2, 50 and Pertusi, *Caduta*, ii, 500.

[62] *Epistolae*, iii, 158–65 and 203–11. Cf. pp. 269–70, *infra*.

[63] Cf. Monfasani, *George of Trebizond*, 118.

[64] Ed. Nogara, *Scritti inediti*, 31–51; cf. *ibid.*, cxxxiv–cxl.

[65] *Ibid.*, 61–71; cf. *ibid.*, cxl–cxli.

European topics,[66] among which the most eloquent were sent immediately after the fall of Constantinople to Pope Nicholas V[67] and Cardinal Nicholas of Cusa,[68] containing his famous lament, in true Renaissance fashion, that Homer and Plato had now suffered a second death,[69] a conceit unmatched in humanist crusading apologetics for its subtle mixture of pathos and erudition.

After Aeneas Sylvius became Pope Pius II on 3 September 1458, he continued to work for a crusade against the Turks with the same dedication as he had shown over the previous quarter of a century, and his pontificate stimulated a further growth of literature on the crusade and the Orient from humanists; indeed, the papal court, where such productions were likely to win appreciation because of their topical subject matter as well as their humanist style and literary forms, helped to set a fashion for crusading and Near Eastern literature in Italian humanist circles and then in the rest of Europe which was hardly to wane for decades to come. Besides the many letters on the crusade which came from the pope himself, humanist epistolography in the years between 1458 and 1464 offers many examples of letters on Near Eastern topics, including the rhetorical letter from Benedetto, archbishop of Mytilene after 1459, to Pius II, calling for the reconquest of the recently captured island of Lesbos,[70] the letters by Lauro Quirini directed from Crete to Cardinal Scarampo-Trevisan on 22 November 1458,[71] describing the enemy terrain to be encountered in the East by Christian forces, and to Pius II on 1 March 1464 urging the pope to hasten his crusade and including the same practical information as in his previous letter to Scarampo-Trevisan,[72] the many letters from Cardinal Bessarion written especially on his various crusading legations to Germany in 1460 and 1461[73] and to Venice after 1463[74] and directed to the city of Augsburg, to Cristoforo Moro, doge of Venice, to Jacopo Ammanati and to Pius II himself,[75] as well as his informative description of the conditions in the Morea contained in a letter addressed to the Francis-

[66] Cf. *Briefwechsel*, iii, ed. Wolkan (*Fontes rerum austriacarum*, xlviii (1918)), 129, 140–1, 188, 216–18, 225–33, 241–5, 248–53, 256, 259–61, 264, 274, 279, 281, 283, 297, 299, 301–2, 346–7, 399–403, 405–6, 412, 414, 417–18, 420–1, 423, 427, 431–32, 440, 444–6, 452, 456, 457, 460, 467, 472–4, 479–84, 488. For his letters as a cardinal (after 18 December 1456), which are similarly preoccupied with this theme, cf. *Opera*, 763–843.
[67] *Briefwechsel*, iii, 199–202.    [68] *Ibid.*, 206–15.
[69] 200. Cf. *ibid.*, 278–85 and 394–5 for two more particularly eloquent letters on this theme.
[70] Ed. C. Hopf, *Chroniques gréco-romanes* (Berlin, 1873), 359–66, where the letter is incorrectly attributed to Leonardo of Chios: cf. Setton, *Papacy*, ii, 239.
[71] Ed. Pertusi, 'Le epistole storiche', in *Lauro Quirini umanista*, 234–40.
[72] *Ibid.*, 241–57.    [73] Cf. Setton, *Papacy*, ii, 216–18.    [74] *Ibid.*, 243ff.
[75] Ed. Mohler, *Bessarion*, iii, 496–530; G. Palmieri, 'Lettere del Bessarione relative alla crociata contro il Turco', *Il Muratori*, iii (1894), 61–6.

can preacher Jacopo della Marca on 20 May 1459,[76] and Flavio Biondo's dedicatory letter of his *Roma triumphans* directed to Pius II in which he declares that not only would the crusaders enlisted by the pope learn lessons of endurance from the example of the Roman soldiers described in his book but also the pope himself would learn from reading about ancient Roman triumphs of the great triumph he would soon enjoy after expelling the Turks from Europe and the holy land.[77] A number of humanist orations on the crusade date from these years, including three delivered at Siena in the presence of Pius II by Ludovico Donato,[78] Tomaso da Rieti's crusading oration delivered to the pope on behalf of Francesco Sforza in 1458,[79] Bessarion's orations during his German legations delivered at Nürnberg and Vienna in 1460,[80] Francesco Filelfo's exhortation to Venice in 1463,[81] and Bernardo Giustiniani's two orations delivered during his French legation on behalf of Venice in January 1462[82] as well as his oration given as a papal consistory in 1463 and devoted to recommending strategy for the forthcoming joint papal–Venetian crusade.[83] The Congress of Mantua, held in 1459 to plan the pope's crusade, was a great forum for humanist crusading rhetoric, occasioning the oration on the assumption of the blessed Virgin delivered on 15 August 1459 by Niccolò Perotti which ended by calling for the liberation of Constantinople,[84] the oration on behalf of the duke of Milan delivered by Francesco Filelfo, where he gave a fuller history of the Turks from their origins up to the time of Mehmed II than in his previous two texts on this subject,[85] an oration on behalf of the college of cardinals by Bessarion, who dwelled particularly on the plunder of Christian churches by the Turks,[86] and two orations, one at the opening[87] and the other at the close of the congress,[88] by Pius II, who, after denouncing Turkish atrocities, offered to join the crusade himself.

[76] Ed. Mohler, *Bessarion*, iii, 490–3; cf. Setton, *Papacy*, ii, 209–10.
[77] *De Roma triumphante*, etc. (Basel, 1531), 1; cf. Setton, *Papacy*, ii, 215.
[78] *Tres orationes habitae Senis apud P. M. Pium II*, Biblioteca universitaria di Pisa, ms. 537; cf. Pastor, *Storia*, ii, 210.
[79] Cf. Flamini, 'Leonardo Dati', 70.
[80] Ed. Mohler, *Bessarion*, iii, 377–403; cf. Pastor, *Storia*, ii, 118.
[81] Cf. O. Raynaldus, *Annales ecclesiastici*, xix (Rome, 1663) ad ann. 1463, 52–6; Setton, *papacy*, ii, 267.
[82] *Orationes* (Venice, 1493), fol. E2v–Fv; cf. Labalme, *Giustiniani*, 166–7, 171–2.
[83] *Orationes* (Venice, 1493), fol. Fv–F5; cf. Labalme, *Giustiniani*, 180–3.
[84] Cf. Mercati, *Per la cronologia della vita e degli scritti di Niccolò Perotti* [Studi e testi, 44] (Rome, 1925), 49–50.
[85] Ed. J. Mittarelli, *Bibliotheca . . . monst. S. Mich. Ven.* (Venice, 1779), 888–93. Cf. Schwoebel, *Shadow*, 151, 172, and Pius II, *Commentaries*, 225.
[86] Ed. C. P. Contarini, in *Anecdota veneta* (Venice, 1757). For a list of eleven manuscripts, cf. Mohler, *Bessarion*, i, 289, n. 1; for a summary of the speech, cf. *ibid.*, 288–9 and Setton, *Papacy*, ii, 212.
[87] Ed. Mansi, *Orationes* (Lucca, 1755–9), ii, 9ff.
[88] Ed. J. Mansi, *Sacrorum conciliorum . . . collectio* (Venice, 1788), xxxv, 113–20.

The principal humanist treatise devoted to the Orient dating from these years is Pius II's *Cosmographia* (also entitled *De asia*), which, completed in 1461, is the most important humanist work on this subject composed in the early Renaissance,[89] but the greatest burst of humanist literary activity inspired by the papal crusade seems to have been in the field of Latin poetry. Some of this verse is addressed to Christian princes such as the duke of Milan, Francesco Sforza, who was exhorted to pursue the crusade by Orazio Romano,[90] and beseeched by Giannantonio de' Pandoni (il Porcellio) not to abandon Rome to the Turks,[91] and whose imminent victory over the Turks was augured by Publio Gregorio Tifernate,[92] or the duke of Ferrara, Borso d'Este, who was the dedicatee of a major crusading poem, Gaspare Tribraco's *Carmen de apparatu contra Turcum*, completed in the spring of 1464, which described Borso's preparations for the papal crusade amidst a wealth of references to classical history and Roman gods and heroes,[93] while Leonardo Dati addressed identical epigrams to Kings Henry VI of England and Louis XI of France, who, he declared, were eagerly awaited by Jerusalem.[94] A series of verse epistles advocating the crusade were composed by the humanist from Novara, Pietro Apollonio Collazio, and dedicated to Emperor Frederick III, Charles VII of France, the Dauphin Louis (the future Louis XI), Ferdinand of Naples, Francesco Sforza and Christendom at large, but pride of place was given by Collazio to Pius II himself,[95] who of course was the principal recipient of crusading verses during his pontificate. Much of this verse is collected in a fifteenth-century manuscript anthology known as *Epaeneticorum ad Pium II. Pont. Max. libri V*;[96] besides several poems with crusading material by the pope himself as well as anonymous authors, this collection includes crusading verses by Porcellio, Orazio Romano, Pietro Ransano, Giovanni Alvise Toscani, Bartolomeo Scala, Antonio Tritentone, Agapito Rustici, Bartolomeo Moriconi, Giacomo da Rieti, Pier Candido Decembrio, Pietro Odi, Niccolò della Valle, Lodrisio Crivelli, Francesco di Antonio Loschi, and Francesco Patrizi;[97] but a number of poets, including Lodrisio

[89] *Opera*, 281–386.
[90] Horatii Romani, *Porcaria . . . cum aliis eiusdem quae inveniri potuerunt carminibus*, ed. M. Lehnerdt (Leipzig, 1907), 53–7.
[91] Cf. R. Avesani, 'Epaeneticorum ad Pium II Pont. Max. libri V', in *Enea Silvio Piccolomini Papa Pio II*, ed. D. Maffei (Siena, 1968), 44–5.
[92] *Opscula* (Venice, 1498), not paginated.
[93] Ed. G. Venturini, *Un umanista modenese nella Ferrara di Borso d'Este* (Ravenna, 1970).
[94] Cf. Flamini, 'Leonardo Dati', 70–1.
[95] Ed. S. Grosso and C. Negroni, *Di Pietro Apollonio Collazio . . . il libro . . . delle epistole a Pio II per la crociata* (Novara, 1877). Cf. A. A. Strnad, 'Studia piccolomineana', in Maffei, ed., *E.S.P.* (Siena, 1968), 376–7, 384; Pastor, *Storia*, ii, 212; Flamini, 'Leonardo Dati', 69–70.
[96] Avesani, 'Epaeneticorum', in Maffei, ed., *E.S.P.*, 15–97.
[97] *Ibid.*

Crivelli,[98] Leonardo Dati,[99] Naldo Naldi,[100] Orazio Romano,[101] Publio Gregorio Tifernate,[102] and Tito Vespasiano Strozzi,[103] composed crusading verses for the pope not included among the *Epaenetica*.

Benedetto Accolti's history of the first crusade is part of this extensive humanist literature of the early Renaissance concerned with Eastern Europe and the Near East; indeed, like many humanists, Accolti was writing to lend support to efforts to launch a crusade in his own day. It was Accolti's hope, so he declares in the preface to *De bello*, that his contemporaries might be moved to follow the example of the first crusaders and wipe out the common blot, which has grown enormously in our time, namely, that the enemies of the Christian religion not only hold His Sepulchre but have extended their power far and wide';[104] Accolti intended to hold up the deeds of the first crusaders to inspire his contemporaries to join a crusade against the Turks. Accolti was not the first humanist to draw on the history of the earlier crusades to rouse enthusiasm for a crusade in his own time; although it was much more usual for humanists to cite examples from Roman and Greek antiquity to inspire crusading militancy among their contemporaries, nevertheless a number of other humanists also looked to medieval history in their crusading apologetics. With a millenarian and providential slant characteristic of his writings on the Orient, George of Treibzond observed that the enemies of Christ had emerged from Africa in the time of Charlemagne and seized Spain, southern France and Palestine, declaring that this had been preordained in order to rouse Christians to the defence of their holy places; the example of Charlemagne, who rescued his contemporaries from destruction at the hands of the Moors, was cited by George to inspire Alfonso of Aragon to save Europe from destruction by African Muslims in his own day.[105] Writing to Pope Nicholas V, Lauro Quirini held up the spectre of Pope Urban III (1185–7), who died disconsolate because Jerusalem had been lost to the Muslims during his pontificate; distorting the history of the third crusade to serve the purpose of his crusading apologetics, Quirini cited the example of Pope Clement III, who, according to him, personally

---

98 Ed. L. F. Smith, 'Lodrisio Crivelli of Milan and Aeneas Sylvius', SR, ix (1962), 46, 48, 51, 56, 59.
99 Cf. Flamini, 'Leonardo Dati', 70.
100 Cf. W. Grant, 'Major poems of Naldo Naldi', *Manuscripta*, vi (1962), 141.
101 Ed. Lehnerdt, 50–3.   102 *Opuscula* (Venice, 1498), not paginated.
103 *Poemata* (Basel, ca. 1535–40), fol. 159v–163r. Cf. Pastor, *Storia*, ii, 212.
104 History, fol. 2r: Quorum [the first crusaders] si extaret memoria, si virtus eorum, laus, nomen per ora hominum volitaret et sepe in libris legeretur, plurimi forsan cupidine laudis vel pudore adducti, vel ob spem celestis felicitatis ad eamdem virtutem excitarentur delerentque communem labem, nostra etate maxime aucta, quod scilicet hostes Christi religionis non modo sepulchrum eius tenent sed longe ac late suum imperium extenderunt (*Recueil*, 530).
105 Cf. Monfasani, *George of Trebizond*, 51, n. 100.

marched at the head of the crusading army to recover Jerusalem, evidently just as he hoped Nicholas V would do in order to recapture Constantinople.[106] Addressing Emperor Frederick III in 1452, Bernardo Giustiniani recalled the deeds of the future Empress Leonora's grandfather, John I of Portugal (1383–1433), who had recaptured Ceuta from the Moors,[107] and speaking before King Louis XI of France on 6 January 1462, he declared that it was almost the French king's destiny to act as the scourge of the infidel: after all, he asked, who made Charles great if not the Saracens in Spain? or Philip [Augustus] great if not Saladin?[108] In the same oration Giustiniani explicitly mentioned the first crusade to rouse enthusiasm for a war against the Turks, pointing out that it was the Muslims who made Godfrey, Baldwin and Hugh the Great famous,[109] and a number of humanists went into even more detail in evoking the example of the first crusade. Petrarch cited Godfrey of Bouillon as one of the only men who had been able, albeit temporarily, to halt the triumphant march of Islam:

> ... the Duke Godfrey came alone,
> To undertake crusade and righteous steps,
>      Who in Jerusalem with his own hands
> Built the nest now bereft of care or guard,
> Whence in my wrath I cry aloud in vain!
>      Live on, ye wretched Christians, in your pride,
> Consuming one the other, caring not
> That the tomb of Christ be in the clutch of dogs!
>      Few men, if any, saw I after him
> Rise to high fame, if I be not deceived,
> Either through arts of peace or arts of war.[110]

In 1438 Bartolomeo da Giano wrote,

O! where now is that most Christian, strong, pious leader Godfrey? or Bohemond, Baldwin and the other princes, glorious for infinite centuries, who liberated Jesus Christ's sepulchre from the hands of the infidel? ... O! therefore, rise up now, since it is time: the example is here ...[111]

Another example comes from the letter to Charles VII of France by Filelfo:

The French, with Godfrey as their leader, came to Asia and defeated the Saracens in battle at Damascus, and at Antioch overcame the Persians and the Turks. They recovered all Mesopotamia and in Syria they drove the Saracens back to the point of extermination. Having stormed the fortifications of the strongest cities, ... they freed the Holy City and all Palestine from shameful servitude to the infidel, retaining

---

[106]   Ed. Pertusi, 'Le epistole storiche', in Krautter *et al.*, *Lauro Quirini umanista*, 227.
[107]   *Orationes* (Venice, 1493), fol. Bv; cf. Labalme, *Giustiniani*, 139–40.
[108]   *Orationes*, fol. E4v; cf. Labalme, *Giustiniani*, 166–7.
[109]   *Orationes*, fol. E4v.
[110]   E. H. Wilkins, tr., *The Triumphs of Petrarch* (Chicago, 1962), 84.
[111]   Mittarelli, *Bibl. ... S. Mich.*, 522.

ing it in possession, to the singular honour of the Christian name, for eighty-eight years, up to the time of Saladin.[112]

Aeneas Sylvius drew attention to the first crusade when in his oration to Nicholas V on behalf of Frederick III in 1452 he argued:

There remains to consider whether it is possible to organize a crusade and what benefit will result from it. There are many, Holy Father, who, when they hear talk of a crusade, will say, 'Behold the old dream, the old delusion, the empty stories.' But when the Eastern Church was suffering persecution from pagans and the Saracens were defiling Jerusalem, your predecessor, Urban [II], moved by the pleas of Alexius [Comnenus], who held power in Constantinople, as well as those of other Christians who lived subject to Turkish tribute, undertook a grave and laborious journey to France, gathered a very great army and into Greece, Asia and Syria sent 300,000 men (according to Otto of Freising, a reliable authority), whom the Saracens were unable to prevent from conquering both Antioch and Jerusalem. For this reason Urban, who called the crusade, and Godfrey, who led it, to this day are both renowned.[113]

Aeneas briefly mentioned the first crusade in his letter to Nicholas of Cusa on the fall of Constantinople[114] and in one of his orations at the Diet of Regensburg in 1454,[115] but he made particularly effective use of this precedent in the oration with which he opened the Congress of Mantua in 1459:

O! if Godfrey, Baldwin, Eustace, Hugh the Great, Bohemond, Tancred and the other strong men who once broke through the Turkish battle lines and recovered Jerusalem by arms were present, they would certainly not allow us to utter so many words, but rising, as once before in the presence of our predecessor Urban II, they would shout with eager voices: It is God's will, it is God's will, but you silently wait for the end of my speech, nor do my imprecations seem to have any effect on you.[116]

Before Accolti published *De bello*, the humanist who made the most extensive use of the first crusade in advocating war against the Turks to his contemporaries was Flavio Biondo. Brief references to this theme occur in his letter to Alfonso of Aragon in August 1453, where he wrote,

It would be extremely easy and secure for a Christian expedition to cross into Asia: . . . hence our Christians at the time of the Roman pontiff, Urban II, under the leadership of Hugh the Great, brother of the king of France, Godfrey of Bouillon and Bohemond, son of Robert Guiscard.[117]

or in his letter a few months later to Pietro Campofregosi, doge of Genoa, in which he drew attention to the Genoese and Pisan role in the first crusade:

You lent not a little aid to the glorious efforts of Pope Urban [II], for the Genoese

---

[112] *Epist. fam.* (Venice, 1502), fol. 56v.    [113] Mansi, ed. *Orationes*, i, 168.
[114] Wolkan, ed., *Briefwechsel*, iii, 211.    [115] *Ibid.*, 545.
[116] Mansi, ed., *Orationes*, ii, 28.    [117] Nogara, ed., *Scritti inediti*, 46.

contributed a fleet of fifty triremes and eight other ships to that most glorious of all expeditions by which Jerusalem was recaptured.[118]

But Biondo dwelled at length on this theme in the crusading oration he delivered to Frederick III and Alfonso of Aragon at Naples in 1452:

In 1094 Urban II, the Roman pontiff, a man filled with the holy spirit . . . in four different places in a single year held councils . . . of which the fourth was in the city of Clermont in the French Auvergne. At that council, going beyond his own intentions as well as those of the fathers present, he strongly deplored an indignity that ought to break the hearts of all Christians – the oppression of holy Jerusalem, which, then as now, the filthy Saracens hold . . . The magnates and peoples of France, Spain, England and Germany were urged by letters from the Council [to attend] . . . Almost innumerable princes and soldiers, many more than those to whom letters were written, came to the Council of Clermont . . . And beyond the hope, opinion and intention of all, with God's cooperation, a crusade was declared and it is known that 300,000 men in a few days vowed to join that crusade. Christian princes, hear, I ask, how miraculously our best Lord aided the will of his faithful! Each soldier pledged to the expedition returned to his own country and everyone in public and private made peace with his neighbour without coercion . . . Nor did Italy lack such blessings from Our Lord . . . William, one of the sons of Robert Guiscard, wanted to keep the kingdom of Italy and Sicily for himself and exclude his brother, Bohemond. Bohemond, however, . . . took very strong objection to this and sailed [from Greece] to Italy with an army of 12,000 cavalry and infantry. He took Bari and Melfi and so terrified his brother William that, fearing for his kingdom in Italy and Sicily, he called 20,000 Saracen mercenaries from Africa into Italy. A war was waged, extremely dangerous to Italy, because it was clear to Bohemond that, if he were repelled by such a force of arms, William also would abandon the kingdom to pillage by the Saracens. But in this emergency God's mercy was present. For the princes and soldiers from France, Spain and England and a large part of the Germans, pledged to the forementioned Christian expedition, shipped to Venice their arms and other equipment, which the Venetians were conveying free of charge to Constantinople; they themselves, unarmed and attired as pilgrims, travelled the length of Italy to Brindisi, where, by Venetian ships, part would go to Dyrrachium, part to Constantinople. When they had passed many continuous days on the Via Appia from Rome to Brindisi, Bohemond, keen to see such a glorious spectacle, joined the road, himself unarmed, not far from Bari. And it happened through God's help that he met the counts of Flanders and St Pol . . . Why shall I linger over events memorable for all time? Bohemond, persuaded to join the Christian expedition, took the vow and accepted the sign of the cross; on the next day, he embarked, leaving his entire paternal inheritance to his iniquitous brother . . . who sent the Saracens back to Africa before harm was done; and so this kingdom which you now possess, glorious King Alfonso, by the divine mercy of which I have spoken, was saved. And it was Bohemond, who took the most powerful [city] of Antioch after a three years' siege, holding it with full authority of Christians, and by taking Jerusalem together with Godfrey of Bouillon, he became so distinguished by his righteousness and in that expedition he performed so many acts of virtue that he can justly be compared to Caius Julius Caesar and the two Scipios . . . [119]

[118] *Ibid.*, 64.
[119] *Ibid.*, 111–13. The first crusade continued to be used as an *exemplum* in crusading

## (iii) Florence and the crusade, 1453–64

With predecessors such as Filelfo, Pius II and Biondo, Accolti could therefore rest assured that the subject he had chosen for his second composition as chancellor could in no way be regarded in Florentine learned society as a theme unworthy of humanist study, but the wish to enhance his reputation in the eyes of the Medici and other Florentine patrons of the humanities was not the only reason that he turned to the history of the first crusade and to crusading apologetics. As first chancellor, Accolti was Florence's official apologist, and his history of the first crusade was intended to support Florence's official diplomacy. It has sometimes been believed that growing commercial interests in the East and hostility to Venice predisposed the Florentines against a war with the Turks after the fall of Constantinople,[1] but in fact Florence had publicly supported efforts to launch a crusade by the papacy in the years after 1453. Behind the scenes there were misgivings in Florence about the prudence of papal crusading projects: some Florentines were reluctant to waste good money on futile holy wars, especially when they saw that other Christian states were often hesitant to come forward; there was a powerful feeling that crusading taxes were a pretext for ecclesiastical extortion; to some extent they feared for their trade in the Orient, now dominated by the Turks; they were particularly loath to give their full backing to a war in which their political and commercial rivals, the Venetians, would take the lead and reap the profits. On the other hand, the claims on Florence of the papacy were powerful too; Florence was a Christian state, which moreover was tied to the papacy by the strongest political and commercial bonds, and a sense of political expediency, if not of Christian duty, would oblige Florence to succumb to a truly determined pope such as Pius II. Indeed, a variety of opinions existed in Florence on the question of the crusade in the years after 1453; there were Florentines who were cynical over the prospects of papal projects and whose hostility to Venice outweighed all other considerations, but there were also Florentines who enjoyed long ancestral associations with the Orient, who genuinely grieved for the plight of their fellow Christians in the East and who with deep sincerity hoped for a crusade to

---

apologetics after Accolti's time: cf. e.g. B. Giustiniani, *Oratio . . . apud Sixtum IV* (2 December 1471) in *Orationes* (Venice, 1493) fol. G3v (cf. Labalme, *Giustiniani*, 197–200); Pietro Mansi's oration to Innocent VIII (25 March 1490) in Sigismondi de'Conti, *Le storie de' suoi tempi* (Rome, 1883), ii, 416, 420, 423 (cf. Setton, *Papacy*, ii, 413).

[1] This has been argued in the two works which discuss in greatest detail Florence's Eastern diplomacy: Pastor, *Storia*, i, 622–3, 702, 715 and ii, 17–18, 53, 56–7, 210–11, 237–9, 242, 253, 265–6; and G. B. Picotti, *Dieta di Mantova*, 74–5, 79–81, 369–72. Setton, *Papacy*, ii, 154, 190, 246–7, 263–4, and F. Babinger, 'Lorenzo de' Medici e la corte ottomana', *ASI*, cxxi, (1963), 307ff. and 'Maometto II, il conquistatore, e l'Italia', *RSI*, lxiii (1951), 489ff., repeat similar views; an earlier attempt to revise this picture was my 'La storia della prima crociata di Benedetto Accolti'.

turn the tide against the advancing Turks. Between these two extremes were the pragmatists who doubted that papal hopes would ever have any practical consequences but who recognized that it was expedient to support the crusade in order to keep the pope's goodwill; privately they may have expressed strong reservations but publicly they gave the pope their full support, and it is clear that such voices were usually predominant in Florence in the years after 1453.

When in early July 1453 the Florentines first learned that Constantinople had fallen to the Turks,[2] they were at war with Venice and some Florentines were said to have rejoiced over losses suffered by their enemies in Constantinople.[3] But Florentines had themselves lost heavily there, and Genoa, to whom they were allied, had probably suffered even more than Venice.[4] As in the rest of Christendom, there was genuine anguish in Florence over the fate of Constantinople; one Florentine chronicler declared that 'it was for Christians an enormous loss, defeat and disgrace',[5] and the official Florentine reaction was given on 17 July 1453 by the Signoria, who wrote to their ambassador in Genoa,

> We cannot express to you how greatly we were overcome with despair at the sad tidings of the loss of Constantinople; all Christian princes . . . should make peace with one another, and all other Christians should dress themselves in mourning to demonstrate their anguish; and they should be so utterly ashamed that they are impelled to recover the lost places. But if they do not, as they will not, all Christendom will be injured and shamed forever.[6]

When in September 1453 it was learnt in Florence that Pera had been lost to Genoa, they again wrote to their ambassador there, declaring that 'the princes and rulers of Christendom should make peace and unite to take vengeance on the Turks, who should endure the same suffering and humiliation that they had inflicted in Constantinople and Pera'.[7] At the same time, when the king of Cyprus sent an ambassador to recount Turkish atrocities and urge peace in Italy as a preparation for a crusade, the Florentines took up his cause with the pope, declaring their anger against the barbarous Turks and stating that if peace were granted to Italy they would be prepared to the best of their ability to meet this threat to Christendom.[8]

Pope Nicholas V felt it was up to him to bring peace to Italy in order to

---

[2]   Cf. Pastor, *Storia*, i, 622–3; Schwoebel, *Shadow*, 3.
[3]   Cf. Pastor, *Storia*, i, 622–3.
[4]   Cf. Jacopo Tedaldi, 'Informations . . . de la prinse de Constantinople', in E.Martène and U. Durand, *Thesaurus novus anecdotorum*, i (Paris, 1717), 1823.
[5]   Buoninsegni, *Istorie*, 103; cf. Cambi, *Istorie*, in *Delizie*, xx, 311.
[6]   Iorga, *Notes et extraits*, ii, 499. Cardinal Isidore of Kiev took it for granted that Florence would sympathize with eastern Christians after the fall of Constantinople: cf. his letter to Florence, published by G. Hofmann, 'Quellen zu Isidore von Kiew', *Orientalia Christiana Periodica*, xviii (1952), 146–8.
[7]   Iorga, *Notes et extraits*, ii, 500.        [8]   Müller, *Documenti*, 178–9.

counter the Turkish menace, and at the beginning of October 1453 he convoked a peace congress in Rome;[9] throughout the long negotiations the
Florentine ambassadors supported a crusade which could result from
peace in Italy, even complaining at the beginning of December that the
pope and the cardinals had 'become very cool to this matter of the
Turks'.[10] Shortly afterwards, in February 1454, they congratulated
Emperor Frederick III for calling a diet at Regensburg to undertake 'the
defence of Jesus Christ against the cruelty and . . . fury of the Turks',
declaring their willingness to join the common effort.[11] However, in
March 1454 the peace talks in Rome collapsed, preventing the Florentines,
so they wrote to the emperor, from attending the diet at Regensburg;[12] it
was finally through secret negotiations between Milan and Venice that
peace was concluded in April 1454,[13] and in the wake of enthusiasm after
the Peace of Lodi the Florentines continued to be eager for war against the
Turks. Another diet had been called by the emperor to meet at Frankfurt-
am-Main in October 1454 and on 29 August 1454 the Florentines
accepted his invitation, thanking God for having inspired the *culmen
caesareum* against the insanity of the savage and bestial Turk and congratulating his majesty for undertaking so glorious an enterprise.[14]
Moreover, on 19 October 1454 they wrote to the pope on behalf of two
Florentine knights hospitaller, who wanted to join the defence of Rhodes
against the Turks. They had not the means, the Signoria stated, to equip
themselves, and so the pope was asked to look with favour on the proposals for raising money to be put to him by the two knights, who were
representing the Florentine people as a whole in the defence of the faith.[15]

At the beginning of the pontificate of Nicholas V's successor,
Callixtus III, Florence was still keen to support the crusade against the
Turks. In their letters congratulating Callixtus on his election, the Florentines declared, 'We are certain a shepherd has been provided by God who
will delight in peace and tranquillity and as defender and champion of the
faithful will devote himself to exterminating the infidel enemies'; on behalf
of the Christian faith, the city of Constantinople and the Eastern Church,
they rejoiced that, like an angel come from heaven, he would drive the
infidel from Europe and the Orient.[16] The ambassadors sent by Florence in
May 1455 to swear obedience to the new pope were instructed to dwell on
the Turkish threat, expressing their joy that the holy church, menaced by
the impious Turk, had found a fervent and mighty protector.[17] At their

[9] *Storia di Milano* (Milan, 1953–66), vi, 55.  [10] Iorga, *Notes et extraits*, ii, 502.
[11] Müller, *Documenti*, 179.  [12] ASF, Miss. 40, fol. 33r–v.
[13] *Storia di Milano*, vii, 56–64; Pastor, *Storia*, i, 628–34.
[14] Müller, *Documenti*, 180.  [15] *Ibid.*, 180–1.
[16] ASF, Miss. 40, fol. 119v, 126r.
[17] ASF, LC, 13, fol. 136v–137r; cf. *Due legazioni al sommo pontifice per il comune di
Firenze presedute da Sant'Antonino Arcivescovo*, ed. C. Guasti (Florence, 1857), 4.

audience in Rome, after the pope had expressed his intention of sacrificing his own life to reconquer Constantinople,[18] the archbishop of Florence, Sant'Antonino, who headed the Florentine embassy, delivered an impassioned oration in favour of the crusade: Callixtus had been chosen to hurl the savage infidel beast into oblivion; now at peace, Italy would crush that angel of Satan, that filthy dog, that perverse antichrist, recovering his conquests and, above all, Constantinople; with the Turks perpetrating new iniquities every day, there could be no delay and therefore the Florentine people placed themselves under the command of the pope in this undertaking.[19] At about the same time, when an ambassador from Thomas Paleologus, one of the despots of the Morea, came to Florence, he was told that the Florentines were willing at any time to take part in a joint crusade,[20] and later in the summer of 1455, at the request of the king of Naples, the Florentines instructed their ambassador in Rome to urge Callixtus III to give the highest priority to the crusade,[21] an intervention which earned the Florentines commendation from the pope.[22]

Moreover, the Florentines helped to raise money for the crusade. During the spring of 1455, in reply to the papal ambassador who had come to Florence to ask for a crusading tithe, the Florentine government declared that Florence would always cooperate with efforts to collect tenths for the holy war,[23] and on 11 August 1455 Callixtus III wrote that he had instructed the Dominican preacher, Giovanni da Napoli, to go to Florence to arrange for crusading subsidies;[24] Giovanni arrived in Florence in early September, requesting the Florentines to allow another *decima* to be collected from their clergy for the crusade, and to specify what their own subsidy would be.[25] They answered that the resources of their clergy had been dissipated by recent wars and by the burden of the previous tenth and if it were not now possible to spare the Florentine clergy, they asked for the new tenth to be postponed; regarding their own subsidy, they declared that, as was their wont, they would not be outdone by other Christian states, and, although they could not yet enter into specifics, they would offer a liberal contribution.[26] This reply did not entirely satisfy Callixtus III, who insisted on a specific answer to Giovanni da Napoli's requests.[27] Moreover, while Giovanni da Napoli was in Florence, Alain de Coëtivy, cardinal of Avignon and papal legate in France for the crusade, arrived in Porto Pisano, where he was met by the Florentine ambassador,

[18] Pastor, *Storia*, i, 667–8.
[19] Sant'Antonino, *Chronica*, III, xii, 16 (Lyons, 1586, iii, 585–9); Guasti, ed., *Due legazioni*, 17–18.
[20] Müller, *Documenti*, 181–2.   [21] ASF, LC, 13, fol. 153r–v.
[22] *Ibid.*, fol. 154v.   [23] *Ibid.*, fol. 137v–38r.
[24] ASF, Resp. 1, fol. 22v.   [25] ASF, LC, 13, fol. 155v–56; Miss. 40, fol. 149v.
[26] *Ibid.*, fol. 149v–50r; cf. also *ibid.*, fol. 155v–156r.   [27] ASF, Resp. 1, fol. 23r–24v.

Giovanni di Cosimo de' Medici, who was instructed to emphasize Florence's obedience to the papacy but in no way to obligate Florence to any specific subsidy to the crusade, declaring only in general terms that the Florentine people would do no less than other Christian states; regarding the clerical tenth, he was to ask for as long a postponement as possible and for the proceeds to be spent in Florentine territory.[28] In the end, however, the Florentines yielded to the cardinal, excusing their seeming reluctance and declaring that they would provide as many galleys as was thought fitting by the pope,[29] who was satisfied with this reply, demonstrating, according to their ambassador in Rome, the greatest affection for the Florentine people.[30] At the end of the year the pope ordered the taxes thus collected or about to be collected to be used to equip four galleys and a ship at Porto Pisano to defend Rhodes[31] and the following summer they joined the papal fleet in defence of the Aegean Islands.[32]

During his visit to Florence in 1455, Giovanni da Napoli had no difficulty in rousing popular enthusiasm for the crusade; during October he preached the crusade in the Florentine cathedral, and in response, beginning on Thursday 16 October and culminating on the following Sunday, great processions numbering as many as 6000 people were formed in the four quarters of the city, with the people dressed in white bearing a red cross on their breasts.[33] Popular feeling was also stirred in Florence, as in the rest of Christendom,[34] by the Christian victory over the Turks at Belgrade in July 1456. The Florentine Signoria wrote to the pope that long thanksgiving processions had immediately been formed and were still continuing as they wrote; they thanked God for providing a scourge of the infidel in the person of the pope, and they reiterated their promise to give whatever subsidy the pope thought fit, declaring that 'pulcrius enim et sanctius est mori quam sub religione falsa vitam ducere'.[35] At about the time of the celebrations of the victory at Belgrade, the Portuguese ambassador arrived in Florence expressing his king's intention to devote himself to the crusade and requesting assistance and safe-conduct for his forces in Florentine territory. The Florentines replied that they would help the king in every way, repeating that their own contribution was to be fixed at the discretion of the pope,[36] a reply which pleased not only the king[37] but also Callixtus III, who hoped that Florentine enthusiasm would

[28] ASF, LC, 13, fol. 158r–159r.    [29] *Ibid.*, fol. 161r.
[30] ASF, Miss. 40, fol. 174r.    [31] ASF, Resp. 1, fol. 25r.
[32] Pastor, *Storia*, i, 686–7; cf. Guasti, ed., *Due legazioni*, 20; Sciambra, Valentini and Parrino, *Il 'Liber brevium'*, 30.
[33] ASF, CStr., ii, 16 bis, fol. 21r; Cambi, *Istorie*, in *Delizie*, xx, 334; Buoninsegni, *Istorie*, 114.
[34] Setton, *Papacy*, ii, 183.    [35] ASF, Miss. 40, fol. 214r–v.
[36] ASF, CP, 54, fol. 39v, 41r–v; Müller, *Documenti*, 183.
[37] ASF, Resp. 1, fol. 41r–v.

confirm the king's crusading ardour.[38] Also in 1456, when the pope protested that Florentine officials in Pisa had subjected some goods intended for use in the crusade to the *gabella*,[39] the Signoria, deeply apologetic, replied that, as soon as the matter had come to their attention and even before they had received his letter, they had ordered the *gabella* to be waived.[40] Again in 1456 Giovanni da Napoli was sent by the pope to preach the crusade in Florentine territory,[41] and in the course of his mission to Tuscany during 1456 and 1457 he was able to collect from the inhabitants of Florence and its dominions a considerable quantity of jewels, silver and money,[42] which he consigned to Callixtus III, who expressed his satisfaction with the results of Giovanni's missions.[43]

In the period from 1453 to 1456, therefore, Florence openly voiced support for papal crusading efforts and contributed the proceeds of tenths collected in their territories to provide galleys, ships and men; however, beginning in 1457 they became markedly less willing to join the holy war, showing themselves to be considerably less amenable to papal influence. One reason for this changed attitude may have been their expanding trade with the Orient; voyages of communal galleys to Turkish Constantinople had resumed in 1456,[44] and protection for Florentine merchants had to be sought from Sultan Mehmed II.[45] Indeed, crusading forces were regarded as a possible threat to Florentine merchants trading in the Orient, as is shown by Florence's request in 1457 to the pope and the king of Naples for their galleys to enjoy safe passage to Constantinople;[46] this was granted by the pope and, although it was refused by the king, the Florentines, with considerable anxiety, allowed the voyage to proceed.[47] Another influence on the Florentines at this time was the apparent indifference of other Christian states to the crusade:[48] in France the king had forbidden the tenth to be collected for two years,[49] and the same was done, in the teeth of papal threats of excommunication, by Federigo da Montefeltro, who actually enjoyed the title of apostolic vicar for Urbino;[50] Perugia failed to make its promised contribution of 4000 florins,[51] the king of Portugal, who had been allowed to keep the Portuguese tenths, never appeared with his promised fleet,[52] and the Ragusans refused to consign the Dalmatian tenths with which they had been entrusted.[53] Moreover, widespread indifference was often turned into outright hostility by not entirely unjustified

[38] Müller, *Documenti*, 184–5.　[39] ASF, Resp. 1, fol. 42r.　[40] ASF, Miss. 41, fol. 6v–7r.
[41] Sciambra, Valentini, Parrino, *Il 'Liber brevium'*, 93, 131.
[42] *Ibid.*, 148.　[43] *Ibid.*, 154.　[44] Mallet, *Florentine Galleys*, 67–8.
[45] Müller, *Documenti*, 182.　[46] ASF, LC, 14, fol. 45r–v.　[47] ASF, Miss. 41, fol. 56r–v.
[48] Setton, *Papacy*, ii, 190–1; Sciambra, Valentini, Parrino, *Il 'Liber brevium'*, 24–32; L. Fumi, 'Il disinteresse di Francesco I Sforza alla crociata di Callisto III contro i turchi', ASL, xxxix [4ª ser., 17] (1912), 101–11.
[49] Pastor, *Storia*, i, 695–9.　[50] Setton, *Papacy*, ii, 190–1.　[51] *Ibid.*, 191.
[52] Pastor, *Storia*, i, 700.　[53] *Ibid.*, 739.

suspicions that crusading funds were being peculated by fraudulent preachers and collectors;[54] in fact, one such case occurred in Florentine territory at the end of December 1456 when an Aretine priest called Leonardo was accused of absconding with money collected as part of the crusading tenth,[55] and doubtless such incidents had repercussions in Florence, where, as elsewhere in Europe during the later 1450s,[56] there was widespread animosity to crusading taxes and crusading preachers. At the beginning of 1457 the pope ordered another tenth to be collected but he now met vehement protests from Florence, whose ambassador to Rome, Guglielmo Benci, was instructed on 18 February to declare that the Florentine had already been subject to three tenths and that any further demands would be 'l'ultimo tuffo'.[57] In subsequent letters they wrote to Benci that, although they were pleased by the pope's fervent dedication to the crusade, this new tenth would be the utter ruination of the Florentine clergy, who had already given to the limits of their ability; a further tenth might be easy to impose but it would be impossible to collect.[58] The pope remained unmoved by these protests and in May it was necessary to send another ambassador to Rome with instructions to declare that crusading preachers had extracted a fortune already from Florentine territory with the help of loose women and thugs; indeed, in the name of the crusade more money had been taken from Florence than from almost all the rest of Italy.[59] For the remainder of Callixtus III's pontificate Florence, like other European states,[60] remained hesitant to make further commitments to the crusade. At the end of 1457 the pope convoked a congress of ambassadors in Rome to discuss the impasse reached by the crusade,[61] and Florence, like other Italian states, was instructed to send its ambassador by the end of the year,[62] but as time elapsed no embassies arrived.[63] In November a papal legate in Florence had announced the coming congress and in reply the Florentines stated that as faithful Christians they would send their ambassadors when the other states had done the same, a decision which was repeated the next month.[64] It was not until the following March that enough representatives had arrived in Rome to enable discussions to begin,[65] but there is no record that the Florentines committed themselves to further subsidies during this final crusading conference of Callixtus's pon-

[54] Setton, *Papacy*, ii, 168.  [55] *Ibid.*
[56] Cf. Fumi, 'Il disinteresse', 110; Setton, *Papacy*, ii, 160, 217.
[57] ASF, LC, 14, fol. 34v–36r.  [58] *Ibid.*, fol. 37v, 38r.  [59] *Ibid.*, fol. 45v–46r.
[60] Setton, *Papacy*, ii, 190–1; Sciambra, Valentini, Parrino, *Il 'Liber brevium'*, 24–32; Fumi, 'Il disinteresse', 101–11.
[61] *Ibid.*, 110–11; Sciambra, Valentini, Parrino, *Il 'Liber brevium'*, 23–4.
[62] *Ibid.*, 180.
[63] Pastor, *Storia*, i, 749.  [64] ASF, CP, 54, fol. 165r–v, 180r–v.  [65] Pastor, *Storia*, i, 749.

tificate.[66] Nevertheless, even at this low point in Florentine commitment to the crusade, they did in fact give indirect help to the defence of the eastern Mediterranean when their galleys transported grain from Cyprus to Rhodes during a food shortage in the summer of 1457.[67]

The Florentines continued to be wary of crusading projects during the first years of the pontificate of Callixtus's successor, Pius II, who, unmatched among Renaissance popes for his dedication to the crusade, wrote to them shortly after his election that he expected their cooperation in his forthcoming expedition against the Turks;[68] however, the Florentine embassy sent to swear obedience to the new pope, although permitted to discuss the crusade, were forbidden to make any binding commitments.[69] Archbishop Antonino delivered an oration, which, however, was noticeably cooler to the crusade than his exhortation to Callixtus III three years before,[70] and when the pope soon afterwards called a preliminary meeting to negotiate subsidies[71] he was dissatisfied with the general promises proffered by the Florentine ambassadors,[72] under orders to hedge from their government, in whose view a great deal of Florentine money had been wasted on futile crusading projects in the past.[73] When in December 1458 the pope once again asked the Florentines to declare their subsidy to the crusade, the question was referred to the *pratica*, where there was some disagreement. Giovannozzo Pitti, although agreeing that Florence should not yet enter into specific commitments, nevertheless felt that they must preserve their good name as Christians and declare their general willingness to come to the church's defence, as they had always done in the past.[74] Other speakers were more reluctant, arguing that Florence was impoverished, that the crusade was more the affair of the Hungarians and Germans than theirs, that Florentine trade would suffer, that only the Venetians would profit, that more money had been taken from Florentine territory in the past for the crusade than from elsewhere, that Florence was weaker than other Christian states, and that, judging from past experience, it was difficult to believe that this money would be spent on its intended purpose.[75] Accepting the majority opinion of the *pratica*, the Signoria instructed the Florentine ambassadors in Rome to say that crusading tenths had been collected in Florence and its ally Milan but not elsewhere and that crusading preachers had extracted vast quantities of money from

[66]  Sciambra, Valentini, Parrino, *Il 'Liber brevium'*, 24, say that only the Venetians did not send ambassadors.
[67]  ASF, Miss. 41, fol. 56r–v.   [68] *Ibid.*, Resp. 1, fol. 64v.   [69] *Ibid.*, LC, 15, fol. 2v, 5v.
[70]  Sant'Antonino, *Chronica*, III, xxii, 17 (Lyons, 1586, iii, 593–8).
[71]  Picotti, *Dieta*, 80; L. Crivelli, *De expeditione Pii Papae II adversus Turcos*, ed. G. Zimolo, RIS², xxiii, pt v, 96ff.
[72]  ASF, LC, 15, fol. 14r; Picotti, *Dieta*, 81.
[73]  ASF, LC, 15, fol. 13r–v.   [74] ASF, CP, 55, fol. 90v.   [75] *Ibid.*, fol. 90r–91v.

their lands; using 'buone parole' with the pope, they should insist that
Florence, poorer than other states, could not be expected to do more than
the rest.[76]

At the beginning of his pontificate Pius II had announced that he would
convoke a congress to organize the expedition against the Turks[77] and
Florentine diplomacy regarding the Congress of Mantua reflected their
ambivalent attitude to the crusade: despite strong private doubts over the
pope's prudence in calling such a conference, in public the Florentines
strove to maintain their reputation as cooperative Christians. As the pope
proposed to stop in Florence on his way from Rome to Mantua, the Florentines instructed their ambassadors in Rome to declare that, although it
would be impossible to honour him adequately, nevertheless everything
possible would be done to make his visit to Florence comfortable,[78] and
later the Signoria wrote to the pope that they eagerly anticipated his arrival
in Florence to carry out a mission which would bring honour, glory and
salvation to Christians but sorrow and destruction to the barbarians.[79]
Despite such public assurances of their support, privately many Florentines wished that the pope had not embarked on this journey to Mantua,
as is clear from the debates of the *pratica* regarding how he was to be
honoured during his visit to Florence.[80] The pope was to be accompanied
by young Galeazzo Maria Sforza, the son of Florence's staunchest ally, the
duke of Milan, and in the *pratica* most speakers placed greater emphasis
on entertaining the son of Francesco Sforza than on honouring the pope
himself.[81] In giving hospitality to the Milanese and papal parties, the
Florentines in the end spent the considerable sum of 13,500 florins,[82] the
knowledge of which the Florentines, in their wish to maintain a reputation
as good Christians, did not hide from the pope, who, however, realized
that most of the money had been spent on Galeazzo, not on himself.[83]

Shortly before his arrival in Mantua Pius II wrote to the Florentines that
he expected their ambassadors to arrive at the congress no later than the
official opening day of 1 June 1459;[84] however, the episode of the election
and despatch of Florence's ambassadors to Mantua indicates yet further
the mixed feelings with regard to the crusade entertained by many Florentines, who, on the one hand, doubted the success of the congress but, on the
other, did not want to be publicly tainted as bad Christians. On 23 May
they elected Bernardo Giugni and Antonio Ridolfi as their ambassadors,

[76] ASF, LC, 15, fol. 16r–17v.   [77] Pastor, *Storia*, ii, 17.   [78] ASF, LC, 15, fol. 16r.
[79] ASF, Miss. 42, fol. 103r–v; cf. *ibid.*, RVdO, 1, fol. 32v–33r.
[80] ASF, CP, 55, fol. 103v–104v.   [81] *Ibid.*
[82] Cf. *ibid.*, 105v–106v; Provv. 150, fol. 8r; LF, 66, fol. 4r–5r for the arrangements to raise
the money before the visit of Pius II and Galeazzo Maria Sforza. These original provisions
were inadequate and so more money had to be raised, in the teeth of considerable popular
opposition: cf. *ibid.*, CP, 55, fol. 112v–117r; Provv. 150, 43v–45r; LF, 66, fol. 12r–18r.
[83] Pius II, *Commentaries*, 166.   [84] ASF, Resp. 1, fol. 75v.

but since the Florentines did not want to be the first to arrive they instructed Giugni and Ridolfi to make their departure on 23 June,[85] which they subsequently postponed to 8 July;[86] in the meantime Pius II had written them two letters, in the second of which he warned of the divine displeasure caused by their continued absence.[87] By the beginning of July the issue of sending Florentine ambassadors to Mantua had become so pressing as to merit a debate of the *pratica*, which was not in complete agreement, showing that the Florentine patriciate remained split over the issue of the crusade. The extreme views were represented on the one hand by Guglielmo Tanagli, who declared that the ambassadors should be sent immediately, and on the other by Ugolino Martelli, who flatly advised against sending them since he had heard that everyone, including the cardinals, was deserting Mantua. The majority view was that they should not be despatched until other ambassadors had arrived but that the restrictions to hold other offices ordinarily imposed on ambassadors should not be lifted to avoid further opprobrium from the pope.[88] Accordingly the Signoria postponed the departure of their ambassadors for another month until 8 August;[89] with regard to the restrictions, no immediate action was taken, but at the end of July the ambassadors were once again made eligible to hold other communal offices.[90] In the meantime, however, the prospects of the congress were improving as Italian and ultramontane embassies began to arrive,[91] and on 28 July the pope sent to Florence a third admonition;[92] by 8 August, the day on which their ambassadors were due to depart for Mantua, the Florentines were in a state of almost complete confusion, and the mixed feelings and divisions within the government over this question are clear from a series of last-minute changes of plan: first it was decided to substitute Franco Sachetti for Bernardo Giugni, then Mariano Salvini, bishop of Cortona, was elected in place of both Sachetti and Ridolfi, then Salvini failed to have his instructions ratified despite successive attempts, and finally Sachetti and Ridolfi were reelected under order to leave Florence by 25 August.[93] In the meantime, the pope was putting the greatest possible pressure on Florence: he ordered the archbishop of Florence, Lorenzo Bonarli, to intervene,[94] and on 16 August he directed a fourth and final admonition to the Florentines, accusing them of looking only to their own self-interest and threatening to denounce them in public and abandon them to God's judgement.[95] The crusade was a cause to which even the most cynical Florentine had to succumb in the end, and so on 14 August Sachetti and Ridolfi were finally

---

[85] Picotti, *Dieta*, 158.  [86] *Ibid.*  [87] ASF, Resp. 1, fol. 75v–76v, 77r–v.
[88] ASF, CP, 55, fol. 131r–134v.  [89] Picotti, *Dieta*, 158.
[90] ASF, Provv. 150, fol. 75r–v; LF, 66, fol. 29v–31v.
[91] Picotti, *Dieta*, 147–9.  [92] ASF, Resp. 1, fol. 79r–v.  [93] Picotti, *Dieta*, 158.
[94] Pastor, *Acta inedita*, 111.  [95] ASF, Resp. 1, fol. 79v–80v.

given their instructions;[96] on 23 August the Florentines were at last able to reply to the pope that their willingness to participate in such a holy undertaking was never in doubt and that they placed the good of Christendom over their own private interests.[97] On 25 August the ambassadors were given their final instructions and, probably owing to the arrangement of last minute details such as the number of horses needed, their departure was postponed until 31 August, but it is clear that they finally left for Mantua that day.[98]

Both the pope and the Florentines themselves had referred to a possible conflict of interests, which clearly meant the two Florentine galleys that had sailed for the Levant in the middle of August 1459. They arrived in Constantinople on 28 September, one of them proceeding to the Black Sea, which was the first voyage of a Florentine galley to that region.[99] The Florentines were attempting to extend the scope of their Levantine commerce and Florentine concern for their galleys is evident in the instructions given to their ambassadors at Mantua. Although given full powers in the public instructions to be read out before the entire diet in compliance with papal strictures, nevertheless they were also provided with a set of private instructions in which they were forbidden to commit Florence in any way without the expressed consent of the Signoria. In this secret mandate they were instructed to say that the Florentines were ardent supporters of the Roman church for whose honour and welfare they had always been and always would be ready to work; although the Florentine people considered no undertaking more glorious and worthy than a war against the infidel, nevertheless they lacked the strength to contribute to the extent they would have wished; all the same, they would contribute to the limits of their ability; finally, they excused their delay in sending their ambassadors to Mantua on the grounds that, as a lesser power, it was appropriate for their ambassadors to arrive after those of the greater states, pointing out that their good faith was demonstrated by the fact that, as everyone knew, they had elected their ambassadors before the official opening of the congress.[100] Their public instructions were written in the same vein, except that more space was devoted to Turkish iniquities and the section nullifying their full powers was, of course, omitted.[101] The Florentine ambassadors arrived in Mantua at the beginning of September and the beginning of their mission presented no difficulties.[102] When, however, at the end of September each Italian state was called upon in a public assembly to declare its subsidy, the Signoria despatched a letter by special courier to

[96] ASF, LC, 15, fol. 26v–30v.   [97] Pastor, *Acta inedita*, 112.
[98] Picotti, *Dieta*, 159; Del Piazzo, *Il protocollo*, 43–4.
[99] Mallett, *Florentine Galleys*, 68.
[100] ASF, LC, 15, fol. 26v–28r.   [101] *Ibid.*, fol. 29v–30v.   [102] *Ibid.*, fol. 31r.

Mantua reminding Sachetti and Ridolfi of the gravity of the negotiations. For the Turks had in their power galleys worth 100,000 florins or more as well as five hundred Florentines, two hundred of whom belonged to the best families; therefore they should put nothing in writing but go to the pope in secret to assure him of their approval of his intentions; provided other Christian states cooperated, the Florentines would play their part, confident that the pope would require a just subsidy from them; however, at that time their merchants were more actively engaged in trading in Turkish lands than those of any other nation, and there were some states previously active in Levantine trade (an obvious reference to Venice), who, having lost their primacy in the East, would stop at nothing to injure the prospects of Florence there; therefore the pope was asked to take personal responsibility for Florence's part in the crusade; if he were unwilling, the ambassadors should ask the duke of Milan to do so as well but it was preferable to keep this between only themselves and the pope; they should delay as along as possible to discover the intentions of the Venetians, but secrecy was paramount, as only six principal citizens in Florence knew of these instructions and any betrayal of the strictest confidence would be punished severely.[103] The Florentines were consumed with anxiety lest any undertaking signed by them should reach the hands of Mehmed II, and so their ambassadors obtained a private papal audience where, in the presence of two cardinals, they pledged Florence to the same contribution as that offered by other states.[104] The assembly of the Italian nation took place on 30 September, when the pope proposed a tenth to be levied on the clergy, a twentieth on the Jews and a thirtieth on the laity for the crusade; everyone present signed the agreement except the Venetians, who said they were still awaiting instructions, and the Florentines, whose agreement was guaranteed by the pope and the duke of Milan.[105] Anxious to avoid public exposure at the Congress of Mantua with their galleys at Constantinople, the Florentines instructed their ambassadors to leave Mantua as soon as possible and they were back in Florence by 10 November.[106]

The Florentines thus agreed, albeit in secret, to the crusading taxes demanded at Mantua, and when Pius II passed through Florence on his way back to Rome in January 1460[107] he pressed the Florentines to say how they were intending to carry out their promises.[108] He was met by four leading citizens, who stressed the difficulty of raising the agreed subsidies, declaring that taxes could not be levied without the approval of the legis-

---

[103]  *Ibid.*, fol. 32v–33v; Del Piazzo, *Il protocollo*, 47.

[104]  Pius II, *Commentaries*, 257.    [105]  Pastor, *Storia*, ii, 63–4.

[106]  ASF, LC, 15, fol. 34v–35r, 36v; Picotti, *Dieta*, 201.

[107]  Picotti, *Dieta*, 370. The Florentines spent 1500 florins entertaining him during his two-day visit: cf. ASF, CP, 56, fol. 26r–29v.

[108]  Pius II, *Commentaries*, 301; ASF, RVdO, 1, fol. 55v–57v.

lative councils, suggesting that the twentieth and thirtieth presented greater difficulties than the tenth, and requesting the Florentine contribution to be deferred.[109] The pope agreed to a postponement, but there was a misunderstanding with regard to which taxes were to be deferred. The Florentines believed that he had postponed all three levies,[110] whereas the pope thought the Florentines had asked for contributions of the laity and Jews only to be deferred.[111] The Florentines were puzzled, therefore, when Pius II, having left Florence for Siena, requested an ambassador to be sent for further discussions of the Florentines' subsidy[112] but, when a papal representative arrived in Florence at the beginning of March to begin collecting the clerical tenth, they were outraged.[113] The *pratica* was immediately summoned, and morning and afternoon for several days there were heated debates raising fundamental issues of church and state. At first everyone agreed that the pope must be made to desist: it was argued that the clergy were subjects of the commune, that the pope was aiming to become ruler of Florence, and that Florentine liberty was being grossly infringed.[114] Pius II's attempts to collect the subsidies agreed at Mantua were being frustrated elsewhere in Italy (especially in Venice),[115] and this example encouraged resistance from the Florentines, who complained in the *pratica* that they were being forced to make the first contribution to the crusade. But soon it became clear that the pope was absolutely determined to have the clerical tenth: he told the Milanese ambassador that he was contemplating grave censures against Florence,[116] and his ambassador made a number of thinly disguised threats in person to the Signoria.[117] Now a number of leading Florentines began to admit that more harm than good might result from continued opposition,[118] and although a few prominent citizens held out against the pope,[119] many of the former champions of communal liberty and ecclesiastical independence had to concede that, since they could no longer present a united front, it was useless to continue their resistance.[120] In the end, everyone agreed that the pope should be allowed to collect the tenth, for, as Dietisalvi Neroni put it,

[109] *Ibid.*; CP, 56, fol. 49v, 51v; Pius II, *Commentaries*, 301; Picotti, *Dieta*, 370.
[110] ASF, CP, 56, fol. 49r, 49v, 51v, 55v, 58v.
[111] ASF, RVdO, 1, fol. 55v–57v; Picotti, *Dieta*, 370.
[112] ASF, CP, 56, fol. 44r; RVdO, 1, fol. 44v.
[113] ASF, CP, 56, fol. 47v; Resp. 1, fol. 69v–70r.
[114] ASF, CP, 56, fol. 47v–57v, 76r–77r.  [115] Setton, *Papacy*, ii, 221–2, 245–6.
[116] Picotti, *Dieta*, 371.   [117] ASF, RVdO, 1, fol. 55v–57v.
[118] In the *pratica* of 18 March 1460, Carlo Pandolfini, Giovannozzo Pitti, Martino Scarfa, Bernardo de' Medici, Ugolino Martelli, Dietisalvi Neroni and especially Otto Niccolini were in favour of yielding to the pope (ASF, CP, 56, fol. 59r–62v).
[119] In the *pratica* of 18 March, Matteo Palmieri, Mariotto Benvenuti, Bartolomeo Lenzi and Antonio Ridolfi were against yielding to the pope (*ibid.*, fol. 60r–63r).
[120] *Ibid.*, fol. 63v–64v.

who can deny that the pope is lord of the clergy[121] and that, in Manno Temperani's words, 'que sunt Cesaris Cesari et Domini Domino dentur'.[122] The much-discussed tenth was collected in Florentine territory during 1460[123] and the Florentines consigned the proceeds to papal representatives in the early months of 1461.[124]

This episode marks another turning point in Florentine diplomacy with regard to the crusade: after 1460 Florence was prepared to go beyond lip-service and make actual contributions to the crusade as they had done before 1457; if some Florentines were not burning with crusading ardour, still they were now prepared to play a part in a joint undertaking of Christendom against the Turks. Pius II was prevented from organizing a large-scale crusade such as had been planned at Mantua by his war against Sigismondo Malatesta as well as by papal involvement in the disputed succession to the Neapolitan throne, but in 1463 the crusade once more became his top priority and so again Florence was called upon to declare its contribution.[125] Since the period of the Congress of Mantua, however, the implications of a crusade for Florentine foreign policy had significantly changed; Florence's rival, Venice, had now abandoned its policy of appeasing the Turks in favour of open war,[126] and in any expedition led by the pope Venice would now play the principal role. On the one hand, therefore, Florence was wary of joining an enterprise which would primarily benefit the Venetians; on the other, the Florentines, worn down by Pius II in 1460 over the issue of crusading tenths, no longer had the heart for intransigent opposition to papal plans. Moreover, Florence's ally, the duke of Milan, firmly opposed resistance to Pius II's crusade, arguing that this would deliver the pope into the hands of Venice and so undermine the Florentine and Milanese diplomatic position in Italy; his plan was to cooperate with the pope in such a way as to ensure that the expedition would not be under sole Venetian leadership, making it possible thereby for any conquered territories to be ruled by the church, not Venice.[127] Florence at first was hesitant, expressing a number of reservations about the probable success and expediency of such a crusade,[128] but, even if their overriding concern was to safeguard their own political position rather than to defend the faith,[129] they eventually had to concede the Milanese

---

[121] *Ibid.*, fol. 64r.      [122] *Ibid.*, fol. 160r.
[123] Cf. ASF, CSopp. 8, n. 23, fol. 183r. I am grateful to Dr Brenda Preyer for this reference.
[124] ASF, CP, 56, fol. 100v, 140v–141v, 160r–v.
[125] ASF, Resp. 1, fol. 116v–117r.
[126] Setton, *Papacy*, ii, 240ff.; Lopez, 'Il principio della guerra Veneto-Turca nel 1463', 45–131.
[127] Pastor, *Acta inedita*, 189–91.
[128] ASF, Resp. 1, fol. 117v; LC, 15, fol. 90r–92r; Pastor, *Acta inedita*, 190–2, 195–9; *idem*, *Storia*, ii, 238; Pius II, *Commentaries*, 812ff.
[129] ASF, LC, 15, fol. 91v.

point that it was in their own political interest as rivals of the Venetians to
support the papal crusade and so deny Venice full disposal of the moral
and material resources of the church.[130]

Florence was prepared to back Pius's crusade by the end of September
1463,[131] but a major diplomatic crisis blew up between Florence and
Venice at the beginning of October 1463, once again placing in doubt
Florentine cooperation in the crusade. The issue was the future of Florentine commerce in the eastern Mediterranean and, in particular, the Florentine communal galleys, which had sailed to Constantinople every year
from 1459 to 1462; at a time when Florence was officially committed to
the crusade, this attempt to continue and even expand their Mediterranean
commerce had led to occasional difficulties, for example, from the pope[132]
and the archbishop of Florence,[133] but these were nothing compared to the
row kicked up by Venice during 1463. In view of deteriorating relations
between Venice and the Turks, a Venetian ambassador, Febo Capella, had
been sent to Florence in March 1463, requesting the Florentines to suspend
their annual voyage to Constantinople of three galleys, which otherwise,
Venice believed, might be commandeered by the Turks into action against
the Venetian fleet;[134] however, Capella was told that the galleys had to
proceed in order to collect Florentine citizens and property left in Constantinople and that, as in the past, the safe conduct given to Florentines was
sure to be respected by the Turks.[135] Venice was by no means satisfied with
this reply,[136] and in September 1463, as the usual time of departure for the
Florentine galleys approached, Capella was sent again to Florence, with
instructions to declare that if the Florentine galleys went beyond the
Dardanelles they were certain to be stopped by the Venetian armada;[137]
just before he reached Florence, the Florentine galleys were despatched[138]
and on arrival in early October Capella was given a deliberately ambiguous assurance which he took to mean that the Florentine galleys would not
pass the Dardanelles.[139] With Florence determined to send the galleys as
far as Constantinople[140] and with Venice's admiral under instructions to
stop them if they went beyond the Dardanelles,[141] the deliberately evasive
diplomacy of both sides could hardly prevent the crisis from worsening,
and when the Venetian ambassador in Milan, Frate Simonetto, declared
that the Venetian admiral would treat the Florentine galleys as enemy ships

[130] Lopez, 'Principio', 89.   [131] *Ibid.*
[132] Picotti, *Dieta*, 487–8; ASF, CP, 56, fol. 141v.
[133] ASF, Miss. 43, fol. 124r–v.
[134] ASF, LC, 15, fol. 81v; ASV, Senato Secreti, 21, fol. 43r.
[135] ASF, LC, 15, fol. 81v–82r.   [136] ASV, Senato Secreti, 21, fol. 186v–187v.
[137] *Ibid.*   [138] ASF, Miss. 44, fol. 111v–112r.
[139] Pastor, *Acta inedita*, 216; ASV, Senato Secreti, 21, fol. 193v.
[140] *Ibid.*, fol. 204v.   [141] *Ibid.*, fol. 189v, 193v.

subject to confiscation or attack,[142] it became inevitable that the crisis of the galleys would affect Florence's attitude to the forthcoming crusade; in mid-October the Florentines declared that they would participate in the crusade alongside Venice only if the Venetians guaranteed the security of their galleys.[143] Frantic diplomatic activity took place in Florence, Venice, Milan and Rome for the rest of October and throughout November involving the pope, Cardinal Bessarion (his legate in Venice), the duke of Milan, the Milanese ambassadors in Rome, Cardinal Scarampo-Trevisan and Bernardo Giustiniani (the Venetian ambassador in Rome), as well as Otto Niccolini, Dietisalvi Neroni and Tommaso Soderini (respectively Florentine ambassadors in Rome, Milan and Venice)[144] but as neither Florence nor Venice would give way over the question of the galleys, the Florentine role in Pius II's crusade remained in doubt.[145]

The crisis was finally overcome through the efforts of Florence's ally, the duke of Milan, whose overriding aim throughout the negotiations of 1463 and 1464 was to cooperate with the crusade and so keep the pope from placing himself entirely in the hands of Venice. The Florentines, who had been won over to the Milanese view in late September 1463, were on the point of committing themselves to the crusade when Venice's opposition to further voyages to Constantinople led to consternation in Florence, and now again in early December the duke of Milan persuaded Florence to accede to the pope's wishes although Venice still refused to guarantee the galleys' safe passage.[146] Again the decisive argument was fear 'lest his holiness should become perturbed or take any displeasure and for this reason place himself entirely at the disposal and behest of others; if he had [already] fallen into this error', Florence now hoped to regain his goodwill.[147] Another reason for Florence's change of stance in early December was that by then their galleys had probably arrived in Constantinople unobstructed by the Venetian armada; although Venice had refused to give them a safe-conduct and had actually instructed their admiral to prevent their passage beyond the Dardanelles,[148] it seems that

[142]  Pastor, *Acta inedita*, 213–16.
[143]  Lopez, 'Principio', 127; Pastor, *Acta inedita*, 213–16.
[144]  *Ibid.*, 218–19, 226–36, 240, 255; ASF, LC, 15, fol. 102v–120r; ASV, Senato Secreti, 21, fol. 199r, 204v. Cf. also P. Clarke, 'A Biography of Tommaso Soderini' (Ph.D., London University, 1982), 83–6, 113–16.
[145]  Pastor, *Acta inedita*, 258–9.
[146]  ASF, Miss. 44, fol. 122v–123v; LC, 15, 120v.
[147]  ASF, Miss. 44, fol. 123r: acciochè la Santità sua non si turbasse o pigliasse sdegno alcuno et per questo rispetto non si mettesse in tutto nella voluntà et arbitrio d'altri et se fusse transcorso in questo errore rivocarlo da quello et ridurlo in tutto alla comune nostra benivolentia.
[148]  ASV, Senato Secreti, 21, fol. 193v.

the three Florentine galleys had given the Venetians the slip,[149] and the Florentines may have felt better disposed to cooperate with the crusade now that the most dangerous part of the voyage had been completed by their galleys. Moreover, the Florentines had always been hesitant to join a crusade without wide support throughout Christendom,[150] but after the publication of the crusading bull on 22 October 1463,

seeing the great stir roused among everyone, wrote the Milanese ambassadors in Rome to Francesco Sforza, . . . the Florentine ambassador told us that in his view it was necessary in every way that the Florentines should also contribute and he said it was certain that . . . the Florentines would do their duty; although before the publications [of the bull] there were many who thought this expedition would go up in smoke and would be impossible, nevertheless . . . seeing that the pope together with the cardinals had put themselves and their money on the line, seeing that the Hungarians and Venetians had committed all their might to the undertaking, and seeing that the duke of Burgundy would soon be arriving in person, he thought that the expedition had solid foundations . . . and that, as long as the pope and the duke of Burgundy lived, this expedition ought to succeed to the great honour of Christendom.[151]

It has often been assumed that rivalry with Venice both in Italy and in the East prevented Florence from supporting Pius II's crusade in 1463 and 1464,[152] but in fact it was Florence's anti-Venetian policy which actually tipped the balance in favour of the crusade at a time when Venetian–Florentine relations were rapidly deteriorating. In January 1464 Florence agreed to contribute whatever the pope and the duke of Milan saw fit,[153] and in view of their forthcoming role in the crusade the Florentines decided not to send galleys to the East in 1464.[154] That spring the Florentines asked the pope to send agents to collect the crusading taxes agreed and subsequently they allowed crusading indulgences to be preached in Florentine territory.[155] With the proceeds of the taxes they agreed to equip a contingent half the size of the force to be sent by the duke of Milan, namely, five hundred infantry and one thousand cavalry for six months.[156] Moreover, when a papal legate came to Florence to buy three unfinished galleys then at Porto Pisano, he was presented with them as a gift,[157] and when the legate who was equipping the papal fleet there was short of men, some prisoners were released from the Florentine gaol to man the galleys.[158] Contrary to what has hitherto been believed, Florence's official policy in

[149] *Ibid.*, fol. 226v (1 February 1464): Galeatias Florentinorum profectas esse Constantinopolim preter id quod fieri debere existimabamus.
[150] ASF, LC, 15, fol. 90v, 92r, 120v; Pastor, *Acta inedita*, 195–9.
[151] *Ibid.*, 229.
[152] E.g. Setton, *Papacy*, ii, 246–7, 264.   [153] ASF, Miss. 44, fol. 132v–133r.
[154] Mallett, *Florentine Galleys*, 70.   [155] ASF, Miss. 44, fol. 140v–141r, 144r–v.
[156] Pastor, *Acta inedita*, 278–9, 287; ASF, Miss. 44, fol. 148r–149r.
[157] ASF, Provv. 155, fol. 9r–9v.
[158] *Ibid.*, fol. 42v–43v.

1464 supported Pius II's crusade, and their promises of aid were not made cynically: the three galleys were in fact despatched to join the papal fleet in Ancona,[159] there is proof that they began collecting the crusading taxes,[160] and their closest ally, the duke of Milan, believed that they would contribute throughout the spring of 1464,[161] when even the embittered Pius II himself accepted their good faith.[162] The cornerstone of Florentine policy was to prevent a papal–Venetian rapprochement, and Florentine bad faith in offering a crusading subsidy would, when revealed, have thrown the pope into the arms of the Venetians, which is exactly what Florence wanted to avoid.

In the course of the summer of 1464 Florence's crusading ardour somewhat cooled: although still committed to the crusade, Florentines became half-hearted in preparing their contingent,[163] but this is hardly remarkable given that, after the duke of Burgundy's defection in April 1464,[164] all their old fears about wasted money on futile and undersubscribed crusades must have returned; what is noteworthy is that they went as far as they did while prospects grew ever bleaker for Pius II. The principal witness to Florence's alleged bad faith in August 1464 was the pope himself,[165] who, like many idealists, was deeply embittered because others did not share his dreams, but although his outburst against Florence,[166] four days before his pathetic death in Ancona, is wholly understandable, nevertheless the unavoidable sympathy roused by his noble self-sacrifice must not obscure the fact that, as an extremely subjective observer, he was not in a fit state physically or psychologically to know Florence's true intentions, which now amounted more to a policy of wait and see than outright hypocrisy. Plague hindered the collection of taxes in the summer of 1464,[167] but the principal reason that Florentines failed to send their promised contingent to Ancona in August 1464 was not bad faith but the illness and death on 1 August of Cosimo de' Medici, who, it will be seen,[168] had been the moving force behind Florence's policy of cooperation with Pius II's admit-

---

[159] Cf. Mallett, *Florentine Galleys*, 35, mentioning that one of the galleys was returned in February, 1465.

[160] Cf. ASF, CSopp. 88, n. 23, fol. 203v: [26 May 1464] Pagammo l'anposta et tassa ci posono i commess. di Papa Pio pe' fatti del Turcho . . . in fl. xxx larghi. I am extremely grateful to Dr Brenda Preyer for this reference.

[161] Cf. ASF, Resp.1, fol. 120v–121r; Pastor, *Acta inedita*, 324.

[162] Pius II, *Opera*, 857: Nec Florentini desunt viri prudentia potentes et opibus: quamvis de his aliquando fuerat dubitatum, nunc certum est eos egregie in Turcos de expeditione laturos opem (8 April 1464).

[163] Cf. ASF, Miss. 44, fol. 144r–v, 155v–156r, 160r–v, 161r; Pastor, *Storia*, ii, 265.

[164] Cf. Pastor, *Acta inedita*, 278–80.     [165] Cf. *Commentaries*, 812–17.

[166] Pastor, *Acta inedita*, 324.

[167] This was the excuse offered by the Florentines (ASF, Miss. 44, fol. 160r–161r) and it was confirmed by the Milanese ambassador in Rome (Pastor, *Acta inedita*, 324).

[168] Cf. pp. 279ff., *infra*.

tedly idealistic dreams; with Cosimo gone, there was no one left who
carried sufficient weight to overcome the widespread and deep-seated feelings,[169] which had come to the surface in the *pratica* debates of 1460, that
crusading taxes were sheer robbery.[170]

### (iv) Accolti's history and Florentine crusading diplomacy

By 1464 when Accolti published his apologetic history, Florence had
come out openly in support of Pius II's crusading project; moreover, their
previous hesitancy, their rivalry with Venice under whose banner they
would now be fighting, and their growing commercial success in the East
caused Florentine commitment to the crusade to be questioned in 1464,
and therefore a humanist work in support of the crusade from the Florentine first chancellor served as further proof of their sincerity in the common
Christian cause under the leadership of the pope. Throughout 1464 the
Florentines made great efforts to maintain their reputation as good
Christians and above all to preserve the goodwill of the pope. They had,
for example, been keen to publicize their gift of galleys to the crusade and
instructed their ambassador in Rome to point out to the pope that 'in order
to demonstrate our filial devotion to his holiness and to find every way not
only of preserving his goodwill but of increasing it, we have decided to
donate the galleys to him without payment'.[1] They wrote in the same vein
to the duke of Milan,[2] and they did not hesitate to declare their fundamental sympathy with the aims of the crusade:

Present yourselves to the holy father, they instructed their ambassadors, and say
that, having regard to the welfare and good of the Christian religion and to his
holiness's goodwill towards us, we have decided to cooperate in this expedition
against the infidel, freely, and according to the discretion and wishes of his holiness, as his devoted sons desiring the universal welfare of all Christians.[3]

Benedetto Accolti was the author of these instructions and of many other
similar letters and mandates as chancellor of Florence, and throughout his
term of office he did not refrain from summoning all the powers of
humanist rhetoric when writing on behalf of Florence in support of the

---

[169] This was the view of the Milanese ambassador in Rome (Pastor, *Acta inedita*, 324).
[170] E.g. cf. CP, 56, fol. 100v.
[1] ASF, LC, 15, fol. 121r: noi per gratificare alla sua beatitudine come buoni figluoli di
quella, et per tenere ogni via non solamente conservare la sua benivolenza ma acrescierla,
abbiamo deliberato donarglele [sc. the galleys] liberamente.
[2] ASF, Miss. 44, fol. 123v.
[3] ASF, LC, 15, fol. 120v: Voi vi presenterete alla presentia del sancto padre et direte noi,
avendo rispetto alla salute et bene della christiana religione et alla benivolenza della
santità sua verso di noi, avere deliberato concorrere in questa impresa degl'infedeli,
liberamente, col parere et voluntà della sua beatitudine come optimi suoi figli di sancta
chiesa et desiderosi della salute universale di tutti e christiani.

crusade. Referring to the Hungarian crusader John Hunyadi in 1458, Accolti declared,

What is better known in the Christian world than the many wars that he waged, the numerous enemies of Christ whom he often defeated and put to flight, the many armies that he destroyed? Indeed, human strength would seem scarcely adequate to accomplish such feats. As a result of these deeds, he was considered the defender of Christendom but the great scourge of the infidel. There is little doubt that, if he had not debilitated the Turks and frequently restrained their attacks, Christians would have suffered a miserable fate and great calamities.[4]

Later that year Accolti praised the Acciaiuoli family,

many of whom long ruled extensive possessions in Greece and often fought successfully against the enemies of Christ, protecting Christian cities and lands; devoted to the Roman church, they also frequently undertook in many places faithful and extraordinary work on its behalf.[5]

Writing to the pope in 1459, Accolti declared,

Who ought to be considered more worthy, honourable or glorious than someone who brings honour, safety and glory for Christians but grief and ruin to barbarians?[6]

That year Accolti praised the Florentine Antonio Frescobaldi, who

against barbarian enemies together with others defended the Christian faith, on behalf of which he has often fought hitherto, refusing neither danger nor labour.[7]

Of another Florentine, Bernardo da Castiglionchio, Accolti declared in 1460,

With his ship, fighting either alone or with the rest of the fleet he often accomplished great deeds against the barbarians on behalf of the Roman church, and among others so much did his virtue shine out that many, and especially the papal legate, both by word and in letters which we have seen, have celebrated him with great commendation.[8]

---

[4] ASF, Miss. 42, fol. 12v: Nam quid est christiano in orbe notius quam ipsum tot confecisse bella, tam multos Christi hostes sepe fudisse ac fugasse, tam magnos exercitus ab eodem esse deletos ut vix ea humanis viribus fieri potuisse videantur. Ob que quidem gesta christianorum defensor, infidelium vero ingens terror est habitus. Nec sane ambigi potest quod si non ipse turchorum vires attrivisset ac sepe illorum frenasset impetus, sevum christiani exitium, magnas calamitates incidissent.

[5] *Ibid.*, fol. 47r: quorum plerique in Grecia longe lateque dominantes, sepenumero adversus Christi hostes felicissime pugnaverunt et christianorum urbes ac loca tutati sunt. Nonnulli etiam Romane sedis devotissimi crebro multis in locis pro ea fidelem et egregiam operam navarunt.

[6] *Ibid.*, fol. 103r–v: Cui enim decus, honor, gloria debuntur magis quam ei . . . qui, posthabitis omnibus, sue valitudinis immemor, caritate flagrans, id incepit virtutis quo christianis honor, salus et gloria ingens pareretur, barbaris is vero luctus ac pernities?

[7] *Ibid.*, fol. 130r: una cum aliis christianam fidem adversus barbaros hostes tueretur, pro qua sepenumero decertans nuncusque nullum periculum aut laborem recusavit.

[8] *Ibid.*, 43, fol. 53v: Is enim cum sua triremi pro Romana ecclesia contra barbaros dimicans vel solus vel cum reliqua classe sepenumero preclara facinora editit, tantumque

Writing of a delegation of ambassadors from oriental states early in 1461, Accolti declared,

Nothing could be sweeter to our ears or more pleasant to our eyes and minds than to have recently seen and heard many legates of oriental kings who adore and also acknowledge Christ as the son of God, and who made such a long journey for no other reason than to urge Christian princes not only to protect the Catholic faith but, together with their kings, to enhance it and bring greater salvation to mankind. What indeed could be more useful to the common welfare, what more glorious, what finally more acceptable to God himself than to become Christian soldiers against the enemy, to rouse the rest of the faithful to the same work by exhortation and warning lest they desert Christ's cause, lest they seem ungrateful or forgetful of the blood of the Redeemer, lest they seem to prefer the terrestrial and perishable to the eternal and celestial, lest they appear to make more of their own comforts than of the common welfare of so many mortals, lest they allow the ruin and shame of our time to grow further, namely that the Catholic faith seems almost forsaken? . . . Therefore as worshippers of the true Christ we are delighted beyond measure and vehemently praise so beneficial and pious an undertaking by the kings, and in the common cause of the faith together with other Christian princes we promise to make neither a late nor a small contribution.[9]

Similarly Accolti wrote in 1464, after the defection of the duke of Burgundy,

it has continually been our idea and intention to omit nothing against the barbarian enemies of Christ which concerns the dignity of this city and our obligations, and although often it seemed to us that we were threatened by many inconveniences, not to mention the greatest dangers, nevertheless we always decided that the common religion must be placed before all else. But if our subsidy could be deferred without danger to the common welfare . . . our citizens without doubt will prefer Christ's cause and the Catholic faith to their own danger, in imitation of their ancestors who were inferior to no men in protecting religion on behalf of the Roman church . . . Nor would they desert the struggle for praise, on behalf of which they fight far more ardently than for comfort or riches, in the belief that nothing is

inter alios enituit sua prestans virtus ut eum permulti, presertim legatus pontificis, tam verbo quam literis quas vidimus ipsi magnis laudibus celebrarent.
9   *Ibid.*, fol. 111v: Nil potuit esse nostris auribus dulcius aut oculis mentique suavius quam nuper vidisse atque audivisse legatos plures orientalium regum qui Christum Dei filium adorant simul et confitentur non aliam ob causam tam longum iter emensos quam ut hortentur christianos principes nedum tueri catholicam fidem sed una cum suis regibus ampliorem illam efficere quo major humano generi salus constituatur. Quid enim ad comunem salutem utilius? quid ad illustrem gloriam maius? quid denique deo ipsi acceptius tentari potuit quam Christi militiam adversus hostes assumere, fideles reliquos ad idem opus pellicere, monendo atque hortando ne Christi causam deserant, ne redempti sanguine illius tanti meriti vel inmemores vel ingrati esse velint, ne terrena celestibus, ne caduca perenibus anteponant, ne pluris faciant commoda propria quam tot mortalium communem salutem, ne sinant amplius crescere labem atque ignominiam nostri temporis, quod scilicet catholica fides pene deserta videatur, utque oblatam dei munere facultatem unanimi voto amplectantur. Itaque nos veri Christi cultores ex ea re supramodum letati eiusmodi regum adeo salubre ac pium opus vehementer laudamus, inque comuni fidei causa una cum reliquis christianis principibus nec senem nec exiguam operam pollicemur, nil omissuri cum aliis . . .

worthier of a free man than to act in such a way as to seem to deserve merit on behalf of the common good rather than for his own benefit.[10]

Again at the very time he was publishing his history Accolti wrote,

it is our intention to omit nothing which is demanded by our faith, or by the dignity of our city or the care of our common religion, which we have always judged to be preferred to everything else . . . We shall lend every favour to this effort on behalf of the holy expedition, on behalf of the Catholic faith and in order to suppress the enemies of Christ.[11]

But the *pièce de resistance* among Accolti's crusading apologetics written officially on behalf of Florence as first chancellor was the public mandate which he composed to be read out in open consistory by the Florentine ambassadors at the Congress of Mantua in 1459.

We, the priors of liberty and Gonfalonier of Justice of the Florentine people, following in the footsteps of our ancestors who always and in every way cherished the Catholic faith and the Roman church, rejoice beyond measure and take delight that it has pleased God for the pastor of the Christian world in our time to think night and day of only cherishing and enhancing Christendom and of averting its perils. All look upon him as the parent of the human race, who, regardless of everything, without concern for his own health, burning with affection, has been impelled by God himself, not relying on others but by himself, to undertake the protection of the faith, calling upon Christian princes to take those steps which cannot be neglected without the greatest shame, without the greatest danger and which, when eventually accomplished, will gain for Christians glory and salvation, but for him himself immortality and glory. What indeed at this time is more useful to the common welfare? What more glorious? What finally could be considered more acceptable to God himself than to take from the hands of the infidel the most noble city of Byzantium and to force the barbarian enemies who threaten Christians to retreat and at length to tremble in fear for their own possessions? Their insane fury has gone so far that they have threatened to attack all Christians and subject them to their rule. O! immortal God, can someone be sufficiently praised for undertaking so great, so beneficial an enterprise? Can any man of the

---

[10] *Ibid.*, 44, fol. 140v: Ea fuit continuo nostra mens et intentio nil unquam prorsus omittere contra barbaros Christi hostes quod ad dignitatem huius urbis et debitum nostrum pertineret. Cumque plerumque animis nostris salus religionis et incommoda multa obversarentur necnon pericula maxima que iam impendere videbantur, semper tamen decrevimus communem religionem cunctis rebus esse anteponendam. Quod si nobis constitisset non posse differri nostrum presidium absque periculo communis salutis atque incommodo sanctitatis vestre, haud dubie cives nostri Christi causam et catholicam fidem suis periculis pretulissent, imitati suos maiores qui nulli hominum generi pro tuenda religione pro Romana ecclesia officio, caritate inferiores fuerunt. Nec profecto laudis certamen deservissent pro qua longe ardentius quam pro commodis aut opibus dimicarunt, rati nihil libero esse dignius quam ita se gerere ut magis de re publica bene mereri quam de se ipsis viderentur.

[11] *Ibid.*, 44, fol. 114r–v: Nos autem respondemus idem esse nostrum propositum, nil scilicet pretermittere quod vel flagitet fides nostra vel dignitas civitatis aut cura communis religionis quam semper omnibus rebus preferendam censuimus . . . Omnem favorem huic rei concedemus, pro sacra expeditione, pro fide catholica, pro reprimendis Christi hostibus.

Christian race do or attempt anything which would seem more fitting, more worthy of his name, more beneficial to God and to all men, more illustrious in fame and reputation? Is there anything which could be more welcome to the faithful of Christ than to see the pope, girded with Christian sgrength, prepare for war in defence of the faith against the enemies of Christ, whom they continually denounce with blasphemies, whose worshippers they persecute with inhuman cruelty, whose sacred churches and shrines they plunder, where, what is worse, in place of God they worship abominable and accursed demons – they who like sheep lead lives without struggling virtuously to overcome vice. Therefore on behalf of so excellent and worthy an enterprise let us not only rejoice but thank God for providing such a pope in the first place and for inspiring the rest with such mind and spirit as to undertake and complete this glorious work.[12]

Benedetto Accolti's *De bello* has many passages of crusading rhetoric similar to those which he composed on behalf of the Florentine Signoria. In his speech at the end of the first book, Bohemond declares to his followers,

Many mortals from everywhere have gathered together in order to take by arms Christ's sepulchre, which the barbarian enemies hold to the shame of the Christian name . . . Nor do the great danger, the long journey, the forthcoming struggle, the attraction of their native land and their children detract from their intention, but, as befits the bravest men, they think that Christian salvation is preferable to all

---

[12] ASF, LC, 15, fol. 29v–30v: Nos priores liberatatis et vexillifer iustitie populi florentini, inherentes maiorum vestigiis qui catholicam fidem et Romanam ecclesiam ita semper omni ex parte coluerunt ut nemo alius magis religiose, magis pie, maiore animi cura, propensiore affectu quam ipsi eas observarit, dilexerit, suppliciterque sit veneratus et ampliores quantum valebant conatus reddere, supramodum letamur gaudemusque divino numini placuisse eum esse Christiani orbis pastorem qui etate nostra solum de illis colendis augendis et christianis propulsandis periculis dies noctesque cogitaret, quem cernent omnes velut parentem humani generis posthabitis omnibus, sue valitudinis immemorem, caritate flagrantem, a deo ipso impulsum non per alios sed per se ipsum fidei tutelam adsumpsisse ad ea provocantem christianos principes que sine maxima ignominia, sine gravi periculo negligi non potuissent et que tandem perfecta christianis gloriam et salutem sint paritura, sibi vero cum gloria ipsa immortalitatem. Quid enim hoc tempore ad comunem salutem utilius? quid ad illustrem gloriam maius? quid denique deo ipsi acceptius tentari potuit quam ut Bizantium nobilissima civitas ex infidelium manibus eriperetur, utque barbari hostes qui christianis cervicibus imminent retro tandem cedere et de suis rebus timere compellantur, quorum vesanus furor eo processerat ut se christianos omnes invasuros et ditionis sue facturos minarentur. Proh deus immortalis! Potestne satis digne laudari qui talem rem adeo magnam, usque adeo salubrem facere adoriatur? Potestne christiani vir generis aliud quicquam aut agere aut moliri quod sibi magis debitum suo nomini magis conveniens ei et hominibus cunctis salubrius fama et opinione illustrius esse videatur? Estne res aliqua que nobis Christi fidelibus iocundior esse possit quam cernere pontificem summum, christianis accinctum viribus pro tutela fidei parere adversus illos bellum qui Christi hostes continuo in illum blasfemias evocarunt, eiusdem cultores immani sevitia persecuntur, sacras suas hedes et sacrorum omnium evertunt, vel, quod deterius est, pro deo in illis nefandos ac scelestos demones venerantur qui, pecudum more ducentes vitam, nullum unquam virtutem inter vitia discrimen habuerint. Itaque pro tam excellenti virtutis opere non solum letamur sed deo agimus gratias qui pontifici primum deinde reliquis eam mentem animumque concesserit ut eiusmodo clarissimam rem perficere adorientur.

things and that it is better to seek death with great glory than to remain alive in shame and ignominy . . . If you refuse to fight, according to what law will you defend your cause? Divine? But the holy scriptures especially command that we place nothing at all before the love of God, and therefore the defence of religion and of the faithful whom the Barbarians oppress cannot be neglected without sin. Or human law? But nothing is thought more worthy of a free man than to strive for virtue and praise, and nothing can be more honest or just than what is proposed, but nothing is more base than for an excellent man to be outdone by his inferiors especially in religion, duty or courage and to prefer base leisure to honest work.[13]

Godfrey of Bouillon, addressing his army before battle in the third book, says,

God will hardly allow those to be conquered whom he has led this far as victors, fighting on behalf of the divine name and for virtue; but if He should decide otherwise and we are frustrated in our near certain hope, you will gain a great reward: indeed, dying for His glory, on behalf of the world's salvation, with our sins expiated, we shall gain celestial glory, which was the cause for the sake of which you preferred the greatest labours, the greatest dangers to peace and leisure; also future generations will gratefully celebrate your name with the highest praises.[14]

But the first book of *De bello* is the richest source of Accolti's crusading apologetics. One notable passage is the very opening of the work, where he wrote,

When under Heraclius Caesar the Roman Empire had for the most part collapsed, there arose a new religion, the ruin and plague of mankind, which almost overturned the empire in the East. This originated from a certain Arab, called Mohammed, who, born in a humble and sordid place, . . . dared to say that he was a prophet sent by God to reveal perennial laws and new rites to mortals, nor did he lack a sharp wit or knowledge of sacred matters which he took from Jews and Christians. And although his morals were depraved, nevertheless he hid his sins artfully . . . adding also feigned prodigies, derisory to behold and to hear, in order

---

[13] History, fol. 25r–26v (*Recueil*, 549–50): Convenere undique multi mortales quo armis redimant Christi sepulchrum, quod cum dedecore christiani nominis barbari hostes occuparunt . . . Nec eos magnitudo periculi, vie longinquitas, propositus labor, patrie caritas, liberique ab instituto revocarunt sed, ut fortissimos decet viros, putant hiis omnibus christianam salutem esse preferendam ac satius fore cum magna gloria mortem oppetere, quam in hac luce cum ignominia dedecoreque versari . . . Vos quoque, si hanc recusetis militiam, quo iure causam vestram tuebimini? Divinone? At littere sacre inprimis iubent ne in deum amori proximumque quicquam omnino preferamus, ideoque religionis defensio et eorum fidelium quos barbari opprimunt non absque scelere negligi potest. An humano? At nil putatur libero dignius quam virtutis certamen ac laudis, quo nullum honestius aut maius quam quod proponitur esse potest. Nil vero est turpius prestanti homini quam committere ut ab alio quolibet inferiore, presertim religione, offitio, magnitudine animi, victus videatur et honesto labori turpe otium anteferre.

[14] History, fol. 58v (*Recueil*, 577): Deus enim quos hucusuque duxit victores pro suo numine, pro virtute pugnantes, minime vinci patietur; quod si aliter statuisset, et spe iam certa frustraremur, ingens accedet vobis premium. Nam pro illius laude, pro mundi salute morientes, expiatis delictis, celestem gloriam consequemur, que causa fuit ut summos labores, pericula maxima paci et otio preferretis; posteri quoque nomen vestrum summis laudibus grata memoria prosequentur.

to increase his credibility among men and enhance the authority of his deeds and laws. Not unaware that the people are more prone to vice than to virtue ... he instituted laws which scarcely seemed strict nor did he order anything which might prevent the gratification of lust, for he believed that many, weary of Christian severity, would forsake their faith and follow his sect ... Nor did the result disappoint those unworthy hopes, for Mohammed, having secured a kingdom by these arts, and energetically using the gifts of fortune, spread this nefarious heresy far and wide.[15]

Accolti goes on to give a lurid description of the moral depravity encouraged by Islam:

In this new way of life, virtue and learning were neither honoured nor at all rewarded, since nothing could be more inimical to a sham religion than virtue and knowledge of the arts and sciences, and so men turned to debauchery and idleness, abandoning the pursuits worthy of a free man; they embraced all the more avidly the pleasures which Christian severity had denied them, and, as if they had tasted the banquet of Circe, with their minds captured and their spirits enervated, they changed their way of life and morals, and, as though long buried in the most profound darkness, they were able neither to lift themselves up nor to behold the light.[16]

Accolti then paints a pathetic picture of the sacrileges done to the holy places and the hardships endured by Christians under Muslim rule:

Nothing was more bitter to good men than [to behold] the capture of the province of Judaea, the profanation of temples and all the places through which Christ had passed, where He had performed His greatest miracles, taught the truth with His words and had suffered so many unspeakable things for the sake of human salvation, and the heinous pollution of the sepulchre which covered his interred body, than which no place in the world is more venerable, no shrine more holy. The disgrace of the thing was increased by the cruelty of the barbarians, who almost

---

[15] History, fol. 3r–v (*Recueil*, 532): Cum sub Heraclio Cesare Romanum imperium magna ex parte concidisset, exorta insuper nova religio clades ac lues humani generis, ipsum pene in oriente subvertit. Ea vero sumpsit exordium ab arabe quodam, Maumetto nomine, qui, humili et sordido loco natus, ... ausus est prophetam se dicere a deo missum qui leges peremnes, novissima sacra mortalibus traderet. Nec acre ingenium illi defuit nec peritia sacrarum rerum quam ex iudeis christianisque hauserat. Et quamvis esset perditis moribus, tamen flagitia quadam arte occultabat . . . addens quoque prodigiorum comenta, ludibrium oculis atque auribus, quo magis cresceret hominum fides et suis gestis legibusque maior inesset auctoritas. Neque ignarus populos magis ad vitia quam ad virtutem pronos esse, . . . eas instituit leges que parum graves videri possent nec fere iuberent quicquam quod explende libidini adversum esset. Sic enim credidit fore ut multi, christiane severitatis pertesi, posthabita illa, suam sectam sequerentur ... Nec improbe spei eventus defuit, nam Maumettus, hisce artibus regnum adeptus, impigre utens fortune munere, nefariam heresim longe lateque diffudit.

[16] History, fol. 3v–4r (*Recueil*, 533): Inque hac nova vivendi norma, cum virtuti aut doctrine nullus honos, nullum penitus premium esset, nam vanitati religionis nil erat infestius quam virtus cognitioque bonarum artium, ad luxum homines desidiamque conversi, studium quodque libero dignum abiecerunt, tanto avidius voluptates amplexi quanto impensius christiana severitas eos compresserat, ac, velut si circeas gustassent dapes, mente capti enervatique animis, vitam ac mores mutarunt suos et, quasi mersi profundis in tenebris, post longa tempora, nec se attollere nec lucem aspicere potuerunt.

exterminated the Christian population in that province; indeed, an example of every kind of cruelty, lust and inhuman arrogance was performed by such men as these. And whatever men survived the slaughter either went as refugees to other lands or, remaining in the same places, were regarded almost as slaves, bearing all kinds of insults and ill-treatment; no one thought it worth speaking to them, no one would walk up to them, no one would give them hospitality, nor would any of them dare to complain of injury, speak freely or even open his mouth; indigent, afflicted and smothered by squalor and filth, they led a life destined to hardship alone. The same was true of those who, stirred by the love of God, migrated to live in those places. Nevertheless, nothing was more embittering to all than to see impure men openly mock Christian rites, contemptuously interfere with solemn ceremonies which they disturbed with savage ferocity, afflict priests with injuries and insults, pollute or destroy shrines and sanctuaries, leaving them with nothing sacred, nothing unprofaned, nor, finally, allowing the rites to be celebrated according to Christian custom. But whoever gathered from everywhere in order to visit the temples and worship the divinity, after which they would return home – these [pilgrims], although they placated the barbarians with money in order to have a safe journey and gain access to the sacred temples, nevertheless suffered numerous injuries.[17]

As far as Accolti's readership was concerned all this was just as applicable to conditions in the Orient during the fifteenth century as it had been to the circumstances which had led to the first crusade, and similarly the great papal oration at Clermont, as reported by Accolti, was intended to rouse the emotions of his contemporaries and lead to a renaissance of that early crusading ardour to which Urban II had given birth in 1095:

Of all the evils which the Christian religion has endured, declared Accolti's Urban II, the greatest, I believe, have been the deadly rites of Mohammed which have crept into the world. Although Christians from the very beginning have suffered grave calamities, oppressed by the wrath of emperors who cherished gods

---

[17]  History, fol. 4v–5r (*Recueil*, 533–4): Nil acerbius fuit bonis omnibus quam capi ab his Iudeam provinciam, templa locaque omnia profanari per que versatus Christus fuerat, in quibus fecit prodigia maxima, verbis edocuit veritatem, totque infanda pro humana salute fuit passus, sepulchrum id nefarie pollui, quod eius corpus humatum texit, quo nullus est augustior locus, nullum in orbe fanum sanctius. Auxit quoque indignitatem rei barbarorum sevitia, per quos in ea provincia christianum genus pene ad internitonem est redactum, ita omnis crudelitatis, libidinis et inhumane superbie in eiusmodi homines editum est exemplum. Et qui superarunt ex cede homines, vel commigrarunt in alias terras vel qui remansere in iisdem locis pene ut servi habebantur, omnes verborum rerumque contumelias ferentes, nemo eos colloquio, nemo aditu, nullus hospitio dignos putabat, nec aliquis de iniuria conqueri, libere loqui aut hiscere audebat, omnes egeni, afflicti, obsiti squalore ac sordibus, vitam ducebant ad solas erumnas reservatam. Par erat prorsus eorum conditio qui, amore in deum commoti, ad habitandum in hec loca migrabant. Nil tamen cunctis erat acerbius quam cernere impuros homines christianos ritus palam eludere, solemnibus sacris contemptim se immiscere, immani ferocia illa turbare, sacerdotes iniuria contumeliisque afficere, fana delubraque polluere aut evertere, nil sanctum illis, nil improfanum relinquere, non denique pati ut more christiano sacre celebrarentur. Qui vero undique confluebant ut, visitatis templis adoratoque numine, domos repeterent licet placarent pecunia barbaros qui tutum illis facerent iter darentque aditum ad sacras edes, tamen crebras iniurias tolerabant.

nd were inimical to change; although many heresies have arisen again and again o rend the church asunder; nevertheless, nowhere did such plagues extinguish the hurch. Nay, after bondage and imprisonment, after savage torture, in the midst of anger, this religion has finally prevailed to go forth ever greater and more illustri-us ... [But] once the world had again been illuminated by the true light which it eemed impossible to extinguish or dim, an old woman's superstition has nearly educed it to oblivion in Asia and Africa. What has ever been harsher than this ane? What more mournful to all good men? What more adverse to human sal-ation? What more loathsome to the Christian name? In the face of such evils, what amentation can be thought adequate? So many peoples who, redeemed by Christ's eath, had recognized the truth, have now denied his power. Overcome by dark-ess, dulled in mind, they resist their own salvation, and thus the greater part of umanity has been damned. O useless labours of ancestors on their behalf! O lood of martyrs shed in vain! O miserable plight of mankind! O intolerable abuse! Alas, all powerful God! Are our transgressions so manifest that you permit for so ong the overturn of countless nations, that you bear the contempt and ridicule of our authority and allow sacrilege to be committed in places where the ancients ffered rightful sacrifice? Pondering this shame, I feel my soul in torment, I am con-umed with grief, I feel pity and shed tears ... I do not speak of the countless laughter inflicted on our people [in Judaea], of the rape of women, of the carnage f good men. I do not recount the enslavement of the population, however much ll this should be lamented, however unworthy and shameful it is. It should rouse very good man to seek vengeance against those who have committed these out-ages. But this especially I bewail, something which above all I believe is deserving f grief, and which in no way should you tolerate: namely, that the barbarians hold he land which Christ consecrated by his presence, birth, teaching and martyrdom, he land in which his religion had its origin; that they have either destroyed the emples dedicated to his name or profaned those that have survived; that the holy epulchre of Christ has been seized and by those very enemies is held, infested and olluted; that the sacred rights have become a mockery; that Christian priests or ny other survivors endure every abuse, every injury; that their children, after aptism, are violently circumcised in the Jewish manner. And a greater injury efalls that child, whose blood, gushing out through their crime, is mixed with ursed water, nor is there any escape for our people who from everywhere gather t the sepulchre itself, unless they bribe the barbarians with money. Surely day would forsake me should I continue to describe what infamies towards God and nan these vile brigands have committed, how proudly, how cruelly they rule our eople, how insolently they consume your patience and their own strength, to what a piteous state they have reduced that province. Let it suffice to have mentioned these few things so that, Christian men, I might stir you from your sleep and reveal the dishonour which is your burden.[18]

18  History, fol. 7v–9r (*Recueil*, 536–7): Ex omnibus malis que Christi religio est perpessa, maximum id fuisse censeo cum Maumetti execrabiles ritus orbi terrarum irrepserunt. Nam, licet ab ipso initio graves christiani tulerint clades, premente illos cesarum ira qui deos colentes nove tum rei adversabantur, quamvis exorte a multis hereses crebro ecclesiam lacerarint nec ubi tamen eiusmodi pestes eam extinsere, quinimmo post vincla et carceres, post cruciatus immanes, inter ipsa pericula, prevalens tandem hec religio maior evasit atque illustrior ... Quibus reiectis, cum lux vera toto in orbe refulsisset nec ea extingui vel minui posse vederetur, anilis pene superstitio eam in Africa atque in Asia delevit. Hac vero pernicie quid unquam fuit acerbius? Quid luctuosius bonis omnibus? Quid humane saluti adversius? Quid christiano nomini fedius? Quis dignus meror pro

Such themes as the cruelty of the infidel and their vices, blasphemies abuse of holy places and maltreatment of Christians have an important place, therefore, in Accolti's history as well as in his official crusading rhetoric on behalf of the Florentine government,[19] and in fact the wording of some of his public writings on the crusade actually resembles passages of his history. For example, in the preface to *De bello* Accolti speaks of the 'communem labem, nostra etate maxime auctam, quod scilicet hostes christi religionis non modo sepulchrum eius tenent, sed longe ac late suum imperium extenderunt';[20] in a letter of the Signoria written on 3 February 1461 Accolti writes of 'labem atque ignominiam nostri temporis, quod scilicet catholica fides pene deserta videatur'.[21] In the same letter Accolti writes, 'quid . . . deo . . . acceptius quam . . . fideles reliquos ad idem opus pellicere, monendo atque hortando ne christi causam deserant . . . ',[22] while in his history he states, 'num exhortando monendoque pellicere posset Christianos principes, ut opus tam salubre aggrederentur'.[23] Two further examples of similar wording are 'nullum periculum aut laborem recusavit' (*missive*)[24] and 'quos nullum laborem aut periculum recusare' (history),[25] and 'quid enim ad comunem salutem utilius, quid ad illustrem gloriam

tantis malis haberi potest? Tot nationes Christi morte redempte post agnitam veritatem illius numen abnegarunt, et tenebris obrute mente obtusa sue saluti adversantur atque hoc modo maxima pars humani generis perdita est. O vanos pro his maiorum labores! O frustra effusum martirum sanguinem! O miserrimam hominum cladem! O contumeliam non ferendam! Proh Deus omnipotens! Itane prestant flagitia hominum, et gentes innumeras tam longo tempore perire sinas ut tuum numen contemni, haberi ludibrio patiaris atque ubi litabant veteres, sacrilegia perpetrentur? Excrucior animo, conficior pre dolore, lacrimas miserans fundo . . . Taceo nunc innumeras cedes nostrorum factas, stupra in feminas, bonorum rapinam, servitutem multorum non recenseo quamvis hec omnia deflenda, indigna, plena dedecoris fuerint, que optimum quemque movere debent ab his penam repetere qui hec flagitia perpetrarunt. Illud vero precipue queror, id in primis dolendum existimo nec ullo pacto a vobis ferendum, quod scilicet barbari terram occupent Christi hospitio, nativitate, doctrina, et sanguine consecratam, in qua eius religio exordium sumpsit, et templa dicata illius nomini vel sunt eversa vel que supersunt prophanantur, quod sacrum Christi sepulchrum iidem hostes occupatum tenent, infestant, polluunt, sacra dum fiunt eludentes, quod sacerdotes christiani aliive, quicunque supersunt, omnia proba, omnes iniurias patiuntur, eorumque liberi, post baptisma receptum violenter iudaico more circumciduntur, quove maior accedat iniuria, manans ab his eo scelere cruor sacrate aque admiscetur, neque aditus patet nostris hominibus, qui undique ad ipsum sepulchrum confluunt, nisi pecunia illum redimant. Dies certe me deficeret si pergam exprimere que impuri latrones nefanda in deum atque homines commisere, quam superbe, quam crudeliter nostris imperitent, quam insolenter patientia vestra et viribus suis abutantur, quo in statu miserrimo provincia illa sit constituta. Satis nunc sit pauca hec retulisse quo vos, viri christiani, velut a somno excitarem doceremque qua ignominia oneremini.

[19] For more examples of similarity of subject matter, cf. pp. 259–63, *supra* and History, fol. 18r–v, 19v, 26r, 43r, 45v, 50r, 75v, 79v, 87v, 88r (*Recueil*, 544, 545, 550, 564, 566, 570, 590, 594, 600, 601).

[20] History, fol. 2r (*Recueil*, 530).      [21] ASF, Miss. 43, fol. 111v.      [22] *Ibid.*

[23] History, fol. 5v (*Recueil*, 534).

[24] ASF, Miss. 42, fol. 130r.      [25] History, fol. 95r (*Recueil*, 607).

naius, quid denique deo ipsi acceptius tentari potuit, quam Christi
militiam adversus hostes assumere' (*missive*)²⁶ and 'quid enim est
gloriosius, quid maiore dignum laude quam pro religione tuenda, pro
salute humani generis bellum suscipere' (history).²⁷ Such resemblances
lend weight to the argument that *De bello* had a place in Florentine diplomacy similar to Accolti's official writings as chancellor. A semi-official history written with the aim of exhorting Christians to fight the Turks would
have enhanced the Florentines' reputation as faithful Christians in the
same way as their gift of galleys to the crusade; moreover, the summer of
1464, a time when they were being cautious in raising their subsidy for
Pius II's crusade, was a particularly propitious moment to publish *De
bello*. Indeed, the Florentines certainly would have welcomed confir-
mation of their sympathy with the papal crusade such as Accolti's history
would have provided.

   Florentine chancellors had often written as private citizens in support of
official policy. Coluccio Salutati wrote many private letters to back up
Florence's diplomatic position;²⁸ his long *Invective in Antonium
Luschum*, moreover, was intended to justify Florentine conduct during
their wars with Giangaleazzo Visconti.²⁹ In answer to charges made
against Florence by the Lucchese chancellor, Leonardo Bruni too wrote a
defence of Florentine conduct during the Lucchese war.³⁰ Nor was Accolti
the first Florentine chancellor to write in support of the crusade. Early in
1455 Poggio wrote to Alfonso of Aragon urging him to lead a naval
expedition against the Turks. Alfonso had agreed to accede to the Peace of
Lodi of 1454, and Poggio congratulated him for securing peace in Italy, so
that finally the Turkish threat could be met and the Sultan could be driven
from Europe with Alfonso at the head of the fleet. He reminded the king
that glory won in a crusade was greater than any gained in another war;
waging a holy war was the surest path to immortality.³¹ Poggio was
writing in the wake of enthusiasm for a crusade inspired by the Peace of
Lodi and by the promising negotiations between Alfonso and the pope at
that time.³² About the same time, Poggio wrote to Emperor Frederick III
urging him to lead a crusade. Under no illusions about his crusading
fervour, he upbraided Frederick for deferring his support and warned of

²⁶ ASF, Miss. 43, fol. 111v.   ²⁷ History, fol. 9v (*Recueil*, 537).
²⁸ *Epistolario*, ii, 11–46, 146ff., 252–64, 375ff., 400ff.
²⁹ Ed. D. Moreni (Florence, 1826); cf. Baron, *Crisis*², 76, 96ff.
³⁰ *Difesa di Leonardo Bruni Aretino contro i riprensori del popolo di Firenze nella impresa
   di Lucca*, ed. P. Guerra, nozze Guerra-Mariani (Lucca, 1864); cf. also Bruni, *Epistolae*,
   ed. Mehus, ii, 43–5.
³¹ *Epistolae*, iii, 158–65. For the date, cf. *ibid.*, 170–1, 173–4; G. Shepherd and T. Tonelli,
   *Vita di Poggio* (Florence, 1825), ii, appendix xxiv, pp. lxix–lxxi; Poggio, *Opera omnia*,
   ed. Fubini, iv, 696.
³² Cf. Pastor, *Storia*, i, 682ff.

the dangers imminent if he delayed any longer. His reputation, though tarnished, might still be vindicated if only he would now lead the expedition against the Turks.[33] It has been seen that in 1454 and 1455 the Florentine government was sympathetic to the crusade,[34] and so Poggio' letters resemble Accolti's history in their support for official Florentin policy.

### (v) Accolti and crusading traditions in Florence and Tuscany

Accolti's history not only served the interests of the Florentine governmen but also reflected crusading traditions going back to the twelfth century in Florence and the rest of Tuscany;[1] although the struggle against Islam could never have been an issue of the same monumental importance in Florence as in Pisa, Genoa or Venice, nevertheless in the thirteenth and fourteenth centuries many Florentines were deeply involved in the East and they were frequently active as crusaders, missionaries and pilgrims o at least sympathetic to the crusading movement in general. The earlies positive evidence of Florentines participating in a crusade comes from a late twelfth-century charter, according to which a number of men took th cross at the Florentine church of San Donato a Torri in 1188 'for the liber ation of Jerusalem';[2] at the beginning of the thirteenth century 'multitudes of Florentines, according to Giovanni Villani, responded to papal calls fo

---

[33]  *Epistolae*, iii, 203–11; for the date, cf. Poggio, *Opera omnia*, ed. Fubini, iv, 716; for the judgement of Poggio on Frederick III, cf. *ibid.*, 249ff.
[34]  Cf. *supra*, pp. 243–5.
[1]  On the crusades, the Near East and Tuscany, cf. F. Cardini, 'L'inizio del movimento crociato in Toscana', in *Studi di storia medievale e moderna per Ernesto Sestan* (Florence 1980), i, 135–57; *idem*, 'Per una edizione critica del Liber secretorum fidelium crucis di Marin Sanudo il Vecchio', *Ricerche storiche*, n.s. i (1976), 191–250, and esp. 216–17, 233; *idem*, ed., *Toscana e terrasanta nel medioevo* (Florence, 1982); R. Manselli, 'Gli italiani alla prima crociata', *Humanitas*, iv (1949), 714–22; N. Rauty, 'Il testamento di un crociato pistoiese (1219–1220)', *Bullettino storico pistoiese*, lxxxii (1980), 15–51; A. Chiapelli, 'Contributo di Pistoia ad una crociata contro i Turchi (1345)', *ibid.*, i (1890), 113–15; A. Castellini, 'I due grandi animatori della crociata: Santa Caterina da Siena e Pio II', BSenSP, n.s. ix (1938), 323–72; F. Donati, 'S. Bernardino predicatore delle indulgenze per la crociata', BSenSP, ii (1895), 130–6; Müller, *Documenti*; S. Calzolari M. Donati, A. Gengaroli, D. Naldi, L. Parigi and D. Sottili, *Viaggiatori e pellegrini italiani in terrasanta fra Trecento e Quattrocento*, 2 vols. (published by the Università degli studi di Firenze, Facoltà di Magistero, Istituto di Storia, 1974–5). For further bibliography on Pisa and the crusades, cf. the article by M. Tangheroni, in *Toscana e terrasanta*, ed. Cardini, 31–55; further bibliography on Italy, the crusades and the holy lands is cited in the review articles by F. Cardini, in RSI, lxxx (1969), 88 and 332–9 and in his 'La crociata nel Dugento', ASI, cxxxv (1977), 101–39. There is also considerable incidental material on Tuscany and the Eastern crusades in a recent work on papal crusades against Christian lay powers, N. Housley's *The Italian Crusades* (Oxford 1982). I have been unable to find a copy of R. Cessi, *L'Italia et le crociate in Terrasanta* (Naples, 1941).
[2]  Müller, *Documenti*, 32.

a crusade,[3] and a 5% tax on ecclesiastical revenues was paid by the Florentine clergy on behalf of the crusade against Egypt of 1217–21, an expedition which many Tuscans seem to have joined.[4] During the thirteenth century it was a frequent custom for Florentines to leave a legacy, sometimes a large sum, for the crusade;[5] the earliest known example of this practice dates from 1220,[6] and between 1275 and 1300 no fewer than fifty such legacies have been found among Florentine testaments.[7] The crusade at this time found widespread support among the Florentine patriciate, as shown again by these crusading legacies, more than half of which were made by members of notable families such as the Buondelmonti, Alamanni, Bardi, Beccanugi and Magalotti.[8] Literary sources reflecting the attitudes of the Florentine elite in this period also demonstrate sympathy with the crusade: Dante condemned Pope Boniface VIII for declaring a crusade against his Roman enemies, the Colonna family, instead of the Saracens or Jews,[9] whereas he celebrated the deeds and glorious death of his ancestor Cacciaguida, who, he says, gave his life in the holy land during the second crusade,[10] and the chronicle by the pseudo-Brunetto Latini devotes considerable space to celebrating the preaching of Urban II and the expedition of Godfrey of Bouillon,[11] as does Malispini, who adds that many cavalry and infantry from Tuscany and Florence joined the first crusade.[12] Florentine crusading spirit was nourished by the profits made by Florentine banks which as early as the turn of the fourteenth century were acting as depositories for crusading funds,[13] but the role of the mendicant orders, established in the great convents of Santa Maria Novella and Santa Croce, was fundamental in winning sympathy for the crusade in Florence. The success of Franciscan preaching is clear from the large number of legacies made in favour of the crusade in the late thirteenth century by Florentines with close connections to Santa Croce,[14]

---

[3] *Cronica*, V, xiii.

[4] Davidsohn, *Storia di Firenze*, ii (Florence, 1956), 85–7.

[5] Cf. P. Pirillo, 'La terrasanta nei testamenti fiorentini del Dugento', in Cardini, ed., *Toscana e terrasanta*, 57–73.

[6] Davidsohn, *Storia*, ii, 86–7; cf. Pirillo, 'La terrasanta', 57–8, n. 5.

[7] *Ibid.*, 59.      [8] *Ibid.*, 60.

[9] *Inferno*, xxvii, 85–90; cf. E. Rotelli, 'La politica crociata dei papi del primo Trecento e il disimpegno delle città toscane visti attraverso i registri pontifici', in Cardini, ed., *Toscana e terrasanta*, 75.

[10] *Paradiso*, xv, 139–48.

[11] Ed. P. Villari, in *I primi due secoli della storia di Firenze*[3] (Florence, 1945), 519–21.

[12] R. Malispini, *Storia fiorentina* (Livorno, 1830), ch. lxiv, pp. 173–5.

[13] Rotelli, 'La politica crociata', 83.

[14] Pirillo, 'La terrasanta', 60–1. On Franciscans as advocates of the crusade in Tuscany, cf. F. Cardini, ' "Nella presenza del Soldan superba". Bernardo, Francesco, Bonaventura e il superamento spirituale dell'idea di crociata', *Studi francescani*, lxxi (1974), 199–250; Donati, 'S. Bernardino', 130–6; A. Benvenuti Papi, ' "Margarita filia Jerusalem". Santa Margherita da Cortona e il superamento mistico della crociata', in Cardini, ed., *Toscana*

whereas Santa Maria Novella is notable for its succession of Dominican missionaries to the East and the holy lands in the thirteenth century.[15] Ricoldo da Montecroce, an important Dominican missionary at the turn of the fourteenth century and author of one of the earliest surviving Italian pilgrims' books,[16] spent the last years of his life at Santa Maria Novella,[17] whence also were despatched to the East a considerable series of friars with affiliations to the Societas Fratrum Peregrinatum, a missionary society formed within the Dominican order at the end of the thirteenth century.[18] Several friars from Santa Maria Novella had been killed by the Muslims at the capture of Antioch in 1268 and of Acre in 1297,[19] and no fewer than seven Florentine Dominicans, no longer content only to preach the crusade, were inspired by the preaching of their fellow Dominican Ubertino de' Filippi da Vacchereccia, to join the crusade against Syria in 1345.[20] The Smyrniote crusade was the climax of active participation in the holy war by Florentines, four hundred of whom, according to Giovanni Villani, went to the East in aid of their fellow Christians;[21] such figures, although large enough to rouse suspicion,[22] are confirmed by the large number of Dominican crusader-preachers who are known to have gone from Florence to the East between 1343 and 1345,[23] as well as by documentary evidence of a large Pistoiese crusading contingent in 1345;[24] moreover, eschatological emotions, such as were nourished by the atmosphere of political, social and economic crisis in Florence during the 1340s,[25] were not infrequently associated with growing crusading ardour as well as with other manifestations of heightened religious fervour.[26]

There were no further incidents of spontaneous mass crusading activity in Florence in the years after 1345, but there remained deeply felt concern

*e terrasanta*, 130–7; K. Hefele, *Der hl. Bernardin von Siena und die franziskanische Wanderpredigt in Italien während des xv Jahrhunderts* (Freiburg im Breisgau, 1912), 60–9.

[15] Cf. M. D. Papi, 'Santa Maria Novella di Firenze e l'*Outremer* domenicano', in Cardini, ed., *Toscana e terrasanta*, 87–101.

[16] Cf. U. Monneret de Villard, *Libro della peregrinazione nelle parti d'Oriente di Frate Ricoldo da Montecroce* (Rome, 1948); A. Dondaine, 'Ricoldiana, Notes sur les oeuvres de Ricoldo da Montecroce', *Archivum fratrum praedicatorum*, xxxvii (1967), 119–79; Papi, 'S. M. Novella', 98.

[17] *Ibid.*  [18] *Ibid.*, 87–92.  [19] *Ibid.*, 97.  [20] *Ibid.*, 99.

[21] *Cronica*, XII, xxxix.  [22] Cf. Setton, *Papacy*, i, 193, n. 158.

[23] Cf. Papi, 'S. M. Novella', 99–100.

[24] A. Chiapelli, 'Contributo di Pistoia ad una crociata contro i Turchi (1345)', *Bullettino storico pistoiese*, i (1890), 113–15; *Storie pistoiesi*, ed. S. Barbi, in RIS², xi, pt 5, 214–16. Cf. M. S. Mazzi, 'Pistoia e la terrasanta', in Cardini, ed., *Toscana e terrasanta*, 107–8.

[25] On the revolutionary events and atmosphere of this decade, cf. Brucker, *Florentine Politics*, 105ff., and M. Becker, *Florence in Transition* (Baltimore, 1967), i, 123ff.; on the religious and social consequences, cf. M. Meiss, *Painting in Florence and Siena after the Black Death* (Princeton, 1951), 61ff.

[26] Cf. Papi, 'S. M. Novella', 98–9.

for the holy lands and widespread support for a crusade; it is all too frequently assumed that the idea of a crusade met with little enthusiasm in Tuscany because of lucrative and expanding commercial interests in the East,[27] but in fact many Florentines as well as other Tuscans preserved their traditional crusading sympathies, were horrified by the rapid advance of the Turks, and felt profound compassion for the growing plight of Eastern Christendom. Indeed, there is evidence to show that their interest in the holy lands may have been growing during the fourteenth and fifteenth centuries. Florentine profits from trade with the Turks are persistently emphasized but it is frequently overlooked that Florentine families such as the Pazzi enjoyed a lucrative position as bankers for the papal crusades in the fifteenth century.[28] A Florentine such as Benedetto Dei to be sure traded in the East with the Turks, for whom he gained considerable sympathy,[29] but another Florentine merchant, Jacopo Tedaldi, manned the barricades at the siege of Constantinople,[30] while a few years later Michele Alighieri, a Florentine merchant resident in Trebizond, returned to Italy to negotiate aid for Emperor David of Trebizond in his struggle against the Turks.[31] Florentines were active in the military orders in the East,[32] where a number also lived as members of religious orders,[33] and two Florentines played a notable role as captains in the papal fleet in the eastern Mediterranean during the 1450s and 1460s.[34] The crusade was preached with great success in Florence during 1455, 1456 and 1457,[35] and it may perhaps have been a theme in the Florentine sermons of San Bernardino of Siena, who was a powerful preacher in Florence as well as an ardent advocate of the crusade;[36] Jerusalem and the holy lands were also mentioned in the sermons of the Milanese Franciscan, Michele

[27] Cf. e.g. F. Babinger, 'Maometto, il conquistatore, e l'Italia', RSI, liii (1951), 489ff.; cf. p. 241, *supra*.

[28] Cf. Sciambra, Valentini and Parrino, *Il 'Liber brevium'*, 29, 32, 107–8, 110, 138, 139, 141, 154, 155, 170, 172, 188, 199, 202.

[29] Cf. the passages from his chronicle edited by G. F. Pagnini, in *Della decima e de varie altre gravezze imposte dal comune di Firenze* (Lisbon and Lucca, 1765–6), ii, 246ff., and also Picotti, *Dieta*, 372–3.

[30] On Tedaldi and his 'Informations', cf. M.-L. Concasty, 'Les "Informations" de Jacques Tedaldi sur le siège et la prise de Constantinople ', *Byzantion*, xxiv (1954), 95–110; Pertusi, *Caduta*, i, 172ff., 408ff.; Schwoebel, *Shadow*, 4–5, 25.

[31] Cf. A. Bryer, 'Lodovico da Bologna and the Georgian and Anatolian embassy of 1460–1461', *Bedi Kartlisa*, xix–xx (1965), 180–1, 185–7, 193–4, 196–8.

[32] Cf. Müller, *Documenti*, 180–1.

[33] Cf. Pertusi, *Caduta*, ii, 30–1; L. Gai, 'La "Dimostrazione dell'andata del Santo Sepolcro" di Marco di Bartolommeo Rustici fiorentino (1441–42)', in Cardini, ed., *Toscana e terrasanta*, 202.

[34] Cf. ASF, Miss. 42, fol. 130r; *ibid.*, 43, fol. 53v; Setton, *Papacy*, ii, 166–7.

[35] Cf. pp. 245–6, *supra*.

[36] On San Bernardino's preaching in Florence, cf. Vespasiano, *Vite*, i, 246–7; on his activities as a preacher of crusading indulgences, cf. Donati, 'S. Bernardino', 130–6.

Carcano, delivered in Florence during 1461.[37] Imitation of the church of the Holy Sepulchre at Jerusalem is evident, it has been argued, in the fifteenth-century Florentine church of Santissima Annunziata in Florence,[38] while the Florentine patrician Giovanni Rucellai had built for himself and his family 'a sepulchre similar to that of Our Lord at Jerusalem' in the Florentine church of San Pancrazio;[39] moreover, the legend of the true cross, which, based on Jacopo da Voragine's *Legenda aurea*, had as a central theme the war between Christians and the infidel, became an important subject in Florentine and Tuscan painting at the turn of the fifteenth century and thereafter.[40] It is hard to deny that such subjects did not demonstrate a literal concern for the holy lands when it is clear that many Florentines, especially from the patriciate, were travelling to the holy lands as pilgrims in the later fourteenth and throughout the fifteenth centuries;[41] indeed, the considerable number of Italian and especially Florentine and Tuscan pilgrims' books which appear in this period, in contrast to their almost complete absence in previous centuries,[42] not to mention the very wide circulation of these new Italian itineraries in manuscript,[43] suggests that Italian and particularly Florentine pilgrimage to the holy lands was increasing during the later middle ages. Many, if not a

---

[37] R. Rusconi, 'Gerusalemme nella predicazione popolare quattrocentesca tra millennio, ricordo di viaggio e luogo sacro', in Cardini, ed., *Toscana e terrasanta*, 286, 293–4.

[38] S. Lang, 'The programme of the SS. Annunziata in Florence', JWCI, xvii (1954), 292ff.

[39] F. W. Kent, 'The making of a Renaissance patron of the arts', in *Giovanni Rucellai ed il suo Zibaldone ii: a Florentine Patrician and his Palace* (London, 1981), 58–60.

[40] E. Borsook, *The Mural Painters of Tuscany*[2] (Oxford, 1982), 93; for bibliography of the legend of the true cross, cf. *ibid.*, 100ff.; Ginzburg, *Indagini*, 41–9.

[41] These Tuscan pilgrims' books include M. Dardano, 'Un itinerario dugentesco per la Terra Santa', *Studi medievali*, ser. 3, vii (1966), 154–96; *Viaggio di Lionardo di Niccolò Frescobaldi . . . in Egitto e in Terra Santa* (Rome, 1818); Mariano da Siena, *Del viaggio in Terra Santa*, ed. D. Moreni (Florence, 1822); Niccolò da Poggibonsi, *Libro d'Oltramare (1346–1350)*, ed. P. B. Bagatti (Jerusalem, 1945); Zanobi di Antonio del Lavacchio, 'Relazione di un viaggio al soldano d'Egitto e in terra santa', ed. G. Corti, ASI, cxvi (1958), 247–66. For the unpublished itinerary of Marco di Bartolommeo Rustici, cf. Gai, in *Toscana e terrasanta*, 189–233; for the unpublished itineraries of Piero Antonio Buondelmonti and Alessandro di Filippo Rinuccini, cf. A. Calamai, 'Il viaggio in terrasanta di Alessandro Rinuccini nel 1474', *ibid.*, 235–56 and B. Bagatti, 'L'inedito itinerario nel 1474 del domenicano A. Rinuccini', *La terra santa*, xviii (1953), 242–5. On these itineraries in general, cf. *Viaggiatori e pellegrini italiani in Terrasanta*, 126–31, 263–313, 244–62, 340–51; F. Cardini, 'Viaggiatori medioevali in Terrasanta: a proposito di alcune recenti pubblicazioni italiane', RSI, lxxx (1968) 331–9; J. Richard, *Les récits de voyages et de pélegrinages* (Turnhout, 1981) [fasc. 38 of *Typologie des sources du moyen âge occidental*, ed. L. Genicot], which includes further bibliography, as does *Viaggiatori e pellegrini*.

[42] J. K. Hyde, 'Navigation of the Eastern Mediterranean in the fourteenth and fifteenth centuries according to pilgrims' books', *Papers in Italian Archaeology I: The Lancaster Seminar*, ed. H. McK. Blake, T. W. Potter, D. B. Whitehouse, in *BAR Supplementary Series*, xli (2) (1978), pt 2, 522.

[43] Cf. R. Delfiol, 'Su alcuni problemi codicologico-testuali concernenti le relazioni di pellegrinaggio fiorentine del 1384', in *Toscana e terrasanta*, 145–47.

majority, of known Florentine pilgrims in this period were from patrician families,[44] and this custom of pilgrimage to the holy land may have been nourished by the chivalric culture with which the Florentine aristocracy was imbued;[45] indeed, it has recently been shown that in this very period of the later fourteenth and early fifteenth centuries one Florentine patrician family, the Pazzi, were provided with a legendary ancestor in the person of a crusading knight who, as the first to scale the walls of Jerusalem during the first crusade, was given for a memento a piece of the holy sepulchre which, brought back to Florence, was used thereafter in the festival of the Scoppio del Carro on Easter Saturday.[46] Moreover, there had always been a close connection between pilgrimage and crusade, and this was no less true in the fifteenth century than before, as is clear, for example, in the pilgrim's book of Mariano da Siena, who passionately advocated a crusade, following in the traditions of his great Sienese predecessors, Saints Catherine and Bernardino;[47] crusade as well as pilgrimage are also prominent themes in the recently studied pilgrim's book by the Florentine goldsmith, Marco di Bartolomeo Rustici, who went to the East in 1441–2 together with two other Florentine pilgrims, Antonio di Bartolomeo Ridolfi and Maestro Leale from the Florentine Servite convent of Santissima Annunziata who himself emerges from this text as an outspoken advocate of a crusade.[48]

Benedetto Accolti was one more Florentine in whom a profound personal concern for the holy lands and their holy remains, as is clear from the central role occupied in his history by the holy sepulchre,[49] was combined with anxiety over the growth of Muslim power, which, he laments, had in his day spread so far and wide;[50] like many Florentines, Accolti's crusading fervour was the fruit of deep religious feelings and interests which, in his case, are clear in his early Italian vernacular poetry[51] as well as in the prominent sections of his dialogue relating to church history and ecclesiology.[52] Accolti's crusading enthusiasm was also nourished in his native city of Arezzo, where, as in other Tuscan cities such as Pistoia,[53] Pisa,[54]

[44] Cf. G. Pinto, 'I costi del pellegrinaggio in terrasanta nei secoli xiv e xv (dai resoconti dei viaggiatori italiani)', *ibid.*, 279–84; *Viaggiatori e pellegrini*, 434–9.
[45] Cf. P. J. Jones, 'Economia e società nell'Italia medievale: il mito della borghesia', in his *Economia e società nell'Italia medievale* (Turin, 1980), 4–189, *passim*.
[46] S. Raveggi, 'Storia di una leggenda: Pazzo dei Pazzi e le pietre del Santo Sepolcro', in *Toscana e terrasanta*, 299–315.
[47] Cf. F. Cardini, 'Nota su Mariano di Nanni rettore di San Pietro e Ovile in Siena', *ibid.*, 182; Castellini, 'Santa Caterina', 323ff.; Donati, 'S. Bernardino', 130–6; *Viaggiatori e pellegrini*, 340–51.
[48] Gai, 'Dimostrazione', in *Toscana e terrasanta*, 204, 218–20.
[49] Cf. p. 224, *supra*.    [50] Cf. p. 237, *supra*.
[51] Cf. pp. 68–70, *supra*.    [52] Cf. pp. 205–8, 216–23, *supra*.
[53] Cf. Mazzi, 'Pistoia', in *Toscana e terrasanta*, 104ff.
[54] Cf. Raveggio, 'Storia di una leggenda', *ibid.*, 315.

Cortona,[55] and Siena,[56] crusading sentiments were still very much alive in the later middle ages. One prominent Aretine citizen and friend of Accolti's, the physician Niccolò Tignosi, was a passionate crusader, as is shown by his treatise on the fall of Constantinople, where an account of the tribulations experienced by Christians in the East is combined with a call for Italy to awaken from slumber and lead an army of vengeance against the Turks.[57] San Bernardino preached at least two important series of sermons in Arezzo, in 1428 and 1440–1,[58] when it is possible that the crusade was one of his themes;[59] he made a great impression there,[60] and it may be significant that he is represented in the famous chapel of the Bacci family in the church of San Francesco in Arezzo,[61] which was decorated by Piero della Francesca with a renowned fresco cycle depicting the legend of the true cross.[62] Even more prominent in this cycle than in other fourteenth- and fifteenth-century representations of this theme are two battle scenes representing successful holy wars, Constantine's victory over the barbarian horde and the triumph of the Byzantine emperor, Heraclius, over the Persian monarch, Chosroes; Piero began decorating the chapel probably at about the time that Constantinople fell to the Turks, and his period of activity there coincides with the pontificates of Callixtus III and Pius II,[63] which, it has been seen, constituted a decade of crusading fervour unprecedented in the fifteenth century. The decorations in the Bacci chapel are open to many different kinds of interpretation,[64] but it is scarcely credible that anyone could have commissioned, designed, painted or beheld these frescoes in the second half of the fifteenth century without calling to mind an issue of such overriding immediacy and urgency as the Turkish menace and the struggle between Christians and the infidel.[65]

---

[55] A. Benvenuti Papi, 'Margarita', *ibid.*, 130ff.

[56] Cf. Cardini, 'Mariano', *ibid.*, 182; Castellini, 'Santa Caterina', 323ff.; Donati, 'S. Bernardino', 130–6.

[57] Cf. ed. Sensi, 'N. Tignosi', 378–82, 423–31.

[58] Cf. D. Pacetti, 'La predicazione di S. Bernardino in Toscana: S. Bernardino ad Arezzo durante la Quaresima del 1428', *Archivum franciscanum historicum*, xxxiv (1941), 261–83.

[59] Cf. Donati, 'S. Bernardino', 130–6.

[60] Cf. P. Delorme, 'Apologie de la dévotion au S. Nom de Jésus', *Archivum franciscanum historicum*, xxxiv (1941), 360; I. Origo, *The World of San Bernardino* (London, 1963), 176–7.

[61] Cf. Borsook, *Mural Painters*[2], 95, 100.

[62] *Ibid.*, 91ff.    [63] *Ibid.*

[64] Cf. Borsook, *Mural Painters*[2], 93–5, 100–1, and Ginzburg, *Indagini*, 15–49, for recent discussions of the iconography.

[65] Borsook's assertion (*Mural Painters*[2], 95, n. 83) that the Bacci family had trading links with the East is based on a mistranscription of ASF, Cat. 202, fol. 404v: Francesco Bacci's twenty-one-year-old son 'inpara' (is learning), not 'in pera' (in Pera). Given the depressed state of the Aretine economy, there was probably little Aretine trade with the Eastern Mediterranean, and this kind of argument has no more validity for Arezzo than similar arguments do for Florence or the rest of Tuscany: a merchant such as Michele Alighieri

## (vi) Accolti, the crusade and the Florentine regime

In his history Accolti not only voiced time-honoured Florentine and Tuscan crusading sympathies but also echoed the opinions of a section of the Florentine ruling elite who supported the crusade. Chief among these Florentine crusading oligarchs was Agnolo Acciaiuoli, one of the three or four most powerful men in Florence during the 1450s and 1460s.[1] The Acciaiuoli were not only a first-rank Florentine political family but also had forged the strongest links to the East of all Florentine families in the fourteenth and fifteenth centuries.[2] Making use of the traditional connection between Florence and the Angevins of Naples, the great Niccolò Acciaiuoli (d. 1365) had formed an intimate alliance with the Latin titular Byzantine imperial family, then resident in Naples, from whom he gained extensive possessions in the Greek Morea, ultimately to become lord of Corinth; his position in Greece was inherited by his nephew Nerio Acciaiuoli (d. 1394) who eventually wrested the duchy of Athens from the Catalans (1388) to become duke of Athens nine months before his death. After an interlude of Venetian rule, the duchy of Athens was reconquered in 1403 by Nerio's bastard son, Antonio I Acciaiuoli, whose thirty-three year rule until his death in 1435 was the longest in Athens's medieval history; Antonio I was succeeded by his cousin Nerio II, whose rule lasted until his death in 1451 except for an interval of about two years from about 1439 to 1441 when his brother Antonio II seized power, and Nerio's young son Francesco succeeded him as duke of Athens until 1455, when his cousin Franco Acciaiuoli was installed in the duchy by Mehmed II. The Acciaiuoli rule of Athens, having lasted over sixty years, finally came to an end in 1456 when the Turks deposed Franco Acciaiuoli, allowing him to take possession of Thebes, but the Acciaiuoli family lost even that token of their once great Greek lordship when in 1460 Franco was murdered at Thebes on instructions from Mehmed II. The Florentine branches of the family, to which Agnolo Acciaiuoli belonged, always retained close ties with their Greek cousins, and when Agnolo suffered exile in 1433 along with other leaders of the Medici party, it was to Greece as the home of his relatives that he was banished.[3] Like the rest of his family, Agnolo could have had little love for the Turks, and during his exile an incident occurred which confirmed his antipathy:

(cf. Bryer, 'Lodovico da Bologna') could act as an ambassador on behalf of the crusade and at the same time have extensive trading links with the Turks.

[1] Rubinstein, *Government*, 127, 134 etc.
[2] For the Acciaiuoli in Greece, cf. K. Setton, *Catalan Domination in Athens 1311–1388* (Cambridge, Mass., 1948), *passim; idem*, 'The Latins in Greece and the Aegean from the Fourth Crusade to the end of the middle ages', *Cambridge Medieval History*, iv, pt 1 (1966), 407, 421ff. with bibliography, 908–38; *idem* and H. Hazard, eds., *A History of the Crusades*, iii (Madison, 1975), 120–277.
[3] Vespasiano, *Vite*, ii, 287.

One day while [Agnolo] was riding near the borders of Turkish territory, he was taken and led to the Turk; because he did not say either who he was or what he was doing, the Turk had him thrown in prison. With the help of a Florentine who was with him, he fled one day and together with his companion he underwent the gravest danger. He later said . . . that this liberation was nothing short of miraculous.[4]

Agnolo, who was second cousin to Duke Antonio I and first cousin to Dukes Nerio II and Antonio II,[5] was probably able to reciprocate the hospitality he had received in Greece during his exile when his cousin Nerio II was living as an exile in Florence from about 1439 to 1441,[6] and Agnolo's intimate connections with the Greek world were put to good use during the Council of Florence when he acted as official guide to the Greek Emperor John VIII Paleologus on an excursion to Pistoia and Prato from Florence.[7] Agnolo always preserved a keen interest in the affairs of Greece and the East, and when the time came in 1458 for Pius II to announce his forthcoming crusade against the Turks, Agnolo, chosen as a member of the Florentine legation to Rome, was outspoken in his sentiments:

We ought to help in this undertaking against the Turks [he wrote to the Gonfalonier of Justice, Otto Niccolini]; it is necessary that we should do our duty, because it would be too greatly to our discredit if all other Christians were to act, and we alone were not to join them . . . It is necessary that you should take counsel with your own self and you should think of what great importance this matter is, when it concerns the defence of our faith for our honour and profit.[8]

During this legation Agnolo reminisced about his youth in Greece, offering advice about Greek geography to facilitate the forthcoming expedition,[9] and although he was under instructions not to commit the Florentine government in any way to the crusade,[10] he seems, in his eagerness to combat the Turks, to have exceeded his mandate by declaring that Florence wanted to be the first to do their share in the pope's holy war.[11] With feelings doubtless even more roused by the final collapse of Acciaiuoli rule in 1460, Agnolo was adamant in his censure of any measure which might impede the success of the papal crusade, and at the beginning of the diplomatic crisis between Florence and Venice in 1463 over the Florentine levantine galleys, Acciaiuoli wrote,

There has not yet been any discussion about despatching our galleys to the East,

---

[4]  *Ibid.*     [5]  Setton, *Papacy*, ii, 63.

[6]  *Idem, Catalan Domination*, 207–8.      [7]  *Idem, Papacy*, ii, 62–4.

[8]  Quoted and translated by Niccolini di Camugliano, *Chronicles of a Florentine Family*, 258–9; I was unable to find the original letter in the Niccolini archives in Florence: cf. p. 104, n. 129, *supra*.

[9]  Cf. the summary of Acciaiuoli's speech in L. Crivelli, *De expeditione Pii Papae II adversus Turcos*, in RIS², xxiii, pt 5 (ed. G. C. Zimolo), 98.

[10]  ASF, LC, 15, fol. 2v, 5v, 13r–v.      [11]  Crivelli, *De expeditione*, 98.

but I believe that they are certain not to be sent; otherwise great damage and inconvenience will result.[12]

As the crisis worsened during the summer of 1463, Agnolo was full of praise for Venice, writing in July that

the Venetians are pursuing their undertaking against the Turks and it will be something useful and worthy, particularly if the Hungarians give them assistance on land, but if the Hungarians cannot or will not move forward and attack the Turk at his heart, the Venetians will not be able to do great things;[13]

at the same time, he criticized the Florentines for not allowing Venice to recruit troops for its crusading army in Florentine territory.[14]

Agnolo Acciaiuoli's relations with Cosimo and Piero de' Medici were at this time deteriorating,[15] and it is clear that one reason for this widening split in the regime was the Medicean attitude to the crusade. There is no doubt that Cosimo de' Medici did not share Agnolo Acciaiuoli's crusading ardour: he considered that Pius II had been foolish for having summoned the Congress of Mantua, and that the entire venture had been undertaken in poor judgement.[16] On the other hand, as a pious Christian, Cosimo could never have been an outspoken opponent of papal crusading plans; he seems to have been not unmoved by the fall of Constantinople,[17] and he paid for the repair and redecoration of the church of the Holy Spirit at Jerusalem.[18] He was anxious to remain on good terms with the pope, and when asked, he refused to intercede in an attempt to persuade the pope to call off the Congress of Mantua; although sceptical about the success of a crusade, he said that the pope was working for the good of Christendom and he would only prejudice his own reputation if he were to stand in the

---

[12] ASF, CStr., i, 352, fol. 63r: Dell'andare delle galee nostre in Romania, non se n'è parla ancora, ma credo che siano certi che le non possino andare, di che sequirà qui danno et inconvenienti assai (dated Florence, 27 May 1463).

[13] ASF, CStr., i, 136, fol. 33v: E venitiani seguitano in questa impresa del turco, la quale sia cosa utile et degna se l'ungharo gli serve per terra; ma se l'unghero non potessi o non volessi farsi inanzi et stare a pecto al Turco, non potranno e Venitiani fare grande cose (dated Milan, 4 July 1463).

[14] *Ibid.*: [the Venetians] mandorono ad Firenze per soldare fanti; fu dineghato, di che e Venitiani si doggono assai. *Ibid.*, fol. 36r: Qui è suto uno cancellieri il quale è dal Monte a San Sovino, et sta a Vinegia . . . et voleva soldare in quello d'Arezzo fanti per menargli contra al Turco. Qui non si consentirà (Florence, 2 June 1463).

[15] Cf. Rubinstein, *Government*, 134–6.

[16] Archivio di stato, Mantua, Gonzaga 1099, fasc. 69, fol. 428r (despatch of Antonio Donato, Mantuan ambassador in Florence, to Lodovico Gonzaga, duke of Mantua, 24 April 1459): [Cosimo de' Medici] conosca che la mossa sua [Pius II's journey to Mantua for the congress of 1459] sia stata cum po' chossiglio. (I am extremely grateful to Dr R. Hatfield for providing me with a transcription of this letter.)

[17] Poggio, *De miseria conditionis humanae*, in *Opera*, 88.

[18] Vespasiano, *Vite*, ii, 180–1.

way of the pope's efforts.[19] Cosimo's refusal to obstruct papal plans was
not entirely disinterested: the Medici had profited during the pontificate of
Callixtus III as papal bankers for the crusade,[20] and they may have had
hopes of continuing to act in this capacity under Pius II.[21] Moreover, it was
paramount for Cosimo to retain good relations with Francesco Sforza,
who at the time of the Congress of Mantua and before the papal–Venetian
rapprochement of 1463 supported papal crusading policy.[22] Sforza was
critical of Florentine objections to collecting clerical tenths for the crusade
in March 1460[23] and it is certain that Cosimo used his authority to overcome Florentine hostility to the collection of these tenths.[24] During the
crisis over the galleys of 1463, Cosimo at first took a hard line against the
Venetians, who, in his opinion, would not be reconciled to the pope
because of their dispute over the town of Cernia on the border between
Venetian territory and the papal states. In this policy Cosimo was opposed
by Agnolo Acciaiuoli and the duke of Milan, as is clear from a letter
written by Agnolo from Milan on 4 July 1463:

I see things growing worse every day between [the Venetians] and us. Cosimo is
helping this business. Indeed, since he saw the pope and the Venetians enter into
this dispute over Cernia, he has been putting as much wood as possible into that
fire, and he would like [the duke of Milan] to take Genoa and he is urging him to
expand, since the Venetians are embroiled with the Turks and he can expect every
assistance from Florence. But in this scheme Florence will not succeed. But I fear
that [Florence] will not make its peace with Venice. [Cosimo] entered into discussions over this with [the duke of Milan] who does not want to hear a word
about it and has taken it very badly . . .[25]

---

[19]  Archivio di Stato, Mantua, Gonzaga 1099, fasc. 69, fol. 428r: Cosimo me dice ancora
      che altri gli hanno ditto che, se'l voleva operarsi, el faria restare el papa qua, e non
      passaria più oltra, et che ha risposto non volerlo fare, perché nostro signore ha tuolto
      questa impresa per ben di tuta la christianitade e gran lezereza seria la sua a tentare che'l
      non andasse, et pareria che'l si fusse mosso per cupiditade del denaro, et utile de questo,
      più tosto che per altra casone, et non voleva per alcun modo impazarsene.
[20]  *Liber brevium*, 29, 32, 205–6.
[21]  They were appointed bankers for the crusade by Paul II in 1464: cf. Setton, *Papacy*, ii,
      275.
[22]  Cf. Picotti, *Dieta*, 442; Setton, *Papacy*, ii, 210–11.
[23]  Picotti, *Dieta*, 372, n. 3.
[24]  The debates of the *pratica* show the leading citizens of Florence opposed to the crusading
      taxation (ASF, CP, 56, fol. 47r–63v, 76r–77r) from 6 to 20 March 1460, until Manno
      Temperani declared (fol. 64r) 'quia intellexit quid in eiusmodi casu Cosma agendum
      censuit, perquirendum in hoc suum iudicium et approbandum dixit' after which speakers
      agreed that the pope must be allowed the tenths (fol. 64r–v). When the matter was raised
      again for a final decision on 4 April 1460, Manno Temperani again said 'intellexisse se
      Cosmam dixisse nonnulla super hoc negotio pontificis que sibi viderentur, cuius con-
      silium velut prudentissimi viri futurum utile civitati exequendum censere se dixit' (fol.
      74r), and all other speakers agreed with this advice (fol. 74r–v). On the collection of the
      tenths following this decision, cf. p. 254, *supra*.
[25]  ASF, CStr. i, 136, fol. 33v: Veggo le cose fra loro et noi ogni dì agravare. Cosimo aiuta
      questa materia, peroché, poiché 'gl 'a veduto il papa essere alterato con loro pel facto di
      Cernia, mette quante legna può in quello fuocho e vorrebbe che il 'lustre signore [the

As the crisis neared its climax in the autumn of 1463 Agnolo was in accord with the duke of Milan, who blamed Florence under Cosimo's domination for undermining the Florentine–Milanese diplomatic position by impeding the papal crusade and risking a total collapse of their interests in Italy:

[the duke of Milan] wants to do nothing which might be a reason for impeding the Venetian war against the Turks and the expedition which the pope and the duke of Burgundy are making. [The duke of Milan] has told [the Florentine ambassador] how greatly the Florentines have been and are in error for having assumed the shameful attitude which has grown up in Italy.[26]

Cosimo finally succumbed to this pressure from Milan in December 1463 but Agnolo was still critical of, in his view, the ignominious way in which Florence under Cosimo's leadership came round to the crusade.[27] From the beginning of 1464 Cosimo was reconciled to the Milanese policy of cooperation in the crusade to forestall a papal–Venetian rapprochement, and in this changed frame of mind he intervened with the Florentine Signoria to obtain the release of prisoners to man the papal galleys[28] and promised to equip a galley for the papal fleet at his own expense.[29] Agnolo Acciaiuoli seems now to have made his peace with the Medici, at least as far as the crusade was concerned, and when Florentine commitment weakened in June and July 1464, leading Agnolo to complain that 'here [in Florence] they are slow to provide money for the thirtieth'[30] for the crusade, it is significant that Agnolo no longer saw Medicean influence as the cause of Florentine reluctance:

duke of Milan] piglassi Genova et confortalo a doversi alargare, essendo e Veneziani inpaciati col Turcho et che sarebbe aiutato ad Firenze d'ogni cosa. Ma questo pensiero di Firenze non gli riuscirebbe. Ma temerei che quella terra non si accordarssi con Viniziani. Hanne facto parlare al 'lustre signore, il quale non vole udirne parola et hallo havuto molto a male (dated Milan, 4 July 1463).

26  *Ibid.*, fol. 32r: per niente lui [the duke of Milan] intende fare cose che fusseno cagione d'impedire la guerra de' Venitiani contro al Turco nela impresa che fa il papa et il duca di Borgogna, et hagli [to Dietisalvi Neroni, the Florentine ambassador to Milan] mostro quanto è stato et è l'errore de' Fiorentini ad havere gittatosi drieto alle spalle gli scandale che sono nati in Italia (dated Milan, 28 November, 1463).

27  *Ibid.*, fol. 30r: Messer Otho [Niccolini, the Florentine ambassador to the pope] tornò a Roma [to conclude Florence's agreement to participate in the crusade despite the Venetian refusal to guarantee the Levantine galleys: cf. p. 356, *supra*] . . . et sono seguitate cose di che ho dispiacere et per honore della città et suo . . . E sse n'è facto caso assai a Firenze et hanno mandato Niccodemo [Tranchedini, the Milanese ambassador in Florence] al duca [of Milan] perché rimedii col papa allo honore della communità il più che si può (dated Milan, 11 January 1464).

28  M. Morici, 'Il Cardinale Niccolò Forteguerri e Giovanni di Cosimo de' Medici', *Bulletino storico pistoiese*, ii (1900), 114.

29  Pius II, *Commentaries*, 848.

30  ASF, CStr. i, 136, fol. 28r: Qui sono molto pigri a provedere a danari della xxx^ma (dated Florence, 16 June 1464).

Our affairs at home could not be in worse order and poorer control. Cosimo and Piero are in bed, and they do what they can, but they cannot do what is necessary for the city.[31]

The meaning of Agnolo's remarks are clear: Cosimo's and Piero's influence has grown so weak that they were no longer able to lead Florence to fulfil its commitments, one of which was to provide crusading taxes for the papal expedition. The Milanese ambassador in Rome had the same view: on 12 August 1464 he warned the pope not to hold out any further hopes of Florentine participation in the crusade, above all else, because of Cosimo's disappearance from the scene.[32] It is evident that Cosimo de' Medici, far from impeding the crusade, had become its prime mover in Florence during the period from January 1464 to his death on 1 August.

The attitude of the Florentine elite to Pius II's crusade was therefore anything but unanimous. On the one hand, there was obviously widespread and deep-seated hostility to further papal crusading taxes, which was particularly manifest in the debates of the *pratica* of 1460;[33] on the other hand, these feelings could be subdued by the Medici, as happened in 1460 and 1464. Moreover, there were Florentine patricians who followed Agnolo Acciaiuoli's lead and fully supported the crusade; one of these was Agnolo's cousin, the renowned humanist, Donato Acciaiuoli, who wrote in 1463:

We understand here that [the Venetians] have mounted a great force in the Morea, and on land they will have 15 to 20 thousand men, and an armada of 44 galleys, which seems, to tell the truth, to be a [veritable] Roman expedition. The pope has sent to Venice [Cardinal Bessarion], and [the Venetians] are giving help to the Hungarians to keep the Turks occupied over there, and in this way their expedition in the Morea is likely to succeed, which would be a great thing.[34]

Donato Acciaiuoli, whom Accolti certainly knew and with whom he shared common interests and acquaintances, was possibly a link between Accolti and Agnolo Acciaiuoli's circle of crusading enthusiasts. Accolti, who according to Vespasiano da Bisticci knew almost every learned man in Florence,[35] had connections with Argyropulos's circle,[36] of which

---

[31]  *Ibid.* Queste nostre cose della terra non potrebbono esser in più cattivo ordine et peggio governare. Cosimo et Piero si stanno nel lecto et fanno quello che possono, ma e' non possono fare quello che bisognerebbe alla città (dated Florence, 16 June 1464).
[32]  Cf. p. 258, *supra*.     [33]  Cf. p. 253, *supra*.
[34]  ASF, CStr. i, 352, fol. 66r: Qui intendiamo che sono volti [the Venetians] con uno grande sforzo nella Morea e per terra arano xv^m in xx^m persone et l'armata di galee 44, che pare, a dire el vero, una impresa romana. El papa ha mandato a Venezia Niceno [Cardinal Bessarion] e loro danno aiuto agli Ungheri per tenere occupato el Turcho di là e per questa via è apto riuscire loro la impresa della Morea, che sarebbe grande chosa (dated Florence, 21 July 1463).
[35]  Vespasiano, *Vite*, i, 597.     [36]  Cf. p. 212, *supra*.

Donato Acciaiuoli was a prominent member.[37] Like Accolti, Donato composed a humanist historical work on the crusade, a funeral oration for the
Hungarian crusader Hunyadi;[38] like Accolti he was involved, with his life
of Charlemagne published in 1461, in historical research on the early
middle ages;[39] and like Accolti he had a deep admiration for Leonardo
Bruni's history of Florence, which he carefully studied and eventually
translated into Italian.[40] Another Florentine who seems to have followed
Agnolo's lead as a supporter of the crusade was Giuliano Portinari, whose
speech in the *pratica* of 7 March 1460 emphasizing the importance and
honour of a holy war contrasted with the prevailing hostility of other
speakers to the crusading taxes;[41] it is certain that the crusade was an issue
between Agnolo Acciaiuoli and the Medici in 1463 and possibly it was a
divisive force within the regime as a whole. When Cosimo reversed his
position in December 1463, he may have hoped to win back the allegiance
of Agnolo Acciaiuoli and his friends, just as he was attempting to regain
the confidence of Francesco Sforza and Pius II, but in doing so he may have
jeopardized his position to some degree with the adamant opponents of the
crusade and the intransigent anti-Venetians, thus perhaps contributing to
that waning of Medicean influence in the few weeks before his death noted
by Agnolo Acciaiuoli.

Against this background, one aim of Accolti's history of the first
crusade with its dedication to Piero de' Medici is clear. Intimacy with the
Medici had thus far eluded him, but now that they had become supporters
of the crusade and reconciled with the crusading sympathizers among the

---

[37] Cf. E. Garin, 'Donato Acciaiuoli cittadino fiorentino', in his *Medioevo e rinascimento*
(Bari, 1954), 235ff.
[38] The autograph manuscript is BNF, Magl. IX, 123, fol. 83r–86r, dated 15 November
1456.
[39] The autograph manuscript is BNF, II, II, 10, fol. 31r–52v; there is also an incomplete
autograph version of an Italian version in BNF, II, II, 325, fol. 14r–20v. Cf. Gatti, ' "Vita
Caroli" ', 230.
[40] Donato Acciaiuoli's copy of the first six books of Bruni's history is BLF, Ashburnham
517 (449): cf. fol. IIv: Donatii Nerii de Acciaiolis est liber Historie florentine, and fol. IIIv,
where he sketched the Acciaiuoli arms. Donato made a careful study of this ms., adding
many marginalia including year dates (omitted by Bruni) for the narrative after 1250,
corrections of the text and references to notable events and persons, especially from the
Acciaiuoli family (e.g. fol. 136v).
[41] ASF, CP, 56, fol. 54r: Julianus Partinari dicit . . . videri sibi materiam hanc mature
examinandam et optimum partitum capiendum ut cum intelligent pontifex et cardinales
deliberationem factam eam laudare compellantur ex quo honor et laus etiam accedet
civitati. Et quia casus iste respicit reverentiam dei et salutem christianorum et si Theucri
perseverant nocere christianis periculis imminere[n]t omnibus, considerandum hoc esse
nec omnino pecunias denegandas sed potius concludendum esse non denigare dominos
solutionem sed differre parumper ut utilius et melius pecunie erogentur. Sic enim agendo
laus et honor eveniet civitati. Et quoniam in aliis solvendis pro eorum causa Florentini ex
primis fuerunt, graviter facturos eos qui dominos redarguant si parumper hanc
solutionem distulerint, et hec se consulere ait pro decore et ornamento civitatis.

Florentine oligarchy, he must have felt the possibility of a new bond, a real
common interest between himself and the Medici. In this sense the work
had the same purpose as his earlier dialogue,[42] and it is not surprising that
Accolti's panegyric of Cosimo in the history recalls the encomium of him
in the dialogue. Once again he praises Cosimo's native intelligence, his
devotion to scholarship, his patronage of learning, his virtuous family life,
his exemplary character, his leading part in public life, his magnificence,
liberality and charity, and his devotion to religion.[43] With Cosimo's death
impending, however, Accolti thought it was time to flatter his successor
and so he enlarged on another theme of the dialogue: 'You have imitated
with great zeal the virtues of this man', he declared to Piero, 'and have
shown yourself to be a son worthy of such a parent in every way, especially
in those attainments which usually win the highest praise.'[44] He goes on to
praise Piero's wisdom, justice, friendship, piety, reverence and modesty,
and it is clear from his reference to Piero as the new protector of 'fatherland, friends and all Tuscany' that Accolti was thinking of his own future
under a regime soon to be headed by Cosimo's son;[45] indeed, with their
newly arisen common interest in the crusade, Accolti seems to have hoped
that even greater prospects might soon await him in Medicean Florence.
On Pius II's death so soon after Accolti completed his history, however, the
crusade dissolved and perhaps with it waned his expectation of a new
intimacy with the Medici.

In a letter to the doge of Venice written on behalf of the Florentine
Signoria on 7 September 1464, Accolti praised the crusading fervour of the
late Pius II, whose death, it was lamented, would delay decisive military
action against the Turks:

In our view it is fitting that you have taken so hard the death of Pope Pius of blessed
memory, who has died at a time in which all good men ought to have wanted him
to live. For he was greatly inspired to protect the Christian religion; he had already
prepared a great fleet, had roused many men, and desired nothing more than turn
arms against the barbarians. His fervour was such that, although weak in body and
old, he declared that he himself would lead the entire force and he would have completed the task undertaken if bitter death had not snatched him from us. Therefore
his death must be lamented, and it must be regretted, as we ourselves have done,
that by this misfortune the thrust of war has been delayed and many preparations
made ready for the occasion have perished, nor will you be able to press the enemy

---

[42] Cf. pp. 184ff., *supra.*     [43] Cf. pp. 225–6, *supra.*

[44] History, fol. 2v: Has tu eximias viri virtutes magno studio imitatus, dignum te parente
filium omni ex parte ostendisti, in his maxime florens artibus que laudem parere
summam consueverunt (*Recueil*, 530).

[45] History, fol. 2v: Nam te quis melior, sapientior, iustior, bonis amicior invenitur aut
habetur? Quis pietate, religione, modestia, et in omni virtute prestantior? Atque ideo te
incolumen et longissimo evo felicem boni omnes esse desiderant, ut postquam Cosma
quod nature debet exsolverit, tu patriam, amicos et omnem Etruriam tuearis (*Recueil*,
530–1).

so vigorously as would have been possible before. For this grave misfortune, however, one great consolation must be that a noble citizen of your city has been created pope, one whose virtue is so outstanding that all kinds of great things are predicted for him; and we believe that he will do everything which in his view will befit his dignity and the common good. We also think you deserve great praise for not losing heart in this crisis; on the contrary, you have begun again to pursue the war and have decided to launch now another fleet against the enemy.[46]

This letter seems to express not only Accolti's own despondency over the tragic death of Pius II but also his renewed hopes for a crusade founded on an alliance between Venice and the new Venetian Pope Paul II. Indeed, perhaps once more Accolti entertained fleeting hopes of a rapprochement with the Medici founded on a rekindled crusading ardour in Piero, who in fact was appointed banker on 16 September 1464 for the papal alum mines at Tolfa, the profits of which were reserved for the crusade; Piero was soon to become official 'depository for the monies of the Holy Crusade',[47] but Accolti's own death on 26 September 1464[48] saved him any further disappointment such as he would have suffered had he lived to witness the pontificate of Paul II and the remainder of Piero's ascendancy in Florence.

[46] ASF, Miss. 44, fol. 168r: Dignumque censemus fuisse et ea [the Venetian doge] prorsus graviter ferret dive memorie Pium pontificem eo tempore diem obisse quo eius vitam boni omnes cupere debuerint. Magno enim erat animo ad tuendam Christi religionem. Iam paraverat magnam classem, multi mortales concitaverat, nilque aliud cupiebat quam ut arma in barbaros verterentur, adeoque flagrabat animo ut eger corpore ac senes ducem se omnium fore apud omnes pronuntiarit et perfecisset ceptum opus ni mors acerba eum nobis eripuisset. Proinde flendus fuit illius obitus dolendumque, ut ipsi fecimus, quod eo casu impetus belli est retardatus, et multa tum ad tempus parata simul etiam periere. Nec excellentie licuit vestre suis viribus premere hostem prout antea licuisset. Eius autem gravis mali magnum solamen esse debet quod is est creatus pontifex nobilis vestre urbis civis cuius ita enituit virtus ut summa in eo esse omnia predicentur, quem facturum omnia credimus que spectare ad illius dignitatem et bonum comune existimaverit. Nos quoque celsitudinem vestram magna laude dignam censemus quod in eo rerum discrimine non defecit sane animo nec remisit studium belli, sed aliam classem contra hostes mittere nunc instituerit.
[47] For these appointments, cf. Setton, *Papacy*, ii, 275.
[48] Cf. p. 335, *infra*.

# 10

# *Accolti and Renaissance historiography*

## (i) Accolti's historical thought

Benedetto Accolti's preoccupation with history impressed his contemporary, Vespasiano da Bisticci, who wrote that he 'had universal knowledge of ... histories',[1] and Accolti was apparently already contemplating and even planning a longer work of history on the crusades – which was to become his *De bello* – while composing the dialogue, where he declares,

Not long ago many Christian princes gathered to recover the city of Jerusalem and Christ's sepulchre from the infidel – how great, how admirable, how similar to the deeds of the ancients would theirs seem if worthy authors had only celebrated them!² 

Accolti's dialogue is itself a work of historical research: besides revealing wide reading of classical authors including Cicero,[3] Livy,[4] Sallust,[5] the elder Seneca,[6] Lucan,[7] Justin,[8] Polybius[9] and Josephus,[10] who were the sources for Accolti's picture of the ancient world, the work also shows the study of patristic authors such as Augustine,[11] Jerome,[12] Athanasius, Basil, Chrysostom and Eusebius[13] for his portrait of the ancient church and of a recent author such as Bruni for modern history.[14] His two completed Latin compositions did not satisfy his historical enthusiasm, as was noted by Vespasiano, who wrote that 'he wanted to pursue history up to his own

[1] Vespasiano, *Vite*, i, 596.
[2] Dialogue, fol. 17v–18r: Convenere iam multi christianorum principes ut Iherosolymam urbem et Christi sepulchrum ab infidelibus recuperarent ... Horum res gestas, si qui auctores digni celebrassent, quam magnae, quam admirabiles, quam veteribus illis similes viderentur! Cf. Galletti, 112.
[3] Dialogue, fol. 23v, 37r, 38v, 40r; Galletti, 114, 120, 121.
[4] Dialogue, fol. 16v, 25r, 26r; Galletti, 111, 115.
[5] Dialogue, fol. 16r; Galletti, 111.     [6] Dialogue, fol. 40r; Galletti, 121.
[7] Dialogue, fol. 27v; Galletti, 116.
[8] Dialogue, fol. 39r, 56r–v; Galletti, 121, 128.
[9] Dialogue, fol. 16r; Galletti, 111.     [10] Dialogue, fol. 16r; Galletti, 111.
[11] Dialogue, fol. 16r, 44v, 47v; Galletti, 111, 123, 124.
[12] Dialogue, fol. 47v, 51r; Galletti, 124, 126.
[13] Dialogue, fol. 47v; Galletti, 124.     [14] Dialogue, fol. 18v–19r; Galletti, 112.

times, part of which he completed having written the history of Godfrey of Bouillon's expedition to the holy land';[15] indeed, at the end of the preface to *De bello*, he himself wrote to Piero de' Medici, 'If you do not regard my work as entirely inept, I shall be encouraged to pursue the study of history more keenly in the future.'[16]

Accolti's dialogue is related to a time-honoured type of historical literature – the collection of short notices about the lives of famous men. An early example of this genre was Suetonius's series of brief notes on the lives of ancient grammarians, orators and poets, which was transformed by Jerome into a series of short notices about the lives of ecclesiastical writers.[17] Jerome's catalogue was followed by several medieval lists composed by Gennadius of Marseilles, Isidore of Seville, Ildefonso of Toledo, Honor of Autun, Sigibert of Gembloux, and Henry of Ghent, all of whom continued and amended Jerome's series of notable ecclesiastical authors.[18] In the Renaissance, this genre of short literary lives remained in use, most notably by Sicco Polenton, whose history of famous Latin authors was a conscious adaptation of Jerome's, Isidore's and Gennadius's lives of ecclesiastical authors.[19] Sicco returned to Suetonius's original intention of a series of literary biographies, and there were other transformations of the genre in the years before Accolti's dialogue. The scope was extended beyond writers by the Veronese Guglielmo da Pastrengo in his catalogue of illustrious men[20] and by Filippo Villani, who, although limiting himself to Florentines, included lawyers, physicians, astrologers, musicians, painters, clowns and soldiers.[21] The earliest humanist to go beyond the limits of one city-state as well as of literature was Aeneas Sylvius Piccolomini,[22] whose example was followed by Bartolomeo Fazio,[23] and both these were the immediate forerunners of Accolti, who in

---

15 Vespasiano, *Vite*, i, 597.
16 History, fol. 2v: Quod si eos tibi videri non prorsus ineptos animadvertero, posthac audacius ad historiam excitabor. Cf. *Recueil*, 531.
17 Ed. J.A. Fabricius, *Bibliotheca ecclesiastica* (Hamburg, 1718).
18 *Ibid.*
19 *Sicconis Polentonis Scriptorum illustrium Latinae Linguae*, ed. B. L. Ullman (Rome, 1928), 216. A Renaissance catalogue of ecclesiastical writers was composed by Johannes Trithemius, who adopted the genre created by Jerome; it is published in Fabricius, *Bibloteca eccl.*.
20 Ed. M. Biondi, as *De origine rerum libellum* (Venice, 1547).
21 Ed. Galletti, 1–42.
22 Published as *Aeneas Sylvius Piccolomineus qui postea Pius II. P. M. De viris illustribus*, in *Bibliothek des literarischen Vereins in Stuttgart*, i (1843), 1–68.
23 Ed. as *Bartholmaei Facii De viris illustribus* by L. Mehus (Florence, 1745). On this *genre* of collections of short lives, cf. M. Miglio, 'Biografia e raccolte biografiche nel Quattrocento italiano', *Atti della Accademia delle scienze dell'istituto di Bologna. Rendiconti*, lxiii (1974–5), 166–99, for further discussion and bibliography; there is also a brief discussion in E. Cochrane, *Historians and Historiography* (Chicago, 1981), 393ff.

his dialogue neither limited himself to authors nor to his famous Florentine compatriots.

In the dialogue Accolti was concerned with the lives of great men because for him, as for other humanists, biography occupied a central place in the study of history. Distinctions could be drawn between biography as the study of character and *mores* and history as the narrative of deeds,[24] but such categories were recognized as anything but clear cut, as was neatly summed up by Matteo Palmieri, who declared, 'History is nothing other than the celebration of illustrious men.'[25] Indeed, it had long been recognized that an understanding of history depended on a critical assessment of biographical method. Sallust had argued that the contrast between Roman and Greek history could be exaggerated by failing to appreciate that the Greeks were far greater biographers than the Romans:

The acts of the Athenians, in my judgment, were indeed great and glorious enough, but nevertheless somewhat less important than fame represents them. But because Athens produced writers of exceptional talent, the exploits of the men of Athens are heralded throughout the world as unsurpassed. Thus the merit of those who did the deeds is rated as high as brilliant minds have been able to exalt the deeds themselves by words of praise. But the Roman people never had that advantage, since their ablest men were always most engaged with affairs; their minds were never employed apart from their bodies; the best citizen preferred action to words, and thought that his own brave deeds should be alluded by others rather than that theirs should be recounted by him.[26]

In the twelfth century Walter Map adapted this Sallustian thought to his defence of modern times:

The results of the industry of the ancients are in our hands; they make the deeds which even in their times were past, present to ours, and we keep mum; and thus their memory lives in us, and we forget our own. A notable wonder! the dead live, and the living are buried in their stead! . . . Yet the excellences of our modern heroes lie neglected and the cast-off fringes of antiquity are raised to honour. This to be sure is due to the fact that while we know how to criticize, we do not know how to compose . . . Think! Caesar lives in the mighty praises of Lucan, Aeneas in those of Maro, largely by their own merits, and yet not least by the alertness of the poets. For us the troupe of buffoons keeps alive the divine fame of the Charlemagnes and Pepins in popular ballads, but of our modern Caesars no one tells: yet their characters, with their fortitude and temperance and the admiration of all, lie ready to the pen . . . great Alexander is my witness that many survive in the descriptions of authors, even all who have succeeded in living amongst men after their death.[27]

---

[24] The variety of humanist opinion is summarized, with texts, by Miglio, 'Biografia e raccolte', 167–76.
[25] *Matthaei Palmerii De captivitate Pisarum liber*, ed. G. Scaramella, RIS², xix, pt 2, 3.
[26] *Bel. Cat.* viii, tr. J. C. Rolfe (Loeb Classical Library, pp. 15–17).
[27] *De nugis curialium*, ed. M. R. James, revised by C. N. L. Brooke and R. A. B. Mynors (Oxford, 1983), 405.

Following Sallust again, Matteo Palmieri too saw the connection between historical understanding and biographical technique:

Glory is gained not by those who perform great deeds but by those whose deeds are well narrated . . . There have been many most noble peoples, many most excellent men who have done great and magnificent things but whose memory has not survived, not because they were unmemorable but because they lacked a biographer.[28]

Similarly, Accolti pointed out how easy it was to exaggerate the contrast between antiquity and modern times and to overemphasize the historical changes since antiquity. Explicitly following Sallust's lead, he links biography and historical analysis in his critique of ancient biographers who, he argues, were unreliable and exploited their literary skills to exaggerate the merits of their subjects; modern men appear inferior to the ancients only because moderns have lacked competent biographers to celebrate their deeds:

According to Sallust the deeds of the ancients were certainly great and magnificent; nevertheless, their writers had such genius that they made mediocre and often trifling deeds seem great through the force of their eloquence . . . Among the Greeks especially, innumerable fables are found in their books; the Latins too are not innocent of this offence. According to Livy . . . there was no limit on the falsehoods contained in history, authors including lies in their works according to their whims without regard for truth . . . How many deeds in these times [sc. the early middle ages] were done in France, Germany, Asia, Spain, Italy of which there remains little or no record? If such deeds had been chronicled by a literary master such as Livy, they would seem very great indeed and not dissimilar to those of the ancients themselves.[29]

As a work of history, the dialogue can be likened to an essay in which Accolti considers the relationship between two historical periods, antiquity and modern times, examining the changes which had occurred since the fall of the Roman Empire. The broad scope and profound analysis characteristic of this work can be seen in Accolti's discussion of why histories similar to Livy's and Sallust's ceased to be composed after the collapse of Rome; for Accolti, changing literary fashions became part

[28] *De vita Nicolai Acciaoli*, ed. G. Scaramella, RIS², xiii, pt 2, 4.
[29] Dialogue, fol. 16r–v: iuxta Sallustii sententiam res nempe antiquorum gestas satis amplas ac magnificas fuisse, verum ea vis ingenii apud earundem scriptores fuit, ut mediocres res plerumque etiam parvas, pro maximis sua eloquentia fecerint videri . . . apud Graecos maxime innumerabiles fabulae in eorum libris reperiuntur; Latini quoque nec talis culpae insontes extiterunt. Apud Livium . . . nullum in hystoria mentiendi modum fuisse; id est, auctores suo pro libito sua litteris mendacia tradidisse, non veritati studentes . . . *Ibid.*, fol. 17v: Quam multa inter haec tempora in Gallia, in Germania, in Asia, in Hispania, in Italia gesta sunt, quorum nulla, aut exigua extat memoria, quae, si Livium scribendi magistrum habuissent, amplissima et vetustissimis illis simillima viderentur (cf. Galletti, 111–12). The same Sallustian theme was taken up shortly after Accolti's dialogue by Cristoforo Landino in his *Proemio al commento dantesco*, published in his *Scritti critici*, i, 106. Cf. R. Cardini's full commentary, *ibid.*, ii, 112–15.

of the wider cultural transformations accompanying the fall of the Empire:

> I think this happened because, with the Roman Empire in decline and then collaps-
> ing, the barbarians who entered Greece and Italy changed the entire pattern of life;
> and, because they were hostile to learning, learned men saw that there would be no
> reward forthcoming and so they preferred to be silent rather than record the deeds
> of their times for posterity . . . Nor do I think there was any lack of learned or
> intelligent men then, for it is manifest that in those days every kind of literature was
> distinguished by men of accomplishment who, if they had applied their minds to
> history, would have been able to write with eloquence not inferior to that of
> previous writers. There was perhaps another cause, namely, that learned men of
> the Christian faith wanted to devote their labour to the deeds of the saints and the
> defence of their religion rather than to this kind of history; and once the tradition
> of writing history had disappeared and men's intellects had been turned time and
> again elsewhere, history was rendered almost mute so that the memory of the most
> eminent men has been obliterated, from the end of barbarian rule up to the present
> day.[30]

In considering the important historical questions posed by the dialogue, Accolti was guided by the traditions of rhetoric, for the comparison of ancients and moderns, which, it has been seen, was a fundamental commonplace of panegyric,[31] was also one of the most important themes of historical thought in antiquity, the middle ages and the Renaissance; the quarrel was a basic tool of historical analysis, enabling historians to consider questions of historical change and the relationship between historical periods. A famous example is the opening of the *Catiline Conspiracy*, in which Sallust drew a comparison between early Rome and the Rome of Catiline's day, showing how Roman society had degenerated since the end of the Punic wars.[32] Similarly, Carolingian historians and biographers such as Einhard and Walafrid Strabo observed that Louis the Pious's reign did not measure up to Charlemagne's, which they regarded as a golden age in contrast to their own times.[33] Thietmar of Merseburg (975–1018) used the terms *antiqui* and *moderni* in his discussion of the history of the Ottonian empire, contrasting the shortcomings of modern times, that is,

---

[30] Dialogue, fol. 16v–17v: idcircor accidisse reor, quoniam nutante iam Romano imperio et in occasum vergente, barbari, Graeciam et Italiam ingressi, omnem vivendi normam mutaverunt, et cum essent litteris infensi, atque illarum periti nullum propositum premium viderent, tacere quam monimentis res sui temporis gestas tradere maluerunt . . . Neque opinor ego tum defuisse ingenia doctissimorum hominum, quoniam liquet per ea tempora multos fuisse claros et in omni literarum genere peritos viros qui, si animum ad hystoriam applicuissent, forsitan non minore quam priores quidam eloquio valuissent scribere. Illa etiam forte suberat causa, quod Christianae religionis homines doctissimi magis in sanctorum rebus gestis et defensione fidei quam in huiusmodi hystoriis laborare voluerunt, et, cum ea scribendi facultas iam obsolevisset, alio iam semel conversis animis, etiam post exactum barbarorum dominatum usque ad haec tempora hystoria pene muta facta est et praestissimorum hominum memoria obliterata. Cf. Galletti, 111.
[31] Cf. pp. 194ff., *supra.*     [32] *Bel. Cat.*, v–xiii.
[33] Einhard, *Vita Karoli Magni*, in *Scriptores rerum germanicarum in usum scholarum* (Hanover and Leipzig, 1911), pp. XXVIII–XXIX, 1–2.

his own age, with the golden age of the ancients, who for him were Emperor Otto I (d. 973) and his contemporaries.[34] The crusading historian William of Tyre described the disintegration of the Latin kingdom of Jerusalem in the twelfth century, contrasting former times when friendship with Egyptian Muslims had brought prosperity to the kingdom with the present day when hostility with neighbours was leading the Latins to the brink of destruction.[35] A similar use of ancients and moderns to present an interpretation of history was made by Giovanni Villani, who, writing in the early fourteenth century, showed how the Florence of his day, riddled with faction and dissent, had degenerated from the good old days of the 1250s, when there had been a true spirit of the common good.[36] Indeed, Petrarch's analysis of the periods of ancient and modern history is perhaps the most famous example in the Renaissance of how the theme of ancients and moderns offered scope for historical reflection and analysis.[37]

Accolti himself used the rhetorical theme of ancients and moderns as a tool of historical analysis not only in his dialogue but in his narrative historical writing. To assess the achievement of Godfrey of Bouillon at the end of his history, Accolti compared him to Alexander the Great, who, he argued, was no more than Godfrey's equal:

I should praise him above Alexander of Macedon, who, driven by a lust for conquest without any just cause, provocation or injury, destroyed the wealth of the Orient, made great carnage of men, reduced many to slavery; he was born not to bring about the salvation of mankind but to wreak enormous calamity. Godfrey, on the other hand, undertook a pious and honest war in order to recover Christ's sepulchre, to spread religion, to lead many to virtue. As the one and only commander, Alexander with the strongest army inherited from Philip, himself always a conqueror, doubtless accomplished great things. Godfrey, without an empire, with untrained troops sharing no common language, customs and race who obeyed him voluntarily, together with other commanders in a short time conquered many provinces and many armies; his virtue stood out so far that the other leaders, although wealthy themselves, freely placed themselves under his authority. There is no record of temerity, pride, cruelty or extravagance on Godfrey's part, but there are many accounts of Alexander's intoxication, wicked fornication, slaughter of friends, of reckless deeds in battle, and he even proclaimed himself a god. Alexander was quick and bold, but Godfrey was considered the strongest man of his age. Godfrey was certainly unlucky because no author distinguished in eloquence and learning had celebrated his deeds, whereas the Greeks, who were

---

[34] Gössmann, *Antiqui und Moderni*, 36–7.
[35] Quoted by C. Haskins, *The Renaissance of the Twelfth Century* (Cambridge, Mass., 1927), 270.
[36] C. Davis, 'Il buon tempo antico', in *Florentine Studies*, ed. N. Rubinstein (London, 1968), 45–69.
[37] E.g. *Fam.*, VI, 2. Cf. T. Mommsen, 'Petrarch's conception of the "Dark Ages"', *Speculum*, xvii (1942), 226–42, reprinted in his *Medieval and Renaissance Studies* (Ithaca, N.Y., 1959), 106–29.

extremely erudite, championed Alexander not only with praise based on truth but even with fiction, without regard for the limitations of history.[38]

Accolti did not conceive of history as distinct from rhetoric; on the contrary, he regarded history and rhetoric as inseparable because it was eloquence which enabled the historian to perform his essential function of rescuing the deeds of great men from oblivion, and moreover, rhetoric gave him the tools of historical interpretation. The influence of rhetoric in his dialogue was not confined to form and style but very much determined the content and nature of his historical thought. For example, the critical judgement used by Accolti to evaluate differences between antiquity and modern times often derived from his attempt to compose a panegyric. This can be seen clearly in his discussion of Dante and Petrarch, which begins with a conventional comparison between them, as modern poets, and Vergil and Homer as the ancients: 'I should think that there were two men, namely Dante and Francesco Petrarch, neither of whom was inferior to Vergil or Homer in elegance, suavity and abundance of wisdom.'[39] Comparing modern and ancient authors was a standard technique of panegyric, and Accolti here was working within a well-established tradition.[40] However, rhetoric could also help the humanists to develop a more critical approach. This could occur when they were praising individuals who, like Dante and Petrarch, had received frequent praise before. In the attempt to compose a better encomium, they formed at the same time a more critical judgement. Sometimes they endeavoured to concede in advance arguments which might otherwise be held to refute their own – a rhetorical figure, known as *hypophora* or *subiectio*.[41] Thus, Salutati conceded that

[38] History, fol. 100r–v: Hunc igitur ego Macedoni Alexandro vera in laude anteferrem: ille libidine dominandi, nulla honesta impulsus causa, non iniuria lacessitus, Orientis opes evertit, magnam fecit hominum stragem, multos in servitutem redegit, non ad salutem hominum natus sed ingentem calamitatem; hic, ut redimeret Christi sepulchrum, religionem amplificaret, multos eliceret ad virtutem, bellum pium et honestum suscepit. Ille unicus belli dux, cum exercitu robustissimo sub Filippo semper victore, magnas res haud dubie gessit; hic, absque imperio, milite cum tirone, lingua, moribus et genere dissono, qui voluntarie illi parebat, una cum aliis multis ducibus brevi multas provincias, magnos exercitus superavit, in quo tanta enituit virtus, ut reliqui duces, licet opibus eminentes, ei sponte protinus cederent. Huius non temeritas in rebus agendis, non superbia, non crudelitas, non luxuries referuntur. Illius vero ebrietatem, nefarios coitus, amicorum cedes, temere multa in bellis gesta, sibi assertam divinitatem plurimi litteris tradidere. Ille manu promptus et audax, hic fortissimus omnium etatis sue habitus est, in eo sane prorsus infelix, quod eius res gestas nemo doctrina et eloquio prestans illustravit. Greci autem, viri eruditissimi, non modo veris laudibus Alexandrum, sed etiam fictis extulerunt, modum historie non servantes. Cf. *Recueil*, 611.
[39] Dialogue, fol. 41v: fuisse in primis duos, Dantem videlicet et Franciscum Petracum, quorum neminem elegantia, suavitate et sententiarum copia Virgilio aut Homero postponendum arbitrarer. Cf. Galletti, 122.
[40] Cf. Pliny, *Ep.*, VI, xxi; Curtius, *European Literature*, 163; Baron, *Crisis*[1], ii, 538–41; idem, *Crisis*[2], 258, 536 n. 24; Galletti, 15, 78; *Prosatori latini*, ed. Garin, 68.
[41] *Rhet. ad Her.*, IV, xxiii, 33; Quintilian IX, iii, 98.

Petrarch's Latin style (*facultas dicendi*) was inferior to that of the ancients;[42] Bruni admitted that Dante's Latin was poor[43] and that Petrarch's was imperfect;[44] and Manetti said that their Latin was inferior not only to the ancients' but to that of many of his contemporaries.[45] Accolti too concedes that, although Dante's *Ecologues* and Petrarch's *Africa* are not entirely without merit, they are nevertheless not equal to many ancient works.[46] A further refinement came by way of the commonplace that Dante and Petrarch were more versatile than the ancients. Thus Salutati, Bruni, Niccoli (in Bruni's *Dialogus*) and Manetti argued that Petrarch was greater than Cicero or Vergil because he excelled in composing both poetry and prose whereas they were proficient in only one or the other genre.[47] This, of course, was a veiled criticism and implied that Petrarch was, as a prose writer, inferior to Cicero and, as a poet, inferior to Vergil. Accolti himself varies this commonplace slightly when he praises Petrarch and Dante for writing in both Latin and Italian, thereby conceding by implication that their Latin was inferior to that of the ancients.[48]

As an historian, Accolti was perhaps most provocative and stimulating in discussing church history, to which he brought critical judgement and wide historical perspective. He criticizes allegations, for example, that modern clerics are corrupt, arguing that, however virtuous a man is, he will always find detractors, and that this is especially true of clerics, whose lives are scrutinized with particular zeal. Denunciations of the modern church must be regarded with caution according to Accolti, for there are many sinners who criticize virtuous clerics in order to draw attention away from their own vices; indeed, not even Christ and the apostles escaped calumny. Moreover, if modern clerics had not been of a high standard, Accolti asks critically, how could the church have survived for so many centuries? In evaluating both the ancient and modern churches, Accolti uses the balanced judgement of an historian: in antiquity there may have been saints, martyrs and scholars, but there were apostates, heretics and illiterates as well; similarly, in modern times there may be wicked clerics but equally there are many saints. Accolti as an historian was able to see the church as a particular historical institution whose character changes in the course of time: poverty may have been appropriate to the primitive church, but riches and luxury are needed by modern clergy to maintain the respect of the people; cardinals and popes as princes of the church need magnificence to make their authority effective. Accolti points out that it is not men but historical circumstances which have changed: if there were

---

[42] Baron, *Crisis*[2], 258.  [43] Bruni, *Vita di Dante*, in *Schriften*, 61–2.
[44] Bruni, *Vita di Petrarca, ibid.*, 65.  [45] Manetti, *Vitae*, in Galletti, 69.
[46] Dialogue, fol. 41v–42r; Galletti, 122.
[47] Baron, *Crisis*[2], 259; *Prosatori latini*, ed. Garin, 92–4; Bruni, *Schriften*, 67; Galletti, 84.
[48] Dialogue, fol. 41v; Galletti, 122.

more martyrs in antiquity, that was because there was more persecution; given the opportunity, men in the modern church would die for their faith. The mendicant orders were founded to revive the customs of the early church, but Accolti with his sense of history realized that they were a novelty of the modern church, different from any religious order of antiquity: from Saints Francis and Dominic 'grew new religious orders the likes of which antiquity never saw'. Particularly impressive is Accolti's sense of the historical evolution of civilization under the influence of Christianity. Modern men, he argues, may not be faultless, but the Christian religion has restrained their vicious inclinations; men have gradually abandoned barbarous religious rituals, indiscriminate slaughter in warfare and cruel pillaging of cities as the influence of Christianity has grown pervasive.[49]

The prevailing opinion during the middle ages and particularly the later middle ages was that the ancient church was superior to modern Christianity; however, it is clear that the modern church had sometimes been defended during the middle ages too. Eleventh- and twelfth-century canonists, for example, often distinguished between ancient and modern ecclesiastical customs without implying that the practices of the primitive church were to be preferred; moreover, canonists occasionally implied that the modern church represented a completion or further development of Christian antiquity and therefore was superior to the primitive church.[50] Similarly, a later medieval theologian such as Gerson looked to Christian antiquity as an ideal for the reform of the modern church, but sometimes he pointed to instances when the modern church had fulfilled the potential of the early church,[51] all of which implied a sense of historical development not dissimilar to Accolti's. Medieval canonists and theologians sometimes demonstrated an acute capacity for historical criticism, as for example in Rufinus's discussion of conflicting interpretations of scripture, in which he resolved an apparent disagreement between Augustine and Jerome on the reliability of exemplars of scripture by referring to divergent manuscript traditions.[52] Moreover, a fundamental principle in the interpretation of canon law and scripture was that attention had always to be paid to circumstances of place, person and time,[53] and so a theologian such as Gerson was by no means adopting an unprecedented method of argument when he maintained, like Accolti, that in the ancient church the success of Christianity was achieved through poverty and simplicity, whereas in the

---

[49] Dialogue, fol. 45v–55r; Galletti, 123–7.
[50] Olsen, 'The idea of the *ecclesia primitiva*', 70–80.
[51] Pascoe, 'Jean Gerson', 380–409.
[52] Olsen, 'The idea of the *ecclesia primitiva*', 77.      [53] *Ibid.*, 73, n. 34.

modern age of materialism it is more appropriate for the ecclesiastical
hierarchy to win respect with magnificence and external splendour.[54]

What distinguishes Accolti's justification of the modern church from
that of a theologian such as Gerson is that his arguments are predominantly historical, whereas Gerson mixes history with logic, analogy and
prophecy, for example arguing that the whole is greater than the parts,
comparing the modern church to a queen brought in splendour to her king,
and citing the prophecy from Isaiah that 'Kings shall be your foster
fathers'.[55] Accolti's predominantly historical outlook derives from
rhetoric, for a fundamental way of praising or blaming an individual was
to place him in an historical context. This is actually praise by reference to
external circumstances, a basic rhetorical commonplace.[56] The humanists
often praised Dante and Petrarch by putting them in historical perspective,
by saying 'they did very well considering when they lived' or 'it must be
remembered that they were the first to revive the study of letters'.[57] Thus
Accolti praises the modern church by reference to external circumstances
when he says that miracles are no longer necessary and criticizes the
ancient church with the same *topos* by pointing out that in antiquity there
were more martyrs because there was more persecution. Similarly, a commonplace of rhetoric was to praise an individual as the sole possessor of a
certain accomplishment: hence Accolti's praise of the mendicant orders as
a unique characteristic of the modern church. Medieval scriptural exegesis
and canonical interpretation was deeply influenced by the classical
rhetorical tradition, particularly after the twelfth century when more
emphasis began to be placed on the literal or historical significance of the
text;[58] this influence of rhetoric is clear for example in the historical
interpretation of the ancient and modern churches offered by Gerson.
What is significant is that medieval theologians and canonists did not offer
such an exclusively historical analysis of the development of Christianity
as did Accolti because they were not professional rhetoricians and so
included philosophical, analogical and prophetic as well as rhetorical
material. As a Renaissance humanist and professional rhetorician, on the
other hand, Accolti developed predominantly historical arguments as a
matter of course in his discussion of the ancient and modern churches.

Interestingly, it was another humanist who like Accolti developed an
almost exclusively historical defence of the modern church in the fifteenth
century. Lapo da Castiglionchio, in his *Dialogus super excellentia curie*

[54] Pascoe, 'Jean Gerson', 408–9.
[55] *Ibid.*, 403–4, 407.
[56] Cf. Quintilian III, vii, 13–14.
[57] For examples by Filippo Villani, Boccaccio, Vergerio, Poggio and Bruni, cf. Baron, *Crisis*[2], 260–8.
[58] Cf. B. Smalley, *The Study of the Bible in the Middle Ages*[3] (Oxford, 1983), 83ff.

*Romane*,[59] insisted that, whereas poverty suited the early church, the modern church needed wealth. Christ has to be poor, Lapo argues, in order to convince the world of his own divinity, because in that materialistic age a rich man would have gone unnoticed. Moreover, Christ had to confute extremely learned opponents, but since reason and argument were inadequate, he had to resort to miracles, which must have seemed all the more wonderful when invoked by a man of neither social background nor position. However, not all periods in history are the same. The church, well established in Lapo's time, needs wealth, for he lives in an age that admires riches and despises poverty. How ridiculous it would be to see the pope riding a donkey![60] Lapo's defence of the modern church does not have the wide range of Accolti's arguments, but it shows clearly that the germ of Accolti's historical interpretation of the modern church came from rhetoric.

One contribution to historical thought made by Accolti and his fellow humanists, therefore, was to move towards a more exclusively historical view of the development of the church; another was to simplify ancient and medieval concepts of historical periods. Implicit in the quarrel of ancients and moderns was a concept of historical change, an idea of contrast between two historical periods, and it was what authors meant by these historical labels – antiquity and modern times – that developed in the course of the quarrel. The contrast between *antiquitas* and *modernitas* is one of the most important themes in medieval thought; what is interesting is that medieval authors had no conventional definitions for these concepts. Sometimes the dividing line between antiquity and modern times was at the birth of Christ, as in John of Salisbury's distinction between *antiquae* and *modernae historiae*[61] or the famous contrast in the writings of the scholastics between the old testament as *fides antiquorum* and the new as *fides modernorum*.[62] Another scheme placed the line of demarcation in late antiquity, contrasting church fathers with medieval philosophers and theologians, the decrees of ancient and modern church councils, and ancient authors including the church fathers with medieval writers.[63] According to yet another concept the new logic of the twelfth century (*logica nova*) was contrasted with the old logic of Boethius (*ars vetus*);[64] along similar lines was the distinction between teachers of the

59   Ed. R. Scholz, *Quellen und Forschungen aus italienischen Archiven und Bibliotheken*, xv (1914), 116–53. Cf. Baron, 'Franciscan poverty and civic wealth', *Speculum*, xiii (1938), 29–30.
60   Ed. Scholz, 148–50.
61   Gössmann, *Antiqui und Moderni*, 70. Cf. *ibid.*, 51 (Augustine), 57 (Hugh of St Victor), 100 (Alexander of Villedieu).
62   *Ibid.*, 102–8, esp. 106–7.
63   *Ibid.*, 23–4 (Gelasius), 27 (Cassiodorus), 30 (Bede), 36 (Hrabanus Maurus), 38 (Berthold of Reichenau), 40 (Vincent of Lerinum), 46 (Humbert), 94–5 (Conrad of Hirsau).
64   *Ibid.*, 67, 73.

trivium and quadrivium as *magistri antiqui* and *moderni*,[65] and the famous contrast between realists and nominalists in the *via antiqua* and *via moderna* of the fourteenth and fifteenth centuries.[66] Another historical scheme, expressed in the concepts of *translatio imperii* and *translatio studii*, emphasized the continuity between antiquity and modern times, maintaining that the heritage of the ancients had been handed on to the moderns.[67] According to eschatological theories of history, the most famous of which derived from Joachim of Fiore, the crucial dividing line was not so much in late antiquity or even at the birth of Christ as in the present or near future.[68] One of the most pervasive concepts of antiquity and modern times in the middle ages derived from antiquity itself. In this scheme, in E. R. Curtius's words, 'from century to century, the line of demarcation shifts'.[69] As Horace wrote:

A writer who dropped off a hundred years ago, is he to be reckoned among the perfect and ancient, or among the worthless and modern? Let some limit banish disputes. 'He is ancient,' you say, 'and good, who completes a hundred years.' What of one who passed away a month or a year short of that, in what class is he to be reckoned? The ancient poets, or those whom today and tomorrow must treat with scorn?' He surely will find a place of honour among the ancients, who is short by a brief month or even a year. I take what you allow, and like hairs in a horse's tail, first one and then another I pluck and pull away little by little . . .[70]

One of the most famous medieval examples of this shifting antiquity comes from Walter Map, who said, 'I call modern times the course of the last hundred years',[71] and this practice of referring to the recent past as antiquity continued throughout the middle ages, for example, in the writings of Einhard, William of Malmsbury, Abbot Suger, Albertus Magnus, Aquinas, Roger Bacon and Rolandino of Padua.[72] This concept of an ever-expanding antiquity continues to be found in the fourteenth century: Dante called the contemporaries of Cacciaguida 'antiqui' in contrast to 'la cittadinanza, ch'è or mista',[73] and Filippo Villani, contrasting the 'saeculi praesentis ignominiam' with 'antiquorum virtutes', still meant by the 'antiqui' the contemporaries of Dante, 'nostri Poetae . . . Concives multi'.[74] Complexity characterized historical thought about antiquity and modern times in the middle ages; indeed, a number of authors, for example, John of Salisbury and Walter Map, used several of these different historical schemes in their writings.[75]

[65] *Ibid.*, 65.  [66] *Ibid.*, 109–16.  [67] *Ibid.*, 49–50, 81–2, 101.
[68] *Ibid.*, 56–62.  [69] *European Literature*, 253.
[70] *Ep.*, II, 1, vv. 34–46, tr. H. Fairclough, *Loeb Classical Library*.
[71] Curtius, *European Literature*, 255.
[72] Cf. Gössmann, *Antiqui und Moderni*, 36, 38, 39, 78, 79, 95; cf. Curtius, *European Literature*, 251–5.
[73] *Paradiso*, XVI, 49, 91.
[74] Galletti, 5.  [75] Gössmann, *Antiqui und Moderni*, 70, 73, 79, 96.

Simplicity, on the other hand, was the hallmark of the Renaissance concept of antiquity and modern times; the ancients, once and for all, had become, in Accolti's words, 'those who flourished once among the Greeks or Macedonians, or among the Carthaginians and Romans, under the republic or shortly afterwards under the Roman emperors'.[76] For Filippo Villani, writing in the medieval tradition, Dante was an 'antiquus',[77] but for Accolti Thomas Aquinas was a man of his own age, a 'neotericus' or modern in the words of Erasmus.[78] From the great variety of medieval schemes of antiquity and modern times, the humanists took one concept, in which antiquity ended some time between the fourth and sixth centuries A.D., and Accolti's dialogue is the clearest example of how the differing views of antiquity and modernity used during the middle ages to represent changes and developments in such fields as philosophy, literature, religion, morals, military practice and political life were simplified by the Renaissance humanists into one comprehensive historical scheme.[79]

### (ii) Historical method[1] in Accolti's 'De bello'

Accolti wrote his history to inspire crusading zeal among his contemporaries, and, in order to serve the Florentine government's diplomatic needs as well as to enhance his reputation as a humanist with the Florentine patriciate, it was important for him to put over this message as forcefully as he could. His history therefore had to be a work of eloquence so

---

[76]   Dialogue, fol. 3v (Galletti, 106): qui vel apud Graecos et Macedones quondam, vel apud Penos Romanosque, vigente republica, vel parum post ea sub Romanis principibus floruerunt.

[77]   Galletti, 5. It is interesting that the letter on ancients and moderns, written by Filippo Villani's contemporary, Giovanni Dondi, still preserves a certain complexity of historical thought reminiscent of medieval writers. In religious history, Dondi places the dividing line at the birth of Christ (Gilbert, 'Dondi', 331–2), whereas in secular history he places it in late antiquity (*ibid.*, 332ff.). Petrarch had placed the dividing line at the Donation of Constantine for both religious and secular history (cf. *Fam.*, VI, 2), and his professional humanist successors such as Salutati (cf. *De seculo et religione*, ed. Ullman, 128–31), seem to have found it easier to follow his lead than amateur humanists such as Dondi or Filippo Villani, who, as a physician and a lawyer respectively, were on the fringes of the humanist movement.

[78]   Curtius, *European Literature*, 251.

[79]   For a discussion of the influence of this historical scheme established by the humanists, cf. Ferguson, *Renaissance in Historical Thought*, 8ff. It is interesting that Ulrich von Hutten, in his *Epistolae obscurorum virorum*, parodied medieval usage of the terms 'ancients' and 'moderns' (cf. K. Gerschmann, 'Antiqui – novi – moderni in den *Epistolae obscurorum virorum*', *Archiv für Begriffsgeschichte*, xi (1967), 23–36; Gössmann, *Antiqui und Moderni*, 143), showing how conscious the humanists were of the changes that they had made in the historical concepts implicit in the quarrel.

[1]   Some works on early humanist historical method are E. Fryde, 'The beginnings of Italian humanist historiography', EHR, xcv (1980), 533–52; F. Gilbert, *Machiavelli and Guicciardini* (Princeton, 1966), 203–26, 332–5; Wilcox, *Development*; Santini, 'Leonardo Bruni Aretino'; Black, 'B.A. and the beginnings of humanist historiography'.

that he could persuasively offer the example of the first crusaders to his contemporaries; indeed, Accolti believed that earlier histories had failed to inspire enthusiasm because they were poorly written:

While reading recently, he wrote, books containing the deeds of those who recovered Christ's sepulchre and all Judaea, which were unsuitably written and lacked the embellishments of eloquence, so that they were little known, I was distressed that such men, by no means the inferiors of [the ancients], . . . had been cast into oblivion . . . If their memory were preserved, if their virtue, praise and name flew through the lips of men and were frequently read about in books, many men, led perhaps by a desire for praise or by shame or in the hope of heavenly felicity, would be inspired to the same virtue.[2]

Accolti was offering these men and their deeds as moral examples to his contemporaries and in bringing home the lessons of his history he regarded eloquence as indispensable. In this view of history as a teacher of virtue, he was following authors since Roman antiquity who agreed that history could not speak as a moral tutor without eloquence.[3] For a Renaissance humanist such as Accolti, eloquence could be achieved only by following the rules for historiography set out by such authorities as Cicero, Quintilian and Gellius and, above all, by imitating the paragons of Latin historical writing, Sallust and Livy.[4]

Accolti's preoccupation with eloquence and classical imitation can be seen in his use of sources. The main source of his history was the French version of William of Tyre's *Historia rerum in partibus transmarinis gestarum*, and he used two other sources, Robert of St Remy's *Historia iherosylimitana* and Marin Sanudo's *Liber secretorum fidelium crucis*.[5] Accolti was critical of these sources, especially because he thought they lacked eloquence and failed to imitate Livy and Sallust.[6] His contempt for William in particular is more easily understood if it is remembered that he was familiar only with the French translation, a popularization which omitted or abbreviated almost all the classical elements, such as quotations

---

[2] History, fol. 1v–2r: Ideo nuper libros legens gesta eorum continentes qui Christi sepulchrum Iudeamque omnem recuperarunt, inepte scriptos absque ornatu orationis, atque ideo paucis notos, egre tuli eiusmodi viros illis non impares quorum gesta prisci tradunt rerum scriptores ita obscuros factos, ut qui fuerint, que gesserint, pene ab omnibus ignoretur, eosque ingratissimos censui, magni certe criminis reos qui, doctrina eloquioque prestantes, hanc historiam non scripsere, illos obliti qui pro tuenda religione, pro salute generis, pro sola virtute dimicarunt, quorum si extaret memoria, si virtus eorum, laus, nomen per ora hominum volitaret et sepe in libris legeretur, plurimi forsan cupidine laudis vel pudore adducti vel ob spem celestis felicitatis ad eandem virtutem excitarentur (*Recueil*, 530).
[3] Cicero, *De oratore*, ii, 36; Aulus Gellius V, xviii, 9; Sallust, *BJ*, iv, 5–6; Livy, *Praef.*, 10; Guarino, *Epistolario*, ii, 462; 'Una lettera di Lapo da Castiglionchio', ed. Miglio, 22–6.
[4] George of Trebizond, *Rhet.*, fol. 82v–84r; Lapo da Castiglionchio, ed. Miglio, 28–9. 28–9.
[5] On Accolti's sources, cf. pp. 322ff., *infra*.
[6] History, fol. 1v; *Recueil*, 530.

from ancient authors, geographical descriptions, speeches and accounts of battles, found in the original Latin version.[7]

It was the lack of such classical details that led Accolti to look beyond William of Tyre; he changed from one source to another according to his idea of what a classical author would have included. For example, speeches in direct discourse were a typical feature of classical histories, and Accolti often sought additional sources to find more details of what a speaker had said. An example is Urban II's oration at Clermont in 1095; the French translation of William (in contrast to the Latin original) contained only the briefest summary of this speech,[8] so that Accolti turned to Sanudo's fuller version for more details.[9] Adhemar of le Puy's oration after the discovery of the true cross was mentioned by neither William nor Sanudo and it was from Robert of St Remy that Accolti learnt of it.[10] Another example is Bohemond's speech to his followers at the end of the first book, which had its source not in William but in Sanudo.[11]

Historians were frequently advised to aim at a flowing style, which was often achieved by Livy through carefully constructed transitions,[12] and Accolti on one occasion achieved such a Livian touch by changing his source. To recount the failure of some Germans and Frenchmen to organize a crusading expedition, he followed William of Tyre,[13] who, however, left the Frenchmen dangling in Apulia and abruptly turned to the departure of Godfrey of Bouillon in Germany.[14] Sanudo, on the other hand, having followed the Frenchmen to Apulia where they joined another crusading force, went on to pursue this new expedition from Apulia to Constantinople.[15] Sanudo used the survivors of the former expedition as a link between two episodes, and Accolti, seeing the literary merits of this version, abandoned William in favour of Sanudo, exploiting to the full the Livian possibilities.[16]

Digressions were commonly used by ancient historians to avoid an otherwise tedious narrative,[17] and Accolti sometimes turned to another source for the sake of this kind of variety. Following William of Tyre's account of the crusaders' journey up to Caesarea in Judaea, for example,

---

[7]  Cf. F. Ost, *Die altfranzösische Übersetzung der Geschichte der Kreuzzüge Wilhelms von Tyrus* (Halle a. S., 1899), 27ff.
[8]  Cf. William of Tyre, 39–42.
[9]  Cf. History, fol. 8v (*Recueil*, 536–7) with Sanudo, 131.
[10]  Cf. History, fol. 67r ff. (*Recueil*, 584ff.) with Robert of St Remy, 829–30.
[11]  Cf. History, fol. 25r ff. (*Recueil*, 549ff.) with Sanudo, 135.
[12]  Quintilian IX, iv, 18; X, i, 32–3, 73, 101; Cicero, *Orator*, 39 and *De oratore*, ii, 64; Lapo, ed. Miglio, 29; George of Trebizond, *Rhet.*, fol. 83r–84r; Walsh, *Livy*, 180–1.
[13]  Cf. History, fol. 22v–23v (*Recueil*, 547–8), with William, 66–9.
[14]  *Ibid.*, 68–9, 71ff.      [15]  Sanudo, 135.
[16]  Cf. History, fol. 23v (*Recueil*, 548), with Sanudo, 135.
[17]  Cf. Walsh, *Livy*, 156–7.

he turned to Robert of St Remy to include some details of Caesarea's history in antiquity.[18] Digressions regarding national character or history were common in classical histories, and Accolti turned the meagre opening sentences of William of Tyre into a full-scale essay on the origins of Islam, the early life of Mohammed and the customs and laws of the Muslims, for which his source was Sanudo.[19] Indeed, this entire digression is reminiscent of Sallust's discussion of Africa and its peoples at the beginning of *Bellum Iugurthinum*.[20]

Another feature of ancient historiography was recounting the careers and characters of leading figures,[21] and on one occasion Accolti turned to another source to include more details of the career of Kilij Arslan, the Seldjuk sultan of Nicea. Kilij Arslan had abruptly dropped out of William of Tyre's narrative after failing to prevent the crusaders from marching from Nicea to Antioch. Sanudo, on the other hand, followed this episode with an account of how, having encountered in his flight some reinforcements, Kilij Arslan discouraged them from engaging the crusaders, and Accolti supplemented his account from William with this material from Sanudo.[22]

Accolti had an overriding concern with the moral message of his history,[23] and so he frequently changed the source he was following to find examples of the crusaders' merits. An example is his account of the oaths sworn by the crusaders to Alexius Comnenus promising to restore any conquered territories formerly belonging to the Empire. For this Accolti turned from William of Tyre to Robert, making a particular point of the crusaders' altruism: 'For they had not taken up arms from a desire for conquest, but in order to liberate the holy sepulchre and Judaea'.[24] Another example is the surrender of Edessa to Baldwin of Bouillon. William of Tyre had said that the Greek ruler of Edessa at first offered Baldwin hospitality, but then, evidently realizing the threat Baldwin posed, plotted to have him killed; eventually, according to William, the Edessans themselves overthrew their lord and elected Baldwin in his place.[25] Sanudo, on the other hand, gave Baldwin no role in this suspect affair and simply said that, having arrived in Edessa after the Greek ruler's death, Baldwin was asked

---

[18] Cf. History, fol. 85v (*Recueil*, 598–9) with William, 310–12 and Robert, 858.
[19] Cf. History, fol. 3r–v (*Recueil*, 532–33) with Sanudo, 124–7.
[20] *BJ*, xvii–xix.
[21] Cf. *De oratore*, ii, 63; Sallust, *BC*, xiv–xvi, liv, and *BJ*, vi–vii, xcv–xcvi; Walsh, *Livy*, 82–109.
[22] Cf. History, fol. 41r–42r (*Recueil*, 562–3), with William, 129–34 and Sanudo, 139–40.
[23] History, fol. 2r; *Recueil*, 530.
[24] History, fol. 31v: Neque enim dominandi libidine ceperant arma, sed quo sacrum sepulchrum Iudeamque liberarent (*Recueil*, 555). Cf. Robert, 748–50.
[25] William, 154–9.

by the citizens to take his place.[26] Accolti chose Sanudo's version, which in contrast to William's, revealed no possible grounds for questioning Baldwin's conduct.

Moreover, Accolti was so preoccupied with classical imitation that when he found his sources not providing the right material, he tried to imagine what Livy or Sallust would have written. It is well known that histories written in the classical tradition included speeches composed by the historians themselves and Accolti's history was no exception.[27] But Accolti went much further and included in the actual narrative of his history long sections for which no source existed and which he himself had invented.

Accolti frequently, for example, took the opportunity to create situations of human interest similar to the pathetic scenes in Livy.[28] Once some stragglers from Peter the Hermit's army were attacked by Bulgarians from Nish. When the main army learnt of the incident, Accolti went beyond his source and imagined their reaction, emphasizing the depth of their anguish:

When this sad news was brought to Peter, he immediately despatched messengers to recall the front ranks of his army. Returning, together with the rest, they went to see the massacre of their comrades, and when they found so many dead, each of them wept aloud, condemning the nefarious deed and execrating such perfidy, then angrily demanded vengeance for this crime, stretching out their hands to heaven and invoking the revenge of God, for whom they were fighting.[29]

Another example is found in Accolti's account of the siege of Nicea, in

---

[26]  Sanudo, 141. For similar methods used by Biondo in the *Decades*, cf. Black, 'B.A. and the beginnings', 45.

[27]  Speeches in *De bello*: History, fol. 7v ff., 25r ff., 34v ff., 50r ff., 58r–v, 67r ff., 98r ff. (*Recueil*, 536ff., 549ff., 557ff., 570ff., 576ff., 584ff., 609ff.). Occasionally some topics in these speeches were taken from Accolti's sources: e.g. Urban II's account of the Muslim abuses of the Christians, the pollution of Christian churches, the violent circumcisions of Christians, their blood left dripping from altars, are based on Sanudo (cf. fol. 8v (*Recueil* 536–7) with Sanudo, 131). But Accolti invented most of the topics in his speeches, constructing them according to the rules of deliberative rhetoric: e.g. in Urban's speech Accolti starts with a *principium a re* and then divides the body (*tractatio*) of his speech into three *topoi*: *utile*, *honestum* and *facile*. In the same way, most of the speeches in *oratio obliqua* were almost entirely invented by Accolti according to deliberative rhetoric with little taken from his sources: e.g. Peter the Hermit's oration to Urban II in favour of a crusade contains only one argument from William of Tyre, the rest being composed using the *topoi necessarium, gloriosum, honestum* and *gratum* (cf. History, fol. 6r–v (*Recueil*, 534–5) with William, 35). For similar methods in Biondo's speeches in the *Decades*, cf. Black, 'B.A. and the beginnings', 48, n. 2).

[28]  Cf. Walsh, *Livy*, 191ff., 212–18.

[29]  History, fol. 15v: Hac re tam tristi ad Petrum delata, idem celeriter misit nuntios, qui ante pregressos revocarent; qui redeuntes et simul cum reliquis ad stragem videndam suorum profecti, cum tot occisos reperissent, quisque ipsorum vehementer flere, rem prorsus nefariam esse dicere, tantam perfidiam execrari, ulciscendum id scelus palam fremere supplices manus ad celum tendere, Deum vindicem invocans, cuius militiam assumpsisse (*Recueil*, 542). Cf. William, 53–4.

which he added details of the part of women and children in defending the
city from the crusaders:

Therefore, since punishment, horrible death, ruin of their city was before their
eyes, not only men of military age but women and children helped beyond the
limits of their bodily and mental strength, handing weapons and stones to the combatants . . . Mothers of families, handing weapons and stones to them, with their
hair dishevelled and weeping, begged the soldiers to use their valour and snatch
their relatives and children from the cruelty of the enemy.[30]

Formalities of diplomacy such as letters, congresses and councils were
important in Livy and Sallust[31] and were often invented by Accolti. One
example is the exchange of letters between Urban II and Alexius at the
beginning of the crusade;[32] another is the correspondence between the
king of Egypt and his subjects in Jerusalem urging them to resist the
crusaders.[33] Accolti said too that letters were sent from the leaders of the
expedition to Raymond of Toulouse to urge him to hurry to Nicea,
whereas his source William of Tyre had not specified that letters were the
means by which the message to Raymond was sent.[34] Accolti also states
that the question of the surrender of Gottschalk's army to the king of
Hungary was referred to a council of crusaders, although no such council
was mentioned in the sources.[35] He also says on his own authority that the
leaders of the plot against Baldwin in Edessa were invited to a council
where they were arrested.[36] William of Tyre said only that Alexius sent his
legates several times to ask Godfrey to come to Constantinople, whereas
Accolti assumes that a full-fledged conference took place.[37] Indeed,
Accolti's preoccupation with classical imitation is clear when he broadens
the scope of the council held on the day after Urban II's oration at
Clermont from a 'council of bishops' to a war council at which secular
princes or their legates were present.[38]

A particular virtue with which Accolti was concerned was concord,[39]
and to demonstrate the benefits of *concordia* and the disadvantages of
*discordia* Accolti frequently made additions to his sources, usually in the

---

[30]  History, fol. 38v–39v: Igitur cum supplicia, mors feda, ruina urbis essent ob oculos, non
   militaris modo etas aut virilis, sed femine puerique supra corporis atque animi vires
   aderant, propugnantibus tela ac saxa ministrantes . . . Matres familie, dum tela vel saxa
   illis porrigunt, passis crinibus, flentes orabant, ut, sua virtute, coniuges, liberos crudelitati
   hostium eriperent (*Recueil*, 560–1). Cf. William, 117–23.
[31]  Walsh, *Livy*, 84, 204–8; Sallust, *BC*, xxxv, xliv, 5, and *BJ*, ix, 2, xxiv, lxx, 5.
[32]  Cf. History, fol. 12v (*Recueil*, 539), with Sanudo, 132.
[33]  Cf. History, fol. 92v (*Recueil*, 604), with William, 335.
[34]  Cf. History, fol. 36v–37r (*Recueil*, 559), with William, 115.
[35]  Cf. History, fol. 22v (*Recueil*, 547), with William, 65.
[36]  Cf. History, fol. 76v (*Recueil*, 591), with William, 284–5.
[37]  Cf. History, fol. 30r (*Recueil*, 553–4), with William, 83.
[38]  Cf. History, fol. 11r (*Recueil*, 538), with Saundo, 131.
[39]  Cf. Walsh, *Livy*, 69–70; Sallust, *BJ*, xli; Cicero, *De officiis*, i, 25. Cf. p. 210, *supra*.

form of disagreements between leaders and followers in the crusading army. For example, he added that the men who were massacred by the people of Belgrade had gone foraging in defiance of Walter the Penniless,[40] and he added too that Peter the Hermit opposed the attack of Maleville in Hungary undertaken by his followers;[41] the result of their disobedience was that when Gottschalk's army, who were the next group of crusaders to follow Peter, passed through Hungary, they were slaughtered by the Hungarians in revenge.[42] On the other hand, when followers remained in harmony with their leaders, disaster did not result; thus Walter the Penniless was able to persuade his followers not to avenge their comrades who were robbed by the Hungarians, so that the army was able to move on in peace.[43]

Roman historians had stressed the role of the individual and especially of the leader in history,[44] and so Accolti emphasized the importance of leaders of the crusade more than his sources had done. The papal legate according to Accolti ordered the crusaders to use the winter after the Council of Clermont to prepare for the crusade, even though his role at that time is not made explicit by the sources;[45] similarly Accolti has the legate choose the new patriarch of Antioch even though William of Tyre does not specify by whom he was elected.[46] He stated that the lowering of Tancred's standard at Tarsus was Baldwin's work, when William of Tyre had stated that the people of Tarsus were responsible.[47] Another example is the plot in which an Armenian guard agreed to betray Antioch to the crusaders: in Accolti's version the crusaders worked out the details, whereas according to William the Armenian was responsible for the planning.[48] Accolti always emphasized Godfrey of Bouillon's virtue: thus he added as an apology a passage accounting for Godfrey's delay in beginning his expedition,[49] and he alone said that Godfrey went without escort to visit the emperor in Constantinople, thereby attributing to him greater courage than his source.[50] Similarly when the emperor's legates came to the army to protest that Antioch had been handed to Bohemond rather

[40] Cf. History, fol. 13r–v (*Recueil*, 540), with William, 48–9.
[41] Cf. History, fol. 14r (*Recueil*, 541), with William, 50.
[42] Cf. History, fol. 22r–v (*Recueil*, 547), with William, 50ff.
[43] Cf. History, fol. 13r (*Recueil*, 540), with William 48.
[44] Livy, *Praef.* 9; Walsh, *Livy*, 82ff.; Cicero, *De oratore*, ii, 63; Sallust, *BC*, xiv–xvi; Guarino, *Epistolario*, ii, 464.
[45] Cf. History, fol. 11v (*Recueil*, 539), with Sanudo, 131.
[46] Cf. History, fol. 73r–v (*Recueil*, 589), with William, 274.
[47] Cf. History, fol. 43v (*Recueil*, 564), with William, 141–2.
[48] Cf. History, fol. 61v ff. (*Recueil*, 579ff.), with William, 220ff.
[49] History, fol. 27v–28r (*Recueil*, 552).
[50] Cf. History, fol. 31r (*Recueil*, 554–5), with William, 87.

than the emperor, Accolti said that Godfrey alone received them, whereas William had said that the leaders as a group had been present.[51]

Related to the moral purpose of history is the exaggerated patriotism typical of Roman historiography;[52] for Accolti, the Romans were replaced by the crusaders, and he sometimes changed the account found in his sources to show them to advantage. One example is the aftermath of the massacre by the Bulgarians of the foragers from Walter the Penniless's army. According to William the main army simply moved on without vengeance, but Accolti, considering this unworthy of the crusaders, fabricated an entire episode showing the crusaders' proper revenge:

When he heard the noise of the fleeing soldiers and their pursuers and saw the cloud of dust caused by such a multitude of men, the commander together with his troops was roused from his camp and, leading his armed cohorts with him, he had not gone far before meeting the fleeing Frenchmen; and after reforming them into a proper battle line, he assailed the enemy, ferocious from their victory, and having put them to flight in a brief battle, he pursued them up to the city, killing many in battle and during their flight.[53]

Accolti also exaggerated the size of crusading armies in order to make the crusades assume the scale of Roman expeditions.[54] Thus Accolti declared that Baldwin took 6000 cavalry and 10,000 infantry on his Armenian expedition, whereas according to Sanudo he took only 200 knights and a 'multitude' of infantry.[55] During the siege of Antioch, Accolti said that 6000 cavalry and 10,000 infantry were put under the command of Godfrey and Baldwin, but William had said they went with only about 700 men.[56] Accolti also exaggerated the numbers of enemy killed in battle by crusaders. In one engagement near Antioch, Accolti said that 15,000 Turks fell, but William, only 2000;[57] in another, Accolti said that 6000 were killed, but William, only 2000.[58] Sometimes when his source did not cite the size of an army, Accolti supplied an exaggerated figure. William did not say how large the Muslim army was when the crusaders were attacked outside Antioch, but Accolti gave the figure of 150,000.[59] Similarly when William did not include the numbers fallen in

---

[51] Cf. History, fol. 83v (*Recueil*, 597), with William, 307–8.

[52] Walsh, *Livy*, 64ff., 144ff., 151ff.; Sallust, *BC*, vi–x, and *BJ*, xli, 2.

[53] History, fol. 13v: Auditus fugientium et insequentium clamor, visusque simul tot hominum cursu sublatus pulvis ducem a castris cum suis excivit, qui, secum ducens expeditas cohortes, non multum progressus, fugientibus Gallis obvius fuit; redactisque illis ad integram aciem, feroces victoria invadit hostes, fusosque levi certamine usque ad urbem est persecutus, multis in prelio et fuga occisis (*Recueil*, 540). Cf. William, 49.

[54] Cf. Walsh, *Livy*, 120–1, 144–5.

[55] Cf. History, fol. 46v (*Recueil*, 567), with Sanudo, 141.

[56] Cf. History, fol. 56v (*Recueil*, 575), with William, 195.

[57] Cf. History, fol. 60r (*Recueil*, 578), with William, 204.

[58] Cf. History, fol. 57r (*Recueil*, 575), with William, 196.

[59] Cf. History, fol. 37r (*Recueil*, 559), with William, 115–16.

battle, Accolti gave large figures. Thus, he added that 50,000 Persians and 3000 crusaders fell in the battle between the crusaders and Kerbogha[60] and in the defeat inflicted on Peter the Hermit by Kilij Arslan he added that the crusaders lost 15,000 men, the Turks, 2000.[61] At one point, Accolti exaggerated the number of casualties and prisoners, saying that 6000 were killed and almost the same number captured, whereas William had cited 4000 killed and a few captured,[62] but even so Accolti apologized for the crusaders' failure to kill even more Muslims:

> The slaughter of those fleeing was smaller, because nearby were woods and mountains which offered shelter to the enemy and impeded our men from pursuing, especially since they were unfamiliar with the terrain.[63]

Portraying the state of mind of historical figures played a major role in classical histories[64] and much of the narrative of Accolti's history is devoted to depicting psychology not found in the sources. Neither William of Tyre nor Sanudo had mentioned Urban II's state of mind on the eve of the Council of Clermont, but Accolti said that he was pleased that the council would be well attended and was sanguine of its success.[65] Nor had William discussed the emperor's thoughts while attempting to force the crusaders to swear homage to him; Accolti added that he was torn between a desire to avenge the injuries his subjects had suffered at their hands, and a fear that they might prevail in open battle.[66] Similarly, Accolti added to his account an interesting analysis of Ridwain of Aleppo's state of mind when he learnt that Godfrey was coming to raise the siege of Asarta. He was undecided, according to Accolti, whether to abandon the siege or to join battle: on the one hand he feared engaging such a renowned leader; on the other, he gained confidence from the thought of his large army.[67] Sanudo had said that Alexius had imprisoned Hugh the Great to force the other crusaders to swear homage to him, but Accolti went further, saying that Alexius was anxious lest, having conquered Asia, the crusaders should overrun his empire, that he especially suspected Hugh as the brother of the king of France, and that he hoped the crusaders would submit to the wishes of a prince of Hugh's stature.[68] Accolti usually expressed his psychological analyses in terms of the *topoi* of deliberative rhetoric. For example, he

[60]  Cf. History, fol. 73r (*Recueil*, 588), with William, 269–73.
[61]  Cf. History, fol. 21v (*Recueil*, 546), with William, 61.
[62]  Cf. History, fol. 38r (*Recueil*, 560), with William, 116.
[63]  History, fol. 38r: Minor cedes fugentium fuit, quod silve proxime montesque, in quos hostes refugerant, nostris impedimento ad persequendum fuere, presertim quia locorum ignari erant (*Recueil*, 560).
[64]  Cf. Walsh, *Livy*, 168ff., 191ff.
[65]  Cf. History, fol. 7v (*Recueil*, 535), with Sanudo, 131 and William, 39.
[66]  Cf. History, fol. 29v (*Recueil*, 553), with William, 80–1.
[67]  Cf. History, fol. 75r (*Recueil*, 590), with William, 280–3.
[68]  Cf. History, fol. 27v (*Recueil*, 551), with Sanudo, 135.

depicted Bohemond's indecision whether to join the expedition in terms of the commonplaces *utile* and *honestum*. It was dangerous to leave his home surrounded by enemies and unsafe to trust himself to the Greeks, who had been expelled from Sicily by his father, Robert Guiscard (*utile*); on the other hand, it was shameful to neglect the faith especially when there were so many others ready to come to its defence (*honestum*).[69] Robert of St Remy had said that the crusaders swore obedience to Alexius because they were entering a foreign land and faced the possibility of a shortage of supplies, but Accolti rewrote their motives in terms of deliberative rhetoric: they had not come to conquer but to free the sepulchre (*honestum*); they did not want to enter Asia with an enemy at their backs (*periculosum*); and they thought it unwise to diminish their numbers by having to garrison conquered cities (*temerarium*).[70]

Elaborately described sieges were typical of classical histories,[71] and these gave considerable scope to Accolti's inventive powers. One example is his version of Kilij Arslan's siege and recapture of a town seized by some German followers of Peter the Hermit, which is entirely fabricated by Accolti, who emphasizes in the Livian manner the psychological state of the besieged, and their desperate condition; equally Livian is the savagery at the end when Kilij Arslan slaughtered all the Germans and mutilated their corpses.[72] In his account of the siege of the Hungarian fortress by the German and French crusaders, Accolti added to William's account a description of the despair felt by the Hungarians after their recent defeat at the hands of the crusaders;[73] another example is the siege of Nicea when a

---

[69] Cf. History, fol. 24v–25r (*Recueil*, 549), with Sanudo, 135.

[70] Cf. History, fol. 31v (*Recueil*, 555), with Robert, 749.

[71] Cf. Walsh, *Livy*, 191–7; Sallust, *BJ*, xxi–xxvi, xxxvii–xxxviii, lvi–lxi, lxxvi, lxxxix–xci, xcii–xciv. Typical features were emphasis on psychology of besieged (cf. Walsh, *Livy*, 191–7; Livy, XXXI, xviii, 6–7 and XXI, xiv, 1); overall strategy of besiegers (cf. Sallust, *BJ*, lvi 1, xxv 9, lxxxix–xci); preparations of besiegers (cf. *ibid.*, xxi 3, xxxiii 1, xcii 7–9); vigorous defence (cf. Walsh, *Livy*, 191–7; Sallust, *BJ*, lvii 5–6, lx 1–6); role of the leader (cf. Sallust, *BJ*, xxiii 1 and xc–xci); and savagery at the end (cf. Livy, VI, iii, 6–9 and XXXI, xxiii, 7–8; Sallust, *BJ*, xci 6; *Aeneid*, ii, 368–9, which is quoted by Accolti in describing the fall of Antioch (History, fol. 62v; *Recueil*, 580)).

[72] Quod ubi Solimanus intellexit (iam enim non procul cum exercitu erat), ulcisci properans cladem acceptam, itineribus magnis ad eos contendit. Cuius adventu Germani attoniti, qui preter spem in hostes inciderant, deficere animis, per vias oppidi velut amentes cursare, tumultuari ad invicem, modo ad defendendum se accingere, modo fugam meditari. Cum vero subire muros viderunt hostem ac totis viribus oppidum aggredi, tum omnes trepidi muros conscendunt, animo ac viribus Persis impares, nec primum impetum eorum ferentes vel cesi sunt in ipsis muris, vel, se ex illis precipitantes, fuge aut latebre locum querebant. Quos persequentes undique hostes, qui iam intus irruperant, omnes ad unum occiderunt, avulsa humeris capita supra pila gestantes, tantum ira ob detrimentum acceptum et in Christianos inexpiabile odium preter sevitiam insitam eos commoverat (History, fol. 19v; cf. *Recueil*, 545, and William, 59–60).

[73] History, fol. 23v; recens victoria [of the crusaders] . . . aliis [the Hungarians] vero iniecerat metum, ut qui erant in arce, brevi spatio illam tutantes, tandem pene defensionem desererent (*Recueil*, 548).

complete blockade led, according to Accolti, to utter despair in the city: all
hope was now lost; no way remained open for flight or rescue; starvation
was inevitable unless Kilij Arslan arrived with relief; nevertheless, fear of
the enemy, regarded as implacable, made them carry on.[74] Another
example of an entire episode of a siege invented in the classical manner is
an unsuccessful assault on Nicea by the crusaders.[75] One classical element
was the emphasis on the besiegers' strategy: to attack the city after the
recent defeat of the Turks, before the citizens could collect themselves;
another, the preparations of the besiegers, investing walls, filling moats,
gathering ladders; a third, the psychology of the besieged: it was better to
die fighting than face capture; a fourth, the vigorous defence by the
besieged in which attackers were killed by weapons hurled from the walls.
Especially classicized was the role of the leader of the besieging army.
Accolti changed the place of Godfrey's feat in which he shot a Turk from
the wall with an arrow from its place in William's narrative after Nicea had
been blockaded to this unsuccessful attack on Nicea, in order to
demonstrate Godfrey's abilities as a leader and soldier. Accolti rewrote
William's account to make Godfrey's actions seem even more noteworthy,
for in William's version it was the Turk, not Godfrey, who had first
wounded many enemy with his bow.

The *pièce de résistance* of a classical history was the battle scene,[76] and

[74] History, fol. 39r (*Recueil*, 561), cf. William, 119–20.
[75] History, fol. 38r–v: Hoc prelio facto, duces rati oppidanos ea clade perculsos egrius
urbem defensuros, si prius eam oppugnent quam illi ex tanto pavore sese colligant,
postero die aggredi menia decreverunt. Ergo, postquam illuxit, instructi omnes subeunt
muros, et brevi momento ex parata materia fossas complent, scaleque multis erigi
partibus cepte, per quas in summum evadere promptissimus quisque studebat. Obsessi
vero, putantes ex se supplicium, non victoriam peti, minus acerbum fore censebant, si
pugnantes occumberent, quam si, diruta urbe, ante ora captarum coniugum
liberorumque, inter verbera et vincula, omnia feda atque indigna passi, expirarent. Igitur
cum supplicia, mors feda, ruina urbis essent ob oculos, non militaris modo etas aut virilis,
sed femine puerique supra corporis atque animi vires aderant, propugantibus tela ac saxa
ministrantes, et ipsi qui erant in muris certamine laboris ac periculi conspectu mutuo
accendebantur. Igitur, quanquam vi summa pugnarent nostri et fessis integri sepe
succederent, multique hostes vulnerarentur, multi etiam caderent, nec per aliquot horas
ulla eis daretur quies, tamen tantus fuit eorum ardor, adeo presens ad pugnam animus,
ut nostros tandem castra repetere coegerint, centum ex illis interfectis, quorum pars
maior, dum scandit muros vel scalas admovet, saxis est obruta. Quos inter nonnulli
fuerunt factis et genere illustres, multi quoque ex prelio saucii discessere. Nec est
silendum in ea pugna Goffredi facinus, qui, cum sagiptis plures barbaros confesisset,
animadvertens quemdam ex muris procero corpore latine loqui, suosque increpare stul-
tos imbelles vocitantem, sagipta eum transfixum precipitem ex muro dedit (*Recueil*,
560). Cf. William, 117–22.
[76] Cf. Walsh, *Livy*, 157–63, 197–204; Sallust, *BC*, lix–lx, and *BJ*, xlviii–liii, lxxiv 2–3, ci.
Battles in classical histories were characterized by such conventional features as a three-
part battle line (cf. Walsh, *Livy*, 161–2, 199), three stages in the fighting (cf. *ibid.*, 198–
9), ambushes and sudden attacks (cf. *ibid.*, 201–3; Sallust, *BJ*, liv 9–10, lv 8, lviii, lix 2–3,
xci 4, xcvii 4–5), an overall scheme of strategy (*De oratore*, ii, 63; Walsh, *Livy*, 197ff.;
Sallust, *BC*, lix, and *BJ*, xlviii–xlix, xcvii 3, xcviii 1–5, ci 3–4), an assessment of the

here Accolti excelled himself. One Livian technique adopted by Accolti was the division of a battle into stages, an example of which is the encounter of Peter the Hermit's army with the Bulgarians near Nish. William does not mention stages in the battle, but Accolti divides the fighting in the Livian manner: first, the front line of the crusaders retreat; then they pull themselves together and join battle; finally after an hour of equally matched combat the villagers retire.[77] Another characteristic of Livy's battle accounts was the division of the army into a three-part battle line, and this formation is frequently imposed by Accolti on troops not described in this way in the sources. An example is the engagement between Peter the Hermit's and Kilij Arslan's forces near Nicea, where William does not mention their battle formation, but Accolti describes a classicized three-part battle line;[78] another example is the battle between the Greeks and crusaders near Constantinople, where Accolti adds that the crusaders drew up a triple battle line.[79]

Classical authors frequently added to the drama of their battle accounts by introducing a subsidiary force, whose sudden intervention turned the tide of the fighting and which frequently took the form of an ambush. Accolti frequently made *insidiae* and sudden attacks important features of battles, even if there was no source for them. An example is the battle between Kilij Arslan and Peter the Hermit's men near Nicea. William of Tyre had said nothing about Turkish cavalry lying in ambush for the crusaders but, according to Accolti, the sultan hid knights in the forest who attacked the crusaders from behind and put them to flight.[80] Another example is Bohemond's march to Constantinople through Macedonia; William had said only that he was attacked by the Greeks, but Accolti turned the attack into a full-scale ambush:

Therefore, determined to execute his order, they placed their soldiers in ambush near a certain river, called the Bagdar then by the inhabitants. And on the next day, seeing that Tancred, Bohemond's nephew, had crossed the river with part of the army, they attacked the others who had remained on this side of the river, and having surrounded them on the front, rear and sides, they assailed the dismayed men so forcefully that they scarcely had an opportunity to collect themselves and prepare their arms.[81]

reasons for victory or defeat (cf. *De oratore*, ii, 63) and an emphasis on the role of the leader (cf. Sallust, *BC*, lx 4).
[77] Cf. History, fol. 16v (*Recueil*, 543), with William, 55–6.
[78] Cf. History, fol. 20r–v (*Recueil*, 546), with William, 61.
[79] Cf. History, fol. 31r (*Recueil*, 554), with William, 84–5.
[80] Cf. History, fol. 20r–21r (*Recueil*, 545–6), with William, 61.
[81] History, fol. 32v: Hi ergo, ad exequendum iussum intenti, prope fluvium quendam, Bagdarum tunc ab incolis dictum, suos milites in insidiis locant. Videntesque, die sequenti, Boamundi nepotem, Tancredum nomine, cum parte exercitus amnem transgressum, in alios qui citra flumen remanserant, impetum fecerant, et a fronte, a tergo, a lateribus circumfusi, ita perculsis institere, ut vix colligendi sui expediendique arma facultatem haberent (*Recueil*, 555–6). Cf. William, 92–3.

Following Cicero's advice and Livy's and Sallust's example, Accolti frequently imposed a scheme of tactics on the account of a battle found in his sources, as for example in his description of the battle between the Turks and the main crusading army before Nicea. After learning that they were about to be attacked, orders were given to the camp to prepare for battle, more guards were posted and each soldier was instructed to remain in his usual post in order to give the Turks the impression that they did not expect an attack. Part of the army was stationed to keep watch over the nearby villages, all baggage and wagons were put aside to facilitate defence; nobody was to mount his horse until the enemy was sighted, keeping their horses fresh to surprise the Turks.[82] Also in line with Cicero's prescriptions, Accolti often specifies the reasons for victory or defeat although they are not explicit in his sources. An example is his account of the battle between the Greeks and Normans in Macedonia, in which Accolti invents reasons why at first the Greeks prevailed but in the end succumbed. Had the fighting been longer, he said, the Greeks would have won because they outnumbered the Latins and their troops were fresher. In the end, they were put to flight by Tancred, whom they had not expected to be present.[83]

Another standard classical feature of battle accounts is an emphasis on the role of the leader, a feature which Accolti added to many of the battle descriptions found in his sources. For example, William did not mention Bohemond's individual role in the battle between his men and the Greeks, but Accolti emphasized his crucial contribution:

But Bohemond was unperturbed in this sudden affair; lacking neither spirit nor ingenuity he urged his men to battle, drew up the battle line insofar as it was possible, sent help to his struggling men; wherever danger was the greatest he was there; in short he neglected no duty of a leader.[84]

Accolti's account here is reminiscent of the part played by Catiline in Sallust's description of the battle against Marcus Petreius,[85] and Accolti draws even closer to Sallust's Catiline in his version of Godfrey's role in the battle with the Turks before Nicea. He adds that Godfrey exhorted his men to hold the line and resist the enemy. He ends by calling him, as Sallust had done Catiline, a great warrior as well as leader: 'he performed the art of not only a leader but a soldier'.[86]

[82] Cf. History, fol. 36v–37r (*Recueil*, 559), with William, 115.
[83] Cf. History, fol. 32v–33r (*Recueil*, 556), with William, 92–3.
[84] History, fol. 32v: At Boamundus, ut in re subita satis impavidus, nec animo neque consilio deficere, sed suos ad pugnam hortari, aciem, prout erat facultas, instruere, subsidia laborantibus mittere, unde maius erat periculum ibi adesse, nullum denique ducis offitium pretermittere (*Recueil*, 556). Cf. William, 92–3.
[85] *BC*, lx, 4. Cf. *BJ*, xcviii, 1–3.
[86] History, fol. 37v: nec ducis modo, sed militis arte fungebatur (*Recueil*, 560). Cf. William, 115–16.

Accolti did not merely adopt a few classical elements in his battle accounts and add them to his sources but almost completely invented many of the battles according to the classical pattern. An example is the battle between Kilij Arslan and Peter the Hermit which William of Tyre only summarized:

When our men were there and those who had not taken guard saw them suddenly, they ran for their lances and swords to avenge the deaths of their brothers. The infidel saw that the outcome was certain and that each man was fighting for his life, so that they assailed them very forcefully. The battle began cruelly, and many were killed here and there and it lasted a long time. But Kilij Arslan had many more cavalry, whom the crusaders on foot were no match for, and they took to the road without their equipment and baggage.[87]

Accolti's version, on the other hand, is very full indeed:

When our men drew near and the trumpets and horns had sounded, the lines joined battle and the noise grew. Soldiers fought and the leaders encouraged them with great vehemence. Our men were easily persuaded that the battle was not only for glory but for salvation; behind them the way back to Greece was closed and on enemy ground there was nowhere safe refuge, so that they had decided courageously to seek death rather than with shame to lose life or liberty. Therefore, although inferior in numbers, they tried their utmost to displace the enemy's battle line, but when he saw that it was disturbed, Kilij Arslan sent help to his struggling men, and ordered his cavalry who were on the flanks to surround the enemy from all sides, which was very easy since they were superior in numbers. And he sent messengers to his cavalry, whom he had hidden in the woods, to attack the enemy from behind. Their noise and especially their furious assault shattered the spirits of men who were hardly sustaining the battle on the front and the flanks, so that the Christians were having the worst of the fighting. For, only a few men had many adversaries, and the greatest part of them were fighting on horseback, using a new kind of tactics unknown to our men, first rushing at the enemy in a tight battle line, then, having dispersed, fighting now in one place, now in another, eluding the Christians, who were weighed down with arms. Another factor was that they were able to move about freely in the vast plain and could surround and weaken the infantry which was the major part of the Christian army and who were certainly having the worst of it. Moreover, on one side there was one commander with an obedient army, on the other, no one had command; whichever men were preeminent in nobility or prudence exercised the office of leader, and so they were not adequately obeyed by the soldiers, nor could they very often agree among themselves. All this caused enormous casualties. Nevertheless, our battle line would have remained firm despite their disadvantage if the enemy had not invaded from behind. At last this attack put them to flight, especially since they had no protection from cavalry.[88]

---

[87] *Ibid.*, 61.
[88] History, fol. 20v–21r: Propinquantibus nostris, cum utrinque tube cornuaque cecinissent, inter se acies, clamore sublato, conflixere. Summa vi pugnabant milites, et duces hortabantur. Nostris facile suasum erat non modo pro gloria, sed pro salute, id esse certamen, quibus mare a tergo viam in Greciam clauderet, et in hostili solo nusquam tutum refugium esset. Itaque decreverant animo mortem potius honeste oppetere, quam cum dedecore vitam aut libertatem amittere. Igitur, licet numero impares, vehementer

Accolti took only three facts from William: that the battle took place in a plain, that the crusaders were outnumbered and that the Turks had superior cavalry. The rest of Accolti's version is invented along classical lines. He emphasized the state of mind of the combatants: the crusaders were fighting not only for glory but for salvation; since they were trapped in a foreign land, they were willing to take on superior numbers. He imposed a scheme of tactics: Kilij Arslan ordered his cavalry, which had been stationed on the wings of the battle line, to surround the enemy. He invented a surprise attack by the Turks from behind, which became the turning point of the battle, and, at this point, he emphasized their psychological reactions. He added a description of the peculiar fighting manner of the Turks, rushing *en masse*, then suddenly thinning ranks; indeed, this was a frequent theme in Accolti's history and recalls the tactics of the Numidians as described by Sallust. At the end Accolti explained the reasons for defeat: they were outnumbered, unaccustomed to the Turks' unusual tactics; the battle was in a plain allowing greater freedom of movement to the enemy's superior cavalry; the Turks had an able commander, but the Christians had none.

Accolti's historical methods were influenced by theories and practices prevailing in the early Renaissance. In some ways, he was critical of his sources. He had access to Sanudo, a later compilation based on William and Robert, and perhaps mindful of Pliny the Younger's dictum that the great difficulty in writing the history of a remote period was collating the chronicles,[89] he was probably grateful for Sanudo's guidance. Neverthe-

---

annixi movere loco hostium aciem, quam ubi Solimanus vidit turbatam, subsidium suis laborantibus mittens, iubet equitibus, qui in cornibus erant, ut, his extensis, undique hostes circumdarent. Quod erat perfacile, cum longe numero prestarent. Misitque ad equites nuntios, quos in silvis condiderant, ut terga hostium invaderent. Quorum acceptus a nostris clamor impetusque maxime fregit eorum animos, cum vix a fronte cornibusque pugnantes iam sustinerent, et sane in multis non equa erat Christianis pugna. Nam pauci multos habebant hostes, et horum pars maxima et equis certabat, novo etiam prelii genere nostris incognito, cum modo agmine densi in hostem ruerent, modo rari dispersique nunc uno in loco, nunc in alio dimicarent, graves armis Christianos eludebant. Accedebat preterea quod in vasta planitie vagandi liberius potestatem habebant, nostrosque omni ex parte circumdandi ac dissipandi protinus pedites, quorum pars maior exercitus erat, qui haud parem cum ipsis in eo loco dimicationem habebant. Ab una item parte dux unus erat ac miles duci maxime fidens, ab altera nemo imperio precellebat; qui vero nobilitate aut prudentia pollebant munere ducum fungebantur, ideoque non satis illis parebant milites, nec ipsi plerunque in idem conveniebant. Que res frequenter ingentium cladium causa fuit. In tanta rerum iniquitate stetisset tamen nostrorum acies, vel saltem diutius fuisset pugnatum, ni hostis a tergo invasisset. Is demum impetus fudit eos, presertim cum ibi nullum equestre presidium esset (*Recueil*, 546). Other examples of classicized battle scenes in *De bello*: History, fol. 40v ff., 49r ff., 55r–55v; 56v ff., 57v ff., 58v ff., 70r ff., 75r–v, 81v, 101v ff. (*Recueil*, 562ff., 569, 574, 575, 576, 577–8, 586ff., 590, 598, 612ff.). For similar classical inventions in Biondo and Bruni, cf. Black, 'B.A. and the beginnings', 51–2.

[89] *Ep.*, V, 8.

less, Sanudo did not supplant the original sources, and Accolti displayed a certain critical awareness in rejecting Sanudo as his main source in favour of William who was nearer to being a contemporary of the events. Accolti's preference for eye-witness or contemporary accounts derived from long-standing assumptions about historical method, originating not from classical theories but from medieval hagiography; few lives of saints opened without affirming that the miraculous events recounted either had been seen by the author or could be verified by the most trustworthy witnesses,[90] and this preoccupation with eye-witness evidence was transformed by Isidore of Seville into a theory of historical criticism:

None of the ancients would write history unless he had been present and had seen what he narrated; we grasp what we see better than what we gather from hearsay. Things seen are not represented falsely.[91]

The most distinguished medieval historians repeated these views,[92] which continued to hold sway among early humanists such as Lapo da Castiglionchio, who praised Biondo in particular for his attention to eye-witness accounts:

You have most diligently obeyed the laws of history, for you have either taken part yourself in the events which you report; or, if you were not present, you have made careful enquiry among eyewitnesses, from whom you have taken your information.[93]

Similarly Valla assumed that wherever possible history should be written by an eye-witness or based on the accounts of participants; although aware of the problems inherent in using eye-witness sources, Valla continued to assume that the historian who took part in events was particularly fortunate and that any difficulties encountered in using this evidence simply proved how difficult it was to be an historian.[94]

Moreover, Accolti attempted to exclude obvious bias from his work. For the humanists, historical truth had a specific meaning derived from Cicero's *De oratore*, where the emphasis was on avoiding personal bias:

For who does not know history's first law to be that an author must not dare to tell anything but the truth? And its second that he must make bold to tell the whole truth? That there must be no suggestion of partiality anywhere in his writings? Nor of malice?[95]

[90] I am grateful to Mr A. Spitzer for this interesting point.
[91] Quoted by B. Smalley, *Historians in the Middle Ages* (London, 1974), 24.
[92] E.g. William of Malmsbury, *De gestis regum anglorum libri quinque*, ed. W. Stubbs (London, 1887–9), i, 3; Robert, 721–3; Fulcher Carnotensis, *Historia iherosolymitana*, in *Recueil des historiens des croisades. Historiens occidentaux*, iii (Paris, 1866), 319.
[93] Lapo, ed. Miglio, 28.
[94] L. Valla, *De laude historiae*, in *Gesta Ferdinandi Regis Aragonum*, ed. O. Besomi (Padua, 1973), 7–8.
[95] II, 62, tr. E. W. Sutton, Loeb Classical Library, i, 243–5.

This definition was paraphrased by Lapo da Castiglionchio in his letter on historiography to Biondo[96] and restated in his well-known treatise on history by Guarino, who was able to develop his entire discussion of historical truth from it, by paraphrasing material from Lucian's *De historia conscribenda*.[97] For his part, Accolti made a considerable effort to omit or alter passages in his sources which showed prejudice; the Western chronicles written at the time of the crusaders were biased against the Greeks, and Accolti went to some lengths to expurgate these prejudices. For example, William of Tyre included this unfavourable account of the rise to power of the Byzantine emperor, Alexius Comnenus:

At this time the emperor in Constantinople was a false, treacherous and disloyal Greek, Alexius Comnenus. He had been most intimate with the previous emperor, Nicephorus Boteniat, so that he had been made his seneschal and had become the most important man in the realm after the emperor. He maliciously conceived evil designs towards his lord, and with the approval of the great men who were close to him, he seized the emperor and held him in his castle for six years when our crusaders arrived there.[98]

Rewriting this passage, Accolti left out all reference to Alexius's treachery and malice: 'The emperor then ruling had deposed Nicephorus, whose minister he had been, and was holding him prisoner.'[99] Similarly, Accolti omitted sections of William's chronicle which depicted the miserable state of the Byzantine Empire at the time of the crusade,[100] as well as those in which William discussed Alexius's treacherous motives for wanting the crusaders quickly to pass beyond Constantinople.[101] Another example is William's unfavourable portrait of Alexius's lieutenant, Tactitius, which is not included in Accolti's history.[102] The imprisonment of Hugh the Great might have given a bad impression of Alexius, so that Accolti added to Sanudo's account that Alexius treated Hugh's men at that time 'with friendship and hospitality'.[103]

Accolti's attitude to historical truth might seem contradictory. On the one hand, he showed his concern for historical truth with his quest for contemporary sources and his attempt to eliminate bias; on the other hand, he seemed oblivious to historical fidelity when inventing much of the material for his history. Moreover, Accolti clearly disdained such simple forms of historical research as checking the accuracy of his sources, and he made no attempt to synthesize the material found in them. For example, in

[96] Lapo, ed. Miglio, 28.    [97] Guarino, *Epistolario*, ii, 461.    [98] William, 79.
[99] History, fol. 18v: Tertiusque ab eo Diogene regnabat princeps, qui Nichoforum, cuius ipse fuerat minister, privatum imperio nexum tenebat. Cf. *Recueil*, 544.
[100] Cf. History, fol. 29r ff. (*Recueil*, 553ff.), with William, 77–9.
[101] Cf. History, fol. 31v–32r (*Recueil*, 555ff.), with William, 90.
[102] Cf. History, fol. 56r ff. (*Recueil*, 575), with William, 186–7.
[103] Cf. History, fol. 27v: amice hospitaliterque (*Recueil*, 551), with Sanudo, 135.

his account of the beginning of the expedition of Raymond of Toulouse, Adhemar of le Puy and Bohemond, Accolti's source was Sanudo and not Robert, who included much not found in Accolti.[104] If Accolti had actually used Sanudo together with Robert, one might expect to find some trace of Robert in Accolti's version, which is almost identical to Sanudo's. Similarly, in the passage narrating the flight of Kilij Arslan after the fall of Nicea, again no details from Robert's account can be detected.[105] Nor did Accolti, when introducing the leaders of the crusade, use any source other than Sanudo, whom he copied almost verbatim, even though he could have gained further information from William's fuller account.[106] Some notable blunders are directly due to Accolti's failure to check his facts. For example, he said that the siege of Nicea lasted thirty days,[107] but if he had consulted Robert he would have found that it lasted fifty-two.[108] Similarly he stated that at the Council of Clermont Adhemar of le Puy had willingly taken charge of the crusade as papal legate,[109] whereas Robert had made a point of saying that Adhemar had been unwilling.[110]

Accolti's attitude to historical truth may appear paradoxical, but humanists took classical concepts of historical truth literally. In antiquity, it was often held that there were two levels of truth in history: on the surface were the simple facts – dates, names and events; below was the whole truth – causes, motives, character, background and strategy. It was this deeper truth which distinguished history from chronicle.[111] Facts alone could not 'make men more eager to defend their country, or more reluctant to do wrong'; only greater profundity could provide the moral force which a humanist such as Accolti sought for his history.[112] Cicero, in a renowned passage of *De oratore*, had been specific about what made up the deeper layers of history,[113] and his words were paraphrased by theorists of history in the early Renaissance.[114] Accolti may have thought that care with original and contemporary sources was worthwhile, but he knew that this was not the ultimate work of the historian. The deeper truth was what mattered and it is not surprising if Accolti disregarded the simpler forms of historical research such as checking the accuracy of his

[104] History, fol. 23v–24r (*Recueil*, 548); Robert, 739–40; Sanudo, 135.
[105] History, fol. 42r (*Recueil*, 563); Robert, 764–6; Sanudo, 139–40.
[106] History, fol. 11v–12r (*Recueil*, 539); Sanudo, 131–2; William, 45–6.
[107] History, fol. 40v; *Recueil*, 562.    [108] Robert, 758.
[109] History, fol. 11v (*Recueil*, 539).
[110] Robert, 731. For similar methods used by Biondo, cf. Black, 'B.A. and the beginnings', 46–7.
[111] Cf. *De oratore*, ii, 51–64; Aulus Gellius V, xviii, 8–9.
[112] *Ibid.*, V, xviii, 9, translated by J. C. Rolfe, Loeb Classical Library.
[113] II, 63.
[114] George of Trebizond, *Rhet.*, fol. 82v; Guarino, *Epistolario*, ii, 463–4; Lapo, ed. Miglio, 28–9.

sources. For his classical preceptors clearly disparaged research aimed at establishing mere facts. 'But between those who have desired to leave us annals, and those who have tried to write the history of the Roman people there was this essential difference. The books of annals merely made known what happened and in what year it happened', wrote Asellio *apud Gellium*.[115] 'For my part I realize that it is not enough to make known what has been done, but that one should also show with what purpose and for what reason things were done.' Reporting the bare facts alone – 'that is to tell stories to children, not to write history'.[116] Guarino as good as invited such inventions as were made by Accolti, evidently not regarding them as violations of historical truth, but as ways of fulfilling Cicero's requirements.[117] Guarino's description of the bare facts as 'naked and insipid' recalls Cicero's and Asellio's disdain for the jejune narrative annals and suggests that a humanist such as Accolti regarded such embellishments as essential elements of history, not as transgressions of the laws of truth.

In rhetorical theory current in the early Renaissance, moreover, truth did not signify adhering scrupulously to the sources but meant what was probable or plausible.[118] In the ancient system of rhetoric as transmitted to the middle ages and Renaissance, fact and what was probably fact were inextricably intertwined. For example, invention or devising what to say was defined as 'the devising of matter, true or plausible, that would make the case convincing';[119] moreover, narration, which 'sets forth the events that have occurred or might have occurred', had to have three qualities – brevity, clarity and plausibility – but not absolute truth.[120] A humanist historian such as Accolti was only following the rules of rhetoric by including in his narrative both fact and invented material which appeared to be fact; indeed, this mixture of fact and the semblance of fact precisely describes the contents of Accolti's history. Moreover, a humanist such as Accolti may actually have believed that the kind of material he added to his sources – causes, strategy, geography, speeches, councils – in itself made his work more plausible: all this subject matter, according to Lapo da Castiglionchio, 'signifies the prudence and diligence of the writer and

---

[115] V, xviii, 8, tr. Rolfe.
[116] *Ibid.*, V, xviii, 8–9 (tr. Rolfe). Cf. *De oratore*, ii, 52ff.
[117] Guarino, *Epistolario*, ii, 463–4.
[118] For the connection between rhetoric and history, cf. *De oratore*, ii, 36; George of Trebizond, *Rhet.*, fol. 84r; Guarino, *Epistolario*, ii, 459.
[119] *Rhet. ad Her.*, I, ii, 3 (tr. H. Caplan, Loeb Classical Library, p. 7); *De inventione*, I, vii, 9. George of Trebizond placed no limits on the range of invention for an historian: nihil inventionis praetermittere historici quoque conentur (*Rhet.*, fol. 82v).
[120] *Rhet. ad Her.*, I, ii, 4 (tr. Caplan, p. 9), and I, ix, 14; *De inventione*, I, xix–xx, 27–8. For the importance of preserving plausibility, but not truth, in narrative, cf. *Rhet. ad Her.*, I, ix, 16, and Guarino, *Epistolario*, ii, 465.

renders his history itself more credible' (ipsam probabiliorem hystoriam reddunt).[121]

Because of their apparent indifference to historical accuracy, humanists such as Accolti have been condemned as second-rate historians and their works have been written off as rhetorical exercises. However, history has never been a mere catalogue of documents, literally recording unquestionable facts; since antiquity it has always been the historian's duty to look beyond the surviving evidence and in this task of recreating the past the role of historical imagination is paramount. In the early Renaissance, under the influence of rhetoric, a concern with the plausible stimulated the humanists' historical imagination. By modern standards the early humanists such as Accolti let their imaginations go too far, but it would be wrong to condemn his work as unhistorical. Accolti regarded history as a medium for displaying his eloquence and demonstrating his ability to imitate Livy and Sallust, and the enthusiasm with which he exercised his historical imagination is the best evidence of his genuine commitment to history.

## (iii) Accolti and Renaissance medievalism[1]

The Italian Renaissance saw a great burgeoning of historical writing, and Renaissance historians not only cultivated fields of historical study well-established in the middle ages but also broke new ground. Not merely the first Byzantinists,[2] the first classical archaeologists,[3] and the first Islamic historians,[4] the Italian humanists became the first medievalists and founded the study of medieval history. It is true that throughout the middle ages, the history of post-classical Europe, from the decline of the Western Empire to the contemporary world of the writer, had been chronicled; the medieval historian ostensibly covered much of the same ground as his Renaissance successor. Nevertheless, there are a number of reasons to suggest that the study of medieval history as a specialized field of historical research did not really exist before the Renaissance.

In the first place, the Renaissance humanists invented the idea of the

---

[121] Lapo, ed. Miglio, 28–9.

[1] The only general treatment of medieval studies in the Italian Renaissance is the inaugural lecture by Giacinto Romano, *Degli studi sul medio evo nella storiografia del Rinascimento in Italia* (Pavia, 1892). For particular aspects cf. also C. Dionisotti, 'Medioevo barbarico e cinquecento italiano', in *Concetto, storia, miti et imagini del medio evo*, ed. V. Branca (Florence, 1973) (*Civiltà europea e civiltà veneziana. Aspetti e problemi*, 7); Gustavo Costa, *Le antichità germaniche nella cultura italiana da Machiavelli a Vico* (Naples, 1977).

[2] Cf. A. Pertusi, *Storiografia umanistica e mondo bizantino* (Palermo, 1967).

[3] Cf. R. Weiss, *The Renaissance Discovery of Classical Antiquity* (Oxford, 1969).

[4] Cf. Pertusi, 'I primi studi'.

middle ages as a time between classical antiquity and their own period of revived classicism,[5] and so it is obvious that they had to be the first students of a period which they themselves had created. The fact that Renaissance scholars were now consciously working in a newly defined historical period had distinctive effects in their writings. Renaissance historians in fact launched the first revolt of the medievalists, anticipating the eighteenth-century Gothic Revival, the Romantic medievalism of the nineteenth century and the denigration of the Renaissance itself by twentieth-century medievalists.[6] Thus, in order to justify their period as one worthy of study, some Renaissance medievalists defined the middle ages, like their successors, as an age of faith in contrast to classical antiquity;[7] they defended the merits of typically medieval fields of learning such as scholasticism and the revival of Roman law, attacking the empty rhetoric of some of their own fellow humanists;[8] they defended the humble medieval chronicle as more reliable than classical or classicized literary history;[9] they pointed to the great medieval religious revival initiated by the Gregorian Reform and continued by the mendicants as the achievements of a strong and vital church;[10] they saw the crusades as the culmination of all that was quintessentially medieval.[11] Despite the large amount of historical writing undertaken during the middle ages themselves, a coherent picture of the medieval period did not emerge until the Renaissance; the portrait of a distinctive middle ages, of medieval culture different yet worthy in its own right, is due to the Renaissance medievalists and their efforts to take a positive view of their particular period of study.

Renaissance medievalists also gave birth to the medieval monograph. Most medieval historical writing took the form of encyclopedias with some historical content, universal histories, ecclesiastical histories, monastic histories, historical biographies, national histories and civic histories;[12] in the middle ages there were writers of monographs who often followed Sallust's model, but like Sallust, such authors wrote about their

---

[5] Cf. G. Gordon, '*Medium aevum* and the Middle Ages', *Society for Pure English, Tract* xix (1925), 3–28; N. Edelman, 'The early uses of *Medium Aevum, Moyen Âge, Middle Ages*', *The Romanic Review*, xxix (1938), 3–25; idem, 'Other early uses of *Moyen Âge* and *Moyen temps*', *ibid.*, xxx (1939), 327–30; H. Weisinger, 'The Renaissance theory of the reaction against the Middle Ages as a cause of the Renaissance', *Speculum*, xx (1945), 461–7. For an early use of *media barbaries* by G. A. Campano, cf. Gatti, ' "Vita Caroli" ', 231.

[6] Cf. Ferguson, *Renaissance in Historical Thought*, 78ff. for these later developments.

[7] Cf. Gilbert, 'Dondi', 331–2.

[8] Cf. Seigel, 'Teaching of Argyropulos', 246ff.; Kristeller, *Studies*, 146, 573, n. 60; Q. Breen, 'Giovanni Pico della Mirandola on the conflict of philosophy and rhetoric', JHI, xii (1952), 384–426; Rinuccini, *Lettere ed orazioni*, ed. Giustiniani, 86–104.

[9] Cf. Landino, *Scritti critici*, ed. Cardini, i, 106; ii, 47–8, 112–14.

[10] Cf. p. 328, *infra*.        [11] Cf. Ch. 9, i, ii, iv, *supra*.

[12] Cf. *Typologie des sources du moyen âge occidental*, ed. L. Genicot (Turnhout, 1972– ).

own time or a period shortly before.[13] In the Renaissance, there was a renewed fashion for the historical monograph, stimulating many such works on contemporary history, but some of these Renaissance monographs were also devoted to the new fields of historical study such as Turkish history[14] and Byzantine history.[15] There were also many monographs now devoted to topics in the remote medieval past such as the origins and early history of cities,[16] the early history of noble families,[17] the lives of great individuals from the early medieval past,[18] medieval wars,[19] and the early history of cities.[20]

During the Renaissance research into the early medieval past reached a new level. For historians in the middle ages, investigation of earlier periods of post-classical history had usually been the prelude to contemporary or recent history, and some of the medieval history undertaken in the Renaissance was similarly a backdrop, sketched in without much interest in the earlier period for its own sake. However, in the Renaissance there also developed a much more wide-ranging investigation of earlier medieval periods: a wide variety of chronicles were consulted, certainly more than were necessary to fill in the background;[21] archaeological[22] and archival materials were used;[23] languages such as old French[24] and Greek[25] were read to provide new sources. On certain key issues such as the foundation of a city, an even wider spectrum of sources was examined, and indeed it

---

[13] Cf. B. Smalley, 'Sallust in the middle ages', in *Classical Influences on European Culture*, ed. R. Bolgar (Cambridge, 1971), 165–75; an example of a Sallustian monograph is Buoncampagno di Signa's *Liber de obsidione Ancone*, ed. G. C. Zimolo, RIS², vi, pt 3.

[14] Cf. Pertusi, 'I primi studi'.      [15] Cf. *idem, Storiografia umanistica*.

[16] E.g. Bernardo Giustiniani's *De origine urbis gestisque Venetorum*, in *Thesaurus antiquitatum et historiarum Italiae*, J. G. Graevius, V, i (Leiden, 1722).

[17] E.g. Giorgio Merula's *Antiquitatis Vicecomitum libri X, ibid.*, III, i (Leiden, 1704).

[18] E.g. Donato Acciaiuoli's *Vita Caroli Magni*, ed. M. F[reher], in *Corpus Franciae Historiae veteris et sincerae* (Hanoviae, 1613), ii, 549–59, and J. B. Mencke, *Scriptores rerum germanicarum*, i (Leipzig, 1728), 813–32; cf. Gatti, ' "Vita Caroli" '. Paolo Giovio included biographies of Atila, Totila, Charlemagne, Barbarossa and Saladin in his *Elogia virorum bellica virtute illustrium* (Venice, 1546).

[19] E.g. Benedetto Mastiani's *De bello Balaerico a Pisanis gesto libri II*, ed. D. Moreni (Florence, 1810).

[20] E.g. Carlo Sigonio's *Historiarum Boneniensium libri sex* in his *Opera omnia*, ed. L. Muratori (Milan, 1732–7), iii.

[21] E.g. cf. P. Buchholz, *Die Quellen der Historiarum Decades Flavius Blondus* (Naumburg, 1881); A. Hessel, *'De Regno Italiae Libri Viginti' von Carlo Sigonio: Eine quellenkritische Untersuchung* (Berlin, 1900). Cf. Aeneas Sylvius's study of Otto of Freising in his *Hist. Frid. III*, in A. F. Kollar, *Analecta monumentorum* (Vienna, 1764), ii, 29, and G. Billanovich, 'Gli umanisti e le croniche medievali', IMU, i (1958).

[22] Cf. Hay, 'Biondo and the middle ages', 111–12.

[23] Cf. Santini, 'Leonardo Bruni Aretino', 50ff.      [24] Cf. pp. 322–4, *infra*.

[25] Cf. Pertusi, *Storiografia umanistica*, 12–24, esp. 21–4.

became a matter of competition among scholars to flaunt how many sources had been consulted over these hotly debated questions.[26]

The pioneers in this new field of medieval history were Leonardo Bruni, Flavio Biondo, Donato Acciaiuoli and Benedetto Accolti. Bruni was not a self-conscious medievalist, and most of his Florentine history is devoted to what for him was the more recent past, namely, the period between 1250 and 1402; nevertheless, he devoted particular care to aspects of Florentine history in the preceding period, especially to the effects of the barbarian invasions on Florence and to Charlemagne's place in Florentine history.[27] Moreover, to his fellow humanists he issued an influential call not to forget their duty to record the history of the post-classical period.[28] Following Bruni, some humanist historians developed deep interests in the middle ages without becoming self-conscious medievalists,[29] and Biondo too took up where Bruni left off and began writing a general modern history of fifteenth-century Italy in the 1430s, which eventually became the third decade of his *Historiarum ab inclinatione Romani imperii decades III*;[30] by the early 1440s, however, no longer satisfied to write only contemporary history, he turned to the earlier middle ages and devoted much of ten years' work and twenty further books to writing the first general medieval history which became the initial two decades of his *Historiae*.[31] The range of his medieval sources and the greater weight given to medieval as opposed to modern history highlight Biondo as the first true medievalist; as is clear from the two distinct phases of his work on the *Decades*, he seems to have distinguished between his activity as a medievalist and as a modernist, and indeed, it has rightly been pointed out that the two sections of his work reveal differences of style and method.[32] Bruni and Biondo did not publish specialized studies in medieval history but Donato Acciaiuoli's life of Charlemagne, dedicated in 1461 to Louis XI of France, was nothing if not a monograph in the history of the early middle ages.[33] Acciaiuoli's emphasis on Charlemagne's deeds, especially in war, as opposed to his character, the pronounced influence of Livy and Sallust on his work, not to mention its substantial historical digressions, show that he intended to write history, not mere biography;[34] moreover, his range of sources,

---

[26] E.g. the controversy over the refoundation of Florence by Charlemagne: cf. D. Wilcox, *Development of Florentine Humanist Historiography* (Cambridge, Mass., 1969), 11–14.

[27] Ed. Santini, 20–6.    [28] *Ibid.*, 3–4.

[29] E.g. Bartolomeo Platina, *Historia urbis Mantuae Gonziacaeque familiae*, in RIS, xx; Pandolfo Collenuccio, *Compendio de le istorie del Regno di Napoli*, ed. A. Saviotti (Bari, 1929).

[30] Hay, 'Biondo', 103–4.

[31] *Ibid.*, 104ff.; cf. Fubini, 'Flavio Biondo', DBI, x, 542–4.

[32] Cf. Hay, 'Biondo', 113ff.

[33] Cf. Gatti, ' "Vita Caroli" '.    [34] *Ibid.*, 245, 249–51, 260–4.

extending from Einhard to Villani, Bruni and the *Liber pontificalis*, demonstrate a genuine historical interest in the early middle ages.[35]

Benedetto Accolti was therefore part of a growing movement among fifteenth-century humanists whose aim was to study and write the history of medieval Europe. He saw his work, in fact, as a direct continuation of what Bruni had begun. In his dialogue, when considering the various worthy but neglected episodes of post-classical history, he mentions first the crusades, which was the topic he was then writing or soon to write about, and then moves to the events narrated in the *Historiae Florentinae*, 'which, if there had been no Leonardo [Bruni], would lie in obscurity and have disappeared entirely from human memory'.[36] He and his famous predecessor were both involved in the same work of saving the great deeds of men, particularly in the post-classical period, from oblivion, and it is no accident that Bruni's call to preserve modern history in the preface to the Florentine history:

Would that erudite and eloquent men from the previous age have preferred to write the history of their own time rather than pass over it in silence! Unless I am mistaken, indeed, it is the particular duty of learned men to celebrate their own age, to snatch it from oblivion and to preserve it for immortality.[37]

became the point of departure for Accolti in his preface to *De bello*:

What good man not entirely lacking in humanity could bear with equanimity that the deeds of so many excellent men . . . should perish entirely, and that their hope [of immortality] should have been in vain . . . Indeed, it is the duty of the good and grateful mind to praise, to commemorate preeminent men who have served the human race with their virtue . . . Therefore, to me it seems ungrateful . . . for those endowed with learning and eloquence to neglect . . . to celebrate their own age, . . . which seems [therefore] entirely destitute of excellent men.[38]

Like Accolti, Donato Acciaiuoli took his inspiration as a medievalist from Bruni, whose Florentine history he copied, annotated and translated[39] and whose work not only influenced the style and character of his life of Charlemagne but also served as one of its principal sources.[40] Indeed, it is likely that Accolti and Acciaiuoli, who were exact contemporaries, encouraged in each other a mutual enthusiasm for the middle ages. Both

[35] *Ibid.*, 243, 260ff.

[36] Dialogue, fol. 19r: Quae omnia, si Leonardus non fuisset, iacerent in obscuro et omnino apud hominum memoriam deperissent. Cf. Galletti, 112.

[37] Ed. Santini, 3.

[38] History, fol. 1r–v: Nam quis ferat equo animo bonus vel humanitatis non expers tot prestantium hominum gesta . . . penitus deperisse ac spem eorum fuisse inanem? . . . Boni enim gratique animi est offitium viros prestantes qui sua virtute humano genero profuerunt . . . memoria retinere . . . Itaque ingrati mihi visi sunt . . . qui doctrina et eloquio prediti . . . neglexerunt . . . suas etates illustrare . . . [quae ideo] prestantium hominum vacuae prorsus fuisse viderentur (*Recueil*, 529–30).

[39] Cf. p. 283, *supra*.      [40] Gatti, ' "Vita Caroli" ', 260ff.

were ardent advocates of a crusade, which helped to inspire Accolti's medievalism, and in fact one of Acciaiuoli's principal interests in Charlemagne was as a champion of Christendom against the infidel who would inspire similar fervour among contemporary princes. Similarly, Acciaiuoli's emphasis on Charlemagne as a great religious leader parallels Accolti's portraits of the crusaders, and especially of Godfrey of Bouillon;[41] moreover, just as Accolti, it has been seen, used the quarrel of the ancients and moderns to praise Godfrey of Bouillon, so Acciaiuoli used the quarrel in his panegyric of Charlemagne, stressing like Accolti the greater merit of having undertaken the defence of Christendom:

If Cicero exalts with supreme praise and commends the Decii, the Fabii, the Marcelli, Scipiones and many others for endeavouring to defend their native land and extend its empire, what would he have to say about that prince who not for one republic, not for the glory of the Roman people, but for the common liberty of all Christians always struggled and for about fifty years made war against their enemies![42]

The principal evidence of Accolti's enthusiasm for the middle ages is the detailed study he made of several of the principal crusading chronicles for his history. His main source was William of Tyre's *Historia rerum in partibus transmarinis gestarum*, originally written in Latin but mainly known in the middle ages in a French translation, which survives in seventy-three manuscripts[43] in contrast to only nine of the original Latin version;[44] indeed, the original Latin text was so little known in the middle ages that Latin translations of the French version were undertaken.[45] In Italy in particular it is clear that William's history was mainly if not exclusively known in the French version. Francesco Pipino of Bologna made a Latin translation of an abbreviated version of the French translation of William at the turn of the fourteenth century,[46] and in 1348 a Florentine called Lorenzo made an Italian translation of the entire French version;[47] Biondo apparently knew only the French version, referring to William as 'ipse scriptor Gallicus'.[48] As William was born and died in the East,[49]

[41] *Ibid.*, 254ff.     [42] Text in Gatti, ' "Vita Caroli" ', 255.
[43] Cf. P. Riant, 'Inventaire sommaire des manuscrits de l'Eracles', *Archives de l'Orient latin*, i (1881), 247–56.
[44] Cf. E. A. Babcock and A. C. Krey, 'Introduction' to the English translation of William of Tyre's *A History of Deeds Done Beyond the Sea* (New York, 1943), i, 39.
[45] Riant, 'Inventaire', 352.
[46] Ed. RIS, vii (Milan, 1725), col. 663ff. Cf. Riant, 'Inventaire', 253; M. L. de Mas-Latrie, 'Essai de classification des continuateurs de l'*Histoire des croisades* de Guillaume de Tyr', *Bibliothèque de l'École des Chartes*, ser. 5, i (21) (1860), 145ff.
[47] BLF, 61, 45; it is clear from the opening sentences that Lorenzo was translating the French, not the Latin version, of William of Tyre: cf. *ibid.*, fol. 12r with William, 9.
[48] *Decades*, 216.
[49] Cf. Babcock and Krey, 'Introduction' to William of Tyre, 6, 25.

Biondo would have had no reason to associate him with France unless he had been acquainted with his history only in French.

Biondo himself may have been put off reading the entirety of William because it was available only in old French; in the *Decades* he made use only of Pipino's abbreviated version in Latin.[50] On the other hand, such linguistic difficulties did not deter Accolti who made direct use of the original French version, and not the less troublesome Latin original. Introducing Peter the Hermit, Accolti describes him as 'magno ingenio, maiore animo preditus',[51] a translation of the French 'de grant cuer et de cler engin'.[52] During Peter's march to the East Accolti says he ordered his men not to attack Nish 'suo ac principum nomine',[53] again a translation of the French 'de par soi et de par les barons de l'ost'.[54] Similarly, during Tancred's quarrel with Baldwin of Bouillon, Accolti says that Tancred yielded to Baldwin, 'iram dissimulans',[55] closer to the French 'il couvri sa pensée' than to the Latin 'motum animi temperans'.[56] Not a literal translation of the Latin, the French version often omits, changes or adds details, so that Accolti's version diverges substantially from the Latin. Thus he states that Urban II instructed Peter the Hermit to preach the crusade in the West before the Council of Clermont,[57] a detail found in only the French version.[58] Similarly Accolti derives from the French version his account of the humiliation of the emperor Romanus Diogenes after the battle of Manzikert in 1071: they both state that the victorious sultan used the emperor's neck to mount his horse, whereas according to the Latin version his entire body was used.[59] Accolti's statement that Nicephorus Boteniat was being held prisoner by Alexius I at the time of the first crusade is also taken from the French, not the Latin version.[60] Pipino's abbreviation sufficed for Biondo but could not have supplied all the detail required by Accolti, who for example includes a full account of the march of Peter the Hermit's army to Constantinople[61] including many details taken from the

---

[50] Cf. Buchholz, *Die Quellen Blondus*, 80–1.
[51] History, fol. 5r; *Recueil*, 534.
[52] William, 32; the Latin text reads: 'major in exiguo regnabat corpore virtus. Vivacis enim ingenii erat.'
[53] History, fol. 16r; *Recueil*, 542.
[54] William, 54; Latin version: 'praecepit districtius, ut nemo . . .'
[55] History, fol. 44r; *Recueil*, 565.        [56] William, 142.
[57] History, fol. 7r; *Recueil*, 535.        [58] William, 37–8.
[59] Cf. History, fol. 18r (*Recueil*, 544), with William, 28.
[60] Cf. History, fol. 18v (*Recueil*, 544), with William, 79. Some other examples: cf. Accolti's account of Peter the Hermit's embassy to Nish, History, fol. 16r (*Recueil*, 542), with William, 54; his account of the beginnings of the siege of Nicea, History, fol. 34r (*Recueil*, 557), with William, 117; his account of the capture of messengers to Nicea, History, fol. 36v (*Recueil*, 559), with William, 114; his account of Godfrey's heroism during an assault on Nicea, History, fol. 38v (*Recueil*, 560), with William, 122.
[61] History, fol. 14r–17r; *Recueil*, 541–3.

complete French translation[62] not found in Pipino's summary.[63] There was also the Italian translation of the French version made by Lorenzo Fiorentino which is still preserved in the Biblioteca Laurenziana,[64] but even if Accolti knew of this version, nevertheless he still made use of the original French version.[65] Thus Accolti states that the men from Nish were the best soldiers in their country,[66] as does the French text, where it is said that they were 'de totes les meilleurs genz de la terre',[67] whereas Lorenzo merely says they were 'buona gente'.[68] Another example is the episode of the mills near Nish that were burnt by some of Peter the Hermit's followers: Accolti's and the French versions agree that the malefactors were German,[69] but Lorenzo merely says, 'In quella compangnia avea iy che molto erano mafacienti', with no reference to nationality.[70]

Accolti's determination to use a French chronicle as his main source impressed Vespasiano da Bisticci, who remarked that his linguistic ability enabled him to become the first humanist historian of the first crusade.[71] Accolti's interest in medieval history not only led him to a detailed study of a French source but also inspired him to supplement his account with a source by a contemporary of the events described, Robert of St Remy's *Historia iherosylimitana*, a work widely circulated in the later middle ages,[72] which was also used by Biondo.[73] One example of Accolti's use of Robert is the homage sworn by the crusaders to Alexius I. William of Tyre does not discuss the oaths taken by the crusaders but Robert devotes a long section to them, upon which Accolti's account is based.[74] During the siege of Antioch the besieged citizens put a number of horses to pasture outside the city; these were captured by the crusaders, 'que res', said Accolti, 'vehementer fregit hostium animos',[75] a paraphrase of Robert's 'quod infortunium cives vehementer attrivit'.[76] Just before the crusading army was to engage Kerbogha, the general sent to reconquer Antioch, Accolti said that the papal legate, Adhemar of le Puy, addressed the host;[77] he was not mentioned as giving a speech on this occasion by William of Tyre, but

[62] William, 50–6.    [63] RIS, vii, col. 671–2.
[64] BLF, 61, 45; cf. *Recueil*, cxxxvi.
[65] Unlike Pipino's summary it is a literal translation of the complete French version, even to the point of including Gallicisms in the text, and is not a corrupt version as is stated *ibid.* The ms. was not part of the Medici collection during the fifteenth century: cf. Piccolomini, *Intorno alle condizioni*, 67ff.
[66] History, fol. 14v; *Recueil*, 541.
[67] William, 51.    [68] BLF, 61, 45, fol. 21r.
[69] Cf. History, fol. 15r (*Recueil*, 541), with William, 52.
[70] BLF, 61, 45, fol. 21r.    [71] Vespasiano, *Vite*, 597.    [72] Cf. Robert, 718.
[73] Buchholz, *Die Quellen Blondus*, 77.
[74] Cf. History, fol. 31v (*Recueil*, 555), with Robert, 748–50.
[75] History, fol. 60r–v; *Recueil*, 578.
[76] Robert, 793.    [77] History, fol. 67r; *Recueil*, 583–4.

Robert included an account of his speech.[78] Another example is Accolti's description of Caesarea in Judaea, which is based on Robert.[79]

Accolti used yet a third source, Marin Sanudo's *Liber secretorum fidelium crucis*, also a work widely circulated in the fourteenth and fifteenth centuries.[80] An example is Accolti's account of the Council of Clermont; he might have derived from Robert that Pope Urban II delivered his oration outside the city[81] or that there was a council held on the day after the pope's address,[82] but Robert mentioned neither the reforms of the Council of Clermont nor the measures enacted there against the anti-pope, both details which Accolti derived from Sanudo.[83] Nor does Robert mention that on the very day of Urban II's oration many pledges were made to join the crusade, as do Accolti and Sanudo.[84] Robert also does not make clear that it was at the council on the day after Urban's oration that Adhemar of le Puy was elected papal legate, another detail which Accolti derived from Sanudo.[85]

Accolti's attitude to Sanudo is revealing of his genuine curiosity about medieval history. Sanudo's account, written in the early fourteenth century, is itself a combination of the same two other chronicles used by Accolti, namely, William of Tyre and Robert of St Remy. The temptation was there, therefore, for Accolti merely to rewrite Sanudo without reference to the earlier sources, but in fact Accolti used all three sources independently. It has been pointed out that there are passages in *De bello* based directly on Robert and not included in Sanudo's account,[86] and similarly, he made direct use of William of Tyre. For example, Sanudo gives only an abbreviated account of how the stragglers from Walter the Penniless's army were robbed by the Hungarians; and whereas Accolti and William say that the victims themselves returned to the main army bringing news of the disaster,[87] Sanudo merely says that 'hoc . . . ad sociorum devenisset notitiam'.[88] Similarly, while Walter's troops were near Belgrade, Sanudo simply states that some of them were killed by natives;[89] Accolti derives his more detailed account from William, who had said that first a group of crusaders were attacked, then those who survived fled, and

---

[78] Robert, 829.
[79] Cf. History, fol. 85v (*Recueil*, 598–9), with Robert, 858.
[80] Cf. F. Cardini, 'Per una edizione critica di Marin Sanudo', *Ricerche storiche*, n.s., i (1976), 214–18.
[81] Cf. History, fol. 7v (*Recueil*, 536), with Robert, 727 and Sanudo, 131.
[82] Cf. History, fol. 11r (*Recueil*, 538), with Robert, 730 and Sanudo, 131.
[83] Cf. History, fol. 7v (*Recueil*, 535–6), with Sanudo, 131.
[84] Cf. History, fol. 11r (*Recueil*, 538), with Sanudo, 131.
[85] Cf. History, fol. 11v (*Recueil*, 539), with Sanudo, 131.
[86] Cf. pp. 324–5, *supra*.
[87] Cf. History, fol. 13r (*Recueil*, 540), with William, 48.
[88] Sanudo, 132.    [89] *Ibid.*

finally some of them, who had taken refuge in huts, were burnt alive by the natives.[90]

Vespasiano da Bisticci suggested that Accolti had wanted to write a comprehensive medieval history,[91] and although he did not live to complete such a work, it is clear from his dialogue that his interests in the middle ages extended beyond the crusades and that he had undertaken wide reading in medieval history during the 1460s. One type of source mentioned is saints' lives,[92] and he actually says that he had recently been studying the chronicles and histories of late antiquity and the beginnings of barbarian rule:

The deeds of Theodosius, a distinguished ruler, and of many other rulers, as well as of Belisarius, Stilicho and many other generals have perished. How many deeds are there in those times, in France, in Germany, in Asia, in Spain, in Italy, of which there exists little or no record! In the hands of a master historian such as Livy, such deeds would seem great and very similar to those of antiquity, as is clear from brief jottings or from fuller histories, which, however, written without skill, without embellishments of eloquence, have remained in obscurity and been circulated in few hands. In these books I have lately read many great things worthy of memory.[93]

It is impossible to say what shape Accolti's medieval interests would have taken, but he possibly would have gone on to study, besides the decline of Rome and the early barbarian kingdoms, the history of the national monarchies in Britain, France and Spain, as is again suggested by the dialogue:

There have also been in our own age and in earlier times distinguished and notable kings, princes, generals in Britain, in France, in Spain, whose memory has almost vanished.[94]

It has been stated that it was only in political, not cultural, history that the humanists were drawn to study the middle ages;[95] however it is clear that the interests of Benedetto Accolti and his fellow fifteenth-century medievalists went beyond politics to the history of civilization in general.

---

[90] Cf. History, fol. 13r–v (*Recueil*, 540), with William, 48–9.
[91] Vespasiano, *Vite*, i, 597.
[92] Dialogue, fol. 17r; Galletti, 111.
[93] Dialogue, fol. 17v: Sic res gestae Theodosii clarissimi principis et plurium aliorum principum ac etiam Belisarii, Stiliconis et plurimorum ducum perierunt. Quam multa inter haec tempora in Gallia, in Germania, in Asia, in Hyspania, in Italia gesta sunt, quorum nulla aut exigua extat memoria, quae si Livium scribendi magistrum habuissent amplissima et vetustissimis illis simillima viderentur; sicut ex his satis constat quae a quibusdam breviter annotata sunt, vel ab his etiam scripta plenius quorum libri sine peritia, sine ornatu eloquentiae conditi in tenebris ipsis remanserunt, in paucorum manus delati, in quibus legi ego iam plura et maxima memoratu digna. Cf. Galletti, 111–12.
[94] Dialogue, fol. 18r–v: Fuerunt etiam aetate nostra et superiori in Brithannis, in Gallia, in Hyspania clarissimi et memoria digni reges, principes, duces, quorum fama pene deleta est. Cf. Galletti, 112.
[95] Ferguson, *Renaissance in Historical Thought*, 19.

Perhaps a first step towards this more positive appreciation of medieval culture was taken by Bruni in his life of Petrarch, where he links a cultural renaissance to the medieval revival of the Italian city-states:

Having then recovered their liberty . . . by defeating the Lombards, the cities of Tuscany and elsewhere began to revive and to turn their attention to culture (*dare opera agli studi*), and somewhat to refine their crude manners (*limare il grosso stile*). And thus little by little they took strength again, but very weakly.[96]

Donato Acciaiuoli, in his life of Charlemagne, stressed not only Charlemagne's political but also his cultural achievements; indeed, he went beyond his principal source, Einhard, to include material on the foundation of the palatine school, on Alcuin and even the legendary account of Charlemagne as the founder of the University of Paris, which,

enhanced and preserved by later kings, has become so worthy and glorious that now, also widely celebrated throughout the entire world, it has become the residence of the most learned men.[97]

Acciaiuoli's praise of the medieval university *par excellence* was echoed in Accolti's defence of scholasticism, which did not merely include his near contemporaries such as Giovanni Dominici and Luigi Marsili but also Thomas Aquinas, Albertus Magnus, Egidius Romanus, Duns Scotus, Alexander of Hales and Paul of Venice, not to mention the Arabic philosophers, Averroes and Avicenna.[98] In some respects, Accolti was outdone as a champion of medieval culture by Cristoforo Landino, who not only praised medieval scholastics such as the rector of the University of Paris, Roberto de' Bardi, but also poets such as Guido Cavalcanti and lawyers such as Accursius.[99] Landino also took Accolti's denunciation of ancient historians as unreliable to its logical conclusion; implicit in Accolti's argument that classical writers were carried away by the force of their own eloquence in recounting the great deeds of the ancients was the view that medieval chronicles, albeit lacking in eloquence, were more truthful and reliable, and this sympathy with the medieval chronicle was made explicit by Landino in the early 1470s:

Our annals, . . . because they were written by men more truthful than eloquent, gain credibility by their very simplicity from those who read them, but they are little read because of their rough style.[100]

Donato Acciaiuoli had emphasized Charlemagne's great importance in the development of the medieval church, but even this prominent feature of his work could not equal the breadth of interest which Accolti showed

[96] Quoted by N. Rubinstein, 'Il medio evo nella storiografia italiana del Rinascimento', *Lettere italiane*, xxiv (1972), 432.
[97] Cf. Gatti, ' "Vita Caroli" ', 272.    [98] Dialogue, fol. 43r–v; Galletti, 122–3.
[99] *Scritti critici*, i, 115ff.   [100] *Ibid.*, 106; cf. *ibid.*, ii, 47–8, 112–14.

for the history of religion in the middle ages. In his dialogue he defends
medieval religious figures such as Vincent of Beauvais, Celestine V,
Gregory X, Joachim of Fiore, St Clare and Bonaventura, but his greatest
praise goes to the founders of the mendicant orders, Saints Francis and
Dominic;[101] indeed, in his history he elaborates upon his source, William
of Tyre, to include a section on the work of the Franciscans in maintaining
the Christian religion in Jerusalem in the midst of the infidel:

[On Mount Sion] is also the church of St Francis, where many men, followers of his
order and his way of life, have lived pure and holy lives, although they dwell
surrounded by barbarous enemies of the faith.[102]

Accolti had a genuine historical vision of the development of medieval
religion, and he anticipates many future historians of the church in seeing
the eleventh century, with the beginnings of the Gregorian Reform, as the
turning point in the development of the medieval church; in the period
before, the church had struggled against its enemies, paganism and
barbarism, but 'now look at the time which has passed over the last four
hundred years' and behold the true flowering of the medieval church in its
greatest splendour.[103] Indeed, with his criticism of the fifteenth-century
church and particularly the Roman curia in the dialogue, it could be
argued that Accolti had developed the beginnings of the concept of the
medieval age of faith in contrast to the corrupt and secular world of the
Renaissance papacy.[104]

Accolti and his fellow medievalists thus formed an idea of the middle
ages, which, albeit embryonic, nonetheless was the nucleus of modern concepts of medieval history. It must be pointed out that the predominance in
medieval studies established by Italians in the fifteenth century did not
remain unchallenged: Aeneas Sylvius had provided the impetus for the
study of the transalpine middle ages in the mid-fifteenth century, but by the
end of the century north Europeans had seized the initiative in the study of
their own medieval past. Northerners soon came to dominate one field of
scholarship on the middle ages: the editing and publication of medieval
chronicles and sources, even those related to Italian history.[105] However,
Italians shared the initiative in the publication of these medieval sources
until the beginning of the sixteenth century,[106] and it is clear that in the

[101] Dialogue, fol. 47r–53v; Galletti, 124–7.
[102] History, fol. 89v: edes etiam divi Francisci, quo in loco multi homines, sectam eius ac
mores secuti, caste integreque vixerunt, quamvis inter medios barbaros fidei hostes
versarentur. Cf. *Recueil*, 602, and William, 322–6.
[103] Dialogue, fol. 48r; Galletti, 125.
[104] Cf. pp. 219ff., *supra*.
[105] Cf. G. Fasoli, 'Medioevo e storiografia del Cinquecento', in *Storiografia e storia. Studi in
onore di Eugenio Duprè Theseider* (Rome, 1974), 313.
[106] All five incunabular editions of Paul the Deacon were published in Italy, as were five out
of six of those incunabular editions of Orosius. All five incunabular editions of Bede's

field of writing the history of the middle ages Italians never relinquished their important place. The works of Bartolomeo Scala on early medieval Florence,[107] of Bernardo Giustiniani on the origins of Venice, of Merula and Tristano Calco on medieval Milan,[108] of Pierfrancesco Giambullari on the history of Europe from 887 to 947,[109] of Benedetto Mastiani on medieval Pisa, and especially of the greatest Renaissance medievalist, Carlo Sigonio, on medieval Bologna and on the kingdom of Italy in the middle ages[110] – all these works show the vitality in the Italian Renaissance of medieval studies, a field of scholarship which Benedetto Accolti had helped to found.

*Ecclesiastical History* were published in Germany, and six out of eight incunabular editions of Vincent of Beauvais were published in Germany and Switzerland, the other two in Venice: cf. *ibid.*, 314–17.

[107] *Historiae Florentinorum libri quinque*, ed. J. Graevius, *Thesaurus Antiquitatum Italiae*, VIII, i (Leiden, 1723).

[108] *Historiae patrie libri xx[ii]*, *ibid.*, II, i (Leiden, 1704).

[109] On his *Historia dell'Europa* (first edition, Venice, 1566; most convenient nineteenth-century edition ed. A. Gotti, Florence, 1856), cf. E. Mele, 'Le fonti spagnuole della *Storia d'Europa* del Giambullari', GStLI, lix (1912), 359–74; G. Kirner, 'Sulla Storia d'Europa di P. G.', *Annali della scuola normale superiore di Pisa*, vi (1889), 245–84.

[110] *Historiarum de regno italiae libri viginti*, in his *Opera omnia*, ed. L. Muratori (Milan, 1732–7), ii. On Sigonio as a medievalist, cf. G. Fasoli, 'Appunti sulla "Historia Bononiensis" ed altre opere di Carlo Sigonio', in her *Scritti di storia medievale* (Bologna, 1974), 683–710.

# *Epilogue*

Accolti's appointment as first chancellor of Florence in 1458 was the turning point of his life. Before then, although married to a member of a prominent Florentine family, he was still an Aretine living in Florence, retaining Aretine citizenship and maintaining the patrimony inherited from his father. He did not hesitate to seek a favourable position outside Florence, as for example at the University of Siena in 1456, and it was still conceivable that he might have given up Florentine residence to further his legal career, following the example of his brother Francesco's success at Siena, Ferrara and Milan. But after Benedetto Accolti's election as chancellor, he and his family undoubtedly became Florentine. He passed the crucial point when he received Florentine citizenship sometime between October 1458 and February 1459. In 1458 he was still subject to the Aretine *catasto*[1] and on 7 October 1458 when his salary as chancellor was increased from 300 to 450 florins, he was referred to as only 'dominus Benedictus olim domini Michaelis de Accoltis'.[2] But on 20 February 1459 when he was reelected chancellor he was called 'dominus Benedictus domini Michaelis de Accoltis de Aretio Civis Florentinus',[3] and on 23 February 1461, when his salary was increased from 450 to 600 florins, he was again referred to as 'dominus Benedictus domini Michaelis de Accoltis de Aretio civis ac primus cancellarius florentinus'.[4] It is not known exactly when Accolti became a Florentine citizen during this time, and apparently no official act of citizenship has survived. He was certainly not *ex officio* a Florentine citizen as chancellor, for not all previous chancellors had become Florentine citizens on election: Leonardo Bruni, although first elected chancellor in 1410, was not made a citizen until 1416,[5] and Salutati did not become a citizen until 1400, after twenty-five years as chancellor.[6]

---

[1]  ASA, Cat. 7, fol. 212v ff.; Lira, 9, fol. 113r; Lira, 12, fol. 57v.
[2]  ASF, Balìe, 29, fol. 60r.   [3]  ASF,Cento, 1, fol. 15v.
[4]  ASF, Provv. 151, fol. 367r. He also began to sign his legal *consilia* as a Florentine citizen: cf. BNF, Panc. 139, fol. 139v.
[5]  Cf. Santini, 'Leonardo Bruni Aretino', 133ff.
[6]  Cf. Martines, *Social World*, 148–9.

Accolti's election to the chancellorship raised his standing in his native city of Arezzo: before 1458 he had been a prominent Aretine living and working in Florence, where he was sometimes useful to his native city as an ambassador or unofficial spokesman or legal adviser, but after becoming chancellor he was regarded as a patron who was now in a position to protect and forward Aretine interests in Florence. Aretines were overjoyed at the news of his success, writing to him on 21 April 1458, four days after he took office, of the 'gaudio et letitia et consolatione ac iocunditate' which the Aretine people and Aretine commune had over his election.[7] Subject towns often attempted to develop a special relationship with individual men of influence in Florence, hoping to use the goodwill so nurtured to their advantage; Aretines had already formed such a relationship for example with Otto Niccolini, who was employed during the 1450s and 1460s by the Aretines as their advocate,[8] and now the Aretine commune sought to put its ties with the new Florentine chancellor to use, recommending 'the community of Arezzo to him' at the end of their letter of congratulations.[9] Indeed, during his chancellorship Accolti retained connections which would not allow him to forget his native city. On 28 March 1460, his cousin, the Aretine notary Agnolo di Grazia Accolti, shortly before his own death on 6 April 1460,[10] made him guardian of his son Matteo.[11] Accolti was also qualified in the Aretine scrutiny of 1462 to hold office as Gonfalonier of Justice (as the Aretine *caput scripte* had come to be known), captain of the Guelf party, official of the guard and member of the general council,[12] and was drawn to serve as Gonfalonier on 26 February 1462,[13] as captain of the Guelf party on 29 October 1462[14] and as official of the guard on 28 August 1463.[15] Although he declined to hold office on these occasions, there is no indication that he thereby aroused ill-will in Arezzo, as had happened in the 1440s; on the contrary, the Aretine commune frequently solicited his help in these years,[16] just as

---

[7] ASA, Provv. 10, fol. 142v: [21 April 1458] dicti domini priores etc. deliberaverunt litteras famosissimo atque clarissimo iuris interpreti domino Benedicto quondam domini Michaelis de Accoltis civi honorabili aretino nuper bene merito electo in cancellarium magnifici potentissimi ac incliti domini florentini de gaudio et letitia et consolatione ac iocunditate quam populus aretinus et comunitas aretina habet de eius electione etc.

[8] He was first appointed on 21 September 1452 for a salary of 10 florins a year: cf. *ibid.*, 9, fol. 153r–154v. For his work as communal advocate, cf. *ibid.*, 10, fol. 207v, 208v, 213r, 217r, 244r–245r, 262r; 11, fol. 126r–v, 150r.

[9] *Ibid.*, 10, fol. 142v: recommictendo eidem comunitatem Aretii.

[10] AFL, 888, fol. 20r.

[11] ASF, Not.A., P. 297 (1456–77), n. 14, not foliated.

[12] ASF, Tratte, 862 (Aretine *reforma*, 1462), fol. 2r, 12r, 17r, 20r; cf. ASA, Provv. 11, fol. 73r, 76r.

[13] ASA, Estr. 12, fol. 126r, 129r.

[14] *Ibid.*, fol. 147v.    [15] *Ibid.*, fol. 169r.

[16] ASA, Provv. 10, fol. 185r, 194r, 217r; 11, fol. 109r–v, 128r, 141r, 145r, 147v, 150r, 159r; Vacch. 1, fol. 7v.

they did from other Florentine patrons such as Luca Pitti, Cosimo and
Piero de' Medici and Otto Niccolini.[17] Indeed, the Aretine commune was
eventually able to repay Accolti, who petitioned them for examption from
Aretine taxation on the grounds that he had recently become a Florentine
citizen and would have to pay taxes in Florence; on 9 March 1460, therefore, Accolti was duly absolved from liability to all Aretine taxes, 'in con-
sideration of the favours and innumerable services had and received from
our Florentine lords through the intercession of the said Messer
Benedetto', not to mention 'those to be obtained in the future'.[18]

After becoming chancellor, therefore, Accolti probably received every
encouragement from Aretine friends to strengthen his ties with Florence,
and he soon began selling his land near Arezzo and buying farms near
Florence, so that eventually all his property in the countryside round
Arezzo, with one minor exception, had been exchanged for property near
Florence. According to his tax return of 1458, all his property was still
located near Arezzo,[19] but he soon began buying land near Fiesole, just
outside Florence. On 16 February 1462 Accolti designated ser Giovanni
Battista di Messer Guido Lamberti, his distant cousin, to act as his
procurator to purchase certain properties from the general of the Servite
order.[20] These were part of a farm which Accolti acquired in the parish of

---

[17] ASA, Provv. 10, fol. 180v, 244r–245r; 11, fol. 147v, 150v; Vacch. 1, fol. 7v. On Accolti's
position as patron of Arezzo equal in status to the leading oligarchs of Florence, cf. ASA,
Provv. 11, fol. 88r (12 March 1462 (ab inc.)): the Aretine priors . . . deliberaverunt
litteras regratiatorias . . . infrascriptis civibus florentinis fautoribus comunis Aretii in
ottenendo gratiam . . . a magnificis dominis nostris . . . : Luce de Pittis, Petro Cosme de
Medicis, domino Ottoni de Sirigattis [Niccolini], domino Benedicto de Acoltis, Antonio
Pucci de Puccis, ser Bartolomeo [Guidi] de Pratoveteri; *ibid.*, fol. 98r (6 June 1463):
Messer Giovanni Roselli, elected Aretine ambassador to Florence, is given letters of
credence to: Luce de Pictis, Petro et Johanni Cosme de Medicis, domino Ottoni de
Nicholinis, domino Benedicto de Acoltis, Karulo de Ghondis, Piero de Malegonellis,
Johanni Antonii Silvestri ser Ristori, civibus honorabilibus florentinis protectoribus et
benefactoribus comunis . . . Aretii.
[18] ASA, Provv. 10, fol. 217v: (9 March 1459 (ab inc.)) Cum propter singularissimas virtutes
et eminentissimam scientiam ac probitatem excellentissimi ac clarissimi iurisconsulti et
eximii legum doctoris domini Benedicti de Accoltis civis nostri arretini per magnificum ac
excelsum populum et commune Florentie idem dominus Benedictus sit effectus civis
honorandus florentinus et accatastatur in dicta civitate Florentie et ibidem subportet
honera ac gravedines occurentes ut alii cives florentini substinent et supportant, et
desideret per commune Aretii fieri a commune Aretii exemptus ac immunis a
gravedinibus et honeribus civitatis Aretii ad hoc, ut pro una eademque re in duobus locis
non sustineat ac supportet prefata honera et consideratis gratiis et innumerabilibus ser-
vitiis habitis et receptis a dominis nostris florentinis mediantibus intercessionibus dicti
domini Benedicti et etiam obtinendis in futurum . . . fuit . . . deliberatum . . . quod
auctoritate presentis generalis consilii dictus dominus Benedictus domini Michaelis de
Accoltis intelligatur esse et sit exemptus et liber in futurum ab omni et toto eo quod posset
cogi aut compelli ad solvendum . . . Accolti had first begun to pay the *catasto* in Florence
in December 1459: cf. ASF, Monte Commune, 1457, fol. 139r.
[19] ASA, Cat. 7, fol. 212v, 218r–221r.
[20] ASF, Not.A., L 189 (1451–66), fol. 226r.

the Badia of Fiesole; the rest of the farm was purchased from Girolamo Giugno and Antonia di Francesco di Sandro.[21] In 1469 the farm was reported to be worth 912 florins.[22] He kept a few pieces of land at Bagnena in the Aretine countryside worth 43 florins, so that the farm at Fiesole constituted by far the largest part of his landed wealth.[23] His wife's family, the Federighi, had been closely associated with Fiesole, and it may have been that connection which led Accolti to purchase land there. In 1427 Accolti's father-in-law, Carlo Federighi, owned a vineyard in the parish of San Pietro a Careggi at the foot of Fiesole,[24] and sometime between 1433 and 1442 he acquired half a house with a vineyard and a piece of land for growing cane in the parish of the Badia of Fiesole.[25] Carlo's brother, Benozzo, was also bishop of Fiesole from 1421 to 1450, having previously been a canon of the cathedral there.[26]

In addition to gaining Florentine citizenship and property, Accolti succeeded in establishing his family in Florentine society. Whereas each of his father's children, except for Benedetto himself, had married an Aretine, each of Benedetto's children married a member of a prominent Florentine family. It is true that Accolti died before any of his children were married; nevertheless, the social position he had secured for his family enabled his children to contract favourable marriages after his death. In 1469 Caterina, Benedetto's eldest daughter, married Bernardo di Paolo Altoviti.[27] The Altoviti were descended from a feudal family who had settled in Florence in the twelfth century,[28] and were prominent in Florentine political, commercial and military life from the thirteenth to the fifteenth centuries.[29] Bernardo di Paolo's line included several well-known public figures and soldiers, but by the fifteenth century it had become a lesser branch of the family, which only with difficulty maintained its place in public life,[30] and Bernardo di Paolo himself played only a minor role in the political life of the commune.[31] Moreover, Bernardo di Paolo's father

---

[21] ASF, Cat. 929, fol. 610r.  [22] *Ibid.*  [23] *Ibid.*

[24] ASF, Cat. 42, fol. 446r; he continued to own this property until his death in 1449: cf. *ibid.*, 671, fol. 376v.

[25] *Ibid.*, 620, fol. 320r; he continued to own this property until his death: cf. *ibid.*, 671, fol. 379r.

[26] Cf. C. Eubel, *Hierarchia catholica medii aevi*, i (Monasterii, 1913), 249; BNF, CPass. 187, fasc. 51, fol. 4r.

[27] BCA, 12, fol. 2r.

[28] N. Ottokar, *Il comune di Firenze alla fine del Dugento*[2] (Turin, 1962), 63; L. Passerini, *Genealogia e storia della famiglia Altoviti* (Florence, 1871), 1ff.

[29] Cf. *ibid.*, 17, 19, 20, 71, 143–46, 150–56; DBI, ii, 573–81; Ottokar, *Il comune*, 62; R. Davidsohn, *Forschungen zur Geschichte von Florenz* (Berlin, 1896–1908), iii, 159, 189; A. Sapori, *Studi di storia economica* (Florence, 1955–67), iii, 110.

[30] Passerini, *Altoviti*, 143–6, 150–56, 158–59, table xi; DBI, ii, 576; ASF, Cat. 38, fol. 331v; *ibid.*, 811, fol. 214v.

[31] Passerini, *Altoviti*, 159; ASF, Mss. 266, fol. 2v ff.

and grandfather were not successful merchants like many of their relatives:[32] according to the *catasti* of the fifteenth century they were barely
able to keep out of debt.[33] The Altoviti name, however, still had considerable weight in Florence, for Bernardo's sisters married members of the
Ridolfi, Rondinelli and Strozzi families.[34] Caterina Accolti did well to
marry Bernardo, who, because his fortune was small, could not have
expected to marry someone from a richer family. The other Florentines
whom Accolti's children married were no richer than Bernardo Altoviti:
Giovanni di Guido Baldovinetti, the husband of Accolti's daughter
Lucrezia; Giovanni di Bartolo Mori, the husband of Lisabetta Accolti; and
Lucrezia di Giovanni Alamanni, the wife of his eldest son Michele, all came
from households no richer than Bernardo Altoviti's.[35] But like the Altoviti,
these families enjoyed high social rank in Florence. The Baldovinetti were
descended from a branch of the Conti Guidi[36] and played a large part in
Florentine political and commercial life, which was cut short by the
triumph of the Medici in 1434.[37] The Alamanni were believed to have
descended from German followers of Frederick Barbarossa[38] and they
were active in communal life as early as the end of the twelfth century.[39] In
the later thirteenth and early fourteenth centuries they became more
involved in business than public affairs, but gained prominence again during the fifteenth century.[40] The Mori-Ubaldini had emigrated from Signa
to Florence during the thirteenth century and had at first encountered
social prejudice,[41] but by the fifteenth century they were as well accepted
as any of the leading Florentine families.[42]

[32] Martines, *Social World*, 361, 373.
[33] ASF. Cat. 38, fol. 331r–v; *ibid.*, 74, fol. 153r; *ibid.*, 916, fol. 497r–498r.
[34] On these families, cf. Ottokar, *Il commune*, 48–51; Brucker, *Florentine Politics*, 32–4
203; Rubinstein, *Government*, 3, 9, 48, 49, 153; Stefani, *Cronaca*, in RIS², xxx, pt 1, 75
78.
[35] On the Baldovinetti, cf. ASF, Cat. 38, fol. 333r–336v; *ibid.*, 74, fol. 38r–39v; *ibid.*, 811
fol. 260r–263v; *ibid.*, 916, fol. 287r–288v. On the Mori, cf. *ibid.*, 10, fol. 393r–394v;
*ibid.*, 75, fol. 253r; *ibid.*, 814, fol. 5r–9v; *ibid.*, 1009, fol. 229r–230r. On the Alamanni,
cf. *ibid.*, 16, fol. 490r–v; *ibid.*, 64, fol. 352r–353v; *ibid.*, 785, fol. 408r–411r; *ibid.*, 992,
fol. 444r–445v; ASF, Decima repubblicana, 1, fol. 534r–535r.
[36] G. Corti, 'Le ricordanze trecentesche di Francesco e di Alessio Baldovinetti', ASI, cxii
(1954), 110; Ottokar, *Il commune*, 63.
[37] Corti, 'Ricordanze', 110–12; BNF, CPass., 185, fasc. 29, pp. 11–12; G. Villani, *Cronica*,
vi, 80; Ottokar, *Il commune*, 62–3; Davidsohn, *Forschungen*, iii, 52, 140; Stefani,
*Cronaca*, 77; Brucker, *Florentine Politics*, 199, 297, 323, 344, 383; *Delizie*, xx, 184–5,
198, 201; Kent, *Rise of Medici*, 160–2, 355.
[38] BNF, CPass. 44, pp. 193–5; U. Verino, *De illustratione urbis Florentiae* (Paris, 1790), iii,
88.
[39] BNF, CPass. 44, pp. 193–6.
[40] *Libro di Montaperti*, ed. C. Paoli (Florence, 1889), 123, 132, 146; Sapori, *Studi*, iii, 87,
110; Davidsohn, *Forschungen*, iii, 159; BNF, CPass. 44, pp. 196–265 *passim*.
[41] Cf. *Paradiso*, xvi, 56–7.
[42] BNF, CPass. 187, fasc. 73; *ibid.* 8, p. 167; *Libro di Montaperti*, 87; *Divina commedia*,
ed. T. Casini (Florence, 1903), 693.

It was one of Benedetto Accolti's achievements, when he died suddenly of dropsy on 26 September 1464,[43] to have established his family firmly in Florence; indeed, it was due largely to the foundations laid by him that his line of the Accolti family emerged as a minor Renaissance dynasty in the sixteenth century. In the short term, however, his family had to face difficulties after death. His wife received moral support from the Aretine commune,[44] which also approved a contribution of thirty florins to his funeral expenses,[45] but she and her eight children, the eldest of whom was twelve, had to live on capital worth about 2500 florins,[46] which would have yielded an annual income of about 175 florins. These were modest

---

[43] ASF, Medici e Speziali, 245, fol. 74v. Accolti was in good enough health on 5 September 1464 to act as godfather to the notary of the Tratte's son: cf. ASF, Acquisti e doni, 11, n. 1, fol. 8v.

[44] ASA, Vacch. 1, fol. 10v (29 September 1464): the priors order two letters to be written 'in nome del nostro chomune, una a ser Giovanni Batista [Lamberti] e l'altra a Andrea di Jacopo di Tome, e quali erano a Firenze, e quali dovessino andare alla donna di Messer Benedetto di Messer Michele Acholti, cancellieri per lo passato de' nostri magnifici Signori . . . e per parte di questa chomunità si dolessero e offerissero tanto quanto a lloro paresse per debito et honore di questo chomunità, et a noi chon presteza avisassero se per onoranza o per altra chosa bisongnasse acioché noi potessimo chon prestezza fare providimento. I am grateful to Mr Frank Dabell for this reference.

[45] ASA, Provv. 11, fol. 172r (6 January 1464 (ab inc.)): In primis cum vir probus, peritus et egregius legum dottor dominus Benedictus de Acoltis de Aretio, venerabilis et dignus consilarius et olim cancellarius magnificorum dominorum nostrorum Florentinorum, qui erat et fuit semper dum vivebat defensor, proteptor et benefactor istius civitatis et hominum et personarum eiusdem in universalibus et particularis, iam plures et plures menses sunt que de ea vita migravit et mortuus . . . est, propterea pro honore istius civitatis erga memoriam ipsius domini Benediciti bonum esset providere et facere aliqua signa gratitudinis et iuxta posse ad faciendum et honorandum funus dicti domini Benedicti prout et sicut reverentiis viris videbitur et placebit . . . Rainaldus Massi domini Landi de Gozaris de Aretio, unus de numero ufitialium custodie, surgens . . . dixit et consuluit quod ex nunc . . . domini priores . . . una cum eorum collegiis habeant auctoritatem . . . nominandi . . . otto cives presentis consilii qui sic eletti habeant autoritatem . . . providendi . . . pro predicto faciendo illam quantitatem denariorum prout eis videretur fore necessarium et non scedendo summam florenorum triginta auri . . . et hoc dixit et consuluit sic et in quanto per heredes domini Benediti seu per Florentinos fieret seu fattum fuerit honor dicto funere domini Benedicti et aliter non. The committee of eight citizens were ser Antonio di Filippo di ser Rosado, Donato di Cosimo Migliorati, Guido di Antonio Camaiani, Catenuccio di Batista Catenacci, ser Stefano di Antonio Apolloni, ser Antonio di Vanni Pecori, Bartolomeo di Nanni di ser Bartolomeo and Bernardo di Mariotto del Camerrino (cf. *ibid.*, fol. 172v–173r; Vacch. 1, fol. 14v). Having died in office as chancellor, Accolti was eligible for a public funeral at the expense of the Florentine commune, as had occurred at the deaths of previous chancellors such as Salutati, Bruni and Marsuppini (cf. Martines, *Social World*, 239–45); the Aretines expected that such a funeral would be provided, as is clear from this provision and the deliberation cited *supra* n. 44, p. 335. There is no positive evidence to explain why the Florentines failed to honour Accolti like previous chancellors, but it seems likely that the question of the future leadership of the city, following the death of Cosimo de' Medici only eight weeks before that of Accolti, was demanding the full attention of the regime; this same preoccupation with fundamental political problems also helps to account for the long delay of seven months in finding a successor to Accolti: cf. Brown, *Scala*, 42ff.

[46] ASF, Cat. 929, fol. 610v.

resources for a large family, making it, for example, impossible to erect in Accolti's memory a monument at a cost of 150 florins in the church of Santissima Annunziata, where he was buried.[47] It was therefore far from easy for them to live 'honourably', as they declared in their *catasto* of 1469,[48] but in the end they prevailed, owing in part to the support they were given by Florentine society, in which their father had firmly rooted his family. Connections with prominent Florentines first established by Benedetto Accolti not only led to the patrician marriages which his children contracted but also meant material assistance, such as Accolti's eldest son Michele received from his mother's family, the Federighi, while establishing himself as a wool merchant in Florence.[49] Accolti's heirs also received help from their prosperous unmarried uncle, Francesco, who probably supervised the university education of several of Accolti's sons[50] and whose large estate they inherited in 1488.[51]

Equally important for Accolti's children was the strong sense of obligation which the Florentine government felt to the family of a chancellor who had given such outstanding service; as the Florentine Otto di Guardia wrote to the captain of Arezzo in 1471:

You must be aware of the respect in which the cherished memory of Messer Benedetto di Messer Michele Accolti of Arezzo is held because of his estimable achievements and exceptional qualities, and you will have heard how much favour, praise and honour he bestowed on this republic, just as, in the same way, his brother Francesco and the other members of their family have done and always do. Therefore the government and citizens of this republic have a clear duty to praise and commend the memory of Messer Benedetto.[52]

---

47 *Ibid.*: Abiamo d'incharicho a fare la sepoltura ne' Servi di Messer Benedetto di spesa di fi. 150. Non s'è fatta perché non ci è stato il modo a spendere.
48 *Ibid.*: Siamo rimasi questi otto figliuoli picholi e popilli e sanza padre, ch'anno assai da potere vivere a onore.
49 *Ibid.*, fol. 610r; *ibid.*, 1024, fol. 131v [1480]: faciamo una bottegha d'arte [d'arte: ms] di lana in nome di Miche[le] di Messer [Benedetto] a mezzo chon Antonio di Messer Carlo Federighi.
50 *Ibid.* (1480): Abiamo 2 fratelli inn istudio, i quali ci costano l'anno assai chome per [sona] ogni sa, de' quali non ne speriamo guadagno nessuno per di qui a un gran tempo: these were Bernardo and Pietro: cf. *ibid.*, fol. 132r. Evidence of Francesco Accolti's esteem for his deceased brother Benedetto appears in a letter he wrote on 16 June 1465 recommending his cousin, Giovanbattista Lamberti, to the Milanese ambassador in Florence: Ser Iohannes Baptista Aretinus, sobrinus meus, vir probus et ad omnia industrius, mihique tum iure sanguinis, tum veteri consuetudine, qua ab adolescentia viximus, coniunctissimus, preterea Benedicto fratri meo adeo carus, ut nihil de re sua familiari sine eo disponeret: BRF, 834, fol. 43r.
51 Cf. Francesco Accolti's will of 18 November 1485, in BCA, 34, pp. 262–6; they are mentioned as his heirs in a notarial act of 16 December 1488: cf. *ibid.*, 268–9.
52 ASA, Provv. 12, fol. 117r–v (30 April 1471): Voi dovete sapere le dengne opere e le grande virtù che rengnano nella recolenda memoria di Messer Benedetto de Messer Michele Accolti d'Arezo et quanto lui fu favorevole a questa re pubblica et quanto honore et laude 'a procurato a quella, comme simulamente sempre stato et è Messer Francesco suo fratello e chosì seguitono gli altri loro attinenti in modo che meritamente s'apartiene

By the end of the fifteenth century Accolti's children were well on the way to prominence not only in Florence[53] but throughout Italy. One of them, Bernardo, who was, like his father, a lawyer and proficient vernacular poet, gained distinction in the papal curia and eventually became lord of the small Romagnol town of Nepi. Another son, Pietro, one of the leading canonists of his day, who was probably responsible for the text of several papal bulls condemning Luther as well as being the author of one of the most authoritative opinions on Henry VIII's divorce, became an influential bishop and cardinal in the early sixteenth century, but his eminence as a prince of the church was surpassed by Benedetto Accolti's grandson, Benedetto, another canonist, who as a cardinal too gained enormous independent authority and wealth as papal vicar in Ancona in the 1520s and 1530s; he became a political magnate in his own right under Clement VII until he was toppled from power by Paul III, ending his life in exile in Florence under the protection of Duke Cosimo I.[54]

a chi reggie et governa questa et qualunche citadino di quella la memoria del prefato Messer Benedetto laudare et commendare.

[53] By 1488 Accolti's sons evidently enjoyed considerable favour in Florence: cf. the Florentine chancellor Bartolomeo Scala's letter about them to the Balìa of Siena (British Museum Add. MS 21, 519, fol. 7r, a transcription of which was very kindly given to me by Mrs Alison Brown): amiamo questi heredi [Benedetto Accolti's sons, the heirs of Francesco Accolti] e per la loro costumateza et meriti sono molto cari e accepti a tutta la città [7 May 1488].

[54] Cf. DBI, i, 101–10.

# Appendix I Letters of Benedetto Accolti

### To the priors of Arezzo, 25 February 1458[1]

Dicta die xxviii et ultima Februarii [1457 (ab inc.)]
(Prudens vir ser Angelus quandam Gratie de Acoltis civis et notarius Aretinus produxit et presentavit coram dictis dominis prioribus populi civitatis Aretii quasdam litteras famosissimi legum doctoris domini Benedicti domini Michaelis de Acoltis tenoris et contientie infrascripte videlicet intus:) Magnifici domini priores. Ho inteso che quelli che furono costà electi sopra la riforma dela cità fecono per loro partito che in caso io fussi tracto capo di scripta dei priori di costà et io non aceptasse[2] e fussi contento che ser Angnolo di Gratia fusse in mio luogo che lui potesse exercitare l'uficio in mio luogo. Et però v'aviso che mia intentione non è quando fussi tracto d'aceptare, non perché l'uficio non sia più degno assai ch'io non merito, ma per le molte mie occupationi et per la absentia, la quale legiptimamente mi scusa. Et per tanto vi priego che se quando si farà la tracta io per sorte sarò tracto, voi diate quello honore a ser Angnolo, che ne so molto contento. Valete feliciter. In Firenze a dì xxv di febraio MCCCCLVII.

Benedictus de Acoltis de Aretio legum doctor

### To Cosimo de' Medici, 30 July 1459[3]

Clarissime vir pater et domine mi precipue. Bernardo da Castiglioncho chiese una lectera al Re Renato, et deliberossi perché Messer Octo mi disse che vi pareva, et disse l'effecto dela lectera. Par melo avere scripto in buona forma et, come vederete, non si confessa in tucto Bernardo esser fuor di colpa, né anche s'accusa. Mandovela, et se vi par da mutar nulla, avisatemi et farassi. Bernardo la sollecita molto et vorrebbela oggi. In ongni modo valete felix et diu. Servitor vester,

Benedictus de Aretio, doctor

[1] ASA, Estr. 12, fol. 39r.    [2] Ms.
[3] ASF, MAP, 138, 19. For Accolti's letter on behalf of King René, cf. ASF, Miss. 42, fol. 146r–147r. The letter attributed to Accolti by Flamini (*Lirica toscana*, 577–8) is by Benedetto di Giovannozzo, another Aretine lawyer.

# Appendix II  Accolti's work as a palace official during his chancellorship[4]

[Officiales catasti comitatus]

MCCCCLVIII

Indictione septima die trigesima mensis septembris. Cum esset compertum quod dictus Jacobus Pagnogi di Ridolfis ut supra electus pro quartario Sancti Spiritus non erat etatis annorum quadraginta complectorum die initii dicti officii prout requiritur secundum dispositionem legis de electione dictorum officialium tractantis, habui ego Albertus Donnini Luce notarius extractionum officiorum communis Florentie colloquium cum eximio legum doctore ac egregiis viris domino Benedicto domini Micaelis di Accoltis de Aretio dignissimo maiori cancellario florentino et ser Bartolomeo ser Guidonis Iacobi Guidi scriba reformationum et ser Antonio Mariani Mutii secundo cancellario dicti communis, ad quos et me simul cum eis pertinet in hoc casu et in similibus nostri temporis iudicare quid esset fiendum, quoniam dictus Jacobus quia non est capax officii ratione minoris etatis et ab illo propterea vacat, et ipse Jacobus et Alexander Filippi de Machiavellis fuerunt simul concurrentes et positi pluries ad partitum ipsi duo soli pro dicto officio pro quartario Sancti Spiritus, an sit redeundum ad scructinandum de novo pro dicto quartario Sancti Spiritus an vero dictus Alexander sit assumendus absque aliqua scructinatione propterea fienda. Et habito inter nos quatuor diligenter examine et visa dicta provisione et intellecta eius dispositione, tandem remansimus, auctore principali prefato domino Benedicto sicut decet et decisore, quod dictus Jacobus ipso iure ab officio vacet et dictus Alexander assumatur, non quia de rigore iuris assummendus sit sed propter observatam simili modo consuetudinem in pluribus similibus casibus preteritis ante assumptionem mei Alberti ad officium extractionum prefatum, que consuetudo vim legis obtinere asseritur. Nam si dictus presens modus non servaretur, et foret causa suscitandi scandala non parva in dictis preteritis casibus et opponendi de nullitate et scilicet irritatione gestorum, et quod hoc simile in omni futuro simili casu pro regula capiatur, cum recordatione tamen quod omnis possibilis diligentia adhibeatur ne error interveniat.

[4] ASF, Tratte, 95, fol. 87v.

339

# Appendix III 'Pratica' concerned with increasing Accolti's salary as chancellor[5]

Die v februarii 1460. Magnificus . . . vexillifer iustitie dixit . . . videri preterea dominis aliquid agendum esse de augendo salario domini Benedicti cancellarii, nec in his quicquam eos decreturos absque illorum assensu et consilio.

Franciscus Ventura . . . super negotio cancellarii dixit gratum esse opus ei salarium augere qui bonam operam prestat nec mercedem bene expensam caram unquam videri posse.

Dominus Mannus [Temperani] . . . super salario cancellarii augendo dixit proverbium esse vulgatum mercedem institoris boni aut discipuli nunquam caram fuisse. Ideoque cum ipse virtuose serviat videri sibi iuxta eius virtutes retributionem fiendam esse ac salarium augendum.

Dominicus Martellus . . . de salario autem domini Benedicti dixit idem videri sibi quod aliis. Neminem enim fuisse in eo loco qui diligentius ac melius se habuerit. Et reliquit exercitium advocationis sibi maxime utile. Et ideo salarium eius omnino augendum esse.

Dominus Otto [Niccolini] dixit . . . de re autem domini Benedicti idem se quod alios sentire, presertim cum reliquerit exercitium advocationis et optime satisfaciat. Et ideo videri sibi centum florenos addendos esse salario veteri.

Johannes Bartolus dixit . . . cumque omnes cives pariter efferant laudibus cancellarium ipsum equum esse ut salarium illi augeatur, cuius officium magis prodest civitati quam sibi.

Franchus Sacchectus ait . . . nec satis de virtute cancellarii digne dici posse cui, cum reliquerit sua exercitia, de maiori salario censere providendum esse, sicut alii dixerunt.

Dietisalvius Neronis . . . cancellarium autem dixit esse hominem valde prestantem. Et ideo nedum sibi pro salario centum florenos augendos esse sed longe maiorem quantitatem, sicut dominis visum fuerit.

Loisius Guiciardinus in cunctis aprobavit aliorum sententiam presertim

---

[5] ASF, CP, 56, fol. 138v–140r.

de cancellario, affirmans cedere ad honorem civitatis maximum talem virum eiusmodi officium gerere. Et ideo salarium eius augendum.

Bartolomeus Lenzius . . . ait . . . addens . . . in officio[6] cancellariatus neminem unquam talem fuisse qualem nunc sit. Et ideo gratitudinem esse magnam salarium illi augere sicut alli dixerunt.

Vannes Oricellarius . . . quantum ad cancellarium ait quotidie magis patere eius virtutem. Et quemadmodum boni principes eriditos viros locupletes reddebant, sic de ipso fiendum esse et ideo salarium eius augendum esse.

Nicola Caponus ait . . . domino Benedicto augendum salarium florenis 150.

Bernardus Medix aprobare se ait aliorum sententiam . . . de cancellario. Fidem enim illius et virtutem emi non posse.

Loisius Rodulfus idem dixit quod alii circa omnes partes consultationis, addens solitum esse dominum Benedictum longe plus lucrari ex patrocinio quod prestare solitus erat quam ex hoc munere publico. Et mereri suam doctrinam omne premium. Nec posse illi satisfieri iuxta meritum.

Mariottus Benvenutus similiter aprobavit aliorum dicta addens quotidie crescere bona opera cancellarii et ideo illa retributionem mereri sicut alii dixerunt.

Matteus Palmerius idem in omnibus aprobavit, affirmans omnia mereri dominum Benedictum et ideo se cum aliis concordem esse ut salarium illi augeatur.

Angelus dela Stufa aprobavit aliorum sententiam, dicens inter alia non posse constitui cancellario[7] dignum premium sue virtutis et consuesse premia impellere homines ad virtutem maiorem capessendam. Et ideo illi augendum salarium ut melior quotidie efficiatur spe premii.

Leonardus Bartolinus confirmare se ait aliorum dicta, presertim quanto ad dominum Benedictum, dicens eum omne salarium mereri.

Petrus Pazius aprobans aliorum sententiam, dixit non posse tantum laudari cancellarium et affici premiis quin etiam maiora mereatur. Et ideo se cum aliis concordem esse ut salarium ei augeatur.

Antonius Puccius aprobavit sententiam aliorum presertim Francisci Venture, addens quoque nunquam in civitate clariorem cancellarium fuisse quam eum qui nunc est. Et ideo salarium sibi omnino augendum esse, sicut alii monuerunt.

[6] ms: officium.    [7] ms: cancellarium.

# Appendix IV   Accolti and the incident of Ponzano, July–August 1463

*The Florentine Signoria to Francesco Sforza, 2 July 1463*[8]

Rendiamo gratie alla excellentia vestra avendo inteso per le sue lettere quanto dimonstra esserli in dispiacere l'ingiurie fatte alla magnifica madonna Catherina da Campofregoso, ma perché ancora el magnifico Jacopo da Losolo [Malespini], il quale prese il castello di Ponzano, quello ritiene non obstante e commandamenti fatti per parte dela prefata vestra excellentia et questo a noi risulta in vergogna perché al tempo che madonna Catherina divenne nostra racomandata da lei si teneva questo castello insieme cogli altri, e quali tucti promettemo conservarli et difendere lei da qualunche ingiuria et oppressione. Siamo constretti di nuovo pregare la vostra sublimità et così con ogni affectione d'animo preghiamo gli piaccia dare opera col prefato marchese Jacopo che in ogni modo il castello di Ponzano sia ristituito a madonna Catherina perché così non seguendo come intende l'excellentia vestra a noi sarebbe vergogna grandissima lasciare la cosa in questi termini e rompere la fede non observando quanto abbiamo promesso con cattivo exemplo agli altri racommandati o a qualunche altro che per alcuno tempo volesse venire sotto la nostra protectione. Et speriamo sanza alcuno dubbio che l'excellentia vestra non meno desiderosa del nostro honore che del suo proprio satisfarà al nostro desiderio. 2 iulii 1463.

*The Florentine Signoria to Marchese Jacopo Malespini, 2 July 1463*[9]

Noi crediamo essere assai noto alla magnificentia vestra la magnifica madonna Catherina da Campofregoso già più tempo essere venuta in confederatione con questa signoria et in nel tempo nel quale teneva il castello di Ponzano et che noi secondo la consuetudine ci obligamo a difendere lei et quelle terre che teneva da qualunche persona. Il perché

[8] ASF, Miss. 44, fol. 91r–v.   [9] *Ibid.*, fol. 91v.

sendo il castello di Ponzano al presente a llei tolto per la magnificentia vestra l'onor nostro, il quale preferiamo ad ogni cosa, richiede non considerare altro che l'oservanza dela fede data dela quale mai siamo consueti mancare; però preghiamo la vestra magnificentia voglia liberamente desistere dala inpresa fatta et restituire il prefato castello alla prefata magnifica madona Catherina imperoché così non seguendo intende chiaramente la vestra magnificentia che a noi sarebbe vergogna grandissima lasciare la cosa in questi termini. Rendiamoci certi che voi arete non meno rispetto alla dignità et honore di questa re pubblica che al interesse vestro particulare. 2 iulii 1463.

### The Florentine Signoria to Francesco Sforza, 7 July 1463[10]

Per altra lettera scrivemo alla excellentia dimostrandoli apartenersi all'onore di questa repubblica che essendo racomandata di quella la magnifica madonna Catherina da Campofregoso gli fusse restituito il castello di Ponzano, el quale possedeva nel tempo che si fece simile confederatione et che se noi lasciassimo el caso suo ne' termini ne' quali al presente si truova ne risulterebbe a noi vergogna grandissima con malo exemplo degli altri racomandati et ancora di quelli e quali per alcun tempo avessono intentione venire sotto la protectione di questa cità pregando la prefata vestra excellentia gli piacesse dare opera con Jacopo da Losolo che restituisse il predicto castello. Di poi abbiamo inteso gli huomini di quello per l'opera del commissario della sublimità vestra avere giurato fedeltà a quella et che parte degli huomini gridano duca! duca! et parte marzocho! come se questi fussono vari nomi et i varii potentie et non una medesima cosa come noi siamo. Il perché credendo noi questo procedere sanza saputa o voluntà della vestra excellentia, la quale mai per alcun tempo non desiderò né desidera cosa alcuna che ritornasse in preiudicio o vergogna nostra perché sarebbe comune a quella, essa instantissimamente con ogni affectione d'animo preghiamo gli sia di piacere fare desistere el mandatario suo et il prefato marchese Jacopo da questa cosa et fare restituire liberamente il dicto castello a madonna Catherina come richiede il debito et honore di questa re pubblica et l'amicitia nostra et riputeremo questo in luogho di piacere singulare. 7 iulii 1463.

### The Florentine Signoria to Francesco Sforza, 30 July 1363[11]

Benché quello che a noi ha exposto per parte della excellentia vestra lo spectabile Nicodemo [Tranchedini] circa la restitutione del castello di

---

[10]  *Ibid.*, fol. 93v.    [11]  *Ibid.*, fol. 97v–98v.

Ponzano alla magnifica madonna Catherina da Serzano assai ci abbia commosso per le cagioni prudentissimamente assegnate et per rispetto della vestra excellentia dal proposito della quale mal volentieri in qualunche cosa benché piccola ci partiremmo, non di meno constretti dala fede data et dal'onore nostro, il quale si debba a qualunche cosa preferire come sempre in ogni tempo 'a observato l'excellentia vestra, restiamo fermi nella prima opinione, cioè che'l debito et honor nostro richieggha il castello di Ponzano a madonna Catherina sia restituito. Imperoché benché aparisca per instrumenti publici il magnifico marchese Jacopo essere già molto tempo suto racomandato alla sublimità vestra inanzi ancora che la prefata magnifica madonna Catherina fusse in nostra protectione, non di meno dapoiché quella fu confederata con questa re pubblica nel tempo che teneva il dicto castello fu fatta lega universale fra la vestra excellentia et molte altre potentie et questa signoria nella quale fu promesso da ogni parte non offendere alcuno degli aderenti et confederati delle sopradette potentie, infra e quali aderenti nostri fu la prefata magnifica madonna Catherina con tutte le terre che in quel tempo possedeva et per qualunche modo o cagione questo ci fusse consentito, pure aparisce ne' capitoli della lega noi essere obligati a conservarla, e quali capitoli essendo noti a quella, non intendiamo con qual faccia, con che ragione possiamo ricusare la difesa sua, maxime perché a essa no[n] furono cogniti altri ragionamenti né altre cose che quelle che ne' capitoli si contengono. Né a tutti gli altri a' quali è nota la racomandigia sua collei potremo in alcun modo satisfare che non fussimo riputati mancatori della fede fuori della nostra consuetudine. Il perché sendo noi richiesti da lei del'oservanza della fede et che diamo opera coll'excellentia vestra a farle restituire Ponzano, non ci pare essere in quelli medesimi termini con lei ne' quali è la sublimità vestra col magnifico Jacopo da Lusuolo. Imperoché per la lega ultimamente fatta ci ritroviamo obligati di conservarla di consentimento et parere della vestra excellentia. Onde preghiamo quella con ogni affectione d'animo che sia contenta levarci questa vergogna et infamia, la quale stimiamo gravissima procedendo dal mancamento della fede con cattivo exemplo apresso ciascuno et secondo la sua optima consuetudine preponga noi e l'onor nostro al desiderio del prefato Jacopo et faccia quella stima di questa re pubblica et della dignità sua, la quale è consueta sempre in ogni caso di fare et giudichi veramente come 'a sempre giudicato la vergogna nostra et iniuria essere a quella comune et più doversi stimare la conservatione dell'onor nostro che'l commodo del marchese Jacopo, il quale giustamente debba avere excustata la excellentia vestra considerate le cagioni sopradette, la quale ultimamente preghiamo gli piaccia in ogni modo satisfare al nostro giusto et honesto desiderio. 30 iulii 1463.

*The Florentine Signoria to Caterina de' Campofregosi, 30 July 1463*[12]

Non pigli admiratione alcuna la magnificentia vestra se ne' casi di quella et circa la restitutione di Ponzano alquanto abbiamo differito perché sempre è ssuto nostro parere che questa materia si debba trattare in forma che ne segua el desiderio vestro con meno scandolo et inconveniente che è possibile stimando sanza alcun dubbio che lo illustre signor duca di Melano amicissimo di questa re pubblica et benivollo alla magnificentia vestra finalmente sarà cagione dell'onore et utile vestro et di buona pace et concordia di cotesto paese. Però confortiamo la magnificentia vestra a prendere buona speranza che sanza molto intervallo di tempo e casi suoi a optimo fine si condurranno maximamente mediante il favore et aiuto del prefato illustre signor duca di Melano et noi dala parte nostra in alcuna cosa a noi possibile et honesta non mancheremo. 30 iulii 1463.

*Nicodemo Tranchedini to Francesco Sforza, 14 August 1463*[13]

Heri sera hebi una vestra de 9. circa ala lettera vi ha scripta questa signoria al facto de Ponzano, quale mostray al magnifico Cosimo. Tandem trovo che questa signoria senza consultacione de Cosimo né mia saputa dissero a Messer Benedecto d'Arezo, loro secretario, che vi scrivesse una lettera iustificata como pareva a luy. Et questo perché parve loro gli strengessi li panni ale spalle, quando me scrivesti l'altra vestra in modo che non seppero ben che se dire; perhò ricorsero al doctore. Cossì passò questa lettera. Pur ne serò con le loro signorie et oltra al dolermi honestamente como posso, gli dirò de novo quanto accade et farò de vedere l'auctentico de l'adherentia de madonna Caterina et per altra mia avisarò vestra sublimità.

*Nicodemo Tranchedini to Francesco Sforza, 22 August 1463*[14]

Ho veduta la recomandisia de madona Catterina Frugosa et domane o l'altro credo havere la copia de quanto appertiene al facto de Ponzano et subito ela manderò a vestra sublimità. Quale accerto che quando me son doluto como da me cum questa excelsa signoria dela lettera vi scripsero, havendomi promesso de respondere, consultati havessero li citadini, trovo che la signoria se ne vergogna et dano la colpa a Messer Benedecto d'Arezo, maxime che Cosimo non ne havesse aviso né io. Messer Benedecto imputa la signoria cum dire gli fo facta la commissione et non gli fo dicto più oltra né luy vi pensò. Tantum est che tucti se ne vergognano

12  *Ibid.*, fol. 98v–99r.    13  ASM, SPEFi, 271, n. 197.    14  *Ibid.*, n. 202.

et hano mi facto recordare del iudicio dede de questa signoria un notabile signore de' Malatesti molti anni fa.

### Nicodemo Tranchedini to Francesco Sforza, 27 August 1463[15]

Ala parte del mandare a vestra sublimità l'adherentia de madonna Caterina Fregosa, dice Cosimo che operarà me sia data autentica como sta al libro loro, quale ho veduta che fo facta nel 1450 d'aprile et son vi specificate dentro tucte le terre de' quelli da Luxolo. La signoria me promise ad questi darmene copia, como per altra mia avisay vestra celsitudine. Poy ellecto che fo Dietesalvi me fecero respondere per lo loro cancelliere, cioè Messer Benedetto d'Arezo, che non me la possevano più dare, perché ne era facta commissione a Dietesalvi. Io me ne dolsi fortemente benché nol scrivessi ad vestra excellentia, dicendo gli havevate mandata la vestra fin qui et che andavate cum loro cum altissima realità che non vano cum vestra excellentia. Poy doledomene cum Cosimo, me disse che quando me la promissero, non sapevano che non me la possevano dare senza il partito de' collegii. Perhò se vergognavano a dirmene el vero, ma che devia bastare ch'io l'havessi veduta etc. Pur vederia ch'io l'havessi.

# Select Bibliography

## MANUSCRIPTS OF ACCOLTI'S DIALOGUE

BLF, 54, 8, the presentation copy to Cosimo de' Medici: cf. Piccolomini, *Intorno alle condizioni*, 92 (ASI, ser. 3, xx (1874), 78). For the scribe, cf. p. 157, *supra*.

BLF, Asburnham 924 (855), a copy of a manuscript dated 1626 and presented by Leonardo and Pietro Accolti to Cardinal Francesco Barberini.

Biblioteca Landau Finaly, 271. When the collection was sold this codex did not become part of the Biblioteca Nazionale in Florence and I have been unable to trace its location. It is described by F. Roediger, *Catalogue des livres manuscrits et imprimés composant la bibliothèque de M. Horace de Landau* (Florence, 1885–90), ii, 137, who maintained it was the presentation copy to Cardinal Barberini.

ASF, C.Str., ser. iii, 102, fol. 252r, a passage of the dialogue praising a member of the Strozzi family, copied by Carlo Strozzi, from a manuscript deriving from the one dedicated to Barberini.

## MANUSCRIPTS OF ACCOLTI'S HISTORY

BLF, 54, 6, the presentation copy: cf. fol. 111v: LIBER PETRI DE MEDICIS COS. F., the dedicatee: Piccolomini, *Intorno alle condizioni*, 84 (ASI, ser. 3, xx (1874), 70); E. Müntz, *Les collections des Médicis au XV$^e$ siècle* (Paris, 1888), 48. For the scribe, cf. p. 157 *supra*.

Paris, Bibliothèque de l'Arsenal, 670 (104 H. L.). Membr. illuminated, xv saec. Cf. H. Martin, *Catalogue des manuscrits de la Bibliothèque de l'Arsenal*, ii (Paris, 1886), 7–8.

New York, Pierpont Morgan Library, 475. Membr. illuminated, xv saec. Cf. S. de Ricci and W. J. Wilson, *Census of Medieval and Renaissance Manuscripts in the United States and Canada* (New York, 1935–40), ii, 1456.

Split, Yugoslavia, Naucna Biblioteka, Shelf Mark M. 169. Membr. xv saec., fragmentary, containing the end of Book i, all of Books ii and iii and the beginning of Book iv. I am grateful to Professor P. O. Kristeller for this description.

Berne, Stadtbibliotek, variants indicated by Bongars in the margins of the Basel 1544 edition of *De bello*, according to a lost manuscript belonging to the English ambassador to Venice in the early seventeenth century: Shelf Mark X.240. Cf. *Recueil*, cxxxvii; H. Hagen, 'Eine neue Handschrift von Benedetto Accoltis Geschichte des Kreuzzuges', *Vierteljahrsschrift für Kultur und Literatur der Renaissance*, i (1885), 134–6.

347

Archivio storico comunale, Genoa, 172. Cart., xviii saec., 153 fols, not numbered. I am grateful to the Director, Dott. Liana Saginati, for this description.

## PUBLISHED WORKS

Girolamo Aliotti, *Epistolae et opuscula*, ed. G. M. Scarmali, 2 vols. (Arezzo, 1769).

Hans Baron, *The Crisis of the Early Italian Renaissance*, 2 vols. (Princeton, 1955). Revised one-volume edition (Princeton, 1966).

'The *Querelle* of the ancients and moderns as a problem for Renaissance scholarship', JHI, xx (1959), 3–22.

Paola Benigni, 'Fonti per lo studio dell'imposizione diretta in Arezzo tra il xiv e il xv secolo', *Studi in onore di Leopoldo Sandri* (Rome, 1983), 107–22.

Flavio Biondo, *Scritti inediti e rari*, ed. B. Nogara, *Studi e testi*, xlviiii (Rome, 1927).

Vespasiano da Bisticci, *Le vite*, ed. A. Greco, 2 vols. (Florence, 1970–6).

Robert Black, 'Ancients and moderns in the Renaissance: rhetoric and history in Accolti's *Dialogue on the preeminence of men in his own time*', JHI, xliii (1982), 3–32.

'Benedetto Accolti and the beginnings of humanist historiography', EHR, xcvi (1981), 36–58.

'La storia della prima crociata di Benedetto Accolti e la diplomazia fiorentina rispetto all'Oriente', ASI, cxxxi (1973), 3–25.

Poggio Bracciolini, *Epistolae*, ed. T. Tonelli, 3 vols. (Florence, 1832–61).

*Opera* (Basel, 1538).

*Opera omnia*, 4 vols., ed. R. Fubini (Turin, 1964–9).

Alison Brown, *Bartolomeo Scala, 1430–1497, Chancellor of Florence* (Princeton, 1979).

Gene Brucker, *The Civic World of Early Renaissance Florence* (Princeton, 1977). *Florentine Politics and Society, 1343–1378* (Princeton, 1962).

Leonardo Bruni, *Epistolarum libri viii*, ed. L. Mehus, 2 vols. (Florence, 1741). *Historiarum florentini populi libri xii*, ed. E. Santini, RIS², xix, 3. *Humanistisch-philosophische Schriften*, ed. H. Baron (Leipzig, 1928).

August Buck, *Die 'Querelle des anciens et des modernes' im italienischen Selbstverständnis der Renaissance und des Barocks* (Wiesbaden, 1973).

Domenico Buoninsegni, *Istorie, o memorie della città di Firenze* (Florence, 1637).

Lauretta Carbone, 'Note sulla formazione e l'attività di un ufficio finanziario: il camarlingo della comunità di Arezzo e l'esazione delle imposte dirette (1384–1529)', *Studi in onore di Leopoldo Sandri* (Rome, 1983), 185–226.

Franco Cardini, ed., *Toscana e terrasanta nel medioevo* (Florence, 1982).

M.-D. Chenu, *Nature, Man and Society in the Twelfth Century*, ed. and tr. by J. Taylor and L. Little (Chicago, 1968).

G. Cherubini, 'Schede per uno studio della società aretina alla fine del Trecento', BollRCA, 867 (1 May 1977), reprinted in *Contributi*. *Signori, contadini, borghesi. Ricerche sulla società italiana del basso medioevo* (Florence, 1974).

*Contributi allo studio della storia di Arezzo*, published by the Rotary Club di Arezzo (Arezzo, 1981).

*Contributi allo studio della storia di Arezzo*, ser. 2, published by the Rotary Club di Arezzo (Arezzo, 1982).

E. R. Curtius, *European Literature and the Latin Middle Ages*, tr. W. R. Trask (New York, 1953).

*Delizie degli eruditi toscani*, ed. Ildefonso di San Luigi (Florence, 1770–89).
A. della Torre, *Storia dell'Accademia platonica di Firenze* (Florence, 1902).
M. Del Piazzo, *Il protocollo del carteggio della Signoria di Firenze, 1459–1468* (Rome, 1969).
Daniela De Rosa, *Coluccio Salutati: il cancelliere e il pensatore politico* (Florence, 1980).
B. Dini, 'Lineamenti per la storia dell'arte della lana in Arezzo nei secoli xiv–xv', BolIRCA, 902 (30 June 1980), reprinted in *Contributi*, ser. 2.
F. Donati, 'S. Bernardino predicatore delle indulgenze per la crociata', BSenSP, ii (1895), 130–6.
Wallace Ferguson, *The Renaissance in Historical Thought* (Cambridge, Mass., 1948).
F. Flamini, *La lirica toscana del Rinascimento anteriore ai tempi del Magnifico* (Pisa, 1891).
'Leonardo di Piero Dati poeta latino del secolo xv', GStLI, xvi (1890), 1–107.
Eugenio Garin, *La cultura filosofica del rinascimento italiano* (Florence, 1961).
ed., *La disputa delle arti nel Quattrocento* (Florence, 1947).
ed., *Prosatori latini del Quattrocento* (Milan, n.d.).
D. Gatti, ' "Vita Caroli" di Donato Acciaiuoli', *Bullettino dell'istituto storico italiano*, lxxxiv (1972–3), 223–74.
George of Trebizond, *Rhetoricorum libri V* (Venice, 1523).
A. Gherardi, ed., *Statuti della università e studio fiorentino* (Florence, 1881).
Neal Gilbert, 'A letter of Giovanni Dondi dall'Orologio to Fra' Guglielmo Centueri: a fourteenth-century episode in the quarrel of the ancients and the moderns', *Viator*, viii (1977), 299–346.
Carlo Ginzburg, *Indagini su Piero* (Turin, 1981).
E. Gössmann, *Antiqui und Moderni im Mittelalter* (Munich, 1974).
L. Gualdo Rosa, 'Il Filelfo e i Turchi', *Annali della Facoltà di lettere e filosofia. Università di Napoli*, xi (1964–8), 109–65.
Guarino Veronese, *Epistolario*, ed. R. Sabbadini, 3 vols. (Venice, 1915–19).
R. Haubst, 'Der Reformentwurf Pius des Zweiten', *Römische Quartalschrift*, xlix (1954), 188–242.
D. Hay, 'Flavio Biondo and the middle ages', *Proceedings of the British Academy*, xlv (1959), 97–128.
*The Church in Italy in the Fifteenth Century* (Cambridge, 1977).
Peter Herde, 'Die Schrift der florentiner Behörden in der Frührenaissance', *Archiv für Diplomatik, Schriftsgeschichte, Siegel- und Wappenkunde*, xvii (1971), 302–35.
D. Herlihy and C. Klapisch-Zuber, *Les toscans et leurs familles* (Paris, 1978).
George Holmes, *The Florentine Enlightenment* (London, 1969).
N. Iorga, *Notes et extraits pour servir à l'histoire des croisades au xv$^e$ siècle*, 6 vols. (Paris and Bucharest, 1899–1916).
E. Jacoboni, 'Le rime di Benedetto Accolti d'Arezzo', *Studi di filologia italiana*, xv (1957), 241–302.
Dale Kent, *The Rise of the Medici* (Oxford, 1978).
F. W. C. Kent, *Household and Lineage in Renaissance Florence* (Princeton, 1977).
P. O. Kristeller, *Renaissance Thought and its Sources* (New York, 1979).
*Studies in Renaissance Thought and Letters* (Rome, 1956).
P. Labalme, *Bernardo Giustiniani* (Rome, 1969).
Cristoforo Landino, *Carmina omnia*, ed. A. Perosa (Florence, 1939).
*Scritti critici et teorici*, ed. R. Cardini, 2 vols. (Rome, 1974).

350 *Select bibliography*

C. Lazzeri, *Aspetti e figure di vita medievale in Arezzo* (Arezzo, 1937).
*Guglielmino Ubertini vescovo di Arezzo (1248–1289) e i suoi tempi* (Florence, 1920).
R. Lopez, 'Il principio della guerra Veneto-Turca nel 1463', *Archivio veneto*, ser. 5, xv (1934), 45–131.
F. P. Luiso, 'Riforma della cancelleria fiorentina', ASI, ser. 5, xxi (1898), 132–42.
Michael Mallett, *The Florentine Galleys in the Fifteenth Century* (Oxford, 1967).
Girolamo Mancini, *Francesco Griffolini, cognominato Francesco Aretino*, nozze Valentini-Faina (Florence, 1890).
Raymond Marcel, *Marsile Ficin* (Paris, 1958).
Giacinto Margiotta, *Le origini italiane de la querelle des anciens et des modernes* (Rome, 1953).
Lauro Martines, *Lawyers and Statecraft in Renaissance Florence* (Princeton, 1968).
*The Social World of the Florentine Humanists* (London, 1963).
Demetrio Marzi, *La cancelleria della repubblica fiorentina* (Rocca San Casciano, 1910).
M. Miglio, 'Una lettera di Lapo da Castiglionchio il giovane a Flavio Biondo', *Humanistica lovaniensia*, xxiii (1974), 1–30 (reprinted in his *Storiografia pontificia del Quattrocento* (Bologna, 1975), 33–59, 189–209).
John Monfasani, *George of Trebizond* (Leiden, 1976).
Giuseppe Müller, *Documenti sulle relazioni delle città toscane coll'oriente e coi Turchi* (Florence, 1879).
K. Müllner, ed., *Reden und Briefe italienischer Humanisten* (Vienna, 1899), reprinted with introduction, bibliography and indices by B. Gerl (Munich, 1970).
G. Niccolini di Camugliano, *The Chronicles of a Florentine Family, 1200–1470* (London, 1933).
G. Olsen, 'The idea of the *ecclesia primitiva* in the writings of the twelfth-century canonists', *Traditio*, xxv (1969), 61–86.
Matteo Palmieri, *Della vita civile*, ed. F. Battaglia (Bologna, 1944).
K. Park, 'The readers at the Florentine Studio', Rin., ser. 2, xx (1980), 249–310.
L. B. Pascoe, 'Jean Gerson: the "Ecclesia Primitiva" and reform', *Traditio*, xxx (1974), 379–409.
Ubaldo Pasqui, ed., *Documenti per la storia della città di Arezzo nel medio evo*, 4 vols. (Florence and Arezzo, 1899–1937).
'Raccolte di codici in Arezzo', AMAPet, viii (1907–8), 122–58.
'Una congiura per liberare Arezzo dalla dipendenza dei fiorentini', ASI, ser. 5, v (1890), 3–19.
and U. Viviani, *Arezzo e dintorni, guida illustrata storica e artistica* (Arezzo, 1925; reprinted Rome, 1981).
Ludwig Pastor, *Acta inedita historiam pontificum romanorum . . . illustrantia* (Freiburg im Breisgau, 1904).
*Storia dei Papi*, tr. G. Mercati (Rome, 1958–64).
Agostino Pertusi, 'I primi studi in occidente sull'origine e la potenza dei Turchi', *Studi veneziani*, xii (1970), 465–552.
*La caduta di Costantinopoli*, 2 vols. (Verona, 1976).
E. Piccolomini, *Intorno alle condizioni ed alle vicende della Libreria Medicea Privata* (Florence, 1875), published without index in ASI, ser. 3, xix (1874), 101–29, 254–81, xx (1874), 51–94, xxi (1875), 102–12, 282–96.

G. B. Picotti, *La dieta di Mantova e la politica de' Veneziani* (in *Miscellanea di storia veneta della R. Deputazione veneta di storia*, ser. 3, iv) (Venice, 1912).

Pius II, *Commentaries*, tr. F. A. Gragg, in *Smith College Studies in History*, xxii (1936–7), xxv (1939–40), xxx (1947), xxv (1951), xliii (1957). *Opera* (Basel, 1571).

Alamanno Rinuccini, *Lettere ed orazioni*, ed. V. R. Giustiniani (Florence, 1953).

Robert of St Remy, *Historia iherosylimitana*, in *Recueil des historiens des croisades. Historiens occidentaux*, iii (Paris, 1866).

Nicolai Rubinstein, *The Government of Florence under the Medici* (Oxford, 1966).

Coluccio Salutati, *Epistolario*, ed. F. Novati, 4 vols. (Rome, 1891–1911).

E. Santini, 'Leonardo Bruni Aretino e i suoi "Historiarum florentini populi libri xii" ', *Annali della scuola normale superiore di Pisa*, xxii (1910).

Marin Sanudo, *Liber secretorum fidelium crucis*, in *Gesta dei per Francos*, ed. J. Bongars, ii (Hanoviae, 1611).

R. Schwoebel, 'Coexistence, conversion and the crusade against the Turks', SR, xii (1965), 164–87.
*The Shadow of the Crescent: The Renaissance Image of the Turk (1453–1517)* (Nieuwkoop, 1967).

M. Sciambra, G. Valentini and I. Parrino, *Il 'Liber brevium' di Callisto III* (Palermo, 1968).

J. Seigel, 'The teaching of Argyropulos and the rhetoric of the first humanists', in *Action and Conviction in Early Modern Europe*, ed. *idem* and T. K. Rabb (Princeton, 1969), 237–60.

M. Sensi, 'Niccolò Tignosi da Foligno, l'opera e il pensiero', *Annali della facoltà di lettere e filosofia dell'Università degli studi di Perugia*, ix (1971–2), 359–495.

K. Setton, *The Papacy and the Levant (1204–1571)*, 2 vols. (Philadelphia, 1976–8).

H. Silvestre, ' "Quanto iuniores, tanto perspicaciores". Antécédants à la querelle des anciens et des modernes', *Recueil commémoral x^e anniversaire de la faculté de philosophie et lettres de l'Université Lovanianum de Kinshasa* (Louvain, 1967), 231–55.

*Statuta populi et communis Florentiae*, 3 vols. (Friburgi, 1778–83).

L. Thorndike, *Science and Thought in the Fifteenth Century* (New York, 1929).

B. L. Ullman, *The Origin and Development of Humanistic Script* (Rome, 1960).

P. Varese, 'Condizioni economiche e demografiche di Arezzo nel secolo xv', *Annuario del R. Istituto magistrale di Arezzo*, i (1924–5), 39–67.

E. Walser, *Poggius Florentinus* (Leipzig and Berlin, 1914).

P. G. Walsh, *Livy* (Cambridge, 1961).

J. N. Warner, 'Political ideas in Matteo Palmieri's *Della Vita Civile*' (London University, unpublished M.Phil. thesis, 1969).

Diana Webb, 'The decline and fall of eastern Christianity: a fifteenth-century view', BIHR, xlix (1975), 198–216.

H. Weisinger, 'Renaissance accounts of the revival of learning', *Studies in Philology*, xlv (1948), 105–18.

H. Wieruszowski, 'Arezzo as a center of learning and letters in the thirteenth century', *Traditio*, ix (1953), 321–91 (reprinted in her *Politics and Culture in Medieval Spain and Italy* (Rome, 1971), 387–474).

William of Tyre, *Historia rerum in partibus transmarinis gestarum (L'estoire de Eracles Empereur et la conqueste de la terre d'outremer)*, in *Recueil des historiens des croisades. Historiens occidentaux*, i (Paris, 1844).

R. Witt, *Coluccio Salutati and his Public Letters* (Geneva, 1976).

G. Zippel, 'Carlo Marsuppini da Arezzo', in his *Storia e cultura del rinascimento italiano* (Padua, 1979), 198–214.

# Index

Tribraco, Gaspare, 236
Tristan, 46
Trithemius, Johannes, 287n
Tritentone, Antonio, 236
true cross, legend of, 274, 276
Tuccerello di Cecco, 8n
Tulliano, 27–8

Ubertini family, 3; of Chitignano, 3
Ubertini, Guglielmo, 3
Urban II, 224, 239–40, 266, 271, 300, 302n, 303, 306, 323, 325
Urban III, 237
Urbano di Guido, 8n
Urbino, 48, 246
da Uzzano family, 209n
da Uzzano, Niccolò, 193n, 194, 209–10

Val d'Arno Casentinese, 27–8, 32
Val di Serchio, 170n
Valla, Lorenzo, 13–14, 81, 187, 198, 200, 206, 217, 313
della Valle, Niccolò, 236
Vallombrosa, 137
Valori, Bartolomeo, 193n, 194, 209n, 210
Valturio, Roberto, 204n
Vanni di ser Niccolò, 8n
Varchi, Benedetto, 198
Varna, battle of (1444), 228, 231
Varro, 168
Vechietti, Luigi, 107–8
Venice, x, 19, 60, 77, 102–3, 130, 143, 185, 193, 227–30, 232, 234–5, 240–3, 248, 252–9, 270, 277–85, 329
Ventura, Francesco, 160n, 174n, 179, 340–1
da Verazano, Lodovico di Cece, 160n

Verdi, faction, 2, 26
Vergerio, Pier Paolo (the elder), 137, 206, 217, 295n
Vergil, 17, 19, 196–7, 288, 292–3; *Aeneid*, 146; *Georgics*, 167n
Verino, Ugolino, 137
Vettori, Agnolo, 164
Vettori, Andrea, 209n
Via degli Orefici, 60
Vicenza, 60
Vienna, 235
del Vigna, Alessandro, 97n
Villani, Filippo, 196, 198, 200, 287, 295n, 297–8
Villani, Giovanni, 136, 270, 272, 291, 321
Villani, Matteo, 137
Vincent of Beauvais, 328, 329n
Vincent of Lerinum, 296n
Visconti, Filippo Maria, 5, 61, 130–1, 185
Visconti, Giangaleazzo, 3, 123–4, 137, 269
Vitelli, Giovanni, 185
Vitéz, Johannes de Zredna, 232
Volterra, 10, 36, 133

Walafrid Strabo, 197, 290
Waldensians, 205
Walter the Penniless, 224, 304–5, 325
War of Eight Saints, 123
Wido of Amiens, 197
William of Malmsbury, 297
William, supposed son of Robert Guiscard, 240
William of Tyre, 291, 299–315, 322–5

Zabarella, Francesco, 18
Zimara, Marcantonio, 197